Multiple Perspectives on Problem Solving
and Learning in the Digital Age

Dirk Ifenthaler · Pedro Isaías · J. Michael Spector ·
Kinshuk · Demetrios G. Sampson
Editors

Multiple Perspectives on Problem Solving and Learning in the Digital Age

Editors
Dirk Ifenthaler
Universität Freiburg
Abt. Lernforschung
Rempartstr. 11
79085 Freiburg
Germany
ifenthaler@ezw.uni-freiburg.de

J. Michael Spector
Learning & Performance Support Lab.
University of Georgia
611 Aderhold Hall
Athens, GA 30602, USA
mspector@uga.edu

Demetrios G. Sampson
Department of Technology in Education
    and Digital Systems
Ctr. Res. and Technology Hellas (CERTH)
University of Piraeus
150 Androutsou St.
185 32 Piraeus
Greece
sampson@iti.gr

Pedro Isaías
Universidade Aberta
86 Rua de Junqueria
1300-344 Lisboa
Palacio Burnay
Portugal
pisaias@univ-ab.pt

Kinshuk
Centre for Science
Athabasca University
Athabasca Alberta
Canada
kinshuk@ieee.org

ISBN 978-1-4419-7611-6   e-ISBN 978-1-4419-7612-3
DOI 10.1007/978-1-4419-7612-3
Springer New York Dordrecht Heidelberg London

© Springer Science+Business Media, LLC 2011
All rights reserved. This work may not be translated or copied in whole or in part without the written permission of the publisher (Springer Science+Business Media, LLC, 233 Spring Street, New York, NY 10013, USA), except for brief excerpts in connection with reviews or scholarly analysis. Use in connection with any form of information storage and retrieval, electronic adaptation, computer software, or by similar or dissimilar methodology now known or hereafter developed is forbidden.
The use in this publication of trade names, trademarks, service marks, and similar terms, even if they are not identified as such, is not to be taken as an expression of opinion as to whether or not they are subject to proprietary rights.

Printed on acid-free paper

Springer is part of Springer Science+Business Media (www.springer.com)

Preface

Research on problem solving and learning has a long tradition in both psychology and education. Cognitive psychologists agree that people have abilities that are essential for processing information and acting successfully in different environments. The nature of human problem solving and learning has been studied by educators and psychologists over the past hundred years. Accordingly, this interesting field of research was always linked with paradigm shifts, e.g. the cognitive revolution. The progress of computer technology has enabled researchers to develop more effective research methodologies and tools for the assessment of problem solving and learning.

This edited volume with selected expanded papers from the CELDA (Cognition and Exploratory Learning in the Digital Age) 2009 Conference (www.celda-conf.org) addresses the main issues concerned with problem solving, evolving learning processes, innovative pedagogies, and technology-based educational applications in the digital age. There have been advances in both cognitive psychology and computing that have affected the educational arena. The convergence of these two disciplines is increasing at a fast pace and affecting academia and professional practice in many ways. Paradigms (such as just-in-time learning, constructivism, student-centered learning and collaborative approaches) have emerged and are being supported by technological advancements such as simulations, virtual reality and multi-agent systems. These developments have created both opportunities and areas of serious concern. Hence, this volume aims to cover both technological as well as pedagogical issues related to these developments.

We organized the papers included in this volume around five themes: (a) instructional design perspectives, (b) cognitive perspectives, (c) assessment perspectives, (d) schooling and teaching perspectives, and (e) virtual environments perspectives. Each of the editors took lead responsibility for reviewing and editing the papers associated with one theme.

In Part I, instructional design perspectives are described and discussed. The authors show how information and communications technology (ICT) tools have completely altered the way museum curators design many of their exhibits and examine the human-computer interaction (HCI) which occurs when people access online museum exhibits (Alwi & McKay, Chapter 2). An ongoing challenge for academics is the choice of which technologies to use and how to effectively integrate them into the curriculum. Accordingly, a framework for guiding the integration of technologies into curricula is introduced in the second chapter (Gosper, Chapter 3). Further, to support the learning process, the usability concept must be extended to include pedagogical considerations. The importance of pedagogical usability in education has been recognized, but not sufficiently researched. Therefore, the author shows how to foster pedagogically usable Web-based learning objects in school education (Hadjerrouit, Chapter 4). The lack of monitoring and expertise transfer tools involves important dysfunctions in the course organization and therefore dissatisfaction for tutors and students. The authors propose a personalized platform, which gives information to monitor activities and supports the acquisition and transfer of expertise (Michel & Lavoué, Chapter 5).

In Part II, chapters focus on cognitive perspectives of problem solving and learning in the digital age. The authors introduce a tool which basic aim is to construct a semantic knowledge base of concepts and relations among them, in order to analyze free text responses, assess concept maps and provide to users a semantic dictionary of concepts categorized according to the structures of that cognitive model (Blitsas, Grigoriadou, & Mitsis, Chapter 6). A new 1st person approach, singular and plural, to educational research and practice is introduced and compared with the traditional 2nd/3rd-person education (Iran-Nejad & Stewart, Chapter 7). A study which validates a theoretical framework for identifying social and cognitive regulation strategies employed by students during the process of joint construction of meaning in cooperative tasks in a university's virtual learning environment is introduced next (López-Benavides & Alvarez Valdivia, Chapter 8). The last chapter of this part presents the new collaborative cognitive tools (CCT) for shared representations. The cognitive tools make a difference by providing a platform for collaborative construction of the school's information strategy with a shared vision and practice-oriented goals supporting its implementation (Orava & Silander, Chapter 9).

In Part III, new assessment methodologies and tools are introduced. The authors present an attempt to validate a computerized tool as it is used to measure evidence of critical thinking for individual participants in discussion forums (Corich, Kinshuk, & Jeffery, Chapter 10). A new integrated framework for assessing complex problem solving in digital game-based learning in the context of a longitudinal design-based research study is introduced next (Eseryel, Ifenthaler, & Ge, Chapter 11). The concept map based adaptive intelligent knowledge assessment system is described which compares a teacher's and a learner's concept map on the basis of graph patterns and assigns score for a submitted solution (Grundspenkis, Chapter 12). Two case studies are presented which show how ttechnologies support the assessment of complex learning in capstone units (McNeill, Chapter 13). Last, a graph-based approach to help learners with ongoing writing is introduced (Pirnay-Dummer & Ifenthaler, Chapter 14).

In Part IV, schooling and teaching perspectives are described and discussed. The authors compare the impact of electronic performance support and web-based training (Klein & Nguyen, Chapter 15). Concepts and applications for moving beyond teaching and learning into a human development paradigm are introduced next

(Reeb-Gruber, McCuddy, Parisot, & Rossi, Chapter 16). Preparation, experiences, and roles in technology implementation for leaders for the 21st Century are critically reviewed in the following chapter (Schrum, Galizio, English, & Ledesma, Chapter 17). A project which examines the impact of an instruction based on the technology, pedagogy, and content knowledge framework on podcasting and vodcasting for preservice teachers in the United States is presented next (Yamamoto, Chapter 18).

In Part V, chapters focus on virtual environments perspectives. The authors explore the degree to which individual learning styles affect pre-simulation attitudes toward teamwork and post-simulation perceptions of the value of the simulation as a learning experience among third-semester university-level participants in a large-scale telematic simulation (Ekker & Sutherland, Chapter 19). Effects of an online social annotation tool which was implemented in the context of utilizing question-answering tasks with reading documents in order to foster students' cognitive development with higher-order thinking, critical analysis, and development of sophisticated arguments in English writing are reported (Kim, Mendenhall, & Johnson, Chapter 20). The development of self-direction indicators for evaluating the e-learning course using students' self reflections with social software are discussed next (Pata & Merisalo, Chapter 21). The next chapter explores the use of the Internet to connect university students in equivalent classes across international borders, completing collaborative assignments requiring student-student virtual dialog and cross-cultural reflection (Poindexter, Amtmann, & Ferrarini, Chapter 22). Last, the virtual campus project ViCaDiS is introduced which facilitates a shift from Institutional Learning Environments towards Personal Learning Environments (Vasiu & Andone, Chapter 23).

This is the second edited volume to result from a CELDA conference. We are convinced that this work covers the current state of research, methodology, assessment, and technology. When we have so many outstanding papers as were presented in Freiburg, Germany 2008 and Rome, Italy 2009, we will certainly seek to also have future edited volumes, as this benefits the entire professional community.

Freiburg, Germany	Dirk Ifenthaler
Athabasca, AB, Canada	Kinshuk
Lisboa, Portugal	Pedro Isaías
Piraeus, Greece	Demetrios G. Sampson
Athens, Georgia	J. Michael Spector

Acknowledgements

We would like to acknowledge the vital role played by the International Association for Development of the Information Society (http://www.iadis.org) and for its continuing sponsorship of CELDA conferences. In addition, we owe our thanks to the over 150 international CELDA committee members for providing thoughtful reviews for all papers submitted to the CELDA 2009 conference. Finally, we owe special thanks to Springer Science-Business Media (http://www.springer.com/) and Marie Sheldon for agreeing to publish the best papers from CELDA 2009 in this edited volume.

Freiburg, Germany	Dirk Ifenthaler
Athabasca, AB, Canada	Kinshuk
Lisboa, Portugal	Pedro Isaías
Piraeus, Greece	Demetrios G. Sampson
Athens, Georgia	J. Michael Spector

Contents

1 **Learning to Solve Problems in the Digital Age: Introduction** 1
  J. Michael Spector and Kinshuk

Part I   Instructional Design Perspectives

2 **Investigating an Online Museum's Information System** 11
  Asmidah Alwi and Elspeth McKay

3 **MAPLET – A Framework for Matching Aims, Processes,
  Learner Expertise and Technologies** 23
  Maree Gosper

4 **Web-Based Learning Objects in School Education** 37
  Said Hadjerrouit

5 **KM and WEB 2.0 Methods for Project-Based Learning** 49
  Christine Michel and Élise Lavoué

Part II   Cognitive Perspectives

6 **Semandix: Constructing a Knowledge Base
  According to a Text Comprehension Model** 67
  Panagiotis Blitsas, Maria Grigoriadou, and Christos Mitsis

7 **First-Person Education and the Biofunctional Nature
  of Knowing, Understanding, and Affect** 89
  Asghar Iran-Nejad and William Stewart

8 **Socio-cognitive Regulation Strategies in Cooperative
  Learning Tasks in Virtual Contexts** 111
  Denisse Margoth López-Benavides
  and Ibis Marlene Alvarez-Valdivia

9 **Collaborative Cognitive Tools for Shared Representations** 127
  Jukka Orava and Pasi Silander

xi

Part III Assessment Perspectives

10 Automating the Measurement of Critical Thinking for Individuals Participating in Discussion Forums 143
Stephen Corich, Kinshuk, and Lynn Jeffrey

11 Alternative Assessment Strategies for Complex Problem Solving in Game-Based Learning Environments 159
Deniz Eseryel, Dirk Ifenthaler, and Xun Ge

12 Concept Map Based Intelligent Knowledge Assessment System: Experience of Development and Practical Use 179
Janis Grundspenkis

13 Technologies to Support the Assessment of Complex Learning in Capstone Units: Two Case Studies 199
Margot McNeill

14 Text-Guided Automated Self Assessment 217
Pablo Pirnay-Dummer and Dirk Ifenthaler

Part IV Schooling and Teaching Perspectives

15 Comparing the Impact of Electronic Performance Support and Web-Based Training 229
James D. Klein and Frank Nguyen

16 Moving Beyond Teaching and Learning into a Human Development Paradigm 243
Sandra Reeb-Gruber, Michael K. McCuddy, Xavier Parisot, and David Rossi

17 Leaders for the Twenty-First Century: Preparation, Experiences, and Roles in Technology Implementation 259
Lynne Schrum, Lyndsie M. Galizio, Mary C. English, and Patrick Ledesma

18 Pedagogy and Content Knowledge Based Podcasting Project for Preservice Teachers 273
Junko Yamamoto

Part V Virtual Environments Perspectives

19 Simulation-Games as a Learning Experience: An Analysis of Learning Style and Attitude 291
Janet Lynn Sutherland and Knut Ekker

20 Implementation of an Online Social Annotation Tool in a College English Course 313
Anne Mendenhall, Chanmin Kim, and Tristan E. Johnson

21	**Self-Direction Indicators for Evaluating the Design-Based Elearning Course with Social Software** 325
	Kai Pata and Sonja Merisalo
22	**Employing Virtual Collaborative Exchanges to Expand Global Awareness** 343
	Sandra Poindexter, Ray Amtmann, and Tawni Ferrarini
23	**Ideas and Concepts of ViCaDiS – A Virtual Learning Environment for Digital Students** 359
	Radu Vasiu and Diana Andone

Index 377

Contributors

Ibis Marlene Alvarez-Valdivia Universitat Autònoma de Barcelona, Barcelona, Spain, ibismarlene.alvarez@uab.cat

Asmidah Alwi School of Business IT and Logistics RMIT University, Melbourne 3000, VIC, Australia, asmidah.alwi@rmit.edu.au

Ray Amtmann Northern Michigan University, Marquette, MI, USA, ramtmann@nmu.edu

Diana Andone "Politechnica" University of Timisoara, Timisoara, Romania, diana.andone@cm.upt.ro

Panagiotis Blitsas I.P.G.S. in Basic & Applied Cognitive Science, National & Kapodistrian University of Athens, Panepistimiopolis, Athens, Greece, pblitsas@di.uoa.gr

Stephen Corich Eastern Institute of Technology Hawke's Bay, Napier, Taradale, New Zealand, scorich@eit.ac.nz

Knut Ekker Information Technology, Nord-Trondelag University College, Steinkjer, Norway, knut.ekker@hint.no

Mary C. English George Mason University, Fairfax, VA, USA, menglis2@gmu.edu

Deniz Eseryel College of Education, University of Oklahoma, Norman, OK, USA, eseryel@ou.edu

Tawni Ferrarini Northern Michigan University, Marquette, MI, USA, tferrari@nmu.edu

Lyndsie M. Galizio George Mason University, Fairfax, VA, USA, lgalizio@gmu.edu

Xun Ge University of Oklahoma, Norman, OK, USA, xge@ou.edu

Maree Gosper Learning and Teaching Centre, Macquarie University, Sydney, NSW, Australia, maree.gosper@mq.edu.au

Maria Grigoriadou I.P.G.S. in Basic & Applied Cognitive Science, National & Kapodistrian University of Athens, Panepistimiopolis, Athens, Greece, gregor@di.uoa.gr

Janis Grundspenkis Department of Systems Theory and Design, Faculty of Computer Science and Information Technology, Riga Technical University, Rīga, Latvia, janis.grundspenkis@cs.rtu.lv

Said Hadjerrouit University of Agder, Kristiansand, Norway, said.hadjerrouit@uia.no

Dirk Ifenthaler Albert-Ludwigs-University Freiburg, Freiburg, Germany, ifenthaler@ezw.uni-freiburg.de

Asghar Iran-Nejad The University of Alabama, Tuscaloosa, AL, USA, airannej@bamaed.ua.edu

Pedro Isaías Universidade Aberta, Lisboa, Portugal, pisaias@univ-ab.pt

Lynn Jeffrey Massey University, New Zealand, l.m.jeffrey@massey.ac.nz

Tristan E. Johnson Florida State University, Gainesville, FL, USA, tristanjohnson@gmail.com

Chanmin Kim University of Georgia, Athens, GA, USA, chanmin@uga.edu

Kinshuk University of Athabasca, Athabasca, AB, Canada, kinshuk@ieee.org

James D. Klein Arizona State University, Tempe, AZ, USA, james.klein@asu.edu

Élise Lavoué Equipe de recherche MAGELLAN, Université Jean Moulin Lyon 3, Lyon, Cedex 08, France, elise.lavoue@univ-lyon3.fr

Patrick Ledesma George Mason University, Fairfax, VA, USA, pledesm1@gmu.edu

Denisse Margoth López-Benavides Universitat Oberta de Catalunya, Barcelona, Catalonia, Spain, dlopezben@uoc.edu

Elspeth McKay School of Business IT and Logistics RMIT University, Melbourne 3000, VIC, Australia, elspeth.mckay@rmit.edu.au

Michael K. McCuddy Valparaiso University, Valparaiso, IN, USA, mike.mccuddy@valpo.edu

Margot McNeill Macquarie University, Sydney, NSW, Australia, margot.mcneill@mq.edu.au

Anne Mendenhall Department of Educational Psychology Learning System, Florida State University, Gainesville, FL, USA, anne.mendenhall@gmail.com

Sonja Merisalo Helsinki Metropolia University of Applied Sciences, Oulu, Finland, sonja.merisalo@metropolia.fi

Christine Michel Laboratoire LIESP, INSA-Lyon, Villeurbanne, France, christine.michel@insa-lyon.fr

Christos Mitsis University of Piraeus, Piraeus, Greece, mpsp09006@students.cs.unipi.gr

Frank Nguyen American Express, USA, frank@frankn.net

Jukka Orava Department of Education, Medical Center, Helsinki, Finland, jukka.orava@hel.fi

Xavier Parisot Champagne Graduate School of Management, Troyes, France, xavier.parisot@groupe-esc-troyes.com

Kai Pata Institute of Informatics, Tallinn University, Tallinn, Estonia, kpata@tlu.ee

Pablo Pirnay-Dummer Albert-Ludwigs-University Freiburg, Freiburg, Germany, pablo.dummer@ezw.uni-freiburg.de

Sandra Poindexter College of Business, Northern Michigan University, Marquette, MI, USA, spoindex@nmu.edu

Sandra Reeb-Gruber INHolland University of Applied Sciences, HB Hoofddorp, The Netherlands, sandra.reebgruber@inholland.nl

David Rossi Reims Champagne Ardenne University, Reims, France, david.rossi@univ-reims.fr

Demetrios G. Sampson Department of Technology in Education and Digital Systems, University of Piraeus, Piraeus, Greece, sampson@unipi.gr

Lynne Schrum George Mason University, Fairfax, VA, USA, lschrum@gmu.edu

Pasi Silander Department of Education, Medical Center, Helsinki, Finland, pasi.silander@hel.fi

J. Michael Spector University of Georgia, Athens, GA, USA, mspector@uga.edu

William Stewart The University of Alabama, Tuscaloosa, AL, USA, airannej@bamaed.ua.edu

Janet Lynn Sutherland English-Speaking Cultures, Languages and Literatures Faculty, University of Bremen, Bremen, Germany, jsuther@uni-bremen.de

Radu Vasiu "Politechnica" University of Timisoara, Timisoara, Romania, radu.vasiu@cm.upt.ro

Junko Yamamoto Slippery Rock University of Pennsylvania, Slippery Rock, PA, USA, junko.yamamoto@sru.edu

Reviewers

Maiga Chang Athabasca University, Canada, maigac@athabascau.ca

Nian-Shing Chen National Central University, Taiwan, nianshing@gmail.com

Jon Dron Athabasca University, Canada, jond@athabascau.ca

Andrew S. Gibbons Brigham Young University, USA, andy_gibbons@byu.edu

Richard Huntrods Athabasca University, Canada, huntrods@athabascau.ca

Dirk Ifenthaler Albert-Ludwigs-University Freiburg, Freiburg, Germany, ifenthaler@ezw.uni-freiburg.de

Pedro Isaías Universidade Aberta, Portugal, pisaias@univ-ab.pt

Tristan E. Johnson Florida State University, Tallahassee, FL, USA, tjohnson@lsi.fsu.edu

Vani Kalloo University of West Indies, Trinidad, vanikalloo@gmail.com

Haralambos Karagiannidis University of Thessaly, Greece, karagian@uth.gr

Kinshuk Athabasca University, Athabasca, AB, Canada, kinshuk@ieee.org

Vive Kumar Athabasca University, Canada, vive@athabascau.ca

Tzu-Chien Liu National Central University, Taiwan, ltc@cc.ncu.edu.tw

Barbara B. Lockee VirginiaTech, USA, lockeebb@vt.edu

Flavio Manganello Università Politecnica delle Marche, Italy, blueflavio@gmail.com

Foteini Paraskeva University of Piraeus, Greece, fparaske@unipi.gr

Demetrios G. Sampson Department of Technology in Education and Digital Systems, University of Piraeus, Piraeus, Greece, sampson@unipi.gr

Rustam Shadiev National Central University, Taiwan, rshadiev@cl.ncu.edu.tw

J. Michael Spector University of Georgia, Athens, GA, USA, mspector@uga.edu

Jie Chi Yang National Central University, Taiwan, yang@cl.ncu.edu.tw

Chapter 1
Learning to Solve Problems in the Digital Age: Introduction

J. Michael Spector and Kinshuk

Abstract This chapter addresses the nature of problem solving in general, how cognitive psychologists believe that problem solving expertise develops, new issues in problem solving that have risen with new information and communication technologies, and some specific technologies and tools that can support the development of problem solving expertise. The chapter concludes with remarks about thorny issues that inhibit progress and mention some things to consider in the future.

Keywords Complexity · Distributed knowledge · Expertise development · Problem solving · Technology affordances

1 Context

The International Association for Development of the Internet Society (IADIS; see http://www.iadisportal.org/) has been sponsoring the International Conference on Cognition and Exploratory Learning in the Digital Age (CELDA) since 2004. Each CELDA conference has focused on issues that arise at the intersection of cognitive psychology and educational computing. There are many issues involved in making effective use of new technologies in learning and instruction (e.g., designing highly engaging online environments, developing mobile learning resources, providing automated personalized feedback, etc.).

Of particular interest at CELDA 2009 was the issue of problem solving in the digital age. Nearly all of the 116 CELDA 2009 papers addressed some aspect of problem solving, as the 22 expanded papers collected in this volume amply illustrate. It is worthwhile to distinguish technologies that support problem solving from technologies that create new problem solving challenges. Most of the papers presented at CELDA 2009, including those collected herein, focused on technologies that promote or enhance problem solving in one way or another. However,

J.M. Spector (✉)
University of Georgia, 611B Aderhold Hall, Athens, GA, USA
e-mail: mspector@uga.edu

D. Ifenthaler et al. (eds.), *Multiple Perspectives on Problem Solving and Learning in the Digital Age*, DOI 10.1007/978-1-4419-7612-3_1,
© Springer Science+Business Media, LLC 2011

technologies have resulted in new problem solving challenges, such as how to find and validate relevant information or how to collaborate effectively with remotely located team members in developing solutions to challenging problems.

In this introductory chapter, we address: (a) the nature of problem solving in general, (b) how cognitive psychologists believe that problem solving expertise develops, (c) new issues in problem solving that have arisen with new information and communication technologies, and (d) some specific technologies and tools that can support the development of problem solving expertise. We conclude with remarks about thorny issues that inhibit progress and mention some things to consider in the future (Dörner, 1996; Salas & Klein, 2001; Rittel & Webber, 1984). Our focus throughout is on complex problems – that is to say, problems that are somewhat ill-structured and known to be particularly challenging for a variety of people with varying levels of prior knowledge and experience. Ill-structured problems are those that are not completely defined – that is to say that there is vague or missing or changing information pertaining to the current state of affairs, desired outcomes, and relevant transformations or procedures (Klein, 1998). It is our belief that educators and instructional technologists already understand how best to support learning relatively simple, well-structured problems where relevant information is completely specified, relevant transformations/procedures are straightforward, and the desired outcomes are clear and operationally specified.

2 Problem Solving

What is the nature of problem solving? The mathematician, George Polya (1945) said that problem solving was a practical skill that was fairly general, that could be learned, and that consisted of four phases or principles: (a) understand the problem (the goal, what is known, what is not known), (b) devise a plan or solution approach, (c) implement the plan and confirm correctness of the implementation, and (d) examine the solution, confirm the result, and consider whether alternate solutions are possible.

One might think that Polya's (1945) seminal work on problem solving is out of date and less relevant today than it was 65 years ago. One could look further back, however, and find Descartes' *Discourse on the Method of Rightly Conducting the Reason and Seeking for Truth in the Sciences* published in 1637 and find quite complementary principles (e.g., avoid haste and prejudice, divide up difficulties, commence with simple problems, and make enumerations that are complete and general). More recently, Jonassen (2004) has developed a taxonomy of problem classes ranging from analogies to dilemmas, along with different instructional approaches appropriate for different kinds of problems. These scholars, and many others (e.g., Brown & Walter, 1983; Dewey, 1933; Newell & Simon, 1972; Tuma & Reif, 1980; van Merriënboer & Kirschner, 2007) believe that there are general problem solving methods that can and should be learned. Others (Ericsson, 2001; Ericsson & Smith, 1991) argue that problem solving skills and strategies are highly domain specific and contextually sensitive. As with many things, the truth is likely somewhere in between the notions that all problem solving skills are domain specific and problem solving skills are generally applicable across a broad set of problems and problem classes. We proceed on that middle ground, especially because it provides an opportunity to assess the progressive development of problem solving expertise.

3 Developing Problem Solving Expertise

People do develop expertise in solving complex problems in a variety of domains. In many cases, such expertise is recognized by a professional community in the form of special credentials and awards. In addition, an individual who has many successfully solved problems to his or her credit becomes known within a professional community and becomes one of a select few who are sought out when especially challenging problems arise. Evidence of resorting to experts when facing a complex problem can be found in many different domains, including the judicial system (e.g., expert witnesses), corporate management (e.g., consultants), engineering design, government agencies (e.g., the National Transportation Safety Board), among many others. Expert problem solvers do exist and many are formally recognized in many different domains.

How did these people become experts? How can experts be formally identified? Can expertise be measured? These questions are of critical concern to the educational research community. Formal education is aimed at developing expertise, among other things. Let's briefly examine these questions before looking at problem solving in the digital age.

Ericsson (2001) argues that expertise is developed by a long period of focused and disciplined practice (see also Ericsson & Smith, 1991). Typically, those who attain the highest levels of performance in a domain have spent more than 10 years practicing and refining their skills on a daily basis – often more than four hours a day. Such a long period of deliberate practice is not within the feasible support of very many educational organizations. Indeed, Ericsson is primarily concerned only with the highest levels of performance. Educational institutions are more reasonably concerned with the development of competence and proficiency (see Dreyfus & Dreyfus, 1986). Still, it is a well-established finding in instructional design research that *time-on-task* or *engaged-time* is a strong predictor of learning (see, for example, Berliner, 1991; Thorndike, 1913).

Given that there is limited time in an educational program, what sorts of activities are likely to contribute to the efficient development of expertise? Milrad, Spector, & Davidsen (2003) argue that a program that begins with orientation to problems followed with structured inquiry-based explorations and concluding with policy development activities is a general framework that works in many different contexts. The framework is called model-facilitated learning and embraces the notion of graduated complexity – that is to say that problems should be realistic and genuine but new learners should be presented less complex problems than more advanced learners. This notion is consistent with cognitive apprenticeship (Collins, Brown, & Newman, 1987). Model-facilitated learning makes problem solving central to the overall process of developing expertise. Problem centered instructional models are also advocated by Merrill (2002), Seel (2003; see also Spector, 2004), and van

Merriënboer and Kirschner (2007). In short, instructional designers generally argue that problem solving expertise can be developed by having learners solve problems – lots of problems, problems that are authentic and similar in nature to what can be expected to be encountered after instruction, and problems that are increasingly challenging and difficult.

There is such wide agreement on this that we will not belabor it further. However, we would like to point out that these and other instructional design frameworks and models can and should be tested. That is to say, these models in general make the claim that a particular form or series of interventions will contribute to the development of expertise. How can such claims be confirmed or refuted? In order to validate these models, what is needed are stable and reliable measures of expertise. In short, we need the means to formally identify and measure expertise. It is not sufficient for educational purposes to follow the Ericsson method of using such credentials as Grand Master Chess Player or Olympic Athlete as measures of expertise. Educators need to develop measures that can be used in a curriculum context to provide formative and summative feedback to learners and program managers.

How to assess the progressive development of expertise is a core concern in instructional design research. This area of investigation is still in its infancy. When the targeted domain involves complex and ill-structured problems, it is clear that knowledge measures alone are not adequate, although they do provide an initial indicator. Performance measures are also problematic as the problems in complex and ill-structured domains can vary a great deal. Demonstration of competent or proficient performance on a particular ill-structured problem may not predict performance on other problems due to inherent differences and the nature of problem solving in real world (Dörner, 1996; Klein, 1998). This is the problem of transfer, generally stated.

It would seem that what is needed is a way to gain access to how experts think about a variety of problem situations and then use that information to assess how less experienced persons are thinking about the same problem situations. In other words, a cognitive measure of expertise is needed to supplement knowledge-based and performance-based tests. This cognitive measure can be accomplished by eliciting a representation of how an expert conceptualizes the problem space and using that as a basis of comparison with how a less experienced person conceptualizes the same problem space. Such a representation can be elicited by asking for the following information when presenting a problem scenario: (a) what are the key factors to consider when developing a solution, (b) briefly describe those factors, (c) indicate how these factors are interrelated, and (d) describe the nature of those relationships (Spector & Koszalka, 2004). After taking a look at problem solving in the digital era, we will discuss a suite of tools that can accomplish this form of measurement.

4 Problem Solving in the Digital Age

Some might be inclined to argue that problem solving has becoming simpler in the digital age. This is not our view. Rather, we are inclined to agree with Dijkstra

(1972) that information and communications technologies have introduced new and challenging problems – namely, learning how to make effective use of these technologies. This is especially true in the world of education.

While it is tempting to point out, for example, that digital repositories and warehouses provide a one-stop place to store and retrieve information on a just-in-time, just-in-need basis, one also finds new dilemmas in the vast information available on the Web. First, there is the challenge of finding exactly what one is seeking in an efficient manner. It is true that search engines have become powerful and sophisticated. However, the amount of information that can be searched has grown significantly over the years. Second, once one does find what appears to be what was sought, there is the issue of verifying that information. Is the source reliable? Is there a way to corroborate the information? One is then likely to conduct still more searches. Third, because there is so much information readily available, when one might have only considered one or two solution approaches to a particular complex problem, the number of apparently possible alternatives to a challenging problem tends to increase dramatically. This creates a new burden on the problem solver – namely, the problem of evaluating the alternative solution approaches that now appear feasible.

We close this section with a final issue, although there are many more challenges that result from the digitization of our universe. When technology is involved in a solution approach, what considerations are relevant for the effective integration of that technology in an ongoing and effective manner over a sustained period of time. We mention this issue because all too often designers and developers will fixate on a particular technology without considering the implications for training the workforce, for transitioning to a new technology, for planning for the next generation of that technology or a subsequent technology, and so on. In short, the human dimension of integrating technologies into problem solutions is a particularly *wicked* problem (Rittel & Webber, 1984; see also Bransford et al., 2000; Fredrickson, 1984).

5 Tools and Technologies

While we believe that technology is indeed a part of many complex and challenging problems that one encounters these days, we also believe that technology can often be part of a solution. With regard to the development of expertise, it is well established that technology can be used to generate many realistic problem solving scenarios and interactive simulations to help learners gain competence and confidence (Dörner, 1996; van Merriënboer & Sweller, 2005). Technology can also provide the means to assess the progressive development of expertise. A suite of Web-based tools called HIMATT (Highly Interactive Model-based Assessment Tools and Technologies; Pirnay-Dummer, Ifenthaler, & Spector, 2010) can elicit problem conceptualizations in response to problem scenarios, either in the form of open text or annotated concept maps. HIMATT can also generate measures of relative expertise in near real-time. These measures can help individual learners see how they are doing and suggest where they might focus their efforts; in that way, such dynamic, formative assessments help learners develop their meta-cognitive skills.

Such measures can help instructional designers identify learning activities that are not particularly helpful for learners. Moreover, such measures can in principle be used to dynamically generate new learning activities, although this aspect of the measures has yet to be realized.

Indeed, technology has great potential to support the mass personalization of learning and instruction (Kalyuga & Sweller, 2005; Kinshuk, Lin, & Patel, 2005). It is now possible for a typical learning management system to create dynamic individual profiles of learners. These profiles can contain relatively stable information such as demographic information (date of birth, native language, etc.) and cognitive traits (working memory capacity, inductive reasoning ability, information processing speed, and associative learning skill) (see, for example, Graf, Liu, Kinshuk, Chen, & Yang, 2009; Kinshuk, Lin, & McNabb, 2006), and highly dynamic and real-time information such as learner's location, context and environment (see Graf et al., 2008), along with information about courses taken, lessons completed, artifacts created, and much more.

Technology provides us these two important tools – the ability to assess the progressive development of problem-solving expertise, and the ability to personalize instruction and select appropriate and meaningful problems using relevant cognitive traits, learning preferences and learning histories.

6 Concluding Remarks

In conclusion, we believe that we only scratched the surface with regard to making effective use of technology to promote the development of problem solving expertise in the digital age. There is a great deal yet to be done. This is true in the short-term with regard to further development of promising tools and technologies such as those discussed above, and it is true in the long-term when we try to envision the kinds of problems that should be the focus of our collective attention as educational researchers and developers. What we have learned thus far is basically that we have a far distance yet to travel when it comes to promoting the development of problem solving skills. Progress in this area can occur. Such conferences as CELDA can promote progress. Such books as this might also promote progress. Ultimately, it is teachers, trainers, educational researchers, and policy makers who will foster sustained progress (or not). We hope this work is a nudge in the right direction.

References

Berliner, D. (1991). What's all the fuss about instructional time? In M. Ben-Peretz & R. Bromme (Eds.), *The nature of time in schools: Theoretical concepts, practitioner perceptions*. New York: Teachers College Press. Retrieved October 14, 2010, from http://courses.ed.asu.edu/berliner/readings/fuss/fuss.htm

Bransford, J. D., Brown, A. L., Cocking, R. R. (Eds.). (2000). *How people learn: Brain, mind experience, and school*. Washington, DC: National Academy Press.

Brown, S. I., & Walter, M. I. (1983). *The art of problem posing*. Hillsdale, NJ: Erlbaum.
Collins, A., Brown, J. S., & Newman, S. E. (1987). *Cognitive apprenticeship: Teaching the craft of reading, writing and mathematics* (Technical Report No. 403). Cambridge, MA: BBN Laboratories. Centre for the Study of Reading, University of Illinois.
Descartes, R. (1637). *Discourse on the method of rightly conducting the reason, and seeking truth in the sciences* [Published in The Harvard classics series edited by C. W. Eliot]. New York: Collier & Son.
Dewey, J. (1933). *How we think: A restatement of the relation of reflective thinking to the educative process*. Boston, MA: Heath.
Dijkstra, E. W. (1972). The humble programmer. *Communications of the ACM, 15*(10), 859–866.
Dörner, D. (1996). *The logic of failure: Why things go wrong and what we can do to make them right* (R. Kimber & R. Kimber, Trans.). New York: Metropolitan Books.
Dreyfus, H. L., & Dreyfus, S. E. (1986). *Mind over machine: The power of human intuition and expertise in the era of the computer*. New York: Free Press.
Ericsson, K. A. (2001). Attaining excellence through deliberate practice: Insights from the study of expert performance. In M. Ferrari (Ed.), *The pursuit of excellence in* education (pp. 21–55). Mahway, NJ: Erlbaum.
Ericsson, K. A., & Smith, J. (Eds.). (1991). *Toward a general theory of expertise: Prospects and limits*. New York: Cambridge University Press.
Frederiksen, N. (1984). Implications of cognitive theory for instruction in problem solving. *Review of Educational Research, 54*, 363–407.
Graf, S., Liu, T.-C., Kinshuk, Chen, N.-S., & Yang, S. J. H. (2009). Learning styles and cognitive traits: Their relationship and its benefits in Web-based educational systems. *Computers in Human Behavior, 25*(6), 1280–1289.
Graf, S., MacCallum, K., Liu, T.-C., Chang, M., Wen, D., Tan, Q., et al. (2008). An infrastructure for developing pervasive learning environments. *Proceedings of the 6th Annual IEEE International Conference on Pervasive Computing and Communications*, Los Alamitos, CA, IEEE Computer Society, 389–394.
Jonassen, D. H. (2004). *Learning to solve problems: An instructional design guide*. San Francisco: Pfeiffer.
Kalyuga, S. & Sweller, J. (2005). Rapid dynamic assessment of expertise to improve the efficiency of adaptive e-learning. *Educational Technology Research and Development, 53*, 83–93.
Kinshuk, Lin, T., & McNab, P. (2006). Cognitive trait modelling: The case of inductive reasoning ability. *Innovations in Education and Teaching International, 43*(2), 151–161.
Kinshuk, Lin, T., & Patel, A. (2005). Supporting the mobility and the adaptivity of knowledge objects by cognitive trait model. In J. M. Spector, C. Ohrzada, A. Van Schaack, & D. Wiley (Eds.), *Innovations in instructional technology: Essays in honor of M. David Merrill* (pp. 29–41). Mahwah, NJ: Lawrence Erlbaum.
Klein, G. A. (1998). *Sources of power: How people make decisions*. Cambridge, MA: MIT Press.
Merrill, M. D. (2002). First principles of instruction. *Educational Technology Research and Development, 50*(3), 43–59.
Milrad, M., Spector, J. M., & Davidsen, P. I. (2003). Model facilitated learning. In S. Naidu (Ed.), *Learning and teaching with technology: Principles and practices* (pp. 13–27). London: Kogan Page.
Newell, A., & Simon, H. A. (1972). *Human problem solving*. Englewood Cliffs, NJ: Prentice Hall.
Pirnay-Dummer, P., Ifenthaler, D., & Spector, J. M. (2010). Highly integrated model assessment technology and tools. *Educational Technology Research and Development, 58*(1), 3–18.
Polya, G. (1945). *How to solve it*. Princeton, NJ: Princeton University Press.
Rittel, H., & Webber, M. (1984). Dilemmas in a general theory of planning. *Policy Sciences, 4*, 155–169.
Salas, E., & Klein, G. A. (Eds.). (2001). *Linking expertise and naturalistic decision making*. Mahwah, NJ: Erlbaum.

Seel, N. M. (2003). Model-centered learning environments. *Technology, Instruction, Cognition, and Learning, 1*(3), 242–251.
Spector, J. M. (2004). Problems with problem-based learning: Comments on model-centered learning and instruction in Seel (2003). *Technology, Instruction, Cognition and Learning, 1*(4), 359–374.
Spector, J. M., & Koszalka, T. A. (2004). *The DEEP methodology for assessing learning in complex domains* (Final report to the National Science Foundation Evaluative Research and Evaluation Capacity Building). Syracuse, NY: Syracuse University.
Thorndike, E. L. (1913). *Educational psychology: The psychology of learning* (Vol. 2). New York: Teachers College.
Tuma, D., & Reif, F. (1980). *Problem solving and education*. Hillsdale, NJ: Erlbaum.
van Merriënboer, J., & Sweller, J. (2005). Cognitive load theory and complex learning: Recent developments and future directions. *Educational Psychology Review, 17*, 147–177.
van Merriënboer, J. J. G., & Kirschner, P. A. (2007). *Ten steps to complex learning*. Mahwah, NJ: Erlbaum.

Part I
Instructional Design Perspectives

Chapter 2
Investigating an Online Museum's Information System

Instructional Design for Effective Human-Computer Interaction

Asmidah Alwi and Elspeth McKay

Abstract Information and communications technology (ICT) tools have completely altered the way museum curators design many of their exhibits. The literature reveals many interesting studies, which explain the unique nature and characteristics of the Web-based environment, to provide many educational advantages. As a consequence, online learning is now an important agenda for many museums. They have become learning institutions in their own right as they enhance their exhibits to leverage the opportunities offered by ICT tools; thereby providing a wider (cognitive) thinking space for their online visitors. Although the role of museums in supporting the formal education of the general population is usually associated with visits to a physical museum, the online museum environment is now playing an important part in providing more information to people, as well as further enriching their life-long learning experiences. Nevertheless not enough is known about the educational effectiveness of online-museum exhibits. This paper describes a doctoral project, underway in Australia that examines the human-computer interaction (HCI) which occurs when people access online museum exhibits.

Keywords Instructional design · Instructional architecture · Web-based learning · Cognitive preferences · Human-computer interaction · Online museums

1 Introduction

The Web-based technologies offer opportunities to enhance the design of online learning environments. As a result, many museums around the world are now adopting information and communications technology (ICT) tools that emphasize the use

---

A. Alwi (✉)
School of Business IT and Logistics RMIT University, Building 108, Level 17, 239 Bourke St, Melbourne, 3000 VIC, Australia
e-mail: asmidah.alwi@rmit.edu.au

of Web-based multimedia to enrich and fulfil their visitors' learning experiences. Nevertheless, awareness of the complexities of human-computer interaction (HCI) presents a new dilemma that challenges the design and development of museums' online learning systems. As tempting as they are, the adoption of these emerging ICT tools for displaying a museum's exhibits needs to align with appropriate instructional strategies to ensure the effectiveness of their visitors' learning experiences. This concept underpins a doctoral research project underway in Australia that is investigating the interactive effects of a museum's online exhibits with students' cognitive style preferences on their participation outcomes.

It is reasonably well known that the teaching style will influence a learner's experience and level of engagement with their subject content (Anderson & Elloumi, 2004). To ensure that online-learning promotes enhanced learning experiences, instructional strategies are needed to differentiate between the 'approach' or 'view' of the online-activities and the supporting instructional architecture. Taking a passive/absorption approach will work best in some circumstances, while at other times there is a need for more interactivity. According to Clark (2003):

The absorption view-of-learning requires clarity about the difference between learning and instruction. Learning in this view, is about assimilating information; while instruction is about providing information to learners. Some call this approach to learning design, a transmission-view of teaching (Mayer, 2001). Courses that rely on lectures or videotapes to transmit information generally reflect this view.

The behavioral view-of-learning was promoted in the first part of the 20th Century. Behavioral psychology promoted a different view: one that considered learning to be based on the acquisition of mental associations. This view-of-learning is about correct responses to questions and instruction; providing small chunks of information followed by questions and corrective feedback. In the process of making many small correct responses, learners generally build large (memory) chains of new knowledge. To promote mental wellbeing this type of behavioral-view can be reflected in programmed instruction.

The cognitive view-of-learning has developed in the last part of the 20th Century, when learning was again re-conceptualized (McKay, 2008). This time, the emphasis concentrates on the active processes learners use to construct new knowledge; construction of this kind requires an integration of new incoming information from the environment with existing knowledge held in a person's memory. In the cognitive-view, learning is about active construction of new knowledge by interacting with new information, while instruction is about promoting the psychological processes that mediate that type of knowledge construction. It is very important in this approach to encourage the student with an apprehension to online instruction (McKay, 2008), to build upon their individuality and enable them to wander around the learning materials at their own pace.

It is essential however to differentiate between the type of learning and the technical means or instructional architecture to support it. Take for example the analogy of designing specifications for building a house. In this scenario there is an overarching purpose to provide specific prescriptions for the building process. When building a family home, we create different rooms for different purposes:

kitchens for our cooking, bathrooms for cleaning our body, and bedrooms for sleeping. Similarly we can describe experiential learning environments, by concentrating on the type of cognitive activities required by a learner to develop knowledge and skills. Although the active construction of knowledge is commonly accepted today as the mechanism for learning, that construction can be fostered through four diverse instructional environments: receptive, directive, guided-discovery, and exploratory (Clark, 2003). Each of these unique instructional architectures reflects different 'views' or 'approaches' to the learning context. They also require different instructional prescriptions to enhance the effectiveness of their particular instructional architecture (McKay, 2008).

- *Receptive architecture*: supports a transmission-view of learning, which is characterized by an emphasis on providing information for a learner. For online museum exhibits this screen-based information may be in the form of words and pictures that are both still and animated. A good metaphor for the receptive architecture is that the learner is a sponge and the instructional strategy pours out knowledge to be absorbed by the receiving learner. In some forms of receptive instruction, such as lectures or video-lessons; learners have minimal control over the pacing or sequencing of their learning environment. In other situations such as a text assignment, learners control the pace and can select the topics in the book of interest to them. Some examples of this architecture include a traditional (non-interactive) lecture, an instructional video, or a text assignment. Sadly, many online/eLearning programmes, which are known as 'page turners', lack interactivity. As such there is no corrective feedback given to the learner. For the student who may feel a little cognitively-fragile, this ability to revisit the instructional content many times (in the privacy afforded by working alone) may be beneficial.
- *Directive architecture*: supports a behavioral-view of learning. The assumption is that learning occurs by the gradual building of skills starting from the most basic and progressing to more advanced levels in a hierarchical manner. The online-lessons should be presented in small chunks of knowledge, providing frequent opportunities for learners to respond to related questions. Immediate corrective feedback should be used to ensure that accurate associations are made. The goal is to minimize the aversive consequences of the learner making errors that may promote incorrect associations. Programmed instruction that was popular in the 1950s and 1960s is a prime example of directive architecture. Such lessons were presented in books originally; with the advent of ICT tools, they migrated to a computerized delivery.
- *Guided-discovery architecture*: using job-realistic problems to drive the learning process, learners typically access various sources of data to resolve problems and receive the instructional support (sometimes called scaffolding) that is available to help them. Unlike the directive architecture, guided-discovery offers learners the opportunities to try alternatives, make mistakes, experience consequences of those mistakes, reflect on their results, and revise their approach. The goal of

guided- discovery is to promote construction of mental models by helping learners experience the results of decisions made in the context of solving realistic cases and problems. Guided-discovery designs are based on inductive models of learning; that is, learning of concepts and principles from experience with specific cases and problems.

- *Exploratory architecture*: also known as open-ended learning, the exploratory architectures rely on a cognitive-view of learning. Clark (2003) identified that out of these four instructional architectures, the exploratory models offer the most effective opportunities for providing high levels of learner control. Instruction should therefore be designed to provide a rich set of instructional/learning resources including: learning content, examples, demonstrations, and knowledge/skills building exercises that are complete with the means to navigate the materials. Architectures of this type are frequently used for online-courseware.

2 Online-Museums

Web-based museum exhibits that are designed to enhance the public's information and knowledge have been found to be extremely successful. For example, Museum Victoria in their 2007–2008 annual report records a triple number of online visits compared to the number of their physical visits. This report also shows a doubled increase in the number of visitations to their 'Discovery Program' compared to the previous year. Another example is Virtual Museum of Canada (VMC) that records millions of visits each year as listed in their website. With such an outstanding result, the potential to promote this type of online-learning environment has become important agenda for many museums around the world (Copeland, 2006). As the virtual museum users/visitors emanate from the formal educational sector (Peacock, Tait, & Timpson, 2009), museum curators need to be mindful of how to present their exhibits to afford effective learning experiences.

The rush towards creating online-museums presents fresh dilemmas and challenges for museum curators and their exhibit designers (Brown, 2006; Marty, 2004; Soren, 2005). As a consequence, they require a deeper understanding of how people interact with the Internet. According to McKay (2003) there are critical design factors which should be in place to ensure effective learning takes place with Web-mediated instructional materials. The HCI literature looks into this dilemma (Elsom-Cook, 2001; Sharp, Rogers, & Preece, 2007). These researchers examine human mental models, describing how human beings process their information. Such research into cognitive ability provides a rich collection of very detailed information and knowledge about how to improve the educational technology design process (Elsom-Cook, 2001).

In general, museums design their interactive exhibits for a broad range of visitors. Instead of seeing how to cater for a diverse number of participants, the literature emphasizes a more formal educational view of such participatory museum visits. Hence, to set the scope for this research the participants will be school students in a specified age range. The principal aim of this doctoral project, (which is underway in Australia at the time of writing), is to investigate the effectiveness of the museum's exhibit information systems interfaces (ISIs), for enhancing school students' cognitive performances. The main objective of the research is to consider how differently human beings process their Web-mediated learning experiences by investigating the online-instructional-strategies implemented as ISIs for the museum exhibits.

2.1 Preparing the Cognitive Space in Online Exhibits

The literature shows that there is previous work relating to the museum context that recognizes the online-environment as a 'cognitive space' in which a museum operates to deliver pertinent information and exhibit their artifacts. This new online-role has also been highlighted in the definition of emerging museum roles as defined by the Museums Australia Constitution in 2002. Historically, the use of ICT tools to enhance the museum learning experience started in the early 1990s. Back then, the potential of interactivity and multimedia were well considered (Schweibenz, 1998) and embedded in the delivery mode of the museum's exhibitions (Witcomb, 2007). Even as the role of museums grow with the advent of their ICT exhibiting tools, we see museums only taking advantage of these tools to merely record their collections in electronic databases or to embed the exhibition itself as an ICT artifact. Instead, we suggest that museums can play a more important role in facilitating the process of learning through the use of the newest Web-mediated ICT media tools which offer new learning opportunities (McKay, 2003).

2.2 Considering Learners' Differences

The differences in human cognitive preferences, which some people call learning styles, are well acknowledged. For instance, Kolb's theory is well known as an example that considers learning styles to assist in the design of museum learning experiences. According to Kolb's theory, there are four learning styles: the divergers who are the 'why' people, the assimilators who are concerned with the 'what,' the convergers who are more interested in the 'how,' and the accommodators who are concerned about 'what happens' (Black, 2005). It is possible to see the characteristics of this model reflected through the various exhibit designs that museums make when constructing their visitors' learning experiences. Taking a generic approach such as this to their instructional decisions is understandable as it is very difficult to design one instructional programme to suit everybody (Schaller & Allison-Bunnell, 2003; Schaller, Borun, Allison-Bunnell, & Chambers, 2007).

The way learners process their information depends upon their individual mental model. Often the discussions in the literature are based on the differences between human cognitive preferences. Others indicate that information representation can be designed in two ways: for instruction (delivery) or for learning (knowledge acquisition) (Berry, 2000; Mayer & Moreno, 2002). Mayer and Moreno (2002) assert that if the learning goal is to promote knowledge construction/acquisition, then the design process should take the cognitive-view rather than an information-delivery-view. Hence the way information is presented to the learner should not only deliver the information but should be designed in such a manner to help the learner to process the information in meaningful ways (Berry, 2000; Inglis, Ling, & Joosten, 1999; Mayer & Moreno, 2002) depending on an individual's mental (information processing) model.

2.3 Cognitive Style Construct

There is a vast amount of literature that discusses the differences in how human beings process information. Cognitive style is understood to be an individual's preferred and habitual approach to organizing and representing information. Measurement of an individual's relative right/left hemisphere performance and their cognitive style dominance has been a target of researchers from several disciplines over the last decade.

Table 2.1 Well known research terms for humans' processing information (McKay, 2000)

Terms describing cognitive differences	Researchers
Levellers-Sharpeners	Holzman and Klein (1954)
Field dependence-Field independence	Witkin, Dyke, Patterson, Goodman and Kemp (1962)
Impulsive-Reflective	Kagan (1965)
Divergers-Convergers	Guilford (1967)
Holists-Serialists	Pask and Scott (1972)
Wholist-Analytic	Riding and Cheema (1991)

Over the years, various terms have been used by other well known researchers to describe the same cognitive (learning) strategies (Table 2.1), into which Riding and Cheema (1991) were able to condense the earlier researchers' style constructs into two families (dimensions) of cognitive style, which Riding called Verbal-Imagery and Wholist-Analytic (Fig. 2.1). The latter describes the way an individual processes the information they receive for recall purposes, while Riding maintains that the Verbal-Imagery dimension represents the information representation strategy an individual may use during thinking. According to Riding, this choice will differ according to the task at hand.

Attempting to address the issues discussed earlier highlights the need for further investigation of the interaction between the effects of learners' cognitive preferences and information representation formats to help to untangle and understand the likely educational outcomes from museum visits. The following conceptual research framework is underway to accommodate the online-museum's instructional strategies (Fig. 2.2).

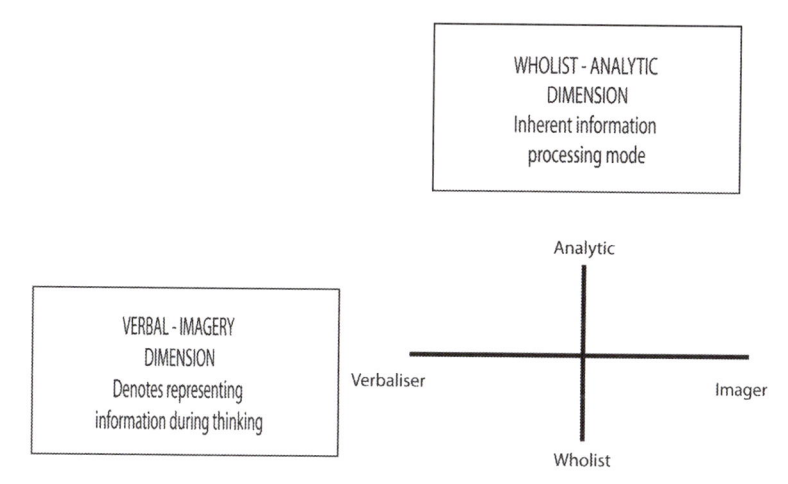

Fig. 2.1 Cognitive styles construct (Riding & Cheema 1991)

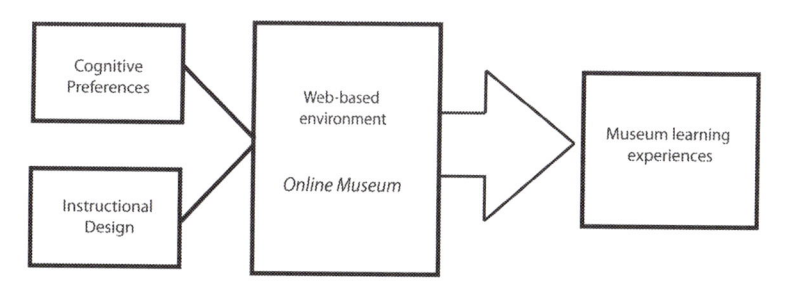

Fig. 2.2 Conceptual research design model

Based on this conceptual framework, this doctoral research aims to investigate how the different instructional strategies adopted by ISIs may facilitate online-museum learning experiences for both cognitive preferences (on the Riding's Verbal and Imagery dimension). It is anticipated that learners' cognitive preferences and the way an exhibit's information is represented may affect the learning experiences in a Web-based environment. We are suggesting that the learning experiences derived from an online-museum may provide a predictable measure of the instructional outcomes, thus providing the much needed finer details to inform the design and development of effective online-museum learning experiences.

3 Experimental Design

We employ a quasi-experimental design and the research will be informed by two independent variables: the ISI media access, which is the information representation formats (online- and physical-museum), and an individual's personal cognitive preference (Verbal-Imagery). A three-phase experimental design will be carried out. The first phase involves a screening test to measure cognitive style using the Cognitive Styles Analysis (CSA) tool, devised by Riding (1991), followed by a pre-test to determine the participant's prior domain knowledge portrayed by the museum exhibits. Based on the CSA ratio, which identifies cognitive style preferences (Verbal-Imagery and Wholist-Analytic), participants will be divided into two museum treatment groups (online or physical visit).

The second research phase will be the actual museum activities (visiting) period in which treatment groups will be given access to either the online-museum or the physical museum respectively. The final research phase will be a post-test to measure any improvement in the cognitive performance (or learning outcomes) derived from the museum's learning exhibits. The experimental design is illustrated in Fig. 2.3.

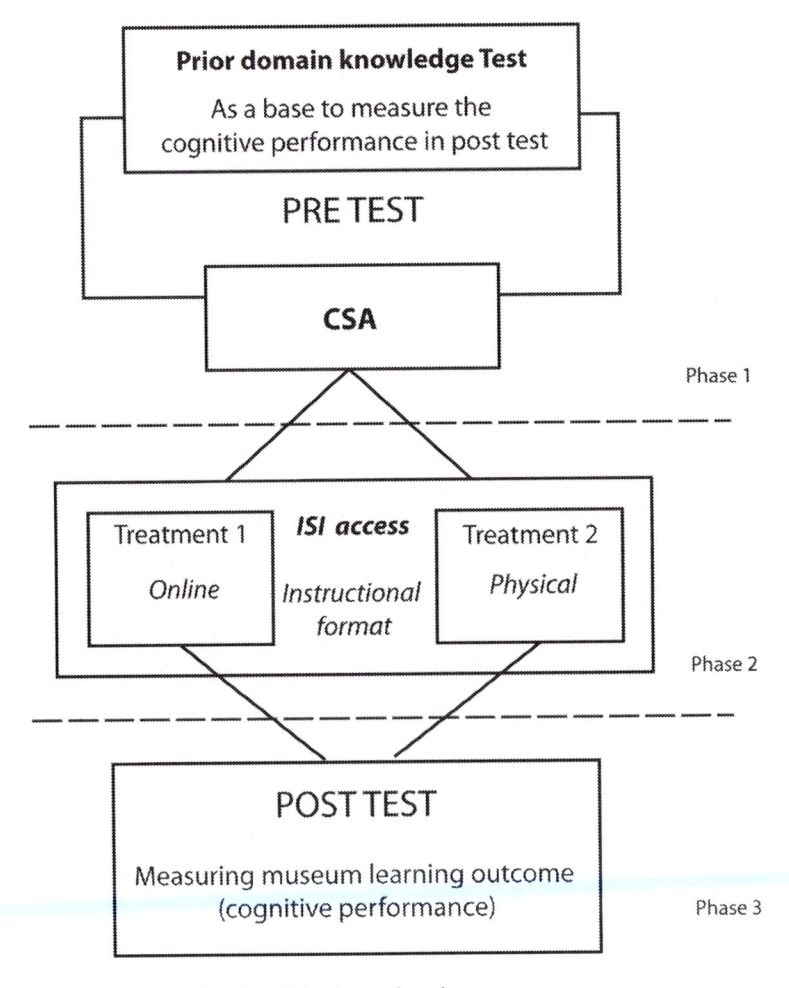

Fig. 2.3 The experimental design of the doctoral-study

Validation and reliability testing (calibration of the test instruments) for both pre-test and post-test will be conducted in a preliminary experiment prior to the main data collection process. This preliminary experiment will provide evidence of whether the test-items can distinguish effectively between those participants who lack knowledge pertaining to the museum's exhibit and the knowledgeable participants. This experiment is also important to test out the research design, to ensure there is enough time for all activities required for the experiment.

4 Discussion and Conclusions

Over the years, museums have been implementing various instructional strategies in the arrangement and organization of their educational programs, with specified learning objectives (Hein, 1998). For instance, museum exhibits have been organized using a transmission view of learning for educational programs with specified learning objectives. If museums wish to achieve discovery learning exhibits they should be arranged in such a way as to allow for knowledge exploration using various active learning modes. Museum curators who implement exploratory exhibit architectures will ensure a typical constructivist environment. In an approach such as this, there is no specific learning path expected. Instead, the exhibit presents a range of points of view that afford the museum visitor to delve into their own experiential learning. With the increased popularity of Web-based ICT tools, understandably, many museums are adopting constructivist learning environments that provide open ended options for their visitors to experience learning events through both their physical and online-visits.

In adopting technologies to support the constructivist-museum context, the roles of ICTs need to be reconceptualized as effective HCI tools for learners to construct their own meaning (Jonassen, Peck, & Wilson, 1999). Fundamentally, technology is used to support the acquisition of knowledge (Inglis, Ling, & Joosten, 1999), involving information a learner receives, stores and retrieves. There is an instructional imperative to understand both how the technology should present information that may be gleaned from museum exhibits, and how a learner's mental model may work in processing screen-based information that is a complex cognitive-environment. Recent research has shown that learning is accepted as an active and ongoing process, as well as being a final outcome (Black, 2005). As information assimilates between the various contexts of a learning experience in a museum, this process may depend heavily on one's mental structure/capacity (Falk & Dierking, 1992). Learning events that are stored within an individual's mental structure might be interpreted in parallel as it potentially matches with their existing prior knowledge or resides as (unprocessed) information until it meets a situation that may turn it into knowledge. Cognitive psychologists say this human-dimension provides valid techniques for us to understand the museum learning process (Hein, 1998). The findings from this doctoral-study will serve to inform museum staff involved in exhibit design and development.

These days, ICT tools provide the means to produce instructional packages with relative ease. Multimedia accentuates a highly graphical (or visual) approach to screen-based instruction. Typically, little consideration is given to the effectiveness of screen-based visual stimuli, and curiously, learners are expected to be visually literate (McNamara, 1988), despite the complexity of human-computer interaction (Dreyfus & Dreyfus, 1986; Tuovinen & Sweller, 1999). However, visual literacy is much harder for some people to acquire than for others (McKay & Garner, 1999).

In the past, verbal (or analytic) ability was taken to be a measure of crystallized intelligence, or the ability to apply cognitive strategies to new problems and manage a large volume of information in working memory (Hunt, 1997), while the non-verbal (or imagery) ability was expressed as fluid intelligence (Kline, 1991). As online-learning environments lend themselves to integrating verbal (textual) and non-verbal (graphical) instructional strategies, which generate novel (or fluid) intellectual problems, more research needs to be carried out to provide instructional designers with prescriptive models that predict measurable instructional outcomes for a broader range of human cognitive abilities. Picking out these important instructional variables (spatial ability, and method of delivery for instance) for some types of instructional outcomes progresses our ability to provide instructional environments for a broader range of novice-learners, thereby giving them a choice of screen-based instructional strategy, and control over their choice of delivery format. Both cognitive-dimensions must be considered for developing tailored instructional strategies for Web-mediated online-museum exhibits of the future.

References

Anderson, T., & Elloumi, F. (Eds.). (2004). *Theory and practice of online learning*. Athabasca: Athabasca University. Retrieved on September 30, 2009 from http://cde.athabascau.ca/online_book/pdf/TPOL_book.pdf. ISBN: 0-919737-59-5.

Berry, L. H. (2000). Cognitive effects of web page design. In B. Abbey (Ed.), *Instructional and cognitive impacts of web-based education* (pp. 41–55). London: Idea Group Publishing.

Black, G. (2005). *The engaging museum: Developing museums for visitor involvement*. London, Routledge.

Brown, S. (2006). Do richer media mean better learning? A framework for evaluating learning experiences in museum web site design. *International Journal of Heritage Studies, 12*(5), 412–426.

Clark, R. C. (2003). *Building expertise: Cognitive methods for training and performance improvement*. Washington, D.C.: International Society for Performance Improvement.

Copeland, C. R. (2006). Out of our mines! A retrospective look at online museum collections-based learning and instruction (1997–2006). *Proceedings Museums and the Web 2006*, Albuquerque, NM.

Dreyfus, H. L., & Dreyfus, S. E. (1986). *Mind over machine: The power of human intuition and expertise in the era of the computer*. New York: Free Press.

Elsom-Cook, M. (2001). *Principles of interactive multimedia*. Berkshire: McGraw-Hill.

Falk, J. H., & Dierking, L. D. (1992). *The museum experience*. Washington DC: Whalesback Books.

Guilford, J. (1967). *The nature of human intelligence*. New York: McGraw-Hill.

Hein, G. E. (1998). *Learning in the museum*. London: Routledge.
Holzman, P., & Klein, G. (1954). Cognitive-system principles of levelling and sharpening: Individual differences in visual time-error assimilation effects. *Journal of Psychology, 37*, 105–122.
Hunt, E. (1997). The status of the concept of intelligence. *Japanese Psychological Research, 39*(1), 1–11.
Inglis, A., Ling, P., & Joosten, V. (1999). *Delivering digitally: Managing the transition to the knowledge media*. London: Kogan Page.
Jonassen, D. H., Peck, K. L., & Wilson, B. G. (1999). *Learning with technology: A constructivist perspective*. New Jersey, OH: Prentice Hall.
Kagan, J. (1965). Individual differences in the resolution of response uncertainty. *Journal of Personality and Social Psychology, 2*, 154–160.
Kline, P. (1991). *Intelligence: The psychometric view*. England: Routledge.
Marty, P. F. (2004). The evolving roles of information professionals in museums. *Bulletin of the American Society for Information Science and Technology, 30*(5), 20–23.
Mayer, R. E. (2001). *Multimedia learning*. New York: Cambridge Press.
Mayer, R. E., & Moreno, R. (2002). Aids to computer-based multimedia learning. *Learning and Instruction, 12*(1), 107–119.
McKay, E. (2000). Instructional strategies integrating cognitive style construct: A meta-knowledge processing model (Doctoral Dissertation, Deakin University, Australia, 2000). Retrieved on September 25, 2009, from http://tux.lib.deakin.edu.au/adt-VDU/public/adt-VDU20061011.122556/
McKay, E. (2003). Managing the interactivity of instructional format and cognitive style construct in web-mediated learning environments. In W. Zhou, B. Corbitt, P. Nicholson, & J. Fong (Eds.), *Advances in web-based learning –ICWL 2003* (Vol. 2783, pp. 308–319). Berlin: Springer.
McKay, E. (2008). *The human dimensions of human-computer interaction: Balancing the HCI equation* (Vol. 3). Amsterdam: IOS Press.
McKay, E., & Garner, B. J. (1999). The complexities of visual learning: measuring cognitive skills performance. Paper presented at the 7th International Conference on Computers in Education: New human abilities for the networked society, held 4–7 November, Japan. In G. Cumming, P. Okamoto, & L. Gomez (Eds.), *Advanced research in computers and communications in education: New human abilities for the networked society* (Vol. 1, pp. 208–215). Amsterdam: IOS Press.
McNamara, S. E. (1988). *Designing visual analysis training for the individual learner: An examination of individual learner differences and training content and procedures*. Published Doctor of Philosophy, Monash University, Melbourne.
Pask, G., & Scott, B. C. E. (1972). Learning strategies and individual competence. *International Journal Man-Machine Studies, 4*, 217–253.
Peacock, D., Tait, S., & Timpson, C. (2009). Building digital distribution systems for school-based users of museum content: New initiatives in Australia and Canada. *Proceedings Museum and the Web*, Indianapolis, IN, USA.
Riding R. J. (1991). *Cognitive Style Analysis*. Birmingham: Learning and Training Technology.
Riding, R., & Cheema, I. (1991). Cognitive styles- an overview and integration. *Educational Psychology, 11*(3 and 4), 193–215.
Schaller, D. T., & Allison-Bunnell, S. (2003). Practicing what we teach: How learning theory can guide development of online educational activities. *Proceedings Museum and the Web*, Toronto, ON.
Schaller, D. T., Borun, M., Allison-Bunnell, S., & Chambers, M. (2007). One size does not fit all: Learning style, play, and online interactives. *Proceedings Museum and the Web*, San Francisco, CA.
Schweibenz, W. (1998). The "Virtual Museum": New perspectives for museums to present objects and information using the internet as a knowledge base and communication system. *Proceedings Internationalen Symposiums fur Informationswissenschaft (ISI 1998), Prag*.

Sharp, H., Rogers, Y., & Preece, J. (2007). *Interaction design: Beyond human computer interaction* (2nd ed.). West Sussex: Wiley.

Soren, B. (2005). Best practices in creating quality online experiences for museum users. *Museum Management and Curatorship, 20*(2), 131–148.

Tuovinen, J. E., & Sweller, J. (1999). A comparison of cognitive load associated with discovery learning and worked examples. *Journal of Educational Psychology, 91*(2), 334–341.

Witcomb, A. (2007). The materiality of virtual technologies: a new approach to thinking about the impact of multimedia in museums. In F. Cameron & S. Kenderdine (Eds.), *Theorizing digital cultural heritage: A critical discourse* (pp. 35–48). Cambridge, MA: The MIT Press.

Witkin, H. A., Dyke, R. B., Patterson, H. F., Goodman, D. R., & Kemp, D. R. (1962). *Psychological differentiation*. New York: Wiley.

Chapter 3
MAPLET – A Framework for Matching Aims, Processes, Learner Expertise and Technologies

Maree Gosper

Abstract With the increasing availability of sophisticated technologies for educational purposes, an ongoing challenge for academics is the choice of which technologies to use and how to effectively integrate them into the curriculum. Too often decisions are based on the available technologies or the latest innovation and the danger of this is that the technologies may not be effective in supporting student learning. After all, it is the activity fostered in learners, not the technology, that ultimately influences learning. This paper introduces the MAPLET Framework for guiding the integration of technologies into curriculum. At its core is a three-phased approach to the development of intellectual skills such as those required for solving problems. The framework provides a learner focused perspective that makes explicit the relationship between the learning processes underpinning the aims and outcomes of the curriculum, the expertise of learners, and the potential of technologies to support learning.

Keywords Technology · Learning · Expertise · Curriculum design

1 Introduction

The ever expanding range of technologies available to teachers offers increasingly sophisticated choices in the tools available to support learning. Learning Management Systems which for many years have been the mainstay of online delivery in the university sector can now be augmented by a range of more specialized learning technologies. Web-based lecture technologies, for example, have been widely adopted to support flexible attendance at lectures and to support learning by enabling students to selectively revisit and review key concepts and ideas in their

M. Gosper (✉)
Learning and Teaching Centre, Macquarie University, Sydney, NSW 2109, Australia
e-mail: maree.gosper@mq.edu.au

D. Ifenthaler et al. (eds.), *Multiple Perspectives on Problem Solving and Learning in the Digital Age*, DOI 10.1007/978-1-4419-7612-3_3,
© Springer Science+Business Media, LLC 2011

own time (Gosper et al., 2008). Blogs, wikis, podcasts, videocasts, virtual worlds, and multiplayer educational gaming tools have opened new opportunities for social networking, self publication and collaboration (Horizon-08, 2008) enabling the learner to become a co-contributor, not merely an acquirer of knowledge (Bower, Hedberg, & Kuswara, 2009). Significantly for both teachers and students, many of these emerging web-based technologies are quite inexpensive or freely available, require little specialist knowledge to use and can provide spaces and materials that can be easily shared.

Not only are there now more technologies to choose from, the technologies are becoming more sophisticated in relation to how they can support learning. Because of this, making decisions about which technologies are most appropriate for supporting teaching and learning in different contexts can pose significant challenges for academic staff, particularly those with little to no formal knowledge of cognition and learning. Where technologies have been adopted because of fashion and without a defensible educational rationale, there is the risk they will quickly reach a 'use-by' date and not be effective in supporting learning.

To make effective choices, rather than simply focusing on the more immediate and eye catching characteristics of the technologies or what they can do, a deeper understanding of how and why technologies can support learning is called for (Burns, 2006). Ellis and Goodyear (2010) maintain that:

> ...when teachers do not focus on the development of student understanding and have poor conceptions of learning technologies, they tend to use e-learning as a way of delivering information bolting it on to course design in an unreflective way. Teachers who focus on the development of student understanding and have richer conceptions of learning technologies, not only integrate e-learning into their approach to teaching, but also stress the importance of the integration of learning across physical and virtual spaces. (Ellis & Goodyear, 2010), p. 104)

The introduction of any new technology into an established learning environment is not an isolated experience and has implications for the relationship between all the elements of the curriculum (Gosper et al., 2008) Moreover, there are cognitive implications for the learner arising from the use of different technologies (Jonassen, 2000a).

When designing curricula, a key tenet is constructive alignment, which Biggs (2003) describes as bringing together the teaching system – what the teacher constructs, and the learning system which is how the student reacts. These two systems interact to form a mutually supportive structure where all aspects of teaching – aims, outcomes, activities and assessment strategies – are aligned and interrelated (Biggs, 2003). Within this alignment, choices need to be made about the most effective technologies to facilitate learning.

From the teaching perspective, an understanding of the cognitive processes underpinning the aims and outcomes of the curriculum can lead to the identification of the types of activities that can facilitate the desired learning. In addition, these same cognitive processes can be used as the criteria by which to analyse different technologies. Thus, making explicit the cognitive processes underpinning learning can optimise the match between learning and technologies.

A critical consideration from the learning perspective is the prior knowledge and skills learners bring with them. Their level of expertise within the particular knowledge domain has been shown to influence the design of learning and teaching activities (Tuovinen & Sweller, 1999). More broadly, an understanding of the learning processes underpinning the development of expertise can assist in organising and structuring the curriculum in ways that can minimise cognitive load on the learner (Paas, Renkl, & Sweller, 2003).

This chapter outlines a framework for the design of curricula which focuses on the development of expertise and makes explicit the links between teaching aims, cognitive processes, learner expertise and technologies. In developing the framework, the acquisition of intellectual skills, such as those used for solving problems is used as the context for learning. This context is highly applicable to the higher education sector where the development of the intellectual skills that enable the critical, conceptual and reflective thinking required for solving problems are key learning outcomes (Toohey, 1999). A case study which illustrates how the framework can be used as a diagnostic tool to analyse existing curricula in order to identify strategies and technologies to enhance student learning will also be discussed.

2 Intellectual Skill Development

Anderson (1982) developed a framework for cognitive skill acquisition which is based on a three-phased approach encompassing the establishment of declarative knowledge, the development of procedural knowledge and the automation of skills. In an adaption of this framework to educational contexts VanLehn (1996) used the development of problem solving skills as the context for learning. In VanLehn's model, the early phase of acquisition is signified by the development of an understanding of the scope of the knowledge domain and involves the introduction of the learner to specific facts, rules, terminology or conventions, definitions, simple concepts and principles. The intermediate or procedural phase is entered when, having established some understanding of the relevant domain, the learner is in a position to use this knowledge in meaningful ways. Domain knowledge is manipulated so that it is directly embodied in procedures required to perform a particular task or problem and in the process the knowledge base is expanded and refined. In the late phase, the knowledge domain is secure and the aim is to improve both speed and accuracy, even though the approach does not change.

In practice, the three-phase approach is an iterative, not a sequential process which means learners can be operating in more than one phase on any given learning task. For example, a student working on a problem in the intermediate phase may need to review or acquire new knowledge to complete the task. A break from the original task is required to become familiar with the required knowledge before it is then integrated back into the problem solving task. Hence, working within the intermediate phase could require concurrent learning events in the early phase (VanLehn, 1996).

The three-phase approach to intellectual skill acquisition exhibits two valuable characteristics that have implications for the design of curricula. The first is that the phases of acquisition reflect the development of expertise in a particular domain. As learners develop, they are able to: store more domain specific knowledge; organise their knowledge in more accessible ways; perceive domain related information and patterns faster and more effortlessly; make use of more complex strategies that permit the contemplation of a wide range of alternatives; and make better use of metacognitive skills (Ericsson & Smith, 1991; Ericsson & Lehmann, 1996). This has implications for the sequencing of the knowledge and skills for development in the curriculum. Relating knowledge and skills to the three phases of acquisition can provide a developmental pathway for learners that is reflective of the progression towards expertise.

The second characteristic is that the three-phased approach can assist in aligning the elements of the curriculum (aims, outcomes, activities and assessment tasks) with the level of expertise of the learner. Each of the phases can be related to specific aims and outcomes. By identifying the cognitive processes underpinning phase specific aims and outcomes, learning activities can be designed to facilitate the desired processing in the learner. In addition, technologies and other resources embedded into the activities can also be chosen on the basis of their ability to facilitate the identified processing. Therefore, aligning learning activities and technologies with the expected level of expertise of the learner should, in theory, minimize cognitive load on the learner (Paas et al., 2003).

3 The MAPLET Framework

The combination of these two characteristics forms the MAPLET Framework – a framework for mapping aims, processes learner expertise and technologies. As illustrated in Table 3.1, and discussed more fully below, the vertical axis represents the phases of acquisition and this provides a guide to the sequencing of knowledge and skills for development in relation to the general principles underpinning the development of expertise. The horizontal axis represents the alignment of the elements of the curriculum with the phases of acquisition. Although assessment strategies would normally be included as one of the curriculum elements, they will not be discussed in this paper. However, a detailed examination of the alignment of learning outcomes with assessment processes can be found in the chapter by Margot McNeill on *Technologies to assess complex learning in capstone units.*

3.1 Alignment Along the Horizontal Axis

In the early phase of acquisition, learning is usually focused on activities such as reading, discussion and the acquisition of basic facts, skills and concepts. These activities are typically associated with the development of lower order knowledge and skills related to remembering and understanding factual and simple conceptual

3 MAPLET

Table 3.1 The MAPLET framework – aligning phases of acquisition with the elements of the curriculum

Phases of acquisition	Aims	Outcomes	Processes	Activities
Early	Recognition of characters and scripts (Kanji, Hiragana Katakana)	Read and understand simple passages using Japanese scripts	Memorising Japanese characters	Flash cards or computer-based exercises and games e.g. *Kantaro*
Intermediate	Develop intercultural awareness and understanding	Communicate in written and spoken forms showing awareness of cultural/social differences.	Perceiving different contexts; analysing different behaviours; discriminating between different behaviours in different contexts; understanding cause and effect in behaviour	Use of exemplars; exposure to authentic experiences, modeling by teachers; communicating with people from different cultures; role playing
Late	Proficiency in written and spoken communication	Communicate easily with native speakers of Japanese	Automating verbal and written responses	Repeated and varied practice

knowledge (Anderson & Krathwohl, 2001). Activities that have been shown to be suited for this purpose are those that exhibit clear objectives, sequenced exercises, and immediate feedback (Fletcher-Flinn & Gravatt, 1995; Kulik & Kulik, 1991). The example shown in Table 3.1 to illustrate the alignment of curriculum elements has been drawn from an analysis of a program in Japanese Studies (Gosper, Woo, Muir, Dudley, & Nakazawa, 2007). The teaching aim in the early phase of skill acquisition is to develop basic knowledge and skills in Japanese characters in order that students can read and understand simple passages. This involves memorisation for quick recall that is aided by the use of flash cards in class and a multimedia CD, *Kantaro,* which has a variety of games, mnemonics and exercise that gave immediate feedback to the user.

The intermediate phase accommodates a great variety of aims and outcomes which usually encompass the development of complex conceptual models; the establishment of the robust interconnected knowledge networks that form problem solving schemas with embedded principles, procedures and heuristics; and the development of metacognitive skills. During this phase, solving problems and working through targeted activities, leads the learner through the processes of refining, testing, challenging, understanding, correcting flaws and establishing complex interrelationships within the body of knowledge. This ultimately leads to a comprehensive understanding of the structure and organisation of the knowledge domain (VanLehn, 1996).

The practical illustration at the intermediate phase shown in Table 3.1 has once again been drawn from Japanese studies. The aim is to develop intercultural awareness and understanding in order that students can communicate sensitively and effectively in written and spoken forms. This involves being aware of different contexts, being able to analyse different behaviours and their implications, and understanding which behaviours are most appropriate. The types of activities that can be used include exemplars of appropriate and inappropriate behaviour, role plays and the analysis of media reports from the internet, newspapers and television.

Not all activities will necessarily lead to the integration of technologies nevertheless, the process of articulating the links between the different curriculum elements can help to identify the options available. An understanding of complex concepts, for example, can be facilitated by the use of simulations (de Jong, 1998), spreadsheets and relational databases (Jonassen, 2000b) and games (Hutchison, 2007; Oblinger, 2006) which have been shown to be effective for establishing theoretical relationships, as well as for testing and demonstrating applicability to real world situations. The Microworlds popular in the nineties (Rieber, 1992) and now surpassed by virtual worlds and multiplayer user interfaces provide new opportunities to emulate real world situations (Boulos, Hetherington, & Wheeler 2007; Dickey, 2005).

A second example can be seen in the development of the organisational and structural knowledge that is fundamental to schema development. The linking and integration of knowledge can be achieved through inference. Effective tools have been shown to be those that exhibit careful sequencing of related ideas, use of thematic sentences, and use of text organizers such as indexes, headings and subheadings (Dee-Lucas, 1996; Mayer & Gallini, 1990). Well designed hypertext environments can be set up to achieve this through their ability to make explicit links between facts, concepts and ideas (Jacobson & Spiro, 1995; Jonassen, 1997; Khalifa & Kwok, 1999). Wiki technologies, for example Wikipedia, illustrate how this can be achieved with the additional benefits of doing so in a collaborative environment (Bower et al., 2009).

In the final phase of acquisition the approach does not change and it is one of refinement and extension. Activities may resemble those of the earlier phases and include extensive practice so that procedures can be fine tuned to an automated state where they can be executed automatically with a minimum of cognitive effort (Anderson, 1982). Transfer to novel contexts can be aided by varying the nature of the examples and practice exercises to include rules and exemplars (Hesketh, 1997; van Merrienboer, Jelsma, & Paas, 1992).

The examples given are not intended to provide a comprehensive account of all the aims, outcomes, cognitive processes and activities at the different phases of acquisition. They do, however, illustrate the critical link between the processing requirements underpinning teaching aims, learning activities and the affordances technologies offer to the achievement of the desired learning outcomes.

3.2 Sequencing Down the Vertical Axis

As well as making explicit the alignment between learner expertise and the elements of the curriculum, the MAPLET Framework can guide the sequencing of the curriculum over a program of study such as an undergraduate degree, in accordance with the developing expertise of the learner. For example, expertise in problem solving involves the development of metacognitive and self-regulated learning skills which is an intermediate phase activity. This is best introduced after foundational knowledge and basic concepts have been established in the early phase of acquisition. The reason for this is that in the intermediate phase, as a higher level of conceptual understanding is attained, spare attentional capacity becomes available and students have a greater ability to develop and use the metacognitive skills associated with self questioning to identify areas of weakness, review important components, and organise and reflect upon performance throughout problem solving (Alexander & Judy, 1988). One of the negative consequences for the learner of introducing metacognitive skills too early is unmanageable cognitive load. Competition for limited cognitive resources may arise if self-monitoring for accurate assessment and regulation takes place at the same time as the development of foundational domain knowledge, in the early phase of acquisition. If, on the other hand, self-monitoring is delayed until the knowledge base becomes more secure, cognitive resources are more likely to be available to undertake self-regulatory processes (Kanfer & Ackerman, 1989).

4 The MAPLET Framework in Action

In practice, the MAPLT Framework can be used for two purposes. The first is as a tool to guide the sequencing of the curricula which has been illustrated in the previous section. The second is as diagnostic tool to analyse existing curricula. As an analysis tool, it is proposed that where there are inconsistencies between the sequencing of knowledge and skills with the phases of acquisition then problems may occur. Likewise, inconsistencies in the alignment of the expected level of expertise of the learner with the cognitive processes underpinning aims outcomes, activities and assessment tasks will also give rise to teaching and learning difficulties. For example, inconsistencies can occur if the expertise level of students is situated in the early phase of acquisition, and students are required to immediately perform tasks and are assessed at the intermediate level without appropriate support. Not all inconsistencies necessarily lead to teaching and learning difficulties and in some cases they could present positive motivational challenges for the learner if they fall within the 'zone of proximal development' (Vygotsky, 1978), that is, the stage at which the learner can master a particular task if given the appropriate support and help (Wertsch, 1991). A careful choice of learning experiences and supporting instructional tools in this instance can elevate performance levels to accommodate the challenges.

The following case study illustrates how the MAPLET framework can be used as a diagnostic tool to analyse an existing curriculum and recommend solutions to enhance student learning.

5 The Case Study

The case study is situated in a first year undergraduate subject, Global Environmental Crises. The subject attracts a diverse range of students from across the university including those majoring in the discipline and those who take the unit for interest. It deals with four themes – the greenhouse effect, urban environments, population growth and deforestation. A challenge for staff teaching on the subject is that students are expected to develop an understanding of the four knowledge domains as well as the interrelatedness of knowledge and skills between each. This is heightened by the need to also make links between other discipline areas such as physics, economics and politics. Often students make intuitive connections, but a more explicit approach to reinforce connections based on an expert view is desired. The development of critical thinking skills and the ability to critique and evaluate the worth of knowledge are important outcomes that are often difficult to achieve.

The aim of the study was to explore these challenges from a learner perspective and develop recommendations that could be put in place to enhance learning.

5.1 Procedure

The MAPLET framework was used as the tool for guiding the analysis and this involved identifying: (1) the expertise of the learner (2) the teaching aims and learning outcomes in relation to the phases of acquisition (3) the teaching and learning experiences and (4) the instructional tools and other resources being used to facilitate the required cognitive processing in the learner. It is proposed that where there is misalignment between these four elements and the phases of acquisition, this would signify areas for attention and intervention.

A structured interview of approximately one hour was conducted with the subject coordinator to explore the points of alignment listed above. In addition, a content analysis of the subject outline was undertaken to obtain additional information about the aims, outcomes, teaching and learning activities and assessment tasks. Information from both sources was synthesised and then reviewed by the subject coordinator to ensure that the interpretations were valid.

5.2 Results

The results of the analysis are summarised in Table 3.2 and discussed more fully below.

Table 3.2 Analysis of global environmental crises guided by the MAPLET framework

Phases of acquisition	Learner expertise	Aims and outcomes	Activities to facilitate processing	Assessment
✓	✓	✓	✓	✓
Early	Starts with expectation for no prior knowledge and skills	Understanding basic concepts and scope of domain	Focussed on activities to support recall recognition and comprehension	Less difficulty with lower order assessment tasks
✓		✓	✗	✗
Intermediate	Ends semester with an expectation for intermediate phase expertise	Extend to critical analysis	Little to no activities to scaffold linking of concepts and ideas, synthesis and analysis	Greater difficulty with higher order critical analysis tasks

5.2.1 Aims and Outcomes in Relation to the Phases of Acquisition

Global Environmental Crises is a first year undergraduate subject which aims to develop a better understanding of the nature of the major environmental crises facing the world today. It deals with the human and physical contexts of global environmental futures, specifically those resulting from the greenhouse effect, urban environments, population growth and deforestation. An understanding of the interaction between biophysical, demographic, political, economic and technological factors is stressed throughout. A familiarity with management issues, including the urgent need for better information and communication, improved technology and greater international cooperation is also expected.

In relation to the phases of acquisition, knowledge and skills for development cover the early phase foundational facts, definitions, and basic concepts progressing into intermediate phase schema development for conceptual understanding and the development of critical analysis skills. This is illustrated in Table 3.2 by the ticked cells. The learning outcomes cover both early and intermediate phases of acquisition which is again consistent with the teaching aims. Outcomes are reflected in the assessment tasks which are a mixture of three written assignments weekly quizzes, a final exam. Collectively these cover both phases and require students to recall and interpret basic facts and concepts, interrelate component parts of information and key concepts from each module and also relate these to real life situations. For example, students are expected to be able to take basic principles and concepts such as deforestation and the greenhouse effect and use these to analyse other environmental issues and concerns.

5.2.2 Learner Characteristics

Students are drawn from all disciplines across the University. Just over half have studied the subject as part of a coherent program whilst the remainder are enrolled for general interest. They are not expected to have any prior expertise in the four knowledge domains. Although students with some background knowledge may be able to attain a successful level of performance at the intermediate level, those with low prior knowledge may not have the cognitive resources available to acquire domain knowledge and at the same time develop and apply the metacognitive skills (Alexander & Judy, 1988; Kanfer & Ackerman, 1989) required for critical analysis. Scaffolding these students in their progression to intermediate phase outcomes was revealed in the analysis as one of the areas for attention.

5.2.3 Activities and Resources

Each of the four modules is of three weeks duration and is taught and assessed independently of the others. The subject is structured around a resource-based approach to the delivery of learning experiences. This approach was adopted for a variety of reasons including the need to find alternatives to the traditional tutorial and to provide students with a flexible approach to learning which would give them real choices in the time and place of study. Computer and internet technologies are comprehensively integrated into all aspects of the subject, with content delivery and communications being coordinated through the subject web site. The subject, and each module, is taught using lectures (face-to-face, or distributed on audiotape, or through the Internet), and a mix of coursework tasks that include weekly practical exercises (some of which are delivered through the Internet), weekly quizzes (delivered through the Internet), and recommended readings. To support these activities, students are provided with, or have access to a study guide, a textbook lecture summaries placed on the Internet outlining the main points, a collection of additional paper-based and Internet-based readings, a multimedia resource package on Forests of Australia (Davis, Gould, Jacobson, & Rich, 1999) and web-based discussion facilities.

Communication is provided through lectures, and personal contact, as well as via email and online discussion facilities. Learning is primarily viewed as an individualistic endeavour, however students can collaborate in computer sessions. Overall the activities and resources are designed to introduce students to the scope of the knowledge domain, the acquisition and testing of concepts and ideas – all of which are situated within the early phase of acquisition. Few activities have been designed to scaffold the intermediate phase expectations which has consequently led to difficulties in the intermediate phase assessment tasks, as shown by the shaded cells in Table 3.2.

5.2.4 Discussion and Recommendations

The analysis revealed that the key point of misalignment arose in progressing students from the early into the intermediate phase of acquisition in the absence of focused activities to scaffold their development. Students were required to develop domain specific knowledge and move into the intermediate level where they were applying their knowledge to critically analyse environmental problems. This level of achievement was expected of individuals with a variety of backgrounds ranging from those with no theoretical or practical knowledge of the subject to those who had some knowledge of all or some of the four modules. The problem of advancing students from an early to an intermediate phase was compounded by having to do this for four separate modules of work, each of three week's duration.

The dilemma in such an approach is that domain specific knowledge is required for higher order skill development (Mayer, 1992; Sweller, 1990), but when time is limited, if too much time and effort is required to acquire the necessary domain knowledge then cognitive resources may not be available for the development of higher order skills.

The challenge for staff is to develop ways of establishing foundational knowledge as well as scaffold the development of higher order skills within a short time span. One way of doing this would be to reduce the number of modules and re-design the curriculum to support the development of critical analysis skills over the duration of the entire subject covering 13 teaching weeks. Instead of having a critical analysis assessment task for each module, activities could be designed to culminate in a final critical review based on the interconnecting themes over all modules. In addition podcasts or learning activities addressing gaps in key concepts and skills could be provided for students on a just-in-time basis. This would also help to cater for those with differing levels of expertise.

A noticeable gap that was evident was in scaffolding the development of intermediate phase organisation and structural knowledge required for the development of critical analysis skills. In particular, helping students to establish links and interrelationships between the theoretical constructs from across the four themes. This was compounded by the learning activities and instructional tools being largely focussed on early phase knowledge and skill development for each particular module. There was little to no specific support provided to make explicit the interrelationships across the themes. Students were expected to intuitively make the required links that represented expert thinking.

With reference to expert performance, one of the characteristics of experts is their ability to recognise the underlying structure, rather than dealing with individual pieces of information. A more explicit articulation of expert thinking to assist students in making structural links was needed. Explicit linking of concepts and ideas has been shown to assist in the development of structural knowledge (Khalifa & Kwok, 1999), conceptual knowledge and transfer to new contexts (Jacobson & Spiro, 1995). This is not necessarily dealt with effectively in traditional teaching approaches. Textbooks, for example, rarely make explicit links and often assume the thinking of experts will be implicitly modelled (Glaser, 1991). As noted earlier, well developed hypertext environments whether created by experts or more collaboratively using wiki software, could be used to link the interconnecting themes that represent the semantic networks which model expert thinking.

The case study illustrates how the framework can be used as a diagnostic tool to identify inconsistencies between the learner and curriculum elements (aims, outcomes, processes, activities, resources, tools and technologies) and to then develop solutions to overcome these inconsistencies. While there may have been more sophisticated solutions available to support the challenges identified for Global Environmental Crises, the suggestions made were based on the need to find solutions compatible with the technologies and support that was available.

6 Conclusion

The MAPLET framework provides a perspective to the design of the curriculum which places the learner and the process of learning at the forefront of decisions. The three-phase approach to the acquisition of intellectual skills that forms the core of the framework provides a developmental procedure that can guide the sequencing of knowledge and skills for development across whole programs of study in relation to the developing expertise of the learner. By making explicit the cognitive processes underpinning phase specific aims and outcomes, links can be made between the needs of learners, teaching and learning activities, and the features of technologies that can support the learning process.

The Framework has focussed on the cognitive aspects of integrating technologies the curriculum. All the same, it is recognised that when choosing technologies consideration must also be given to a range of influences covering: student motivation; socio-cultural factors such as cultural and language background; and institutional factors relating to the delivery mechanisms, access arrangements, hardware and software, institutional resources, and teaching and learning support (Gosper et.al., 2007)

The MAPLET Framework has the potential to make a valuable contribution to the field of curriculum design. It can assist in advancing our understanding of the inter-relationships between teaching, learning and technology, particularly how different technologies support the process of learning and consequently which technologies are best suited to supporting specific learning outcomes.

References

Alexander, P. A., & Judy, J. E. (1988). The interaction of domain-specific and strategic knowledge in academic performance. *Review of Educational Research, 58*(4), 375–404.

Anderson, J. R. (1982). Acquisition of cognitive skill. *Psychological Review, 89*(4), 369–406.

Anderson, L. W., & Krathwohl, D. R. (2001). *A taxonomy for learning, teaching, and assessing: A revision of Bloom's taxonomy of educational objectives.* New York: Longman.

Biggs, J. (2003). *Teaching for quality learning at university.* Philadelphia, PA: SRHE and Open University.

Boulos, M. K., Hetherington, L., & Wheeler, S. (2007). Second life: An overview of the potential of 3-D virtual worlds in medical and health education. *Health Information and Libraries Journal, 24*(4), 233–245.

Bower, M., Hedberg, J., & Kuswara, A. (2009). Conceptualising Web 2.0 enabled learning designs. In *Same places, different spaces: Proceedings for ascilite Auckland 2009*. Retrieved on November 5, 2010 from http:www.ascilite.org.au/conferences/auckland09/procs/bower.pdf

Burns, M. (2006). *Educational Leadership December 2005-January 2006*, 48–53.

Davis, J., Gould, S., Jacobson, C., & Rich, D. C. (1999). *Forests of Australia*. Sydney: Macquarie University.

de Jong, T. (1998). Scientific discovery learning with computer simulations of conceptual domains. *Review of Educational Research, 68*(2), 179–201.

Dee-Lucas, D. (1996). Effects of overview and structure on study strategies and text representations for instructional hypertext. In J. R. Rouet, J. J. Levonen, A. Dillon, & R. J. Spiro (Eds.), *Hypertext and cognition*. Mahwah, N J: Lawrence Erlbaum, pp. 73–108.

Dickey, M. (2005). Three-dimensional virtual worlds and distance learning: Two case studies of active worlds as a medium for distance education. *British Journal of Educational Technology, 36*(3), 439–451.

Ellis, R., & Goodyear, P. (2010). *Students' experiences of E-learning in higher education: The ecology of sustainable innovation*. London: Taylor and Francis.

Ericsson, K. A., & Smith, J. (1991). *Towards a general theory of expertise*. Cambridge: Cambridge University Press.

Ericsson, K. C., & Lehmann, A. C. (1996). Expert and exceptional performance: Evidence of maximal adaptation to task constraints. *Annual Review of Psychology, 47*, 273–305.

Fletcher-Flinn, C. M., & Gravatt, B. (1995). The efficacy of computer assisted instruction (CAI): A meta-analysis. *Journal of Computing Research, 12*(3), 219–242.

Glaser, R. (1991). The maturing of the relationship between the science of learning and cognition and educational practice. *Learning and Instruction, 1*, 129–144.

Gosper, M., Green, D., McNeill, M., Phillips, R. A., Preston, G., & Woo, K. (2008). *Final report: The impact of web-based lecture technologies on current and future practices in learning and teaching*. Sydney: Australian Learning and Teaching Council. Retrieved on November 5, 2010 from http://www.altc.edu.au/carrick/webdav/site/carricksite/users/siteadmin/public/grants_project_webbasedlecture_report_aug08.pdf

Gosper, M., Woo, K., Muir, H., Dudley, C., & Nakazawa, K. (2007). Selecting ICT based solutions for quality learning and sustainable practice. *Australasian Journal of Educational Technology, 23*(2), 227–247.

Hesketh, B. (1997). Dilemmas in training for transfer and retention. *Applied Psychology: An International Review, 46*(4), 317–339.

Horizon-08. (2008). *The 2008 Horizon report*. Austin, TX: The New Media Consortium.

Hutchison, D. (2007). Video games and the pedagogy of place. *Social Studies, 98*(1), 35–40.

Jacobson, M. J., & Spiro, R. J. (1995). Hypertext learning environments, cognitive flexibility, and the transfer of complex knowledge: An empirical investigation. *Journal of Educational Computing Research, 12*(4), 301–333.

Jonassen, D. H. (1997). Instructional design models for well-structured and ill-structured problem-solving learning outcomes. *Educational Technology Research and Development, 45*(1), 65–94.

Jonassen, D. H. (2000a). Toward a design theory of problem solving. *Educational Technology Research and Development, 48*(4), 63–85.

Jonassen, D. H. (2000b). *Computers as mindtools for schools* (2nd ed.). New Jersey: Prentice Hall.

Kanfer, R., & Ackerman, P. L. (1989). Motivation and cognitive abilities: An interactive/aptitude-treatment interaction to skill acquisition. *Journal of Applied Psychology, 74*(4), 657–690.

Khalifa, M., & Kwok, R. C.-W. (1999). Remote learning technologies: Effectiveness of hypertext and GSS. *Decision Support Systems, 26*(3), 195–207.

Kulik, C. C., & Kulik, J. (1991). Effectiveness of computer-based instruction: An updated analysis. *Computers in Human Behaviour, 7*, 75–94.

Mayer, R. E. (1992). *Thinking, problem solving and cognition* (2nd ed.). New York: W.H. Freeman.

Mayer, R. E., & Gallini, J. K. (1990). When is an illustration worth ten thousand words? *Journal of Educational Psychology, 82*(4), 715–726.

Oblinger, D. (2006). Games and learning. *Educause Quarterly, 29*(3), 5–7.
Paas, F. G., Renkl, A., & Sweller, J. (2003). Cognitive load theory and instructional design: Recent developments. *Educational Psychologist, 38*(1), 1–4.
Rieber, L. P. (1992). Computer-based microworlds: A bridge between constructivism and direct instruction. *Educational Technology Research and Development, 40*(1), 93–106.
Sweller, J. (1990). Cognitive processes and instructional procedures. *Australian Journal of Education, 34*(2), 125–130.
Toohey, S. (1999). *Designing courses for higher education*. Philadelphia, PA: Open University Press.
Tuovinen, J. E., & Sweller, J. (1999). A comparison of cognitive load associated with discovery learning and worked examples. *Journal of Educational Psychology, 91*(2), 334–341.
van Merrienboer, J. J. G., Jelsma, O., & Paas, F. G. (1992). Training for reflective expertise: A four component instructional design model for complex cognitive skill. *Educational Technology Research and Development, 40*(2), 23–43.
VanLehn, K. (1996). Cognitive skill acquisition. *Annual Review of Psychology, 47*, 513–539.
Vygotsky, L. S. (1978). *Mind in society the development of higher mental process*. Cambridge, MA: MIT Press.
Wertsch, J. V. (1991). *Voices of the mind: A sociocultural approach to mediated action*. Cambridge, MA: Harvard University Press.

Chapter 4
Web-Based Learning Objects in School Education

Pedagogical Usability Issues

Said Hadjerrouit

Abstract The added value of Web-based learning objects (WBLOs) lies in supporting learners to acquire the right knowledge and skills in order to function as active and collaborative learners. To realize this, WBLOs must be both technically and pedagogically usable. Technical usability in itself is not sufficient. To support the learning process, the usability concept must be extended to include pedagogical considerations. The importance of pedagogical usability in education has been recognized, but not sufficiently researched. In addition, little research has been done to evaluate the pedagogical value of WBLOs. The main goal of this paper is to show how to foster pedagogically usable WBLOs in school education. The article also reports on students' perceptions of WBLOs by means of survey questionnaires

Keywords Learning theory · Pedagogical usability · Technical usability · Web-based learning objects · WBLO

1 Introduction

Technical usability as defined by Nielsen (2000) is an important criterion for WBLOs, but not sufficient to support learning processes. WBLOs must be pedagogically usable in order to support learning. The goal of technical usability is to minimize the cognitive load, resulting from the interaction with the WBLO in order to free more resources for the learning process itself. The concept of pedagogical usability is related to the learning utility of WBLOs (Nokelainen, 2006). Hence, technical and pedagogical usability of WBLOs cannot be considered as separate activities. On the contrary, they are related to each other. However, while technical usability is a self-evident requirement for WBLOs, it is not necessarily

S. Hadjerrouit (✉)
University of Agder, Serviceboks 422, 4604 Kristiansand, Norway
e-mail: said.hadjerrouit@uia.no

conductive for learning (Mayes & Fowler, 1999). WBLOs are considered beneficial for the learners if they contribute to the learning process, and not if they simply support efficient execution of software functions (Tselios, Avouris, & Komis, 2008). It follows that the pedagogical usability of WBLOs cannot be approached as a conventional task that can be solved only with techniques developed by work in Human-Computer Interaction (Mayes & Fowler, 1999). For this reason, the pedagogical usability of WBLOs must be re-defined and related to its learning utility (Elliot, Jones, & Barker, 2002; Sedig, Klawe, & Westrom, 2001).

2 Literature Review

WBLOs as educational tools offer learners access to well-structured and easily-updatable study materials, task-based activities, online resources, and tutorial support. In spite of these benefits, however, learners may be left disappointed, because WBLOs do not sufficiently address their needs. WBLOs have been developed mainly by software developers with a high level of technical expertise, but without knowledge about learners' needs (Nam & Smith-Jackson, 2007). For instance, difficulties may arise when graphics is over-emphasized to the detriment of pedagogical aspects, so that a WBLO looks attractive, but is difficult to use in educational settings (Brinck, Gergle, & Wood, 2002). In addition, in certain cases, increased technical usability could influence negatively the pedagogical usability of WBLOs, since high level of technical usability does not contribute necessarily to the learning outcome (Tselios, Avouris, & Komis, 2008). Clearly, there still exist a number of important issues that need to be addressed in WBLO design and evaluation.

First, WBLOs are still the domain of software experts rather than teachers, educators, and learners (Nam & Smith-Jackson, 2007). As a result, most WBLOs basically emphasize technical usability as defined by Nielsen (2000). However, technical usability is not necessarily conductive for deep learning. For instance, according to Ingram (2003), the degree and rapidity of navigation, which is a crucial characteristic of WBLOs, does not necessarily measure the pedagogical quality of WBLOs in terms of learning, since the aim is to determine whether learners can effectively navigate through WBLOs, for example the number of links learners had to follow to find specific information, perform an assignment, answer questions, or survey questionnaire. Clearly, navigation is supposed to measure task performance, not learning.

Second, to support learning, a number of researchers (Kukusska-Hulme & Shield, 2004; Laurillard, 2002; Leacock & Nesbit, 2007; Nokelainen, 2006) suggest that the usability concept must be extended to capture elements that are pertinent to pedagogy. However, little attention has been paid to this dimension, which is a critical factor to the success of WBLOs in classroom. From the viewpoint of pedagogical usability, current WBLOs lack a number of features that would make them more flexible, interactive, motivating, and collaborative. Research literature reveals that WBLOs with advanced features are difficult to design, and therefore current systems are still limited in their pedagogical usability. Martinidale, Cates, and Qian (2005) stated that it is substantially more difficult to create WBLOs that accommodate the demands of constructivist learning. Likewise, Liu, and Johnson (2005) found a lack of fit between existing WBLOs and what teachers, educators, and learners need, as well as a lack of connection between WBLO design and educational standards.

Third, the pedagogical value of WBLOs lies in helping learners discover and explore things for themselves through interactive, flexible, differentiated, and motivating activities. Unfortunately, most WBLOs are developed without a previous analysis of learners' needs. In addition, a learner-centered approach to WBLOs requires a change from teacher-centered instruction to an environment that emphasizes the learners' needs (John & Sutherland, 2009). However, Maddux (2005) indicated that such a change demands a massive shift in values related to school culture, teaching, and learning, as well as an intensive commitment to individualized learning. In line with this view, Belland (2009) and Jamieson-Proctor et al. (2007) do not attribute the lack of technology integration to insufficient post-teacher education in digital skills or lack of software resources and infrastructure, which are very present in most classrooms, but to obstacles related to cultural issues and folk pedagogies formed through home, school education, and experience. These obstacles are very difficult to change, unless technology integration is of longer duration, integrated into content and methods, and incorporates pedagogical modeling.

Finally, in contrast to higher education, little research has been done evaluating students' perceptions of WBLOs in school education (Kay & Petrarca, 2009). In addition, exhaustive instruments, e.g. (Squires & Preece, 1999) are not suitable to evaluate WBLOs, which tend to be smaller and more numerous (Leacock & Nesbit, 2007). Furthermore, traditional evaluation frameworks (Nielsen, 1993) are intended for software environments rather than WBLOs in which learner-centered user interface systems should be developed to support users' activities. Another problem with evaluating WBLOs is that relatively few are currently being used in schools. ITU Monitor (2009) reports that the selection of digital learning resources is limited, and that developing WBLOs, which provide added value in learning and teaching, is very demanding and time consuming. Nevertheless, some schools have made considerable progress in the use of digital learning resources, but many of them still have much to do to develop and use subject-specific digital learning resources.

3 Pedagogical Usability Criteria

WBLOs are considered beneficial for learners only if they contribute to the learning process and not if they simply support the cognitive load and technical execution of software functions. To support the learning process, the usability concept must be extended to include pedagogical issues. The concept of pedagogical usability has been addressed by Nokelainen (2006) in relation to the design of digital learning resources. For this purpose, Nokelainen defined a set of ten criteria: Learner control, learning activity, collaborative learning, goal orientation, applicability, added value, motivation, previous knowledge, flexibility, and feedback. These criteria can be adapted to the specificities of WBLOs with slight modifications, because the criteria cannot be used in exactly the same terms as for digital learning resources that are developed in other contexts. Hence, Nokelainen's definition of pedagogical usability has been expanded to include the criteria of understandability, autonomy, multiple representation of information, and variation. In addition, interactivity is similar to the criterion of feedback. Finally, some criteria (applicability, previous knowledge, and added value) are self-evident requirements that are explained in greater details in (Nokelainen, 2006). These are not taken into consideration in this work. Accordingly, the key criteria that influence the pedagogical usability of WBLOs are:

Understandability. WBLOs should provide a well-structured description of the subject information using a clear and understandable language. The content should be clear and concise so that it is easy understandable.

Goal-orientation. This criterion is related to the learning utility of WBLOs in terms of the learning goals set by the teacher and the curriculum.

Learner-control. Learner-control describes the students' ability to control the order in which they would like to perform activities.

Time. WBLOs must allow students to learn the subject information within a limited period of time. It should take less time to learn the subject information with WBLOs than with traditional resources.

Interactivity. WBLOs should provide support for interactivity through easy and user-friendly accessibility of the subject information. Interactivity allows students to be actively involved in problem solving.

Multiple representation information. WBLOs should provide multiple representation of information using various multimedia elements. Students should feel that their learning is enhanced through the use of multimedia.

Motivation. The material provided by WBLOs should contain intrinsically motivating tasks. Motivation is goal oriented and facilitates students' higher levels of engagement with the study material.

Differentiation. This criterion involves fitting the subject information to the characteristics of the students, taking into account their age, abilities, gender, language, needs, motivation, prior knowledge, and computer skills.

Flexibility. Flexibility means that WBLOs provide different levels of difficulty and contain diverse tasks that are tailored to all students, so that their individual differences are taken into account.

Autonomy. This criterion means that students are able to work on their own using WBLOs without being completely dependent on the teacher. The knowledge provided by WBLOs should be potentially powerful to enable the student to become less dependent on the teacher.

Collaboration. This criterion is important because learning is considered as an inherently social activity as good solutions are developed not in isolation; instead they involve collaboration with other students.

Variation. Students are able to use other learning resources in combination with WBLOs. Variation of learning resources is considered as important to learning, because of different students' preferences.

4 WBLO Architecture

WBLOs exist at the intersection of content, pedagogy, and technology. From a technological point of view, a WBLO is defined as 'self-contained, discrete piece of instruction or resource material that is designed for viewing on the Web' (Liu & Johnson, 2005). From a pedagogical point of view, WBLOs are defined as 'interactive Web-based tools that support learning by enhancing, amplifying, and guiding the cognitive processes of learners' (Kay & Petrarca, 2009). From the content point of view, WBLOs are computer-based implementations of a specific topic that is aligned with a given curriculum in school education, its objectives and competence aims (Liu & Johnson, 2005). Hence, the core of WBLOs is the integration of content, technology, and pedagogy into a system that supports learning.

To achieve this goal, WBLOs are divided into components with one or many pages and subpages. The navigation through the WBLO from one page to another is flexible with many entries. A number of pages are interactive and designed with multimedia elements. Students have the possibility to control the order of the activities they do. They may skip and revisit pages. This way of using the WBLO engages the students in flexible navigation paths and nonlinear learning. Flexible design is important, because some students learn the topics before doing exercises, while other students prefer working with interactive tasks rather than reading theoretical topics. Some students prefer WBLOs that open up for many entries, while others are satisfied with one or two entries. The following figure (Fig. 4.1) gives an overview of the main functionally of WBLOs.

The technologies used for implementing WBLOs are the scripting languages JavaScript and PHP, Macromedia Flash, HTML/CSS, and diverse tools for recording video film, sounds, and other multimedia elements. WBLOs are tested in a heterogeneous computing environment that includes multi-platforms and multi-browsers.

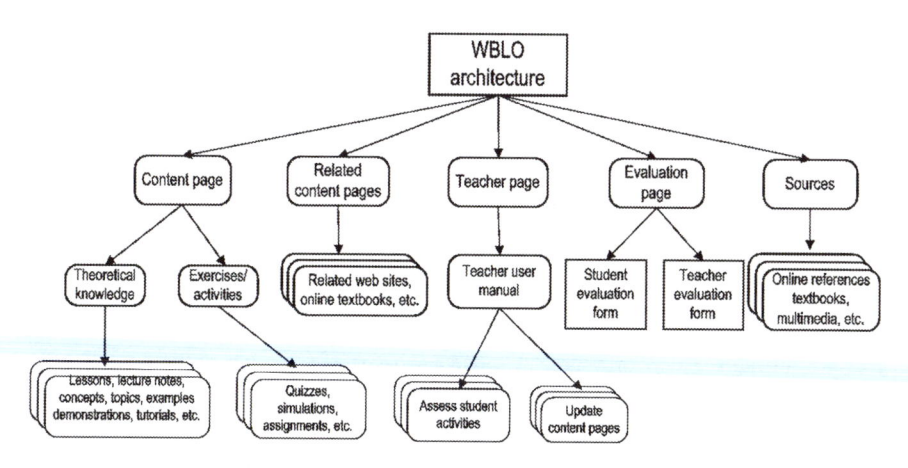

Fig. 4.1 WBLO architecture

5 Case Study

A case study is used to evaluate the pedagogical value of WBLOs. The case study was situated within teacher education in collaboration with a middle school, where three WBLOs were developed by trainee teachers.

5.1 Learning Objectives

The learning objectives that needed to be achieved with the WBLOs were aligned with the National Curriculum for schools and the competence aims that are specified for each subject. The main reason for using WBLOs was the increased focus on digital literacy skills in the curriculum, which now defines digital literacy as a key area of competence (Erstad, 2006). The situation, in which the WBLOs were developed, is listed in Table 4.1. Each row refers to the class, the school subject, the grade, and the number of participating school students. The school subjects were taught in three different classes in a middle school.

Table 4.1 School subjects and associated WBLOs

Class	School subject	Grade	No. student
Class 1	Language and culture	10th	18
Class 2	Water – A vital resource	8th	24
Class 3	Volcanoes, tsunamis, and earthquakes	8th	23

The WBLO in class 1 was designed to support students in the 10th grade to explore the Norwegian language from an historical, cultural, and linguistic perspective. The WBLO in class 2 was conceived to help students in the 8th grade to explore water as a vital resource from a natural science, societal, and political perspective. Finally, the objective of the WBLO in class 3 was designed to help students in the 8th grade to explore the characteristics of volcanoes, tsunamis, and earthquakes in different regions of the world.

5.1.1 Methods

Data from the case study came from sixty-five (65) students between 14–16 years from three different classes with 18, 24, and 23 students respectively. The data were collected by means of survey questionnaires that were delivered to the students at the end of the teaching sessions with the WBLOs. To measure their responses, a five-point Likert scale from 1 to 5 was used, where 1 was coded as the lowest and 5 as the highest (5 = 'Strongly Agree'(SA); 4 = 'Agree' (A); 3 = 'Neither Agree or Disagree' (NAD); 2 = 'Disagree' (D); 1= 'Strongly Disagree' (SD)). The students were asked to respond by placing a cross 'X' in the appropriate box using the scale provided. The survey questionnaire across the three classes focused on what the students had to say about the pedagogical usability of WBLOs. The items of the survey questionnaire were:

1. *Understandability.* The content of the WBLO is easy to understand.
2. *Goal-orientation.* It is more instructive to use such WBLOs to learn the subject matter than textbooks.
3. *Learner control.* I learn mostly from using this WBLO.
4. *Time.* It takes less time to learn the subject matter using the WBLO than the textbook.
5. *Interactivity.* The activities of the WBLO are interactive, instructive, and informative.
6. *Multiple representation of information.* The animations, graphics, and pictures provide support for understanding the subject matter.
7. *Motivation.* The WBLO is exciting to use, motivating, and interesting.
8. *Differentiation.* The WBLO is adapted to my age, development, and interests.
9. *Flexibility.* The WBLO provides different levels of difficulty, and can be tailored to all students.
10. *Autonomy.* I do not ask the teacher for help when I use the WBLO.
11. *Collaboration.* I collaborate with my fellow students when I use the WBLO.
12. *Variation.* I use the textbook in combination with the WBLO.

In addition, the students were asked to respond to two open-ended questions and comment what they liked and disliked about the WBLOs, as well as what they think should be improved.

13. Describe shortly with your own words what you liked and disliked about the WBLO.
14. Describe shortly with your own words what you think should be improved with the WBLO.

6 Findings

The findings describe the students' perceptions of WBLOs in their respective classes by means of descriptive statistics across the range of values of the five-point scale. The statistical analysis shows that the majority of the students strongly agreed or agreed that the WBLOs were pedagogically well-designed with respect to the first twelve items of the survey questionnaire (Table 4.2).

More specifically, the findings pointed out that almost 89% of the students did not ask the teacher for help when they used the WBLOs (Autonomy criterion). In contrast to autonomy, only 3.2% strongly agreed or agreed that they collaborated with fellow students when they used the WBLOs (Collaboration criterion). In stark contrast, 84.1% disagreed or strongly disagreed that they collaborated with fellow students. Finally, the overwhelming majority (93.8%) did not use other resources than the WBLOs (Variation criterion). Hence, the degree of students' independence

Table 4.2 Students' perceptions of pedagogical usability (in percent)

	SA	A	NAD	D	SD
1. Understandability	46.2	33.8	15.4	4.6	0.0
2. Goal-orientation	36.9	35.4	21.5	4.6	1.5
3. Learner control	27.7	29.2	36.9	4.6	1.5
4. Time	22.2	34.9	31.7	9.5	1.6
5. Interactivity	27.7	50.8	18.5	3.1	0.0
6. Multiple representation	42.2	39.1	17.2	1.6	0.0
7. Motivation	27.0	52.4	9.5	11.1	0.0
8. Differentiation	31.2	40.6	25.0	3.1	0.0
9. Flexibility	32.8	25.0	31.2	10.9	0.0
10. Autonomy	62.9	25.8	9.7	1.6	0.0
11. Collaboration	1.6	1.6	12.7	34.9	49.2
12. Variation	1.6	1.6	3.1	14.1	79.7

from the teacher was high, in stark contrast to the low level of collaboration with fellow students, and the low degree of variation regarding learning resources.

Finally, it must be taken into consideration that 36.9% of the students neither agreed nor disagreed that they learned mostly by using the WBLOs (Learner control criterion). Likewise, it must be considered that 31.7% of the students neither agreed nor disagreed that it takes less time to learn the subject matter using the WBLOs than textbooks (Time criterion). This is also the case of 31.2% of the students who neither agreed nor disagreed that the WBLOs provided different levels of difficulty, and can be tailored to all students (Flexibility criterion).

In addition to the descriptive statistics analysis, students commented the value of the WBLOs they used in their respective classes (items 13 and 14). Basically, most students agreed that they liked the WBLOs, but there were some differences between the classes.

Class 1: Language and culture. Most students in this class liked the content provided by the WBLO, especially the combination of written and recited text with audio recording. A typical comment was: '*It was very good that we did not need to read all the text, but just to listen to the audio recording. Everything was well arranged and well done. The content of the text was varied, informative, and easy to understand*'. Most students preferred the WBLO than textbooks. Only one student expressed concerns about the difficulty of the topic. Even though the majority of the students were satisfied with the WBLO, some students expected more interactive animations, audio recording of text, and video films.

Class 2: Water - A vital resource. Globally, the students in this class pointed out very clearly that they liked very much this kind of WBLO, especially sound recording, quizzes, and the content. A typical student's response was: '*I liked that there was audio recording of the text and motivating quizzes. It was easier to understand the text without reading. Nice quizzes*'. Most students did not think that the WBLO should be improved, but some expected more interactive exercises. One commented that the crossword exercises were not quite understandable. Another student did not like the blue color as background.

Class 3: Volcanoes, tsunamis, and earthquakes. Likewise, the students in this class liked very much the resources, especially the content, animations, and quizzes. However, most students think that there is a need for more interactive animations and recited text with audio recording. One typical student's comment was: '*I liked very much the animations. There were fine and easy to understand. I liked audio recording of the text, but you should have done this for all the text*'. Some students expressed some concerns about the time needed to download the graphics and the technical design of the video films, which did not always work as expected.

As a result, a number of students think that there is a need for more interactive animations and exercises, recited text with audio recording of text, and video films.

7 Discussion

Looking at the different dimensions of pedagogical usability some implications can be drawn. First, students pointed out that the degree of learning activities was satisfying, but the tasks provided, were not sufficient to really engage the students in constructivist learning as they do not cover the entire knowledge level of a number of students, who demonstrated strong motivation in the topics being taught. Advanced learning activities can be achieved only with increased integration of motivating and advanced multimedia elements. According to John and Sutherland (2009), advanced features require a change from an educational philosophy based on teacher-centered instruction to an environment that emphasizes the learners' needs and constructivist learning.

Second, differentiation is an important concept for any WBLO. It includes different ways of interacting with the WBLOs while giving special consideration to differentiation between students according to their ability, the different ways students learn, and the different speeds at which they learn. Since it cannot be expected to develop WBLOs with a high degree of differentiation within a limited period of time, it implies that the students' perceptions of differentiation cannot be generalized even though most students pointed out that they were satisfied with the level of differentiation and flexibility of the learning material. Nevertheless, designers of WBLOs should take into account the students' preferred learning styles and knowledge levels.

Third, motivation measures the degree of engagement of the students with the subject matter when using the WBLOs. Accordingly, WBLOs cannot be considered as highly motivating if they are not adapted to the students' age, development, and interests. Student satisfaction with a WBLO is, of course, a subjective phenomenon, but one that is important in keeping students engaged with the school subject. According to Nokelainen (2006), enhanced motivation can be achieved in many ways, for example through self-regulation, performance or learning goals, as well as extrinsic or intrinsic goal orientation, such as meaningful and interesting study material provided by the WBLOs.

Furthermore, collaboration is important because learning is considered as an inherently social activity. It fits well with the socially situated learning theory, which assumes that learning occurs as learners improve and reflect on their understanding of the subject matter through discussion with fellow students (Vygotsky, 1978). Accordingly, it is important that WBLOs contribute to increase the learning by collaboration in a higher degree, and allow the students to engage in levels of activity that could not be managed alone using the WBLO, without collaboration with fellow students. However, WBLOs can contribute to collaboration, only if students and teachers perceive the value of collaborative learning. This was not the case as the findings clearly indicate.

Then, the findings reveal that most students worked independently from the teacher, and were satisfied with the degree of autonomy provided by the WBLOs. The criterion of autonomy can reveal the quality of the learning material provided by the WBLO. However, WBLOs can contribute to independent learning only if their added value is well-perceived by students and teachers. Nevertheless, WBLOs are potentially limited in their capabilities to support learning, and beyond a certain level, they cannot contribute to the learning process alone, unless students are engaged in level of activity that they cannot manage alone without the assistance of a more knowledgeable person. Vygostky's theory of Zone of Proximal Development (ZPD) can be a useful construct to understand the tension between learning independence and collaboration with others (Bowler et al., 2005). Students' learning development, according to Vygotsky, should not be assessed by what they can learn independently with the WBLO alone, but rather by what they can do with the assistance of others.

Finally, the added value of WBLOs lies in enhanced cultural usability, which is to a certain degree implicitly connected both to technical usability through graphics, colors, and symbols, and pedagogical usability through the students' characteristics, e.g. their age, preferred learning styles, and language. However, the catalogue of usability criteria does not explicitly address cultural usability, which is a relatively new research perspective (Li, Sun, & Zhang, 2007). Cultural values are connected to folk pedagogies formed through home, school education, and society. A number of students expressed their preferred cultural values through the comments they made by means of survey questionnaires. As a result, WBLOs cannot be considered as a value-neutral technology (Gadanidis & Schindler, 2006). On the contrary, cultural values are embedded within WBLOs, which in turn can potentially affect teaching and learning processes, how students use WBLOs, and what they learn from them.

8 Conclusion

Although students were globally satisfied with the WBLOs, there are a number of limitations that need to be addressed. First, the primary objective of this work was to investigate the pedagogical value and students' perceptions of WBLOs in three classes. Despite positive perceptions, the results of this work cannot be generalized, because of various factors, such as the small sample size ($N=65$), the small number of classes ($N=3$), the limited capabilities of the WBLOs, and the limited number of teaching subjects.

In addition, the survey questionnaire, as conducted, is questionable as to whether all students were able to understand all the items of the survey. Hence, an important concern of this work is the reliability and validity of the method used to collect students' responses. Moreover, one single survey questionnaire may not be sufficient to adequately measure the students' perceptions of pedagogical usability issues. Hence, various, both qualitative and qualitative methods, such as interviews, observations, and eventually supplementary survey questionnaires, pre- and post test experiments, and their triangulation, may be more powerful to measure students' perceptions of WBLOs. Hence, it may be necessary to refine the instrument for measuring students' perceptions of WBLOs.

Future work will focus on the refinement of the pedagogical usability concepts. It is also planned to perform new evaluation experiments with WBLOs in order to generate a more complete picture of usability issues and what constitutes WBLOs in school education.

References

Belland, B. R. (2009). Using the theory of habitus to move beyond the study of barriers to technology integration. *Computers & Education, 52*, 353–364.

Brinck, T., Gergle, D., & Wood, S. D. (2002). *Usability for the web: Designing web sites that work.* San Francisco: Morgan Kaufman.

Bowler, L., Large, A., Beheshti, J., & Nesset, V. (2005). Children and adults working together in the zone of proximal development: A concept for user-centered design. *Proceedings of Annual CAIS/ACSI conference 2005.* Retrieved October 29, 2009, from http://www.cais-acsi.ca/proceedings/2005/bowler_2005.pdf

Elliott, G.J., Jones, E., & Barker, P. (2002). A grounded approach to modeling learnability of hypermedia authoring tools. *Interacting with Computers, 14*, 547–574.

Erstad, O. (2006). A new direction? Digital literacy, student participation and curriculum reform in Norway. *Education and Information Technologies, 11*, 415–429.

Gadanidis, G., & Schindler, K. (2006). Learning objects, Type II Applications, and embedded pedagogical models. *Computers in the Schools, 21*(1), 19–32.

Ingram, A. (2003). Usability of alternative web course structures. *Computer in the Schools, 19*(3), 33–47.

ITU Monitor (2009). The digital state of affairs in norwegian schools. Retrieved September 20, 2009, from http://www.itu.no/ITU+Monitor.9UFRDSXH.ips

Jamieson-proctor, R., Watson, G., Finger, G., Grimbek, G., & Burnett, P. C. (2007). Measuring the use of information and communication technologies (ICTs) in the classroom. *Computers in the Schools, 21*(1), 167–184.

John, P., & Sutherland, R. (2009). Teaching and learning with ICT: New technology, new pedagogy? *Education, Communication & Information, 4*(1), 101–107.

Kay, R., & Petrarca, D. (2009). Exploring teachers perceptions of web-based learning tools. *Interdisciplinary Journal of E-Learning and Learning Objects, 5*, 27–50.

Kukulska-Hulme, A., & Shield, L. (2004). Usability and pedagogical design: Are language learning web sites special? *Proceedings of ED-MEDIA (World Conference on Educational*

Multimedia, Hypermedia & Telecommunications), Lugano, Switzerland, June 21–26, 2004. Retrieved September 2, 2009, from http://www.editlib.org/p/11686, 4235–4242.

Laurillard, D. (2002). *Rethinking university teaching: A conversational framework for the effective use of learning technologies* (2nd ed.). London: Routledge.

Leacock, T. L., & Nesbit, J. C. (2007). A framework for the quality of multimedia resources. *Educational Technology & Society, 10*(2), 44–59.

Li, H., Sun, X., & Zhang, K. (2007). Culture-centered design: Cultural factors in interface usability and usability tests. *Proceedings of IEEE Societie's ACIS International Conference on Software Engineering, Artificial Intelligence, Networking, and Parallel/Distribute Computing* 1084–1088, Washington, DC, IEEE Computer Society.

Liu, L., & Johnson, D. L. (2005). Web-based resources and applications. *Computer in the Schools, 21*(3), 31–147.

Maddux, C. D. (2005). The web in K-12 education. *Computers in the Schools, 21*(3), 149–165.

Martinidale, T., Cates, W. M., & Qian, Y. (2005). Analysis of recognized web-based educational resources. *Computers in the Schools, 21*(3), 101–117.

Mayes, J. T., & Fowler, C. J. (1999). Learning technology and usability: A framework for understanding courseware. *Interacting with Computers, 11*(5), 485–497.

Nam, C. S., & Smith-Jackson, T. L. (2007). Web-based learning environment: A theory-based design process for development and evaluation. *Journal of Information Technology Education, 6*, 23–44. Retrieved September 15, 2009, from http://www.jite.org/documents/Vol6/JITEv6p023-043Nam145.pdf

Nokelainen, P. (2006). An empirical assessment of pedagogical usability criteria for digital learning material with elementary school students. *Educational Technology & Society, 9*(2), 178–197.

Nielsen, J. (2000). *Designing web usability: The practice of simplicity*. Indianapolis, IN: New Riders Publishing.

Nielsen, J. (1993). *Usability engineering*. Boston: Academic.

Sedig, K., Klawe, M., & Westrom, M. (2001). Role of interface manipulation style and scaffolding on cognition and concept learning in learnware. *ACM Transactions on Computer-Human Interaction, 8*(1), 34–59.

Squires, D., & Preece, J. (1999). Predicting quality in educational software: Evaluating for learning, usability and the synergy between them. *Interacting with Computers, 11*, 467–483.

Tselios, N., Avouris, N., & Komis, V. (2008). The effective combination of hybrid usability methods in evaluating educational applications of ICT: Issues and challenges. *Education and Information Technologies, 13*, 55–76.

Vygotsky, L. S. (1978). *Mind and society: The development of higher mental processes*. Cambridge, MA: Harvard University Press.

Chapter 5
KM and WEB 2.0 Methods for Project-Based Learning

Meshat: A Monitoring and Experience Sharing Tool

Christine Michel and Élise Lavoué

Abstract Our work aims to study tools offered to students and tutors involved in face-to-face or blended project-based learning activities. To better understand the needs and expectations of each actor, we are especially interested in the specific case of project management training. The results of a course observation show that the lack of monitoring and expertise transfer tools involves important dysfunctions in the course organisation and therefore dissatisfaction for tutors and students (in particular about the acquisition of knowledge and expertise). To solve this problem, we propose a personalised platform (according to the actor: project group, student or tutor), which gives information to monitor activities and supports the acquisition and transfer of expertise. This platform is based on Knowledge Management (KM) and Web 2.0 concepts to support the dynamic building of knowledge. KM is used to define the learning process (based on the experiential learning theory) and the way the individual knowledge building is monitored (based on metacognitive concepts). Web 2.0 is used to define the way the experience is shared. We make the hypothesis that this approach improves the acquisition of complex skills (e.g. management, communication and collaboration), which requires a behavioural evolution. We aim to make the students become able 'to learn to learn' and evolve according to contexts. We facilitate their ability to have a critical analysis of their actions according to the situations they encounter.

Keywords Project-based learning · Monitoring tools · Metacognition · Experience sharing · Acquisition of expertise · Web 2.0

1 Introduction

Project-based learning is often applied in the case of complex learning (i.e. which aims to make students acquire various linked skills or develop their behaviour). In comparison to traditional learning, this type of learning relies on co-development,

C. Michel (✉)
Laboratoire LIESP, INSA-Lyon, 21 avenue Jean Capelle, 69621 Villeurbanne, France
e-mail: christine.michel@insa-lyon.fr

collective responsibility and cooperation. Students are the principal actors of their learning. A significant enrichment arises from their activity, both for them and all the other students. A consequence of this approach is the segmentation of the class into sub-grouped projects, monitored by tutors. We generally observe that the coordination and harmonisation of tutors' activities are extremely difficult to operate when each group works autonomously, on different subjects and in real and varied environments (for example enterprises). It is even more difficult when the project is conducted over a long period (more than four weeks). In this context, the perception of individuals' and groups' activity is also very difficult, especially if no technical support for information and communication is used. Finally, the implementation of project-based learning in engineering schools, universities or professional training do not benefit from all its capacities (Thomas & Mengel, 2008). Indeed, this learning should implement an educational model based on the Kolb's cycle (Cortez, Nussbaum, Woywood, & Aravena, 2009), composed of four phases: concrete experience, reflective observation, abstract conceptualisation and active experimentation. However, it is often action (via the articulation conceptualisation-experimentation) which is favoured to the detriment of concrete experience and reflective observation (Thomas & Mengel, 2008).

To better understand the type of tool necessary to improve this training, we have studied a project management training course (Michel & Prévot, 2009). This course is supported by a rich and complex organisation, especially for tutors that we detail in Section 2. We have used KM methods to identify all the problems encountered by students and tutors and identify the following three main problems.

1. Difficulties in students acquiring some skills (e.g. project management organisation, use of monitoring tools and groupwork) and autonomy.
2. A lack of information so that tutors can monitor and evaluate students individually and by group.
3. A lack of tutors' communication and coordination so that they develop their expertise, knowledge and competences.

   In Section 3, we study existing tools which can help to solve these problems, especially monitoring and experience sharing tools. We then observe that no existing tool could solve all these problems on its own. Therefore we propose a new tool named MEShaT (Monitoring and Experience Sharing Tool) before finally concluding with the future directions offered by this work.

2 Case Study: A Project Management Training Course

2.1 The Course Organisation

The course is composed of a theoretical presentation of the principles and methods of project management and their practical application to a project (called 'PCo' for 'Collective Project') carried out by groups (12 groups of 8 students which answer to different industrial needs). Envisaged by Patrick Prévôt (Michel & Prévot, 2009), the project management course lasts six months and corresponds to an investment of approximately 3000 students' working hours per project. The instructional objectives are to acquire hard competences (e.g. knowing how to plan the project (Gantt's chart), project management, managing resources, controlling quality) and soft competences (e.g. social competences of collaboration and communication, empathy, consideration of others, leadership). The pedagogical team (see Fig. 5.1) is composed of 24 tutors (a technical and a management tutor per group), two managers (technical and management) in charge of the coordination of the technical and management tutors' activities, one teacher who presents the theoretical concepts and one director responsible for the organisation of the training of all groups.

The project is composed of four phases:

1. November: answer to the call for tender (formalisation of the client's requirements).
2. December: elaboration of a master plan (means, tools and organisation of the team project), definition of tools to drive the project (dashboard) and rules to test the deliverables quality (rules of receipt).
3. January to March: development of a product or a study.
4. Until mid-April: delivery of a technical report which describes the product and management report (a project closure report which is an analysis, from the student's point of view, of the flow and problems of the project). The project is closed by one dramatised presentation in front of all the actors of the project.

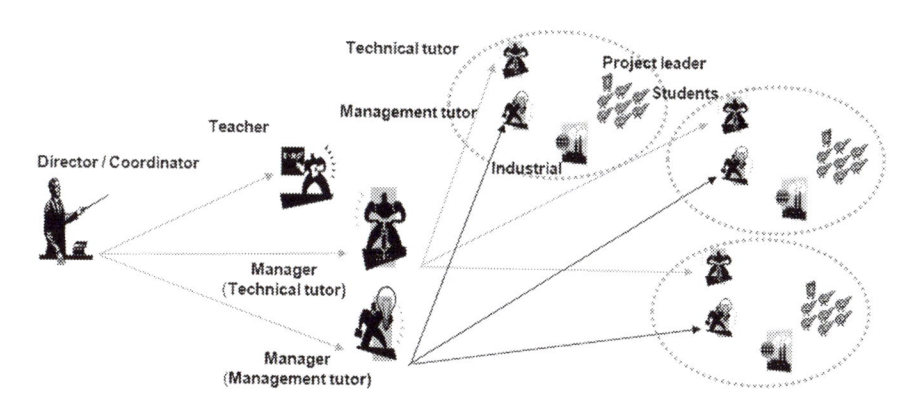

Fig. 5.1 Pedagogical team and course organisation

The course has been designed according to the experiential learning theory, well-known in KM, and is based on the expanded learning circle proposed by Berggren and Söderlund (2008). This circle is based on the learning circle developed by Kolb and Kolb (2005), which consists of concrete experience, reflective observation, abstract conceptualisation and active experimentation, in combination with the different learning styles. Berggren and Söderlund (2008) expanded this model and propose a social twist of experiential learning (see Fig. 5.2):

```
          Diffusion and implementation         Personal Experience
                  ↗     ↘                            ↗     ↘
         Enaction          Personal                     Articulation
                  ↖       and social              ↖
                           Action
                  ↘     ↗                            ↘     ↗
            Investigation                         Reflection
```

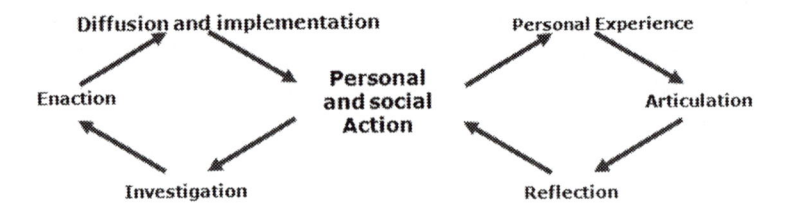

Fig. 5.2 The expanded learning circle (Berggren & Söderlund, 2008)

- The processes of *articulation* and *reflection* allow for the abstraction of knowledge.
- The processes of *investigation* and *enaction* contribute to the social character of knowledge and the diffusion of experience developed within the educational programmes.

In the framework of the project, the *personal experience* of the student is a result of the education process constructed by following the right circle of the model (see Fig. 5.2). The *articulation* phase corresponds to debriefing discussions and debate driven by the tutors (one face-to-face discussion per week). The teacher presents the 'soft' and 'hard' concepts to students during the course. During the realisation of the project, students discuss 'soft' concepts with their management tutor and 'hard' concepts with the technical tutor so as to analyse and understand them. Tutors therefore play the role of animators. This work is strongly linked with the *reflection* phase (especially *reflective observations*). Reflective observation can occur in a tacit way after these discussions with tutors or in a more formal way by realising the management report or other deliverables. Students choose, alone or according to tutors' instructions, the *personal and social actions* useful for the project or relevant according to the teaching objectives. It helps them build a unique experience, not well formalised by the teaching team. In this case, reflection is articulated with the *personal and social actions* and helps to apply 'hard' and 'soft' concepts and to build competences. It is also an occasion for each individual to express their personal experience.

Another characteristic of our project design is to promote, on the one hand, the processes of *investigation* and *enaction*, and, on the other hand, the process of *diffusion*. The courses in project management usually consist of realising a well-known project (a case study). In our case, the *investigation* process is emphasised by the fact that students have to solve an industrial problem without a predefined solution. It provides a real challenge that facilitates the construction of knowledge and improves *enaction*. The *diffusion* process is realised in the form of dramatised representations. Students present their good/bad practices and their feelings and judgments about the training and the tutors. These representations take part in a KM diffusion process, between the project team, the teaching team and the department. They also aim to support the reflection and conceptualisation processes necessary for students to realise the experience they gain by working in a group.

This combination of activities go with an evolution of behaviour in terms of skills (management, communication, collaboration and all 'soft' competences) and natural reactions (to be able to learn how to learn and to evolve in surprising or unknown situations) by supporting the students' capacity for self-critical analysis. This capacity mainly results from the training activities carried out with the tutors. Indeed the tutors play various roles which depend on the type of skills the students have to acquire. According to Garrot's taxonomy (Garrot, George, & Prévôt, 2009), for the acquisition of soft skills, tutors are social catalysts (by creating a friendly environment to incite students to participate), intellectual catalysts (by asking questions and inciting students to discuss and to criticise), 'individualisers' (by helping every student to overcome their difficulties, to estimate their needs, difficulties, preferences) and 'autonomisers' (by helping students to regulate their learning and to acquire autonomy). For the acquisition of hard skills, tutors are relational coaches (by helping students to learn how to work in a group and to become a leader), educationalists (by redirecting groups' activities in a productive way, clarifying points of methodology, supplying resources), content experts (by answering questions on the course contents), evaluators (by evaluating students and groups' productions and participation) and 'qualimetrors' (by measuring and giving feedback on the quality of the course).

Tutors monitor a unique and non-reproducible project. They work with students most of the time face-to-face and no organisation, communication or capitalisation tool is proposed. For example, no specific tool is currently proposed to the tutors for the monitoring of students' activities or for their evaluation. The appreciation of students' activity is made in an implicit way, according to the number and the quality of face-to-face student–tutor interactions. In terms of communication and coordination, each tutor works individually with their group and does not communicate much with the other tutor of the same group (management or technical) in order to have a complete vision of the group's activity.

2.2 The Observed Problems

The observation methodology is adapted from the Method for Knowledge System Management (MASK) approach (Benmahamed, Ermine, & Tchounikine, 2005). This method, starting from documents produced by an organisation and talks with actors, allows the modelling of complex industrial systems by identifying and interrelating various concepts: product, actor, activity, rules and constraint. Each concept is defined on a card; the Information, Constraint, Activity, Rule, Entity (ICARE) cards describe any *object* precisely intervening in the process. The Reuse, Improve and Share Experiment (RISE) cards describe any *problem* occurring during the process and specify the contexts, suggested solutions or recommendations. The elements described in the ICARE and RISE cards are organised overall in a *chart*, which shows their interrelationships (the method is completely described in (Michel & Prévot, 2009)).

For this research, we analyse results from RISE cards. The observation data are various experience feedbacks from students and tutors and were collected by 62 students in the fifth year of engineering school. The observed students are 23 males and 18 females who are between 22 and 25 years old. Thirty-eight of them have carried out the project management course the previous year, three of them are currently 'project leaders'. Observation consists of direct feedbacks made by interview of the course director, of six tutors and of three students currently 'project leaders' and by self-observation for the other 38 students. Indirect feedbacks are based on various groups' experience and analyses expressed in their 'management report', which is one of the projects deliverables. Twenty-four management reports have been considered (each one relating to the experience of a group). By this observation we have identified 36 different types of problems described in RISE cards.

The type and frequency of the observed problems are presented in Fig. 5.3. The majority of cards (57%) relate to a problem with the management of the teamwork by the team itself. More precisely, 29% relate to a lack of project management skills, 18% relate to difficulties working in group, 10% relate to problems with some students who think they are not responsible enough. Meanwhile, 31% of the problems concern tutors' activity and impact on the teaching organisation of the project. Indeed, 13% concern a lack of coherence, coordination and communication between tutors, which involves problems of information diffusion. For example, the instructions given to the project groups were described as ambiguous or contradictory. About 5% concern a lack of communication between tutors and students or a lack of presence of some tutors; 13% concern a lack of information for tutors on the teaching objectives or on the knowledge and skills they have to teach to students.

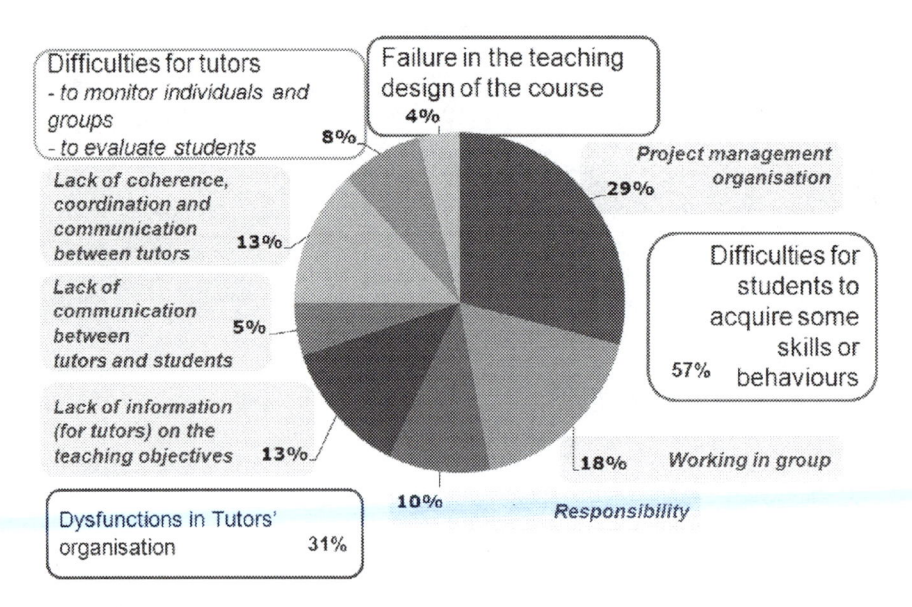

Fig. 5.3 Observed problems

Indeed, students feel alone when they have to learn using some tools or when they have to apply theoretical project management concepts. Students sometime do not understand the role tutors play and the help they can bring them. Moreover, 8% of the problems concern failure in the teaching design of the course (not enough time to work, a not adapted calendar and too short timing for the deliverables). Finally, many groups and tutors express the same problem concerning the monitoring of individuals' or groups' activity and students evaluation (4% of the problems). The students express a feeling of injustice concerning the individual evaluation because the notation is the same for all members of a project (with about + or –2 points according to their investment), even if the students are involved more or less than the others. All the tutors also express their difficulties in evaluating the students individually. These difficulties are explained by the intuitive and tacit character of the evaluations, by the lack of traceability of students' actions, and by the lack of discussion with their colleagues.

It is possible to partially solve problems concerning the course design and the course organisation by changing the timing and the teachers' and coordinators' responsibilities. Nevertheless many problems remain and most of them are directly or indirectly bound to tutors' activity. That is why we aim to help tutors, on the one hand, to monitor and to evaluate the students and the groups and, on the other hand, to exchange information, coordinate and develop their skills and expertise. Although the pedagogical context is not distance learning, we hope to benefit from using tools to support this activity. In the next part, we study knowledge management and Web 2.0 tools which are suitable for our case. We focus on monitoring tools and expertise sharing tools.

3 Tools to Support Learning Activities

In this part, we detail existing tools to help tutors to monitor students' activities and to communicate with the other tutors. We study how these tools can help tutors and solve the problems identified in the previous part. We finally show that none of them answer all the needs and therefore we develop our own tool.

3.1 Monitoring Tools

Many tools have been developed to support tutors in the monitoring of distant and synchronous students' individual activities. ESSAIM (Després, 2003) gives a global view of a student's progress in the course and tutors have a perception of the activity with reference to the path, the actions and the productions of each student. FORMID (Guéraud & Cagnat, 2006) offers a tutor interface with a global view of a class during a session (e.g. students' login, their progress in the course) or a zoom-in on a precise course stage (successfully validated or not by the class, by a student or by a group of students so as to identify their difficulties). These tools work in a synchronous environment with automatically generated tracks. They are thus only meant for tutors and do not offer the possibility for students to regulate their learning for a long period. Furthermore, they are not meant for asynchronous learning situations for which tutors need information on students' activities over a long period.

Other tools are meant to help tutors to monitor asynchronous activities and entice students towards their autonomy or to regulate their learning by determining themselves the state of their progress in the course. Croisières (Gueye, 2005) offers services which individually support students in their learning progress and assist them in autonomy situation. Students select their learning activities according to their objectives and learning strategies. Reflet (Després & Coffinet, 2004) is a tool meant for showing the state of progress of a student or a class. It supplies information to the tutors who monitor the students in distance training and to the students who have feedback on their progress with regard to the learning objectives and the other students. Students determine their state of progress in the course with regard to the tasks they have to carry out and tutors can deny students the validation of some of their tasks.

There are also tools to monitor the activities of groups, not simply individuals. SIGFAD (Mbala, Reffay, & Anyouzoa, 2005) offers a support for actors' interactions in restricted groups (8–15 persons) in distance learning. It helps tutors to hold the groups, to boost them and indeed to conduct the course well. The interaction statistics allow one to model and to show the collaboration into groups, to estimate the group's life and evolution. SIGFAD supplies three main categories of estimations: at the level of the group (present, absent or still persons, the state of the group with regard to the realisation of the activities), at the level of individuals (their productivity in terms of the realisation of activities and their sociability which indicates their level of communication with the other members of the group) and at the level of the activity (level of realisation of an activity by all participants). TACSI (Laperrousaz, Leroux, & Teutsch, 2005) offers more specifically a perception of the individual students' activity into the activity of their group. It distinguishes the perception of students' activity in an individual task (individual productions), the perception of students' activity in a collective task (their contributions in the collective activities and their contributions to the discussions) and the perception of students' situation in the group dynamics (social behaviour and sociometric status). The LCC (Learning to Collaborate by Collaborating) collaborative activity software (Cortez et. al., 2009) is used for teaching and measuring teamwork skills using technologically supported face-to-face collaborative activities. LCC allows seven variables to be measured: the first variables measure the activity score (i.e. the group's efficiency in performing the task assigned), while the last variables measure teamwork (corresponding to core components (skills) of teamwork like team orientation (TO), team leadership (TL), monitoring (MO), feedback (FE), back-up (BA) and coordination (CO)). Communication has not been included in the measurable variables.

The individual and collective indicators for the monitoring of students and project groups offered by these tools are relatively well adapted to our context. We especially adopt those proposed within the LCC framework (Cortez et al., 2009) for the development of our own monitoring tool. However, the course which interests us does not use instrumented activity and thus does not allow using automatically collected tracks of students' activity which is why we have to think about other ways of collecting information on their activities.

The tools which help students to acquire autonomy incite them to evaluate their progress in the course, according to the tasks they have achieved and those they have to achieve. However, these tools are not adapted because they do not help students to build an individual reflection neither on the relevance of the knowledge they acquire and the modalities of this acquisition nor on their behavioural changes. These self-regulatory processes are individual and mainly result from the activities carried out with the tutors. We think it useful (Michel & Prévôt, 2009) to support these processes by using a metacognitive tool (Azevedo, 2007) which takes into account students' point of view of cognition (e.g. activating prior knowledge, planning, creating sub-goals, learning strategies), metacognition (e.g. feeling of knowing, judgment of learning, content evaluation), motivation (e.g. self-efficacy, task value, interest, effort) and behaviour (e.g. engaging in help-seeking behaviour, modifying learning conditions, handling task difficulties and demands).

All the tools studied in this part are exclusively centred on students' activity and help neither students nor tutors to have reflections on their activity. In our context, in which the roles played by tutors are extremely varied, it is essential to have a base structuring this reflection. For example, Berggren and Söderlund (2008) propose to use a 'learning contract' defined as 'a number of fairly simple questions, such as: What do I want to learn? How will I learn this? Who can give support? When can I start? How will I know that I have learned? How will others realise that I have learned?' This contract could be useful not only for students but also for tutors.

Furthermore, all the tools do not help tutors to understand or interpret what they observe. They supply useful information for tutors but this information is rather quantitative than qualitative and thus does not allow the evaluation of the quality of the contributions or productions, or to explain students' behaviour neither individually nor inside the group. These tools can be useful for tutors only if they know how to use them, how to interpret the supplied information and how to react effectively and in an adapted way. Finally, these tools address every tutor individually and do not allow them to coordinate at the level of monitoring of the same project group and to exchange on their activity so as to acquire more expertise. All of which is why we go on to study in the next section the tools which support exchanges between tutors to allow them to help each other and to develop their skills.

3.2 Experience Sharing Tools

The results of a previous study (Michel, Garrot, & George, 2007) about tools supplied to tutors shows that they do not have adapted tools to exchange or formalise their experience as allowed, for example, by Knowledge Based Systems (KBS) or experience booklets (Kamsu Foguem, Coudert, Béler, & Geneste, 2008).

Furthermore, we observed that tutors are rather structured in a hierarchical way within the organisation and do not have coordination tools or dedicated spaces for meeting between peers.

To compensate for a lack of training and formal help, Communities of Practice (CoPs) of tutors emerge. Web technologies (e.g. forums, blogs, wikis) have allowed the emergence of online CoPs (Cuthell, 2008; Pashnyak & Dennen, 2007). CoPs gather tutors together in an informal way because of the fact that they have common practices, interests and purposes (i.e. to share ideas and experiences, build common tools, and develop relations between peers). Members exchange information, help each other to develop their skills and expertise and solve problems in an innovative way. They develop a community identity around shared knowledge, common approaches and established practices and create a shared directory of common resources (Wenger, 1998; Garrot-Lavoué, 2009). The use of technology does allow the accumulation of exchange, but these are relatively unstructured and not contextualised. Web tools such as blogs, mailing lists, chat and email, allow discussions without building concrete knowledge (only forums bring a slightly higher degree of explicit emergence, thanks to the spatial representation as discussion threads which highlights relations between messages).

Numerous works aim to answer the question by supplying tutors with tools to support specific activities. Some tools work through member participation and sociability, for example by offering a virtual 'home' like the Tapped In environment (Schlager & Fusco, 2004), others by supporting collaboration between members like CoPe_it! (Karacapilidis & Tzagarakis, 2007). Other tools favour the creation of contextualised resources and contextual search facilities such as the learning environment doceNet (Brito Mírian, da Nóbrega, & de Oliveira, 2006). However, all these environments either favour sociability (engaging members to participate) to the detriment of the reification of the produced resources, or they favour the accumulation and indexation of contextualised resources, but to the detriment of sociability and member participation.

We have developed the TE-Cap platform (Garrot-Lavoué, 2009) so as to support a good structuralisation of the information without decreasing member participation (for example communication). Indeed, the tutors have discussions by way of contextualised forums: they associate tags with the discussions to describe the context. These tags are subjects of a tutoring taxonomy, shown in an interactive and evolutionary way (the tutors can propose new subjects for the taxonomy). This platform, associated with a monitoring tool, could answer our needs of knowledge and skills acquisition and capitalisation about the realisation of tutors' activity and about the use of the monitoring tools.

4 A Platform for Tutors and Students

We have designed a customised platform called MEShaT (see Fig. 5.4). It proposes different interfaces according to the learning actor: a project group, a student or a tutor. Every interface consists of the following.

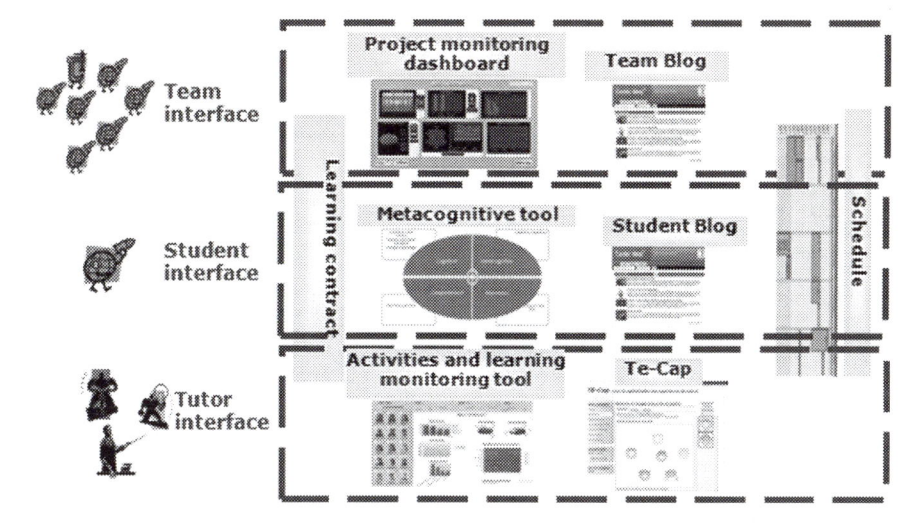

Fig. 5.4 MEShaT: Monitoring and experience sharing tool for project-based learning

1. A monitoring tool (on the form of a dashboard) which helps the concerned actor to have a global view of their activity.
2. A publication tool which allows the spread of their experience.

Three dashboards are offered; two for students (one to monitor the progress of their project and the other one to monitor their own learning process) and one for tutors (to monitor students' and groups' activities and students' learning).

- The project monitoring dashboard is a project management tool meant for the group and shows various indicators: the group's frame of mind (e.g. motivation, satisfaction, relationship with the client), the Gantt diagram, tasks to realise and the percentage of realisation, the working time of each member, the deliverables to produce and the delays. This tool is dedicated to the group leader for the project steering, to the members to situate themselves regarding the others and to express themselves. The indicators provide information to students for the metacognitive processes described below and to tutors for the monitoring of teamwork.
- The metacognitive tool takes into account students' individual point of view of their cognition, metacognition, motivation and behaviour so as to build reflexive indicators. Concerning cognition, students evaluate themselves in relation to the target competencies in project management (hard and soft) as well as to the ones necessary for the project realisation. They define the planning, the sub-goals and the learning strategies required to acquire these competencies. Regarding metacognition, students express their feeling about competencies and knowledge acquisition (level, form, context, judgment). Students more precisely describe their motivation about their self-efficacy, the value and the interest of the tasks and the required effort. They also formalise their behaviour by explaining how

they engage in help-seeking strategy and the way they handle task difficulties and demands. We consider that it is important to reflect all these indicators to students so as to help them to build an individual reflection on the relevance of the knowledge they acquire, on the modalities of this acquisition and on their behavioural changes.

- The activities and learning monitoring tool is meant for tutors and shows information on the individual students' activity and the groups' activity thanks to indicators such as the group orientation, leadership, monitoring, feedback and coordination. These indicators are built thanks to the information given by students in the individual and group dashboards described above. Tutors therefore have access to all the information on student and group activities and can intervene when needed. The history helps them to understand the individual and group processes, to intervene with the students in an adapted way and to assess the students' work.

The publication tools are blogs and TE-Cap.

- Blogs (one per student and one per group) are spaces where students can freely describe, for example, the realisation contexts of their actions and their frame of mind. These blogs help the group members and the tutors to understand the project context, to explain the value of some indicators (as delays or the group's frame of mind) and so to anticipate or to solve problems more quickly.
- TE-Cap is offered to tutors to allow the emergence of a CoP composed of all the tutors who monitor a project. The indexation model is built on three main subjects, corresponding to the different types of expertise required for tutors: (1) their roles and tasks; (2) the project calendar (so as to coordinate); and (3) the specific progress of every group. By exchanging, tutors will acquire expertise on their roles and knowledge on their application ground. TE-Cap can be considered as an expertise transfer tool.

A fixed section shows information accessible by all the actors: the schedule and the learning contract. The schedule helps students and tutors, of the same or different groups, to coordinate their activities. The learning contract defines simple questions for students such as: 'What do I want to learn? How will I learn this? Who can give support? When can I start? How will I know that I have learned? How will others realise that I have learned?' These questions are defined at the start of the project and are used to focus students' attention on the educational objectives throughout the project. This contract could be useful not only for students but also for tutors. Tutors can also refer to these kinds of questions to refocus on their roles. It is a means to coordinate tutors who have to implement the same educational means.

The information on the dashboards can be modified by their owner(s) and are not visible for everybody. Students can modify their blog and their individual dashboard by means of a data entry interface. The groups' dashboard is updated by the project leader, using individual information. Leaders confirm the data and decide what is published on the blog. The tutors' dashboard is directly updated by them and automatically updated according to the information entry on the groups' and students' interfaces. Tutors also contribute directly to the CoP. Tutors have access to the groups' and students' interfaces. The project leaders have no access to the individual dashboards of their group members. The learning contract cannot be modified during the course progress. It is updated at the end of the project, according to the events which were related on blogs and on TE-Cap.

MEShaT is meant for the complex educational context of project-based learning, using the Kolb's learning process. The metacognitive tool, the blogs, TE-Cap and the learning contract, favour the reflexive observation and concrete experience phases of the Kolb's cycle, the monitoring tools help action phases (conceptualisation and experimentation). Moreover, MEShaT solves some of the problems identified in Section 2.2. Monitoring tools and blogs facilitate groupwork, group cohesion and the professionalism of students by making the consequences of their acts more tangible and by informing them. Metacognitive tools and blogs help students to acquire knowledge and reinforce their motivation (by a better understanding of what they have to do and why they do it). If these phenomena do not naturally appear, tools will help the tutors to make them emerge. Indeed, MEShaT reinforces the tutor-student link by allowing the continuous monitoring of the knowledge acquisition process. It also helps tutors to assume some of their roles, like their roles of relational coach and social catalyst (concerning groupwork or leadership), their role of intellectual catalyst (by asking precise and conceptualised questions to incite students to discuss or ask critical questions) and their roles of expert and pedagogue. Moreover, the association of Te-Cap with the learning contract offers tutors a space for refining or developing their expertise.

5 Conclusion and Future Directions

Our work aims to study how KM methods and Web 2.0 tools can be useful in face-to-face or blended project-based learning activities. We propose to make use of them to design a monitoring and expertise transfer tool proposed to tutors and students. To understand better the needs and expectations of each actor, we are especially interested in the case of project management training. Indeed, this type of learning is complex since it has for an objective the acquisitions of soft and hard knowledge and relies on rich and varied social organisations. In the first part of this article we described a course that has been designed according to the experiential learning theory and based on an expanded learning circle. We then expose the observed problems, like the lack of monitoring and expertise transfer tools, which involve important dysfunctions in the course organisation and therefore dissatisfaction for tutors and students (in particular about the acquisition of knowledge and expertise). The study of existing tools highlights two points:

1. There is no tool which helps both tutors and students.
2. There are no clear strategies proposed to acquire, transfer and capitalise on the actors' experience.

Indeed, studied tools do not offer metacognitive functions, formal or informal publication tools (such as knowledge books or blogs) or tools to support CoP.

Therefore, to solve this problem, we propose to associate personalised monitoring tools (one for the project group, one for the student and one for the tutor) with tools for the transfer of experience and the acquisition of knowledge. Regarding the monitoring: the 'team feedback' is a dashboard for the project management, the 'student feedback' is a metacognitive tool and the 'tutor feedback' is a monitoring tool for individuals' and groups' activity. The tool for the acquisition of knowledge considers two types of knowledge: the acquired experience is formalised in a kind of knowledge book called a 'learning contract', the experience being acquired is revealed and capitalised in blogs (for students and project groups) and within a CoP supported by TE-Cap (for tutors). We describe their articulation in a platform: MEShaT. This platform is dedicated to project management education but can also be used to support different types of face-to-face project-based learning activities. Indeed, all the phases of the Kolb's cycle are taken into account. Furthermore, it supports the acquisition of various experiences: those of the individuals (students and tutors) and those of the social organisations (project group, CoP of tutors). Our future work will consist of testing this platform over a long time so as to experimentally validate our hypotheses. We will also observe how the actors (students, tutors and course designer) appropriate this type of technology and how they participate in the redefinition of their roles.

Acknowledgement The authors would like to thank René Peltier, director of Airbus KM service (Toulouse) until 2007, for his help in the adaptation of KM methods for our context.

References

Azevedo, R. (2007). Understanding the complex nature of self-regulation in learning with computer-based learning, an introduction. *Metacognition Learning, 2*, 57–65.

Benmahamed, D., Ermine, J.-L., & Tchounikine, P. (2005). From MASK knowledge management methodology to learning activities described with IMS – LD. *Proceedings of the PKM International Conference, Workshop on Learner-Oriented Knowledge Management & KM-Oriented E-Learning (LOKMOL 2005)*, (pp. 165–175), Kaiserslauten, Germany, Springer LNCS.

Berggren, C., & Söderlund, J. (2008). Rethinking project management education: Social twists and knowledge co-production. *International Journal of Project Management, 26*(3), 286–296.

Brito Mírian, C. A., da Nóbrega, G. M., & de Oliveira, K. M. (2006). Integrating instructional material and teaching experience into a teacher's collaborative learning environment. *Proceedings of the First European Conference on Technology Enhanced Learning (EC-TEL 2006)*, (pp. 458–463), Crete, Greece, Springer LNCS.

Cortez, C., Nussbaum, M., Woywood, G., & Aravena, R. (2009). Learning to collaborate by collaborating: A face-to-face collaborative activity for measuring and learning basics about teamwork. *Journal of Computer Assisted Learning, 25*(2), 126–142.

Cuthell, J. P. (2008). The role of a web-based community in teacher professional development. *International Journal of Web Based Communities, 4*(2), 115–139.

Després, C. (2003). Synchronous tutoring in distance learning. *Proceedings of the AIED Conference*, (pp. 271–278), Sydney, Australia.

Després, C., & Coffinet, T. (2004). Reflet, un miroir sur la formation. *Proceedings of the Conférence TICE 2004*, (pp. 19–24), Compiègne, France.

Garrot, E., George, S., & Prévôt, P. (2009). Supporting a virtual community of tutors in experience capitalizing. *International Journal of Web Based Communities, 5*(3), 407–427.

Garrot-Lavoué, E. (2009). Interconnection of communities of practice: A web platform for knowledge management. *Proceedings of the International Conference on Knowledge Management and Information Sharing,* (pp. 13–20), Madeira, Portugal.

Guéraud, V., & Cagnat, J. (2006). Automatic semantic activity monitoring of distance learners guided by pedagogical scenarios. *Proceedings of the First European Conference on Technology Enhanced Learning (EC-TEL 2006),* (pp. 476–481), Crete, Greece: Springer LNCS.

Gueye, O. (2005). *Instrumentation des activités du tuteur en ligne le cas de CROISIERES, dispositif de Formation Ouverte et à Distance en langues,* PhD Thesis, University of Maine, Le Mans, France, 365p.

Harlow, H. F. (1983). Fundamentals for preparing psychology journal articles. *Journal of Comparative and Physiological Psychology, 55,* 893–896.

Kamsu Foguem, B., Coudert, T., Béler, C., & Geneste, L. (2008). Knowledge formalization in experience feedback processes: An ontology-based approach. *Computers in Industry, 59*(7), 694–710.

Karacapilidis, N., & Tzagarakis, M. (2007). Web-based collaboration and decision making support: A multi-disciplinary approach. *International Journal of Web-Based Learning and Teaching Technologies, 2*(4), 12–23.

Kolb, A. Y., & Kolb, D. A. (2005). Learning styles and learning spaces: Enhancing experiential learning in higher education. *Academy of Management Learning & Education, 4*(2), 193–212.

Laperrousaz, C., Leroux, P., & Teutsch, P. (2005). Analyzing a collaborative writing activity in order to improve tutor's perception of individual contributions of learners. *Proceedings of the IEEE International Conference on Advanced Learning Technologies (ICALT 05),* (pp. 182–184), Kaohsiung, Taiwan.

Mbala, A., Reffay, C., & Anyouzoa, A. (2005). Supporting distributed collaborative learning with usage analysis based systems. *Proceedings of the International Workshop on 'Usage analysis in learning systems', in Conjunction with the AIED'2005 International Conference on Artificial Intelligence and Education,* (pp. 111–112), Amsterdam, Netherlands.

Michel, C., Garrot, E., & George, S. (2007). Instrumented Collective Learning Situations (ICLS): The gap between theoretical research and observed practices. *Proceedings of the 18th International Conference on Society for Information Technology and Teacher Education (SITE 2007),* (pp. 895–901), San Antonio, TX, USA.

Michel, C., & Prévot, P. (2009). Knowledge management concepts for training by project: An observation of the case of project management education. *Proceedings of International Conference on Knowledge Management and Information Sharing Portugal,* (pp. 129–134).

Pashnyak, T.G., & Dennen, V.P. (2007). What and why do classroom teachers blog? *Proceedings of IADIS Web Based Communities Conference,* (pp. 172–178). Salamanca, Spain.

Schlager, M., & Fusco, J. (2004). Teacher professional development, technology, and communities of practice: Are we putting the cart before the horse? In S. Barab, R. Kling, & J. Gray (Eds.), *Designing for virtual communities in the service of learning* (pp. 120–153). Cambridge: Cambridge University Press .

Thomas, J., & Mengel, T. (2008). Preparing project managers to deal with complexity – Advanced project management education. *International Journal of Project Management, 26*(3), 304–315.

Wenger, E. (1998). *Communities of practice: Learning, meaning, and identity.* Cambridge: Cambridge University Press.

Part II
Cognitive Perspectives

Chapter 6
Semandix: Constructing a Knowledge Base According to a Text Comprehension Model

Panagiotis Blitsas, Maria Grigoriadou, and Christos Mitsis

Abstract The current chapter presents a computational semantic tool called Semandix, which is based on a cognitive text comprehension model. The basic aim of this tool is to construct a semantic knowledge base of concepts and relations among them, in order to analyze free text responses, assess concept maps and provide a semantic dictionary of concepts categorized according to the structures of that cognitive model. Thus, its basic modules are: the 'Semantic Dictionary', the 'Text Analyzer', the 'Concept Map Assessor', and the 'Administrator'. The enrichment of Semandix knowledge base is being realized through XML format files, extracted from concept mapping tools, as CmapTools, and 'machine-readable' dictionaries, as WordNet through the Visdic Editor. So far, Semandix implements some of the basic modules of a proposed free-text response assessment system. Future plans are the Semandix extension, in order to implement the other modules of the proposed system, and the formalization of the semantic content constructed to enrich its knowledge base.

Keywords Concept mapping · Knowledge base · Text comprehension model · WordNets

1 Introduction

Many systems for information extraction from texts (Rinaldi et al., 2002; Graesser & Tipping, 1999), free-text evaluation (Kanejiya, Kumar, & Prasad, 2003) and text classification and summarization (Steinberger & Ježek, 2004) have been developed. Most of them are based on the LSA Theory (Landauer & Dumais, 1997), and less

---

P. Blitsas (✉)
I.P.G.S. in Basic & Applied Cognitive Science, National & Kapodistrian University of Athens, Panepistimiopolis, Athens 15784, Greece
e-mail: pblitsas@di.uoa.gr

are based on Cognitive Psychology theories upon the text comprehension (Kintsch, 1992; Kintsch, 2001).

Latent Semantic Analysis (LSA) is a computational model based on word similarities and the automated analysis of huge corpora and reproduces the kind of the text that people have been exposed to. Its basic idea is that the meaning of the words can be inferred from the contexts in which these words occur in raw texts, provided that enough data are available (Landauer, 2002). LSA analyzes the co-occurrence of words in large corpora to draw semantic similarities. In order to facilitate the measurement of similarities between words, LSA relies on very simple structures to represent word meanings; all words are represented as high-dimensional vectors. The meaning of a word is not defined but its relations with all the others determine it. For instance, instead of defining the meaning of the concept 'bicycle' in an absolute way, e.g. by its properties, function, or role, as in semantic networks, it is defined by its degree in which it is associated to other words, e.g. very close to bike, close to pedals, ride, wheel, but far from duck, eat. LSA supports that this semantic information can be drawn from raw texts.

The main drawback of the systems using LSA is that they are not flexible enough, because every concept, in fact, is defined and restricted by the large text bodies transformed into semantic vectors. They do not work well (Landauer, 2002; Perfetti, 1998), in cases that two words could be considered similar, even though they do not co-occur. For instance, two words – road and street – have been mentioned that almost never co-occur in their huge corpus, even though they are almost synonyms (Burgess & Lund, 1997). Finally, LSA cannot be used for proposing any kind of tutoring advice, in case of misconceptions appeared within a free-text response.

In some cases, LSA has been used for marking a free-text response, which is transformed to a vector, exactly like the semantic vectors constructed by the huge corpora. A simple cosine between the two vectors (free-text response vector and the reference huge corpora vector) can measure the degree of similarity, returning this way the percentage, in which the frequencies of the words in the free-text response meet the frequencies of the same words within the huge corpora.

The need of diagnosing alternative conceptions presented in a free-text response, rather than just marking it in a statistical way, leaded to a proposed free-text response assessment system (Blitsas & Grigoriadou, 2008), which:

- is based on the semantic analysis of the concepts within a text and
- provides the possibility of a direct and gradual enrichment of itself with new concepts and semantic relations.

This chapter aims to describe a semantic tool called Semandix, which implements some basic modules of the proposed free-text response assessment system mentioned previously, and gives a boost to:

1. an automated assessment of a free-text response, by extending its knowledge-base concepts and relations among them under the precious contribution of a concept mapping tool and computational semantic dictionaries, and

2. an automated diagnosis of the alternative conceptions presented in this response, according to the Text Comprehension Model.

Section 2 describes the semantic tool 'Semandix' and the functionality of its modules. Furthermore, it gives a description of the semantic tools needed for constructing and extracting semantic content, which could be used to enrich Semandix Knowledge-Base. Finally, Section 3 discusses the proposed system, whose basic modules are implemented by Semandix, and our future plans regarding to the extension of Semandix, in order for it to implement the rest of the modules of the proposed system.

2 Semandix Description

Semandix (*Seman*-tic *Dix*-ionary) is a semantic tool constructing a knowledge base by using as a basis the cognitive Baudet-Denhière text comprehension model. Semandix gives the capability of investigating concepts and relations appeared among them within a free text and its ultimate goal is to automatically assess and diagnose free-text responses by exploring alternative conceptions appearing within them always according to the same text comprehension model.

According to this model (Baudet & Denhière, 1992), for the representation constructed by learners during the comprehension process of a text, primary role should be attributed to the understanding of the cognitive categories: *entity*, *state*, *event* and *action*. The term *entity* refers to the atoms, units or persons participating in the representation structure. The term *state* describes a situation, in which no change occurs in the course of time. The term *event* refers to an effect, which causes changes but is not provoked by human intervention. The event can be coincidental or provoked by non-human intervention, e.g. by a machine. An *action* causes changes but is originating by a man. Text comprehension is considered as the attribution of meaning to causal relations between occurrences in the text. Learners construct a representation of the text, which contains the above cognitive categories. For the interpretation of learners' cognitive processes their discourse is analysed, in order to trace the recognition (or not) of the cognitive categories.

Furthermore, text analysis in relation with the cognitive categories does not suffice. The organization and structure of a cognitive representation should involve three structure types: *relational structure*, *transformational structure* and *teleological structure*. The relational structure represents a state, in which there are entities of the possible world and no change occurs in the course of time, whereas part/all relations define a hierarchy in the structure of the system. The transformational structure represents complex events of the world or events sequences, which provoke transformation of the static states. When a transformational structure is causal then it is described as a causal path among events. When it is temporal the changes are temporal and not necessarily causal. Part/all relations among events and macroevents define a hierarchy in the system. The teleological structure is organized in a tree of goals and/or subgoals and within a time period its initial state, defined by the present entities, their relations and the values of their properties, changes turning into a final state performing in that way the predefined goal.

The structure of the cognitive representation should also be examined on micro and macro-level. On the micro-level scale, the creation of a text that allows a precise description of a technical system and facilitates readers in constructing its microstructure representation must involve the description of (i) the units that constitute the system based on the causal relations which unite them and (ii) the events sequence taking place on these units in respect to causes affecting them as well as to changes that bring the system from one state to another. On the macro-level scale, the development of the macrostructure by readers is achieved through the reconstruction of the microstructure and the establishment of a hierarchical structure with goals and subgoals. The creation of a text, which facilitates readers in constructing its macrostructure representation for a technical system, must involve the teleological hierarchical structure of goals and subgoals of the various operations as well as their implications. A technical system containing a set of associated units, which are fixed by hierarchical relations of all/part-of type and can be organized as a tree of goal/subgoals is called a 'Functional System'.

Semandix has been developed in Visual Basic .Net. For its database building, Semandix uses the RDBMS of Microsoft SQL Server, and more specifically the Express version. Alongside, the tool Microsoft SQL Server Management Studio Express is available for free and helps to mount an already-prepared database dictionary in our program. The existence of Microsoft .NET Framework 2.0 is prerequisite in order to use Semandix. The basic modules of Semandix are described in the following subsections.

2.1 Knowledge-Base Administration Module

The most important module of Semandix is the Administration module (Fig. 6.1). This module gives the knowledge base administrator the capability of:

a. Adding individual concept and relation with another concept, identifying the type of model structure that relation refers to. In case the triad (concept, relation, concept) already exists the administrator is able to remove it or add a new definition for that concept (Fig. 6.1a).
b. Enriching the knowledge base with content of concept maps and wordnets by adding XML format files extracted by CMapTools software and Visdic, respectively (Fig. 6.1b).
c. Enriching massively the system knowledge base with relations referring to every structure of the text comprehension model separately, in order for the tool to automatically categorize the incoming content to the right structure (Fig. 6.1c).
d. Resetting the whole knowledge base of the system (Fig. 6.1d).

For every new concept incoming to the knowledge base by the previous means, there is a parsing mechanism, which compares it with the existing concepts in the

6 Semandix

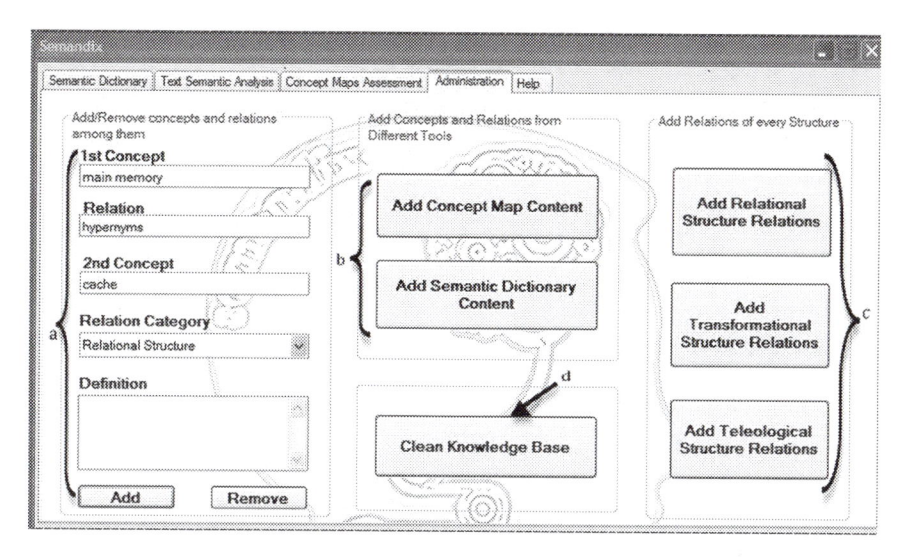

Fig. 6.1 Semandix administration options

base, in order to eliminate wrong spelling or different case of the word expressing the concept. We have to mention that for all our examples here we have enriched the knowledge base with content of concept maps and wordnets created in Greek, except for the enrichment of the base with individual concept-relation-concept triplets, which is in English.

The procedures of constructing this semantic material by concept mapping and wordnet dictionaries are following in Sections 2.1.1 and 2.1.2 respectively. We have to mention that in Section 2.1.1, the constructed concept maps examples have been translated in English for easier understanding.

2.1.1 Concept Map Constructing Procedure

In educational settings, concept mapping is a teaching and learning valuable tool providing an explicit learners' knowledge structure representation and promoting meaningful learning (Novak & Musonda, 1991; Novak & Gowin, 1984; Blitsas, Papadopoulos, & Grigoriadou, 2009).

A *concept map* is a set of nodes, which represent concepts and relations among them. These concepts and relations are organized into hierarchical, circular or hybrid structures as a whole, in order to describe the central concept of a map, which is the root of the nodes. One of the key tools of concept mapping is CMapTools (http://cmap.ihmc.us/), which enables the user to export a concept map created in XML file. Figure. 6.2 presents an example of constructing a concept map concerning the relational structure (is_a type relations) of a Computer Science domain subject.

For the semantic analysis and mapping, in order to have concept map XML files example expressing expert's knowledge, scientific technical texts on Computer Architecture subject were used (Brookshear, 2006).

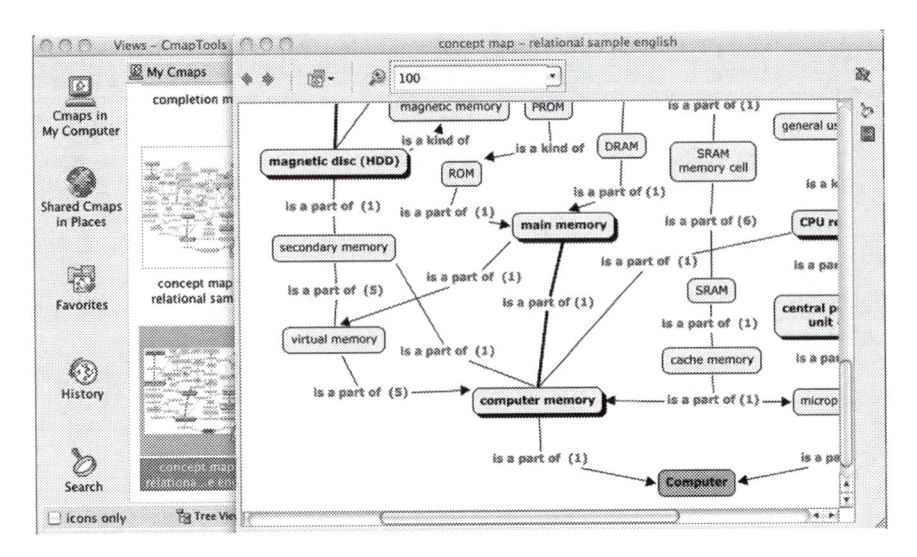

Fig. 6.2 Example of concept map constructed by Cmaptools

The analysis was conducted according to the semantic relations supporting the three structures of the cognitive model. The description of the most important relations, according to the international literature, is following:

Hyponymic and Hypernymic Relations: A concept B is a kind of a concept A of type H or M when B is a kind of H and hyponym of A. For example 'an Ambulance is a kind of a Car'

Meronymic Relations: The meronymic relations is expressed by the phrase 'is a part of' or 'is constituted by'; for example, the proposition "X is part of Y" or "Y is constituted by X". Examples of meronymic relations are the phrases: "The head is a part of the body", "One part of the bicycle is made of (constituted by) aluminum", "The valve is a part of the machine", "An appointment is a part of adolescence", etc. Many studies have been made about the types of meronymic relations. In Fig. 6.6, the six main categories of meronymic relations (Winston, Chaffin, and Herrmann, 1987) are shown. The discrimination among these six different types follows three criteria:

- *Function*. When parts of an object has a specific temporal or spatial position in relation to the other parts and/or to the whole. For example, the wheel of a car can be used in one particular position in relation to the other parts of the car and the whole car itself.
- *Homoeomeria*. When parts of an object are of the same kind with each other and with the whole. For example, a grain of salt is of the same kind with another grain and with a larger amount of salt.
- *Separability*. When members of a set can be separated naturally from the ensemble to which they belong. For example, the wheel can be separated from the car while the aluminum is not resolvable with respect to the bicycle.

6 Semandix

Table 6.1 Different types of meronymy

α/α	Meronymic relation	Example	Function	Homoeomeria	Separability
1	Component-integral object	Pedal – bicycle	Yes	No	Yes
2	Member-collection	Member – committee	No	No	Yes
3	Portion-mass	Slice – pie	No	No	Yes
4	Stuff-object	Flour – cake	No	No	No
5	Feature-activity	Swallowing – eating	Yes	No	No
6	Place-area	Oasis – desert	No	Yes	No

Considering the above categories of meronymic relations and how they are separated, the summary Table 6.1 is presented. Several other semantic relations such as spatial, class are often misread as being meronymic.

Spatial Inclusion Relations: One relation that may be confused as meronymic is that between a container-region and an object, which is cached in it. Examples of such relations are: "Wine is in the refrigerator", "The prisoner is in jail", "West Berlin is in East Germany".

Attribute Relations: Some relations link an object meaning with its characteristics. Examples of such relations: "The towers are tall", "The joke was funny".

Expert's Relational Structure Representation

The expert's relational structure knowledge representation through concept mapping is shown in Fig. 6.3 and describes part of the ontology of the subject "Computer System and Storage Units", where the main concept is the concept "computer". Because each technical text contains implicit knowledge, which is not mentioned explicitly in it, it was necessary to add concepts and relations among them implied, where there was a lack of continuity in the ontology created. On the meronymic relations of the Fig. 6.3, numbers identify the type of each meronymy.

Examples of these meronymic relations are:

- **Magnetic disk** *is constituted by [stuff-object type]* **Magnetic material.**
- **Computer Memory** *is constituted by [component-integral_object type]* **Main memory**
- **Central Processing Unit** *is constituted by [place-area type]* **CPU registers.**

The entities "computer memory", "MDR" and "MAR" participate in the expert's transformational structure described in the following subsection.

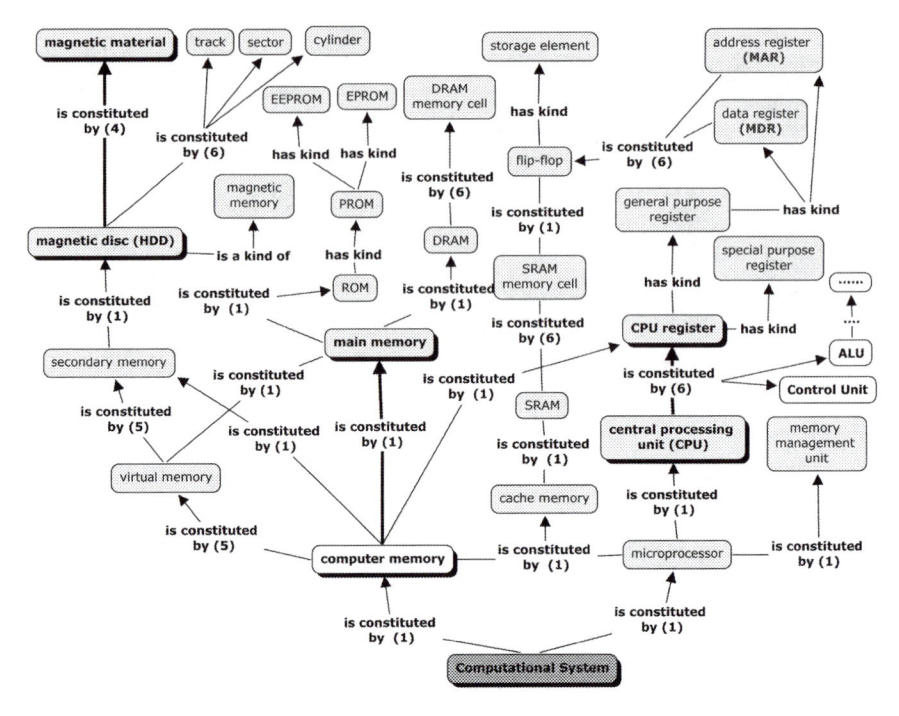

Fig. 6.3 Concept map describing different kinds of meronymy

Expert's Transformational Structure Representation

Constructing an expert's transformational structure representation example, there was a need to use other specific relation types. Some relations used in the transformational structure (Fig. 6.4) are:

- *Has event*: This relation is used to indicate the functions (or events) by which a macroevent is constituted. Each event has a purpose, which must be achieved for the system to change from a system state to another, in order to reach the final one. The purpose of the event has met in the final state alone. In Fig. 6.4 this kind of relation is not shown because of design economy. In, fact this kind of relation is a meronymic relation of Feature-Activity type (Table 6.1).
- *Causes*: There is a causal relation between two events.
- *Follows*: This relation indicates that one event follows another. That is, for an instruction to be executed, the system must first pass by an event, which not necessarily causes the second one.

In Fig. 6.4, where the main concept is the concept "DRAM-read operation", we see the transformational structure describing the macroevent of reading from DRAM memory. In particular, it appears that at the initial state of the system the processor is idle, while at the final state and after the execution of the event sequence, a CPU general purpose register R contains the content of a specific address of

6 Semandix

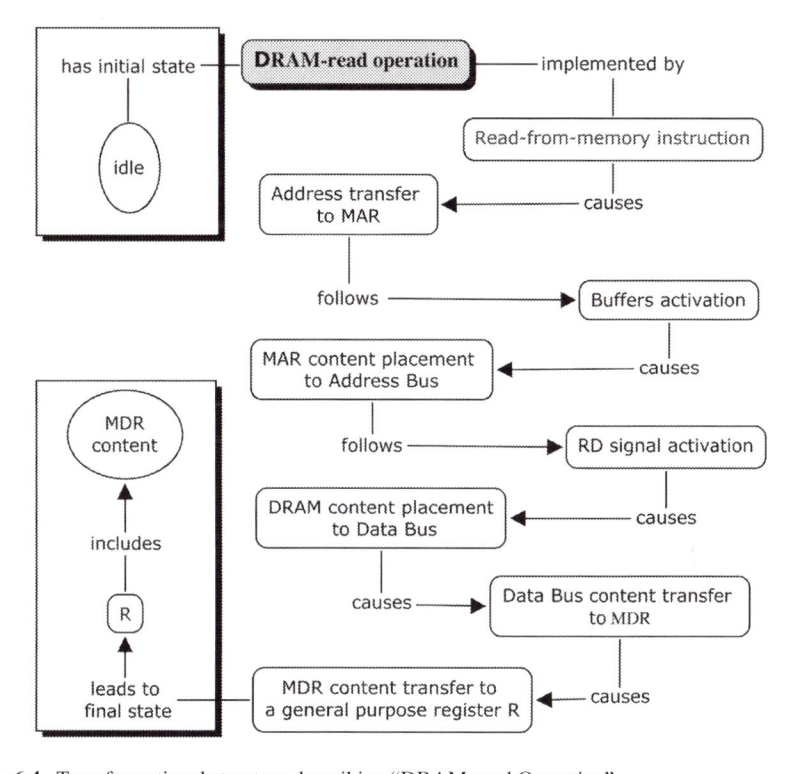

Fig. 6.4 Transformational structure describing "DRAM-read Operation"

DRAM. In fact, these states reflect the relational structure before and after the events sequence of the transformational one. The difference between the two states lies into the different values that the attributes of the entities have for the time instances.

The macroevent, therefore, is constituted by a sequence of events to be performed in a specific order to reach the desired final system state.

The events involved in reconstructing the transformational structure have temporal and causal relations between them. All of them have temporal relations between them, because they run sequentially, but only those that cause one another have causal relations through the automatic management of the CPU control unit, which generates the control signals. The temporal relations represented as links "follows" while the causal relations as type "causes" links. This means that, when describing a macroevent, beyond the statement of its events, which in fact are related to the macroevent through meronymic relations of Feature – Activity type (Table 6.1), the temporal and causal relations are needed, in order to be clear that the events involved in completing a macroevent do not run in parallel.

Expert's Teleological Structure Representation

Seeking the main goal that the Computational System (main map concept) was implemented for, the "application execution" was the first in the row with the high speed and the low cost as well. Thus, expert's teleological structure of the particular Informatics subject, which is the key objective, presents, as the main goal of a computational system, the need of executing applications in a quick and cheap way. The "application execution", in turn, has several subgoals/presuppositions, in order to be achieved, such as the "automatic instruction execution" and the "program storage and reading" (Fig. 6.5). Macroevents that the system needs for achieving the subgoals are the leaves of the hierarchical teleological structure.

Some relation types to be used in order to represent this structure are:

- *Has goal* or *has subgoal/presupposes*: This relation is used to state the purpose of a particular entity/unit of the system or the presupposition of a subgoal, in order for it to be achieved, respectively. Relations of this type are located on the upper levels of the hierarchy of the technical system.
- *Is implemented by*: The relation of this type is actually the link connecting the teleological structure with the transformational structure.

Figure 6.5 also highlights the system macroevents through which its goals/subgoals are getting fulfilled, e.g. the "dynamic reading" is implemented by

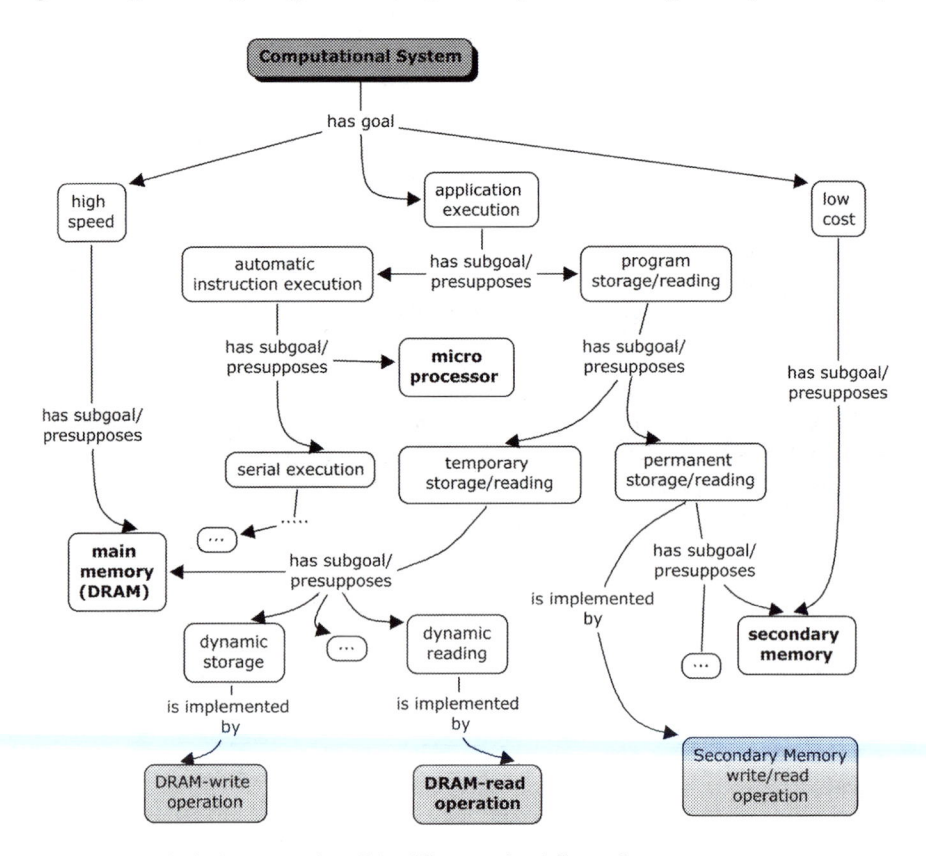

Fig. 6.5 Teleological structure describing "Computational System"

the macroevent "DRAM-read Operation". Figure 6.4 depicts the transformational structure of this macroevent.

2.1.2 WordNet Extension Procedure

Except for the construction of concept map examples of the three structures of the model, the (Greek) WordNet XML files were extended, in order for it to be used as content for Semandix enrichment. Respective WordNet extensions have been already done for the domains of Psychology and Computer Science (Kremizis et al., 2007), but not based on the text comprehension model described here.

Commonly used *electronic dictionaries* are already printed dictionaries converted to electronic form, so that they can be easily searchable on a computer. The *computational lexicons* or *machine readable dictionaries* have completely different function. They include, apart from definitions and examples of the words/entities use, relations among these words. Their creation is resulted by the need of usage in applications in the field of *Linguistic Technologies*, such as *Machine Translation, Information Retrieval & Extraction from Corpora, Summary Construction,* etc. Most of these dictionaries do not rely on text comprehension models but merely on language use standards, such as *grammar rules*, *multilingual terms recognition*, etc., statistical modeling, such as *use of word frequency, cohesion,* or a combination of these. One category of these dictionaries is the "semantic dictionaries".

Wordnet (http://wordnet.princeton.edu/wordnet/) is a computational semantic lexicon organized semantically and containing verbs, adjectives and adverbs grouped into sets of synonyms (synsets). A synset is a set of words, which in a given environment may be used in place of one another. Another important feature of Wordnet is the separation of concepts in domains. A word may belong to several synsets in many domains. Each synset in each domain has its own interpretation by semantic correlations of hypernym, hyponym, holonym and meronym with other concepts, e.g. the word "memory" is presented in separate WordNet synsets in Psychology & Computer Science. Figure 6.6 presents an example of searching hypernyms of the concept "network" on English WordNet, in different domains.

Visdic editor (http://nlp.fi.muni.cz/projekty/visdic/) constitutes a graphical application for browsing and editing "machine readable" dictionaries in different languages and is structured in XML format. In Fig. 6.7 an example of searching the related concepts of the concept "memory" in several scientific domains is presented.

The WordNet extension implementation for the enrichment of Semandix took place in four stages:

At the first stage, the texts concerning the scientific subject were found, read and comprehended. Through these texts, terms, definitions and relations to be used were identified. During searching the terms- definitions within the texts, the need to find new terms not existed within them was revealed. In order to extend the Greek WordNet database, the book "Computer Science: An Overview" (Brookshear, 2006) was used.

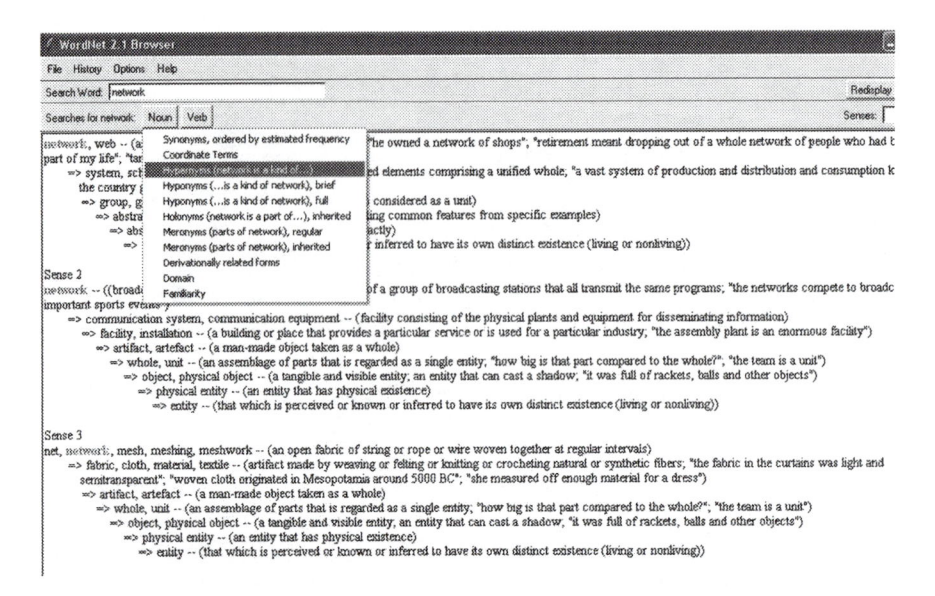

Fig. 6.6 Example of searching a concept and its hypernyms on wordnet, in different domains

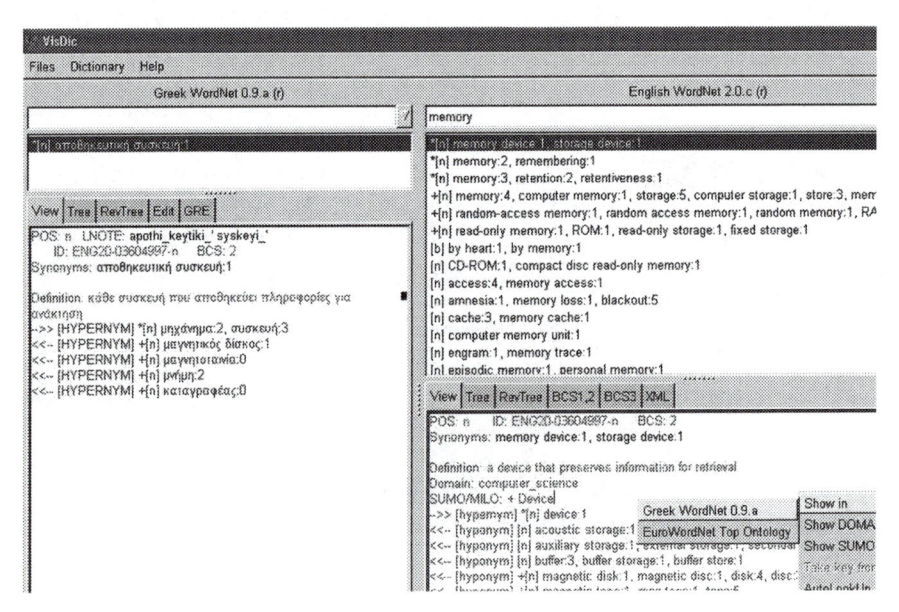

Fig. 6.7 Example of searching concepts and their hyper and hyponyms on Visdic editor, in both English and Greek

At the second stage, the «Dictionary of Modern Greek» issued by the Modern Greek Studies Institute of Aristotle University of Thessalonica was used, as an additional source, in order to get these terms that are not explicit within the text abstracts and cover "semantic gaps".

6 Semandix

At the third stage, the new and necessary relation types based on the text comprehension model were manually added. Adding relations into the Greek WordNet was realized under the help of VisDic Editor. In detail, the XML file that contains the final enriched relations was created. A new directory gre_db was created in the path of VisDic software. The files of the directory contained in the Greek WordNet were copied to the new directory. Additionally, the new enriched .inf file, which contains the new relation sets of synonyms, must have been copied. The new records/rows were added by the name of each new relation type under the default relations. Examples of new relation types according to the model structures that were added are shown on the Table 6.2 and an indicative enriched relation file, where each new relation is marked in bold characters, is presented in Fig. 6.8. We consider that the relations "has_function" and "has action" are synonyms, as well as the relation types "has_a_goal" and "intends_to".

At the fourth stage, the Greek WordNet was manually enriched with new terms concerning the Computer Science domain. The entry was made through the interface of the VisDic Editor. The words/terms not existed in the Greek WordNet were

Table 6.2 New relation types examples

RS		*has_attribute*	X *has_attribute* Y,
			e.g., main memory *has_attribute* high speed.
TrS		*has_function*	X *has_function* or *has_action* Y,
		has_action	e.g., main memory *has_function* storing.
		has_input	X *has_input* or *has_output* Y,
		has_output	e.g., adding *has_input* number
TeS		*has_a_goal*	X *has_a_goal* or *intends_to* Y,
		intends_to	e.g, main memory *has_a_goal* temporary storing.

```
...SYNSET.SNOTE
SYNSET.ILR.TYPE
HOLO_MEMBER          Relational
HOLO_PART            structure
HOLO_PORTION
HOLO_SUBSTANCE
HYPERNYM
NEAR_ANTONYM         Transformational
HAS_ATTRIBUTE        structure
HAS_ACTION
HAS_FUNCTION
HAS_INPUT
HAS_OUTPUT           Teleological
INTENDS_TO           structure
HAS_A_GOAL
...
```

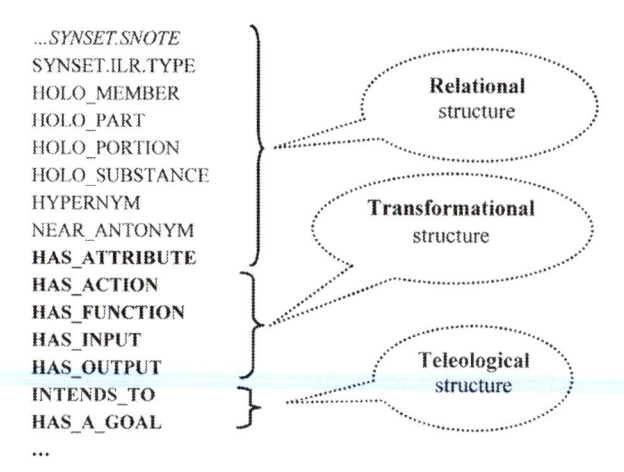

Fig. 6.8 Relations enrichment examples on inf file

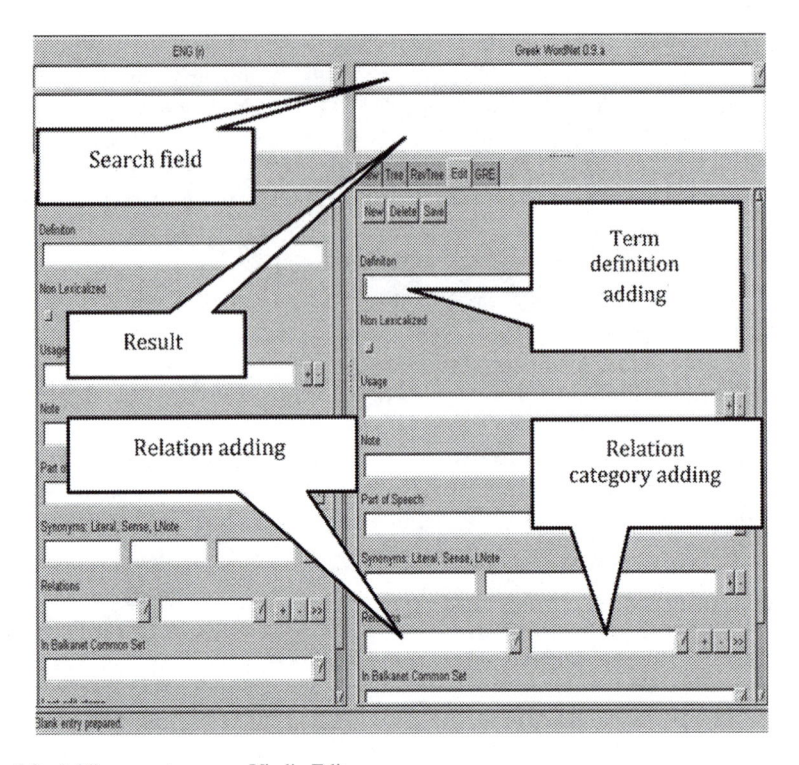

Fig. 6.9 Adding new terms on Visdic Editor

registered. In order to browse the enriched Greek WordNet by the VisDic Editor, the entire director of the dictionary was attached, and the .inf file should be modified, in order for the new relations and terms to be defined in VisDic Editor.

Figure 6.9 shows a screenshot of Visdic editing environment and explains the fields to be filled in. In the field of word searching in the Greek WordNet, the new term is being added by selecting the option "New", and associated to other words/terms. In the Definition field, a definition of the same word is added. In the field "Part Of Speech", the appropriate part of speech of the new added word is being recorded (e.g. verb, adjective, noun). Finally, in the field "Synonyms", the word/term is being added, and in the field "LNote", the Latin form of the word is mapped. Additionally, any synonyms of the term are added into this field. In the field "Relations", the association of the added word with other words is being declared.

Figure 6.10 shows the result of the search entry "Βελτιστοποίηση ερωτήματος "(Query Optimization) of the Data Bases domain, under VisDic Editor "Tree tab". On the same figure, examples of new added relations among the new terms referring to "Query Optimization" are presented.

Example 1 describes the transformational structure relation "βελτιστοποιητής ερωτήματος (query optimizer) – *has action* – βελτιστοποίηση ερωτήματος (query optimization)". Example 2 describes the transformational structure relation

6 Semandix

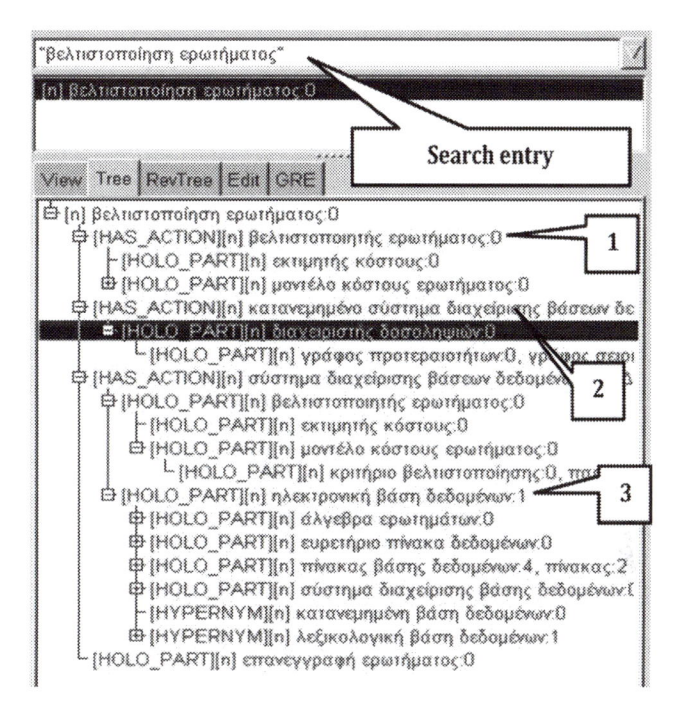

Fig. 6.10 Search entry example of data bases

"κατανεμημένο σύστημα διαχείρισης δεδομένων (distributed data base administration system) – *has action* – βελτιστοποίηση ερωτήματος (query optimization)". Example 3 describes the relational structure relation "ηλεκτρονική βάση δεδομένων (electronic data base) – *is holo part* – κατανεμημένο σύστημα διαχείρισης δεδομένων (distributed data base administration system)".

Respectively, Fig. 6.11 (next page) shows the result of the search entry "ζεύξη" (link) of the Computer Networks domain, under VisDic Editor "View tab" and "Tree tab". On the same figure, examples of new added relations among the new terms referring to *link* are presented. Example 4 describes the relational structure relation "ζεύξη επικοινωνίας (communication link) – *is a hypernym* – ζεύξη (link)". Example 5 describes the teleological structure relation "μέσο μετάδοσης (transfer mean) – *has a goal* – ζεύξη επικοινωνίας (communication link)". Example 6 describes the transformational structure relation "ζεύξη επικοινωνίας (communication link) – *has function* – μετάδοση πληροφορίας (information transfer)". Example 7 describes the teleological structure relation "διασύνδεση συσκευής (device connection) – *has a goal* – ζεύξη (link)".

During enriching the Greek WordNet with new relations, circular paths within the graph of the terms associations revealed. An example of this kind of "semantic cyclic reference", which would be considered a semantic analog to the phenomenon of the "cyclic definition" (Namjoshi & Kurshan, 1999) is following:

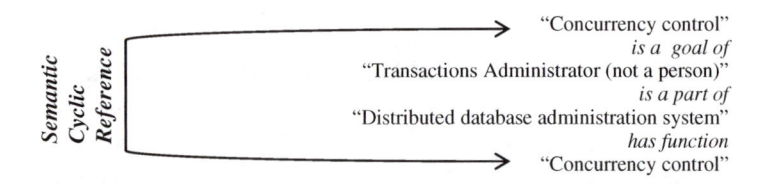

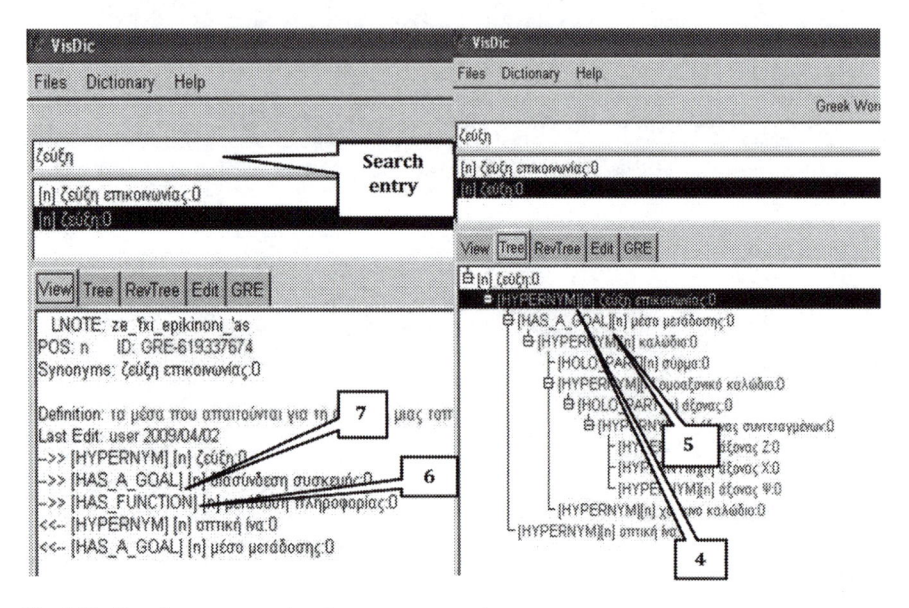

Fig. 6.11 Search entry example of computer networks

In this example, it is not clear if "Concurrency control" is the final goal of Distributed database administration system, a function of the same software or, if semantically valid, of both of them.

In fact and in many cases, semantic analysis is a very difficult task, especially in terms of the Computer Science, because it is necessary to elaborate all the semantic relations among the concepts expressed by the dictionary definitions in a high efficiency grade. So, this is a very important factor that somebody has to be aware of, while constructing or extending this kind of dictionaries, and constitutes one of our future plans.

2.2 Semandix Semantic Dictionary

Another main module of Semandix tool is that of the Semantic dictionary (Fig. 6.12), which gives the possibility of searching a concept in the knowledge-base of the system and presenting all relations referring to the different structures of the cognitive model and the associated concepts with the searched concept. For example, searching the concepts that are related to the concept "main memory"

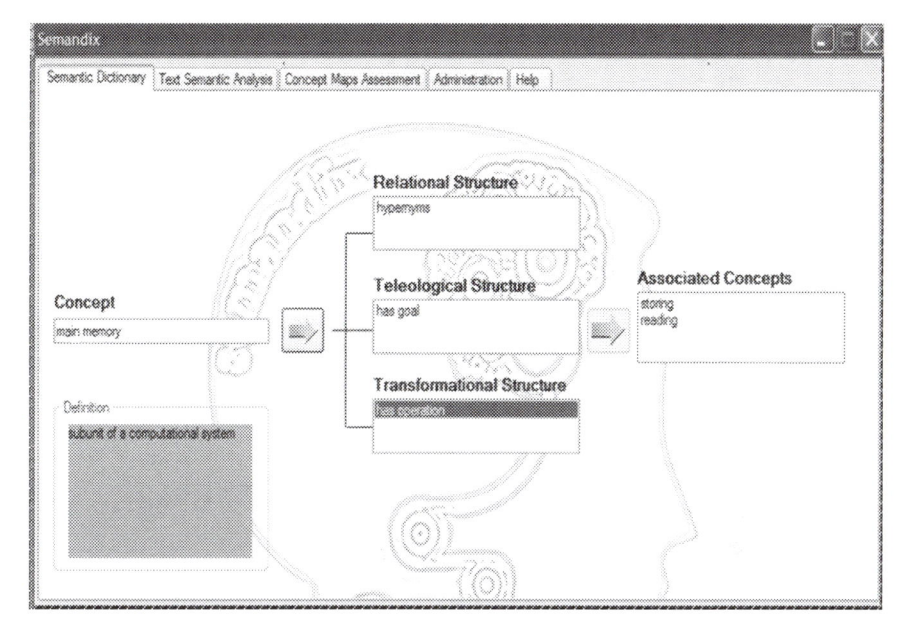

Fig. 6.12 Example of a concept searching in the semantic dictionary

in Computer Science domain, Semandix presents all the relations appeared in the knowledge base and are associated to that concept. Selecting the relation of the transformational structure "has operation", the associated concepts "storing" and "reading" will appear in the respective box, which are the operations of a computer main memory.

2.3 Text Semantic Analysis

Another Semandix module is the Text Semantic Analysis module. So far, it gives a user the capability of analyzing semantically the content of a short free-text response. This semantic analysis is constituted by the recognition of the concepts presented in the text given by the user and highlighting the relations among them. In Fig. 6.13 a two-sentence response example is presented in Greek. This module has to be further elaborated, in order to extract a diagnosis of the alternative conceptions the user presents on his/her free-text response.

2.4 Concept Map Assessment

Besides the text semantic analysis, Semandix includes a module responsible for assessing propositions of a concept map created by a user (Fig. 6.14). The assessment process outputs a list of the propositions presented on the map. For each proposition there is a result "Right", whether the same proposition appears in the

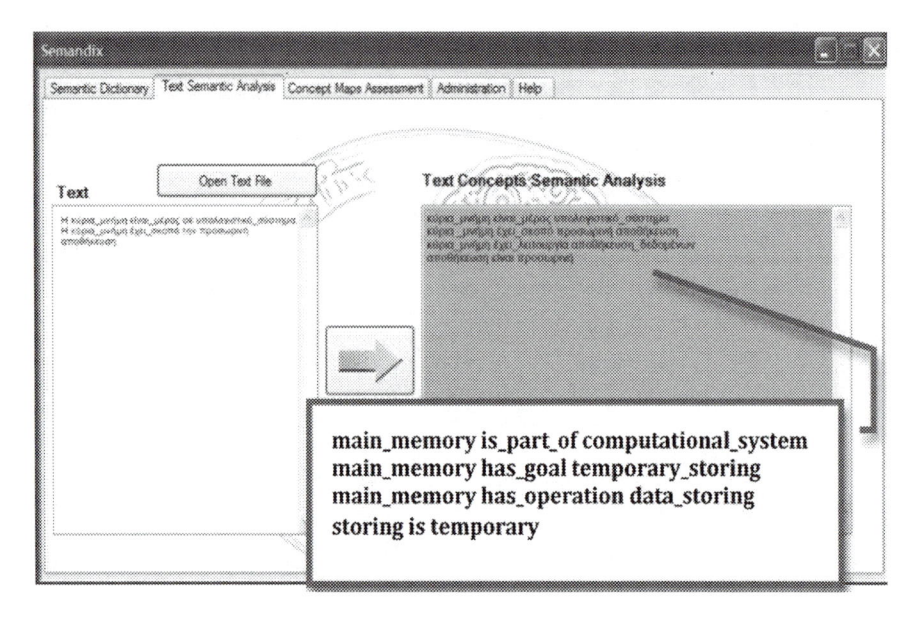

Fig. 6.13 Example of a short text semantic analysis

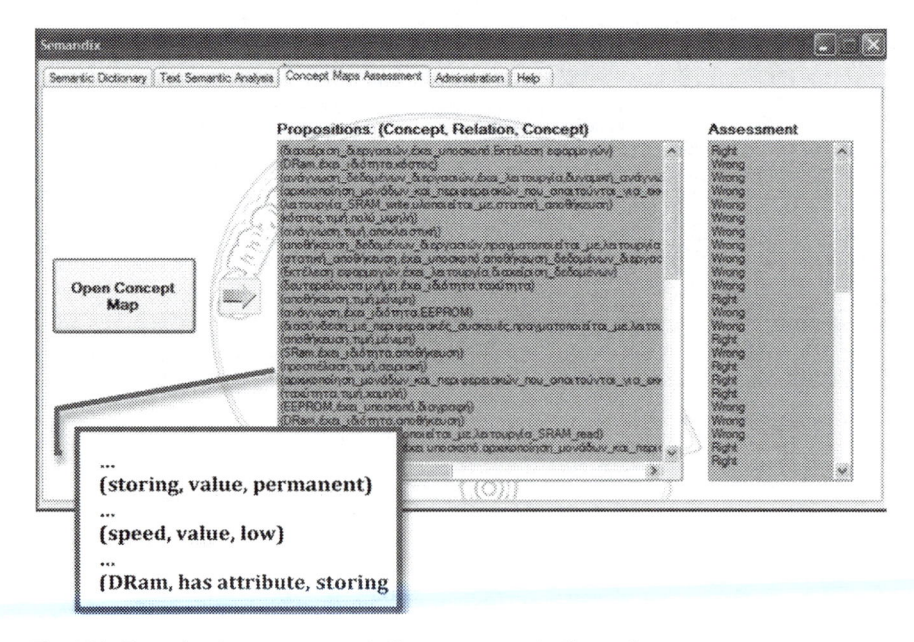

Fig. 6.14 Example of a concept map shallow assessment by Semandix

knowledge base, or "Wrong", whether there's not such a proposition in it. This assessment is shallow enough, but gives the opportunity of estimating the map correctness, in a quantitive way, without taking into account the alternative conceptions appeared on it.

Semandix does not yet categorize the propositions according to the structure of the Baudet-Denhière model.

3 Discussion – Future Plans

As mentioned in the introduction, Semandix constitutes some basic modules of a proposed free-text response knowledge-based assessment system (Blitsas & Grigoriadou, 2008). Figure 6.15 displays the architecture of this system.

Its basic modules are the following:

- Normalization Module (NoM): conversion of a student's free-text response into normalized response through Natural Language Processing.
- Functional System Module (FSM): ontology of the basic structures of the expert's knowledge representation, namely relational, transformational structure

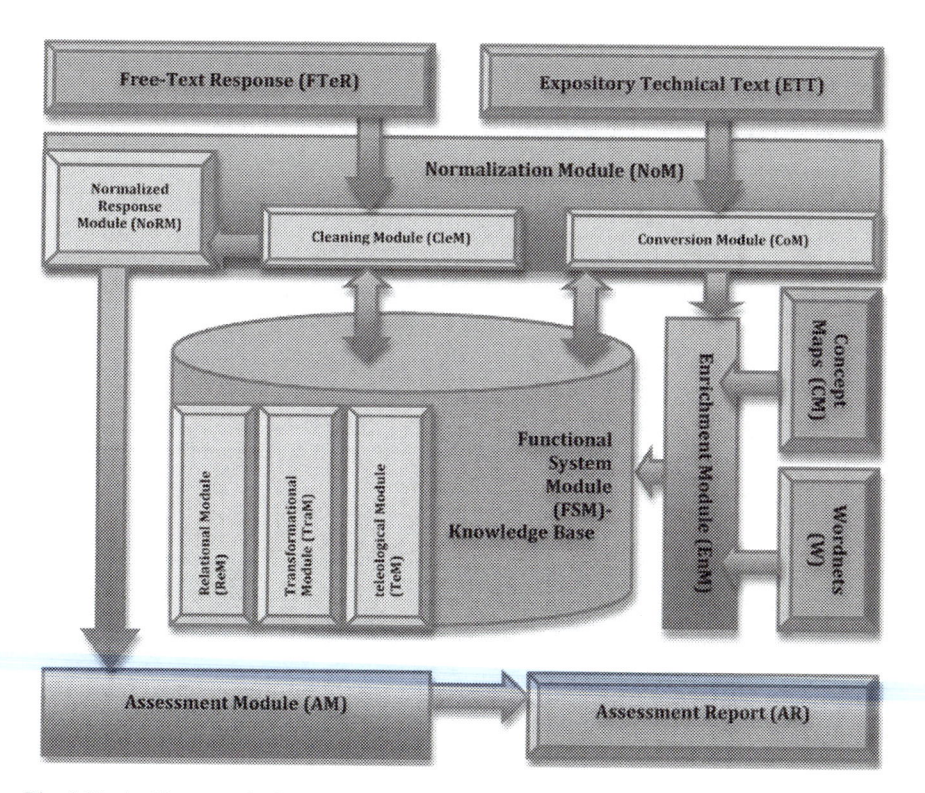

Fig. 6.15 Architecture of a free-text response assessment system

and teleological structure, depicted in the expository text referring to Computer Science domain.
- Enrichment Module (EnM): enrichment of the system Knowledge Base with content from expository texts, concept maps and/or wordnets.
- Assessment Module (AM): assessment of NoM normalized response.

So far, Semandix implements the Functional System and the Enrichment Module (except for enriching FSM with Expository Technical Text). In order for it to implement the whole system, it would be necessary to:

1. Implement the Normalization Module (NoM), for accepting this way as an input a free-text response and normalize it, and
2. Elaborate Assessment Module (AM), for diagnosing alternative conceptions appeared, regarding the three substructures of the model, on the normalized responses with FSM knowledge base that includes the scientific expert's conceptions.
3. Introduce systematic frameworks for designing concept maps and extending WordNet dictionaries, according to the cognitive text comprehension model. Namely, there is a need of setting up a stricter frame of relations concerning the three structures and implementing easier concept map and WordNets constructing tools focused on the relational, transformational and teleological structure.

For implementing NoM, Natural Language Processing tools must be used, such as a grammar/syntax analyzer to obtain the grammatical and syntactic role of the terms/words included in the free-text responses. A simple interface requires the Semandix to promote the grammar/syntax analyzer to analyze the text's words and each word to be returned to Semandix Normalization Module, in order to "construct" the normalized response (NoRM). This analyzer, in fact, will be responsible for implementing the Cleaning (CleM) and Conversion (CoM) sub-modules of NoM of the proposed system (Fig. 6.15). Diagrammatic interconnection between the Semandix Normalization Module and the Grammatical/Syntax Analyzer is presented in Fig. 6.16. We are in progress of elaborating grammar and syntax analyzers (Lovins, 1968; Hull, 1996; Papakostas & Stavropoulos, 2009), in order to integrate it to Semandix.

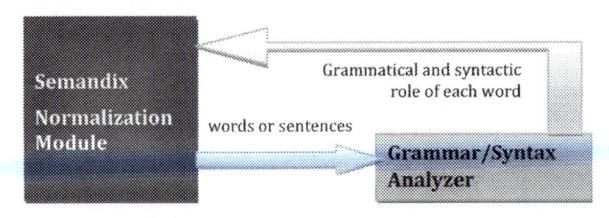

Fig. 6.16 Interconnection between Semandix normalization module and the grammatical/syntax analyzer

On the other hand, for elaborating Assessment Module (AM), there must be an automated enrichment of Semandix Knowledge Base with content expressing the alternative conceptions that readers may have during reading expository texts of the domain of Computer Science. These conceptions could be in a propositional form through concept mapping assessment procedure (Fig. 6.14) or coming from free-text responses by such texts readers through the text semantic analysis (Fig. 6.13), namely the system could "learn" during its use. To this end, a survey was conducted at the department of Informatics, where students were called, after reading expository technical text related to the computer memory, to answer open-ended questions. The experimental data are being processed. The purpose of this research is to reflect the possible alternative concepts that Informatics technical text readers have, in order to further develop the assessment/diagnose system module based on these conceptions.

Most of the handbook texts focus on the relational structure, namely the description of the computer units, but less on the transformational structure, i.e. the way they operate, and even less on the teleological structure. From pedagogical point, therefore, such a kind of system, beyond the assessment and diagnosis through a free text response, could be used as an additional auxiliary tool for students of Computer Science subjects. Through the assessment of free text responses and concept maps students will have the opportunity to rethink their level of understanding and redirect themselves towards the structures that they have not constructed in the right way.

Further implications of the proposed system could be:

- Its connection to the Internet, in order for it to search for semantic information based on the three structures of the model, for example searching on the Internet for information relating to computational units according to the purpose they have to achieve etc.
- Its assessment module integration with a module for assessing/diagnosing answers on closed questions (e.g. multiple-choice questions).

As soon as Semandix will be fully developed, it must be evaluated and its efficiency will be compared with other similar computational/semantic tools, so that we could estimate the degree, under which it performs in meeting its objectives.

References

Baudet, S., & Denhière, G. (1992). *Lecture, comprehension de texte et science cognitive*. de France, Paris: Presses Universiteraires.

Blitsas, P., & Grigoriadou, M. (2008). Towards a knowledge-based free-text response assessment system. *Proceedings of the IADIS international conference in cognition and exploratory learning in digital age (CELDA 2008)*, pp. 37–44, Freiburg, Germany, October 13–15, 2008.

Blitsas, P., Papadopoulos, G., & Grigoriadou, M. (2009). How concept mapping can support technical systems understanding based on Denhière-Baudet text comprehension model. *Proceedings of the 9th IEEE international conference on advanced learning technologies (ICALT 2009)*, pp. 352–354, Riga, 14–18 July 2009.

Brookshear, G. (2006). *Computer science: An overview*. Pearson Addison Wesley, 9th Edit, ISBN 0321387015, Harlow United Kingdom.

Burgess, C., & Lund, K. (1997). Modeling parsing constraints with high-dimensional context space. *Language and Cognitive Processes, 12*, pp. 177–210.

Graesser, A., & Tipping, P. (1999). Chapter 24: Understanding texts. In: W. Bechtel & G. Graham (Eds.), *A Companion to cognitive science*. Malden, MA: Blackwell.

Gruber, T. (1995). Toward principles for the design of ontologies used for knowledge sharing. International Journal of Human Computer Studies, 43, pp. 907–928.

Horák, A., & Smrž, P. (2004). *VisDic–Wordnet browsing and editing tool. Proceedings of the 2nd international wordnet conference – GWC 2004*, pp. 136–141, Brno, Czech Republic: Masaryk University, ISBN 80-210-3302-9.

Hull, D. A. (1996). Stemming algorithms: A case study for detailed evaluation. *Journal of the American Society for Information Science*, pp. 70–84.

Kanejiya, D., Kumar, A., & Prasad, S. (2003). Automatic evaluation of students' answers using syntactically enhanced LSA. *Proceedings of the HLT-NAACL workshop on building educational applications using natural language processing* (pp. 53–60). Edmonton, Canada.

Kintsch, W. (2001). Predication. *Cognitive Science, 25*, pp. 173–202.

Kintsch, W. (1992). A cognitive architecture for comprehension. In H. L. Pick, P. van den Broek, & D. C. Knill (Eds.), *The study of cognition: Conceptual and methodological issues* (pp. 143–164). Washington, DC: American Psychological Association.

Kremizis, A., Konstantinidi, I., Papadaki, M., Keramidas, G., & Grigoriadou, M. (2007). Greek WordNet extension in the domain of psychology and computer science. *Proceedings of the 8th Hellenic European research computer mathematics and its applications conference (HERCMA 2007)*, Economical University, Athens. Retrieved February 2008, from http://www.aueb.gr/pympe/hercma/proceedings2007/.

Landauer, T. K. (2002). On the computational basis of learning and cognition: Arguments from LSA. In B. H. Ross (Ed.), *The psychology of learning and motivation: Advances in research and theory* (Vol. 41, pp. 43–84). San Diego, CA: Academic.

Landauer, T., & Dumais, S. (1997). A solution to plato's problem: The latent semantic analysis theory of acquisition, induction and representation of knowledge. *Psychological Review, 104*(2), pp. 211–240.

Lemaire, B., Denhière, G., Bellissens, C., & Jhean-Larose, S. (2006). A computational model for simulating text comprehension. *Behavior Research Methods, 38*(4), pp. 628–637, Psychonomic Society Publication.

Lovins. J. B. (1968). Development of a stemming algorithm. *Mechanical Translation and Computational Linguistics, 11*, pp. 22–31.

Namjoshi, K., & Kurshan, R. (1999). Efficient analysis of cyclic definitions. *Proceedings of the 11th international conference on computer aided verification*, pp. 394–405 ISBN 3-540-66202-2.

Novak, J., & Gowin, B. (1984). *Learning how to learn*. New York: Cambridge University Press.

Novak, J., & Musonda, D. (1991). A twelve-year longitudinal study of science concept learning. *American Educational Research Journal, 28*(1), pp. 117–153.

Papakostas, E., & Stavropoulos, S. (2009). *Ispell*. Distribution under usage licences GPL/MPL/LGPL. Retrieved November 2009, from http://elspell.math.upatras.gr/ (in greek).

Perfetti, C. A. (1998). The limits of co-occurrence: Tools and theories in language research. *Discourse Processes, 25*, pp. 363–377.

Rinaldi, F., Dowdall, J., Hess M., Molla, D., Schwitter, R. (2002). Towards response extraction: An application to technical domains. In F. van Harmelen (Eds.), *Proceeding of the 15th European conference on artificial intelligence*, pp. 460–464, Amsterdam: IOS Press.

Steinberger, J., & Ježek, K. (2004). Using latent semantic analysis in text summarization and summary evaluation. In *Proceedings of ISIM 2004, Roznov pod Radhostem, Czech Republic, April 2004*, pp. 93–100.

Chapter 7
First-Person Education and the Biofunctional Nature of Knowing, Understanding, and Affect

Asghar Iran-Nejad and William Stewart

Abstract This chapter outlines a new 1st-person approach to educational research and practice and compares it with the traditional 2nd/3rd-person education. The chapter also reports three studies in support of the hypothesis that the acquisition of 2nd/3rd-person knowledge engages different processes from the acquisition of 1st-person knowledge. Second/third-person knowledge acquisition may be defined as internalization of external knowledge by means of such cognitive processes as elaboration, application, and evaluation all of which presuppose, rather than cause, understanding. First person knowledge acquisition, by contrast, may be defined as the reorganization of the learner's own biofunctionally-embodied intuitions resulting in new-understanding outcomes such as realization, revelation, and insight. A noteworthy implication is that 1st-person knowledge acquisition, remembering, acquisition of surprising knowledge, and acquisition of insightful knowledge all involve essentially the same knowledge acquisition processes. Any differences may be attributed, e.g., to whether the prerequisite understanding is routine or new with extensive, affectively-rich, biofunctional reorganization.

Keywords Knowing · Understanding · Affect · Biofunctional embodiment · Intuition · 2nd/3rd-person education · 1st-person education

1 Introduction

As a rule, today's educational objectives are not designed for learners to gain their own 1st-person knowledge. Rather, taxonomies of educational objectives are specifically written to instill 2nd/3rd-person knowledge in learners and use testing to make learners accountable for someone else's knowledge (Bloom, Englehart,

---

A. Iran-Nejad (✉)
The University of Alabama, 309 Carmichael Hall, Tuscaloosa, AL 35487, USA
e-mail: airannej@bamaed.ua.edu

Furst, Hill, & Krathwohl, 1956). This of course is necessary if learning defined as internalization of someone else's knowledge and meaningful, if we as educators take the expert/novice perspective on education in which learning, educational goals, the expert adult, the novice learner, and testing are determined as shown in Table 7.1. In this table, learning (2nd/3rd-person) knowledge, the quantity and quality of which (a) is, as a rule, teacher-determined in accordance with some taxonomy of educational goals and objectives and (b) ranges from retention of knowledge to its understanding defined hierarchically at varying levels of higher-order thinking. Sources like affect, biology, or interest are seldom considered to be reliable contributors to the quality of education. Learners are accountable for the acquisition of someone else's knowledge by means of teacher-determined testing. The ultimate, expected source of the 2nd/3rd-person knowledge is the educational scientist who is likely to share the same 2nd/3rd-person assumptions.

Table 7.1 Essential elements of 2nd/3rd-person education

Definition of Learning: Internalization of someone else's knowledge by rote memorization or constructive elaboration. The someone else is the expert adult represented by the teacher, the curriculum writer, or the scientist, whom the student can address as you, he, she, or they.

Definition of Knowledge: Domain-specific content inclusive of disembodied text-based, schematic, and situated content (or mental software) storable in some external medium for which the learner can be made accountable.

Definition of Understanding: A quality of knowing that ranges from source-explicit (or shallow) to source-implicit (or deep) knowledge demonstrable by the ability, as determined by the expert adult, to actively reproduce in one's own words (or actions) domain-specific content in its most elaboratively concise, complete, and error-free form while guarding faithfully against plagiary or intrusion. This includes using one's own words to engage in sequestered problem solving that enables application, transfer, and evaluation of domain-specific content, the so-called higher order thinking.

The Goal of Education: To turn novice learners into experts in 2nd/3rd-person knowledge:

- Novice Learner: 1st-person who is not ready for the profession and, to get ready, must be shown by means of testing to have:
  (a) Internalized *concepts and principles* of the profession articulated and communicated by experts in the profession in the form of educational objectives and classroom instruction.
  (b) Made concept-to-concept connections rotely or elaboratively.
  (c) reached beyond shallow level or source-explicit to deep level or source-implicit knowledge (i.e., understanding) of 3rd/2nd-person knowledge in order to be able to use that knowledge to achieve higher level educational objectives.
- Expert Adult: Person who has passed accountability tests of knowledge and understanding for the profession.
- Accountability Testing: Testing to determine achievement in 3rd/2nd-person knowledge.
- 2nd/3rd-Person Source of Knowledge: Scientific technical rationality.
- Other Educational Goals Not Considered Consistently: Affect, interest, and biological nature of the learner.

Digital Age Advantage: Digital age technology is used for predominantly disembodied 3rd/2nd-person knowledge acquisition and symbolic knowledge management.

7 First-Person Education

In the past two decades, we have been practicing a 1st-person alternative to 2nd/3rd-person education in teaching undergraduate and graduate classes as well as in an experimental teacher education program (Iran-Nejad & Gregg, 2001; Iran-Nejad et al., 1995). Comparison of Tables 7.1 and 7.2 shows that the two approaches make opposing assumptions about the nature of learning, knowledge, understanding, goals of education, the educator-learner relationship, sources of learner self-regulation, and evaluation of learning.

Table 7.2 Essential components of 1st-person education

Learning: Wholetheme reorganization of the learners own biofunctionally embodied self-awareness.

Wholetheme Biofunctional Reorganization: There are two major kinds of biofunctional reorganization: reorganization in ongoing biofunctional activity (OBA), which is nonsegmental in nature, and momentary constellation firing (MCF), which is segmental in nature. Wholetheme reorganization involves an antithetical diverging-converging alternating OBA in which divergence radiates toward a most enduring wholetheme that is comprehensive of all possible domains and convergence radiates toward a most changing theme that is highly domain-specific. Whereas OBA is a nonsegmental, 1st-person, theme-revealing biofunctional activity, MCF is a segmental 1st-person idea-revealing biofunctional activity. The two types of biofunctional activity join complementarily in a body-mind cycle of adaptation/reflection. In this cycle wholetheme biofunctional reorganization takes two complimentary forms: nonsegmental-to-segmental understanding and segmental-to-nonsegmental understanding.

Understanding: Tacit, 1st-person theme-revelation resulting from wholetheme biofunctional (OBA) reorganization (nonsegmental understanding) and explicit 1st-person idea-revelation resulting from biofunctional (MCF) reorganization (segmental understanding). Nonsegmental understanding is inherently attention-free or attention unbending and segmental understanding is inherently attention-grabbing or attention-prepared.

Nervous System as the Organ of Understanding: The nervous system is the organ of understanding just as the respiratory system is the organ of respiration and the immune system is the body's defense system.

Knowledge: Explicit 1st-person idea-revelation resulting from segmental understanding. Ideas pop out of the wholetheme as a function of multiple-source self-regulation in the context of the biological person's developmental ecosystem.

Sources of Self-Regulation: External (material ecological world), internal dynamic (material biofunctional world), and internal active (mental 1st-person awareness world) sources that regulate wholetheme reorganization of the biological person's intuitive knowledge base.

The Goal of 1st-Person Education: To make as real-worldly an environment as possible, using first and second life digital and other technology, in which the development of 1st-person self-regulation can thrive as spontaneously and naturally as possible.

- Education as Wholetheme, Developmental, 1st-Person Self-Regulation. The backbone of 1st-person education is developmental 1st-person self-regulation, singular and plural.
- Knowledge in 1st Person Education: 2nd/3rd-person knowledge acquisition is never the direct objective. Rather it is left to serve as a tool in the 1st-person hands of the developing learner to go through 1st-person self-regulation for knowledge acquisition: 2nd/3rd-person knowledge → 1st-person wholetheme reorganization → 2nd/3rd-person knowledge.

Table 7.2 (continued)

- Focus on 1st-Person Development: 2nd/3rd-person education→developmental 1st-person education→enhanced 1st-person development.
- Wholetheme Developmental Education: 1st person developmental education is whole-person-embodied education in the 1st-person biofunctional ecosystem that the learner steadily makes for the learner in the material/social world of the learner's lived experiences. This includes simultaneous development of understanding, affect, interest, knowledge, and so forth.
- Multiple-Source Self-Regulation. Multiple material world, social world, biological world, and mental world sources impact 1st-person development, which the learner must learn to regulate as the common denominator of the 1st-person of the developing learner.
- Accountability: Ideally, the learner develops the capacity of producing the artifacts prerequisite for evaluating the learner's developmental progress with the educational system providing the necessary digital or real-world multimedia. In today's increasingly technology rich real world, the challenge is likely to be surmountable.

Digital Advantage: The key concepts for integration of digital technology are 1st-person self-regulation as in Second Life (see www.secondlife.com), understanding as nonsegmental mind-body integration of virtual and actual reality, multiple-source biofunctional embodiment inclusive of multimodal sensory activity, self-regulation, lifespan education, and professional artistry in the learner's own area of creative interest.

1.1 Knowledge Acquisition in 2nd/3rd-Person Education

Many of the assumptions of 2nd/3rd-person education have their origin in a theory of knowledge acquisition widely investigated in the 1970s (see Iran-Nejad, 1980, 1987b). This theory may be illustrated using Bransford and Johnson's (1972) classic study, with which many readers of this chapter are likely to be familiar. The phrase *contextual prerequisite* in the title of this study refers to prior knowledge schemas or permanent memory structures normal learners are assumed to have in their long-term memory stores. The term *understanding* refers to comprehension of paragraph-length passages the experimenters had prepared for their subjects to comprehend and memorize. The passages were about typical everyday scenarios (e.g., doing the laundry) that ordinary subjects were expected to have stored in their long-term memory. The passages themselves, however, were difficult to understand. In preparing these text paragraphs, the experimenters had carefully removed the concrete domain-specific content so as to make the passages fully unrevealing of the typical everyday scenarios they were about. As predicted by their 2nd/3rd-person education schema theory, the experimenters hypothesized and confirmed with their results that, if prodded, their subjects would access their previously-stored abstract schemas and use them to comprehend these otherwise impossible to comprehend paragraphs, as measured by recall of the concrete text content and rated understanding.

To stay as closely as possible to the predictions of their 2nd/3rd-person education theory, the experimenters told their subjects that "they were going to hear a tape-recorded passage" that they were "to attempt to comprehend and remember." They further reiterated, both before and after the subjects heard the passage, that they were to "recall the passage as accurately as they could" (pp. 719–720). If "they could not

7 First-Person Education

remember it word for word, they should write down as many ideas as possible" (p. 720).

As predicted, the subjects who were told, before they heard the passage, that the text was going to be about washing clothes demonstrated higher recall and comprehension scores. Consistent with the theory shown in Table 7.1, the experimenters suggested that the title "washing clothes" accessed for the subjects an abstract, domain-specific (or segmental), memory schema and these subjects actively used that schema to breathe concrete doing-the-laundry content into the otherwise difficult-to-understand passage. The theory outlined in Table 7.2 implies something very different: that the words "washing clothes" caused a routine, 1st-person reorganization in the *nonsegmental* understanding of the experimental subjects. It was this change in prior understanding that helped the subjects in the experimental group to perform better than the control groups. This might seem like a slight departure in wording from the explanation provided by the 2nd/3rd-person education theory. However, as shown in Table 7.2 and described below, the implications are highly consequential. For instance, the 1st-person theory eliminates the need for segmental memory schemas altogether. In short, the experimental setting, driven by 2nd/3rd-person education theory, maximized the conditions for the acquisition of someone else's knowledge, and minimized those for the contributions of the 1st-person factors.

1.2 From 2nd/3rd-Person Prior Knowledge to 1st-Person Prior Understanding

The critical consideration is that the approach shown in Table 7.1 makes learners accountable for storing someone else's knowledge and suggests that the longer the borrowed knowledge is held in static segmental status in long-term memory the better. This, we believe to be an unreasonable demand, given the possibility that people's capacities have been evolution-sculpted, not as a memory system but as a figure-ground navigation system (Iran-Nejad, 2000). By contrast, the theory outlined in Table 7.2 assumes that it is only reasonable to hold learners accountable at best for their own, dynamic, ever-changing understanding, which seems to be more in line with an evolution-tested, figure-ground-navigation endowment (Iran-Nejad, Marsh, & Clements, 1992). How to make learners accountable for their 1st-person understanding, their own lifespan education, and professional artistry in their own area of creative interest without committing them to someone else's static knowledge defines the challenge of 1st-person education.

One of the most widely investigated predictions of the 2nd/3rd-person education theory is the prior knowledge hypothesis. It is important to note how reinforcing Bransford and Johnson's (1972) prerequisite-knowledge results were for the proponents of the 2nd/3rd-person education. For example, in a chapter entitled "The notion of schemata and the educational enterprise: General discussion of the conference" published in a book titled *Schooling and the acquisition of knowledge*, Richard C. Anderson (1977), the Director of the Center for the Study of Reading

(CSR) at the University of Illinois, featured the Bransford and Johnson article and, based on the data it reported and similar findings, made the pronouncement that "abstract schemata program individuals to generate concrete scenarios" (p. 423).

Elsewhere, we have referred to this theory as the structural schema theory of knowledge acquisition on the account that the theory postulates that static long-term memory structures program learners to generate situational scenarios. As such, structural schemas have been identified as the (segmental) building blocks of knowledge in long-term memory. Additionally, they are assumed to be available, ready-made, for retrieval and use in text comprehension (Anderson & Pichert, 1978; Pichert & Anderson, 1977; Rumelhart, 1975, 1976, 1980; Rumelhart & Ortony, 1977).

1.3 Structural and Biofunctional Schema Theories of Knowledge Acquisition

The popularity of structural schema theory heightened in the 1970s. The first author of this chapter was then a student at the CSR and was actively pursuing the cause of 1st-person education and an alternative to structural schema theory called the functional schema theory of understanding (Iran-Nejad & Winsler, 2000), which was later described as biofunctional schema theory (Iran-Nejad & Ortony, 1984). In a technical report published first by the CSR entitled, "The schema: A structural or a functional pattern" (Iran-Nejad, 1980) which was the precursor to the 1st-person education theory shown in Table 7.2, this author challenged the idea, among others, that people store program-like long-term memory structures ready to be accessed and used in understanding. Schemas, on the other hand, were themselves concrete, transient, and domain-specific reorganizations that depended for their momentary existence on (nonsegmental) understanding made possible by ongoing biofunctional activity (OBA) in the nervous system (Iran-Nejad, 1980; Iran-Nejad & Ortony, 1982, 1984).

Exactly how did the biofunctional schema theory for 1st-person understanding manage to do away with the hypothesis that structural 2nd/3rd-person schemas programmed people to generate concrete scenarios and explain Bransford and Johnson's (1972) results? How could biofunctional reorganization in nonsegmental understanding work? Perhaps, rather than prodding ready-made schemas, the separate words like those in the title 'washing clothes' caused momentary constellation firing (MCF) in a distributed set of previously unconnected episodes (Iran-Nejad & Ortony, 1984). Iran-Nejad (1980) used a light bulbs analogy to show how ongoing biofunctional activity (OBA) and momentary constellation firing (MCF) involved in nonsegmental understanding and segmental knowledge production might work. Ongoing biofunctional activity, analogous to the lights staying on over time, would be the direct cause of nonsegmental understanding and momentary constellation firing, analogous to the lights flashing, would cause knowledge production. The momentary constellation firings of the distributed episodes caused by the separate words in a phrase, a sentence, or paragraph would then combine postfunctionally, by the principle of form following function as opposed to form accessing function, to create the concrete scenario, e.g., of doing the laundry (Iran-Nejad & Ortony, 1984). As suggested by Table 7.2, the critical difference is that form following function is a nonsegmental-to-segmental understanding process (Iran-Nejad & Ortony, 1984) but function-following-form is a schema retrieval and instantiation process (Ausubel, 1963; Ausubel, Novak, & Hanesian, 1978).

Structural schema theorists at the Center for the Study of Reading must have been swayed implicitly by the arguments of their critics (Anderson, 1984; Rumelhart, 1984). For example, soon after the biofunctional schema theory of understanding appeared in print, Anderson used the occasion of his 1984 AERA presidential address to demote what he called the strong version of his too abstract structural schema theory to a more concrete weak schema theory (.Anderson, 1984). Similarly, Rumelhart (1984) abandoned what he called his earlier symbolic schema theory in favor of a subsymbolic schema theory (cf., segmental and nonsegmental understanding in biofunctional schema theory).

1.4 Understanding as Embodied Form Following Function

Iran-Nejad and Ortony (1982, 1984) defined biofunctional schemas as segmental forms following function. A schema was segmental because it was a momentary episode of constellation firing in the ground of the ongoing biofunctional activity in the nervous and bodily systems. There are several advantages to this dynamic form following dynamic function (i.e., nonsegmental-to-segmental clicks of understanding) over active retrieval of static memory from some long-term store (i.e., segmental-to-segmental activation of static memory). First, the biofunctional schema theory implies that the dynamic production of domain-specific schemas (i.e., nonsegmental-to-segmental understanding) works essentially the same way in both comprehension and remembering. In both cases, it is the wholetheme, nonsegmental ground of understanding maintained over time by ongoing biofunctional activity (OBA) of the nervous and bodily systems that serves as the causal ground for the 'pop out' production of segmental schemas. Second, the same form-following-function can explain normal and insightful knowledge acquisition. In other words, normal and insightful knowledge acquisition scenarios both involve nonsegmental-to-segmental knowledge acquisition. The difference lies in that normal knowledge acquisition relies on prior understanding with no or little biofunctional reorganization and insightful knowledge acquisition involves new understanding with significant biofunctional reorganization and an extraordinary click of understanding (Iran-Nejad, 2000; Prawat, 2000). Third, and most remarkably, the biofunctional schema theory explains how normal, insightful, and surprising knowledge acquisition are different. Whereas, they all involve the same nonsegmental-to-segmental understanding, they are different in the extent of biofunctional reorganization and the triggering sources that cause it. In normal (or being simply informed) knowledge acquisition, the triggering source is external and very little reorganization occurs; in insightful knowledge acquisition, the perceived triggering source is internal and a great deal of reorganization occurs; and in surprising knowledge acquisition, the triggering source is external and a great deal of reorganization takes place.

1.5 Wholetheme, Whole-Body, Biofunctional Activity

Traditionally, a distinction is common between the so-called irrational or animalistic affect/emotion, on the one hand, and the rational or intellectual knowing and understanding, on the other. The irrational is said to occur in the lower subcortical regions of the nervous system and the rational in the cerebral cortex (Barrett et al., 2007; Panksepp, 1989, 1998; Sperry, 1970). Biofunctional schema theory implies that evolution has sculpted the nervous and bodily systems to work in a fashion too integrated for irrational/rational or cortical/subcortical distinctions to be meaningful. Thus, biofunctional schema theory of 1st-person education predicts that insightful and surprising cases of knowledge acquisition differ from normal because extensive biofunctional reorganization in them tends to make them both affectively and intellectually integrated. In other words, in such cases, whole-person or wholetheme reorganization makes knowledge acquisition take the form of highly striking revelations or insights that encompass multimodal sensory, affective, and other biological systems.

Iran-Nejad (1980, 1987b) illustrated this using a surprising story (Thurmond, 1978). The story was about a nurse, Marilyn, who left the hospital where she worked one late night. She got in her car and, when on the freeway, she noticed that she was running out of gas, she became frightened and decided to go for gas at her usual gas station run by someone called Gabriel. He filled the tank and then invited Marilyn to go inside the station office to see a birthday gift his sister had given him. Reluctantly, she follows him into the office. Once inside, he turned around, locked the door, and grabbed a gun out of the drawer. She panics and begins experiencing the symptoms of shock. As she comes to, she notices Gabriel's lips to be moving as he was apologizing for having had to scare her like that because, as he was pumping the gas and cleaning the windows around the car, he noticed someone lying down in the back of her car. Iran-Nejad used this story to reject the notion of structural schemas as inflexible long-term memory structures, reasoning that such spontaneous reorganizations involving opposing perspectives like Gabriel first being perceived as a wolf in sheep's clothing to an eventual Good Samaritan could not possibly occur by active retrieval of a static memory schema and its instantiation with previously read story events.

Acquisition of surprising knowledge of this kind has been a challenge structural schema theory has never, to our knowledge, met successfully. Blanchard and Iran-Nejad (1987) showed that the statement of Gabriel's apology took less than two seconds to read when it was surprising and about only 800 ms longer than when it was not surprising. Therefore, the data showed, consistent with the biofunctional schema theory, that the biofunctional reorganization from one perspective to its opposite perspective must have occurred dynamically without the involvement of the kind of active schema retrieval and instantiation that is postulated by structural theory. Iran-Nejad (1987a) showed that surprising knowledge acquisition is highly interesting compared to the same knowledge when it is not surprising. Moreover, the resulting striking revelations intensify positive or negative affect depending on the valence of the content of the knowledge acquired. These findings lend support to the biofunctional schema theory.

2 Overall Methodology

The present study tests the participants' first person intuitions about knowing, understanding and affect. We hypothesize that understanding is what the nervous system does biofunctionally and that domain-specific knowing is a mental function for cognitive differentiation. The three experiments that follow examine the immediate implications of these general hypotheses:

1. Being biofunctional by nature, comprehensive understanding processes work without knowing-how on the part of the knower. Thus, participants will find it to be intuitively consistent to assert that understanding has happened while also asserting that they do not know how to engage turn around in understanding processes.
2. Being cognitive by nature, domain-specific knowing processes work by reflection on knowing on the part of the knower.
3. Comprehensive understanding and domain-specific knowing processes behave differently and, as a result, tend not to correlate.
4. Being both biofunctional by nature, comprehensive understanding and affective processes tend to behave similarly and, therefore, correlate with one another and not with knowing.
5. Domain-specific knowing by revelation and understanding by reflection work in a complementary fashion (Iran-Nejad & Gregg, 2001) making it possible for the knower to 'turn around' on his or her own revelations (cf., Bartlett, 1932) and, thereby, control the course of his or her comprehensive understanding.

Three experiments are reported that examine how certain understanding, knowing, knower, and affective statements relate to the biological person's intuitive judgments of acceptability of those statements. Consider the understanding statement (1) *I know how to have insights*, and the knowing statement (2) *I know how to drive a car*. We assume that the two statements point to fundamentally different biofunctional and cognitive processes (Iran-Nejad, 1978). Biology 'knows,' metaphorically speaking, the businesses of understanding and the mind does not, literally speaking. On the other hand, the mind knows the business of driving a car and biology does not, literally speaking. Thus, the first statement is analogous to (3) *I know how to have a fever in response to an infection*. Statement 2 is more like (4) *I know how to open a door in response to someone knocking on it*. We assume that, like having a fever, having an insight is a biofunctional process comprehensive of all relevant domains to the analogous extent that fever is a biofunctional response to all infectious diseases.

It is revealing to compare the biofunctional "knowing how" of understanding with the cognitive "knowing how" of driving. Cognitive psychologists have defined cognitive know-how of driving as procedural knowledge. It is reasonable to say that biofunctional "know-how" is neither procedural nor declarative. This is why we referred to biofunctional "know how" as being metaphorical and to cognitive know-how as being literal knowing.

2.1 Experiment 1

The purpose of Experiment 1 was to explore possible differences in participants' first person-related intuitions about knowing, knower, and understanding processes.

2.1.1 Participants, Design, and Material

Participants were 62 undergraduates (52 females and 10 males) enrolled in an educational psychology course for teacher education majors. They received course credit for participation in this study. The experimental design was 3×10 with 3 levels of statement type (knowing, knower, and understanding) as a within-subjects factor and 10 levels of statement order as a between-subjects factor. The statements were presented in 10 random orders.

Experimental material consisted of three types of statements. These were statements involving knowing processes, knower processes, and understanding processes. An example of a knowing statement is *I know that I drive a car even though I do not really know myself how to drive a car*. This statement is predicted to be intuitively unacceptable because it asserts and subsequently negates one's knowing capacities in the same complex sentence. An example of a knower statement is *I know that I elaborate even though I do not really know myself how to elaborate*. This statement was also predicted to be intuitively unacceptable because it asserts and negates the knower's cognitive capacity of elaboration. An example of an understanding statement is *I know that I understand even though I do not really know myself how to understand*. This statement was predicted to be intuitively acceptable because it presumably asserts capacities (i.e., those of understanding) that occur in biology outside the knower's realm of knowing altogether. As a result, asserting what people know cognitively is unlikely to conflict with what is performed in biology.

2.1.2 Procedure

The experiment was run in participants' regular classrooms. They read and signed an informed consent form and were handed the experimental package. The package contained the rating instructions, followed by the fully randomized set of experimental statements. Participants were asked to rate and mark on a scantron answer sheet the intuitive acceptability of each statement using a four-point Likert scale comprising *strongly disagree* (1), *disagree* (2), *agree* (3), and *strongly agree* (4).

2.1.3 Results

The data from each of the 10 randomizations was reorganized into the original order of the statements. For each subject, three means were calculated, one for each of the three types of statements. These mean ratings were used in subsequent analyses.

A 10×3 repeated measures ANOVA was conducted to examine the effects of the independent variables of statement type and randomization on the ratings. Neither the main effect for order, $F(9, 52) = 1.03$, $MSE = 0.70$, $p > 0.05$, nor the statement x order interaction, $F(9, 52)$, $MSE = 0.19$, $p > 0.05$, was significant. However, as predicted, the main effect for statement type was highly significant, $F(1, 52) = 156.00$, $MSE = 0.19$, $p < 0.001$.

As predicted the understanding statements were rated as the most intuitively acceptable ($M = 2.54$), followed by the knower statements ($M = 2.14$), and the knowing statements ($M = 1.56$). Repeated measures t-tests showed a highly significant difference between knowing and understanding statement types, $t(61) = 12.30$, $p < 0.001$, as well as between knowing and knower statements, $t(61) = 10.08$, $p < 0.001$. As expected, highly significant as well was the difference between knower and understanding statements, $t(61) = 5.93$, $p < 0.001$.

Pair-wise Pearson correlations among the three statement type conditions were also confirmative (see Table 7.3). The correlation between knowing and knower statements was high and significant, $r(58) = 0.71$, $p < 0.001$, and remained high and significant even after controlling for the contribution of understanding processes, $r(58) = 0.66$, $p < 0.001$, By contrast, the relationship between knowing and understanding statements was relatively low and, although significant initially, $r(58) = 0.37$, $p < 0.01$, dropped to non-significant levels after controlling for the contribution of the knower statements, $r(58) = -0.07$, $p > 0.05$. Consistent with the understanding by reflection hypothesis, the correlation between knower and understanding processes was also significant, $r(t8) = 0.57$, $p < 0.001$, and remained high after the impact of the knowing processes was partialed out, $r(58) = 0.48$, $p < 0.001$.

Table 7.3 Pair-wise Pearson correlations among knowing, knower, and understanding processes in Experiment 1 ($N = 62$). Inside parentheses are partial correlations between the two conditions controlling for the third condition

Statement type	Knowing processes	Knower processes
Knower processes	0.71* (0.66)*	
Understanding processes	0.37* (0.07)	0.57* (0.48*)

Note: * $p < 0.001$

2.1.4 Discussion

The results of Experiment 1 supported the hypotheses derived from the theory that knowing and understanding are fundamentally different but complementary, as opposed to overlapping, processes. All of the statements in Experiment 1 used the same syntactic frame. Nevertheless, statements portraying understanding processes behaved significantly differently, under subjects' intuitive judgments of acceptability, from statements representing knowing and as well as knower processes. This supports the knowing-by-revelation prediction of the body-mind revelation-reflection spiral, implied by the a priori prediction that knowing is revealed to knower as the outcome of the biological 'know-how' of understanding that occurs outside the sphere of the mind of the knower. This was confirmed by both inferential and correlational statistics. Similarly, there was a robust difference as well as correlation between understanding and knower processes. This confirms the a priori understanding-by-reflection predication of the body-mind revelation-reflection spiral, suggesting that engaging knower processes has reflective impacts on biofunctional understanding processes (Iran-Nejad, 1978; Iran-Nejad & Gregg, 2001). Not surprisingly, the correlation between knower and knowing processes was also significant. However, as predicated by the a priori hypothesis that they are fundamentally different, knowing and understanding processes did not correlate at all.

The idea that understanding processes are some sophisticated form of knowing processes has long held its monopolizing hegemony over psychological and educational sciences. One possible reason for this is a tendency to base theorizing about knowing and understanding on second and third person definitions of knowing and understanding invariably used by researchers. However, the results of Experiment 1 suggest substantial merit for basing theorizing about knowing and understanding on participants own intuitions. In this vein, the results for Experiment 1 supported the hypothesis that understanding and knowing are different human capacities. What do they tell us about the nature of this difference? Subjects seem to be willing to agree that they only know that understanding occurs after the click of understanding occurs but they do not know what goes on, presumably in biology, before the outcome of understanding is revealed to the knower in the form of domain-specific knowledge (Iran-Nejad, 2000; Prawat, 2000). At least two additional questions remain that can lend support to the prediction that the knower's biology is, but the knower's cognition is not, privy to how understanding occurs in the biological person. First, would the first-person intuitions of the knower allow the knower to acknowledge this difference – that biological and cognitive know-how belong to different realms? Second, at minimum, would the subjects be more willing to agree that understanding occurs in biology, as opposed to the mind. The purpose of the next two experiments was to address these questions.

2.2 Experiment 2

For Experiment 2, the statements were framed to make explicit use of biological concepts. Moreover, the present experiment included affective statements in line with the hypothesis that understanding, like affect and unlike knowing, belongs to the realm of biological 'know-how,' which the knower might treat like third-person know-how. Like the first experiment, participants rated three statement types. Two of these were designed to reflect knower and understanding processes. The third type of statements reflected affective processes. Aside from the general hypothesis that knowing and understanding are different, this study was intended to test two more specific hypotheses. These were (a) that knower and understanding statements would appeal differently to participants' intuitions, replicating the findings of the first experiment, and (b) that understanding statements would behave more like affective statements than knower statements.

2.2.1 Participants

Participants in this study were 40 undergraduates in an educational psychology class. Thirty-eight participants were women and two were men. Thirty-six participants were white, two were African-American, and two were Hispanic.

2.2.2 Materials, Design, and Instrument

A total of 30 statements were used to measure participants' reflective intuitions. There were knower (10), understanding (10), and affective (10) statements. An example of a knower statement is: *I can apply what I know to real life, but I do not know how to apply; only my brain and body somehow do.* An example of an understanding statement is: *I can gain insights into new or old problems; but I do not know how to gain insights; only my brain and body somehow do.* An example of an affect statement is: *I can be filled with joy; but I do not know how to fill with joy; only my brain and body somehow do.*

Participants were asked to rate the degree of internal consistency of each statement–that is, the consistency across the different parts within the same sentence–on a scale ranging from *very inconsistent* (1), *inconsistent* (2), *somewhat inconsistent* (3), *consistent* (4), *very consistent* (5).Specifically, if a participant rated, roughly speaking, the statement *I can use what I know to evaluate things, but I do not know how to evaluate; only my brain and body somehow do* less than 3 this would mean that the participant felt it is intuitively inconsistent to be able to evaluate things without knowing how to evaluate things, in the cognitive sense of the term. Conversely, if a participant rated the statement *I can understand the things I know; but I do not know how to understand; only my brain and body somehow do* more than 3, this would mean that the participant felt it is intuitively consistent to understand without knowing cognitively how to understand. The possibility of divergent ratings for knowing statements and understanding statements is significant because all statements were syntactically identical.

2.2.3 Procedure

The study was conducted using an online data collection application **SurveyMonkey** (for more information see www.surveymonkey.com). Participants received an e-mail informing them of the opportunity to participate in the study and with a link to the study. Clicking on the link took the participant to an informed consent, the 30-item scale presented in one random order for all participants, and a set of demographic items.

2.2.4 Results

For each participant, means were computed for each of the three statement types. A one-way repeated measures ANOVA was conducted on the data to examine any differences in participants' ratings across the knower, understanding, and affect statements. The main effect for statement type was significant, $F(2, 78) = 23.85$, $MSE = 0.27$, $p < 0.001$. Figure 7.1 plots the means for knower, ($M = 2.47$, $SD = 0.54$), understanding ($M = 3.15$, $SD = 0.72$), and affect ($M = 3.18$, $SD = 0.83$) processes. Pair-wise comparisons showed that knower processes were significantly different from understanding processes, $t(39) = 5.51$, $p < 0.001$, and affective processes, $t(39) = 5.20$, $p < 0.001$, but understanding and affective processes were not different, $t(39) = 0.36$, $p > 0.01$. As predicted, understanding processes behaved like affective processes and unlike knower processes in appealing to participants' reflective intuitions.

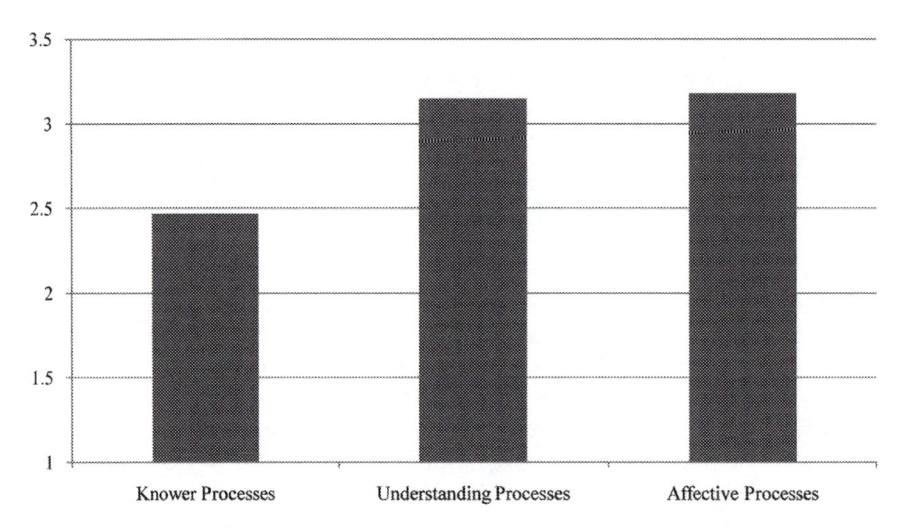

Fig. 7.1 Mean consistency ratings for knower, understanding, and affective processes in Experiment 2

2.2.5 Discussion

This study replicated the findings of the first experiment showing that participants differ in their intuitions about the 'how' processes that underlie knowing and understanding. To the extent that the underlying processes functioned similarly, one would have expected similar ratings. However, in two experiments, the mean ratings were different. There were also noteworthy differences between the two experiments. Experiment 2 shifted the focus toward how the processes underlying understanding and affect behaved similarly in response to participants' reflective intuitions. Traditionally, affective processes have been viewed as being irrational and localized in the lower or animal brain centers (Barrett et al., 2007; Panksepp, 1989, 1998).

7 First-Person Education

The finding that the processes underlying affect and understanding elicited similar ratings suggests that affective and intellectual processes may not be as different as they have been traditionally assumed. We must either admit that understanding processes are irrational or affective processes are as rational as understanding processes. Alternatively, the conventional dichotomy may point to the differences between cognitive and biofunctional processes. The implications of these possibilities are noteworthy. However, a more immediate step is to replicate the findings with more data.

2.3 Experiment 3

The purpose of Experiment 3 was to replicate the results of Experiment 2 with both undergraduates and graduate students.

2.3.1 Participants, Material, and Procedure

The participants were 17 undergraduate and 19 graduate students from educational psychology classes. The majority (32) were female. Twenty three participants were white, eleven African-American, and one Asian. The material and procedure were identical to those for Experiment 2.

2.3.2 Results

A repeated measures ANOVA revealed no significant main effect for education level (undergraduate, graduate), $F(1, 34) = 0.14$, $MSE = 1.23$, $p > 0.05$. The main effect of statement type was highly significant, $F(2, 68) = 22.41$, $MSE = 0.26$, $p < 0.001$. The interaction between statement type and student level was not significant, $F(2, 68) = 1.89$, $MSE = 0.26$, $p > 0.05$. Therefore, the data were combined across the two student levels for further comparisons. As expected, pairwise t-tests showed significant differences between knower statements ($M = 2.39$) and understanding statements ($M = 3.14$) as well as between knower and affective statements ($M = 3.05$). The t-tests were $t(35) = 5.48$, $p < 0.001$ (knower vs. understanding) and $t(35) = 4.57$, $p < 0.001$ (knower vs. affective). However, the t-test between understanding and affective statements was not significant, $t(35) = 1.29$, $p > 0.05$. Therefore, the data replicated exactly the findings of Experiment 2 and generalized to a higher education level.

In order to investigate further the relations among the three types of statements, the data for Experiments 2 and 3 were combined and correlations were conducted. These correlations are presented in Table 7.4. Understanding and affect correlated highly and, as the partial correlation in parentheses show, their relationship did not change after controlling for knower processes. Understanding and affect also correlated similarly with knower processes, even though the corresponding partial correlations dropped to nonsignificant levels. Table 7.5 shows illustrative

Table 7.4 Pair-wise Pearson correlations among knower, understanding, and affective processes for combined data from Experiments 2 and 3 ($N = 76$). Partial correlations controlling for the third variable are presented in parentheses

Statement type	Knower processes	Understanding processes	Affective processes
Knower processes	1.00		
Understanding processes	0.31* (0.09)	1.00	
Affective processes	0.32* (0.12)	0.82* (0.80)	1.00

Note. * $p < 0.001$

Table 7.5 Pair-wise Pearson correlations among marker knower (evaluate, apply), understanding (understanding, gaining insights) and affect (joy, elation) processes using combined Experiments 2 and 3 data ($N = 76$)

	Knower		Understanding		Affect	
	Evaluate	Apply	Understand	Insight	Elated	Joy
Evaluate	1.00					
Apply	0.47*	1.00				
Understand	–0.05	0.11	1.00			
Insight	0.14	0.21	0.32*	1.00		
Elated	0.17	0.15	0.48*	0.31*	1.00	
Joy	0.22	0.18	0.39*	0.37*	0.43*	1.00

Note. Correlations significant at $p < 0.001$ are indicated by *

correlations among marker knower (evaluate, apply), understanding (understanding, insight), and affect (joy, elation) statements. The two knower statements correlated among themselves but neither with understanding nor with affective statements. By contrast, understanding statements correlated both among themselves and with affective statements and vice versa. These findings cast doubt on the common conception of the relations among knowing, understanding, and affect.

3 Conclusion

Biology and cognition contribute differently to intellectual and affective functioning, just as biology and thinking contribute differently to recovery from infectious diseases. Accordingly, the studies reported here supported the notion that understanding is the nervous system's special function; and understanding processes work more similarly to affective than knowing processes. Genuine understanding processes of the kind postulated here are different from domain-specific knowing processes (e.g., washing clothes). This conclusion is supported by the observation that participants rated understanding and affective statements as having similar levels of intuitive consistency in contrast to knower statements. This finding occurred despite the fact that all statements were structurally identical. Moreover, genuine understanding processes are also different from knower processes such as rehearsing, elaborating, applying, and evaluating that presuppose understanding comprehensive of all typical and atypical problem solving situations.

There is a tendency on the part of researchers and practitioners in education and psychology to think that cognition is prerequisite to understanding. This is true when it comes to understanding by reflection but not for knowing by revelation or insight, which may rely fundamentally on biological processes as the results of the studies reported suggest. Therefore, the immediate significance of the new perspective in this paper is that it suggests researchers may have largely missed the true nature of understanding and its intimate relationship with knowing, on the one hand, and with affect, on the other. Also, this new perspective implies that, by focusing inordinately on knowing, educators may have been working against the development of understanding on the part of their students. Thus, additional research is needed to learn more about people's intuitions regarding their own knowing, knower, understanding, and affective processes. The implications of such intuitions for strategic learning are highly promising. For example, this research could shed light on how people's intuitions regarding their own understanding and affective processes might be similar such that affective processes could be engaged in the service of understanding. More applied research could then focus on developing affectively meaningful educational methods.

This article has been contrasting 2nd/3rd-person education with 1st-person education. This does not mean that 2nd/3rd-person education should be kept out of educational research and practice. It is critical, however, to consider the possibilities for 2nd/3rd-person education through the lens of 1st-person education just as it is vital to examine the possibilities for 1st-person education through the lens of 2nd-3rd-person education. In this light, it is noteworthy that in the widely open arena of traditional 2nd/3rd-person education, phenomena such affect, insight, and surprising information have been, for the most part, overlooked (Iran-Nejad, Clore, & Vondruska, 1984). The traditional focus in education has been on knowledge acquisition. Even in the area of understanding progress has been limited (Gardner & Boix-Mansilla, 1994a, 1994b). By contrast, the 1st-person education approach can readily account for the evidence gathered in the context of the traditional theory as well as generate its own kind of research in diverse enough areas to be fitting for the whole-person and wholetheme brand of education (Diener & Iran-Nejad, 1986; Iran-Nejad, 1978, 1987a, 1987b, 1989a, 1989b, 1990, 1994; Iran-Nejad & Marsh, 1993; Iran-Nejad et al., 1995; Iran-Nejad, McKeachie, & Berliner, 1990; Iran-Nejad & Pearson, 1999; Thompson & Iran-Nejad, 1994).

We conclude by drawing the attention of the reader to Fig. 7.2, which contrasts traditional 2nd/3rd-person education (lower cone) with a wholetheme 1st-person approach (upper arrow). Needless to say, the 1st-person approach must explain the acquisition of 2nd/3rd-person knowledge in the manner described in Table 7.2 rather than Table 7.1. Briefly, the cone starting from no domain knowledge at all gradually

Educational Practice Approaches	Lifespan Education
1st-Person Developmental	Repeated reorganization of learner's own intuitive self-awareness → INTUITIVE FLEXIBILITY and TECHNICAL FACILITY Y
2nd/3rd-Person Instructional	Storable knowledge internalization → EXPERT-LIKE THINKING

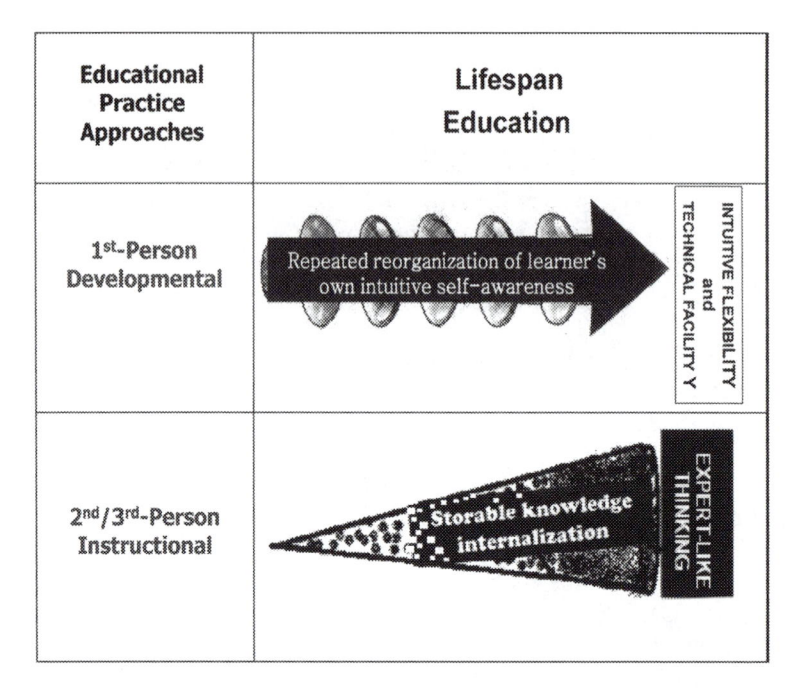

Fig. 7.2 A thematic organizer for two approaches to educational practice (Iran-Nejad, 1994)

accumulates basic concepts of a discipline through what is usually described as introductory, intermediate, and advanced knowledge of a specific field of expertise. This creates an abysmal gap between human development and knowledge acquisition. The process consists of the establishment of gradual interconnections among the segmental pieces of knowledge and the formation of procedural skills in the manner described by J. R. Anderson (1982) and others Dreyfus, Dreyfus, & Athanasiou, (1986); Shuell, (1990). This process of segmental acquisition of knowledge ends when it reaches the state of expertise and the learners pass their comprehensive exams on the knowledge of their fields. By contrast, the top arrow shows a 1st-person developmental approach with repeated reorganizations of the learner's own embodied intuitions. (The basic elements of the two approaches shown in Fig. 7.2 are those compared in Tables 7.1 and 7.2). A notable difference is that the cone ends in a domain-specific state of knowledgeable expertise but the arrow is an always changing lifespan process in which the colored rings represent wholetheme biofunctional reorganizations.

Acknowledgements Correspondence about this chapter may be sent to Asghar Iran-Nejad, Ph. D., University of Alabama, 309 Carmichael Hall, Box 870231, Tuscaloosa, AL 35406; e-mail: airannej@bamaed.ua.edu. An early draft of this paper was presented (and published in the proceedings) of the CELDA 2009 conference as Iran-Nejad, Steward, & Parizi, (2009). Knowing, understanding, and affect: A first person perspective. Proceeding of the IADIS International Conference, Cognition and Exploratory Learning in Digital age, November 20–22, Rome, Italy. The authors thank two anonymous reviewers for their insightful comments.

References

Anderson, J. R. (1982). Acquisition of cognitive skill. *Psychological Review, 89*, 369–406.
Anderson, R. C. (1977). The notion of schemata and the educational enterprise: general discussion of the conference. In R. C. Anderson, R. J. Spiro, & W. E. Montague (Eds.), *Schooling and the acquisition of knowledge* (pp. 415–431). Hillsdale, NJ: Erlbaum.
Anderson, R. C. (1984). Some reflections on the acquisition of knowledge. *Educational Researcher, 13*(9), 5–10.
Anderson, R. C., & Pichert, J. W. (1978). Recall of previously unrecallable information following a shift in perspective. *Journal of Verbal Learning and Verbal Behavior, 17*, 1–12.
Ausubel, D. P. (1963). *The psychology of meaningful verbal learning*. New York: Grune & Stratton.
Ausubel, D. P., Novak, J., & Hanesian, H. (1978). *Educational psychology: A cognitive view* (2nd ed.). New York: Holt, Rinehart & Winston.
Barrett, L. F., Lindquist, K. A., Bliss-Moreau, E., Duncan, S., Gendron, M., Mize, J., et al. (2007). Of mice and men: Natural kinds of emotions in the mammalian brain? A response to Panksepp and Izard. *Perspectives on Psychological Science, 2*, 297–312.
Bartlett, F. C. (1932). *Remembering: A study in experimental and social psychology*. Cambridge: Cambridge University Press, UK.
Blanchard, H. E., & Iran Nejad, A. (1987). Comprehension processes and eye movement patterns in the reading of surprise ending stories. *Discourse Processes, 10*, 127–138.
Bloom, B. S., Englehart, M. D., Furst, E. J., Hill, W. H., & Krathwohl, D. R. (1956). *Taxonomy of educational objectives, handbook 1: The cognitive domain*. New York: Longman.
Bransford, J. D., & Johnson, M. K. (1972). Contextual prerequisites for understanding: some investigations of comprehension and recall. *Journal of Verbal Learning and Verbal Behavior, 11*, 717–726.
Diener, E., & Iran-Nejad, A. (1986). The relationship in experience between various types of affect. *Journal of Personality and Social Psychology, 50*, 1031–1038.
Dreyfus, H. L., Dreyfus, S. E., & Athanasiou, T. (1986). *Mind over machine: The power of human intuition and expertise in the era of the computer*. New York: The Free Press.
Gardner, H., & Boix-Mansilla, V. (1994a). Teaching for understanding in the disciplines–and beyond. *Teachers College Record, 96*, 198–218.
Gardner, H., & Boix-Mansilla, V. (1994b). Teaching for understanding within and across disciplines. *Educational Leadership, 51*, 14–18.
Iran-Nejad, A. (1978). *An anatomic account of knowing. Unpublished master's thesis equivalency paper*. Urbana-Champaign, IL: University of Illinois.
Iran-Nejad, A. (1980). *The schema: A structural or a functional pattern*. (Technical. Report. No. 159). Washington, DC: National Institute of Education. (ERIC Document Reproduction Service No. ED182735).
Iran-Nejad, A. (1987a). Cognitive and affective causes of interest and liking. *Journal of Educational Psychology, 79*, 120–130.
Iran-Nejad, A. (1987b). The schema: A long-term memory structure or a transient functional pattern. In R. J. Tierney & J. N. Anders (Eds.), *Understanding reader's understanding* (pp. 109–128). Hillsdale, NJ: Erlbaum.
Iran-Nejad, A. (1989a). A nonassociative schema theory of cognitive incompatibility. *Bulletin of the Psychonomic Society, 27*, 429–432.
Iran-Nejad, A. (1989b). A nonconnectionist schema theory of understanding surprise-ending stories. *Discourse Processes, 12*, 127–148.

Iran-Nejad, A. (1990). Active and dynamic self-regulation of learning processes. *Review of Educational Research, 60,* 573–602.

Iran-Nejad, A. (1994). The global coherence context in educational practice: A comparison of piecemeal and whole-theme approaches to learning and teaching. *Research in the Schools, 1*(1), 63–76.

Iran-Nejad, A. (2000). Knowledge, self-regulation, and the brain-mind cycle of reflection. *The Journal of Mind and Behavior, 21,* 67–88.

Iran-Nejad, A., Clore, G. L., & Vondruska, R. J. (1984). Affect: A functional perspective. *The Journal of Mind and Behavior, 5,* 279–310.

Iran-Nejad, A., & Gregg, M. (2001). The brain-mind cycle of reflection. *Teachers College Record, 103,* 868–895.

Iran-Nejad, A., & Marsh, G. E. (1993). Discovering the future of education. *Education, 114*(2), 249–257.

Iran-Nejad, A., Marsh, G. E., & Clements, A. C. (1992). The figure and the ground of constructive brain functioning: Beyond explicit memory processes. *Educational Psychologist, 27,* 473–492.

Iran-Nejad, A., Marsh, G. E., Ellis, E. S., Rountree, B. S., Casareno, A. B., Gregg, M., et al. (1995). Educating multiple abilities with wholetheme constructivism. *Canadian Journal of Special Education, 10*(1), 87–103.

Iran-Nejad, A., McKeachie, W. J., & Berliner, D. C. (1990). The multisource nature of learning: An introduction. *Review of Educational Research, 60,* 509–515.

Iran-Nejad, A., & Ortony, A. (1982). *Cognition: A functional view.* Rockville, MD: ERIC Clearinghouse.

Iran-Nejad, A., & Ortony, A. (1984). A biofunctional model of distributed mental content, mental structures, awareness, and attention. *The Journal of Mind and Behavior, 5,* 171–210.

Iran-Nejad, A., & Pearson, P. D. (1999). Introduction: Welcome to the threshold of a new science of education. In A. Iran-Nejad & P. D. Pearson (Eds.), *Review of research in education* (Vol. 24) pp. Xi–Xiv. Washington, DC: American Educational Research Association.

Iran-Nejad, A., Stewart, W., & Parizi, M. I. (2009). *Knowing, understanding, and affect: A first person perspective.* Paper presented at and published in the Proceedings of IADIS International Conference on Cognition and Exploratory Learning in Digital Age, Rome, Italy, November 20–22.

Iran-Nejad, A., & Winsler, A. (2000). Bartlett's schema theory and modern accounts of learning and remembering. *The Journal of Mind and Behavior, 21,* 5–35.

Panksepp, J. (1989). The psychobiology of emotions: The animal side of human feelings. In G. Gainotti & C. Caltagirone (Eds.), *Emotions and the dual brain* (Vol. 18 Experimental Brain Research Series, pp. 31–55). Berlin: Springer.

Panksepp, J. (1998). *Affective neuroscience: The foundations of human and animal emotions.* New York: Oxford University Press.

Pichert, J. W., & Anderson, R. C. (1977). Taking different perspectives on a story. *Journal of Educational Psychology, 69,* 309–315.

Prawat, R. S. (2000). Keep the solution, broaden the problem: Commentary on Knowledge, self-regulation, and the brain-mind cycle of reflection. *The Journal of Mind and Behavior, 21,* 89–96.

Rumelhart, D. E. (1975). Notes on a schema for stories. In D. G. Bobrow & A. Collins (Eds.), *Representation and understanding: Studies in cognitive science* (pp. 211–236). New York: Academic.

Rumelhart, D. E. (1976). *Toward an interactive model of reading*: (CHIP Technical Report No. 56). Center for Human Information Processing, University of California, San Diego.

Rumelhart, D. E. (1980). Schemata: The building blocks of cognition. In R. J. Spiro, B. C. Bruce, & W. F. Brewer (Eds.), *Theoretical issues in reading comprehension* (pp. 33–58). Hillsdale, NJ: Erlbaum.

Rumelhart, D. E. (1984). The emergence of cognition from subsymbolic processes. In *Proceedings of the sixth annual conference of the cognitive science society* (pp. 59–62), Boulder, CO, USA.

Rumelhart, D. E., & Ortony, A. (1977). The representation of knowledge in memory. In R. C. Anderson, R. J. Spiro & W. E. Montague (Eds.), *Schooling and the acquisition of knowledge* (pp. 99–135). Hillsdale, NJ: Erlbaum.

Shuell, T. J. (1990). Phases of meaningful learning. *Review of Educational Research, 60*, 531–547.

Sperry, R. W. (1970). An objective approach to subjective experience: Further explanation of a hypothesis. *Psychological Review, 77*, 585–590.

Thompson, S., & Iran-Nejad, A. (1994). *Altering cultural bias through authentic cultural simulation*. Paper presented at the annual meeting of the Mid-South Educational Research Association, Nashville, TN. (ERIC Document Reproduction Service No. ED382625).

Thurmond, P. J. (1978). If cornered, scream. *Ellery Queen's Mystery Magazine, 71*(1), 66–68.

Chapter 8
Socio-cognitive Regulation Strategies in Cooperative Learning Tasks in Virtual Contexts

Denisse Margoth López-Benavides and Ibis Marlene Alvarez-Valdivia

Abstract This study validates a theoretical framework for identifying social and cognitive regulation strategies employed by students during the process of joint construction of meaning in cooperative tasks in a university's virtual learning environment. The study explored the regulation strategies of five groups of students, during two cooperative tasks. These tasks were based on written argumentation, supported by virtual discussions and its completion was defined through a written report. Through a case study methodology and by means of discourse analysis, three modes of regulation during cooperative tasks: self-, external and co-regulation were identified. Students' interactions revealed how they alternated and combined the use of strategies to regulate the social and the cognitive dimension of their behavior. Moreover, it was possible to identify four models of interaction; which reflected social and cognitive regulation strategies at different stages of cooperative work. We believe this theoretical framework opens up possibilities for educational intervention during the execution of cooperative activities, since it offers clues to evaluate these mechanisms and to promote them.

Keywords Cooperative learning · Socio-cognitive regulation · Virtual learning environments · Higher education

1 Introduction

Recently, there has been a growing interest in understanding the intricacies of the cooperation and collaboration process. A shared concern among researchers that attracts attention is about the mediating factors and the interpsychological mechanisms involved in the effectiveness of cooperative learning (e.g., Durán & Monereo, 2005; Järvela, Jarvenoja, & Veermans, 2008; Salonen, Vauras, & Efklides, 2005).

D.M. López-Benavides (✉)
Universitat Oberta de Catalunya, Barcelona, Catalonia, Spain
e-mail: dlopezben@uoc.edu

Beyond the discussion about the cooperation and collaboration concepts, in the practice, both processes are referred to active and interactive learning, where more similarities than differences can be found (Panitz, 1996).

Collaborative learning is student centered and focuses on the process of students working together and sharing the authority to empower themselves with the responsibility of building on their foundational knowledge. Here, an exact answer is not required and the final results cannot be anticipated. In contrast, when learning cooperatively, the authority remains with the instructor, who retains ownership of the task. In this situation students are employed to produce a designated solution based on the instructor's requirements (Raitman, Zhou, & Nicholson, 2003).

Possibly, the confusion arises when we look at processes associated with each concept and see some overlap or inter-concept usage. For this reason and for the purpose of analysis of this study we will refer to the term cooperation throughout the paper, leaving aside the theorical controversy.

Cooperative learning is a coordinated activity, a continued attempt to construct and maintain a shared conception of a problem, hence the co-regulatory nature of participation in a work group. In an online learning environment students need not only to interact but to think collectively, integrate ideas in a creative way, so that result comes out from the effort of a joint activity more than just of the sum of the parts (Lipponen, 2002).

The interpretation of Vygotsky's ideas highlights the role of mutual engagement and co-construction of meaning. According to this perspective, learning is more a matter of participation in a social process of knowledge construction than an individual endeavor. 'Knowledge emerges through the network of interactions and is distributed and mediated among those (humans and tools) interacting' (Cole & Wertsch, as cited in Lipponen, 2002, p. 3).

In this sense, co-regulation centers on gradual comprehension of shared problems and tasks by means of the cooperative tasks' typical mechanisms: establishment of psychosocial relations, positive interdependence and joint construction of meaning (Johnson & Johnson, 1999). In virtual and asynchronous contexts, this learning situation becomes more complex (Kirschner & Kreijns, 2003).

From this point of view, it seems of great importance to investigate the influence of factors related to behavior regulation during the development of cooperative tasks, paying special attention to the peculiarities of communication in these environments.

According to Hung and Der-Thanq (2001), from the perspective of situated cognition, the notion of construction of meaning is a basic notion that integrates aspects of cognition and interaction present during the learning process in virtual learning environments. This notion is closely related to the notions of collaboration and co-regulation.

In cooperative learning tasks, language is the basic tool to collectively understand, co-regulate, make proposals, negotiate and construct meaning (Lipponen, Rahikainen, Hakkarainen, & Palonen, 2002; Mercer & Littleton, 2007; Wegerif, Mercer, & Dawes, 1999).

By means of language and social interaction, behavior regulation becomes increasingly more self-regulated. In a learning situation, from the very beginning, behavior requires expert or external regulation; which serves to lead to and assist in achieving autonomous and adaptative behaviors.

Various theories have contributed to understand regulation within Computer Supported Collaborative Learning (CSCL). From the constructivist and socio-cultural approach to learning, the attributes specific to text-based communication stand out as advantages, because of promoting reflection and critical discourse (i.e., Dillenbourg, Schneider, & Synteta, 2002; Garrison & Anderson, 2003; Salmon, 2002).

This theoretical perspective is derived from Vygotsky's (1978) theory, and highlights the importance of dialogue and social mediation in the development of psychosocial processes such as learning. In this context learning is seen as an active process, where the learner engages intentionally in the construction of meaning by interacting with others. During the interactions language plays a fundamental role, since it constitutes a tool to express ideas, reasoning, to share and re-construct meaning.

In the context of cooperative learning activities, the regulation process may oscillate between situations in which a person is temporarily in charge of supplying information to the group, metacognitive situations and more balanced performances in which various members of the group are involved (i.e., Salonen et al., 2005; Weinberger & Fischer, 2006; Zimmerman, 1997). From a more practical perspective, it is worth clarifying some of these issues.

a) *External regulation may be an important guiding factor in cooperation*: the term external regulation is applied to situations in which there is unevenness in understanding within the group. The students performing external regulation feel more familiarized with the task and take on an instructive role so as to promote, correct, inhibit or elicit the actions being performed (i.e., Järvelä, Näykki, Laru, & Luokkanen, 2007)

b) *Cooperating requires self-regulating the behavior within the group*: working with others efficiently in order to solve a cooperative task depends greatly on the ability to self-regulate behavior. Self-regulation is a cyclical, recursive, and active process encompassing motivation, behavior, and context (Winters, Greene, & Costich, 2008); which consists of carrying out a task without having to be directed by anyone else, making decisions on their own, being able to seek and take on help and even knowing when and how to request it (i.e., Whipp & Chiarelli, 2004; Zimmerman & Tsikalas, 2005).

c) *Cooperating requires interdependence*: Whilst a student carries out or keeps control over an activity, others get involved with activities that support the task. Shared regulation at a cognitive level presupposes that the participants' previous knowledge becomes manifest and combines during the task. In this sense the term 'shared regulation' results to be the most effective mode of co-regulation (Volet, Summers, & Thurman, 2009) and refers to multiple members constantly monitoring and regulating the joint activity (Vauras, Iiskala, Kajamies, Kinnunen, & Lehtinen, 2003).

It is worth pointing out that delineating the above modalities is merely an analytical recourse, since in reality they appear intermingled, though asymmetrically, and they may even show evidence of styles of dyadic interaction. It is as though both aspects were the two sides of a single coin, where the interlinked faces always come up together, in an ever changing, ever oscillating, relationship (Covarrubias & Estrevel, 2006).

The purpose of reviewing theory is to clarify the psychological mechanisms that underlie the construction of meaning in cooperative learning tasks in virtual and asynchronous learning environments. It is of our particular interest to highlight the role of students' behavior regulation during this process.

Recently, Volet et al. (2009) have examined the nature and process of collaborative learning in student-led group activities at university level. A situative framework combining the constructs of social regulation and content processing was developed to identify instances of productive high-level co-regulation. Inspired by their results, a research carried out by López-B (2009) explored the strategies employed by university students to regulate their behavior in a university's virtual learning environment, whilst carrying out cooperative learning tasks with argumentative demands, from a double perspective–social angle of cooperation– and joint construction of meaning–cognitive angle. Four regulation models were identified showing low- or high-level of self- and external regulation; low- or high-level shared regulation (see Fig. 8.1).

Each quadrant created by the intersection of the two dimensions represents the dominant form of social regulation (building and maintaining social relationships) and cognitive regulation (content processing) that may be observed during group learning episodes with similar tasks as the ones analyzed.

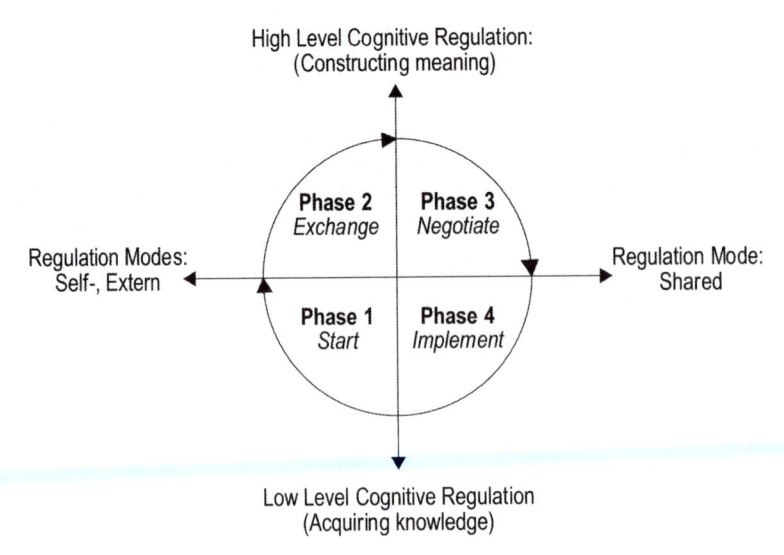

Fig. 8.1 A theoretical framework for regulated learning in cooperative learning tasks in a virtual learning environment

The regulation models correspond to the phases of cooperative work identified during the learning process (Gunawardena, Lowe, & Anderson, 1997). These phases are progressive and strongly dependent on the previous ones. The process of cooperative work begins in Phase 1: *Start* in the third quadrant, continuing to Phase 2: *Exchange* in the fourth quadrant, then Phase 3: *Negotiate* in the first quadrant and ending in Phase 4: *Implement* in the second quadrant.

This twofold theoretical perspective in the study of regulation opens up possibilities for educational intervention during the execution of cooperative activities, since it offers clues to evaluate these mechanisms and to promote them. Having outlined the theoretical framework, the present study is aimed at its empirical validation.

2 Method and Procedure

2.1 Data

The data involved virtual debates during two cooperative learning tasks in a 3 ECTS (European Credit Transfer System) semester course of a Master program in E-learning from the Universitat Oberta de Catalunya (UOC) in Spain. This University has been fully online since its foundation (more information about the pedagogic and assessment model of the UOC can be found on the university's website: http://www.uoc.edu).

The course presents 3 case studies about teaching Process Planning with ICT (Information and Communication Technologies) in face-to-face, blended and virtual learning environments.

This study analyzed the results of the working process of 25 university graduates (5 groups) after having solved two different tasks (A and B). These tasks were based on written argumentation, supported by virtual debates and its completion was defined through a written report.

The groups kept the same configuration in both tasks, received the same instructions and documentation with orientations for reading comprehension, writing reports and the development of debates, as well as guidelines for self- and co-assessment; and had a period of 4 weeks to accomplish each task.

Apart from giving them instructions, the instructor also intervened either with suggestions, explanations about the tasks or social reinforcements, if required.

Messages from the virtual debates were recovered from the debating space of each group from the UOC's virtual learning environment. Additionally, documents exchanged during the collaborative work within the learning spaces of the groups, were gathered and analyzed.

2.2 Categorization Unit, Coding System, Inter-judge Reliability

2.2.1 Categorization Unit

Written language is the base of communication and interaction in Computer Supported Collaborative Learning (CSCL) situations where communication is asynchronous; therefore it was important for us to understand the regulation process during the joint construction of knowledge by means of discourse analysis (Garrison, Anderson, & Archer, 2000).

In order to observe groups' regulation and identify discourse categories through their virtual cooperative discourse, it was essential to select a unit of analysis which different coders would be able to recognize reliably.

Fixed units such as words or whole messages are recognized objectively, but they do not always encompass properly the construct being investigated. However, units of meaning do adequately delineate the construct, but can lead to a subjective identification of the unit (Rourke, Anderson, Garrison, & Archer, 2001).

As the basic unit of categorization we chose the thematic unit (TU) introduced by Henri (1992), namely a 'unit of meaning'; which is similar in form to the conventional thematic unit described as '… a single thought unit or idea unit that conveys a single item of information extracted from a segment of content' (Budd, Thorp, & Donohue, as cited in Garrison & Anderson, 2003, p. 193). A total of 1434 TU were identified from the groups during the analyzed tasks, and subsequently codified using the software Atlas.ti (Version 6).

2.2.2 Coding System

Keeping consistency with the theoretical framework and with the chosen unit of analysis, we proceeded to create a coding system. Its creation resulted from the combination of a deductive analysis and an inductive one.

For the first analysis we revised different research studies and literature referring to (a) face-to-face and virtual education that have contributed with definitions of categories in cooperative discourse (i.e., Arvaja, Salovaara, Hakkinen, & Järvelä, 2007; Boakaerts & Minnaert, 2006; Dillenbourg & Fischer, 2007; Järvelä & Hakkinen, 2002; Vauras et al., 2003, Volet et al., 2009; Wegerif, Mercer, & Dawes, 1999); and (b) categories, models and characteristics of behavior regulation in cooperative and written argumentative tasks, specified for groups and individual cases (i.e. Angeli, Valanides, & Bonk, 2003; Reznitskaya, Kuo, Glina, & Anderson, 2008; Salonen, et al., 2005; Weinberger & Fischer, 2006; Zimmerman, 1997).

The inductive analysis resulted from the exploration of data, where categories emerged. These categories went through a process of definition, adjustment, redefinition, combination, exclusion or precision until achieving the present uniform system consisting of 14 categories shown in Tables 8.1 and 8.2.

2.3 Inter-judge Reliability

In order to establish the reliability of the coding system, one of the groups' sequences was selected at random and evaluated by three external judges (university professors with experience in face-to-face and virtual learning). The judges received training in the coding system, in relation to their definitions, regulation modes (self-, extern and shared) as well as regulation types (social and cognitive).

8 Socio-cognitive Regulation Strategies in Cooperative Learning

Table 8.1 Categories of social regulation with descriptors

Regulation modes	Descriptor
External	Structuring the task (OrT): Questions and suggestions on the organization, procedure, roles, resources, timing, format text, control of the task, etc..
	Social Reinforcements (RS): Emotive interventions supporting the ideas or performances of others because they positively impact on cognition or motivation of the rest of the group.
Self-	Self-evaluation (AeV): Interventions showing assessment of previous knowledge or experience; which may contribute to the successful completion of the task or showing what solving the task will mean in terms of meeting the demands of their daily context.
	Situating the learning process itself (SA): Students understand the objective of the task, relate it to previous knowledge and consider what they need to do in order to achieve the objective.
	Individual Planning (PI): Students consider the available time and resources they have, in order to determine their contribution and voluntarily take on responsibilities.
	Monitoring participation (MI): Controlling management of their own participation.
Shared	Call for accountability/ participation from others (IR): Interactions requesting help or collaboration from their peers, in keeping with the organization and development of the task.
	Mutual perspective (PM): Interactions communicating a mutual agreement, an idea is considered, evaluated and reinforced.
	Short and quick consensus (Ccr): Interactions showing agreement or neutrality with a suggested idea.

Table 8.2 Categories of cognitive regulation with descriptors

Regulation modes	Descriptor
External	Clarifying the task (ExT): Non-argumentative interactions around the common objective. The objective of the task is analysed, clarified, reformulated, and reviewed.
Self-	Exteriorising (EX): Non-argumentative interactions offering information with textual content or expressing points of view on the content to analyse, without making any reference to previous statements.
Shared	Elicitation (Eli): Interventions which directly or indirectly demand a reaction from another peer, in keeping with the content of the task.
	Negotiating meaning (NS): Reasoned interventions offering proposals, alternatives and complements to the information exchanged, with the intention of reaching an agreement.
	Integration aimed at consensus (IoC): Reasoned interventions showing consensus by integrating own reflections with the information offered by other peers.

The sequences were organized by phases of cooperative work, guided by the work of Gunawardena et al. (1997); and by discussion threads. This served to explore in depth each sequence of interaction and identify the purposes, intentions and scope of the expressions in each phase.

The selected sequence included 124 TU and corresponded to one of groups' B, a group built by four students. The sequence was reduced to a 55% (69 TU) from its original extension, keeping a proportional amount of data for applying the different categories. This reduction was consented with one of the judges who was the course instructor and was familiar with the case studies and the working process of each of the groups.

Together with the external judges, we established what would signal agreement: the concurrence on the identification of codes on the same thematic units. Each of the judges categorized independently, taking into account that each thematic unit had to be coded either into one category or, in special cases, into a combination of two categories. In this process, each coding discrepancy was resolved through discussion, ideas were exchanged on the least precise categories, some definitions were improved and others were complemented with more examples. The judges concurred on the codification of 55 TU, representing a 81% agreement.

3 Findings and Discusion

3.1 Regulation Models During Cooperative Tasks in Virtual Learning Environments (VLE)

After examining messages within interaction sequences during the cooperative working process of the groups in both tasks (A and B), and after delimiting and analyzing the thematic units in each message, it was possible to explore four regulation models corresponding to each of the four phases of cooperative work.

In order to determine which regulation strategies, here categories, prevailed over the phases of cooperative work from the 1434 TU, we analyzed single and possible co-ocurrent categories for the thematic units codified in the four phases. As a result, 40 cases including single and co-ocurrent categories were identified using the software Atlas.ti (Version 6), however only 11 of the cases met the selection criteria, namely (1) to be present in both of the tasks and (2) to show a frequency of use higher than 15 times in any of the tasks. The number 15 results from having an average of 3 times of frequency of appearance in each of the groups, where 3 was considered to be the minimum number of turns for action-reaction schemes for an ongoing discussion, whereas one or two times are likely to disappear after the current interaction sequence.

Table 8.3 presents the result of the most representative regulation strategies employed by the students during the four phases of cooperative work in tasks A and B. Five categories represent social regulation, four categories represent cognitive regulation and two represent co-ocurrent categories combining social and cognitive regulation.

8 Socio-cognitive Regulation Strategies in Cooperative Learning

Table 8.3 Regulation strategies used by students during cooperative work

Phase	Task	Social					Cognitive				Social and Cognitive combined	
		OrT	MI	RS	PI	IR	IoC	NS	ELi	EX	AEV EX	PM EX
1	A	27	–	22	26	–	–	–	16	19	–	–
	B	6	–	13	11	–	–	–	6	1	–	–
2	A	–	18	–	–	–	–	–	19	44	15	–
	B	–	11	–	–	–	–	–	13	10	2	–
3	A	–	32	–	–	–	61	35	27	87	–	16
	B	–	17	–	–	–	17	17	21	18	–	4
4	A	22	47	52	47	28	–	–	21	2	–	–
	B	13	38	62	23	15	–	–	28	18	–	–

$N = 1434$ TU

Note. Column 1, Rows 1–4 correspond to the phases of cooperative work identified during students' group work. A and B in column 2 refer to the analyzed tasks. Numbers represent the frequency of appearance of the categories in the dimensions of social and cognitive regulation in each of the phases of cooperative work. Code abbreviations and descriptions can be revised in Tables 8.1 and 8.2.

This analysis provided further insights into how the variables of a cooperative group in a virtual learning situation regulate one to another. The structure and demand of the task strongly determine the particularities of the cooperation process. Understanding how language varies according to the phase of cooperation the group is at, in some phases more intense than in others, allows to interpret its purpose of regulation: social or cognitive.

While strategies of social regulation are present during the whole process of cooperation for establishing and maintaining relationships as well as for keeping a friendly working environment, strategies of cognitive regulation concentrate on meeting the demands of the task, strongly taking place at Phases 2 and 3 of the cooperative work. It is interesting though, to note that two of the cognitive regulation strategies prevailed over the four phases of cooperative work. This is the case of languages linked to the strategy Elicitation (ELi), in the mode of shared regulation, and the strategy Exteriorising (EX), in the mode of self-regulation. These categories aim at different purposes throughout the phases: in Phases 1 and 4 they focus on the organizational part of the task, and in Phases 2 and 3 on the very cognitive part of it. This observation is similar to the ones of Volet et al. (2009) in a study about collaborative learning in student-led group activities at university level in a face-to face learning environment.

By applying the two before mentioned categories during the resolution of the task, students show how they intentionally engage in the learning process. Individually but within the group, students request contributions from their peers but also freely express their ideas, thoughts, points of view in order to promote dialogue; which in some of the cases clearly lead to a joint construction of meaning.

This result confirms the importance of discourse analysis during the learning process contextualized in the interactions (Lipponen et al., 2002; Mercer, 2004). Utterances should not be attributed to a single participant, they must be understood as a product of the interaction between the participants; consequently as a product of the social situation from which they arose. Thus, as stated by Vygotsky (1986) a 'thought' is not expressed in the word, it is there where it takes place.

Social strategies in the mode of self-regulation such as Monitoring participation (MI) and Individual Planning (PI) are present along the learning process. The employment of these strategies showed different regulation purposes: students make their presence known in the group, they let others know which responsibilities they have voluntarily assumed, they express the great importance they give to group work and they also justify each one of their carried out actions. This findings validate revised thesis about the role of self-regulation in the learning process (e.g., Winters et al., 2008; Whipp & Chiarelli, 2004; Zimmerman, 1997; Zimmerman & Tsikalas, 2005).

Languages linked to the strategy of Social Reinforcements (RS), in the mode of shared regulation, are very valuable and important in virtual contexts (Casanova, 2008) and in our analysis, together with the strategy Structuring the task (OrT), they show to be strongly connected to the cooperative Phases 1 and 4. In these phases groups are concentrated either on getting organized as a group, or on collecting agreements from previous phases in order to create the final product. The strategy Call for accountability/ participation from others (IR), in the mode of shared regulation, was only observed during Phase 4 and it was directly related to formal aspects of the written report such as: missing references, font style, text formatting, among others.

A very interesting finding is the emergence of strategies that combine social and cognitive categories in single thematic units. This is the case of Self-evaluation (AeV) and Exteriorising (EX), both in the mode of self-regulation; and also the case of Mutual perspective (PM), in the mode of shared regulation, and Exteriorising (EX), in the mode of self-regulation. The first combined strategy, although low in frequency, was found to be employed in the beginning of the second phase of cooperative work. Here, students assessed themselves based on previous knowledge or experience and expressed to the group what they could bring for helping accomplish the task. In the second combination of strategies, students show agreement with something exposed and complement it from their point of view.

We believe that a higher use of the first combination of strategies Self-evaluation (AeV) and Exteriorising (EX) as well as the strategy Situating the learning process itself (SA) (this last one showed no relevant frequency of use in this analysis), could promote a better development in the consecutive phase of cooperation: Phase 3; which requires high concentration towards meeting the specific objectives of the task.

As for the cognitive strategies there are also important findings. The strategies Integration aimed at consensus (IoC), Negotiating meaning (NS) only appear in the third phase of cooperative work, whereas Elicitation (ELi), in the mode of shared regulation, and Exteriorising (EX), in the mode of self- regulation appeared in each

8 Socio-cognitive Regulation Strategies in Cooperative Learning

of the phases. A possible explanation for this fact is the relation to the purpose of the phase, where construction of meaning takes place. The strategy Integration aimed at consensus (IoC) seemed to be a very essential one when constructing meaning. The use of this strategy indicates that other strategies have been previously employed such as: Exteriorising (EX), Elicitation (ELi) and Negotiating meaning (NS).

Integration means to synthesize different contributions, relate them with other references and with own reflections and finally bring all these ideas together into a concrete position. This shows how behavior regulation becomes increasingly more self-regulated.

Having distinguished the regulation strategies employed by students to regulate their contributions during the process of cooperative work, with the structure and characteristics of this particular cooperative task, we proceed to present the four regulation models explored.

We will briefly describe the characteristics in each phase of cooperative work and present some examples with either individual or grupal contributions in a discourse (original discourse is in Spanish). Separators (|) indicate the segmentation, square brackets with three dots ([...]) indicate an omission of text in the example, codes are represented within curly brackets ({XX}). Code abbreviations can be revised in Tables 8.1 and 8.2.

Phase 1 (Start): Group members get to know each other, they integrate and start to get organized. The task is defined and ideas on how to focus on its realization arise. The regulation strategies in this phase show assumption of compromises and/or promote ways to integrate with other group members through discourses that generate social dialogue. Following examples are single contributions from different group members:

> **Jim:** |[...]|Well here I am, ready to work with you in this case study. {PI}|
> **Lia:** |It seems our group is complete, How do we begin? Perhaps brainstorming, set dates, ...? {OrT}|
> **Zoe:** |It's just great to work with someone you already know. I welcome everybody else in the group! {RS}|
> **Xen:** |Case study 3 is quite related to my current job, that's why I chose it" {EX}|
> **Clark:** |Have you all seen how group 2 has started to collect information? {Eli}|

Phase 2 (Exchange): Group members share opinions, information, reflections and/or points of view on the tasks' content. The information exchange is predominantly cumulative and contributions are mainly non critical and non argumentative. There is evidence of students relating previous knowledge and experience with the actual task, and students who estimated the benefit that the outcome of the task would bring to their everyday context. Following examples are single contributions from different group members:

> **Ria:** |I apologize for my absence, I said I was going to share my opinions yesterday, but I couldn't. {MI}|
> **Jhon:** |I hope is ok for everyone that I start writing the things I consider to be important [...].{ELi}|
> **Mike:** | I've checked the official site of the entity and read some articles explaining that [...].{EX}|
> **Kate:** | I believe I've read something similar about this in other course. Let me find my notes, this could bring us a bit further with our decisions [...].{AEV-EX}|

Phase 3 (Negotiation): The main focus of this phase is to meet the objectives set for the task. The group filters information gathered from previous phases through critical analysis, argumentative statements, alternative ideas and self-reflections. Messages show openness encouraging dialogue, joint construction of meaning and group consensus.

The following example shows a reduced part of the interaction between 4 group members, while negotiating on a proposal made by Karl.

> **Karl:** |For the task, I propose to use the elaboration theory since [...]. To achieve the objectives we could [...]. By doing it this way we could help teachers [...].{NS} |Looking forward to your comments!{Eli}|
> **Sven:** |The proposal from Karl is congruent and I thank him [...]. {PM–RS}| Point 1 of our task says [...], {ExT}| from my point of view I [...]{EX}|This is why I suggest that based on what Karl has presented, we do a [...]; which would complement others' ideas. {IoC}| On the other hand, I don't completely agree with a part of Karl's proposal, because these tools should be used everyday[...].{EX / Eli}| Can't it be seen like [...]? {NS}|.
> **Karl:** |I did think about using them every day, that's why at the end I wrote "[...]".{PM / IoC}|I put it like this since [...].{EX}| About using Wikis instead of Blogs is because [...], this way we can guarantee[...]. {NS}|What do you and the others think? {ELi}|
> **Eve:** |I Agree with Karl's proposal in this point [...] and having into account that [...] as he says, there're no other possibilities. I think that [...]{PM / EX}|. Based on what Sven's has specified about [...] and on the references proposed by Karl, we would meet the criteria of [...].{IoC}| About the use of Wikis or Blogs I think [...] {EX}|and to dynamize its use I suggest [...], we also need to consider [...] because [...] {NS}|
> **Rose:** |I have been tracking the discussion even if I just appear now. {MI}| I attach a document with a possible structure based on what it has been discussed until now.{IOC–NS}| If anything, let me know {Eli}.|

Phase 4 (Implementation): The principal goal of this last phase is to implement and specify the final product: a written report. Interventions communicate perseverance and commitment from each member. There is evidence of cognitive assertions showing an alteration of cognitive schemas due to group interaction.

The next example shows a reduced part of the interaction between 4 group members in the implementation phase. Lei has began to write the final report.

> **Lei:** |With all our contributions I've started to write the official document.{MI}|I'm attaching it here so that everyone can read it {Eli}|
> **Kai:** |Great Lei! you are really quick {RS}|, the structure is adequate and the content is getting a shape, we should check the name of the tables. {OrT}| Besides, Jan and Mel need to add their references {IR}|
> **Jan:** |I'll be off today, but tomorrow morning I'll upload the references plus more contributions {PI}|
> **Mel:** |Ok, Kai, I will do that immediately. {PI}|Through the realization of the task I now feel confident with this complex topic {EX}| This wouldn't have been possible without your effort, thanks everyone. {EX–RS}|

4 Conclusions

The proposed theoretical framework for regulated learning, combining the constructs of social and cognitive regulation, was found to be useful for identifying the strategies employed by university students in order to regulate their performance during the development of cooperative tasks in virtual environments.

The quality of the interactions can only be judged by analyzing the messages that constitutes them, and from observing the intention of each of the thematic units that constitute each message. Additionally, this should be judged based on what the group intend to reach or construct with the interaction.

Our exploratory qualitative analysis of the evolution of the interactions during the cooperative tasks allowed us to identify the particularities of regulation during a cooperative task in a virtual, asynchronous and written environment. We found that in their interactions, students alternate and combine strategies to regulate the social and cognitive dimensions of their performance. We also observed that the regulatory modes of participation vary according to what phase of cooperation the group is at.

In the cooperative phases of exchange and negotiation, cognitive regulation prevails, whilst in the commencing and applying phases social regulation intensifies. In terms of cognitive regulation, the following strategies stood out: expressing previous knowledge and viewpoints (self-regulation), clarifying the task (external regulation), eliciting opinions and questioning, negotiating meaning and making an effort to integrate contributions with the objective of reaching consensus (shared regulation). In terms of social regulation, the following strategies play an important role:

situating the learning process itself, carrying out self-evaluation, monitoring participation, individual planning (self-regulation), structuring the task, offering social reinforcements (external regulation), contributing to a short and quick consensus, mutual perspective, call for accountability and / or participation from others (shared regulation).

As stated by Zimmerman (1997), these aspects form a system involving more personal factors (self), factors derived from their behavior and external factors, related to the learning context or environment. In the learning situation, diverse components of the task and the context integrate each other and configure a type of regulated action which is relevant to the objective of the task.

Finally, whilst our research allowed us to corroborate the conceptual presuppositions taken as a starting point, its application requires further research; which would allow to contrast these observations in other cooperative tasks, with the participation of other teachers and other students. A more focused observation of the interactions in each cooperative phase will allow for the delineation of indicators to evaluate the contributions made by regulation to the construction of learning, whilst at the same time helping to clarify the model we have presented in this research for more practical educational objectives, such as, for example, producing guidelines to support tasks or clues to help the students to regulate their participation during the development of the cooperative task. Likewise, it would be worthwhile to take into account teachers' opinions about our proposal.

Regardless of this constraint, we expect this theoretical framework to be practical for identifying and promoting regulation models, as well as contributing to the emergence and maintenance of the desirable interactions as the cooperative activity evolves in a virtual learning environment.

References

Angeli, C., Valanides, N., & Bonk, C. J. (2003). Communication in a web-based conferencing system: The quality of computer-mediated interactions. *British Journal of Educational Technology, 34*(1), 31–43.

Arvaja, M., Salovaara, H., Hakkinen, P., & Järvelä, S. (2007). Combining individual and group-level perspectives for studying collaborative knowledge construction in context. *Learning and Instruction, 17*(4), 448–459.

Boakaerts, M., & Minnaert, A. (2006). Affective and motivational outcomes of working in collaborative groups. *Educational Psychology, 26*(2), 187–208.

Casanova, M. (2008). Cooperative learning in a virtual university context of asynchronous communication: A study on the process of peer interaction through discourse analysis (Doctoral dissertation). Retrieved October 14, 2010, from http://www.tdx.cat/TDX-0331109-134502/

Covarrubias, M. A., & Estrevel, L. B. (2006). Some affective-cognitive elements involved in the constructive process of self-regulation. *Psicología y Ciencia Social, 8*(002). Retrieved October 14, 2010, from http://redalyc.uaemex.mx/redalyc/src/inicio/ArtPdfRed.jsp?iCve=31480203

Dillenbourg, P., & Fischer, F. (2007). Basics of computer-supported collaborative learning. *Zeitschrift für Berufs- und Wirtschaftspädagogik, 21*, 111–130.

Dillenbourg, P., Schneider, D., & Synteta, P. (2002). Virtual learning environments. In A. Dimitracopoulou (Ed.), *Proceedings of the 3rd Hellenic conference on information & communication technologies in education* (pp. 3–18). Greece: Kastaniotis Editions.

Durán, D., & Monereo, C. (2005). Styles and sequences of cooperative interactions in fixed and reciprocal peer tutoring. *Learning & Instruction, 15,* 179–199.

Garrison, D., & Anderson, T. (2003). *E-learning in the 21st century.* London: RoutledgeFalmer.

Garrison, D., Anderson, T., & Archer, W. (2000). Critical thinking in a text-based environment: computer conferencing in Higher Education. *The Internet and Higher Education, 2* (2–3), 87–105.

Gunawardena, C., Lowe, C., & Anderson, T. (1997). Analysis of a global online debate and the development of an interaction analysis model for examining social construction of knowledge in computer conferencing. *Journal of Educational Computing Research, 17* (4), 395–431.

Henri, F. (1992). Computer conferencing and content analysis. In A. Kaye (Ed.), *Collaborative learning through computer conferencing* (pp. 117–136). London: Springer.

Hung, D., & Der-Thanq, Ch. (2001). Situated cognition, Vygotskian thought and learning from the communities of practice perspective: implications for the design of web-based E-learning. *Educational Media International, 38*(1), 3–12.

Järvelä, S., & Hakkinen, P. (2002). Web-based cases in teaching and learning–the quality of discussions and a stage of perspective taking in asynchronous communication. *Interactive Learning Environments, 10*(1), 1–22.

Järvelä, S., Näykki, P., Laru, J., & Luokkanen, T. (2007). Structuring and regulating collaborative learning in higher education with wireless networks and mobile tools. *Educational Technology & Society, 10*(4), 71–79.

Johnson, D., & Johnson, R. (1999). *Learning together and alone: Cooperative, competitive, and individualistic learning* (5th ed.), Boston: Allyn and Bacon.

Kirschner, P., & Kreijns, K. (2003). The sociability of computer-mediated collaborative learning environments: Pitfalls of social interaction and how to avoid them. *Educational Technology & Society 5* (1), 8–22.

Lipponen, L. (2002). Exploring foundations for computer-supported collaborative learning. *Proceedings from Computer Supported Collaborative Learning 2002* (pp. 72–81). Boulder, Colorado.

Lipponen, L., Rahikainen, M., Hakkarainen, K., & Palonen, T. (2002). Effective participation and discourse through a computer network: Investigating elementary students' computer-supported interaction. *Journal of Educational Computing Research, 27*(4), 353–382.

López-B, D. (2009). Behavior regulation during joint construction of meaning in cooperative tasks within virtual written and asynchronous learning environments (Master's thesis). Retrieved October 2010, from http://openaccess.uoc.edu/webapps/02/handle/10609/1921

Mercer, N. (2004). Sociocultural discourse analysis: Analyzing classroom talk as a social mode of thinking. *Journal of Applied Linguistics, 1*(2), 137–168.

Mercer, N., & Littleton, K. (2007). *Dialogue and the development of children's thinking.* London: Routledge.

Panitz, T. (1996). *Collaborative versus cooperative learning: A comparison of the two concepts which will help us understand the underlying nature of interactive learning* [On-line] Retrieved October 2010, from http://home.capecod.net/~tpanitz/tedsarticles/coopdefinition.htm

Raitman, R., Zhou, W., & Nicholson, P. (2003). Exploring the foundations of practicing online collaboration. In W. Zhou, P. Nicholson, B. Corbitt, J. Fong (Eds.), *Advances in web-based learning–ICWL 2003: Second international conference* (pp. 532–541). Berlin: Springer.

Reznitskaya, A., Kuo, L.-J., Glina, M., & Anderson, R. (2008). Measuring argumentative reasoning: What's behind the numbers? *Learning and Individual Differences, 19*(2), 219–224.

Rourke, L., Anderson, T., Garrison, D., & Archer, W. (2001). Methodological issues in the content analysis of computer conference transcripts. *International Journal of Artificial Intelligence in Education, 12*(1), 8–22.

Salmon, G. (2002). Mirror, Mirror, on my screen. Exploring online reflections. *The British Journal of Educational Technology, 33* (4), 383–396.

Salonen, P., Vauras, M., & Efklides, A. (2005). Social interaction – what can it tell us about metacognition and coregulation in learning? *European Psychologist, 10*(3), 199–208.

Vauras, M., Iiskala, T., Kajamies, A., Kinnunen, R., & Lehtinen, E. (2003). Shared-regulation and motivation of collaborating peers: A case analysis. *Psychologia, 46*(1), 19–33.

Volet, S., Summers, M., & Thurman, J. (2009). High-level co-regulation in collaborative learning: How does it merge and how is it sustained. *Learning and Instruction, 19*(2), 128–143.

Vygotsky, L. (1978). *Mind in society: The development of higher mental processes*. Cambridge, MA: Harvard University Press.

Vygotsky, L. (1986). *Thought and language*. Cambridge, MA: MIT Press. [Original work published 1934].

Wegerif, R., Mercer, N., & Dawes, L. (1999). From social interaction to individual reasoning: an empirical investigation of a possible socio-cultural model of cognitive development. *Learning and Instruction, 9*(6), 493–516.

Weinberger, A., & Fischer, F. (2006). A framework to analyze argumentative knowledge construction in computer-supported collaborative learning. *Computers & Education, 46*(1), 71–95.

Whipp, J., & Chiarelli, S. (2004). Self-regulation in a web-based course: A case study. *Educational Technology Research and Development, 52*(4), 5–22.

Winters, F., Greene, J., & Costich, C. (2008). Self-regulation of learning within computer-based learning environments: A critical analysis. *Educational Psychology Review, 20*(4), 429–444.

Zimmerman, B. (1997). Becoming a Self-Regulated Writer: A social cognitive perspective. *Contemporary Educational Psychology, 22,* 73–101.

Zimmerman, B., & Tsikalas, K. (2005). Can computer-based learning environments (CBLEs) be used as self-regulatory tools to enhance learning? *Educational Psychologist, 40*(4), 267–271.

Chapter 9
Collaborative Cognitive Tools for Shared Representations

The Missing Link Between the National Information Strategy for Education and Its Practical Implementation in Schools

Jukka Orava and Pasi Silander

Abstract There has long been a missing link between the National Information Strategies for Education and its implementation into teaching practices in schools. In this chapter we present the new collaborative cognitive tools (CCT) for shared representations. The cognitive tools make a difference by providing a platform for collaborative construction of the school's information strategy with a shared vision and practice-oriented goals supporting its implementation. Collaborative cognitive tools work as mediators in a transformation process from the traditional school culture, where teachers work alone, to the new culture of teachers' collaboration and teamwork. In addition, they provide an instrument for pedagogical leadership for school principals.

Keywords Cognitive tools · Shared representations · Information strategy · Pedagogical leadership

1 Introduction

This study investigates the influence of collaborative cognitive tools (CCTs) on the strategy process, where schools construct their own development goals and action plans concerning the pedagogical and innovative use of information and communication technology (ICT) in education. In order to react to the developing needs of the surrounding information society and national policies, information strategies are constructed in schools. A collaborative strategy process, and professional development as an ongoing process in schools, are needed in order to get teachers committed and empowered to using ICT in their teaching in pedagogically meaningful ways

J. Orava (✉)
Department of Education, Medical Center, P.O.Box 3010, Helsinki 00099, Finland
e-mail: jukka.orava@hel.fi

(Carlson & Gadio, 2002). Because teachers are the gatekeepers of students' access to educational technology and educational resources, they cannot be bypassed in the information strategy process.

The Finnish National Information Strategy for Education and Research (Ministry of Education, 1995), which defines the outlines of the information and communication policy for education, training and research in the twenty first century, was launched in 1995 and updated in 2000 (Ministry of Education, 1999). The next step nationally was to define the Information Society Programme 2004–2006 (Ministry of Education, 2004), which continued the previous strategies and incorporated a wider social view. The Information Society Program was envisioned to produce the necessary changes in the culture of education so that information society skills and competences could be produced for all learners.

As yet, the strategy has not been realized in the form of renewed teaching and learning practices in educational institutes in Finland, as expected. Even though each school has created its own information strategy based on the policies of the national strategy, the influences of the strategies have been, so far, minimal on teachers' educational practices in classrooms (RESU, 2007). Up to now, the effects of information strategies at the school level can be identified only as developed technical infrastructures and internet connections; from the teachers' viewpoint the information strategy was more about technical devices in classrooms and computer labs than a pedagogical document guiding teaching practices.

Even though there have been good experiences of information strategy processes on a school level (Kylämä & Silander, 2000), the development of the strategy process in educational institutes in terms of the necessary evolving of pedagogical leadership and knowledge management in schools remains a major challenge. Knowledge management in schools is related to the issue of how the role of the school as an institution is seen (OECD, 2004), and this reflects the conceptions on learning and learning theories of the teachers and principals. The use of information technology in schools should follow the current knowledge on the nature of learning, which should, in turn, form a basis for planning how to use ICT in education (Watson, 2001) – a basis for the information strategy process. In addition, ideally teachers' own ICT skills develop in schools through developing information strategies (European Commission, 2002).

In 2008 the Education Department of Helsinki City revised its educational institutions' information strategy process into a continuous Collaborative Annual Action Planning Process (CAP) in which the entire pedagogical staff is incorporated into the collaborative process in order to realize the information strategy and shared vision for an educational institute In order to facilitate the process in educational institutes we have developed a tool kit consisting of CCTs for creating a school's information strategy as a part of the school's annual action planning process. The idea of CCTs is to scaffold the process and work as an instrument for collaboratively shared representations. A background for the tool kit was laid in the Support and Resources for Teachers' Professional Development Initiative in City of Helsinki, in which teachers' professional development in the use of ICT is planned and implemented through a collaborative process.

The CAP containing the information strategy process was introduced to 54 schools in the City of Helsinki in 2009. All 140 schools in the City of Helsinki will have it in use by 2010. For the first time, 54 schools constructed their information strategy through a CAP using CCTs.

2 Information Strategy Process and Collaborative Cognitive Tools

Schools participating in the CAP construct their information strategy with the CCTs as a part of their annual action plans and reports. The essence of the schools' processes (see Fig. 9.1) is that schools themselves evaluate, as a teachers' collaborative process, how the goals of the national curriculum concerning the use of ICT have been realized in their school's teaching practices and its own curriculum. Based on this collaborative self-evaluation, schools set their own development goals with actions for their practical implementation.

School principals were trained for the CAP with the CCTs in one afternoon lecture (3 h). They were provided with complete electronic and paper versions of the CCTs, accompanied by illustrated tutorials and detailed instructions. The school principals' training was focused on the role and meaning of collaborative tools in a collaborative process and how to lead the process in schools. In addition, a training day for teachers who were members of schools' management teams or information technology teams was organized. Training was relatively similar to the school principals' training, but there was more time to get deeper into the strategy process and

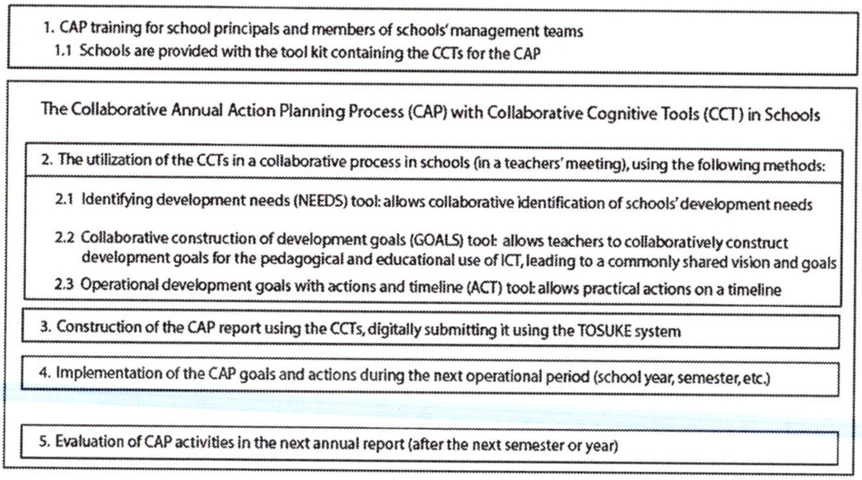

1. CAP training for school principals and members of schools' management teams
1.1 Schools are provided with the tool kit containing the CCTs for the CAP

The Collaborative Annual Action Planning Process (CAP) with Collaborative Cognitive Tools (CCT) in Schools
2. The utilization of the CCTs in a collaborative process in schools (in a teachers' meeting), using the following methods:
2.1 Identifying development needs (NEEDS) tool: allows collaborative identification of schools' development needs
2.2 Collaborative construction of development goals (GOALS) tool: allows teachers to collaboratively construct development goals for the pedagogical and educational use of ICT, leading to a commonly shared vision and goals
2.3 Operational development goals with actions and timeline (ACT) tool: allows practical actions on a timeline
3. Construction of the CAP report using the CCTs, digitally submitting it using the TOSUKE system
4. Implementation of the CAP goals and actions during the next operational period (school year, semester, etc.)
5. Evaluation of CAP activities in the next annual report (after the next semester or year)

Fig. 9.1 Collaborative annual action planning process (CAP) with collaborative cognitive tools (CCT) in schools

the backgrounds of the collaborative process and tools. The task of the trained principals and teachers was to carry out the process of evaluation, setting development goals and actions in schools as a collaborative process for all teachers. The schools then described the outcomes of the process in their annual report and action plan by using the web-based TOSUKE system.

3 Cognitive Tools for Collaborative Shared Representations in a Strategy Process

In challenging situations, in this case the implementation of the National Information Strategy on a school level and the renewal of existing teaching practices regarding ICT, a commonly shared vision and common goals among teachers play major roles (see e.g. Lavonen, Latto, Jutti, & Meisalo, 2006). The practical realization of the strategy and national policies are naturally affected by each of the teachers in a school. In order to gain a common vision and goals that are really shared by each member of the educational organization, social interaction and pedagogical discourse are needed. In order to achieve a common vision and goals applicable on the implementation level, the goals and vision should ideally be constructed by a collaborative process within the school's community of teachers. In addition, the collaborative construction process empowers teachers and teams of teachers on a school level (Carlson & Gadio, 2002); however, pedagogical discourse and the collaborative construction process of shared vision and goals is not an every day practice in a school community and therefore the construction process need to be scaffolded (Wood, Bruner, & Ross, 1976; Bruner, 1985) and facilitated. In this process, we used cognitive tools as the approach (and instruments) with which to facilitate and guide the strategy process in schools.

Cognitive tools are instruments that support humans' cognitive processes by offering a platform for physically distributed cognition (Perkins, 1993; Karasavvidis, Kommers, & Stoyanova, 2002), thereby extending the limits of human cognitive capacities and working memory (see e.g. Pea, 1993; Jonassen & Reeves, 1996). Cognitive tools or mind tools can be physical objects (like an abacus) or computer applications that facilitate cognitive processing and scaffold the process of externalization and problem solving (see e.g. Kommers, Jonassen, & Mayes, 1992; Pea, 1985).

In addition to an individual's physically distributed cognition, we needed to integrate the collaborative aspect and socially shared cognition (see e.g. Schegloff, 1992) into the cognitive tools developed for the collaborative strategy process. The importance of the CCTs (see Fig. 9.2) is to facilitate the processes of creating a common vision and setting up common goals in schools by scaffolding the social cognitive processes and creating a framework for constructing shared representations. Collaborative shared representations are the first step towards a commonly shared vision and common goals. In order for teaching practices regarding ICT to

9 Collaborative Cognitive Tools for Shared Representations

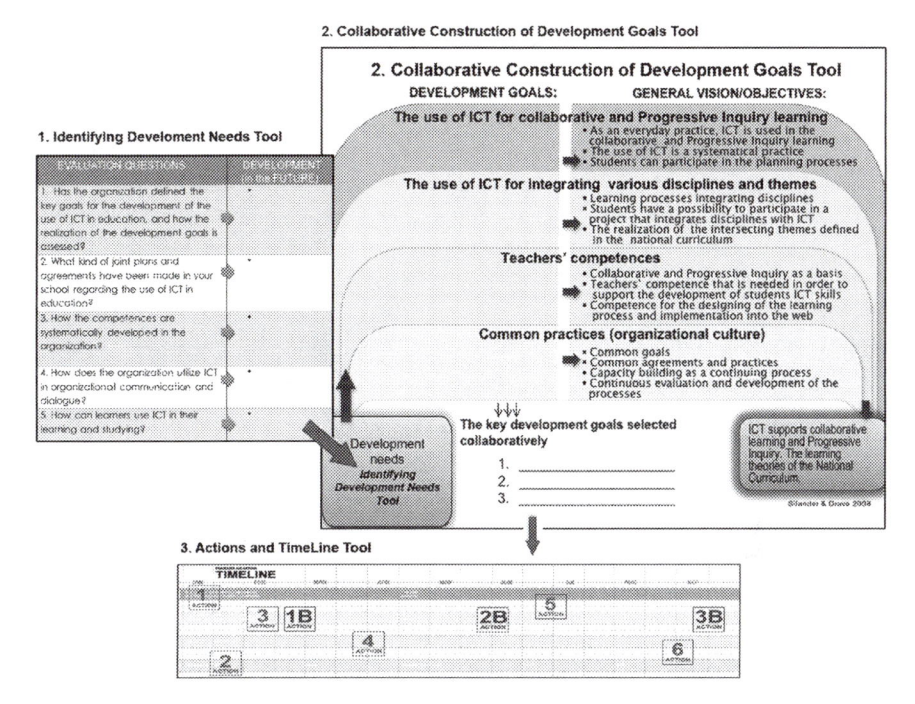

Fig. 9.2 A collaborative strategy process in schools consisting of the use of the three collaborative cognitive tools

change, commonly shared goals need to be practically aligned with actions, practical steps for teachers to take and teachers' teams.

3.1 A Tool for Identifying Development Needs

The identifying development needs (NEEDS) tool (see Fig. 9.2) can be used to evaluate how a school's curriculum, syllabus and teaching practices support the pedagogical use of ICT. The tool facilitates a school's teaching community in collaboratively identifying and formulating development needs concerning the pedagogical use of ICT and the school's curriculum. The evaluation process is conducted via the identification of the development needs on a practical level. The questions used in the process are focused on the ways in which, and issues regarding, how organizational practices and teaching practices with ICT could be development – not on criticism of the past (see e.g. Higgins, 1994). In order to for a school's curriculum and teaching practices to be renewed, it is very important to construct a commonly shared view about the items that should be development via future actions. When the development needs are constructed collaboratively, new development goals and actions will arise from various aspects.

3.1.1 Cognitive Functions – Design Principles Behind the Tool

The design principle behind this cognitive tool was to create an orientation and a context for the whole information strategy process done in schools that enables reflection on the goals and practices related to the pedagogical use of ICT. In this way the tool works as a 'cognitive activator'. When using the tool as part of the process, a gap springs up between an individual teacher's conceptions and the conceptions of the other teachers in a community or the conceptions in the curriculums. From this gap between different conceptions emerges a dynamic need for reflection and development of one's own conceptions (Chan, Burtis, & Bereiter, 1997). The tool is primarily designed to promote and to focus a dialogue and socially shared cognitions towards construction of shared ideas on development needs via future actions. This tool, as well as the thoughts and ideas externalized by the tool, works as an input for the next phase of the process and for the next tool.

3.2 A Tool for Collaborative Construction of Development Goals

The development goals (GOALS) tool is a tool to facilitate the collaborative process, whereby teachers in schools collaboratively construct development goals for the pedagogical use of ICT. The development needs identified earlier in the process (see Section 3.1) work as a ground for setting the development goals, although development needs and goals should not necessarily straight forwardly meet each other.

In the GOALS tool, categories of objectives and goals are divided metaphorically using the curves of a rainbow, forming four layers (see Fig. 9.2) which work as a semi-structured framework for setting development goals collaboratively in schools. The target is for the goals of the national curriculum concerning the pedagogical use of ICT to be described at the right hand end of the rainbow while the left hand end, the beginning of the rainbow, is reserved for the school's development goals that will (eventually) lead to the goals of the national curriculum. Various development goals are constructed collaboratively in a teachers' meeting and they are visualized on the rainbow of the cognitive tool projected on a whiteboard. The development goals visualized on the layers of the rainbow are prioritized by teachers and the most essential goals are selected for the action plan for the next semester. The tool coaches the teachers' community through the collaborative process of setting common goals by providing a semi-structured framework.

3.2.1 Cognitive Functions – Design Principles Behind the Tool

The GOALS tool provides a scaffold for setting development goals that lead to the vision and goals of the pedagogical use of ICT defined in the national curriculum. The key role of the cognitive tool is to visualize the collaboratively constructed goals and the goals of the national curriculum; the tool thereby works as an instrument for analyzing them and for collaborative reflection. The visualization and scaffolds in the cognitive tool build up a shared representation during the process that describes the commonly shared goals and vision in a school's teaching community. The tool brings out the layers in which development goals are identified in a school community and thereby widens the focus.

The GOALS tool is designed to guide a collaborative process as well as to guide externalization and sharing of ideas and thoughts by its structured format. The externalized thoughts and development goals constructed via the tool enable the process of confrontation and reflection when the goals of the school are compared to the national curriculum. This confrontation and reflection process, as well as the process of prioritization, encourages discussion to emerge on the school's educational values. The discussion on values can be seen as one factor in creating teachers' understanding of and commitment to using ICT in education.

3.3 A Tool for the Practical Alignment of the Development Goals

The actions and timeline (ACT) tool facilitates the alignment of development goals with practical development actions distributed along a timeline. The cognitive tool consists of a timeline divided into four layers corresponding to the GOALS tool (see Section 3.2) and to a ready-made pattern of actions. The actions can be graphically dragged and dropped to the layers of the timeline. The layers, with different colors on the timeline, help to illustrate in which category the planned actions are. The pattern of actions works as a set of easy steps when designing what kind of actions and steps must be taken in order to put the development goals into practice. The tool can be used on a computer or on paper. When a collaboratively constructed timeline with actions is pinned on the wall of the teachers' lounge, the goal-oriented development actions of the school are visible and transparent to the whole teaching community.

3.3.1 Cognitive Functions – Design Principles Behind the Tool

The ACT tool enables the teaching community to collaboratively analyze and practically align development goals with practical actions. When goals are aligned with practical actions the goals start to come alive in the minds of the process' participants. This supports teachers' commitment to the process and empowers them to plan their own work. The tool is designed to describe development goals as meaningful and concrete actions, helping teachers to realize and achieve them. The ACT tool enables visual and multimodal operations when collaboratively drafting actions on the four layers corresponding to the development goals constructed earlier. The collaborative construction of the actions as processes on the timeline supports both socially and physically shared cognition and manipulation of shared representations. In addition, the ready-made pattern of development actions works as a scaffold (Wood et al., 1976) for the process. The development goals and actions externalized by the ACT tool are cognitively present in everyday operations become the target of processing and discussion when the timeline as a whole, with goals and actions, is printed out and pinned on the wall of the teachers' lounge, where most of the teachers' professional discussions take place.

3.4 A Tool for Mapping Teachers' Combined Pedagogical Skills in the Use of ICT

The web-based self-evaluation questionnaire was created in order to support the development of the teachers' combined pedagogical skills in the use of ICT. The outcome of the questionnaire is a school-specific summary containing analyses on combined teachers' pedagogical skills, needs for the teachers' skills development and in-service training. Schools can use the results to identify training needs and to plan teachers' professional development process. The results are presented to the teachers and they collaboratively plan what kinds of actions are needed in order to develop teachers' skills. In addition, the schools create a development plan for increasing teachers' pedagogical ICT skills that guides teachers' participation in in-service training.

The Finnish national curriculum defines students' ICT competences that schools should provide. The questionnaire is based on these ICT competences through which the teacher's skills are approached. These competences are listed and teachers self-evaluate competence by competence their own capacity to produce the required competence. A six step self-evaluation scale is used to identify the level of teacher's capability to produce the described competence. The scale starts from technical ability and continues to pedagogical implementation. In addition, teachers mark on each competence whether they want to have in-service training regarding the competence. The questionnaire containing six thematic sections and total of 48 questions was designed so that the answering took approximately 15–20 min. The thematic sections are: practical ICT skills; information skills; interaction, collaboration, information security and ethics; advanced ICT skills; and collaborative inquiry learning. There are three separate questionnaires for teachers working in different educational levels: a primary school (year 1–6) questionnaire, a secondary school (year 7–9) questionnaire and a high school and vocational education (year 10–12) questionnaire.

Optimally, the self-evaluation questionnaire is done prior to collaborative action planning process (CAP). Answering the questionnaire can work as an orientation for the CAP process. The summary of the results can be utilized efficiently in the process when combined with the tool for identifying development needs (NEEDS) and tool for collaborative construction of development goals (GOALS).

The summary of the results of the self-evaluation questionnaires provides firm foundation for collaborative development of pedagogical ICT skills. In addition, school principals can utilize results and the questionnaires in annual appraisal interviews and when recruiting new personnel.

In addition, schools were provided with a tool for constructing a school-specific skills development plan, and a tool for designing learning processes and the integration of various disciplines in students' projects.

4 Analysis: From the Organization's Presentations to the Collaboratively Created and Shared Representation – Meaning and Relevance

We analyzed those parts of the reports concerning the pedagogical use of ICT often schools participating in the process in spring 2009 (see Fig. 9.1). We analyzed goals which were constructed as a result of the collaborative processes by using the CCTs for shared representations. The annual reports were updated in the TOSUKE database by the schools.

Our findings are based on an analysis of the text of the annual reports, including content analysis of the development goals as set collaboratively by teachers in each school. In addition, we analyzed the use of cognitive tools as part of a school's process. The grounded theory (Glaser & Straus, 1967; Straus & Corbin, 1994) was used in order to create classes in the analysis process. The development goals in the annual reports/action plans were firstly classified based on the focus (and role) of the development goal. Secondly, the development goals constructed by schools were examined more closely in order to investigate what kinds of implications they had on the implementation of the National Information Strategy and national policies regarding teaching and learning practices.

Most of the development goals were related to the development of teachers' skills and collaborative working practices in schools (see Table 9.1). Skills development in schools was supported, in addition, by a tool for mapping the combined skills of the teaching community concerning the pedagogical use of ICT. Nine out of ten schools also mapped their teachers' pedagogical skills in using ICT during the strategy process. Development goals focused directly on students were identified by seven of the ten schools, while goals focused on technology where mentioned by only four schools. Development goals concerning the sharing of best practices and collegial support were set by four schools.

The schools' focus on working culture and collaborative work practices in their development goals implies that they have at least started the transformation process from the traditional organizational culture, where teachers work alone, to a

Table 9.1 The focuses of the development goals set by schools ($n=10$)

Focus of the development goals	Freq
Skills development (pedagogical methods, ICT supported collaborative learning)	9
Development of teachers' collaborative working practices	9
Teaching methods and projects with students (classroom practices)	7
Common agreements, practices and rules in the organizational culture	4
Sharing of best practices and collegial support in professional development	4
Utilizing technology without explicit pedagogical implications (technology oriented)	4

culture in which collaborative planning and collaborative development processes are emphasized and members of the teaching community are committed to long term development goals.

4.1 Implications for the Implementation of the National Information Strategy and Policies

The experiences regarding the use of the CCTs in the schools' information strategy processes in 2009 imply that the collaborative use of the tools creates substantial conditions for the implementation process of the National Information Strategy in teaching practices (see Table 9.2).

Table 9.2 Conditions created for the implementation of the national information strategy in schools

Conditions for the implementation
1. Commonly shared vision
2. Common goals for development
3. A view on the actions needed in order to achieve the development goals
4. Acceptance of collaborative and cooperative working practices
5. Focus on the development of combined competences of the teaching community or teams

In this study, all analyzed annual reports of the schools express their commonly shared vision and common development goals, whereas analysis of the 2004 information strategies (RESU, 2007) stated that vision and goals were totally missing in the information strategies of several schools. If a school has not set goals for the pedagogical use of ICT, it is naturally difficult or even impossible to include relevant development actions in an information strategy or annual action plan. In 2004, most of the schools' information strategies were focused on describing existing technical environments in schools (e.g. how many computers they had) (RESU, 2007), whereas the development goals analyzed in this study were focused beyond that, on the development of collaborative practices and systematic skills development in teaching communities.

The analysis of the information strategies in 2004 (RESU, 2007) also reveals that schools' principals and teaching communities were not participating in a collaborative strategy process in which teachers could build a shared vision, goals or new ideas together. This is a major difference, when comparing the strategies in 2004 to those done in 2009 as a part of the CAP report. In the revised strategy process done in 2009, school principals were leading the process and promoting collaborative discussion by using the CCTs for creating shared representations.

In order to get a closer insight, we examined one case in a more detailed way and analyzed the use of cognitive tools and shared externalized thoughts achieved via the tools. Based on a qualitative analysis of the case, we identified the focus on various individual development goals formed by using the CCTs in the school. All the individual goals, both long term and short term, presented via the tool, can be divided into the following three categories: 1) renewal of teachers' work and profession; 2) development of teachers' skills; and 3) creation of a new working culture and practices. The individual goals constructed in the cognitive tool were, for example, *to allocate more time for teachers' collaborative planning, to make common agreements and rules visible, to foster student responsibility, to organize training in web-based learning environments for teachers.*

These development goals did not target technology, software, or hardware, but concentrated on building up prerequisites for work, operations, and practices concerning the pedagogical use of ICT. This can be seen as a remarkable step away from the old-fashioned way of emphasizing technology as the main point without pedagogical implications. In addition, the development goals in the analyzed case were not focused on the individual pedagogical settings or events; they were more general. As a summary, this case illustrates that development goals and actions in the information strategy should ideally be far away from describing the technical environment; they are goals and actions that emphasize the collaboration and shared activities of the teaching community in a school.

We conclude that the use of cognitive tools in the strategy process has substantially enhanced the quality of the strategies. The results show that the developed cognitive tools have shifted strategy work in schools from organizational presentations to the collaboratively created and shared representation–meaning and relevance. Through the collaborative process teachers have found the meaning and relevance of a strategy to be a tool for developing their own work and practice.

5 Discussion

Educational institutes need to achieve genuine and systematic pedagogical benefit from ICT. In addition, the development of the virtual and media world (e.g. social media and web 2.0) creates new needs for education. The pedagogical challenge of schools is to combine contemporary youths' media world and the knowledge-building culture of social media communities with the school culture of knowledge construction, in which learners' own knowledge culture becomes a part of their skills development in the classroom. This challenge regarding renewing the teaching and learning culture can be addressed in schools through collaboratively constructed information strategies.

We have introduced the collaborative cognitive tools (CCTs) developed for the strategy process in schools and educational institutes. In our exploration we have found that the role of CCTs for shared representations which enhance the strategy process is obvious. The information strategies of the schools have transformed from technically oriented documents to meaningful instruments of development containing commonly shared vision and goals. The policies of the National Information

Strategy for education have been effectively implemented in the practices of the school communities. In addition, operational planning becomes a part of strategic planning as a continuous practice, including self-assessment of activities.

The findings imply that providing school principals with instruments for pedagogical leadership renews teachers' working culture in schools. The CCTs for shared representations facilitate pedagogical leadership, which has not before been supported in the information strategy processes of the schools. The role of the school principal seems to be changing from the traditional manager to the strategic coach of a teaching community in which the teachers are empowered.

The process and the CCTs are applicable to other contexts in strategic planning and development processes. The cognitive tools externalize the community's thinking, making it visible and working as an instrument for creating shared representations that enable reflection and assessment as a natural part of the process. In addition, strategies and action plans constructed in a process along with the cognitive tools can be utilized as a decision support system.

CCTs for shared representations in the strategy process of schools are still their early stages of development. More exploration of the tools' direct effects on shared cognitive processes and collaborative constructed shared representations in the strategy process of the schools and educational institutes is needed. In addition, examination of user reactions and experience can be used to enrich evaluation. Multidisciplinary research is required combining computer science, cognition science, organizational psychology, and design sciences. The next step in our research agenda is to examine how adaptive scaffolding, supporting the construction of shared representations, could be implemented in the CCTs. In addition, the major challenge is to find new ways in which students could also be involved in a strategy process with cognitive tools.

References

Bruner, J. (1985). Vygotsky: A historical and conceptual perspective. In J. Wertsch (Ed.), *Culture, communication, and cognition*. Cambridge: Cambridge University Press.

Carlson, S., & Gadio, C. T. (2002). Teacher professional development in the use of technology. In W. D. Haddad & A. Draxter (Eds.), *Technologies for education: Potential, parameters and prospects*. Paris and Washington, DC: UNESCO and AED.

Chan, C., Burtis, J., & Bereiter, C. (1997). Knowledge building as a mediator of conflict in conceptual change. *Cognition and Instruction, 15*(1), 1–40.

European Commission. (2002). *eEurope 2005: An Information Society for all*. Retrieved on July 6, 2009 from http://ec.europa.eu/information_society/eeurope/2002/news_library/documents/eeurope2005/eeurope2005_en.pdf

Glaser, B., & Strauss, A. (1967). The *discovery of grounded theory. Strategies for qualitative research*. New York: Aldine De Gruyter.

Higgins, J. M. (1994). *101 Creative problem solving techniques: The handbook of new ideas for business*. Winter Park, FL: The New Management Publishing Company.

Jonassen, D. H., & Reeves, T. C. (1996). Learning with technology: Using computers as cognitive tools. In D. H. Jonassen (Ed.), *Handbook of research for educational communications and technology* (pp. 693–719). New York: Macmillan.

Karasavvidis, I., Kommers, P., & Stoyanova, N. (2002). Preface: Distributed cognition and educational practice. *Journal of Interactive Learning Research, 13*(1), 5–9.

Kommers, P., Jonassen, D. H., & Mayes, T. (Eds.). (1992). *Cognitive tools for learning.* Heidelberg FRG: Springer.

Kylämä, M., & Silander, P. (2000). Constructing information society in education – the model of ICT learning centre. *Proceedings of the EDEN 4th Open Classroom Conference,* Barcelona, Spain, November 19–21.

Lavonen, J., Lattu, M., Juuti, K., & Meisalo, V. (2006). Strategy-based development of teacher educators' ICT competence through a co-operative staff development project. *European Journal of Teacher Education, 29*(2), 241–265.

Ministry of Education. (1995). *Finnish national information strategy for education and research 1995–2000.* Helsinki: Ministry of Education.

Ministry of Education. (1999). *Education, training and research in information society, a national strategy for 2000–2004.* Helsinki: Ministry of Education.

Ministry of Education. (2004). *Finnish information society programme for education, training and research 2004–2006.* (2004:14), Publications of the Ministry of Education, Finland. Helsinki: Ministry of Education.

OECD. (2004). *Completing the foundation for lifelong learning. An OECD survey of upper secondary schools.* Retrieved on April 3, 2009 from http://browse.oecdbookshop.org/oecd/pdfs/browseit/9604011E.PDF

Pea, R. D. (1985). Beyond amplification: Using the computer to reorganize mental functioning. *Educational Psychologist, 20*(4), 167–182.

Pea, R. D. (1993). Practices of distributed intelligence and designs for education. In G. Salomon (Ed.), *Distributed cognitions: Psychological and educational considerations* (pp. 47–87). New York: Cambridge University Press.

Perkins, D. N. (1993). Person-plus: A distributed view of thinking and learning. In G. Salomon (Ed.), *Distributed cognitions: Psychological and educational considerations* (pp. 88–110). New York: Cambridge University Press.

RESU. (2007). *E-oppimisen resurssikeskusten yhteistyöverkosto.* Retrieved on January 25, 2009 from http://www.edu.hel.fi/tietostrategiat

Schegloff, E. A. (1992). Conversation analysis and socially shared cognition. In L. Resnick, J. M. Levine, & S. D. Teasley (Eds.), *Perspectives on socially shared cognition* (pp. 150–171). Washington, DC: APA.

Strauss, A., & Corbin, J. (1994). Grounded theory methodology: An overview. In N. Denzin & Y. Lincoln (Eds.), *Handbook of qualitative research* (pp. 273–285). Thousand Oaks, CA: Sage.

Watson, D. M. (2001) Pedagogy before technology: Re-thinking the relationship between ICT and teaching. *Education and Information Technologies, 6*(4), 251–266.

Wood, D., Bruner, J., & Ross, G. (1976). The role of tutoring in problem-solving. *Journal of Child Psychology and Psychiatry, 17*(2), 89–100.

Part III
Assessment Perspectives

Chapter 10
Automating the Measurement of Critical Thinking for Individuals Participating in Discussion Forums

Stephen Corich, Kinshuk, and Lynn Jeffrey

Abstract The use of discussion forums in an educational setting is increasing. However the extent to which discussion forums contribute to learning is subject to debate. A review of the literature reveals some evidence of researchers attempting to develop models that measure indicators of critical thinking for group participation within a discussion forum; however, there is little evidence of research aimed at measuring the critical thinking of individuals. This paper builds on previous studies presented by the authors which have reported on the use of a computerized tool designed to measure evidence of critical thinking among participants in a discussion forum. The paper presents an attempt to validate the computerized tool as it is used to measure evidence of critical thinking for individual participants. The validation process involved comparing the results obtained using the tool against the results obtained from administering a recognized critical thinking skills assessment.

Keywords Critical thinking · Discussion forums · Content analysis

1 Introduction

Computer conferencing as an environment for encouraging collaborative learning has become accepted practice in the blended delivery and online educational sectors (Romiszowski & Mason, 2004). Kanuka and Anderson (1998) suggest that discussion forums are increasingly being used to promote critical thinking and knowledge construction. A review of the literature provides evidence that a number of researchers have attempted to measure evidence of critical thinking among discussion forum participants (Garrison, Anderson, & Archer, 2001; Goodell & Yusko, 2005; Hara, Bonk, & Angeli, 1998; Kanuka, 2002; Meyer, 2003). However, previous

S. Corich (✉)
Eastern Institute of Technology Hawke's Bay, 501 Gloucester Street, Napier, Taradale, New Zealand
e-mail: scorich@eit.ac.nz

research is not comprehensive and fails to address the development of critical thinking of individuals over time and through interventions, including group discussion forums.

The Business Dictionary (2009) defines critical thinking as an objective examination of assumptions and underlying current beliefs to assess their correctness and legitimacy, and, thus, to validate or invalidate those underlying beliefs. John Dewey (1933) encouraged the reformation of the educational system and emphasised the importance of active learning over the delivery of knowledge. As far back as 1967, Raths, Jonas, Rothstein and Wassermann (1967) decried the lack of emphasis on thinking in the schools. Today critical thinking is recognized as an essential outcome of the educational process, and critical thinking skills are being added to most high school and college level curricula.

This paper defines critical thinking and identifies the dispositions which are used as indicators of levels of critical thinking. The paper investigates some of the traditional tools that are used to measure evidence of critical thinking and then concentrates on models and tools that have been designed to measure critical thinking within discussion forums. The paper introduces an Automatic Content Analysis Tool (ACAT) and describes how it has been used to automate the process of measuring critical thinking for groups and individuals participating in discussion forums. The paper concludes by describing a study in which an attempt was made to validate the use of the ACAT system by comparing the results of those obtained using the ACAT system with the results obtained using a traditional critical thinking skills assessment test.

2 Critical Thinking

Peter Facione (2010) in his paper entitled 'Critical Thinking: What It Is and Why It Counts' suggests that education should be a public good that benefits society. He provides a model for education that values and encourages thinking and informed decision making. In support of his view on the value of critical thinking he provides the following guidance:

> Teach people to make good decisions and you equip them to improve their own futures and become contributing members of society, rather than burdens on society. Becoming educated and practicing good judgment does not absolutely guarantee a life of happiness, virtue, or economic success, but it surely offers a better chance at those things. And it is clearly better than enduring the consequences of making bad decisions and better than burdening friends, family, and all the rest of us with the unwanted and avoidable consequences of those poor choices. (Facione, 2010, p. 2).

Peter Facione is not alone in his quest to improve critical thinking skills. A number of educators agree that critical thinking skills are essential for the knowledge age (see, for example, Abrami, Bernard, Borokhovski, Wade, Surkes, Tamin, & Zhang, 2008; Doherty, Hansen & Kaya, 1999; Bereiter, 2002). The view that critical thinking is a fundamental aim and overriding ideal of education is supported by Bailin and Siegel (2003). Critical thinking is now recognized as an essential component of education and a vital resource in personal and civic life (Facione, Facione, & Giancarlo, 1997; Halpern, 1996; Myers, 2001). Over the last two decades, American educators and politicians have acknowledged critical thinking as a desired outcome in both K-12 and post secondary education (Facione, 1990; Mayer, 1997; U.S. Department of Education, 1990). The importance of critical thinking has now been recognized in New Zealand and has been embedded as a key competency in the New Zealand Curriculum (New Zealand Ministry of Education, 2007).

Critical thinking has its roots in the Socratic Method. Plato described Socrates as someone who encouraged his students to reflectively question common beliefs, analyse basic concepts and to carefully distinguish beliefs that are reasonable and logical from beliefs that lack rational foundation (Paul, Elder, & Bartell, 1997). Klein, Spector, Garbowski, and de la Teja (2004) suggest that Socrates challenged his students with probing questions to reveal inconsistencies in their thinking.

John Dewey, an American philosopher, psychologist and educator is widely accepted as the 'father' of modern critical thinking (Fisher, 2001). Dewey called it reflective thinking any defined it as:

> Active, persistent, and careful consideration of any belief or supposed form of knowledge in the light of the grounds that support it and the further conclusions to which it tends (Dewey, 1933. p. 118).

Dewey emphasised reflective thinking as being active rather than passive and stressed the importance of questioning the basis of supposed forms of knowledge. Dewey (1933) suggests that reflection involves an active exploration of experiences to gain new or greater understanding.

Today, definitions of critical thinking abound. The Delphi Report (1990), compiled by a panel of more than forty of the worlds leading critical thinking experts, defines critical thinking as:

> purposeful, self-regulatory judgment which results in interpretation, analysis, evaluation, and inference, as well as explanation of the evidential, conceptual, methodological, criteriological, or contextual considerations upon which that judgment is based. (p. 2).

While definitions of critical thinking are the subject of academic debate, there appears to be a consensus of agreement surrounding the dispositions of critical thinkers. Robert Ennis (2004) suggests that critical thinkers have a tendency to:

- be clear about the intended meaning of what is said, written, or otherwise communicated
- determine & maintain focus on, the conclusion or question
- take the total situation into account
- seek and offer reasons
- try to be well-informed
- look for alternatives
- seek as much precision as the situation requires
- try to be reflectively aware of one's own basic beliefs
- be open-minded: seriously consider other points of view and be willing to consider changing one's own position

- withhold judgement when the evidence and reasons are sufficient to do so
- use one's critical thinking abilities
- be careful
- take into account the feelings and thoughts of other people

When attempting to identify evidence of critical thinking, researchers look for indicators of critical thinking dispositions such as those enumerated by Ennis (2004). A number of tools have been developed to identify evidence of critical thinking dispositions. Some of the more commonly used critical thinking tools include:

- The California Critical Thinking Skills Test: College Level (1990) by Peter Falcione.
- The California Thinking Dispositions Inventory (1992) by Peter and Norren Facione.
- Cornell Critical Thinking Test, Level Z and X (2005) by Robert Ennis and Jason Millan.
- Critical Thinking Interview (1998) by Gail Hughes and Associates.
- The Ennis-Wier Critical Thinking Essay Test (1985) by Robert Ennis and Eric Wier.
- ICAT Critical Thinking Essay Examination (1996) by International Centre for Assessment of Thinking.
- Cambridge Thinking Skills Assessment (2003) by Cambridge University.

These critical thinking tools report on various critical thinking characteristics and have been used to measure an individual's level of critical thinking in both educational and vocational environments.

3 Discussion Forums

The increased use of online discussions in recent years within courses that are exclusively online or that use online technologies to enhance on-campus courses is clearly identified (Meyer, 2004). One of the benefits associated with the use of online discussions is that a written record of activity is created that can be referred to by students for reflection. These written records can also be studied by academics who may wish to investigate the types of interactions between and among participants.

Researchers investigating the use of asynchronous discussion forums have adopted the use of quantitative content analysis (QCA) as a tool to identify evidence of critical thinking. White and Marsh (2006) describe content analysis as a highly flexible research method that has been widely used in library and information science studies. They also suggest that content analysis is a systematic and rigorous approach to analyzing documents obtained or generated in the course of research. Content analysis is well suited as a tool for analysing the transcripts produced from discussion forum participant contributions.

In its simplest form, QCA involves breaking transcripts into units, assigning the units to a category and counting the number of units in each category. QCA is described by many who have used it as difficult, frustrating, and time-consuming (Rourke, Anderson, Garrison & Archer., 2001, p. 12). Agreement between coders varies considerably and very few researchers are able duplicate their original models and studies to validate their findings.

A number of content analysis models have been developed to attempt to identify evidence of critical thinking. The more commonly cited researchers include Henri (1991), Gunawardena, Lowe, and Anderson (1997), Newman, Webb, and Cochrane (1995), Garrison, Anderson, and Archer (2000, 2001), and Hara et al. (1998). All the models developed by these researchers used content analysis methods to measure levels of critical thinking of the aggregate group of discussion forum participants.

While there is an abundance of evidence of researchers manually coding models to identify evidence of critical thinking among discussion forum participants, there is little evidence of computers being used to automate the coding process. McKlin, Harmon, Evans and Jones (2002) document one such occurrence, describing the successful use of an automated tool that used neural network software to categorize messages from a discussion forum transcript. One significant advantage of an automated tool would be the elimination of differences among raters categorizing the content. Having a standard and reliable way to categorize content would allow for replication studies and studies across multiple groups, classes, and contexts.

Corich, Kinshuk, and Hunt (2004, 2006) describe the development and use of an automated content analysis tool (ACAT) which was designed to automate the process of identifying critical thinking among discussion forum participants. The ACAT tool used the Garrison et al. (2001) model to automatically code transcripts and achieved results similar to those produced by human coders. In 2007, Corich, Kinshuk & Jeffrey reported on the use of the ACAT system, once again using the Garrison et al. (2001) model to identify evidence of critical thinking for individual participants. The ACAT system was able to produce results similar to human coders; however the results indicated that while the Garrison et al. (2001) model was able to identify critical thinking for the aggregate group it was not able to successfully identify critical thinking characteristics of individual participants. The result was not unexpected as the Garrison et al. (2001) model, often referred to as the Practical Inquiry Model, relies on group interactions and community based discourse to encourage participants to share experiences and construct knowledge. With the Garrison et al. (2001) model, critical thinking requires interaction with a community, drawing upon the resources of the community to test individual contributions. When considering the individual contributions to critical thinking, the individual interactive aspects of the communication process were not considered.

This paper describes how the ACAT tool was used to measure evidence of critical thinking for individual participants using a model developed by Perkins and Murphy (2006). The Perkins and Murphy (2006) model was specifically designed to measure individual participation, and, like the Garrison et al. (2001) model, it classifies participant contributions against four critical thinking indicators. Table 10.1

Table 10.1 Critical thinking models

Model	Garrison et al. (2001)	Perkins and Murphy (2006)
Step 1	Triggering events	Clarification
Step 2	Exploration	Assessment
Step 3	Provisional	Inference
Step 4	Resolution	Strategies

Table 10.2 Model for identifying engagement in critical thinking

Clarification

All aspects of stating, clarifying, describing (but not explaining) or defining the issue being discussed.

| Proposes an issue for debate. | Analyses, negotiates or discusses the meaning of the issue. | Identifies one or more underlying assumptions in a statement in the discussion. | Identifies relationships among the statements or assumptions. | Defines or criticizes the definition of relevant terms. |

Assessment

Evaluating some aspect of the debate; making judgments on a situation, proposing evidence for an argument or for links with other issues.

| Provides or asks for reasons that proffered evidence is valid. | Provides or asks for reasons that proffered evidence is relevant. | Specifies assessment criteria, such as the credibility of the source. | Makes a value judgment on the assessment criteria or a situation or topic. | Gives evidence for choice of assessment criteria. |

Inference

Showing connections among ideas; drawing appropriate conclusions by deduction or induction, generalizing, explaining (but not describing), and hypothesizing.

| Makes appropriate deductions. | Makes appropriate inferences. | Arrives at a conclusion. | Makes generalizations. | Deduces relationships among ideas. |

Strategies

Proposing, discussing, or evaluating possible actions.

| Takes action. | Describes possible actions. | Evaluates possible actions. | Predicts outcomes of proposed actions. |

indicates the different categories used for both the Garrison et al. (2001) model and the Perkins and Murphy (2006) model.

When coding transcripts, both the ACAT system and the manual coders look for indicators that suggest activities within each of the model categories. Table 10.2 shows the indicators used for each of the four categories associated with the Perkins and Murphy (2006) model.

A model dictionary was prepared for the Perkins and Murphy (2006) model and added to the ACAT system. The model was then applied to the transcript of each individual participant and the ACAT system produced a report for each participant showing the number of sentences coded against each category of the Perkins and Murphy (2006) model.

To test the validity of the ACAT system, a human coder was employed to code the transcripts of each individual participant against each category of the Perkins and Murphy (2006) model and correlation coefficients were calculated to compare the results from the two systems.

To further test the validity the results of the ACAT, system using the Perkins and Murphy (2006) model, were compared to a traditional critical thinking test was used to measure the critical thinking skills of the discussion forum participants and results for the two systems were compared.

4 Methodology

The discussion forum transcripts used in this study were obtained from a discussion forum used in a third year undergraduate Web Development course which took place in the first semester of 2007. The transcripts were obtained with ethical approval of the institute and involved sixteen students, aged between 18 and 36, and of varying academic abilities. All participants signed consent forms agreeing to participate in the study. The course was delivered using a blended learning environment, combining traditional face-to-face activities with web publishing, on-line review and discussion forum activities. The discussion forum activity was assessed and given a 15% weighting for the final assessment allocation. Students were asked to discuss 'Web Hosting Environments,' and they were informed that they would be expected to demonstrate aspects of critical thinking in their posts. Prior to the commencement of the discussion forum activity, students were given a marking rubric that indicated the type of activities that would be recognized as contributing to the four different levels of critical thinking (clarification, assessment, inference and strategies).

The software used to support the discussion forum was an integral part of the Moodle learning management system, which allows the discussion forum transcripts to be exported and individual participation to be identified. The transcript exported from Moodle had to be manually parsed to separate the individual contributions and to create individual text files for each participant. The individual text files were then imported into the ACAT system and results were obtained for each individual participant. All students had previously used the Moodle learning management system and most students had participated in an assessed discussion forum earlier in their studies.

During the 3-week period when students were expected to post to the forum, an instructor monitored postings on a daily basis. The instructor provided encouragement, added pedagogical comments and provided reinforcement and expert advice. Of the 16 students, only 12 participated in the discussion and then went on to participate in the critical thinking test. 142 student posts were made which generated 436 sentences for coding. The resulting transcripts were reviewed by a human coder who removed 148 of the sentences which were viewed as being social in nature or not contributing to the discussion topic, leaving 288 sentences for manual and automatic analysis.

The human coder then manually coded the sentences for each individual using a rubric based on the Perkins and Murphy (2006) model, where sentences are categorized as belonging to one of the clarification, assessment, inference and strategies categories. The 288 sentences were imported into the ACAT system, and the system was used to categorise the postings and produce individual reports for each of the participants.

Following the completion of the discussion forum exercise the 12 students who had participated in the discussion forum were asked to complete the Cambridge Thinking Skills Assessment demonstration test.

5 Results and Findings

The tables below (Tables 10.3 and 10.4) show the results of the analysis of the 288 sentences obtained from the discussion forum transcripts after the social and non-contributing sentences had been removed. Table 10.3, represents the individual

Table 10.3 Human coder: Individual participant classification as a percentage using the Perkins and Murphy (2006) model

Participant	Sentences	Clarification	Assessment	Inference	Strategies
1	18	27.8	27.8	22.2	22.2
2	26	30.8	23.1	26.9	19.2
3	19	26.3	26.3	36.8	10.5
4	21	23.8	28.6	28.6	19
5	24	29.2	29.2	29.2	12.5
6	28	32.1	39.3	14.3	14.3
7	30	26.7	30	20	23.3
8	19	31.6	26.3	31.6	10.5
9	27	33.3	37	18.5	11.1
10	25	28	28	24	20
11	31	32.3	32.3	19.4	16.1
12	20	30	30	30	10
Mean	24	29.32	29.82	25.12	15.72

Table 10.4 ACAT system: Individual participant classification as a percentage using the Perkins and Murphy (2006) model

Participant	Sentences	Clarification	Assessment	Inference	Strategies
1	18	27.8	33.3	16.7	22.2
2	26	30.8	26.9	23.1	19.2
3	19	26.3	26.3	36.8	10.5
4	21	28.6	23.8	23.8	23.8
5	24	29.2	25	33.3	12.5
6	28	28.6	39.3	21.4	10.7
7	30	30	26.7	23.3	20
8	19	31.6	21.1	36.8	10.5
9	27	33.3	33.3	18.5	14.8
10	25	28	24	28	20
11	31	25.8	32.3	22.6	19.4
12	20	30	30	35	5
Mean	24	29.17	28.5	26.61	15.72

participants critical thinking classifications, as a percentage, as agreed by the human coder.

Table 10.4, represents the individual participants critical thinking classifications, as a percentage, coded by the ACAT system.

The coefficient of reliability between the manually coded results and the automatically coded results was 72% which compares with the earlier results of 71% (Corich et al., 2006) and 73% (Corich et al., 2007). Like the 2007 study sentences which were viewed as being social in nature or not contributing to the discussion topic were removed prior to analysis, and the manual coders listed them as uncategorized. For the 2006 study no sentences were removed and the automatic system placed them into the category with the highest matching probability.

Like the 2007 study, the results produced by human coders for individual are similar to those produced by the ACAT system. This would tend to reinforce the suitability of the ACAT system for providing useful information about the critical thinking activities of individual participants within a discussion forum.

Unlike the 2007 study, this study indicates differences in levels of critical thinking between different individual participants. This tend to supports the findings made by Perkins and Murphy (2006) that the model they had developed to specifically measure evidence of critical thinking for individuals provided a better indicator of an individual's critical thinking than the Garrison et al., Community of Enquiry model.

Like the results obtained by Perkins and Murphy (2006) the group as a whole tended to engage more in clarification, assessment and inference, and less in strategy. Unlike the Perkins and Murphy study the results for this study show very similar levels clarification, assessment and inference. With the exception of participant number 1, participants making the higher number of postings tended to have the highest scores in the strategies category. This result is similar to that reported in the Perkins and Murphy study.

Table 10.5 Cambridge thinking skills assessment demonstration test results

Participant	Score
1	65
2	60
3	51
4	65
5	55
6	48
7	64
8	55
9	52
10	63
11	61
12	45

Table 10.5, represents the results of the Cambridge Thinking Skills Assessment demonstration test for the same individuals that participated in the discussion forum activities.

The scores from the Cambridge Thinking Skills Assessment demonstration test would suggest that the participants in the study varied in their critical thinking skills abilities. The results obtained from the manual coding and automated coding of transcripts also indicated different levels of critical thinking. Since the results from the manual coding and the ACAT coding do not indicate an overall critical thinking score which can be compared to the Cambridge Thinking Skills Assessment results, an algorithm was used calculate a score that recognizes higher levels of critical thinking for the ACAT system produced results. The algorithm applies weightings to each of the four categories (lower weightings for the lower level categories and higher weightings for the higher level categories), multiplies the percentages in each category by the weightings and totals the result to arrive at a cumulative score for each participant. Table 10.6 shows the calculated total score for the ACAT system results.

Table 10.6 Calculated cumulated score for the ACAT system

Participant	Score
1	222.2
2	207.7
3	173.7
4	238.1
5	179.2
6	157.1
7	213.3
8	168.4
9	174.1
10	220
11	212.9
12	135

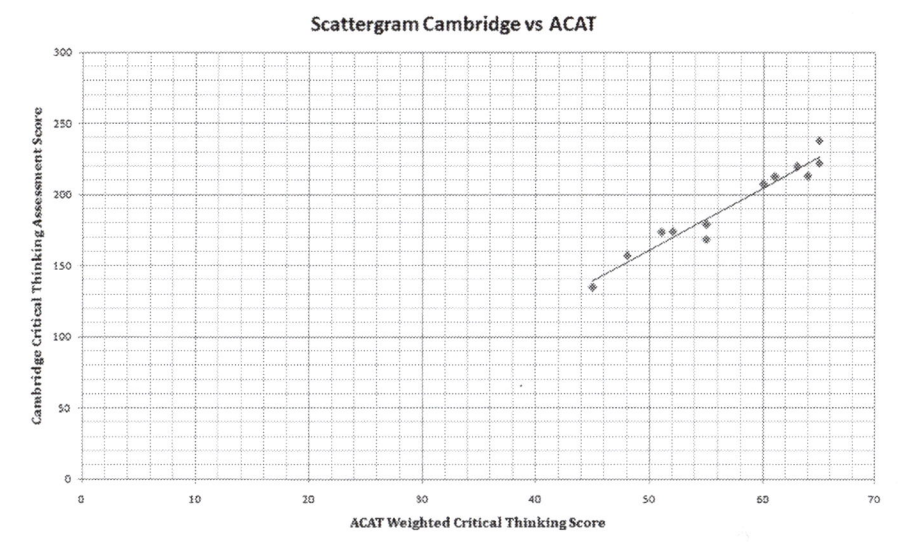

Fig.10.1 Scattergram of Cambridge thinking skills assessment score and the ACAT system weighted score

Figure 10.1 represents a scattergram showing the relationship between the Cambridge Thinking Skills Assessment score and the ACAT system weighted score. The chart suggests a strong correlation between the two sets of results.

Having established that a relationship existed between the Cambridge Thinking Skills Assessment score and the ACAT system weighted score, a statistical test was conducted to determine the strength of the correlation. Two of the most commonly used measures of correlation between two sets of data are the Pearson's product moment correlation coefficient and the Spearman's rank correlation coefficient. Since the two data items are measures of physical quantities that can be ranked and the two variables are not jointly normally distributed, the Spearman's Rank Correlation Coefficient was selected as the most appropriate measure of correlation or association for the study.

The Spearman correlation coefficient was 0.961 suggesting a strong correlation between the scores for the Cambridge Thinking Skills Assessment and the ACAT system. According to SPSS the correlation is significant at the 0.01 level suggesting a one chance in a hundred the correlation could have happened by coincidence.

6 Discussion

The purpose of this study was to evaluate if an automated content analysis tool could be used to identify levels of critical thinking by individual participants in a discussion forum and to validate the results against a traditional measure of critical thinking. Since the sample size was small, generalizations cannot be made on the basis of the findings. The results however do suggest that the use of automated tools for identifying levels of critical thinking in discussion forums is worthy of further research. The automated tool was able to produce results that are similar to those obtained by human coders and also comparable to results obtained using more traditional critical thinking measurement tools.

The strong correlation between the results obtained using the ACAT system with the Perkins & Murphy model and the results obtained using the Cambridge Thinking Skills Assessment (Spearman coefficient = 0.961) suggest that the ACAT system provides an indication of critical thinking that is similar to that produced by the Cambridge Thinking Skills Assessment.

The study adds credibility to the Perkins & Murphy model and reinforces the findings described in the paper presented in the Educational Technology & Society Journal in 2006. The model proposed by Perkins & Murphy and tested with both human coders and the ACAT system does appear to be able to differentiate different levels of critical thinking for individuals participating in discussion forums. The close correlation between the results obtained using the Perkins & Murphy model and the results obtained using the Cambridge Thinking Skills Assessment provide strong evidence to validate the model.

The validity of the results obtained from analysing the discussion forum transcripts could be questioned, since students participating in the study were given a rubric indicating how levels of critical thinking can be measured and they were informed that their discussion forum participation was being tested for evidence of critical thinking. Knowing how critical dispositions towards critical thinking were being measured could have influenced the way that students contributed towards the forum discussion. However, the comparisons with the results obtained using the Cambridge Thinking Skills Assessment would suggest that the impact of informing the participants had little effect. The strong correlation between the two systems would suggest that the provision of the marking rubric had minimal impact on the level of critical thinking identified.

The small sample size (12 participants) means that the results of the study cannot be generalized to a larger population, however the findings do provide the basis for further studies with larger and more randomly selected samples. It should also be noted that since there was only one human coder participating in the study, questions could be raised about the coders knowledge of the ACAT system and the possibility of a subsequent correlation between the manual and the automated systems results. In this study the human coder, did have previous experience of coding using the Perkins & Murphy model, however the coder was not involved in the development the ACAT system. To avoid any suggestions of coder bias, future studies could involve the use of multiple human coders.

While the studies involving the ACAT system have to date involved small sample sizes and audiences of convenience, there is the potential for further studies involving larger and more randomly selected samples. Since the studies conducted using the ACAT system involved participants selected as an audience of convenience the results cannot be generalised beyond the actual participants. The findings do however provide strong supporting evidence of the potential of using an automated tool to measure evidence of critical thinking.

There are a number of immediate improvements that could be made to improve the functionality of the ACAT system. The current version of the ACAT system does not have the functionality to allow it to automatically parse the transcripts exported from Moodle and produce individual transcripts; also the system does not automatically calculate individual results from a consolidated transcript. The ability to automatically analyse transcripts produced by a system such as Moodle and identify critical thinking scores for individuals would improve the tool and make it easier to use. The ACAT system could also be developed further allow it to be integrated directly into a learning management system such as Moodle, to provide a facility that automatically identifies postings from individuals and is able to categories posting against any selected model.

The current research associated with the use of the ACAT system has focused on the provision of a tool that can indicate different levels of critical thinking among participants of discussion forums for the aggregate group and for individual participants. Studies indicate that the tool has the potential to provide useful feedback on the critical thinking abilities of participants. The long term vision for the research is to enhance the tool so that it can provide a mechanism that allows discussion forum participants immediate feedback on the quality of their postings and provides guidance on how the level of critical thinking could be improved. Once fully developed and tested the ACAT system could provide a tool that allows students participating in discussion forums to develop their critical thinking skills on the basis of the feedback provided by the system. The same tool could allow faculty staff to identify individual students requiring assistance to improve the quality of their critical thinking abilities. If used over a period of time the tool could be used to monitor the improvement of critical thinking of individuals as they progress from year to year within an educational institute.

While the ACAT system has been designed for use with discussion forum transcripts, it has the potential to be used with any text that can be saved in a digital format. Future iterations of the ACAT system could be applied to a variety of electronically produced texts such as blogs, twitter postings and wiki contributions.

References

Abrami, P. C., Bernard, R. M., Borokhovski, E., Wade, A., Surkes, M. A., Tami, R., et al. (2008, December). Instructional interventions affecting critical thinking skills and dispositions: A stage 1 meta-analysis. *Review of Educational Research, 78*(4), 1102–1134.

Bailin, S., & Siegel, H. (2003). Critical thinking. In N. Blake, P. Smeyers, R. Smith, & P. Standish (Eds.), *The Blackwell guide to the philosophy of education* (pp. 181–193). Oxford: Blackwell.

Bereiter, C. (2002). *Education and mind in the knowledge age*. Mahwah, NJ: Lawrence Erlbaum.

Corich, S. P., Kinshuk, & Hunt, L. M. (2004). Assessing discussion forum participation: In search of quality. *International Journal of Instructional Technology and Distance Learning, 1*(12), 1–12.

Corich, S. P., Kinshuk, & Hunt, L. M. (2006). Measuring critical thinking within discussion forums using a computerised content analysis tool. *Proceedings of the fifth international conference on networked learning 2006*, Lancaster University, UK, April 10–12, Lancaster, UK. Retrieved on August 1, 2007, from http://www.networkedlearning conference.org.uk/abstracts/pdfs/P0720Corich.PDF

Corich, S. P., Kinshuk, & Jefferey, L. (2007). Changing focus from group to individual: using an automated tool to measure evidence of critical thinking in discussion forums. *CELDA 2007. Proceedings of the IADIS international conference on cognition and exploratory learning in digital age*, 7–9 December, Algarve, Portugal.

Dewey, J. (1933). *How we think: A restatement of the relation of reflective thinking to the educative process.* Boston, MA: D.C. Heath.

Doherty, J. J., Hansen, M. A., & Kaya, K. K. (1999). Teaching information skills in the information age: The Need for Critical *Thinking. Library Philosophy and Practice, 1,* 2. Retrived on April 8, 2010, from http://www.webpages.uidaho.edu/~mbolin/doherty.htm.

Ennis, R. H. (2004). Applying soundness standards to qualified reasoning. *Informal Logic, 24*(1), 23–39.

Facione, P. A. (1990). *California critical thinking skills test manual.* Millbrae, CA: California Academic Press.

Facione, P. A. (2010). *Critical thinking: What it is and why it counts.* Millbrae, CA: California Academic Press.

Facione, P. A., Facione, N. C., & Giancarlo, C. A. (1997). The motivation to think inworking and learning. In E. A. Jones (Ed.), *Preparing competent college graduates: Setting new and higher expectations for student learning—New directions for higher education* (Vol. 96, pp. 67–79). San Francisco: Jossey-Bass.

Garrison, D. R., Anderson, T., & Archer, W. (2000). Critical thinking in a text-based environment. Computer Conferencing in higher education. *Internet in Higher Education, 2*(2), 87–105.

Garrison, D. R., Anderson, T., & Archer, W. (2001). Critical thinking, cognitive presence, and computer conferencing in distance education. *American Journal of Distance Education, 15*(1), 7–23.

Goodell, J., & Yusko, B (2005). Overcoming barriers to student participation in online discussions. *Contemporary Issues in Technology and Teacher Education, 5*(1), 77–92.

Gunawardena, C., Lowe, C., & Anderson, T. (1997). Analysis of a global on-line debate and the development of an interaction analysis model for examining social construction of knowledge in computer conferencing. *Journal of Educational Computing Research, 17*(4), 395–429.

Hara, N., Bonk, C. J., & Angeli, C. (1998). Content analysis of online discussion in an applied educational psychology course. *Instructional Science, 28*(2), 115–152.

Halpern, D. F. (1996). *Thought and knowledge: An introduction to critical thinking* (3rd ed.). Mahwah, NJ: Lawrence Erlbaum.

Henri, F. (1991). Computer conferencing and content analysis. In A. R. Kaye (Ed.), *Collaborative learning through computer conferencing: The Najaden papers* (pp. 116–136). Berlin: Springer.

Kanuka, H. (2002). A principled approach to facilitating distance education: The Internet, higher education and higher levels of learning. *Journal of Distance Education, 17*(2), 70–86.

Kanuka, H., & Anderson, T. (1998). On-line interchange, discord, and knowledge construction. *Journal of Distance Education, 13*(1), 57–74.

Klein, J. D., Spector, J. M., Grabowski, B., & de la Teja, I. (2004). *Instructor competencies: Standards for face-to-face, online and blended settings.* Greenwich, CT: Information Age Publishing.

Mayer, R. E. (1997). Incorporating problem solving into secondary school curricula. In G. E. Phye (Ed.), *Handbook of academic learning: Construction of knowledge—The educational psychology series* (pp. 473–492). San Diego, CA: Academic.

McKlin, T., Harmon, S. W., Evans, W., & Jone, M. G. (2002). Cognitive presence in web-based learning: A content analysis of students' online discussions. *American Journal of Distance Education, 15*(1), 7–23.

Meyer, K. (2003). Face-to-face versus threaded discussions: The role of time and higher-order thinking. *Journal of Asynchronous Learning Networks, 7*(3), 2003. Retrieved August 1, 2007, from http://www.sloan-c.org/publications/jaln/v8n2/pdf/v8n2_meyer.pdf

Meyer, K. A. (2004, April). Evaluating online discussions: Four different frames of analysis. *Journal of American Learning Networks, 8*(2), 101–114.

Myers, M. T. (2001). Preparing students for an uncertain future. *Liberal Education, 87*(3), 22–25.

Newman, G., Webb, B., & Cochrane, C. (1995). A content analysis method to measure critical thinking in face-to-face computer supported group learning. *Interpersonal Computing and Technology, 3*(2), 56–77.

New Zealand Ministry of Education. (2007). *The New Zealand curriculum.* Wellington, New Zealand: Learning Media Limited.

Paul, R. Elder, L., & Bartell, E. (1997) *California teacher preparation for instruction in critical thinking: Research findings and policy recommendations.* Sacramento, CA: California Commission on Teacher Credentialing. Retrieved October 12, 2010, from http://www.eric.ed.gov/ERICWebPortal/contentdelivery/servlet/ERICServlet?accno=ED437379.

Perkins, C., & Murphy, E. (2006). Identifying and measuring individual engagement in critical thinking in online discussions: An exploratory case study. *Educational Technology & Society, 9*(1), 298–307.

Raths, L. E., Jonas, A., Rothstein, A., & Wassermann, S. (1967). *Teaching for thinking, theory and application.* Columbus, OH: Charles E. Merrill.

Romiszowski, A. J., & Mason, R. (2004). Computer-mediated communication. In D. H. Jonassen (Ed.), *Handbook of research on educational communications and technology* (2nd ed.) (a Project of the AECT). Mahwah, NJ: Lawrence Erlbaum.

Rourke, L., Anderson, T., Garrison, D. R., & Archer, W. (2001). Methodological issues in the content analysis of computer conference transcripts. *International Journal of Artificial Intelligence in Education, 12*(1), 8–22.

U.S. Department of Education. (1990). *National goals for education.* Washington, DC: Government Printing Office.

White, M. D., & Marsh, E. E. (2006) Content analysis: A flexible methodology. *Library Trends, 55*(1), 22–45.

Chapter 11
Alternative Assessment Strategies for Complex Problem Solving in Game-Based Learning Environments

Deniz Eseryel, Dirk Ifenthaler, and Xun Ge

Abstract The central thesis of this chapter is that emerging technologies such as digital games compel educators, educational researchers, and instructional designers to conceptualize learning, instruction, and assessment in fundamentally different ways. New technologies, including massively multi-player digital games offer new opportunities for learning and instruction; however, there is as yet insufficient evidence to support sustained impact on learning and instruction, apart from the case of military training based on large simulated war games. Technologically sophisticated design and assessment frameworks are likely to facilitate progress in this area, and that is our focus in this chapter. Specifically, we provide an integrated framework for assessing complex problem solving in digital game-based learning in the context of a longitudinal design-based research study.

Keywords Game-based learning · Assessment · Complex problem-solving

1 Introduction

In the mid-1990s, Koschmann (1996) identified computer-supported collaborative learning as a new paradigm in instructional technology, characterized by collaborative learning and integrating social issues into the foreground as a central phenomena for study, including understanding language, culture, and other aspects of the social setting surrounding the learning experience. There continues to be new technologies that offer new possibilities for computer-supported learning and instruction. For instance, massively multiplayer online games (MMOGs) combine the power of traditional forms of role-playing games with a rich, 2- or 3-D graphical simulated world allowing individuals to interact with both the

---

D. Eseryel (✉)
College of Education, University of Oklahoma, 820 Van Vleet Oval, Norman, OK 73019, USA
e-mail: eseryel@ou.edu

simulated environment and with other game players through their digital characters or avatars. These games enable players to cooperate and compete with each other on a grand scale while solving complex problem scenarios in the game. The emergence of game spaces provides players with new opportunities for learning (Thomas & Brown, 2007). Thus, MMOGs have been receiving increasing attention from educational researchers because of their motivational power as well as their potential in promoting complex problem solving and critical thinking skills.

With the increasing popularity of games and the widespread use of emerging technologies, Koschmann's (1996) work reminds us that we should focus not only on descriptive aspects of applications involving new technologies but that we ought to pay attention to paradigm shifts and innovations in both theory and practice. Accordingly, we should ask such questions as these in addition to conducting descriptive research: (a) What does game-based learning in the digital age mean? (b) What knowledge and skills should students learn in game-based learning? (c) How should we design game-based learning environments to facilitate intended knowledge and skill acquisition? These questions are the motivation behind this chapter.

The purpose of this chapter is two-folds. First, we elaborate on the new perspectives of learning and instruction proposed by the proponents of digital game-based learning. This first section includes review of empirical studies in peer-reviewed journals to arrive at an instructional design framework for effective learning in digital game-based learning environments. Emerging computer-based technologies such as digital games enable the creation of much-needed learning laboratories to systematically study the requirements and strategies for designing learning environments that can facilitate desired higher-order learning outcomes. However, as our literature review points out, lack of validated methodologies for assessing complex problem solving processes and outcomes is what impedes progress in this regard.

Therefore, the second main goal of this chapter is to propose an integrated assessment framework to guide the research and practice on digital game-based learning. We also illustrate how this integrated assessment framework was used to help us collect and analyze data in the context of a longitudinal study, the results of which have provided us with valuable information about the feasibility and value of various instructional design strategies in a MMOG–based learning environment.

2 Game-Based Learning in the Digital Age

Let my playing be my learning and my learning be my playing.
– Johan Huizinga

It took several millennia for games to evolve from one being played in a playground to one being played in a virtual world. It has taken only a couple decades for virtual games to progress from moving dots and lines (e.g., *Pong*) to massively multiplayer online role-play games with 3-D graphical avatars (e.g., *World of Warcraft*). At one time, the term 'games' referred largely to games played in a video arcade. However, in today's context, the term 'games' may refer to different types of games, including digital games playable on a portable computer.

In some sectors, the term 'serious games' (Michael & Chen, 2006) or 'epistemic games' (Shaffer, 2006) are used to distinguish games that are designed for training and instruction from those developed for entertainment purposes. However, the concept of serious or epistemic games is not new. Elementary and secondary teachers are no strangers to using games in the classroom. For a long time, board games, card games, and role-playing games have been commonly used within a classroom setting as a teaching aide to help explain or reinforce learning.

What is new today is the *medium* of games and the arguments of the proponents of game-based learning to rebuild education for the postindustrial, high-tech world by thinking about learning in a new way (see Gee, 2003; Prensky, 2001, 2006; Shaffer, 2006). These arguments are typically based on the well-intentioned discussions in educational circles in the United States about the critical role of vision in the creation of educational system that properly address twenty-first century needs (see Papert & Caperton, 1999). twenty-first century people, it is argued, require different skills, often called the twenty-first century skills, which include (1) complex problem solving skills; (2) collaboration skills; (3) communications skills; and (4) information literacy as these skills are fundamental to the success of knowledge workers in an ever-changing, global society. Riding on these arguments of the educational policy makers, in the United States, the proponents of digital game-based learning promoted the unique affordances of the game-based learning environments to facilitate the acquisition of the twenty-first century skills (see Galarneau & Zibit, 2007).

In addition, proponents of the digital game-based learning argued that game spaces have enabled play and learning merge in fundamental ways, which is quite different from what we have come to consider as standard pedagogical practice (Thomas & Brown, 2007). In the traditional paradigms of instruction, learning concerns with *learning about* whereas these new forms of learning deal with knowledge through the dynamic of *learning to be,* that is, spaces where work and play, convergence and divergence, and reality and imagination intertwine, and where students become involved in communities of practice and learn how to be realize the things they imagine. The notion of *learning to be* is supported by the situated learning theory, in which students not only learn how to apply knowledge and solve problems, but also take on an identity by learning to think like professionals, historians, engineers, or scientists in situ, that is, in communities of learners and practice (Barab & Duffy, 2000; Brown, Collins, & Duguid, 1989). The virtual worlds of games make it possible to develop situated understanding in a *virtual practice world* (Schön, 1987) contributing to *staged learning opportunities* (Macy, Squires, & Barton, 2009) replicating real-life. When designed this way, educational games can facilitate development of twenty-first century skills in the context of real-life complex knowledge domains, such as engineering. But do they? How do we know?

Facilitating learning in and about complex knowledge domains is a challenging and fascinating instructional design problem (see Sterman, 1994 for a detailed review on the difficulties of learning in and about complex domains). Central to learning about a complex knowledge domain is the requirement for effective complex problem-solving skills.

In an attempt to arrive at a design framework for educational games that can effectively promote such higher-order learning and problem-solving skills, we reviewed the empirical research on digital educational games with specific emphasis on MMOGs. Peer-reviewed journals in ERIC and PsycINFO databases were reviewed with the search terms of 'game' and 'learning.' Most of the research conducted in the area of educational MMOGs discussed underlying design features and instructional strategies embedded in educational MMOGs, such as Quest Atlantis and River City (e.g., Squire, 2004; Tuzun, 2004; Warren & Dondlinger, 2009), focusing on engagement, relationship, social interactions, and identity. Unfortunately, little or no empirical evidence was provided in support of those proposed design features and instructional strategies.

Even fewer empirical studies exist with regard to digital game-based learning, especially in the area of problem solving acquisition. Our literature review resulted with only 24 journal articles reporting empirical studies (qualitative or quantitative) on the effect of game-based learning. Overall, the findings regarding the educational benefits of games are mixed. Some of these studies claiming positive outcomes appeared to be making unsupported claims since they only utilized learner's self-report of their learning outcomes or satisfaction surveys without a measurement of their actual learning performance.

Other measures that were used to study game-based learning included: performance on game; time to complete the game; visual attention; and knowledge tests. Only one study measured performance improvement on pre- and post-tests. It should be noted that seven of these studies focused on content understanding, one focused on collaboration, and sixteen focused on domain-specific problem solving outcomes, with one also involving on communication. No studies looked at complex problem solving skill acquisition, although it is one of the most important reasons for digital-game based learning as argued by its proponents (see Barab, Tomas, Dodge, Carteaux, & Tuzun, 2005; Dickey, 2005; Gee, 2003; Prensky, 2001, 2006; Shaffer, 2006).

Despite the arguments for the potential of digital game-based learning, the empirical evidence for their effectiveness is scant. If *learning to be* is an important game-based learning experience, then assessing the dynamic game-playing (and the underlying complex problem solving) processes is equally important as, or even more important than solely assessing the learning outcomes. Therefore, we argue for the need to systematically study, which instructional design strategies work in game-based learning environments to take full advantage of what these emerging technologies can offer for education and training. Towards this goal, a scientific attitude with regard to the design of educational MMOGs requires validated measures of learning outcomes and the associated assessment methodologies in order to determine which design elements work best, when, and why.

3 Assessment of Game-Based Learning

Educational assessment is the systematic and theory-based collection and preparation of knowledge, skills, attitudes, and beliefs with the aim of justifying, controlling and optimizing conclusions and procedures. Furthermore, the assessment of change and the detailed investigation of why and how change takes place are of particular interest. Investigating changes of cognitive structures and understanding how to influence them is the key to well-designed and effective learning environments (Ifenthaler, 2008; Scandura, 1988). Moreover, learning is not a simple matter of information retrieval. It is regarded as an active process (Ifenthaler, 2010a) and key learning goals are regarded as skills, not as facile declarative knowledge (McFarlane, 2003). Additionally, aligning learning goals with goals of the game is a challenging task for instructional designers and educational psychologists. In particular, the digital age and its new technologies have created both opportunities and areas of serious concern for learning, instruction, and assessment. Accordingly, an educational assessment in the digital age requires a flexible setting in which skills are dynamically captured, particularly those of problem solving (Almond, Steinberg, & Mislevy, 2002).

According to Newell and Simon (1972), solving well-structured problems is a linear process and consists of two distinct stages: (a) the generation of a problem representation or problem space (i.e., problem solver's view of the task environment); and (b) a solution process that involves a search through the problem space. The representation of a problem consists essentially of the solver's interpretation of the problem, which determines how easily a problem can be solved (Chi & Glaser, 1985). The solver extracts information and attempts to understand the problem or connect it to existing knowledge to form an integrated representation (Gick, 1986). If schema can be activated during problem representation, the solution process is schema driven, with little search for solution procedures. If appropriate schema cannot be activated, the problem solver goes back to an earlier stage and redefines the problem or uses another method to solve the problem (Gick, 1986). More recent research concluded that (1) processes underlying complex, ill-structured problem solving are different than processes underlying well-structured problem solving (Eseryel, 2006; Jonassen, 1997); (2) performance in solving well-defined problems was independent for ill-structured tasks (Dunkle, Schraw, & Bendixen, 1995), and (3) solving ill-structured problems required different skills than those used for well-structured problems (Hong, Jonassen, & McGee, 2003; Seel, Ifenthaler, & Pirnay-Dummer, 2009).

The digital age has originated significant developments in the field of educational assessment. However, the implementation of assessment features into game-based learning environments is only in its early stages because it adds a very time-consuming step to the design process (Chin, Dukes, & Gamson, 2009). Additionally, the impact on learning and quality criteria (e.g., reliability and validity) of technology-based assessment systems are still being questioned (Pellegrino, Chudowsky, & Glaser, 2003). Closely related to educational assessment of problem solving skills is the requirement for adequate and immediate feedback while playing a game. Feedback is considered to be any type of information provided to learners (see Wagner & Wagner, 1985). Feedback plays a particularly important role in highly self-regulated game-based learning environments because it facilitates the development of mental models, thus improving expertise and expert performance (Johnson-Laird, 1989). However, this requires the learner to be sensitive to characteristics of the environment, such as the availability of certain information at a given time, the ease with which this information can be found in the environment, and the way the information is structured and mediated (Ifenthaler & Seel, 2005). However, not only do new developments in computer technology enable us to dynamically generate simple conceptual models and expert representations, but also direct responses to the learner's interaction with the learning environment (Ifenthaler, 2009b). Nevertheless, dynamic feedback within a game-based learning environment presupposes a reliable and valid educational assessment.

Generally speaking, there are two possibilities for educational assessment within game-based learning environments: Assessment after the game has been completed (outcome) and assessment while playing the game (embedded or stealth). Assessment after learning in a game-based environment often focuses on the outcome. However, such an assessment method may neglect important changes during the learning process. Accordingly, instructors and teachers can only compare the individual outcome with previous outcomes, check against other learners or experts. Still, this assessment method does not allow conclusions on the cause of a possible incorrect result. Did the learner not understand the task? Was the task too difficult? Was he or she too excited? Was it a matter of motivation? In addition, an educational assessment after playing the game cannot involve instant feedback while playing the game.

In contrast, assessment while learning in a game-based environment mostly focuses on the process. The benefits of this assessment method are manifold. Firstly, assessing learners while playing a game will provide detailed insights into underlying learning processes. Secondly, tracking motivational, emotional, and metacognitive characteristics while playing a game will help us to better understand specific behavior and the final outcomes. Thirdly, immediate feedback based on the embedded or stealth assessment can point to specific areas of difficulties learners are having while playing the game (Shute & Spector, 2010). Finally, assessment of *clickstreams* (Chung & Baker, 2003; Dummer & Ifenthaler, 2005) could point out strengths and weaknesses of the game design. Hence, an embedded and process oriented assessment must always include multiple measurement procedures which raises the question of reliable and valid ways of analyzing such longitudinal data (Ifenthaler, 2008; Willett, 1988) and provide instant feedback based on the individual assessment (Ifenthaler, 2009b). Such an intelligent assessment and feedback would result in an adaptive game environment, which changes in response to the learner's activity.

Then, how do we assess learning within games? Basically, we distinguish between (1) external and (2) internal assessment of game-based learning. External assessment is not part of the game-based environment whereas internal assessment is part of it. Next, we discuss some selected methods for external and internal game-based assessment.

3.1 External Assessment

External assessment can be implemented before, during, and/or after playing the game. However, as external assessment is not part of the game-based environment it will interrupt playing the game, which is not desirable. A standard method of external assessment is a so-called debriefing session, which follows right after finishing the game. Debriefing sessions could be implemented as paper-and-pencil tests or as computer-based assessment scenarios (Chin et al., 2009). In order to track changes, a briefing session (also realized as paper-and-pencil test or computer-based assessment scenario) before the game functions as a pretest (Ifenthaler, 2009c; Klabbers, 2008).

Debriefing sessions use paper-and-pencil or computer-based *concept-mapping tools* in order to diagnose a person's individual structural and semantic knowledge (Mandl & Fischer, 2000). A concept map consists of different concepts that are connected with named relations. The collected data of a *concept-mapping tool* can be processed directly for further analysis (Johnson, Ifenthaler, Pirnay-Dummer, & Spector, 2009). Concept mapping is a useful method to show one's conceptual knowledge, which is an appropriate measure of domain knowledge and how the domain specific concepts are related to each other. However, concept maps are less useful as measures of problem solving performance.

One method that has been used in various studies to assess problem solver's structural knowledge about the complex knowledge domains is the *think-aloud method* (Ericsson & Simon, 1993). The think-aloud method basically involves providing solver a problem scenario and asking him or her to think-aloud while solving the problem. However, the dual requirement of both solving or reflecting on a complex problem and verbalizing the cognitive processes represents an unfamiliar situation for the test person. Therefore, the test conductor has to ask for detailed information about the test person during the experiment. The data collected represents only a small amount of the cognitive processes, which occur when one solves a complex problem. One problem with the *think-aloud protocol* method is the insufficient and imprecise verbalization of the test person. Furthermore, the quantification of the collected data and the explicit relation of verbal data to cognitive processes call the validity and reliability of this method into question (Nisbett & Wilson, 1977). However, Chi (1997) and Ericsson and Simon (1980) have developed practicable procedures for quantifying verbal data known as protocol analysis. Since then, think-aloud method has been argued as a valid and reliable method to assess a solver's problem space in various studies (e.g. Tarciani & Clariana, 2006).

The *Dynamic Evaluation of Enhanced Problem-solving* (DEEP) method was developed as a web-based knowledge mapping method for problem-based assessment (Spector & Koszalka, 2004). The test persons are provided with a problem scenario in which they are asked to represent their models of the problem space. Spector and Koszalka (2004) report five steps for constructing these models: (1) Listing key facts and causal factors influencing the problem situation, (2) documenting each factor – what it is and how it influences the problem, (3) constructing a graphical depiction of how these factors are linked, (4) making annotations of each node and link, (5) indicating other considerations or approaches. The *DEEP method* identifies gaps between novice and expert decision-making in complex domains. Spector, Dennon, and Koszalka (2005) discuss their initial findings with the *DEEP method* in three different problem domains – engineering design, environmental planning, and medical diagnosis. The findings show that the *DEEP method* enables researchers to identify differences between novice and expert thinking and problem solving.

From a methodological point of view, other forms of external assessment of game-based learning are possible (e.g. reflection papers, learning journals, retrospective interviews, etc.). Additionally, writing plays an important role for external assessment of game-based learning. Writing is not merely a strategy for externalizing and therefore fixing our current knowledge and sharing it with other learners; it also leads to the reorganization and continual construction of knowledge (Eigler, 2005). Automated knowledge assessment tools allow us to produce instant feedback on semantic and structural aspects of the written text after playing the game and thereby promote the learner's self-regulated writing skills (Pirnay-Dummer & Ifenthaler, 2010; Pirnay-Dummer, Ifenthaler, & Rohde, 2009). However, the most important aspect of external assessment is the definition of the assessment goals: What knowledge, skills, attitudes, and beliefs should be measured after playing the game?

3.2 Internal Assessment

Internal assessment could be implemented before, during, and/or after playing the game. In contrast to external assessment methods, internal assessment is part of the game-based environment and will therefore not interrupt playing the game. Optimally, assessment is part of the action or tasks within the game-based environment. Automated assessment tools which are part of a game-based environment allow us to produce instant assessment as well as feedback and thereby promote the learner's self-regulated problem-solving skills (Ifenthaler, Pirnay-Dummer, & Seel, 2010). Depending on the assessment method, these systems are based on different scoring methods (see Baker, Chung, & Delacruz, 2008): (1) expert-based scoring (comparing experts' and learners' solutions), (2) data-driven methods (learner's performance is subjected to statistical analysis or machine learning), and (3) domain-modeling methods (learner's knowledge and skills are modeled for specific subject domains). With regard to practicability in game-based environments, we will focus only on expert-based scoring.

The first method compares an expert performance (considered as a referent standard) against a learner's performance. Frequently used applications are concept, causal, or knowledge maps which are automatically scored and compared to an expert's solution (Herl, Baker, & Niemi, 1996; Ifenthaler, 2010b). Various measures are generated on the fly which focus on structural and semantic features (Ifenthaler, 2010c). Numerous studies report the high potential of this scoring approach (e.g. Baker et al., 2008; Chung & Baker, 2003; Herl et al., 1996; Ifenthaler, Masduki,

& Seel, 2009; Ruiz-Primo, Schultz, Li, & Shavelson, 2001; Tarciani & Clariana, 2006). Recently developed tools allow an instant assessment of written text, which includes full sentences and a minimum of 350 words (Pirnay-Dummer & Ifenthaler, 2010; Pirnay-Dummer, Ifenthaler, & Spector, 2010). Written text is regarded as a more natural way of externalizing knowledge within a game-based environment than the application of concept, causal, or knowledge maps. Additionally, a comparison with an expert map or written text is also possible. Even cross-comparisons between written text and graphical representations are possible (Ifenthaler, 2009a; Ifenthaler & Pirnay-Dummer, 2009). Finally, it is important to define what is seen as an expert. Not every expert solution is a good instructional model that should be followed when it comes to training of novices. Hence, the goals of the game-based environment should be defined precisely before an expert-solution is considered for assessment purposes.

The implementation of expert-based scoring, data-driven methods, and domain-modeling methods into a game-based environment is still a challenge and most often very costly and labor intensive. Yet again, the most important aspect of internal assessment is the definition of the assessment goals: What knowledge, skills, attitudes, and beliefs should be measured after playing the game.

4 Methods for External and Internal Game-Based Assessment

Following the discussion of various possibilities and methods for assessing the effectiveness of game-based learning, we now further illustrate those concepts and methods through a specific example of a longitudinal study evaluating the effects of playing a MMOG on students' learning outcomes and complex problem-solving skills. Through this illustration, we also attempt to exemplify how various methods are used adaptively to assess digital game-based learning for various purposes and questions. Additionally, data analysis is discussed.

4.1 A Study on Surviving in Space

Surviving in Space is a MMOG designed for 8th and 9th grade students. In this game, students are asked to play the role of researchers set in a survivor story mode where gamers explore an uninhabited, uncharted island to test their skills at finding necessary resources. Through a series of task scenarios, student teams must work together to apply math, bioscience, geography and geology to maneuver through the game. The goal of the game is to successfully complete these series of task scenarios and become the winning team, which would be sent into outer space to explore colonization of other planets. The scenarios constituted complex problem tasks, which were designed to be aligned with Science, Technology, Engineering, and Mathematics (STEM) related process skills as outlined by the State Department of Education. The game was designed in such a way that it complemented State

STEM curriculum and provided teachers with a game-based learning environment to support their classroom instruction so that their students could apply and practice the process skills they learned in the class as part of the game play. Directions and hints for completing the problem solving tasks were embedded in the game.

A longitudinal study (see Eseryel et al., 2009; Miller, Eseryel, & Ge, 2009; Swearingen & Eseryel, 2010) was carried out to investigate the effects of an educational MMOG, called *Surviving in Space* in a rural high school in the Midwest of the United States. 349 ninth-grade students were randomly assigned to one of the nineteen classes. Out of these nineteen classes, ten were randomly assigned to treatment (game group) condition and nine were randomly assigned to control (no game group) condition. The students in the game group played *Surviving in Space* in teams of four for 2 days per week (50 min per day) during class hour for 16 weeks, while the students in the no-game group participated in a class that was specifically developed to facilitate students' interdisciplinary learning and improving their leadership, management, and decision-making skills. The purpose of the study was to examine the impact of Surviving *in Space* on (1) students' complex problem solving skill acquisition; (2) mathematics achievement; and (3) students' motivation. In order to achieve the assessment goals, both external and internal assessment strategies were adopted, which are illustrated in details below.

4.2 External Assessment Strategies

To assess students' learning outcomes in the areas of problem solving, mathematics, and motivation, some typically external assessment strategies were used in this study.

First, a pretest and posttest design were used to track changes over time and comparisons were made between the treatment and the control group. One week before and after the implementation of the game, students in both groups took the mathematics achievement tests and responded to three motivation surveys, which measured intrinsic motivation, competence, choice, pressure, and relatedness. These two kinds of pretest and posttests were conducted in the traditional paper-and-pencil format. The comparison of the pretest and the posttest and between the treatment group and the control group provided us with information about learners' changes in mathematics and motivation over time and allowed us to collect data on the effects of the game.

The students' complex problem-solving skills were also assessed across time by comparing the pretest scores and the posttest scores and by comparing the two conditions. Instead of simply using paper-and-pencil format, the pretest and posttest scores in complex problem solving were obtained through engaging students in a complex problem-solving task through a problem scenario. The data was assessed through two specific assessment methods: annotated causal representation and think-aloud protocols.

4.2.1 Problem Scenario

A problem scenario is an important means for eliciting students' cognitive processes and problem-solving skills for complex problem solving. For the purposes of evaluating problem-solving acquisition skills, the students were presented with the following problem scenario:

> Suppose you are chosen as the lead scientist of a team of experts by Jonathan McLarin of McLarin International. Your team is sent to space to explore Earth-like planets outside of our solar system. Your team has been traveling in space for about 6 months. Your ship's sensors have just identified a planet, which has sufficient oxygen levels in its atmosphere for humans to be able to breath. You have decided to land on this planet and survey the area. Initial explorations show that the planet has similar characteristics to an island on earth. Your team decided to live on this planet and identify resources needed to survive. This will allow you to complete your mission. As the lead scientist, your task is to guide your team. Before you proceed, you must write a report to Jonathan McLarin to inform him of your team's discovery. The guidelines you received from Mr. McLarin suggest that your mission report must have certain information. Your first step is to report your observations of the planet. Further steps and additional information will be required. Use the space provided on the next page to complete your report and submit it to Jonathan McLarin.

Students were asked to respond to this scenario playing the role of a researcher in a scientific team exploring an Earth-like planet outside our solar system. Problem solving was measured through four separate but sequential tasks: (1) writing their initial observations of the planet, (2) creating a causal representation presenting the situational analysis of the factors likely to influence human survival along with a report elaborating each of the factors that had been identified, (3) elaborating on the relationships among the factors, and (4) providing specific recommendations for ensuring survival on the planet.

4.2.2 Think Aloud Protocol

In this study, the think-aloud method was implemented by asking students to write down on the report sheet what came to their minds in Task 1, 3, and 4 by following the outlines of the report. For example, in Task 1 (Step 1), the students were asked to imagine that they are walking around on this new planet to explore its characteristics and asked them to write a report to Mr. McLarin of their initial observations of the planet. This first step was intended to provide us with information regarding students' background and assumptions related to the complex problem-solving task.

In Task 3 (Step 3), the students were asked to write a descriptive paragraph explaining why the factors they listed in Step 2 were important and how they related to each other. The data collected from Step 3 provided us with more information about students' problem space and were also used to check the alignment with the annotated causal representation developed in Step 2.

Finally, in Step 4, the students were asked to provide recommendations for solution by listing the steps to be taken to allow their team to build a settlement area for humans to live on this new planet and ensure their survival. They were also asked to write in this report to Mr. McLarin how confident they felt of their plan including any concerns they had or any possible problems they expected and what they would do if these problems would arise. Data collected from Step 4 not only provided us with the solution strategies of the students for the complex problem task scenario but we were also able to collect data on whether the students were able to justify their solution approach by providing plausible argumentation and whether they were able to assess possible weaknesses and strengths in their solution strategy.

Complex problem-solving tasks in real world contexts typically involve more than one viable solution approaches. Experts in complex knowledge domains are distinguished from the novices by their ability to view all possible solution approaches but settling on the most viable one while provide plausible arguments and a contingency plan (Eseryel, 2006). Therefore, justification and assessment of possible solution approaches are important for successful complex problem solving in real life contexts.

Students' written verbalization, that is, the think-aloud protocols, were later graded with scoring rubrics, which will be discussed specifically in 4.4.1. The purpose of think-aloud method was to elicit students' performance in problem representation, elaboration, justification and argumentation, as well as generating solutions in response to problems that have been identified.

4.2.3 Annotated Causal Representation

Annotated causal representation is the second problem-solving step or task. The students were prompted to think about what humans need to survive and were asked to make a list of each of these factors in paper. When they finished identifying all of the important factors, they were asked to develop an annotated causal representation by, first, arranging each factor so that related factors are close to each other, then by drawing arrows between the factors they thought were related; and annotating their causal representation by writing on each arrow how the two factors were related. At any point, the students were free to add new factors or delete any factor they previously listed. Students' annotated causal representation provided us with information related to their structural knowledge of the complex problem-solving task.

4.3 Internal Assessment Strategies

Since annotated causal representation and think-aloud methods were used as means to gather information about students' structural knowledge and problem-solving performance during the pretest and the posttest outside the MMOG – *Surviving in Space*, the resulting scores in the areas of annotated causal representation and think-aloud can be treated as external assessment. However, we argue that the causal representation could also be implemented as an internal assessment method. In order to provide empirical evidence for our argumentation, we compared the results of the elicited students' structural knowledge with the annotated causal representation of the problem domain with the elicited students' responses to the problem-solving task of the think-aloud method. Our preliminary results suggested that the two assessment methods provided similar results on students' structural knowledge (Eseryel et al., 2009). Accordingly, in a further step of game development we would use the advantage of the annotated causal representation by embedding it in the game-based learning environment. Moreover, HIMATT automated tools can be integrated to measure the progression of students' problem solving over time as they are engaged in the game scenario and provide them instant feedback (Ifenthaler, 2009b; Shute & Spector, 2010).

In addition, the game-environment was able to automatically track students as they were playing the game. Students' log files included details such as the path each student followed during the game-play, which tasks they completed, how much time they spent in each task, which reports they completed and so on. In addition, the game environment also automatically collected students' chat logs, the reports they wrote to McLarin International, and the spreadsheets they completed as part of their field work in the game (such as their measurements of the Ph-levels from different water sources). All of this data was automatically fed into the teacher application so that each teacher could use those to assess student performance, as they deemed necessary.

4.4 Coding and Analysis

4.4.1 Coding and Analysis of Problem-Solving Protocols

Students' protocols were analyzed by the first research team of three using problem-solving rubrics in two categories: (a) *problem representation* and (b) *generating solutions*, which served as the two dependent variables (Chi & Glaser, 1985; Ericsson & Simon, 1980). Scoring rubrics were developed, which focused on these two dependent variables. We went through an iterative process of developing and refining the rubrics. First, we had a meeting with a group of experienced K-12 teachers, who served as subject matter experts for designing *Surviving in Space*. This group of teachers discussed and worked through the same problem scenario to generate solutions. The experts' problem representation, analysis, justification, and solutions served as critical criteria for developing the rubrics for the two dependent variables. Second, based on the experts' responses we discussed and identified a list of key features important for each of the problem solving tasks, developed descriptors and criteria. Then, we tested the scoring rubrics with a small sample of students' responses, which served as important feedback for us to revise and improve the scoring rubrics. It took the research team several rounds of discussions to reach an agreement on the rubrics with 85% interrater reliability.

Regarding the criteria of problem representation, we measured (a) the number of categories of items a student listed that were needed for survival on the planet, which were compared with those categories generated by the experts (e.g., habitability, terrain, vegetation, and animal life), and (b) how well the student describe and elaborate those items in relation to survival. The criteria of generating solutions includes four areas: (a) whether the students had made a recommendation by listing the measures or actions, (b) whether those solutions were aligned with their previous analysis and problem representations, (c) whether they have made a justification of their recommendation, and (d) how confident they felt about their recommendations.

4.4.2 Coding and Analysis of Annotated Causal Representations

The second research team of three analyzed students' annotated causal representations, which served as the dependent variable of *structural knowledge* (see Funke, 1985; Ifenthaler, 2008; Scheele & Groeben, 1984; Seel, 1999). Analysis began with open coding, which is the examination of the written responses of the students' to the given problem scenario. The language of the participants guided the development of category labels, which were identified with short descriptors, known as in vivo codes, of the concepts in the causal representations. These categories were systematically compared and contrasted, yielding increasingly complex and inclusive categories. Categories were sorted, compared, and contrasted until saturated–that is, until analysis produced no new categories. The coding schema for the categories was developed from the causal representations of the group of K-12 teachers who served as subject matter experts for designing *Surviving in Space*. Experts also reviewed and participated in developing the coding schema. Thirty percent of students' causal representations were coded by three researchers with an interrater reliability (kappa) of 0.96. Then, two of the principle investigators completed the rest of the coding according to the coding schema.

Each students' coded causal representations were compared with expert causal representation on the six dimensions as suggested by the HIMATT method (Pirnay-Dummer et al., 2010) for measuring structural and semantic levels of graphical representations: (1) *surface structure*, which compares the number of propositions (concept – relation – concept) within two representation; (2) *graphical matching*, which compares the diameters of the spanning trees of the representation, which is an indicator for the range or complexity of conceptual knowledge; (3) *density of concepts*, or *gamma*, describes the quotient of terms per concept within a representation; (4) *structural matching*, which compares the complete structures of two representations (expert and subject) without regard to their content; (5) *concept matching*, which compares the sets of concepts within a representation to determine the use of terms (semantic correctness); and (6) *propositional matching*, which compares only fully semantically identical propositions between the two representation. Surface, graphical matching, gamma, and structural matching refer to organizational structure of a representation while concept, and propositional matching measures indicate how semantically similar a student's causal representation is to that of the experts' in the respective category.

5 Discussion and Future Directions

Significant developments in the field of game-based learning have been made. However, the implementation of assessment features into game-based learning environments is only in its early stages because it adds a very time-consuming step to the design process. Also, the impact on learning and quality criteria (e.g. reliability and validity) of technology-based assessment systems are still being questioned. We identified two possibilities of educational assessment within game-based learning environments: Assessment after the game has been completed (outcome) and assessment while playing the game (embedded or stealth). Additionally, we distinguish between two assessment strategies in digital game-based learning: (1) external (assessment that is not part of game-play) and (2) internal (assessment part of the game-play).

The think-aloud method is a prominent assessment approach that could be implemented to assess the outcome of a game. Additionally, the think-aloud method could also be used while playing the game. However, the data collected when playing the game represents only a small amount of the cognitive processes that occur when one solves a complex problem. Another problem of think-aloud protocols for game-based assessment is that this method cannot be embedded in the game as an internal assessment. Hence, the learner will always be interrupted for assessment when playing the game. In addition, the quantification of the collected data and the explicit relation of verbal data to cognitive processes call the validity and reliability of this method into question.

Domain-based knowledge tests are primarily used to assess the outcome of a game. Surely, embedded domain-based knowledge test exist. However, they should be designed in a way that the flow of the game is not interrupted. Accordingly, internal assessment using domain-based knowledge tests is principally possible if the system allows instant feedback on the results of the test. If this is not the case, domain-based knowledge tests are classified as an external assessment method.

Concept maps, knowledge maps, or causal representations realized as web-based knowledge mapping methods open up unique possibilities for assessment and analysis in game-based learning. They are accepted methods to illustrate the meaning of locally discussed information (Eliaa, Gagatsisa, & Demetriou, 2007; Hardy & Stadelhofer, 2006; Ruiz-Primo et al., 2001). Additionally, they can be easily embedded into a game scenario and therefore do not interrupt the game play. Of course, knowledge mapping methods can also be applied as external assessment while playing the game (e.g. for representing the understanding of the problem to be solved) or after playing the game (e.g. for representing the learning outcome). Using HIMATT, which is a newly developed analysis technology (Ifenthaler, 2010c; Pirnay-Dummer et al., 2010), provides a powerful automated and on-the-fly technique which produces results and feedback with regard to expert solutions or other game players. Embedding HIMATT into a game-based learning environment could have many benefits for learners, educators and researchers.

Click-streams or log-files assess the behavior of learners while playing the game. The extensive data has to be analyzed and reported back to the player, which makes this method impossible in most cases. Accordingly, internal assessment can be easily realized with logging all user data. However, a meaningful analysis of the collected data is often not possible. Nevertheless, this data could be a good basis for researchers to learn more about effective design of educational games.

Other promising assessment methods are chat- or forum-logs. This method tracks all communication during game-play. Accordingly, this internal assessment method provides in-depth views of the learner's thinking and learning processes. However, analysis of these logs, when done with classical qualitative approaches, are very time consuming. However, we implemented an automated text-based analysis function into HIMATT which enables us to track the association of concepts from text which contain 350 or more words directly (see Pirnay-Dummer & Ifenthaler, 2010). The algorithms produce quantitative measures and graphical representations which could be used for instant feedback within the game or for further analysis (see Pirnay-Dummer & Ifenthaler, 2010).

Accordingly, many approaches require extensive resources in time and people; therefore, scalability to large number of students within the limited resources of a single teacher is problematic. Especially in school settings, approaches to assessment of learning in complex, ill-structured domains mainly concentrate on assessing domain knowledge, largely through standardized tests. However, previous research in complex knowledge domains such as medicine show that possessing required domain-based knowledge is a necessary but not a sufficient condition for successful complex problem solving performance. Hence, our research study focused on the adaptation and verification of a method for assessing and analyzing progress of learning in complex problem solving that can be ubiquitously embedded in game-based learning environments.

We used two different methods to assess student's progress of learning in complex problem solving. The first method *adapted protocol analysis* (Ericsson & Simon, 1980) to analyze students' responses to the given problem scenario within the framework of the think-aloud method. As discussed above, this method was not embedded into the game. However, the findings will be used to validate and support the results of the second assessment method. The second method utilized *HIMATT method* (Pirnay-Dummer et al., 2010) to analyze students' causal representations. The fully automated assessment and analysis tool could be easily implemented into web-based games. External and internal assessments are both possible.

Future technological developments will enable us to easily embed assessment and analysis methods into game-based learning environment. Internal assessment and instant analysis including personalized feedback will be implemented in a new generation of educational games. However, it is up to educational research to provide theoretical foundations and empirical evidence on how these methodologies should be designed and implemented. We have just arrived in the digital age. It is up to researchers, technologists, educators, and philosophers to make sense of these powerful technologies.

References

Almond, R. G., Steinberg, L. S., & Mislevy, R. J. (2002). Enhancing the design and delivery of assessment systems: A four process architecture. *Journal of Technology, Learning, and Assessment, 1*(5), 3–63.

Baker, E. L., Chung, G. K. W. K., & Delacruz, G. C. (2008). Design and validation of technology-based performance assessments. In J. M. Spector, M. D. Merrill, J. van Merrienboer, & M. P. Driscoll (Eds.), *Handbook of research on educational communications and technology* (pp. 595–604). New York: Taylor & Francis Group.

Barab, S. A., & Duffy, T. (2000). From practice fields to communities of practice. In D. H. Jonassen & S. M. Land (Eds.), *Theoretical foundations of learning environments* (pp. 25–56). Mahwah, NJ: Lawrence Erlbaum Associates.

Barab, S. A., Tomas, M., Dodge, T., Carteaux, R., & Tuzun, H. (2005). Making learning fun: Quest Atlantis, a game without guns. *Educational Technology Research and Development, 53*(1), 86–107.

Brown, J. S., Collins, A., & Duguid, P. (1989). Situated cognition and the culture of learning. *Educational Researcher, 18*(1), 32–42.

Chi, M. T. H. (1997). Quantifying qualitative analyses of verbal data: A practical guide. *The Journal of the Learning Sciences, 6*(3), 271–315.

Chi, M. T. H., & Glaser, R. (1985). Problem solving ability. In R. J. Sternberg (Ed.), *Human abilities: An information processing approach* (pp. 227–257). San Francisco: W. H. Freeman & Co.

Chin, J., Dukes, R., & Gamson, W. (2009). Assessment in simulation and gaming: A review of the last 40 years. *Simulation & Gaming, 40*, 553–568.

Chung, G. K. W. K., & Baker, E. L. (2003). An exploratory study to examine the feasibility of measuring problem-solving processes using a click-through interface. *Journal of Technology, Learning and Assessment, 2*(2). Retrieved April 22, 2010, from http://www.jtla.org.

Dickey, M. D. (2005). Engaging by design: How engagement strategies in popular computer and video games can inform instructional design. *Educational Technology Research and Development, 53*(2), 67–83.

Dummer, P., & Ifenthaler, D. (2005). Planning and assessing navigation in model-centered learning environments. Why learners often do not follow the path laid out for them. In G. Chiazzese, M. Allegra, A. Chifari, & S. Ottaviano (Eds.), *Methods and technologies for learning* (pp. 327–334). Sothhampton: WIT Press.

Dunkle, M. E., Schraw, G., & Bendixen, L. D. (1995). *Cognitive processes in well-structured and ill-defined problem solving*. Paper presented at the Annual Meeting of the American Educational Research Association, San Francisco, CA.

Eigler, G. (2005). Textproduzieren als Wissensnutzungs- und Wissenserwerbsstrategie. In H. Mandl & H. F. Friedrich (Eds.), *Handbuch Lernstrategien* (pp. 187–205). Göttingen: Hogrefe.

Eliaa, I., Gagatsisa, A., & Demetriou, A. (2007). The effects of different modes of representation on the solution of one-step additive problems. *Learning and Instruction, 17*(6), 658–672.

Ericsson, K. A., & Simon, H. A. (1980). Verbal reports as data. *Psychological Review, 87*, 215–251.

Ericsson, K. A., & Simon, H. A. (1993). *Protocol analysis: Verbal reports as data*. Cambridge, MA: MIT Press.

Eseryel, D. (2006). *Expert conceptualizations of the domain of instructional design: An investigative study on the DEEP assessment methodology for complex problem-solving outcomes*. Unpublished doctoral dissertation, Syracuse University.

Eseryel, D., Ge, X., Law, V., Hayes, T., Guo, Y., & Ifenthaler, D. (2009). *The effects of an educational massively multiplayer online game on students' complex problem solving skill acquisition*. Paper presented at the Annual Convention of Association for Educational Communications and Technology, Louisville, KY.

Funke, J. (1985). Steuerung dynamischer Prozesse durch Aufbau und Anwendung subjektiver Kausalmodelle. *Zeitschrift für Psychologie, 193*(4), 443–465.

Galarneau, L., & Zibit, M. (2007). Online games for 21st century skills. In D. Gibson, C. Aldrich, & M. Prensky (Eds.), *Games and simulations in online learning: Research and development frameworks* (pp. 59–88). Hershey, PA: Information Science Publishing.

Gee, J. P. (2003). *What video games have to teach us about learning and literacy*. New York: Palgrave-Macmillan.

Gick, M. L. (1986). Problem-solving strategies. *Educational Psychologist, 21*(1&2), 99–120.

Hardy, I., & Stadelhofer, B. (2006). Concept Maps wirkungsvoll als Strukturierungshilfen einsetzen. Welche Rolle spielt die Selbstkonstruktion? *Zeitschrift für Pädagogische Psychologie, 20*(3), 175–187.

Herl, H. E., Baker, E. L., & Niemi, D. (1996). Construct validation of an approach to modeling cognitive structure of U.S. history knowledge. *Journal of Educational Research, 89*(4), 206–218.

Hong, N. S., Jonassen, D. H., & McGee, S. (2003). Predictors of well-structured and ill-structured problem solving in an astronomy simulation. *Journal of Research in Science Teaching, 40*(1), 6–33.

Ifenthaler, D. (2008). Practical solutions for the diagnosis of progressing mental models. In D. Ifenthaler, P. Pirnay-Dummer, & J. M. Spector (Eds.), *Understanding models for learning and instruction. Essays in honor of Norbert M. Seel* (pp. 43–61). New York: Springer.

Ifenthaler, D. (2009a). Bridging the gap between expert-novice differences: The model-based feedback approach. In Kinshuk, D. G. Sampson, J. M. Spector, P. Isaias, & D. Ifenthaler (Eds.), *Proceedings of the IADIS international conference on cognition and exploratory learning in the digital age* (pp. 49–60), Rome: IADIS Press.

Ifenthaler, D. (2009b). Model-based feedback for improving expertise and expert performance. *Technology, Instruction, Cognition and Learning, 7*(2), 83–101.

Ifenthaler, D. (2009c). Using a causal model for the design and development of a simulation game for teacher education. *Technology, Instruction, Cognition and Learning, 6*(3), 193–212.

Ifenthaler, D. (2010a). Learning and instruction in the digital age. In J. M. Spector, D. Ifenthaler, P. Isaías, Kinshuk, & D. G. Sampson (Eds.), *Learning and instruction in the digital age: Making a difference through cognitive approaches, technology-facilitated collaboration and assessment, and personalized communications* (pp. 3–10). New York: Springer.

Ifenthaler, D. (2010b). Relational, structural, and semantic analysis of graphical representations and concept maps. *Educational Technology Research and Development, 58*(1), 81–97.

Ifenthaler, D. (2010c). Scope of graphical indices in educational diagnostics. In D. Ifenthaler, P. Pirnay-Dummer, & N. M. Seel (Eds.), *Computer-based diagnostics and systematic analysis of knowledge* (pp. 213–234). New York: Springer.

Ifenthaler, D., Masduki, I., & Seel, N. M. (2009). The mystery of cognitive structure and how we can detect it. Tracking the development of cognitive structures over time. *Instructional Science*. Retrieved October 18, 2010, from http://www.springerlink.com/content/y62024472v394468/

Ifenthaler, D., & Pirnay-Dummer, P. (2009). Assessment of knowledge: Do graphical notes and texts represent different things? In M. R. Simonson (Ed.), *Annual proceedings of selected research and development papers presented at the national convention of the Association for Educational Communications and Technology (32nd, Louisville, KY, 2009)*, (Vol. 2, pp. 86–93). Bloomington, IN: AECT.

Ifenthaler, D., Pirnay-Dummer, P., & Seel, N. M. (Eds.). (2010). *Computer-based diagnostics and systematic analysis of knowledge*. New York: Springer.

Ifenthaler, D., & Seel, N. M. (2005). The measurement of change: Learning-dependent progression of mental models. *Technology, Instruction, Cognition and Learning, 2*(4), 317–336.

Johnson-Laird, P. N. (1989). Mental models. In M. I. Posner (Ed.), *Foundations of cognitive science* (pp. 469–499). Cambridge, MA: MIT Press.

Johnson, T. E., Ifenthaler, D., Pirnay-Dummer, P., & Spector, J. M. (2009). Using concept maps to assess individuals and team in collaborative learning environments. In P. L. Torres & R. C. V. Marriott (Eds.), *Handbook of research on collaborative learning using concept mapping* (pp. 358–381). Hershey, PA: Information Science Publishing.

Jonassen, D. H. (1997). Instructional design models for well-structured and ill-structured problem-solving learning outcomes. *Educational Technology Research and Development, 45*(1), 65–94.

Klabbers, J. H. (Ed.). (2008). *The magic circle: Principles of gaming & simulation*. Rotterdam: Sense.

Koschmann, T. (Ed.). (1996). *CSCL, theory and practice of an emerging paradigm*. Mahwah, NJ: Lawrence Erlbaum Associates.

Macy, M., Squires, J. K., & Barton, E. E. (2009). Providing optimal opportunities: Structuring practicum experiences in early intervention and early childhood special education preservice programs. *Topics in Early Childhoos Special Education, 28*(4), 209–218.

Mandl, H., & Fischer, F. (2000). Mapping-Techniken und Begriffsnetze in Lern- und Kooperationsprozessen. In H. Mandl & F. Fischer (Eds.), *Wissen sichtbar machen – Wissensmanagement mit Mapping-Techniken* (pp. 3–12). Göttingen: Hogrefe.

McFarlane, A. (2003). Editorial. assessment for the digital age, *Assessment in Education: Principles, Policy & Practice, 10*, 261–266.

Michael, D., & Chen, S. (2006). *Serious games: Games that educate, train, and inform*. Boston: Thomson Course Technology PTR.

Miller, R. B., Eseryel, D., & Ge, X. (2009). *Surviving in space: The effects of a massively multiplayer online game (MMOG) on students' motivation*. Paper presented at the Annual Meeting of the American Educational Research Association, San Diego, CA, USA.

Newell, A., & Simon, H. A. (1972). *Human problem solving*. Englewood Cliffs, NJ: Prentice-Hall.

Nisbett, R. E., & Wilson, T. D. (1977). Telling more than we can know: Verbal reports on mental processes. *Psychological Review, 84*, 231–259.

Papert, S., & Caperton, G. (1999). *Vision for education: The Caperton-Papert platform*. Paper presented at the 91st Annual National Governor' Association Meeting. Retrieved April 22, 2010, from http://www.papert.org/articles/Vision_for_education.html

Pellegrino, J. W., Chudowsky, N., & Glaser, R. (Eds.). (2003). *Knowing what students know. The secience and design of educational assessment*. Washington, DC: National Academy Press.

Pirnay-Dummer, P., & Ifenthaler, D. (2010). Automated knowledge visualization and assessment. In D. Ifenthaler, P. Pirnay-Dummer, & N. M. Seel (Eds.), *Computer-based diagnostics and systematic analysis of knowledge* (pp. 77–115). New York: Springer.

Pirnay-Dummer, P., Ifenthaler, D., & Rohde, J. (2009). Text-guided automated self-assessment. In Kinshuk, D. G. Sampson, J. M. Spector, P. Isaias, & D. Ifenthaler (Eds.), *Proceedings of the IADIS international conference on cognition and exploratory learning in the digital age* (pp. 311–316). Rome: IADIS Press.

Pirnay-Dummer, P., Ifenthaler, D., & Spector, J. M. (2010). Highly integrated model assessment technology and tools. *Educational Technology Research and Development, 58*(1), 3–18.

Prensky, M. (2001). *Digital game-based learning*. New York: McGraw-Hill.

Prensky, M. (2006). *Don't bother me mom–I'm learning*. St. Paul, MN: Paragon House.

Ruiz-Primo, M. A., Schultz, S. E., Li, M., & Shavelson, R. J. (2001). Comparison of the reliability and validity of scores from two concept-mapping techniques. *Journal of Research in Science Teaching, 38*(2), 260–278.

Scandura, J. M. (1988). Role of relativistic knowledge in intelligent tutoring. *Computers in Human Behavior, 4*(1), 53–64.

Scheele, B., & Groeben, N. (1984). *Die Heidelberger Struktur-Lege-Technik (SLT). Eine Dialog-Konsens-Methode zur Erhebung subjektiver Theorien mittlerer Reichweite*. Weinheim: Beltz.

Schön, D. A. (1987). *Educating the reflective practitioner: Toward a new design for teaching and learning in the professions*. San Francisco: Jossey-Bass.

Seel, N. M. (1999). Educational diagnosis of mental models: Assessment problems and technology-based solutions. *Journal of Structural Learning and Intelligent Systems, 14*(2), 153–185.

Seel, N. M., Ifenthaler, D., & Pirnay-Dummer, P. (2009). Mental models and problem solving: Technological solutions for measurement and assessment of the development of expertise. In P. Blumschein, W. Hung, D. H. Jonassen, & J. Strobel (Eds.), *Model-based approaches to learning: Using systems models and simulations to improve understanding and problem solving in complex domains* (pp. 17–40). Rotterdam: Sense.

Shaffer, D. W. (2006). *How computer games help children learn?* New York: Palgrave Macmillan.

Shute, V. J., & Spector, J. M. (2010). *Stealth assessment in virtual worlds*. Retrieved April 22, 2010, from http://www.adlnet.gov/Technologies/Evaluation/Library/Additional%20Resources/LETSI%20White%20Papers/Shute%20-%20Stealth%20Assessment%20in%20Virtual%20Worlds.pdf

Spector, J. M., Dennen, V. P., & Koszalka, T. A. (2005). Individual and collaborative construction of causal concept maps: an online technique for learning and assessment. In G. Chiazzese, M. Allegra, A. Chifari, & S. Ottaviano (Eds.), *Methods and technologies for learning* (pp. 223–227). Southampton: WIT Press.

Spector, J. M., & Koszalka, T. A. (2004). *The DEEP methodology for assessing learning in complex domains (Final report to the National Science Foundation Evaluative Research and Evaluation Capacity Building)*. Syracuse, NY: Syracuse University.

Squire, K. (2004). *Replaying history*. Unpublished doctoral dissertation, Indiana University, Bloomington, IN.

Sterman, J. D. (1994). Learning in and about complex systems. *System Dynamics Review, 10*(2–3), 291–330.

Swearingen, D., & Eseryel, D. (2010). *The effects of massively multiplayer online games on high school students' mathematics achievement*. Paper presented at the Annual Meeting of the American Educational Research Association, Denver, CO, USA.

Tarciani, E. M., & Clariana, R. B. (2006). A technique for automatically scoring open-ended concept maps. *Educational Technology, Research, & Development, 54*(1), 65–82.

Thomas, D., & Brown, J. S. (2007). The play of imagination: Extending the literary mind. *Games & Culture, 2*(2), 149–172.

Tuzun, H. (2004). *Motivating learners in educational computer games*. Unpublished doctoral dissertation. Indiana University, Bloomington, IN.

Wagner, W., & Wagner, S. U. (1985). Presenting questions, processing responses, and providing feedback in CAI. *Journal of Instructional Development, 8*(4), 2–8.

Warren, S. J., & Dondlinger, M. J. (2009). Designing games for learning. In R. E. Ferdig (Ed.), *Handbook of research on effective electronic gaming in education* (pp. 1183–1203). Hershey, PA: IGI Global.

Willett, J. B. (1988). Questions and answers in the measurement of change. *Review of Research in Education, 15*, 345–422.

Chapter 12
Concept Map Based Intelligent Knowledge Assessment System: Experience of Development and Practical Use

Janis Grundspenkis

Abstract Concept maps (CMs), as pedagogical tools, have well established uses to support teaching, learning, and knowledge assessment. This chapter focuses on the use of CMs as knowledge assessment tools. The CM-based adaptive intelligent knowledge assessment system (IKAS) is described. The kernel of the IKAS is the intelligent knowledge assessment agent which is implemented as a multi-agent system consisting of the agent-expert, the communication agent, the knowledge evaluation agent, and the interaction registering agent. The knowledge evaluation agent compares the teacher's and the learner's CMs on the basis of graph patterns and assigns score for a submitted solution. Five-year long experience of developing and using IKAS has resulted in improvements and extensions of the system's functionality and adaptivity. Evolution of IKAS and its characteristics are summarized. This chapter presents student opinions elicited from questionnaires about CMs as knowledge assessment tools. The results of the practical use of four versions of IKAS in different study courses are described.

Keywords Concept map · Knowledge assessment · Adaptive intelligent knowledge assessment system · Multi-agent system

1 Introduction

The purpose of this paper is to represent a 5-year experience and lessons learnt from the development and practical use of the adaptive intelligent knowledge assessment system (IKAS, in brief) created at the Department of Systems Theory and Design of Riga Technical University (Grundspenkis & Anohina, 2009; Grundspenkis, 2008a,

---

J. Grundspenkis (✉)
Department of Systems Theory and Design, Faculty of Computer Science and Information Technology, Riga Technical University, 1 Kalku Street, Riga LV-1658, Latvia
e-mail: janis.grundspenkis@cs.rtu.lv

2008b). The system has been improved using student feedback about its functionality and operation. This chapter is organized as follows. Section 2 is devoted to CMs as knowledge assessment tools. Underlying principles of the IKAS development, its operation scenario and evolution are described in Section 3. Section 4 presents results of the practical use of IKAS and student opinions collected from questionnaires. The paper ends with conclusions and an outline of future work.

A generally accepted view is that modern information and communication technologies (ICTs) substantially influence and change the educational process because ICTs enable student-centered, one-to-one and group learning in traditional as well as in computational environments (Waterhouse, 2004). A plethora of technology-enhanced educational systems, including intelligent tutoring systems (ITSs) with unarguable advantages (Grundspenkis & Anohina, 2005), have been developed and many others are under development. Research in the area of ITSs has been in progress for about 40 years since SCHOLAR for teaching South America's geography appeared. Intelligent tutoring systems like WHY for teaching causal knowledge and reasoning (Stevens & Collins, 1977), SOPHIE for physics (Brown, Burton, & de Kleer, 1982), BUGGY (Brown & Burton, 1978) and WEST (Burton & Brown, 1982) both for mathematics, LISP Tutor for programming language LISP (Anderson & Reiser, 1985) and GUIDON for infectious disease diagnosis and therapy selection (Clancey, 1982) have established a common viewpoint that modern ITSs must include knowledge on what and how to teach, and knowledge on qualities of learners. The above-mentioned examples share a common functional architecture which nowadays has become the core of every ITS: the domain knowledge module, the tutoring module, and the student diagnosis module. The domain knowledge module represents an expert model with objects and relationships to be learned using the ITS. The tutoring module holds teaching strategies and instructions needed to implement learning activities. The tutoring module is able to present and solve problems in a particular domain. The student diagnosis module is able to infer what the student knows and does not know within a particular domain. The student model makes it possible to tailor learning activities to meet the needs of each individual learner. In addition, an ITS will typically have a communication module (an interface) to support interactions between the system and various learners.

The functional architecture of ITSs supports the following tasks: monitoring of learner's actions and appropriately responding to them, selection and presentation of learning material, ensuring feedback and help, adaptation of teaching strategy, and assessment of learner's knowledge level (Grundspenkis & Anohina, 2005). Regardless of some 40 years of development and use, the intelligent support in an ITS still lags far behind that provided by a capable human tutor, in particular concerning knowledge assessment. Analysis of available publications reveals that developers have paid too little attention to regular assessment of learner's knowledge and adaptation to each learner's knowledge level (Grundspenkis & Anohina, 2009). Moreover, a general conclusion has been drawn that with the dissemination of technology-enhanced learning, assessment has become a constant concern (da Rocha et al., 2008).

In computer-assisted assessment systems including ITSs, knowledge assessment, as a rule, is based on objective tests ("Computer-assisted assessment", 2004), adaptive tests (Papanastasiou, 2003) or subjective tests in the form of essays and free text responses. Analysis of test based computer-assisted assessment systems (Lukashenko & Anohina, 2009) shows that objective and adaptive tests allow assessing learner's knowledge only at the first four levels of Bloom's taxonomy (Bloom, 1956), and don't allow assessing student's knowledge structure (Grundspenkis, 2008a, 2008b). The latter shortcoming may be eliminated using concept maps (CMs) (Novak & Gowin, 1984; Novak, 1998).

The theoretical basis of CMs is cognitivism which in recent years has served as the foundation of preferred learning theories. Most cognitive theories share the assumption that concept interrelatedness is an essential property of knowledge (Ruiz-Primo & Shavelson, 1996). As students acquire expertise through learning, training and/or experience, their knowledge becomes increasingly interconnected.

CMs as pedagogical tools represent a person's cognitive structure, revealing his/her particular understanding of a specific knowledge area or problem situation (Novak & Gowin, 1984; Novak, 1998). The representation of a knowledge structure is a quality of a CM that provides significant potential for assessment, including intelligent and automated assessment within the context of an ITS.

CMs have been more frequently used as instructional tools than as assessment tools, though this situation is beginning to change. The research review reveals that several systems have made use of CMs for assessment since 2000. Systems like RFA (Conlon, 2006), Java Mapper (Hsieh & O'Neil, 2002), Verified Concept Mapper (Cimolino et al., 2003), COMPASS (Gouli, 2004), IKAS (Grundspenkis & Anohina, 2009; Grundspenkis, 2008a, 2008b), HIMATT (Pirnay-Dummer et al., 2008), and an approach based on domain ontologies and genetic algorithms (da Rocha et al., 2008) are a few examples of CMs being used as assessment tools.

2 Concept Maps as Knowledge Assessment Tools

The cognitive theory underlying concept mapping grew out of Ausubel's Assimilation Theory (Ausubel, 1968, 2000) and Deese's Associationist Memory Theory (Deese, 1965). The former postulated a hierarchical memory structure, whereas the latter postulated a network of concepts which may also include a hierarchy. In educational settings, CMs have become valuable tools for teaching, assessment and learning, as they enhance learning, promote reflection and creativity, and enable students to externalise their knowledge structure (Novak & Gowin, 1984). CMs are a viable and theoretically sound solution of the problem of expressing and assessing students' learning results (da Rocha et al., 2008).

CM-based knowledge assessment systems offer a reasonable balance between objective and subjective tests because CMs are computable. That is, the assessment of students' answers given in the form of CMs is based on some scoring system (Ruiz-Primo & Shavelson, 1996). Like in case of objective tests, educational environments based on CMs use automated parts of this process and decrease the amount of work required of the teacher. Whereas, answers in subjective tests, such as essays or free text responses, require natural language processing and, as a rule, in practice are evaluated only by humans.

2.1 Representation of Concept Maps

CMs are semi-formal knowledge representation tools visualized as graphs. Natural language is used to define concepts or relationships between concept pairs. In general terms, CMs represent semantic knowledge and its conceptual organization (structure). Mathematically, a CM is either an undirected or a directed graph (Figs. 12.1 and 12.2, respectively) consisting of a finite, non-empty set of nodes representing concepts and a finite, non-empty set of arcs (undirected or directed) representing relationships among concepts.

Graphs representing CMs may be homogeneous if the arcs have the same weights (Figs. 12.1, 12.2 and 12.3), or heterogeneous if the weights are different (Fig. 12.4).

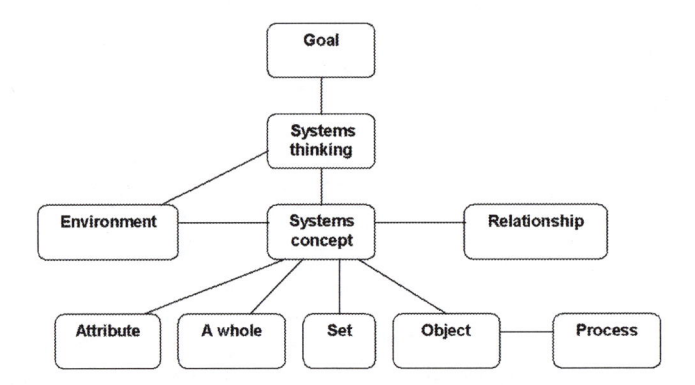

Fig. 12.1 Concept map represented as an undirected graph

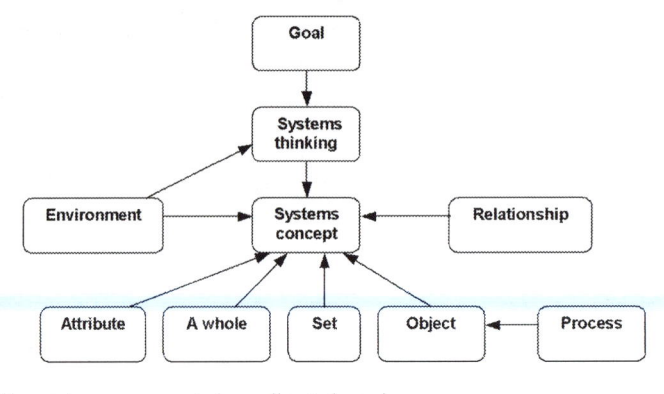

Fig. 12.2 Concept map represented as a directed graph

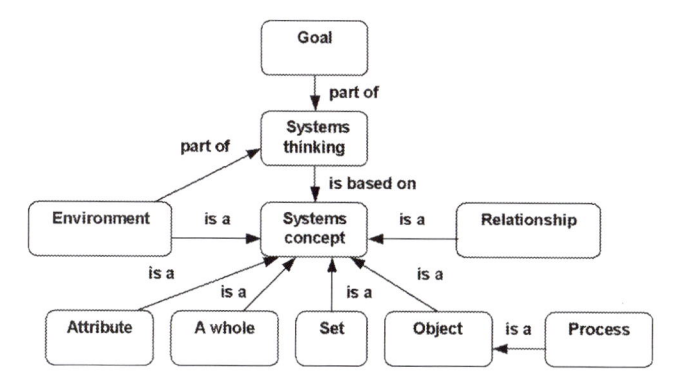

Fig. 12.3 Concept map represented as a homogeneous attribute graph

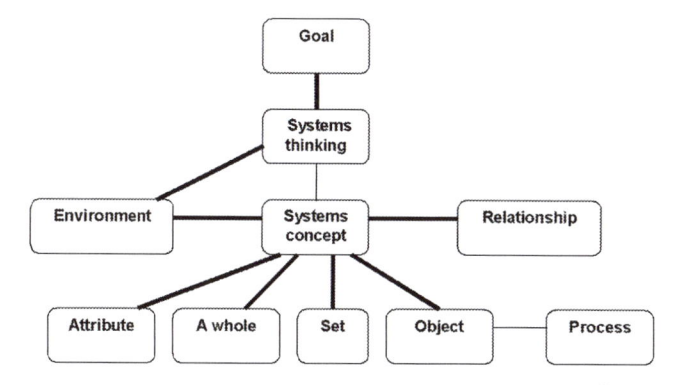

Fig. 12.4 Concept map represented as a heterogeneous graph

The latter (unevenly weighted arcs) reflects the notion that some relationships may be viewed as having more influence or significance than others (Ahlberg, 2004). Moreover, a CM may be represented as an attribute graph. In this case arcs have labels or the so called linking phrases specifying the kind of relationship between a concept pair (de Souza et al., 2008). A homogeneous attribute graph is shown in Fig. 12.3. The semantic unit of CM is a proposition, that is, a concept-attribute-concept triple which is a meaningful statement about objects or events in a problem domain (Cañas, 2003). Examples of propositions represented in Fig. 12.3 are the following: "systems thinking is based on systems concepts", "attribute is a systems concept", and "goal is a part of systems thinking".

2.2 Concept Map Tasks

In accordance with a framework for conceptualisation of CMs as potential assessment tools, CM tasks vary with regard to task demands, task constraints and the content structure of tasks (Ruiz-Primo & Shavelson, 1996). Task demands are related to demands made on students in generating their CMs and determine two commonly used classes of tasks: fill-in-the-map tasks and construct-the-map tasks. For the first class of tasks students, as a rule, receive correct structure of CM with blank nodes where concept names must be inserted. Tasks where students must define linking phrases or both, concepts and linking phrases, also belong to this class. For the second class of tasks students themselves must draw CMs.

Other task demands refer to such tasks as "rate relatedness of concept pairs", "organize cards", "write an essay", "respond to an interview" (Ruiz-Primo & Shavelson, 1996, p. 578).

Task constraints refer to the restrictiveness of the task. The latter, in turn, depends on constraints that are defined for the concept set C_S and for the linking phrase set LP_S. For both sets constraints determine four categories – C – "complete", P – "partial", F – "full up", and E – "empty". If constraints determine the complete set C_S (category C) then students receive a list of all needed concepts which they must put into a given CM's structure (fill-in-the-map task) or use during CM production (construct-the-map task). If the set C_S corresponds to category F ("full up"), students receive a list of concepts which includes also unnecessary (misleading) ones. In fact, there are two subsets – a subset of correct concepts, and a subset of incorrect concepts. If constraints determine a partial set C_S (category P) then only a definite part of concepts is given (these concepts may have already been inserted into correct places in a CM or given as a list) while remaining concepts must be defined by students themselves. Finally, if the set C_S corresponds to category E then students must define all necessary concepts. Besides, in this case students may be allowed to use synonyms of the concepts. All four cases for categories of LP_S are the same as described above for the set C_S. For example, if both sets C_S and LP_S correspond to category C, students receive lists of correct concepts and linking phrases. If it is fill-in-the-map task then there may be at least three different tasks: (1) all concepts have already been inserted into correct nodes and students need only to put all linking phrases; (2) all linking phrases have already been inserted and students must insert correct concepts into blank nodes; (3) part of the concepts and linking phrases is included in the CM, but the remaining part must be filled in by students. If the set C_S corresponds to category F and the set of linking phrases LP_S corresponds to category P then one of the tasks is as follows: students must choose correct concepts from a redundant list of given concepts and define the full list of linking phrases (only standard categories of linking phrases such as "is a", "part of", "instance of", "has value", "has attribute" may be used, too).

The content structure of tasks refers to the intersection of the task demands and task constraints with the structure of the subject domain to be mapped (Ruiz-Primo & Shavelson, 1996).

2.3 Response Format and Scoring System

Response format refers to the response that student makes solving a given CM task (Ruiz-Primo & Shavelson, 1996). For example, students may solve fill-in-the-map tasks, draw CMs, or participate in an oral examination explaining items of a CM. Characteristics of the response format are related to characteristics of the task. For example, if it is a fill-in-the-map task, students receive a correct structure (graph) of a CM. If a construct-the-map task is offered, the format includes only a blank where a CM must be drawn. For both classes of tasks the given elements of concept sets C_S and linking phrase sets LP_S correspond to predefined constraints. There are the following response modes: paper and pencil, oral and computer-based. It is easy to see that all possible combinations of the response mode and characteristics correspond to a wide variety of response formats that can be generated. However, it is still an open question how to determine which format and for which task is the most preferable.

The scoring system is a systematic method used for the evaluation of students' CMs. Existing alternative scoring systems can be classified into three general scoring strategies: (a) score the components of student's CM (for instance, propositions, hierarchy, crosslinks, and examples as proposed in (Novak & Gowin, 1984)), (b) compare student and expert CMs (different methods have been developed, their overview is out of the scope of this paper), (c) use of combination of both strategies. More details about a number of developed scoring systems are given in (Ruiz-Primo & Shavelson, 1996), but novel scoring systems can be found in numerous publications.

3 Overview of the IKAS

3.1 Basic Principles of the IKAS

The design of the IKAS started in 2005 with the goal of supporting student-centered systematic knowledge assessment. Under IKAS framework the teacher divides the course into several stages. Learners have to acquire certain concepts at each stage. The teacher must include concepts and relationships learned during the first stage in the first CM and then use that CM as a basis for knowledge assessment. At the second stage, new concepts and relationships are introduced, and the teacher must add them to the first CM. So each new CM, which can be used as a basis for knowledge assessment, is an extension of the CM of the previous stage. At the last stage, the final CM includes all concepts and relationships introduced during the course (Anohina & Grundspenkis, 2006). So IKAS framework differs from the approach where the teacher may create an entirely new CM at each stage. Ideally, various CMs are extensions of the first one or linked to previous CMs in some way. Again, each new CM can be used as a basis for knowledge assessment.

The IKAS employs five computer generated response formats (three for fill-in-the-map tasks and two for construct-the-map-tasks). In fill-in-the-map tasks a CM's structure with blank nodes is handed out. A given concept set C_S corresponds to category C, i.e., students must fill in blanks with appropriate concepts. Tasks differ according to task constraints. For the first task a heterogeneous attribute graph is given, i.e., a linking phrase set LP_S corresponds to the category C and all linking phrases are already inserted in relationships. For the second task an undirected heterogeneous attribute graph is given. A linking phrase set LP_S corresponds to the category E, i.e. linking phrases are not used at all. For the third task a directed heterogeneous graph is given and a linking phrase set corresponds to the category C. Thus, in this fill-in-the-map task students must place concepts and linking phrases from the given lists. In both construct-the-map tasks students must relate concepts from a given list, i.e., the concept set C_S corresponds to category C. Concerning a linking phrase set LP_S both construct-the-map tasks are similar to the second and the third fill-in-the-map tasks described above.

From a systems viewpoint, the IKAS is embedded in the environment that consists of two types of human agents – teachers (experts) and learners (students) who use corresponding modules. The teacher's module supports the construction of CMs. Its main functions are editing and deleting of CMs. The learner's module includes tools supporting all five response formats needed for the solution of CM tasks given by the teacher and for viewing feedback after a solution is submitted. The system also includes the administrator's module that allows to manage data about the users (learners and teachers) and study courses providing functions of data input, editing and deleting. The kernel of the IKAS is the intelligent knowledge assessment agent which is implemented as a multi-agent system that consists of four software agents, namely, the communication agent, the interaction registering agent, the agent-expert and the knowledge evaluation agent. The IKAS and its environment (learners and teachers) are shown in Fig. 12.5.

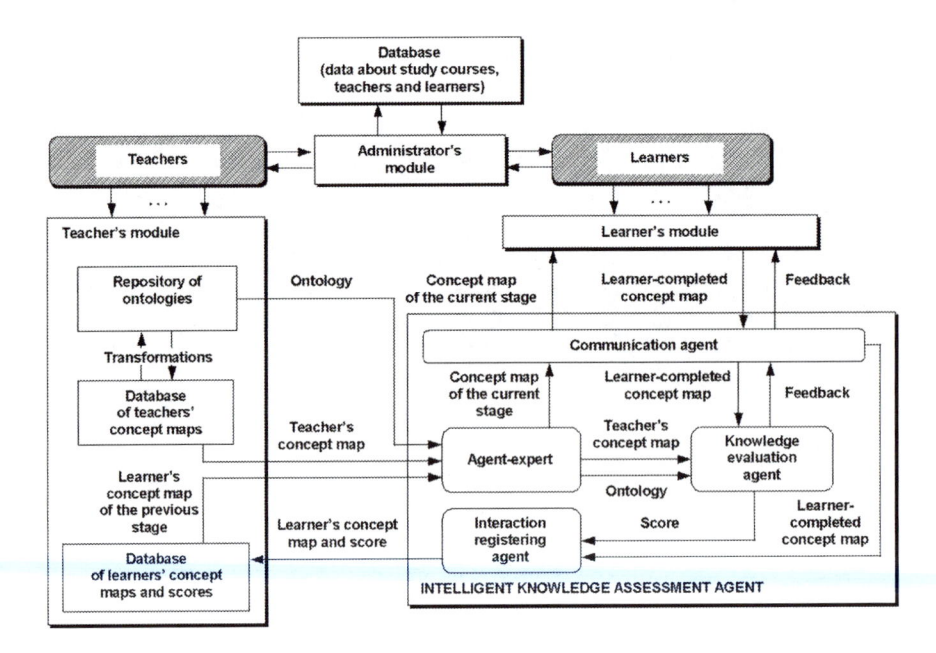

Fig. 12.5 The IKAS and its environment

3.2 Operation Scenario

The created system supports the following scenario. Using the graphical user interface, the teacher prepares a CM for each stage (the system supports teacher's actions for drawing CMs on the working surface). In order to make his/her work easier, existing ontologies of study courses may be transformed into CMs (Graudina & Grundspenkis, 2008). During knowledge assessment learners get a CM task that corresponds to the current stage of learning. After completing the CM task, the learner confirms his/her solution, the communication agent sends it, and the knowledge evaluation agent compares the learner's and the teacher's CMs on the basis of the so called graph patterns.

Graph patterns are subgraphs or, in other words, sets of paths or cycles of limited length (Grundspenkis & Strautmane, 2009; Grundspenkis & Anohina, 2009). The descriptions of some graph patterns shown in Fig. 12.6 are given in Table 12.1. Pattern 1 (Fig. 12.6a) represents a correct solution because all three concepts are inserted correctly, types of relationships and linking phrases are correct, too. Pattern 5 (Fig. 12.6b) represents an incorrect linking phrase defined for the relationship between correctly inserted concepts. Pattern 8 (Fig. 12.6c) corresponds to the solution where the type of relationship and the linking phrase are incorrect. All three patterns are compared with the CM shown in Fig. 12.3 that is considered to be the teacher's CM.

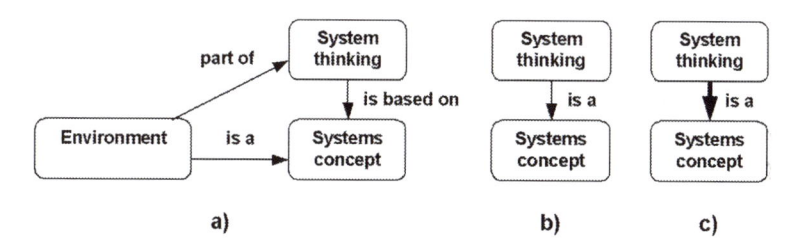

Fig. 12.6 Examples of graph patterns

Table 12.1 Some examples of graph patterns

Pattern no	Description	Score
Pattern 1	Perfectly correct (conforms with the teacher's CM): concepts are in correct nodes and the types of relationships and the linking phrases are correct	S_{max} (maximal number of points, i.e. 5 for an important relationship and 2 for a less important relationship)
Pattern 5	Both concepts are in correct nodes but the linking phrase is incorrect	$0.7\ S_{max}$
Pattern 8	The relationship defined by the learner is in the teacher's CM but both the type of the relationship and the linking phrase are incorrect	$0.5\ S_{max}$

For each graph pattern the knowledge evaluation agent assigns a score which characterizes the level of its correctness. This agent also calculates the final score for the whole CM submitted by the learner and sends it to the interaction registering agent, and as part of feedback containing information about the correctness of the solution to the communication agent. Comparison and assessment of CMs is performed by a developed comparison algorithm. Complexity of this algorithm has increased from one IKAS version to another concurrently with the number of recognized graph patterns (see also Table 12.2). The number of graph patterns depends on task demands and task constraints. In the first two versions of the IKAS when only fill-in-the-map tasks were used, links had only two weights and a graph was undirected (linking phrases were added in the second version), the comparison algorithm recognized 5 and 9 graph patterns, respectively. In the third version the number of patterns increased to 36 because construct-the-map tasks were added and undirected and directed graphs with standard linking phrases from the set R = {"is a", "instance of", "has attribute", "has value", "part of"} were used. In the fourth version learners have more freedom defining concepts and linking phrases. So the number of graph patterns is even higher because synonyms of concepts and linking phrases as well

Table 12.2 Evolution of CM based IKAS

Characteristics	Number of version			
	1st (2005)	2nd (2006)	3rd (2007)	4th (2008–2009)
Tasks for learners	F-M[a]	F-M	F-M, C-M[a]	F-M, C-M
Scoring (number of patterns)	5	9	36	>36
Types (number of weights) of relationships	2	2	2	2
Linking phrases	–	+	+	+
Directed arcs	–	–	+	+
Synonyms and standard linking phrases	–	–	+	+
Drag-and-drop technique	–	+	+	+
Use of student model	–	–	–	+
Changing the degree of task difficulty	–	+	+	+
Insertion of additional concepts	–	+	+	+
Feedback (the score)	+	+	+	+
Feedback (learner's CMs with highlighted mistakes)	+	+	+	+
Feedback (checking propositions)	–	–	–	+
Help (explanation of concepts)	–	–	–	+
Statistics about differences between teacher's and learner's CMs	–	+	+	+
Client/server architecture	2-tier	2-tier	2-tier	3-tier

[a]F-M – fill-in-the-map tasks; C-M – construct-the-map tasks
"+" – a characteristic is implemented
"–" – a characteristic is not implemented

as so called "hidden relationships" (Grundspenkis & Strautmane, 2009) are recognized. At present the used scoring system is rather immature. A significant amount of work should be done to improve it. The final goal is the development of a scoring system which can evaluate students' CMs accurately and consistently.

Other operations are as follows. The agent-expert forms a CM of a current stage using the teacher's CM and the learner's CM of the previous stage, and passes it to the communication agent for visualization. The agent-expert also delivers the teacher's CM and corresponding ontology to the knowledge evaluation agent that finds synonyms if students have used them. The communication agent perceives learner's actions and is responsible for changing the degree of task difficulty and the form of feedback (described below), as well as for the visualization of CMs received from the agent-expert, and for the output of feedback received from the knowledge evaluation agent. After receiving the learner's solution and its assessment the interaction registering agent stores them into database.

The IKAS has a capacity for adaptation to each learner's current knowledge level. The capacity of adaptation refers to a computer-generated response format and is realized in two ways (for details see Grundspenkis & Anohina, 2009). First, the degree of task difficulty may be changed initiated by the learner or by the IKAS. For a fill-in-the-map task the learner can receive an easier task if he/she asks the IKAS to insert a chosen concept into a correct node of CM. The learner may also ask the IKAS to replace the current task with an easier or more difficult one. For example, if the current task is from the fill-in-the-map class of tasks where a CM's structure is given and both the concept set C_S and the linking phrase set LP_S corresponds to category C (complete), the learner can ask to replace this task with a more difficult construct-the-map task or with an easier fill-in-the-map task where the linking phrase set LP_S corresponds to category E (is not used at all).

Second, the learner can choose a form of feedback containing help for those concepts which cause difficulties for him/her. For each concept the IKAS can give a definition, a short description or an explanation. The learner can choose the initial form of explanation and change it during the solution of a CM task. Moreover, the IKAS keeps track of learner's actions and determines which form of help has the greatest value for a particular student in his/her efforts to create a correct graph pattern (Grundspenkis & Anohina, 2009).

The IKAS is based not only on the ideas of the developers but to a considerable extent also on the feedback from students who voluntarily used this system for their knowledge self-assessment in a number of courses. The main characteristics of the IKAS that reflect its evolution are presented in Table 12.2.

The architecture of the IKAS started as a two-tier structure (used in the first three versions) and was altered to a three-tier structure that includes three conceptual elements: the database server, the client application, and the application server Apache Tomcat. Three-tier structure improved response speed and operation security. The IKAS has been implemented using the following technologies: Eclipse 3.2, Apache Tomcat 6.0, Postgre SQL DBMS 8.1.3, JDBC drivers, Hibernate, VLDocking, JGoodies and JGraph.

4 Results of Practical Use of the IKAS

4.1 Organization of Practical Testing

Developers of the IKAS have 5 years' experience of practical use of the system mainly for different computer science courses for third-year bachelor students at two higher education institutions – Riga Technical University (RTU) and Vidzeme University College (VUC). The important point is that in these courses learning was not based on CMs. So students had no work experience with CMs. All initial information about the essence of CMs and operation of the IKAS was provided in a special instructional (teaching) file. At the end of each semester the IKAS was offered to students for voluntary self-assessment of the acquired knowledge. The desire to get unbiased opinion of novice users of CMs and the IKAS led to the use of above-mentioned approach. Developers accumulated experience during the development and use of four versions of the IKAS. In addition, students' opinions were collected and it was a significant driving force to improve the system. After the final CM task was solved students handed in questionnaires. All questions may be divided into four groups. Questions of the first group are focused on CMs as learning and knowledge assessment tools. Questions of the second group refer to the quality of interface, and functionality and operation of the IKAS. Questions of the third group are aimed at obtaining student opinions about the usefulness of reduction of the degree of task difficulty and operation of this mechanism. Questions of the fourth group are centred on the quality of the received feedback and help.

Numerical data of practical testing of the IKAS are the following:

- The first version (2005) was tested for 3 computer science and one pedagogical course at RTU, and 2 computer science courses at VUC; 95 students participated and 84 questionnaires were received.
- The second version (2006) was tested for 2 computer science and one pedagogical course at RTU, and 2 computer science courses at VUC; 74 students participated and 63 questionnaires were received.
- The third version (2007) was tested for one computer science course at RTU; 40 students participated and 37 questionnaires were received.
- The fourth version (2008) was tested for one computer science course at RTU; 36 students participated and the same number of questionnaires were received.
- The improved fourth version (2009) was tested for 3 computer science courses at RTU; 19 students participated and 17 questionnaires were received.

4.2 Student Opinions About CMs as Knowledge Assessment Tools

The most informative questions of the first group (selected from 12 questions) and the percentage of student answers are given in Table 12.3. Students said they

Table 12.3 Questions from the first group

No	Question	Answer	1st	2nd	3rd	4th	4th (improved)
1.	Do you like CM as a knowledge assessment tool?	Yes	69	78	84	92	52
		Neutral	–	11	0	8	24
		No	31	11	16	0	24
2.	Does CM task promote better understanding of the material?	Yes	63	71	41	58	29
		Partly	–	–	51	36	42
		No	37	29	8	6	29
3.	Do you want to use CM in other courses?	Yes	33	71	62	50	18
		Probably	55	22	27	47	58
		No	12	7	11	3	24
4.	Are CM tasks difficult or easy?	Difficult	52	59	49	69	53
		Very difficult	7	11	8	0	18
		Easy	37	24	43	28	29
		Very easy	4	6	0	3	0

liked using CMs for knowledge assessment as it helped them to systematize their knowledge, develop knowledge structure and promote logical and analytical thinking. Thus, the theoretical viewpoint about advantages of CMs was confirmed. Students also pointed out that CMs being graphical objects are easy to perceive, and that it is a fast and convenient way of knowledge checking and assessment. Explaining their negative attitude towards CMs students answered that this approach required an unusual way of thinking and ability to see "the whole picture" but at the same time allowed only superficial assessment of knowledge. Some students mentioned that this is only one of the possible ways of knowledge representation, that it basically requires understanding of relationships between concepts not their essence and applications, and that probability of making mistakes is rather high because the assessment makes students to construct their knowledge in a way that mimics the knowledge constructed by the teacher. It is interesting to note that the latter was mentioned as a serious drawback of CMs in (da Rocha et al., 2008) where it is stated that CM based approach does not address the fact that humans construct knowledge in a number of differing ways.

The majority of students found that CM tasks helped them to understand better the material (at least partly) regardless of their opinion that CM tasks for them are difficult or even very difficult. The following reasons which caused difficulties were mentioned: the idea of CMs is unclear, solutions of CM tasks are time consuming, students had insufficient knowledge and/or no work experience with diagrams. It is worthwhile to stress that the latter reason was pointed out mainly by students of the pedagogical study programme who showed considerably worse results comparing with computer science study programme students. The encouraging factor for further development of the IKAS and extension of its functionality was that overwhelming majority of students expressed a wish to use CMs in other courses.

4.3 Improvements of Functionality of the IKAS

Answers to questions of the second group led to improvements of the IKAS, too. After testing the first version, students suggested implementing the drag-and-drop technique. Regarding functionality they suggested to improve system's feedback, to include help facilities and to increase system's response speed and operation security. Students also pointed out that textual format of feedback in the first version was not informative enough and did not help understanding mistakes; it should contain information about missing knowledge units and should show mistakes in graphical form. All of these suggestions were taken into account and implemented in the second version of the IKAS. Testing results of this version showed that students want (a) to see a correct and complete CM at the end of each stage, (b) to receive more detailed explanations about their mistakes, and (c) to be assigned scores they can verify and understand. They wished to see their progress (the number of correct patterns) and to have information on the elements of the final score. These were impulses for further improvements implemented in the third version. The most frequently mentioned suggestion was to have additional materials available when CM task solving causes difficulties and the inclusion of descriptions of mistakes. Both were added in the fourth version.

4.4 Change of the Degree of Task Difficulty

Starting from the second version the mechanism of changing the degree of task difficulty was introduced. In the second version the system offered to place a limited number (chosen by the student) of concepts in appropriate nodes. In the third and the fourth versions the option to reduce or increase the degree of task difficulty by choosing an easier or more difficult fill-in-the-map or construct-the-map task was offered, too (Anohina, Pozdnakovs, & Grundspenkis, 2007).

Practical use of the IKAS revealed unexpected response from the students. Less than 50% of them used the option to change the degree of task difficulty regardless of the difficulties they met during the CM task solution. Questionnaires helped to find the reasons: some of the students were confident about their knowledge and wished to meet the challenge of solving the task without any help, while others did not want to lower their scores.

Several questions from the third group were aimed at clearing up correctness of the mechanism of changing the degree of task difficulty (see Table 12.4). Collected data give conclusive proof that this mechanism built in the fourth version of the IKAS is working correctly. The system offers an easier task if the student has problems, and the reduction of task difficulty enables further solution of CM tasks. If the student achieves good results, the system reacts by offering a new, more difficult type of task.

Table 12.4 Questions from the third group

No	Question	Answer	2nd	3rd	4th	4th (improved)
1.	Does reduction of the degree of task difficulty make the task execution easier?	Yes	80	25	81	55
		Partly	–	50	19	27
		No	20	25	0	18
2.	Is the task offered by the system easier than the previous task?	Yes	–	50	74	67
		Neutral	–	25	15	33
		No	–	25	11	0
3.	Does the system offer a new more difficult type of task at the next stage?	Yes	–	50	86	20
		No	–	50	14	80
4.	Is the new task more difficult than the task at the previous stage?	Yes	–	58	84	50
		Neutral	–	16	10	50
		No	–	26	6	0

Percentage of answers / Number of version

4.5 Feedback Provided to Students

Continuous improvement of feedback provided to students was accomplished step-by-step from the beginning of the development of the IKAS. In the first two versions feedback only informed students about their final score and showed his/her mistakes in graphical form without any explanations. In the third version the score was shown for each correctly or incorrectly inserted concept and/or relationship, and linking phrase. In the fourth version which was tested in 2008 and 2009 feedback contained explanation and help facilities. Around 51% of students used explanation facilities which were provided in three forms: (1) a definition, (2) a short description, (3) an example. Decision making about the initial form of explanation is up to the learner, it is added to the student model, and may be changed by the learner during his/her work with the IKAS. The system, in its turn, keeping track of learner's actions, offers to change the explanation form if the initial form chosen by the learner does not match the form with the greatest contribution determined by the IKAS. Statistics showed that 42% of students used definitions of concepts, 26% used descriptions and 32% used examples.

The fourth group of questions has the question: "which form of explanation is the most informative?" Student answers showed that for 59% it was definitions, for 41% it was short descriptions but nobody put examples in this category. Fifty percent of students answered "yes", and fifty percent – "partly" to the question: "did explanation make the task execution easier?"

Checking the correctness of chosen proposition was included as a new help facility in the fourth version. If this option was chosen, the system checked correctness of proposition and provided explanation (tutoring) if the proposition was not correct. Questionnaires showed that only 32% of students used this option (others answered that they did not want to lower their scores or they delayed the usage of this option "till the moment when there would be a situation when absolutely nothing comes to my mind how to solve the task"). From those who used the abovementioned option 57% answered that it helped to solve the task, and 43% answered that it helped only partly.

An alternative form of help is automatic insertion of concepts into a CM. The student feeling that the task presents difficulties can ask the system to insert the chosen concept. Around 28% of students used this opportunity, and 51% of them answered that it made task solving easier.

Students who worked with the fourth version of the IKAS ranked alternative ways of help provided by the system in accordance with the criterion: "the most useful way which makes CM task solving easier". The result in 2008 was as follows: (1) change of the degree of task difficulty, (2) explanation facilities, (3) checking proposition correctness, (4) insertion of chosen concepts into a CM, in 2009 the first and second rank was the same, but the third and the fourth rank were exchanged.

Students may view a correct CM where their mistakes are marked. For 47% of them it helped to understand their mistakes. The same percentage answered that it helped only partly, but for 6% this information was useless. The IKAS, in its turn, uses information about mistakes of a particular student and offers an individual plan for revision (57% of students found information about it, but only 17% really used their individual plans to reach better results).

In the fourth version a special instructional file was added with the purpose of getting acquainted with the essence of CM based knowledge assessment and operation of the IKAS. Eighty percent of the users found that this instructional file is informative enough and helps in their work with the system. At the end let us remark that only part of the information elicited from questionnaires is represented in this section of results obtained from the practical use of the IKAS.

5 Conclusions

The paper reflects longitudinal experience of development and practical use of an adaptive multi-agent IKAS based on CMs. Practical use of four versions of the IKAS and their testing results allow to make the conclusion that the number of students who liked the usage of CMs as knowledge assessment tools is high (averaging around 75%), irrespective of which university was teaching the tested courses and the courses themselves. Moreover, regardless of numerous improvements (a more convenient interface, faster response, more informative feedback, explanation and help facilities, etc.) the percentage of students who consider the CM tasks as difficult or even very difficult is rather high (ranges from 57 to 71%). Students agreed that CMs help the systematisation of knowledge, development of knowledge structure, and promotion of logical and analytical thinking. At the same time the student opinion is that CMs may be used not only as knowledge self assessment tools which was the initial goal of the IKAS development but also as knowledge assessment tools for "pass/fail" assessment and for intermediate assessment thereby supporting the process oriented learning. The students argue that for a final assessment oral explanation of CM elements should be used.

Evolution of the IKAS resulted in its transformation from a knowledge assessment tool into an intelligent tutoring system which provides adaptive feedback and help for each particular student if he/she has difficulties in solving CM tasks.

Future work is directed towards a further extension of the IKAS. A new CM comparison algorithm based on a large set of graph patterns is under development. The conception of agent based student modelling shell AGENT-UM is being worked out (Lukashenko & Grundspenkis, 2009). The purpose of the shell is the construction of a complete student model. Concurrently the agent based intelligent tutoring system MIPITS for the study course "Fundamentals of Artificial Intelligence" has been created (Lavendelis & Grundspenkis, 2010). At the moment all needed learning objects for the MIPITS are under development. Both the AGENT-UM and the MIPITS, as well as the algorithm for transforming study course ontology into CMs will be integrated with the IKAS. Research is going on to develop a scoring system which can evaluate students' CMs accurately and consistently taking into account such factors as the number of changes of the degree of task difficulty initiated by the learner or by the system, the number of student requests for checking the correctness of propositions, the number of requests for help, and some others.

References

Ahlberg, M. (2004). Varieties of concept mapping. *Proceedings of the First International Conference on Concept Mapping, (Vol. 2, pp. 25–28), September 14–17, 2004, Pamplona, Spain*. Retrieved March, 30, 2010, from http://cmc.ihmc.us/papers/cmc2004-206.pdf

Anderson, J. R., & Reiser, B. J. (1985). The Lisp tutor. *Byte, 10*, 159–175.

Anohina, A., & Grundspenkis, J. (2006). Prototype of multiagent knowledge assessment system for support of process oriented learning. *Proceedings of the 7th international Baltic conference on databases and information systems*, (pp. 211–219), July 3–6, 2006, Vilnius, Lithuania.

Anohina, A., Pozdnakovs, D., & Grundspenkis, J. (2007). Changing the degree of task difficulty in concept map based assessment system. *Proceedings of the IADIS international conference "e-learning 2007", (pp. 443–450), July 6–8, 2007, Lisbon, Portugal.*

Ausubel, D. P. (1968). *Educational psychology: A cognitive view (p. 685)*. New York: Holt, Rinehart and Winston.

Ausubel, D. P. (2000). *The acquisition and retention of knowledge (p. 232)*. New York: Kluwer.

Bloom, B. S. (1956). *Taxonomy of education objectives. Handbook I: The cognitive domain (p. 207)*. New York: David McKay.

Brown, J. S., & Burton, R. R. (1978). A paradigmatic example of an artificially intelligent instructional system. *International Journal of Man-Machine Studies, 10*, 323–339.

Brown, J. S., Burton, R. R., & de Kleer, J. (1982). Pedagogical, natural language, and knowledge engineering techniques in SOPHIE I, II and III. In D. H. Sleeman & J. S. Brown (Eds.), *Intelligent tutoring systems*. London: Academic.

Burton, R. R., & Brown, J. S. (1982). An investigation of computer coaching for informal learning activities. In D. H. Sleeman & J. S. Brown (Eds.), *Intelligent tutoring systems*. London: Academic.

Cañas, A. J. et al. (2003). *A summary of literature pertaining to the use of concept mapping techniques and technologies for education and performance support. Technical report submitted to the chief of naval education and training* (p. 108). Pensacola, FL: Florida Institute for Human and Machine Cognition.

Carbonell, J. R. (1970). AI in CAI: An artificial intelligence approach to computer-assisted instruction. *IEEE Transactions of Man-Machine Systems, 11*(4), 190–202.

Cimolino, L. et al. (2003). Incremental student modelling and reflection by verified concept-mapping. *Supplementary proceedings of AIED 2003: Learner modelling for reflection* (pp. 219–227), July 20–24, 2003, Sydney, Australia.

Clancey, W. J. (1982). Tutoring roles for guiding a case methods dialogue. In D. H. Sleeman & J. S. Brown (Eds.), *Intelligent tutoring systems*. London: Academic.

Twomey, E., Nicol, J., & Smart, C. (2004). *Computer-assisted assessment: Using computers to design and deliver objective tests*. Computers in Teaching Initiative. Retrieved March 30, 2010, from http://etudeedl.free.fr/annexes/assess.pdf

Conlon, T. (2006). Formative assessment of classroom concept maps: The reasonable fallible analyser. *Journal of Interactive Learning Research, 17*(1), 15–36.

da Rocha, F. E. L. et al. (2008). An approach to computer-aided learning assessment. *Proceedings of the third international conference on concept mapping* (pp. 170–177), September 22–25, 2008, Tallinn, Estonia and Helsinki, Finland.

Deese, J. (1965). *The structure of associations in language and thought*. Baltimore, MD: Johns Hopkins Press.

de Souza, F. S. L. et al. (2008). An approach to comparison of concept maps represented by graphs. *Concept mapping – connecting educators, proceedings of the third international conference on concept mapping (pp. 205–212), September 22–25, 2008, Tallinn, Estonia & Helsinki, Finland.*

Gouli, E. et al. (2004). COMPASS: An adaptive web-based concept map assessment tool. In A. Cañas, J. Novak, & F. González (Eds.), *Concept maps: Theory, methodology, technology. Proceedings of the first international conference on concept mapping, (pp. 128–135), September 14–17, 2004, Pamplona, Spain.* Retrieved March 30, 2010, from http://cmc.ihmc.us/papers/cmc2004-128.pdf

Graudina, V., & Grundspenkis, J. (2008). Concept map generation from OWL ontologies. *Concept mapping – Connecting educators. Proceedings of the third international conference on concept mapping, (pp. 173–180), September 22–25, 2008, Tallinn, Estonia & Helsinki, Finland.*

Grundspenkis, J. (2008a). Development of concept map based adaptive knowledge assessment system. *Proceedings of IADIS international conference on e-learning* (pp. 295–402), *July 22–25, 2008, Amsterdam, The Netherlands.*

Grundspenkis, J. (2008b). Knowledge creation supported by intelligent knowledge assessment system. *Proceedings of the 12th world multi-conference on systemics, cybernetics and informatics (pp. 135–140), June 29-July 2, 2008, Orlando, Florida, USA.*

Grundspenkis, J., & Anohina, A. (2005). Agents in intelligent tutoring systems: State of the art. *Scientific Proceedings of Riga Technical University, 5th Series, Computer Science, Applied Computer Systems, 22*, 110–121.

Grundspenkis, J., & Anohina, A. (2009). Evolution of the concept map based adaptive knowledge assessment system: Implementation and evaluation results. *Scientific Proceedings of Riga Technical University, 5th Series Computer Science, Applied Computer Systems, 38*, 13–24.

Grundspenkis, J., & Strautmane, M. (2009). Usage of graph patterns for knowledge assessment based on concept maps. *Scientific Proceedings of Riga Technical University, 5th series Computer Science, Applied Computer Systems, 38*, 60–71.

Hsieh, I.-L., & O'Neil, H. (2002). Types of feedback in a computer-based collaborative problem-solving group task. *Computers in Human Behaviour, 18*, 699–715.

Lavendelis, E., & Grundspenkis, J. (2010). MIPITS: An agent based intelligent tutoring system. *Proceedings of the 2nd international conference on agents and artificial intelligence (ICAART 2010) (Vol. 2, pp. 5–13), January 22–24, 2010, Valencia, Spain.*

Lukashenko, R., & Anohina, A. (2009). Knowledge assessment systems: An overview. *Scientific Proceedings of Riga Technical University, 5th series Computer Science, Applied Computer Systems, 38,* 25–36.

Lukashenko, R., & Grundspenkis, J. (2009). A conception of agents-based user modelling shell for intelligent knowledge assessment system. *Proceedings of the international conference "e-learning 2009", June 17–20, 2009* (pp. 98–140), *Algarve, Portugal.*

Novak, J. D. (1998). *Learning, creating, and using knowledge: Concept maps as facilitative tools in schools and corporations* (p. 272). Mahwah, NJ: Lawrence Erlbaum Associates.

Novak, J. D., & Gowin, D. B. (1984). *Learning how to learn* (p. 150). New York: Cornell University Press.

Papanastasiou, E. C. (2003). Computer-adaptive testing in science education. *Proceedings of the 6th international conference on computer based learning in science,* (pp. 965–971), July 5–10, 2003, Nicosia, Cyprus.

Pirnay-Dummer, P. et al. (2008). Highly integrated model assessment technology and tools. *Proceedings of IADIS international conference on cognition and exploratory learning in digital age (CELDA 2008)* (pp. 18–28), *13–15 October, 2008, Freiburg, Germany.* IADIS.

Ruiz-Primo, M. A., & Shavelson, R. J. (1996). Problems and issues in the use of concept maps in science assessment. *Journal of Research in Science Teaching, 33*(6), 569–600.

Stevens, A., & Collins, A. (1977). The goal structure of a Socratic tutor. *Proceedings of the national ACM conference,* (pp. 256–263), January 1977, Seattle, WA.

Waterhouse, S. (2004). *The power of e-learning: The essential guide for teaching in the digital age* (p. 228). Boston, MA: Allyn & Bacon.

Chapter 13
Technologies to Support the Assessment of Complex Learning in Capstone Units: Two Case Studies

Margot McNeill

Abstract Capstone or final year units in a program of study ideally provide an opportunity for students to integrate the knowledge and learning experiences from their whole degree program. These units have the potential to scaffold students to synthesise their discipline knowledge with intellectual skills to equip them for dealing with complex situations in the next phases of their careers, whether their transition is to the workplace or further study. While these intentions may be clear, the task of designing the learning and assessment activities can be challenging for academics; firstly in managing an already crowded curriculum and secondly in devising assessment strategies that adequately reflect students' achievements in complex domains. This chapter examines two case studies from an Australian research-intensive university which use a range of technologies to support and assess complex learning in different domains. Characteristics of capstone units are first explored. The case studies are then explained, in terms of the learning outcomes addressed, scaffolding during the unit and the assessment strategies used. A framework for describing the affordances of a range of technologies in supporting and assessing complex learning in capstones or other units is presented.

Keywords Educational technologies · Assessment · Complex learning · Capstone units

1 Introduction

Equipping university graduates to cope with complex problems is on the agenda of many higher education stakeholders. As suggested by a recent consultation paper developed by the Australian Qualifications Framework Council (2009):

M. McNeill (✉)
Macquarie University, Suite C3B, Room 407, Sydney, NSW 2109, Australia
e-mail: margot.mcneill@mq.edu.au

D. Ifenthaler et al. (eds.), *Multiple Perspectives on Problem Solving and Learning in the Digital Age*, DOI 10.1007/978-1-4419-7612-3_13,
© Springer Science+Business Media, LLC 2011

> Higher education qualifications are becoming more focused on the world of work and many descriptions of university courses show an increased emphasis on work related or work integrated learning and practice (p. 14).

This focus on the development of skills to equip students for the complexities they will encounter in their transition to the workplace or further study is also evident in the graduate capabilities acknowledged by many universities. Stephenson and Yorke (1998) suggest that capable graduates:

> ...have the confidence to apply their knowledge and skills within varied and changing situations and to continue to develop their specialist knowledge and skills long after they have left formal education...Taking effective and appropriate action within unfamiliar and changing circumstances involves ethics, judgments, the self-confidence to take risks and a commitment to learn from the experience. (p. 3)

These themes are reiterated by Williams (1999) who suggests that the opportunity for graduates to develop confidence and self-awareness is critical in preparing them for transition into the workplace and the subsequent changes they will experience in their professional lives.

Over recent years, Macquarie University in Sydney, Australia has been developing a suite of graduate capabilities desirable in our graduates, such as critical thinking, problem solving and creativity. The Curriculum Renewal Program currently underway at the University involves faculties mapping these and other graduate capabilities to ensure they are embedded into each program. The development of capstone units for each degree was seen as an opportunity to integrate all these requirements and to embed assessment of many of the graduate capabilities into final year units.

1.1 Capstone Units

Capstone units are final year units in a program of study which provide an opportunity for students to bring together their knowledge and experiences and prepare them for the next stages of their careers, whether in further study or the workplace (Gardiner, 1999). As part of this transition, it is important that students are provided with the opportunity to integrate the material covered in the whole program, understand how it fits together, and focus on how what they have learned equips them for their next step, whether this is to a next level of study, or into the workforce (Collier, 2000; Dunlap, 2005).

Components of capstone units often include

- integrating and synthesising the technical knowledge and skills from across multiple and diverse topic areas gained during the course of study (Collier, 2000; Dunlap, 2005);
- preparing a portfolio to display the acquired graduate capabilities such as problem solving, creative thinking or teamwork;

reflecting on the development of these graduate capabilities and how these have been achieved within the degree;

in professional degrees, undertaking a professional preparation program (Humphrey Brown & Benson, 2005).

If the design of students' learning experiences across their program is seen as cumulative, from an induction into university learning in first year through to a consolidation of learning in the final year, they will ideally encounter increasing complex and ambiguous tasks, along with process-oriented scaffolding to guide the application of their learning (van Gog, Paas, & van Merriënboer, 2004). VanLehn's (1996) three- phase approach to skill development can be used to describe this cumulative learning; from the acquisition phase of familiarization with the key concepts of the domain, through the intermediate phase of applying concepts and establishing the complex interrelationships within the body of knowledge, to the capacity to use this knowledge to solve complex problems in the expertise phase.

With this cumulative learning as a focus, learning outcomes for capstone units typically target higher order skills such as

appreciation of complex, competing issues in graduate jobs;
extension of analytical and strategic thinking;
application of theory into practice;
consolidation of higher-level applied communication skills, such as professional level written and oral presentation skills;
application of employment-related teamwork skills;
demonstration of early professional dispositions and ethical stance.

These outcomes are situated within the intermediate to the late phase of VanLehn's framework strengthening the interconnectedness of knowledge networks, problem solving skills and metacognitive capability.

In his taxonomy to provide a framework for describing learning outcomes as cognitive processes, Bloom (1956) also acknowledged the importance of designing learning to target higher order thinking. The six categories in Bloom's taxonomy were *knowledge, comprehension, application, analysis, synthesis and evaluation* arranged in ascending order beginning with *knowledge*. Williams (2006) describes higher order learning as the highest levels of learning in the cognitive domain of Bloom's taxonomy *analysis, synthesis* and *evaluation*.

In revising Bloom's original taxonomy, Anderson and colleagues (2001) included a *creation* category to the Cognitive Process Dimension and reformatted the nouns to verbs to signify learning as activity. They also developed a matrix by adding a *knowledge* dimension. The matrix format was selected to highlight the array of possible objectives and the relationship between them. Of particular interest in this study are the lower right hand categories, denoted by the diagonal pattern in Table 13.1.

Table 13.1 The revised Bloom's taxonomy (Anderson et al., 2001)

The knowledge dimension	The cognitive process dimension					
	Remember	Understand	Apply	Analyze	Evaluate	Create
Factual knowledge						
Conceptual knowledge						
Procedural knowledge						
Meta-cognitive knowledge						

While skills such as problem solving, leadership, innovation and creativity; all higher order learning according to Anderson et al., taxonomy, are increasingly acknowledged by universities (Bath, Smith, Stein, & Swann, 2004), devising assessment strategies that adequately reflect students' achievements in complex domains (Jonassen & Campbell, 1994) has been challenging for academics (Astleitner, 2002; Burns, 2006; Clarkson & Brook, 2007; Race, 2001, 2006). As suggested by Shepherd (2009):

> Many universities identify the attributes that they hope their graduates will aspire to, but (and perhaps particularly where these attributes relate to affective characteristics) these attributes are rarely assessed with the same level of objectivity as those described by intended learning outcomes (p. 387).

Similarly, Bryan and Clegg (2006) lamented that the focus of much of our assessment is on testing knowledge and comprehension and ignores the challenge of developing and assessing judgments (p. 3).

Part of this continued focus on assessment of lower order skills may lie in academics attitude to the role of assessment. A study conducted by Samuelowicz and Bain (2002) suggests that academic perspectives about the role of assessment might influence whether they design their units to address higher order learning outcomes. Samuelowicz and Bain (2002) analysed academics' orientations toward assessment using a framework developed to describe their beliefs about the role of assessment and feedback, about what should be learned and assessed; and finally about the differences between good and poor answers. They found perspectives ranging from assessment as requiring reproduction of important knowledge, procedures and skills to a focus on challenging students' perceptions. Academics with an orientation toward 'reproduction' were likely to require this in their assessments; students were tasked with reproducing the understandings they had been given. Depending on the level of these understandings, appropriate assessment tasks could range from multiple choice questions testing understanding of facts, to open-ended questions testing students' ability to apply principles to a given, familiar situation (Samuelowicz & Bain, 2002). Conversely, if academics perceived assessment as part of the learning required to challenge existing knowledge, then they were more likely to design tasks requiring higher order tasks such as evaluation and creation of new solutions (Samuelowicz & Bain, 2002).

In addition to academics' perspectives, the assessment technologies themselves may contribute to this tendency toward assessing lower order rather than more complex learning, maintaining rather than challenging the status quo.

2 Technologies to Support Assessment

The prospect of new technologies as enabling a reconsideration of assessment has been raised by researchers in the past (Philips & Lowe, 2003; Zemsky & Massey, 2004). Jonassen and Reeves (1996) were among those who saw computers as having the potential to transform learning and assessment to a focus on higher order rather than lower order learning outcomes. Since then, the opportunities offered by technologies to support the design, delivery and administration of diagnostic, formative and summative assessment have been well documented in the literature (Crisp, 2007).

Despite these examples, assessment has been an area slower to adopt new technologies than other aspects of teaching and learning (Byrnes & Ellis, 2006; Ellis & Goodyear, 2010). There is a preconception that technology-based assessment is best suited to objective testing which targets lower order skills (Biggs, 2003; Crisp, 2007; Nicol & Milligan, 2006; Northcote, 2003).

Advocates of the emerging social networking tools such as blogs and wikis have raised their potential to capture both the processes of student learning and the final artifacts to be submitted, in either collaborative or individual contexts (Boulos, Maramba, & Wheeler, 2006; Churchill, 2007; Hewitt & Peters, 2006). Shepherd raises the possibility that the use of these technologies could enable higher education to 'better assess aspects of learning that have proved difficult to assess using more conventional means' (2009, p. 386). As suggested by Gosper in 2, however, the activity fostered in learners, not the technology, is what ultimately influences learning. Effective curriculum design requires alignment between the unit aims, processes, learner expertise and technologies, the MAPLET framework.

This optimism about the new tools and the theoretical frameworks to evaluate them for use in teaching contexts raised questions about how academics are using technologies in their units, especially with the increasing focus on higher order learning in capstone units and the inherent assessment challenges.

3 The Study

A series of case studies was developed as part of a wider study undertaken at Macquarie University to explore academic practice in the use of technologies to support assessment of learning, specifically

> The types of outcomes convenors envisaged for their students and how these were reflected in the unit outlines;
> The alignment of assessment strategies with these intended outcomes; and
> The selection of technologies in relation to these intended learning outcomes and assessment strategies.

The study was designed using an exploratory mixed methods approach (Creswell & Piano Clark, 2007). In phase one of the study, academics convening online units were surveyed about their curriculum design and assessment practices, including any uses of technologies. The initial survey indicated that the areas academics found most difficult to assess were often related to the higher order, graduate capabilities of communication, evaluation, creativity, metacognition (McNeill, Gosper, & Hedberg, 2008).

The second stage of the study involved a series of ten case studies to explore the issues emerging from the survey. The case studies were developed from a series of semi-structured interviews where convenors were asked to describe aspects of their units including

> The learning outcomes as stated in the unit outline;
> Those outcomes they intended for their students' learning and where these fit in relation to outcomes and processes described in Anderson and Krathwohl's (2001) framework;
> Their perspectives on the role of assessment and feedback in the learning process, in relation to Samuelowicz and Bain's framework (2002);
> Their assessment strategies and how these related to the intended learning outcomes; and
> Any technologies used to support assessment.

The transcriptions were then analysed using a coding scheme based on Anderson and Krathwohl's (2001) taxonomy and Samuelowicz and Bain's (2002) orientations toward assessment. Each of the interviews was written up as a case study with rich descriptions of the specific curriculum context, assessment strategies and the use of technologies, using a template developed from the initial analysis of the results.

While all of the ten case studies employed technologies in some aspect of their delivery or assessment, these two case studies involving capstone units were the only examples from the sample where higher order outcomes and processes were designed specifically into the curriculum. The cases are described in the next section. Although generalisability was not an aim of their development, the case studies do provide examples of uses of technologies to support the development and assessment of complex learning, elements of which may be applicable to other contexts.

4 Case Study One: Computing Science

Capstone exemplar one is a capstone unit for a Computing Science degree. The aim of the unit is to prepare students for working in teams in industry by producing a complete solution from initial problem statement, bringing together the knowledge they have acquired throughout their degree.

It is conducted over two semesters, with four seminar sessions each semester.

4.1 Learning Outcomes

The learning outcomes of the unit reflected the emphasis on graduate capabilities and the integration of knowledge and skills covered in previous units. When asked what she intended as learning outcomes for the students, the convenor described higher order skills such as

> Critical analysis analysis and application of principles and models of software development;
> Performance of the stages of the software engineering life-cycle (requirements analysis, design, construction, testing) in an authentic context;
> Demonstration of an understanding of the influence of group effectiveness and strategies for supporting effective co-operation;
> Demonstration of the capacity to work effectively in a software development team;
> Effective communication of the results of the software development process (in both written and oral form)

When examined in relation to Anderson and Krathwohl's (2001) framework, these outcomes were coded as higher order outcomes such as applying, analysing, and evaluating conceptual, procedural and/or metacognitive knowledge.

The unit was taught using a project-based methodology. The projects which form the major assessment focus of the unit were informed by industry contacts, who provided input into developing authentic tasks for students to work on. There were also opportunities for students with a high Grade Point Average (2.75) to participate in an industry-based project.

4.2 Scaffolding

The unit was designed to scaffold and monitor students' progress in a range of ways. The seminars and lectures were structured to provide students with frameworks for making design decisions and synthesizing content from previous units. There were no workshops or tutorials and students arrange times for their teams to meet, either virtually or face-to-face. Therefore, it was seen by the convenor as important for students to be able to access resources as required by their project teams. There were resources available for just-in-time access in the online site including

- Mini-lectures and assigned readings on the foundations of software and systems engineering;
- Template reminders on how to prepare a project proposal and plan;
- A guide to undertaking an extended group project;
- Information on how to prepare intermediate and final project deliverables and progress reports.

In this unit, both the process of learning and the product of the project were seen as important. As described by the convenor during the interview:

> They need to learn the value of a process. In second year, they hear about this process a number of times, but each assignment they get in other units is just an individual thing and they don't need to think too much about it beforehand... They certainly wouldn't have to write everything down and get it reviewed and go through this whole process.

Formative feedback from teachers and peers was seen by the convenor as an important part of scaffolding towards expertise. Students were encouraged to post questions in the online discussion forum, so that all students could benefit from the answers provided by their peers or the unit convenor. The first assignment was designed to be submitted early in the semester to enable formative feedback to be given early to guide students' subsequent learning.

4.3 Assessment

The assessment was designed as cumulative over two semesters, targeting both the products developed incorporating the students' knowledge and the team processes, through

- Project planning documentation;
- Discussion forum contributions on issues around the software development process and teamwork;
- Personal blog to capture reflection on their own performance as a team member;
- Presentation of the interim and final reports ;
- Final examination.

The assessment was designed to focus attention on the process and the product, as the convenor described:

> I want them to see how to go from a problem in the real world to (producing a) technology-based solution to it in the end. The thing is that many of them don't (want to do this). There

are more people wanting to do the modeling, the design, the analysis part of it and not very many wanting or able to do the actual implementation. I think it's very important and I've certainly had feedback from students that it was valuable for them to see what the challenges were at the different phases, even if they didn't do the programming themselves.

Teams of four were allocated a question either based in an industry context or simulating an industry requirement. They worked to produce a series of interim reports on their plans and processes. They were also required to document their process in the reflective blog and contribute to the discussion forum. There was a presentation component and a final exam, as the convenor described:

> One of the final (exam) questions is always something along the lines of "You've applied for a job as a software engineer. You'll be required to work in a team. What can you say from your experience this year?" That can be worded in lots of different ways, but it is trying to get at what did they learn from this unit.

When the tasks were analysed against Samuelowicz and Bain's (2002) framework, they were coded as

> Assessing students' ability to reproduce structured knowledge and apply it to modified situations
> Assessing students ability to integrate, transform and use knowledge purposefully

Many of the convenor's comments suggested that she saw assessment as important in both rewarding effort and guiding students learning:

> I think from the students' point of view, we need to make use of (assessment as) an incentive for them to do the work and achieve the learning outcomes that we're after. We also have to assess whether they've achieved the learning outcomes so this is feedback to us and to them. It's a way of keeping track of how well they know what they should know...

The use of assessment as feedback for teaching practice was discussed during the interview, as illustrated by the comments above. The feedback comments and also student results were used in informing teaching practice to structure the unit and determine where gaps in student learning needed to be addressed.

Helping students' learning was also raised, in the context of providing timely feedback:

> They give (their work) to me on Friday and I give it back to them on Monday, because one (task) builds on the other. The whole thing is about learning a cycle, a learning a process. In software projects there're two parts to it. There's the process- what are we going to do, what standards are we going to follow, what document layouts and lifecycle methodology. And then there's the product to be delivered.

4.4 Technologies

The convenor's attitude that assessment and feedback were important in scaffolding student learning influenced her use of technologies in the unit. She used a range of tools including

> An online space where students could access supporting resources on project management, teamwork and report writing;
> A discussion forum for student collaboration during the projects. There were separate sections on project development and team issues;
> A reflective blog for capturing their individual learning journeys;
> Online submission of interim and final reports
> Online rubrics available for students from the beginning of the unit, which were used by the convenor to provide formative feedback.

These tools were used to scaffold students' progress during the learning process as well as to collect evidence of increasing expertise. The inclusion of online delivery of content such as guidelines for report writing and managing team issues were used in recognition of students' need for support while they worked on their projects. While not expressly focused on student learning, some provided efficiencies for students or the convenor, or both, such as online submission of assignments.

5 Case Study Two: Child Development

This unit was being piloted for a final year practicum subject to form a capstone for BEd and MTeach undergraduate programs in early childhood. The unit aimed to support students in integrating their prior learning as well as honing communication skills. The unit convenor realized that a specific problem needed to be addressed; the difficulty of providing timely and focused feedback on student learning. Early childhood students need to be able to develop responsive interaction skills with infants and young children (dyadic interactions) and are often dependent on feedback from others, for example their supervising teachers. Feedback from supervising teachers was often global rather than having a focus on specific details, making it difficult for the students to modify their own behaviour in response to feedback.

The solution was to design the curriculum with integrated assessment tasks to support students in evaluating their own performance by videoing and analyzing their own dyadic interactions.

5.1 Learning Outcomes

The learning outcomes focused on the honing of communication skills with children and parents, encouraging students to reflect on their own strengths and weaknesses. Specific capabilities were in critically evaluating dyadic interactions and applying procedures to their own practice;

examining the use of environment rating scales to consider how quality in child analyzing factors within urban environments that might enhance or inhibit dyadic interactions.

When analysed against Anderson et al., (2001) framework these outcomes were coded as applying, analyzing and evaluating concepts, procedures and/or metacognitive knowledge. During the interview, the convenor acknowledged the difficulty of assessing these higher order outcomes, and although she had redesigned the unit, higher order outcomes were still considered to be a challenge:

> I wanted a lot more procedural. I think the procedural and metacognitive are the areas where we don't really do enough of. It is hard. Even though nobody likes to go through the struggle, I think that it's also part of getting a degree. If it comes easily then it's not actually adding anything to what you know.

5.2 Scaffolding

The unit provided a practical opportunity for students to demonstrate and hone the skills they have learned in previous units. Scaffolding strategies included recapping on foundation principles addressed in earlier units and applying these to increasingly complex contexts. For example, in previous semesters students encountered the theory underpinning dyadic interactions and had read transcriptions with coding attached. At the beginning of this unit they could undertake training in how to analyse their own interactions with children. They initially practised coding the behaviour exhibited in animations (made using Xtranormal software (http://www.xtranormal.com/) to reduce complexity. Use of the coding scheme was demonstrated in class, with an online discussion thread available to support continued dialogue. There were also demonstrations on how to use the specific coding technology (NVivo) and the animations and coding schemes were available for students to practice. To support students in making links and to relevant information, a central space was available on the unit web site for access to related articles on theories and strategies linked to the coding of interactions.

The videos of student performance were seen as important in providing feedback during the learning process and supporting the development of self-regulatory learning skills (Butler & Winne, 1995). Students could critique their own performance, consider the contextual factors that compromise interactions and map the process of change. Feedback was available when the videos were shared with supervisors in the workplace or with the unit convenor.

Dialogue with the teacher and between students was seen by the convenor as an important part of scaffolding. The convenor has established a routine of virtual office hours, when she is available, usually twice per day, to respond to student queries and comment on discussions. During semester, the development of the portfolio of work was discussed at intervals. Students were reminded to collect evidence of activities during the unit which demonstrate their developing skills and knowledge, for example documents which may be of interest to potential employers and these were discussed online.

5.3 Assessment

A portfolio, complied by the students, of the evidence of their learning and reflections was used for assessment. It included

> Evidence of their reflections on their coding of dyadic interactions, both from the demonstration animation and their own practice;
> Examples of their use of the different environment rating scales, including ITERS and ECERS-R;
> Their reflections on a range of urban environments and the effects of factors enhancing or inhibiting dyadic interactions;
> An annotated bibliography, filed notes and recommendations, or information sheets for parents and staff about one of the three focus areas of the unit (dyadic interactions, environment rating scales or urban environments).

The convenor described having designed these tasks to overcome issues in earlier designs of the unit, for instance students' inability to analyse and evaluate articles:

> Part of the assessment was an annotated bibliography. Even though it was around describing research, I really wanted students to understand research because a lot of students, even the good students, said to me that their strategy is normally to cherry pick and build an argument around that. They (said) that the annotated bibliography made them think much more deeply about how research methods relate to the conclusions that researchers draw.

Based on these assessment tasks, her orientation toward assessment was coded as

> Assessing students' ability to reproduce information presented in lectures and textbooks
> Assessing students' ability to reproduce structured knowledge and apply it to modified situations
> Assessing students ability to integrate, transform and use knowledge purposefully

Some of her comments also reinforced this coding:

> It is good when you set an assignment; especially where students are saying that it's difficult and they're complaining about it; and then at the end they say "Now that I've been through the whole process I can see why it is important". I think that is rewarding.

When asked about her beliefs about the role of assessment, her comments were coded as rewarding effort and guiding students' learning:

> I think first and foremost it should help the student master the material, to come to terms with the material, deepen their knowledge and conceptual understanding. You can achieve everything else but if you're not achieving that then you're not doing it correctly. (Also) it should give the student some feedback about where they are in that unit; whether they should feel confident that they can build on that knowledge or that they should be revising that material before they move onto the next level.

Feedback was seen by the convenor as valuable in helping students learning and also challenging them:

> It's challenging them and helping them get to the new level. Also the thing that I think I often forget to do, is telling the students what they're doing well. It's easy to assume that they know what they're doing well but they probably don't.

Another example of this focus on challenging students' existing views was in her description of some of the attitudes they may bring to university:

> Often students will have a negative view. It might be about a particular ethnic group or people from a particular socio economic (background). (I) really want to get them to think about the goals of those parents; the different sort of beliefs of those parents and also to think about the different things that children bring to say a long daycare centre. Sometimes students can be very judgmental.

She provides individual feedback, which she acknowledges is possible with a small cohort size:

> What I try to do is to have a look at their responses and pick out areas that are strengths and weaknesses for a student who's not doing so well. So I can focus on (those gaps). It might be the theoretical parts of things where they're having difficulties.

She acknowledged that she found some difficulties with feedback on her students' learning:

> The thing that I find hard to get right in feedback, which I remember as a student, (is) if somebody probably very kindly wrote I need to be doing this, I always read it as [stern tone] "You need to be doing this".

5.4 Technologies

Technologies played an important role in capturing both the process and products in this unit and the convenor saw confidence in their technological literacy as valuable for students. A range of technologies were used, including

- An online space in the University LMS which provided access to readings and supporting resources such as the Xtranormal animations to demonstrate features of simple dyadic interactions;
- A discussion forum for communication between students and with the teacher;
- Video for students to capture examples of their own practice for their own analysis and for use by their teacher or supervisor in providing feedback;

NVivo 8 text analysis software, easy to use and freely available under the University license. Student used this tool to evaluate their own interactions;

An e-portfolio or portfolio where students could collect and present their folio of work using digital or paper-based means. Included were:

Notes and reflections
Images (if permitted)
Articles and student created annotated bibliographies
Documentation on interaction changes
Student reports for colleagues
Assessment guidelines and feedback rubrics
Student information for parents

While the technologies were used by many students, they could choose the extent to which they engaged with the tools. For those students preferring to use less technology, alternatives were provided such as manually coding descriptions of the behaviours and collecting print-based portfolios.

The unit's focus on collecting evidence of learning for transition purposes drove the selection of an e-portfolio to showcase students' work. The convenor's choice of these technologies also reflected her attitude toward the importance of feedback in the learning and assessment process. In addition to the artifacts, the portfolio captured students' learning journeys and sections were available for the supervisor in the workplace to provide feedback. The convenor used online rubrics to both guide students learning prior to the assessment tasks and afterwards to provide comments for future improvement.

6 Common Themes

Although they formed capstones for different disciplines, the units shared a focus on the late phase of acquisition according the VanLehn's (1996) categorization. Both of the convenors recognized the importance of building on foundations from previous units and challenging students' existing ideas as part of the process of mastery. In each unit the learning activities and the assessment strategies were designed to scaffold students' learning, especially in synthesizing discipline knowledge and honing graduate capabilities. The unit convenors each took a student-centred approach to designing the curriculum to guide students towards the next stage of their careers. Higher order learning processes as well as outcomes were designed into the curriculum and assessment of each unit.

The case studies demonstrated the use of a wide range of technologies to support learning and assessment. As suggested by the MAPLET framework from Chapter 3, there was intentional alignment between the higher order unit aims, processes designed to scaffold the learners toward expertise and technologies to capture both process and outcomes.

Between them, these case studies provide illustrations of technologies used to support the assessment of complex learning as typified in capstone units

Supporting the scaffolding of student learning regardless of the learning context or the time. Although capstones are designed to focus on more complex learning, students may require reminders about the foundation concepts or procedures they need to apply. Examples include the resources, housed on the unit LMS site, to guide students in planning their projects, formatting their final reports, resolving conflicts or negotiating within their teams. Rubrics for grading criteria were made available by both convenors early in the semester and used to provide feedback during the process.

Supporting socially constructed learning by providing a web-based space for dialogue in dispersed environments. Opportunities for dialogue with their peers can provide a forum for self explanations, to encourage verbalisation and active engagement in the examination of what is happening (Berardi-Coletta, Buyer, Dominowski, & Rellinger, 1995; Salmon, 2000). Examples included the use of the online discussion tool to provide a forum for communication between and across teams. The asynchronous nature of these tools can be especially helpful when students are working in industry-based contexts and may feel isolated from their teachers and peers. Students don't need to fit in with a predetermined schedule to discuss issues, ask questions or share ideas.

Chronicling the learning journey to make the metacognitive processes more explicit. Examples include the capturing of students' reflections in blogs or individual learning journals. Documenting the journey and the collaborative process can enable students to reflect on their learning, important for the development of metacognitive, self regulatory skills (Butler & Winne, 1995).

Storing learning artifacts in portfolios for storing and sharing assessment products. Examples include digital portfolios to house the various stages of the project for collecting formative feedback, or showcasing the final products for the marker, peers and potential employers. Compiling and sharing resources has the added benefit of enabling student to make explicit links between facts, concepts and ideas; a process which helps in establishing interrelated knowledge networks (Khalifa & Kwok, 1999)

While higher order outcomes may typically be the target of capstone units, students' confidence in lower order processes such as their ability to apply basic procedures as part of the development of expertise is also important. There is then scope to capture the journey on to higher order skills such as evaluation and meta-analysis. The framework demonstrates an inherent focus on the learning outcomes and the learning processes, both lower and higher order, as the drivers for decision-making rather than the technologies themselves.

7 Concluding Comments

These case studies formed part of a wider study into the relationship between intended learning outcomes, assessment strategies and technology uses. While they were not intended to form the basis of generalisable conclusions, they raise issues and challenges which will be explored in later phases of the study.

Among these is the recognition of the affordances of technologies to support the assessment of higher order learning. While technologies have typically been associated with the assessment of lower order outcomes or processes, the requirements of capstone can provide a catalyst for re-thinking this status quo. These final year units can provide opportunities for students to integrate the knowledge and skills they have acquired during their whole program, yet assessing this complex learning has proven a challenge for academics. The two case studies exemplify the use of a range of technologies which can be used to support the assessment of both process and outputs as students develop expertise.

Although they illustrate capstone units in particular, some of the uses may be relevant to complex learning in other units; reflecting the principles of curriculum alignment and authentic assessment. They also provide exemplars of the benefits of considering the technologies in the wider curriculum context; making decisions about what is required in the unit rather than how best to use the new tools. As illustrated by the case studies, however, the technologies need to be embedded in a curriculum designed to elicit higher order outcomes. This can not be provided by the technologies themselves and needs to be driven by academics' attitudes toward the learning outcomes they target and the role of assessment and feedback during the learning journey.

References

Anderson, L., Krathwohl, D., Airsasian, P., Cruikshank, K., Mayer, R., Pintrich, P., et al. (Eds.). (2001). *A taxonomy for learning, teaching and assessing: A revision of Bloom's taxonomy of educational objectives.* New York: Longman.

AQF, C. (2009). *Strengthening the AQF: A proposal.* Retrieved June 2, 2009, from http://www.aqf.edu.au/pdf/Strengthening%20the%20AQF%20Consultation%20Paper.pdf

Astleitner, H. (2002). Teaching critical thinking online. *Journal of Instructional Psychology, 29*(2), 53–75.

Bath, D., Smith, C., Stein, S., & Swann, R. (2004). Beyond mapping and embedding graduate attributes: bringing together quality assurance and action learning to create a validated and living curriculum. *Higher Education Research and Development, 23*(3), 313–328.

Berardi-Coletta, B., Buyer, L. S., Dominowski, R. L., & Rellinger, E. R. (1995). Metacognition and problem solving: A process-oriented approach. *Journal of Experimental Psychology: Learning, Memory and Cognition, 21*(1), 205–233.

Biggs, J. (2003). Teaching for Quality Learning at University (2nd Ed). London: Open University Press.

Bloom, B. S. (Ed.). (1956). *Taxonomy of educational objectives: The classification of educational goals.* New York: McKay.

Boulos, M. K., Maramba, I., & Wheeler, S. (2006). Wikis, blogs and podcasts: A new generation of Web-based tools for virtual collaborative clinical practice and education. *BMC Medical Education, 6*(41).

Bryan, C., & Clegg, K. (Eds.). (2006). *Innovative assessment in higher education.* Abington: Routledge

Burns, M. (2006). Tools for the mind. *Educational Leadership, 63*(4), 48–53.

Butler, D. L., & Winne, P. H. (1995). Feedback and self regulated learning: A theoretical synthesis. *Review of Educational Research, 65*(3), 245–281.

Byrnes, R., & Ellis, A. (2006). The prevalence and characteristics of online assessment in Australian universities. *Australasian Journal of Educational Technology, 22*(1), 104–125.

Churchill, D. (2007). *Blogs, other Web 2.0 technologies and possibilities for educational applications.* Paper presented at the 4th international conference on Informatics, Educational Technology and New Media, Sombor, Serbia, March/April, 2007.

Clarkson, B., & Brook, C. (2007). Achieving synergies through generic skills: A strength of online communities. *Australasian Journal of Educational Technology, 23*(4), 248–268.

Collier, P. (2000). The effects of completing a capstone course on student identity. *Sociology of Education, 73*(4), 285–299.

Creswell, J., & Piano Clark, V. (2007). *Designing and conducting mixed methods research.* Thousand Oaks, CA: Sage.

Crisp, G. (2007). *The e-assessment handbook.* New York: Continuum International.

Dunlap, J. C. (2005). Problem-based learning and self-efficacy: How a capstone course prepares students for a profession. *Educational Technology, Research and Development, 53*(1), 65–85.

Ellis, R. A., & Goodyear, P. (2010). *Students' experiences of e-learning in higher education: The ecology of sustainable innovation.* New York: Routledge.

Gardiner, J. (1999). *The senior year experience* (Vol. March/April 1999). San Francisco: Jossey-Bass.

Hewitt, J., & Peters, V. (2006, June 2006). *Using wikis to support knowledge building in a graduate education course.* Paper presented at the World Conference on Educational Multimedia, Hypermedia and Telecommunications (EDMEDIA) 2006 Chesapeake, VA.

Humphrey Brown, A., & Benson, B. (2005). Making sense of the capstone process: reflection from the front line. *Education, 125*(4), 674–692.

Jonassen, D. H., & Campbell, J. P. (1994). Learning with media: Restructuring the debate. *Educational Technology Research and Development, 42*(2), 31–39.

Jonassen, D. H., & Reeves, T. (Eds.). (1996). *Learning with technology: Using computers as cognitive tools.* New York: Macmillan.

Khalifa, M., & Kwok, R. C.-W. (1999). Remote learning technologies: Effectiveness of hypertext and GSS. *Decision Support Systems, 26*(3), 195–207.

McNeill, M., Gosper, M., & Hedberg, J. (2008). *Engaging students with higher order learning (or not): insights into academic practice.* Paper presented at the ATN Assessment Conference, Adelaide, South Australia. November, 2008

Nicol, D. J., & Milligan, C. (2006). Rethinking technology-supported assessment in terms of the seven principles of good feedback practice. In C. Bryan & K. Clegg (Ed.), *Innovative assessment in higher education.* London: Taylor and Francis Group.

Northcote, M. (2003). Online assessment in higher education: The influence of pedagogy on the construction of students' epistemologies. *Issues In Educational Research, 13.* pp. 66–84

Philips, R., & Lowe, K. (2003). *Issues associated with the equivalence of traditional and online assessment.* Paper presented at the 20th Annual Conference of ACSILITE: Interact, Integrate, Impact, Adelaide, South Australia, December, 2003

Race, P. (2001). *The lecturer's toolkit: A practical guide to learning, teaching and assessment.* London: Kogan Page.

Race, P. (2006). *The Lecturer's Toolkit* (3rd ed.). London: Routledge.

Salmon, G. (2000). *E-moderating: The key to teaching and learning online* (pp. 22–35). London: Kogan Page.

Samuelowicz, K., & Bain, J. (2002). Identifying academics' orientations to assessment practice. *Higher Education Research and Development, 43*, 173–201.

Shephard, K. (2009). E is for exploration: Assessing hard-to-measure learning outcomes. *British Journal of Educational Technology, 40*(2), 386–398.

Stephenson, J., & Yorke, M. (Eds.). (1998). *Capability and quality in higher education*. London: Kogan Page.
van Gog, T., Paas, F., & van Merriënboer, J. (2004). Process-oriented worked examples: improving transfer performance through enhanced understanding *Journal Instructional Science, 32*(1), 83–98.
VanLehn, K. (1996). Cognitive skill acquisition. *Annual Review of Psychology, 47*, 513–539.
Williams, D. (1999). Transitions: managing personal and organisational change. *ACDM Newsletter*.
Williams, J. (2006). The place of the closed book, invigilated final examination in a knowledge economy. *Educational Media International*, 43(2), 107–119.
Zemsky, R., & Massey, W. (2004). Why the e-learning boom went bust. *The Chronicle of Higher Education, 50*(44), B6–B8.

Chapter 14
Text-Guided Automated Self Assessment

A Graph-Based Approach to Help Learners with Ongoing Writing

Pablo Pirnay-Dummer and Dirk Ifenthaler

Abstract Writing plays an important role in institutionalized learning environments. However, it has to be monitored in several ways in order to be successful. We developed automated knowledge assessment tools which allow us to produce instant feedback on a text during the writing process in order to promote self-regulated writing skills. The tools may serve as a complement to human tutoring approaches in learning settings in which individual face-to-face coaching is not possible. To generate text feedback, we used natural language oriented knowledge assessment strategies based on mental model theory and graph theory. Different types of text feedback are then automatically created on the basis of graphs and presented to the learner both for reflection and preflection. So far, we have succeeded in implementing the crucial parts of the coaching into computer-based technology as well as developing and implementing both static and dynamic feedback. Hence, a study of a text-guided assessment tool is presented and discussed. Finally, limitations on the volitional level of the toolset will have to be addressed in future studies.

Keywords Self-assessment · Writing · Automated online-coaching · Learning progression · Feedback · Reflection · Preflection

1 Introduction

Writing plays an important role in institutionalized learning environments such as schools and universities. Writing is not merely a strategy for externalizing and fixing our current knowledge and sharing it with other learners; writing also leads to the reorganization and continual [re-]construction of knowledge (Eigler, 2005). Previous inquiry into the writing process itself (e.g. Graham & Dolores, 2007; Haswell, 2008; Lavelle & Zuercher, 2001; Rose, 1985; Taylor & Beach, 1984)

P. Pirnay-Dummer (✉)
Albert-Ludwigs-University Freiburg, Rempartstr. 11, Freiburg 79098, Germany
e-mail: pablo.dummer@ezw.uni-freiburg.de

and into its technological issues (e.g. Cho & Schunn, 2007; Glaser & Brunstein, 2008; Kintsch, Steinhart, & Stahl, 2000) has been broad and interdisciplinary. Flower and Hayes (1981) described the foundation for a cognitive process theory of writing and divided the writing process into three main stages: *planning*, *translating*, and *reviewing*. Additionally, the learner has to monitor all three steps in order to reflect on them and improve competence in one or more of these three areas.

Automated knowledge assessment tools allow us to produce instant feedback on semantic and structural aspects of the text at all times during the writing process. Such dynamic and timely feedback can promote a learner's self-regulated writing skills. While this supporting strategy has already been shown to be successful in a pilot study, we present a study which evaluates the prototype of a new tool, TASA (*T*ext-Guided *A*utomated *S*elf *A*ssessment). TASA was developed on the basis of our prior experiences with face-to-face coaching.

2 From Coaching to Self-Assessment

Face-to-face coaching, like that performed in a previous study (reference required here), is not always possible due to a lack of time or expertise or other constraints. As a result, self-assessment is a frequently used alternative (Boud, 1995). The idea of self-assessment is to give students tools which enable them to monitor their own progress during learning without a human supervisor (e.g. Chan & Lam, 2010; Fetterman, Kaftarian, & Wandersman, 1996; Koedinger & Aleven, 2007). If the tools are sophisticated and based on sound theoretical foundations, they may serve as a good complement to human coaching and feedback. Based on our previous research and development with regard to analyzing text (include references here), we further developed our work to include on-demand, online automated feedback to learners This new software is called TASA (Text-guided Automated Self-Assessment).

3 TASA: Text-Guided Automated Self-Assessment

TASA is a Web-based online tool for self assessment. It embeds parts of T-MITOCAR (Text Model Inspection Trace of Concepts and Relations; Pirnay-Dummer & Ifenthaler, 2010) which are necessary to generate a graph from the user's text directly after the upload. It is based on mental model theory (Seel, 2003). The uploaded text provides the user with an association net in a format which non-experts have been shown to be able to interpret (see Figs. 14.1 and 14.2). Additionally, TASA serves both as a reflection and a preflection tool for the user.

14 Text-Guided Automated Self Assessment

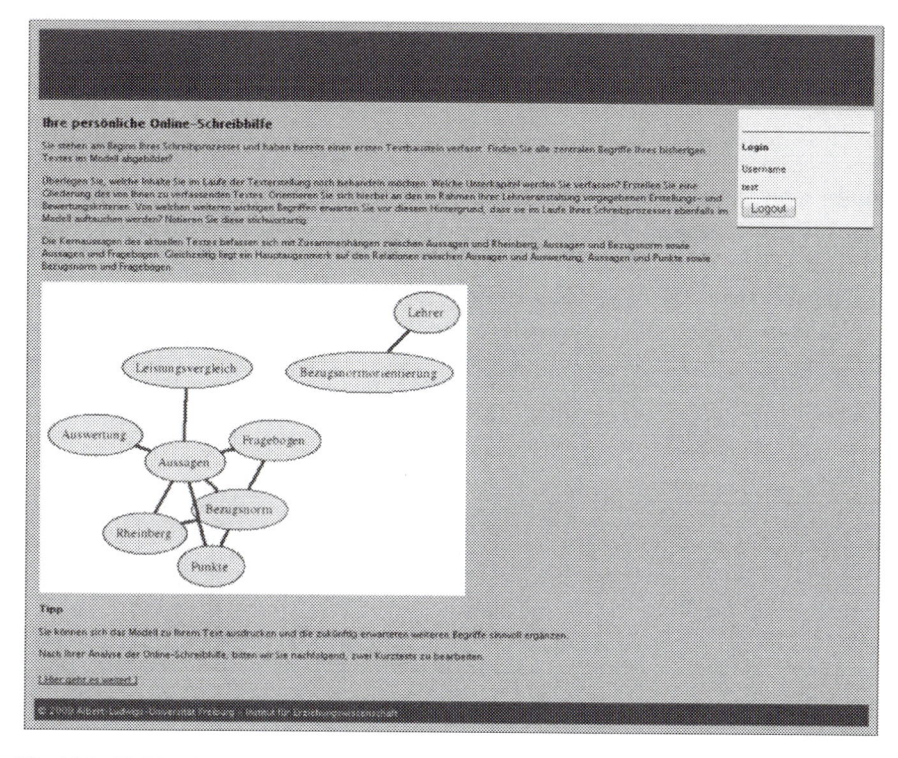

Fig. 14.1 TASA reflection output, including dynamic written text and graphical representation

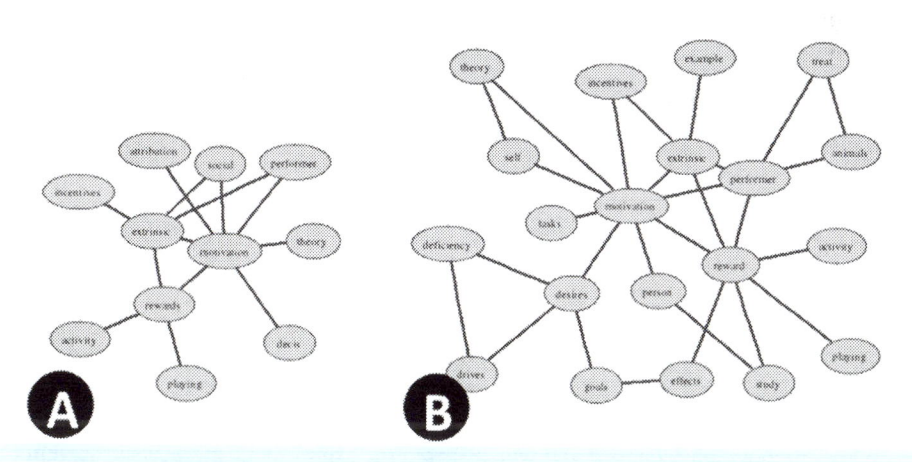

Fig. 14.2 Two models from two different time points from a text on motivation (TASA Output)

3.1 Reflection

After the upload is finished, the users receive written feedback on the text. The text provides information on the key concepts, the ways in which they are connected, and concepts and connections which may be circumstantial but still have some significance for the meaning of the text. TASA uses information from the T-MITOCAR graph to generate this feedback. TASA's reflection screen can be seen in Fig. 14.1.

To generate the feedback text, additional information is taken from the graph – namely the associative strengths between links, which are integral parts of the T-MITOCAR text-to-graph representation process. If the graphs are intended for research, this information is usually noted on the links, and the color of the links resembles the degree of pairwise association. If the output is intended as feedback for learners, then this information is left out in order to minimize extraneous cognitive load for learners. Association link strength information is used to cluster the links in preparation for text output. Links with stronger associations are considered first. The ranked list is split into sets of three propositions. The last two sets vary between two and four propositions, depending on the overall number of links. For the first set an initial phrase is selected randomly from the database in order to embed the propositions in a natural language sentence as follows:

1. Initial phrase from database: *Your text focuses on the relations between* $P_{1,2,3}$.
2. Propositions ($P_{1,2,3}$): *{painting, art, color}*
3. Resulting feedback sentence: Your *text focuses on the relations between painting, art, and color.*

    There is a set of phrases for starting the feedback and another set which continues the feedback on the following subsequent sets of any $P_{a,b,c}$, e.g.
4. Continuing phrase from database: *Moreover, the text also concentrates on* $P_{a,b,c}$.
5. Propositions ($P_{4,5,6}$): *{oil, canvas, texture}*
6. Resulting feedback sentence: *Moreover, the text also concentrates on oil, canvas, and texture.*

The concepts involved in the propositions in the text will be listed and the last one will be connected by "and." Afterwards, they are input into the randomly selected initial (1–3) and continuing phrases (4–6). Thus, the TASA-generated text is different every time the user gets more feedback (another round/week). The feedback is composed of the current model of the users' text and the available phrases. If there are less than four significant propositions in the model then only the initial phrase is used. Figure 14.2 shows an example of the same text at different time points. Which propositions changed and which stayed the same can be more easily seen in Fig. 14.4.

As we mentioned before, there is also feedback on the progress from the second time point on. To generate this feedback on the basis of two compared models, the software considers three additionally available graphs:

14 Text-Guided Automated Self Assessment

1. The intersection set model. This model contains all propositions which have not changed in the underlying model since the last text upload.
2. The left-out difference model. This graph contains all propositions which were in the last model but are no longer part of the current graph.
3. The new difference model. This model contains all propositions which have been added since the last upload.

Like in the single model description, the text feedback is constructed of randomly selected phrases and sets of propositions. From the three models, the learner receives feedback on what has changed and on what has remained the same since the last upload. Figure 14.3 shows the whole process, from graph information and phrases to model-based text feedback.

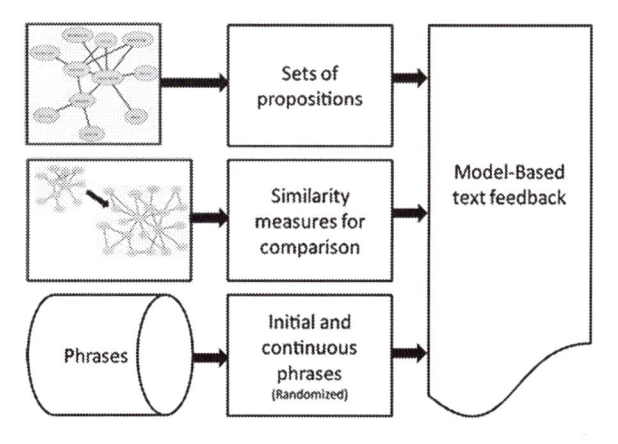

Fig. 14.3 TASA's text feedback composition modules – from graphs and phrases to text

Additionally, any changes in model properties are also part of the feedback. The model may have changed in three ways since the last upload. It may have (1) the same amount, (2) more, or (3) less propositions. If the current text has more words and its model contains fewer propositions then the current text is usually more concise. This usually happens when the learners invest time to revise, edit, and redact the text. If the text also has more words and there are more propositions then this is a good indicator for more broadness. In most cases this happens when new sections or chapters on new content are introduced. The level of conciseness and broadness is considered to be constant if the amount of propositions does not change between two models. This may happen even if a change in the model is visible, such as when the learners think about and change their terminology. Figure 14.4 shows the intersection and difference models from the example provided in Fig. 14.2.

We changed the feedback in the course of the coaching sessions from text-only feedback to text plus graphical feedback. In the latter case, the user is presented with an image of the graph. Otherwise he or she would only get the text feedback (which is provided at every session). From the second time point on, the user interacts with

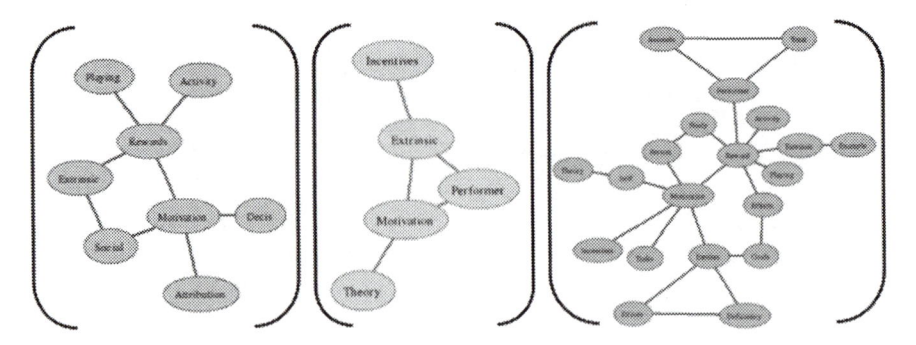

Fig. 14.4 Three different set models as derived from the graph in Fig. 14.2 (TASA Output)

the system and also receives feedback on what has changed since the last upload. Additionally, TASA tracks the time the user has already spent using the system and generates general prompts from this information. The general prompts were selected from the pieces of advice provided most frequently during the face-to-face coaching sessions.

3.2 Preflection

If there is a group of learners which is working on the same task or topic, TASA may also be used as a preflection tool. Preflection has the notion that learners can plan their actions based on what they have already done and know the overall task or goal to be accomplished. Most often, preflection is an unexplored of learner decision making. The general hypothesis is that learners who are better skilled in preflection (i.e., better able to select appropriate tasks) will make faster progress toward mastering overall learning goals (include a reference for this). Once all members of the group have uploaded their text, TASA generates a list of the most common terms from all texts throughout the group. TASA uses the T-MITOCAR modules to generate the list. As a first step, the group model is reconstructed once all of the texts are uploaded and available. As a prerequisite to compute such a model, T-MITOCAR needs to find the list of the most frequent terms. Stemming is used to select the base word so as to prevent multiple entries of unnecessary terms due to variations within the text (e.g., chair, chairs). After the stemming has been completed, the frequency list can be obtained. To present the users real words instead of sometimes weird-looking word stems, the most frequent inflexion of the stem is used to create the list. The learners are then asked which five terms from the whole list they would like to have in their underlying model when they upload their work the next time. The users select from a list of 30 terms. In this way, each user can benefit from the other learners' conceptions.

4 Evaluation of Learning Progression Within the TASA Environment

Since changes in learning and thinking take place continuously, educational research needs to move beyond the traditional two-wave design in order to capture these changes more precisely (Willett, 1988). It is therefore necessary to conduct multiwave longitudinal experiments when complex changes over time are of central interest (Ifenthaler, 2008; Ifenthaler & Seel, 2005). Accordingly, in an initial study we evaluated the estimated learning progression within the TASA environment. Subsequent to each reflection and preflection phase, we had the participants fill in an abridged version of HILVE (Heidelberg Inventory for Course Evaluation; see Rindermann & Amelang, 1994) in order to determine the effectiveness of the automated coaching. The following section describes the methodology and results of the study and discusses the findings.

4.1 Method

Forty students (29 female and 11 male) participated in the study. Their average age was 22.6 years ($SD = 2.5$). The automated coaching was realized as a design experiment, fully embedded in a learning environment. It took place in two undergraduate courses. A written research paper was the major assignment of the courses.

The longitudinal research design was realized in the final 5 weeks of the semester. Each week participants uploaded parts of their research paper in progress. All participants received automated feedback (TASA reflection) and were asked to complete the TASA preflection feature. Subsequent to each coaching session, we had participants fill in an abridged version of HILVE (Rindermann & Amelang, 1994) in order to determine the effectiveness of the teaching. HILVE is a standardized questionnaire for the evaluation of courses that is divided into 14 dimensions (Cronbach's alpha $r = 0.74$ to $r = 0.88$). Each dimension consists of two to four items. The abridged version of HILVE applied in the present study included eight items which were combined as one factor: *effectiveness of learning*. In weeks 1, 3, and 5 the graph was embedded into the feedback. In the remaining cases (2 and 4) we only provided the feedback text in order to see if it made a difference whether the model graph was available to the learner or not.

4.2 Results

We computed a repeated-measure MANOVA with the *effectiveness of learning* at five measurement points as a within-subjects factor. The sphericity assumption was not met ($\chi^2(9) = 36.193$, $p < 0.001$), so the Greenhouse-Geisser correction was applied. The difference between the measurements was significant,

Table 14.1 Means and standard deviations of effectiveness of learning for the five measurement points ($N = 40$)

	M	SD
MP 1	3.69	1.12
MP 2	3.17	1.07
MP 3	2.92	1.06
MP 4	2.72	0.93
MP 5	2.60	0.80

$F(2.67, 104.69) = 17.50$, $p < 0.001$, $\eta^2 = 0.310$. Table 14.1 shows the means and standard deviations of the five measurement points.

4.3 Discussion

The main purpose of our initial study was to determine the effectiveness of the automated coaching of TASA. Participants rated the effectiveness of learning after each of the five coaching sessions on eight abridged items of the HILVE. Our results indicate that the TASA tools' effectiveness decreased during the 5 weeks of our design experiment. There are several possible explanations for this. One explanation is that the participant's motivation might have dropped during the 5 weeks. Additionally, we assume that the pressure caused by other course requirements also had a negative effect on the evaluation of the effectiveness of learning. In a follow-up study we will test the participants' achievement motivation using the short version of the LMI-K (Leistungsmotivationsinventar; achievement motivation inventory). Schuler and Prochaska (2001) report high reliability scores for the LMI-K (Cronbach's alpha $= 0.94$). Therefore, this test should fit in well with our future research design.

5 Conclusion

It is a long way from face-to-face coaching to automated tools of self-assessment – and this is clearly no surprise. So far, we have succeeded in implementing the crucial parts of the coaching into computer-based technology. We were able to develop and implement both static and dynamic feedback. The main limitations so far are on the volitional level. We will concentrate our future studies on this aspect and also consider several covariates on the learners' side. With the additional data at hand, we should be able to make the tool more stimulating. TASA is applicable to any learning task which involves writing. It may be used for short writing assignments. However, its strength clearly unfolds in long-term writing assignments, in which the students may continuously monitor their own progress and make their own decisions when using both the reflection and the preflection tools.

References

Boud, D. (1995). *Enhancing learning through self assessment*. London: Kogan Page.
Chan, J. C. Y., & Lam, S.-F. (2010). Effects of different evaluative feedback on students' self-efficacy in learning. *Learning and Instruction, 38*, 37–58.
Cho, K., & Schunn, C. D. (2007). Scaffolded writing and rewriting in the discipline: A web-based reciprocal peer review system. *Computers and Education, 48*(3), 409–426.
Eigler, G. (2005). Textproduzieren als Wissensnutzungs- und Wissenserwerbsstrategie. In H. Mandl & H. F. Friedrich (Eds.), *Handbuch Lernstrategien* (pp. 187–205). Göttingen: Hogrefe.
Fetterman, D. M., Kaftarian, S. J., & Wandersman, A. (1996). *Empowerment evaluation knowledge and tools for self-assessment & accountability*. Thousand Oaks, CA: Sage.
Flower, L., & Hayes, J. R. (1981). A cognitive process theory of writing. *College Composition and Communication, 32*(4), 365–387.
Glaser, C., & Brunstein, J. C. (2008). Förderung selbstregulierten Schreibens. In W. Schneider & M. Hasselhorn (Eds.), *Handbuch der Pädagogischen Psychologie* (pp. 371–380). Göttingen: Hogrefe.
Graham, S., & Dolores, P. (2007). A meta-analysis of writing instruction for adolescent students. *Journal of Educational Psychology, 99*(3), 445–476.
Haswell, R. H. (2008). Teaching of writing in higher education. In C. Bazerman (Ed.), *Handbook of research on writing. History, society, school, individual, text* (pp. 331–346). New York: Lawrence Erlbaum.
Ifenthaler, D. (2008). Practical solutions for the diagnosis of progressing mental models. In D. Ifenthaler, P. Pirnay-Dummer, & J. M. Spector (Eds.), *Understanding models for learning and instruction. Essays in honor of Norbert M. Seel* (pp. 43–61). New York: Springer.
Ifenthaler, D., & Seel, N. M. (2005). The measurement of change: Learning-dependent progression of mental models. *Technology, Instruction, Cognition and Learning, 2*(4), 317–336.
Kintsch, E., Steinhart, D., & Stahl, G. (2000). Developing summarization skills through the use of LSA-based feedback. *Interactive Learning Environments, 8*(2), 87–109.
Koedinger, K. R., & Aleven, V. (2007). Exploring the assistance dilemma in experiments with cognitive tutors. *Educational Psychology Review, 19*(3), 239–264.
Lavelle, E., & Zuercher, N. (2001). The writing approaches of university students. *Higher Education, 42*(3), 373–391.
Pirnay-Dummer, P., & Ifenthaler, D. (2010). Automated knowledge visualization and assessment. In D. Ifenthaler, P. Pirnay-Dummer & N. M. Seel (Eds.), *Computer-based diagnostics and systematic analysis of knowledge* (pp. 77–115). New York: Springer.
Rindermann, H., & Amelang, M. (1994). *Das Heidelberger Inventar zur Lehrveranstaltungs-Evaluation (HILVE). Handanweisung*. Heidelberg: Asanger.
Rose, M. (1985). The language of exclusion: Writing instruction at the university. *College English, 47*(4), 341–359.
Schuler, H., & Prochaska, M. (2001). *Leistungsmotivationsinventar*. Göttingen: Hogrefe.
Seel, N. M. (2003). Model-centered learning and instruction. *Technology, Instruction, Cognition and Learning, 1*(1), 59–85.
Taylor, B. M., & Beach, R. W. (1984). The effects of text structure instruction on middle grade students' comprehension and production of expository text. *Reading Research Quarterly, 68*, 277–321.
Willett, J. B. (1988). Questions and answers in the measurement of change. *Review of Research in Education, 15*, 345–422.

Part IV
Schooling and Teaching Perspectives

Chapter 15
Comparing the Impact of Electronic Performance Support and Web-Based Training

James D. Klein and Frank Nguyen

Abstract This paper reports on a study conducted to examine the effect of an electronic performance support system (EPSS) and web-based training (WBT) on user performance and attitudes, use of EPSS, and time on task. Employees from several different multi-national companies completed a tax preparation procedure using an EPSS, a WBT course, or a combination of the two interventions. Findings revealed performance scores for participants receiving the EPSS-only and those receiving EPSS and WBT were significantly higher than scores for participants who received the WBT-only. Attitudes for the two groups receiving performance support were also significantly higher than attitudes for the training-only condition. Results also indicated a positive correlation between performance and use of the EPSS. Findings further showed that WBT-only users spent significantly more time completing the task than their counterparts in other treatment groups leading to a negative correlation between time on task and performance. Implications for the design and implementation of electronic performance support and web-based training interventions are provided.

Keywords Performance interventions · Electronic performance Support · Web-based training

1 Introduction

As a result of the tremendous time and monetary costs that can be incurred with formal training, learning organizations have increasingly searched for ways to reduce expenditures and to minimize the time users spend away from their job. The advent of the Internet has led to the introduction of new digital tools such as e-Learning, podcasting, and virtual classrooms. While these technologies can help reduce the

---

J.D. Klein (✉)
Arizona State University, Payne Hall 302/Box 0611, Tempe, AZ 85287-0611, USA
e-mail: james.klein@asu.edu

D. Ifenthaler et al. (eds.), *Multiple Perspectives on Problem Solving and Learning in the Digital Age*, DOI 10.1007/978-1-4419-7612-3_15,
© Springer Science+Business Media, LLC 2011

overall cost of training by eliminating travel, classroom facilities, and even the instructor, they still require employees to take time away from their job to participate in training for hours, days, or even weeks.

Another technology has emerged to address these persistent costs: electronic performance support systems (EPSS). EPSS provides users with 'individualized on-line access to the full range of...systems to permit job performance' (Gery, 1991, p. 21). In other words, EPSS can provide users with the information and tools that they require to do their job, on the job. This capability has led many performance technologists to pursue EPSS in the hope of reducing or eliminating the costs of attending in-class and online training.

To guide performance technologists pursuing the adoption of EPSS, it is important to examine what is currently known about these systems. Although EPSS has been discussed for almost two decades, very few empirical studies have been conducted to measure its effectiveness. The literature can be divided into two distinct areas: theoretical beliefs about EPSS and research on EPSS. Below we discuss both these areas.

In 1995, Gery theorized a widely adopted classification scheme for EPSS. She asserted that performance support systems fall into one of three categories: external, extrinsic and intrinsic support. External systems store content used to support task performance in an external database. This content is not integrated within a user's work interface. As a result, users are forced to manually locate relevant information in an external EPSS. Common examples of external performance support systems include search engines, frequently asked question pages, and help indexes. In addition, external performance support 'may or may not be computer mediated' (Gery, 1995, p. 53).

Extrinsic performance support 'is integrated with the system, but is not in the primary workspace' (Gery, 1995, p. 51). In other words, extrinsic systems integrate with the user's work interface in such a way that the EPSS can identify their location in a system or even the exact task that they may be working on. With this contextual information, the extrinsic system can intelligently locate content that may be relevant to support the task at hand. Like external performance support systems, though, the content used to support a task is external to the work interface.

In contrast, intrinsic systems provide users with task support that is incorporated directly within their work interface. Due to this direct integration with the interface, Gery asserted that intrinsic EPSS provides 'performance support that is inherent to the system itself. It's so well integrated that, to workers, it's part of the system' (Gery, 1995, p. 51). Under this rather broad definition, examples of intrinsic performance support systems can range from tools that automate tasks and processes, user-centered design of work interfaces to reduce complexity and improve usability, or embedded knowledge that is displayed directly in a work interface.

Some authors have theorized that highly integrated intrinsic performance support systems are better than those that are disconnected from the user's work interface. Carroll and Rosson (1987) argued that novice users who require the most support are least inclined to use non-integrated support systems. Raybould (2000) contended that 'as support moves further from the tool, it becomes less powerful and more expensive to use' (p. 34). Based on these assumptions, Gery (1995) provided designers with the guideline that 80% of support systems should be intrinsic, 10% extrinsic, and the remaining 10% external. However, almost no empirical data have been collected to validate this heuristic.

Nguyen (2006) theorized that the decision to choose a type of EPSS to address a performance problem should vary depending on the expertise of the user. He suggested that while all performers would likely benefit from highly integrated EPSS, more experienced users and experts could likely cope with the challenges presented by non-integrated systems. He further speculated that using their prior knowledge, experts could more easily locate content in external system such as search engines or frequently asked questions than a novice. As a result, while 'more integrated types of EPSS such as intrinsic and extrinsic would likely have a positive effect on the performance of experts, the increase may not be as dramatic as that seen in novice users' (Nguyen, 2006, p. 11).

In addition, Laffey (1995) theorized that in the future, 'performance support systems will be tailored to the work environment...dynamic in their knowledge and expertise' (p. 34). In other words, continually evolving technology will offer ways for performance support systems to recognize the user, identify what they are doing, and adapt content based on their requirements.

While literature does exist to help us understand the types of performance support systems that are possible, it is largely based on the beliefs and opinions of individual authors. Few of the aforementioned suppositions have been empirically tested. Below we review some of the research-based findings related to EPSS.

A few studies have been conducted to validate the notion that implementing performance support can significantly improve user performance. Hunt, Haynes, Hanna, and Smith (1998) reviewed studies on the use of clinical decision support systems in the medical field. Results indicated that user performance improved in 42 of the studies reviewed, was not significantly changed in 19 cases, and decreased in only 7 instances. Furthermore, Nguyen, Klein, and Sullivan (2005) examined the most effective types of performance support systems by testing three different types that aligned with Gery's intrinsic, extrinsic, and external EPSS categories. Results from their study indicated that users provided with extrinsic and intrinsic performance support systems performed significantly better on a software procedure compared to a control group with no EPSS. In addition, all users provided with an EPSS had significantly more positive attitudes than the control group.

A few case studies have demonstrated that EPSS can be applied to wide range of settings and performance problems. Brush, Knapczyk, and Hubbard (1993) developed a performance support system to improve collaboration among teachers in rural communities. Dorsey, Goodrum, and Schwen (1993) applied performance support systems to support sales employees. Huber, Lippincott, McMahon, and

Witt (1999) provided three examples of how intrinsic, extrinsic, and external EPSS were applied to automobile manufacturing, insurance, and civil engineering. Kasvi and Vartiainen (2000) demonstrated four different ways EPSS were employed for use in factories. In addition, a survey conducted by McManus and Rossett (2006) showed that performance technologists have applied EPSS to problems ranging from vessel tracking in the United States Coast Guard to coaching restaurant managers.

In addition to the performance support systems that have been used in the past, Nguyen (2005) examined the types of EPSS that users may want in the future. Results revealed the most highly rated performance support systems were those that are aware of a user's job role or location in a software system and are then able to deliver appropriate information. External performance support systems that rely on visuals to navigate to support content, such as equipment diagrams or business processes, were also rated highly.

In summary, performance technologists can take some comfort that a few performance support systems have been empirically tested. Some case studies have also demonstrated that EPSS can be applied to many different settings, and that integrated support systems tend to be better than those that require users to search for information.

While these results are important, they do not answer some of the most basic questions that we face when choosing to design and implement a performance support system. For example, one of the most widely held notions about EPSS is that implementing such on-the-job support can reduce or even eliminate the amount of training that is necessary to address a performance problem. This notion of reducing training through EPSS and enabling day-one performance has been a major attraction for performance technologists.

Two previous studies that attempted to validate this assumption have produced conflicting results. Bastiaens, Nijhof, Stremer, and Abma (1997) explored the effectiveness of different combinations of computer-based and paper-based performance support with computer-based and instructor-led training. The researchers conducted a study with insurance agents and separated them into five treatment groups: software tool with computer-based training (the EPSS treatment), software tool with instructor-led training, software tool with no support, paper-based form with manuals, and paper-based form with instructor-led training. They found that the users preferred the paper-based forms over the electronic software tool as well as the instructor-led training over computer-based training. They did not find significant differences on test achievement scores, performance, or sales results over a 1 year period.

Mao and Brown (2005) also examined the difference between EPSS and training. These researchers provided one group of novice database users with 1 h of instructor-led training on topics ranging from tables, queries, forms, and reports. Another treatment group was provided with a wizard-type EPSS that could be configured either as an intrinsic system intelligently providing content to users as they performed tasks or as an external system presenting content only when searched for. Users then completed self-paced practice activities where they attempted 'exercises to be completed with the help of the EPSS (Mao & Brown, 2005, p. 35). Results indicated that users provided with the EPSS performed significantly better on an achievement test than those provided with training. A significant difference between the two groups on a procedural task was not found.

Thus, research examining the intersection between training and performance support systems yields few clear and satisfying answers. In addition, research conducted to date has produced conflicting results. The lack of concrete information on the relationship between performance support and training is problematic to performance technologists, instructional designers, and trainers. Furthermore, no evidence-based guidelines can currently be offered on how to best combine performance support and training to maximize user performance.

2 Purpose

The current study examined the effect of implementing EPSS, web-based training, and a combination of these two performance interventions. It has been assumed that implementing performance support alone is preferable to a training intervention. In fact, some have asserted that it may be possible to abandon training altogether when a performance support system is properly implemented. The researchers sought to challenge these assumptions by addressing the following three research questions: (1) What combination of performance support and training maximizes user performance? (2) What combination of performance support and training do users prefer? (3) What combination of performance support and training minimizes the time to complete a task?

3 Method

3.1 Participants

Seventy-eight employees from various multi-national companies completed the study. Some participants were identified by their direct managers. Additional volunteers for the study were also solicited from the American Society for Training & Development (ASTD) and the International Society for Performance Improvement (ISPI). Participants involved in the study represented a broad array of educational backgrounds: 39 obtained a masters degree, 28 held a bachelors degree, six obtained a doctoral degree, three were high school graduates, and two held an associates degree. The participants represented a diverse range of job roles: 33 were involved in the education and training industry, 16 identified themselves as software developers or IT professionals, 15 were in human resources, six were involved in manufacturing, three worked in customer service, and five worked in other professions.

3.2 Materials

Materials in this study included a task software application, web-based training course, performance support system, task scenario, and pre-task demographic survey.

A web-based software application based on a corporate tax return form was used by all participants in the study. As part of the process to submit a tax return, companies are required to submit data regarding revenue, profit, costs, and other financial information. While these data are typically recorded on paper-based forms, participants in this study were asked to record data and calculations into an online tax form. The tax software application included a series of open text fields that required the participant to input relevant data using information provided in the task scenario. In total, the corporate tax scenario required 58 participant inputs. Data entered into the tax software application were stored in an isolated database for analysis at the conclusion of the study.

In addition to the tax form, a web-based training course was used to teach processes, procedures, and principles that are required as part of the corporate tax preparation task. If the participants were assigned to the WBT-only or WBT & EPSS groups, then the tax software application required them to complete the WBT activity before attempting the corporate tax performance task.

The web-based training course included contained nine introductory screens, forty-nine information screens, twenty-four practice screens, and five concluding screens. In total, the course included 87 screens and took approximately 1 h to complete. The course was divided into five modules; each one addressed a specific instructional objective. Each module began with an introductory screen informing the learner of the objective for the module. In addition, this screen referenced a diagram of the corporate tax process which served as an advance organizer for the content. Each line in the tax form was addressed by one or more instructional screens. Instructional screens included a brief amount of content which includes tax concepts, rules, procedures that must be completed in tax form and examples where relevant. After the instructional sequence, each module provided scenario-based practice activities with the exception of Module 1 which provided matching and multiple-choice practice activities for factual objectives. All practice activities included appropriate feedback for correct responses or remediation feedback for incorrect responses.

The web-based training course was authored in Adobe Captivate. Instructional screens included images, animations and text. Audio and video were excluded from the WBT course due to usability issues when the content was used for performance support and due to bandwidth concerns over the Internet. Participants navigated within modules using a VCR-like toolbar located at the bottom of each screen. They navigated between modules using a menu located on the upper left corner of the screen. This navigation sequence was chosen as it is a user interface design that is common among current learning management systems.

The tax software application was also equipped with a performance support system for participants in the EPSS-only and WBT & EPSS treatments. The EPSS used was an extrinsic context-sensitive help system which was found in previous studies to be an effective method to deliver on-the-job support (Nguyen, Klein, & Sullivan, 2005). The opening screen of the tax software application provided a brief set of instructions demonstrating how to access the support system. Help buttons in the form of a question mark were inserted throughout the tax software application. When participants clicked on the buttons, their request was recorded in a database and a new window opened displaying support information associated with the task.

To avoid any effects due to content differences between the WBT and EPSS, the content used for the EPSS was derived from the WBT course. WBT courses can be developed into modular, reusable learning objects. These learning objects are granular components of a training course such as individual modules, lessons, screens, practice activities, or media elements. These objects can exist independently from the original WBT course, which then allows them to be accessed as isolated single learning offerings or be combined in different ways to create new training courses.

As mentioned previously, the WBT course contained 49 screens where participants received instructional information. These information objects were linked directly to individual help buttons embedded in the tax software application. By using this approach, identical components from the WBT course could be reused for performance support purposes. Since the actual learning objects were identical between the two treatments, any differences due the quality of the content could be eliminated.

The task scenario portrayed a realistic issue that a new employee might face. It included information that a manager might provide to a new finance employee when preparing federal tax submission for a company. Corporate tax preparation was chosen as the basis of the scenario due to the complexity of the task. The first section prompted the participant to imagine that they have recently been hired as a financial analyst for a small manufacturing company. The second portion of the task scenario contained an email that was sent to the participant from their imaginary new manager. In the email, their manager asked the participant to prepare a tax return for the company. To support this task, the email contained detailed financial information including income, expenses, payroll, and other company information. The participant used these data and any training and support information to complete the tax return using the tax software application.

3.3 Criterion and Enroute Measures

User performance on the task was measured by evaluating the number of correct items the participants submitted to the tax software application. As mentioned earlier, the tax scenario required 58 user inputs or selections. Data entered by the user into the tax software were stored in a database and subsequently evaluated by the researcher. Participants received one point for each correct input with a maximum of 58 points possible. The total amount of time participants spent completing the performance task was measured by calculating the difference between the time at which participants logged into and out of the tax software application. The total amount of time participants spent in the WBT course was measured by calculating the difference between the time at which participants logged into and out of the WBT course.

An eight-item survey was administered to measure participant attitudes towards the effectiveness of the training and support interventions provided in aiding them to complete the task. For most questions, respondents used a 4-point Likert scale (4 = *strongly agree*, 1 = *strongly disagree*) to rate their attitudes regarding the effectiveness of the interventions. One question asked respondents to rate the amount of time they spent learning how to perform the task. As a result, respondents were provided with only three options: *about right, too much,* and *too little.* Cronbach's alpha reliability coefficient for the attitude survey was .81.

3.4 Procedures

Since the participants in the study worked in different companies and were geographically dispersed, various corporate training managers and chapters of ASTD and ISPI were asked to recruit participants from their respective organizations. An email invitation was sent to study participants. The email instructions advised participants to allocate a 2 hour block of time to complete the study. During this time, they were asked to avoid distractions from phone calls, email, or co-workers once they had started the study. They were instructed to complete the task using only the information provided by the task scenario and any training or support that may be provided by the system. The participants were instructed to submit the information as soon as they felt they had completed the task.

The email instructions directed participants to the location of the research materials on the Internet. Prior to the implementation of the treatments, participants completed a demographic survey that was used to screen for prior knowledge of corporate tax preparation. Any individual currently working in a finance-related role, with a finance-related degree, or with tax or accounting certifications were not selected to participate in the study.

If the participant did not have any finance background, the system randomly assigned them into one of three treatment groups (WBT-only, EPSS-only, WBT & EPSS) and displayed the appropriate intervention. Participants were not aware that they were assigned to a different treatment group or that their system was configured with a different WBT or EPSS intervention. If the participants were part of the WBT-only group, they were first directed to take the WBT course. If the participants were part of the EPSS-only group, the opening screen of the tax software application was presented providing a brief set of instructions demonstrating how to access the support system. If the participants were part of the WBT & EPSS group, they first took the WBT course and were then provided with the performance support system instructions.

4 Results

The first research question investigated the effect of EPSS, WBT, and a combination of these two interventions on user performance while completing a tax preparation task. The mean scores for user performance were 46.54 (80%) for the WBT & EPSS group, 43.92 (76%) for the EPSS-only group, and 39.92 (69%) for the WBT-only group. A one-way analysis of variance using the Welch test revealed a significant overall difference, $F(2, 46) = 22.37$, $p < .01$. The strength of the relationship between the treatments and the performance scores was large, $\eta^2 = .31$.

Post-hoc tests were conducted to determine significant differences in mean performance scores. Multiple comparisons conducted using the Tukey method revealed that participants in the WBT & EPSS group and those in the EPSS-only group had significantly higher scores on the task than those in the WBT-only group.

The second research question investigated the effect of EPSS and training interventions on the attitudes of participants. The average overall attitude rating was 3.07 for the training & EPSS group, 2.59 for the EPSS-only group, and 1.91 for the training-only group. A MANOVA was conducted on attitude items to test for significant differences. The overall means were significantly different across the three treatment groups, Wilks' $\wedge = .18$, $F(18, 134) = 13.14$, $p < .01$. The strength of the relationship between the treatments and user attitude scores was strong, $\eta^2 = .57$.

Follow-up one-way analyses of variance revealed significant differences between treatment groups on all seven survey items. Therefore, post-hoc tests were conducted on these items. Pairwise comparisons revealed 20 significant differences between groups. On all seven Likert-type questions, participants in the EPSS-only group and those in the training & EPSS group had significantly more positive attitudes than participants in the training-only group. In addition, participants in the training & EPSS group had significantly more positive attitudes than those in the EPSS-only group on four questions. The eighth item on the survey included three choices that measured the participants' perception towards the amount of time they spent learning how to perform the tax scenario. A total of 38 participants (49%) thought that the amount of time they spent learning was about right, 23 participants (29%) thought that they had spent too little time, and 17 (22%) thought that they had spent too much time. Closer examination of the data shows that the majority of participants in both the training & EPSS group (81%) and in the EPSS-only group (65%) thought that the time they spent learning how to do the task was about right. Meanwhile, no participants in the training-only group indicated that the amount of time they spent learning how to perform the task was about right. Sixteen participants in the training-only group (62%) thought that they spent too much time learning while the remaining ten participants (38%) thought that they did not spend enough time. A chi square test revealed that the difference in proportions between the treatment groups was significant, $X^2(2, N = 78) = 9.00$, $p < 05$.

The third research question investigated the effect of treatment on total time to complete the task scenario. This was measured by calculating the difference between the time at which participants logged into and out of the tax software application. The EPSS-only group spent an average of 27 minutes on the task; the WBT & EPSS group spent 32 minutes; and the WBT-only group spent 61 minutes. A one-way analysis of variance using the Welch test was conducted on the time on task data. This test revealed a significant overall difference, $F(2, 45) = 11.20$, $p < .01$. The strength of the relationship between the treatments for time on task was strong, $\eta2 = .32$. The correlation between time on task and performance on the task scenario was significant at $-.36$, $p < .01$.

Post-hoc tests were conducted to determine significant differences in mean time on task scores. Multiple comparisons conducted using the Tukey method revealed that the WBT-only group spent significantly more time on the task scenario than both the EPSS-only and WBT & EPSS groups. The difference in time on task between the EPSS-only and WBT & EPSS groups was not significant.

The amount of time that participants spent in training was recorded by calculating the difference between the time that the participants logged into and out of the WBT course. The data revealed that the WBT & EPSS group spent an average of 42 minutes in the WBT course while the WBT-only group spent 35 minutes. A one-way analysis of variance conducted on time in training yielded no significant overall difference between the mean scores.

5 Discussion

Findings from the current study support the notion that electronic performance support systems can have a significant impact on user performance. Results revealed performance scores for participants receiving the EPSS-only and those receiving EPSS and WBT were significantly higher than scores for participants who received the WBT-only. One potential reason why participants who received WBT-only had significantly lower performance scores may be due to a transfer gap between the WBT course and the task. The WBT included instructional content that covered portions of the tax preparation procedure. Instructional sequences were followed by practice activities which provided participants with a scenario and asked them to complete that portion of the tax procedure. To minimize participant attrition, no additional practice activity or assessment was provided at the end of the WBT to tie the entire tax procedure together into one whole task.

This lack of part-task to whole-task transfer could have had some effect on the WBT-only participants' lower performance on the task. van Merriënboer (1997) suggested that designers should begin their instructional sequences with part-task procedural practice and then evolve into whole-task problem solving exercises. In addition, 'more and more complex versions of the whole cognitive skill' should then be introduced (van Merriënboer, 1997, p. 8). The use of this instructional design strategy could have increased the effectiveness of the WBT treatment.

Another potential reason for the lower performance of the WBT-only group is the volume of information that participants were required to memorize, recall, and apply at task performance. The WBT course used in this study included 87 navigation, instructional, practice, and transitional screens which included facts, concepts, and procedures on how to complete the corporate tax preparation task. Another compounding factor could be the participants' behavior while in training. Participants spent an average of 39 minutes reviewing the content in the 87 screens of the WBT course prior to completion of the tax procedure – an average of 27 s per screen. This seemingly short period of time in the WBT course suggests that participants 'skimmed' the WBT and only learned the information at a superficial level. This strategy would put WBT-only participants at a disadvantage as compared to EPSS-only and WBT & EPSS participants who could quickly reference and apply information at the moment of need.

Participants in the EPSS-only and training & EPSS groups had significantly more positive attitudes than the training-only group. This finding can be attributed to the fact that participants in the training group were not provided with any on-task support or guidance. Participants in this study indicated a strong preference for the performance support system that was embedded inside of the tax software application. One participant commented, 'The information I needed was where I needed it, when I needed it.' 'Anytime I didn't know what information to put in there, I clicked on the online help.' These data align with previous research conducted by Nguyen, Klein, & Sullivan (2005) and further validate the notion that providing EPSS to support task performance is preferable to having none at all.

The training & EPSS group had significantly more positive attitudes than the EPSS-only users on four survey questions: (1) It was easy to find the information I needed to complete the tax scenario, (2) The learning support was at the appropriate level of detail to aid in completing the tax scenario, (3) I received enough training to successfully complete the tax scenario, and (4) In the future, I would like to use learning support such as the one demonstrated in this study. These positive statements in favor of the training & EPSS treatment are consistent with results for the performance variable. The preference to have training and performance support as combined interventions can likely be attributed to the fact that participants were introduced to the information during the training treatment, could quickly refresh their working memory using the performance support system, and then immediately apply the content to the task scenario.

The WBT-only group spent significantly more time completing the task scenario than participants in the WBT & EPSS and EPSS-only groups. In fact, participants provided only with the WBT intervention spent roughly 1 h more or nearly triple their EPSS-equipped counterparts. A closer examination of the time on task data showed that a sizeable number of WBT-only participants spent 2–3 h completing the task.

The tax software application was programmed to prevent participants from moving backwards through the research materials. After the conclusion of the study, two WBT-only participants reported frustration with this design. In an attempt to obtain information to help them complete the task, these WBT-only participants (and potentially others) attempted to return to the WBT course for reference. Attempting to move backwards in the software resulted in reported loss of information entered into the tax software application. As a result, certain WBT-only participants had to restart the tax scenario from the beginning even though they may have already spent a considerable amount of time in the task.

In considering the fact that WBT-only participants spent nearly three times as much time on the task as those in the EPSS-only and WBT & EPSS groups, it is interesting to note that the WBT-only participants scored significantly lower on the performance task than participants in the other two groups respectively. Correlation tests between the factors revealed a negative correlation between time on task and performance of $-.36$. In short, despite any additional time WBT only participants may have invested in completing the tax preparation activity, they did not perform any better than their counterparts. In fact, they performed worse.

The findings from this study have important implications for performance technologists who are considering web-based training or EPSS as performance interventions. The increase in performance for the participants who received EPSS over their WBT-only counterparts suggests that performance technologists should consider performance support systems to help mitigate information-related performance problems.

When considering EPSS and WBT as performance interventions, it is important consider the amount of time that is available to deliver prescribed interventions and the desired level of performance. For example, participants in the EPSS-only group spent an average of 26 minutes in the tax preparation task with an accuracy level of 76%. Meanwhile, participants in the WBT & EPSS group spent an average of 74 minutes taking training, using the EPSS, and completing the performance task. Despite the additional time invested, they achieved a proficiency level of 80% – just slightly more than the EPSS-only participants. These data suggest that, if a performance problem is very critical and conditions allow sufficient time to develop and deliver multiple interventions, then it may be worthwhile to invest heavily in both web-based training and EPSS interventions. If time is a constraint or incremental increases in performance are not necessary, then the benefits derived from a robust training intervention may not be worth the time or cost invested.

It is also important to note that the development of an electronic performance support system has been demonstrated to be costly from both a time and monetary perspective. In this particular study, the integration of the EPSS into the tax software application added an additional 40–50 h of work. This number does not factor in the cost to develop content for the EPSS. Since learning objects from the WBT course were reused for the EPSS, no specialized content development was required to deliver just-in-time support. When performance technologists are considering EPSS as an intervention, they should weigh the potential benefits on user performance against the time and monetary investment that will be required.

The increased use of electronic performance support systems and web-based training in actual practice requires that performance technologists conduct empirical research to determine the best ways to employ these interventions. As was done in the current study, additional research should examine the impact of knowledge support interventions such as EPSS and web-based training on the performance and attitudes of users in real world settings.

References

Bastiaens, T. J., Nijhof, W. J., Streumer, J. N., & Abma, H. J. (1997). Working and learning with electronic performance support systems: An effectiveness study. *International Journal of Training and Development, 1*(1), 72–78.

Brush, T., Knapczyk, D., & Hubbard, L. (1993). Developing a collaborative performance support system for practicing teachers. *Educational Technology, 33*(11), 39–45.

Carroll, J. M., & Rosson, M. B. (1987). Paradox of the active user. In J. M. Carroll (Ed.), *Interfacing thought: Cognitive aspects of human-computer interaction* (pp. 80–11). Boston: Bradford Books/MIT Press.

Dorsey, L. T., Goodrum, D. A., & Schwen, T.M. (1993). Just-in-time knowledge performance support: A test of concept. *Educational Technology, 33*(11), 21–29.

Gery, G. (1991). *Electronic performance support systems*. Tolland, MA: Gery Associates.

Gery, G. (1995). Attributes and behaviors of performance-centered systems. *Performance Improvement Quarterly, 8*(1), 47–93.

Huber, B., Lippincott, J., McMahon, C., & Witt, C. (1999). Teaming up for performance support: A model of roles, skills and competencies. *Performance Improvement Quarterly, 38*(1), 10–14.

Hunt, D. L., Haynes, R. B., Hanna, S. E., & Smith, K. (1998). Effects of computer-based clinical decision support systems on physician performance and patient outcomes. *Journal of the American Medical Association, 280*(15), 1339–1346.

Kasvi, J. J., & Vartiainen, M. (2000). Performance support on the shop floor. *Performance Improvement, 39*(6), 40–46.

Laffey, J. (1995). Dynamism in electronic performance support systems. *Performance Improvement Quarterly, 8*(1), 31–46.

Mao, J., & Brown, B. (2005). The effectiveness of online task support versus instructor-led training. *Journal of Organizational and End User Computing, 17*(3), 27–46.

McManus, P., & Rossett, A. (2006). Performance support tools delivering value when and where it is needed. *Performance Improvement, 45*(2), 8–16.

Nguyen, F. (2005). Oops, I forgot how to do that: A needs assessment of electronic performance support systems. *Performance Improvement, 44*(9), 33–39.

Nguyen, F. (2006). What you already know does matter: Expertise and electronic performance support systems. *Performance Improvement, 45*(4), 9–12.

Nguyen, F., Klein, J. D., & Sullivan, H. (2005). A comparative study of electronic performance support systems. *Performance Improvement Quarterly, 18*(4), 71–86.

Raybould, B. (2000). Building performance-centered web-based systems, information systems, and knowledge management systems in the 21st century. *Performance Improvement, 39*(6), 69–79.

van Merriënboer, J. J. G. (1997). *Training complex cognitive skills*. Englewood Cliffs, NJ: Educational Technology Publications.

Chapter 16
Moving Beyond Teaching and Learning into a Human Development Paradigm

Concepts and an Application

Sandra Reeb-Gruber, Michael K. McCuddy, Xavier Parisot, and David Rossi

Abstract For decades higher education has been dominated by two models: the Teaching Centered Model (TCM) and, more recently, the Learning Centered Model (LCM). Neither model alone is deemed as sufficient to satisfactorily address the educational needs and challenges of learners in our modern, global society. This paper describes a conceptual framework that can help guide the creation and implementation of teaching/learning approaches that are based on the universal phenomenon of human development – a phenomenon that transcends both the TCM and LCM. This conceptual framework – called the Development Centered Paradigm (DCP) – seeks to capitalize on the benefits of the TCM and LCM while going beyond them. This paper also describes a demonstration project in an interdisciplinary biotechnology management course at a graduate school of management in France; this demonstration project shows how the DCP can be implemented in higher education, building on the positive features of the TCM and LCM.

Keywords Teaching centered model · Learning centered model · Development centered paradigm · Human development · Biotechnology education

1 Introduction

For decades higher education has been dominated by two models: the Teaching Centered Model (TCM), with a centuries-long tradition, and the Learning Centered Model (LCM), of more recent vintage. The TCM focuses on the instructor's role, behaviors, and impacts. This model makes the instructor the focal point of the educational process; it is about the transmission of information – and hopefully,

S. Reeb-Gruber (✉)
INHolland University of Applied Sciences, Saturnusstraat 2-24, HB Hoofddorp 2132,
The Netherlands
e-mail: sandra.reebgruber@inholland.nl

knowledge – from the wise, omniscient sage to eager students clamoring for pearls of wisdom. The LCM focuses on cultivating students' capacities to: solve problems within the context of the learning goals and learning environment that are designed by the teacher/facilitator/coach; guide their own learning (especially on a life-long basis); and seek information on an as-needed basis.

In recent years the format and quality of higher education has received an increasing amount of attention on a global scale. With various nations having ambitions to become innovative knowledge economies in order to stay ahead of the competition, the role of higher education in achieving these ambitions has become an important topic of discussion, raising questions regarding the 'ideal' format and content of higher education. Achieving these ambitions requires people who are critical yet innovative thinkers, pragmatic thinkers and doers, socially responsible, mature, self-directed, flexible, independent, etc. A crucial question for institutions of higher education is: 'Do the current educational models meaningfully contribute to 'producing' these types of people?'

We believe that neither model (TCM or LCM) on its own does a sufficiently satisfactory job of 'producing' graduates with the aforementioned characteristics. We assert there is a need for a new educational model – one that combines, or rather transcends, both the TCM and LCM in order to bring about the changes inherent in the aforementioned global ambitions.

2 The Teaching Centered Model (TCM) of Education

Criticism of the Teaching Centered Model is revealing and abundant. 'We are still putting students in a classroom with an authority figure who lectures for prescribed periods of time. We have progressed very little from the educational paradigm used by Socrates and his followers. Education in colleges and universities is now like a prison sentence' Pelton (1996) observed two-and-a-half millennia after the age of Socrates, Plato and Aristotle. Others have recently compared TCM to factories striving to optimize efficiency by way of regimented processes (Brown, 2003).

In the TCM the teachers assume responsibility for thinking, not the students. The students' responsibility is to memorize and recite information that is given and structured by the teacher; control of learning is in the hands of the teacher as he or she uses content expertise to help learners make connections (Brown, 2003). In the TCM, students 'have mastered a set of rules that privileges teacher action: get the right answer (the teacher's answer); expect every action to merit some tangible reward from the teacher (points or extra credit); work just enough to earn the grade you desire, as defined by the teacher's standards' (Mezeske, 2004).

The primary emphasis of the TCM is the transmission of knowledge (Brown, 2003). Samuelowicz and Bain (2001) provide an amplified perspective that draws on a review of empirical research; this research demonstrates that the TCM includes imparting information, transmitting structured knowledge, and providing and facilitating understanding.

Dehler and Welsh (1997), writing in the *Journal of Management Education*, warn of the problems that can arise in TCM-type education. They contend that, as the students are not responsible for thinking, they might 'know' something, but have little insight as to where it comes from, why it is important, or how to use it.

Franz (1998) presents a critical yet realistic view of teacher- and teaching-centered education: 'We can design programs, deliver courses, give lectures, and grade papers, but we can't compel our students to learn. We, the faculty, will be judged (by society's stakeholders) for the quality of our graduates, but we are not solely responsible for, nor should we be held accountable for, their success.' Successful application of the TCM – with respect to the students' acquisition of knowledge – depends on the abilities, skills, and efforts of the students, but unfortunately 'teachers are driven to meet accountability standards and often sacrifice the needs of the students to ensure exposure to the standards' (Brown, 2003).

Still the role of the teacher in education is paramount, as they are the single most important factor in the school's influence on learning (Darling-Hammond, 2008). Kunkel (2002), arguing in favor of the TCM, states: 'students need tremendous structure or they panic, [being] confused as to how to be successful in the course.'

However, Pelton, who argued that little progress has occurred in society's approach to education since the times of Socrates, Plato, and Aristotle, offers an interesting perspective on the need for educational reform – not just within a given nation, but globally. Pelton (1996) observes that 'the challenge of reforming, improving, and extending quality education and training to the entire global population is huge: Global reform of education to overcome the constraints of the traditional educational model is a more awesome undertaking than the Apollo Moon Project, the Great Wall of China, and the Great Pyramids of Egypt combined.' The Learning Centered Model of education, which we shall explore in the next section, is an important, major step in the direction of needed and meaningful educational reform. However, as we shall discuss later on, even this important, major step falls short of what is needed in educational reform – indeed, higher education must move *beyond teaching and learning*!

3 The Learning Centered Model (LCM) of Education

In the 1950s, as 'the complexity of understanding humans and their environments became increasingly apparent' (Bransford, Brown, & Cocking, 2000) the Learner Centered or Learning Centered Model[1] emerged and led to new approaches regarding the design of the curriculum, teaching, and assessment. Based on research findings from this era we could say that the TCM is not suitable for all learners, only those who have an apparent talent for learning. In order for a larger group of

---

[1] Learner centered instruction or education refers to the learner as the focal person in the instructional process. Learning centered instruction or education refers to the various learning activities engaged in by the focal person and facilitated by the teacher.

learners to develop a deep understanding of important subject matter, new ways to impart knowledge to students are needed. Facts are important for problem solving, but don't lead to problem solving on their own. Understanding is a key to moving from just knowing to genuinely contributing to society and learning.

Prior knowledge, skills, beliefs, and concepts influence what individuals notice about their environment and how they organize and interpret it, and this has a strong effect on an individual's ability to remember, reason, solve problems, and acquire new knowledge (Bransford & Stein, 1993). From this perspective it follows that teaching should engage students' prior knowledge and understanding in order for them to really learn, instead of just memorizing and not internalizing what has been imparted to them. 'Deep understanding of subject matter transforms factual knowledge into usable knowledge' (Bransford & Stein, 1993); more knowledge and deeper understanding allows the individual to build a conceptual framework from which he can draw when presented with new information (Bransford & Stein, 1993). Teaching, therefore, should in addition to focusing on the learners' prior knowledge also elicit from students how they use this prior knowledge in new situations (*i.e.*, make their thinking visible) and provide a conceptual framework for the students.

Another important finding in research into the human mind and learning is that the ability to transfer knowledge, skills, and attitudes to new settings and events increases when individuals are allowed to take control of their own learning (Palinscar & Brown; Scarmadalia, Bereiter, & Steinbach; and Schoenfeld, as reported in Bransford & Stein, 1993) and develop strategies to assess whether they understand or need more information.

Other characteristics of LCM-based instructional approaches include the following:

- Confronting students with the work and tasks of an actual professional during their studies by working on authentic problems or case studies and hence getting more insight into why they need to learn certain things (De Bie & De Kleijn, 2001; Van Merriënboer, 1997);
- Transferring some of the power in the classroom to students, making them co-participants in and co-responsible for the learning process (Brown, 2003; Dehler & Welsh, 1997; Mezeske, 2004; Paris & Combs, 2006);
- Development of expertise on the students' part (Samuelowicz & Bain, 2001).
- Teachers' roles shifting from being an expert or 'sage on the stage' to being a 'guide on the side' (McCuddy, Pirie, Schroeder, & Strasser, 2002; Morse, 2007);
- Providing a variety of instructional methods and techniques to help students construct their own learning and develop a system for applying the knowledge acquired (Brown, 200);
- Using evaluation and assessment to promote learning, not simply to generate grades (Mezeske, 2004).
- Putting learner needs, characteristics, experiences and development at the center of the learning process in order to engage learners (Brown, 2003; McCombs & Whisler, 1997; Paris & Combs, 2006);

- The use of flexible curricula to stimulate students to use their creativity and to become intimately involved in their education (MacDonald, 1998).

The various findings regarding how the human mind works and what facilitates human learning have been incorporated into a variety of LCM-based approaches, including inquiry-based learning, competency-based learning, constructivist designs of curricula, project-based learning, etc.

4 Transcending TCM and LCM with DCP

Recently, McCuddy and Reeb-Gruber (2008), in arguing the case for moving beyond the teaching and learning models that dominate higher education, introduced a possible solution, known as the Development Centered Paradigm (DCP), which has at its core the learners' natural curiosities and interests as well as the fundamental universal process of how human beings develop into functionally mature individuals. The DCP moves beyond the TCM and the LCM through how it addresses the purposes and beneficiaries of education as well as the cultural transcendence of education.

Considering the purposes of education. From the perspective of the DCP, the purpose of education is variously described as: 'to help people develop their capacities to deal with future uncertainties,' or 'to help people develop the capacity to balance their pursuit of self-interests with their obligations to the broader societal community,' or 'to help people develop their capacities for guiding and leading people and change,' or 'to help people develop the capacity to transcend cultural boundaries in a global society' or 'to help people develop into the best that they can be.' The key operative word here is *develop*! Development goes well beyond transmitting information and knowledge – as is the case in the TCM – or imparting competencies and skills for being self-directed and self-sufficient learners – as in the LCM. Development focuses on facilitating the learner's movement toward becoming a functionally mature individual (McCuddy & Reeb-Gruber, 2008). We define a *functionally mature individual* as a person who has developed into a mature personality – intellectually, morally, psychologically, and emotionally – such that she/he can function effectively in contemporary society. A functionally mature individual knows who she/he is, knows what she/he wants, and is not afraid to go out and get it without forgetting to consider others or the bigger picture.

Considering the beneficiaries of education. Again, from the perspective of the DCP, the beneficiaries of education are more diverse and inclusive than occur with either the TCM or LCM. In the DCP, *multiple direct beneficiaries* exist – including students themselves, educational institutions, prospective employers, and the broader community/society. Properly recognizing the multiple direct beneficiaries of education also begs for a conception of higher education that goes beyond the TCM and LCM – a conception that embraces and fosters human development for the betterment of individuals, organizations and institutions, and societies. If the community/society as a whole is a direct beneficiary of education, then the need for every individual to meet a certain standard (or be 'held back' at that level) disappears. Development becomes a combined effort in which every individual provides the best that he/she has to offer. The starting point becomes what the individual learner is good at and wants to learn. Development then depends on each individual's initial educational capacities and the outcomes are diversified. Not trying to make every learner fit into a certain standard 'mold', – an innovation which is part of the DCP, – also leaves ample room for encouragement to achieve more, instead of pointing out to students their position relative to the standard goal.

Considering cultural transcendence in education. Human beings, regardless of where they reside in the world, originally develop in much the same way. They develop the capacity to walk and talk in a quite predictable fashion, without regard to the nation in which they reside. They also move from being dependent creatures to being independent ones, from having few ways of behaving to having diverse behaviors, from being self-centered to having the capacity to balance self-interest with the interests of the broader community, etc. In short, human development is a universal phenomenon that can be used to reconceptualize and restructure the teaching/learning enterprise while effectively accommodating individual differences in facilitating the development of learners into functionally mature individuals.

4.1 The Development Centered Paradigm (DCP)

The DCP proposes an educational world with a strong emphasis on natural human development and facilitation of that process – and doing so just-in-time. Development is a process of 'figuring out' – a child suddenly figures out how to put one foot before the other without losing balance. The first human-made fire was an accident and someone figured out how to replicate the accident; gravity was discovered by accident and then figured out; and so forth. Development also is fueled by curiosity and disbelief – without curiosity and disbelief the world would still be flat. These are among the many mysteries that the natural world presents to human beings. Many mysteries from the social world also confront humans. Humans can and do 'figure out' solutions to these mysteries. The existence of these mysteries, in conjunction with the fact that humans are born with curiosity and the irresistible urge to explore and 'figure out', provides the foundation for the DCP. Moreover, this curiosity and urge to understand the world is universal, not culturally or nationally bound.

Human educational development starts when we are born and is, at least until we go to school, automatic. Until recently most psychologists believed that an infant's mind was a *tabula rasa* on which experiences were impressed over time and that structured guidance and teaching was necessary to understand these experiences and convert them into learning. Not until a child had mastered language was he able to have abstract thought and develop knowledge (Bransford & Stein, 1993). However, recent research has shown that 'very young children are competent, active agents of their own conceptual development' (Bruner, Carey, & Gelman; Gardner, Gelman & Brown; Wellman & Gelman, as reported in Bransford & Stein, 1993).

16 Moving Beyond Teaching and Learning into a Human Development Paradigm

The active role that children take in their own development was also emphasized later by Vygotsky (as reported in Bransford & Stein, 1993). Unfortunately, the educational process, as reflected in the TCM and to a lesser extent in the LCM, diminishes the extent to which students are active agents of their own learning.

The DCP uses the student's interests, curiosity, and talent as a starting point, as opposed to LCM, which is structured from the institution's/designer's point of view and then tries to take the students' prior knowledge and experiences into consideration in the application of the course. The assumption is that learning is easier and more enjoyable when this is the starting point; if a person is talented or interested in something, s/he probably has some prior knowledge of it, even if it's subconscious. Adding a conceptual framework to that knowledge will not take a lot of effort as the learner (subconsciously) already understands or has a 'gut feeling'. The individual's conceptual framework serves as a personal confirmation and becomes the key to making him or her consciously competent. 'Scientific discoveries don't exist without a curious mind that refuses to let itself be restricted by impossibilities. Learning starts with curiosity, with investigating hypotheses oneself and believing in the possibilities' (Hart, 1983).

The DCP is also defined by its emphasis on capitalizing on the naturally and universally occurring process of human beings developing into functionally mature individuals. Although space limits the extent to which we can explore this aspect here, suffice it to say that all human beings move from a state of immaturity to a state of maturity during their physical, psychological, moral, emotional, and intellectual development. The DCP seeks to build on this developmental process by creating educational opportunities that begin with the learners' interests and curiosities and then, through active personal management of their own learning, move toward fuller attainment of the capacity to live as functionally mature individuals (McCuddy & Reeb-Gruber, 2008).

Another important aspect of the DCP is a focus on positive reinforcement. Positive reinforcement leads to self-confidence and motivation, both of which have proven to help considerably in learning (Lazeron, 2007). 'Discoveries are often made not in response to impasses or failures but rather in the context of successful performance' (Bransford & Stein, 1993).

The DCP also draws on multiple disciplines and multiple perspectives within a given discipline. This is illustrated by the time-honored, comprehensive, multidisciplinary approach to human development taken years ago by Lugo and Hershey (1974), in which they discuss numerous theories about becoming fully human and explore major behavioral processes that are involved in becoming fully human. Their major theoretical emphases include: productive orientation; social interest and feeling; accurate perception of people; affirmation of one's will; courage to be; the human as a person; and I-thou relationships. The basic behavioral processes which they discuss include learning, maturation, perception, motivation, emotion, and thinking. Transcending these specific theories and behavioral processes are three distinctive points of view – psychoanalytic, behavioristic, and humanistic – for exploring human development. Lugo and Hershey assert that all three perspectives should be employed to have a better understanding of the processes involved in becoming more fully human.

In another classic theory of personality development, Chris Argyris, writing in the seminal book *Personality and Organization* (1957), provides an instructive foundation for understanding human beings' transformation from immaturity to maturity. His theory of personality development, known appropriately as immaturity-maturity theory, argues that human beings exhibit predictable behavioral and attitudinal changes as they grow into maturity. Argyris identifies seven characteristics that differentiate between the immature personality and the mature personality. From the perspective of human development, each of these characteristics is an important element of a person's transformation into a functionally mature individual. We assert that appropriate and meaningful educational practices, as manifested in the DCP, can contribute in varying ways and to varying degrees to this developmental transformation of students into functionally mature individuals.

In another seminal work, *Pattern and Growth in Personality*, Gordon W. Allport (1961), identified several defining characteristics of people with a mature personality. These characteristics include, but are not limited to: a sense of security, freedom of choice, self-awareness, the development of non-egotistical interests, the capacity to love others non-possessively and unselfishly, and treating other people with respect and being aware of their needs and desires.

Another perspective that reflects the development of human beings into functionally mature individuals is provided by theories of cognitive moral development as articulated by Jean Piaget (1932/1965), Lawrence Kohlberg (1976, 1984), and Carol Gilligan (1982). As Parker (1998) argues, moral development involves 'the growth of moral understanding in individuals. In this respect it concerns a person's progressive ability to understand the difference between right and wrong, to care about the difference between them, and to act on the basis of this understanding' (Parker, 1998).

The DCP is intended to foster the intellectual, moral, psychological, and emotional development of adult learners in a manner similar to or the same as the process by which children's natural curiosity, actions, and development occurs. By using the curiosity, interest, needs, and experiences of the learners, which are culturally neutral, but individually diverse, as the focal point of 'teaching' and the methods used, education would serve every individual's, and hence society's, developmental needs and would help them to more fully develop their potential. By doing so they are moving – sometimes lurching forward haltingly, other times racing ahead vigorously – toward strengthening their potential, developing their character, and becoming functionally mature individuals.

5 A Demonstration Project Applying the DCP

In order to test the practical viability of the conceptually vibrant and theoretically appealing DCP, we conducted a demonstration project in an interdisciplinary management of biotechnology course at a graduate school of management in France. Being a country with a relatively strong degree of uncertainty avoidance (Hofstede, 2001) – especially compared to The Netherlands and the United States, the creation of interdisciplinary courses on biotechnology management is still rare in France. Moreover, the dominant educational model in France, fitting its relatively high power distance (Hofstede, 2001), is the TCM. These characteristics, as well as the fact that these graduate school of management students have little scientific or technical knowledge and tend to have limited – or skewed – representations of biotechnology, pose an interesting challenge when it comes to developing an innovative knowledge economy and introducing a movement toward a new educational paradigm like the DCP.

However, with biotechnology being transversal, the market has an increasing need for graduates with 'dual competence' – meaning that graduates must be competent in the field of business management as well as in the field of biotechnology (two very different areas of expertise), and be able to make the right connections between the two (*i.e.* combine the two competencies in a meaningful way for the market). The TCM has proven to be of little operative value in the context of accelerating the cycle of knowledge in biotechnology management. The LCM seems to overcome some of the pitfalls of TCM although it is not sufficient to ensure the effectiveness of teaching and learning. The LCM is still being structured by teachers/educational designers and learning in the LCM should still lead to predefined and specific, knowledge, skills, and behaviors. Considering a controversial subject like biotechnology (genetic engineering, for instance), this predefinition of outcomes (*i.e.*, accepting biotech applications) leads to (or at least does not diminish) resistance. Taking students' prior knowledge, needs, and characteristics into consideration does not influence the predefined outcomes of the course. In that sense, the LCM learning process is designed more to manipulate than to let students figure things out for themselves and grow into mature thinkers and individuals. Therefore, in the teaching of biotechnology management, it is necessary to transcend TCM and LCM to stimulate the development of a dual competence and mature thinking by students, taking into consideration the impact of social representations – which are very important in France – in the educational process.

Considering these French challenges, we chose to introduce the DCP in a graduate business school in France through an adapted version of problem based learning (PBL), using Kolb's (1984, 2001) learning cycle, Argyris and Schôn's (1989) reflection in action theories, and Watzlawick, Weakland, Fish, Erickson (1974) model of change. This last model distinguishes incremental changes from changes causing a disruption in the way of thinking; the teaching of the management of biotechnology to students in a graduate school of management entails disruptive change in order to be effective.

By using the DCP, we brought about a process of reflexivity[2] through students' various practical experiments. Once the theoretical gaps are filled, a first synthesis leads to the development of a common questionnaire to be used in conducting

---

[2]Reflexivity here is used in both senses of the term: personal reflexivity and epistemological reflexivity. Personal reflexivity refers to how a person's values, beliefs, acquaintances and interests influence his or her research or work. Epistemological reflexivity attempts to identify the foundations of knowledge and the implications of any findings.

interviews in a company. The comparison of student representations with those of specialists allows the construction of a vision aggregating around reality and theoretical concepts. The course thus involves all four stages of Kolb's learning cycle (1984) without necessarily following the order in which it is usually applied. The act of repeating the key steps of this cycle of learning facilitates the acquisition of profound knowledge (Bransford et al., 2000). Moreover, this repetition enhances the scope of 'reflection in action' – which is one of the methods used here as a fundamental basis of pedagogy/andragogy (Finger & Asun, 2001; Argyris Putman, Smith, 1985).

5.1 A Description of the Demonstration Project

The application of this method is standardized over a period of one semester or 40 contact hours per student. It was repeated over two semesters with 6 groups of students. The groups contained between 6 and 10 members. The total number of students included in this study is 50 individuals. The distribution of students is specified in Table 16.1.

Table 16.1 Distribution of student enrollment between the years and programs

Course	2007	2008	Total
BIO201 Master 1	8	9	17
BIO301 Master 2	10	10	20
BIO202 Master 1	6	7	13
Total	24	26	50

The entire demonstration project was supervised by a teacher with a double competence profile in both biotechnology and business. The educational approach was interdisciplinary. It linked the technical aspects of bioproducts to the markets in which they are distributed. Particular care was given to the dissemination of knowledge.

Consistent with the spirit of the DCP, students chose the course from several options. They were all therefore volunteers and motivated by the subject being explored and the educational approach being used. However, the course was structured in advance regarding content and educational approach. The course originated outside the students' interests, but started with the needs of another stakeholder: the professional field.

Within the context of the Development Centered Paradigm, and attempting to combine the best elements of the Teaching Centered Model and the Learning Centered Model, the demonstration project implemented in this business school may be visually summarized as shown in Fig. 16.1.

As Fig. 16.1 shows, the DCP, TCM, and LCM (by way of PBL) (Savin-Baden & Howell, 2004) were combined as follows:

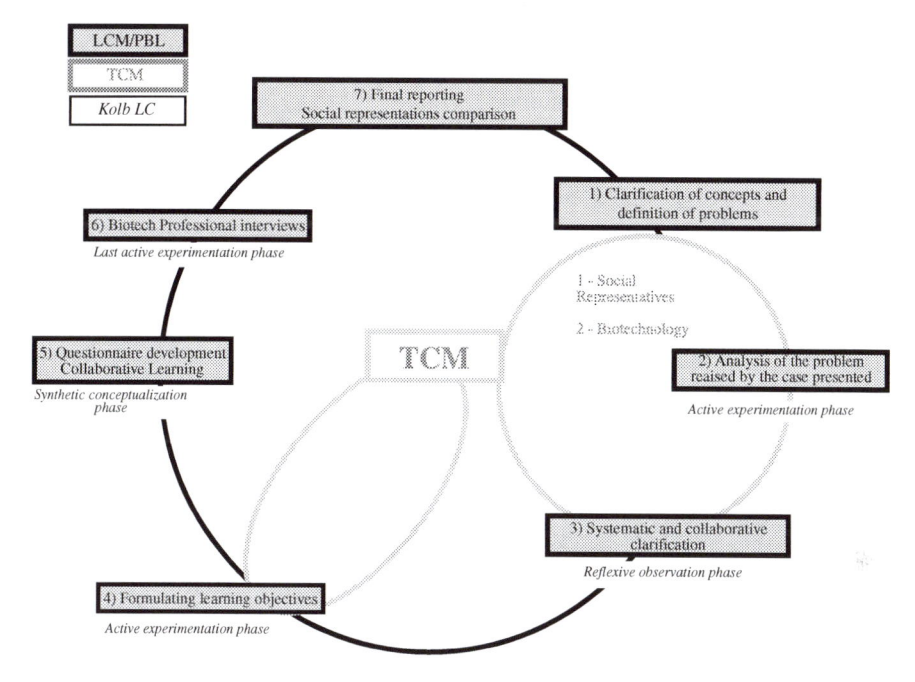

16 Moving Beyond Teaching and Learning into a Human Development Paradigm

Fig. 16.1 Visualization of the DCP-based structure of the management of biotechnology course

1. Students are invited to define the problem set in the case presented and to investigate the concepts underlying the problem, hence developing a pattern of understanding (Bransford & Stein, 1993; Bransford et al., 2000; Wlodkwoski & Ginsberg 1995) [draws on LCM and DCP]. At the end of this stage, the teacher discusses the students' results, clarifies concepts and – if needed – puts students on the right track, offering a theoretical and conceptual structure on which they can elaborate [draws on TCM].
2. Students work together in small groups to analyze the problem raised by the case presented, based on prior knowledge and the results of the discussion and TCM intervention in stage 1, thereby learning by accumulation (Bransford et al., 2000) [draws on LCM and DCP]. This step corresponds to the phase of active experimentation in Kolb's learning cycle (1984). Again, at the end of this stage, the teacher leads a discussion on the results, positively reinforcing their efforts and achievements [draws on DCP] and adding structure if necessary [draws on TCM].
3. During the reflexive observation and synthetic conceptualization phase (Kolb, 1984), the student groups systematically clarify the concepts underlying the problem in a group presentation [draws on LCM]. In doing so they 'feed back' the knowledge they have acquired during the first two stages to the teacher, allowing him to see if his teachings were effective [draws on TCM].

These first three stages are repeated twice. The first cycle introduces students to theories on social representations by mobilizing theoretical knowledge in the field of consumer behavior. Students are also encouraged to investigate their own social representations regarding biotechnology and to identify obstacles these representations might present during the course [draws on LCM]. The second cycle mobilizes students around specific issues raised by biotechnology. Thus, the technical and social fields are connected in order to promote a systemic view, which is essential for the proposed case to be solved adequately: essentially, 'impact analysis of social representations on the market penetration of bioproducts.' The initial separation of the two theoretical fields allows us to measure the potential resistance expressed first in response to a change in educational approach and also against biotechnology. In addition, the repetition of this cycle helps us to identify the knowledge that should be strengthened in the theoretical fields covered.

4. Now the students have a clear view of gaps in their knowledge and encumbering social representations they might have regarding the subject. This allows them to formulate learning objectives [draws on LCM]. To overcome the lack of knowledge expressed by students, the instructor will resort to using the TCM. Its purpose is twofold: (a) to structure and clearly indentify the knowledge gathered; and (b) to facilitate the use of selected technical data in order to develop a questionnaire to collect the representations of professionals in the biotech sector in a semi-directed interview. This step corresponds to the active experimentation phase in Kolb's learning cycle (1984).

5. Students develop the questionnaire on their own and report their results in a group presentation. The discovery of a lack of knowledge is a reflexivity stage to move from concrete experimentation to a synthetic conceptualization in Kolb's learning cycle (1984).

6. The completed questionnaire is then used in the framework of interviews with professionals in the biotechnology sector. Qualitative analysis is made of the representations expressed on the basis of the transcripts of interviews. This step corresponds to the last phase of concrete experimentation in Kolb's learning cycle (1984).

7. Students present a final report on the empirical observations made. At the same time they are invited to look back at the social representations and knowledge base they had (or thought they had) regarding biotechnology at the beginning of the assignment and to reflect on how these have changed over the course of the assignment [draws on DCP].

Structuring the management of biotechnology course in this fashion provides an important step on the journey toward fuller implementation of the DCP. Specifically, the course contributes to the students' development into functionally mature individuals: they are provided the opportunity to form their own opinions on biotech and its applications, and to explain/justify these opinions. In other words, the students are required to approach the subject in a mature way. Also, reflecting on their own social representations and doing research (*i.e.*, interviews with practitioners who know a lot more about the subject than they do) contributes to their maturation. By allowing students to form their own opinions of biotechnology and its uses (in a mature way), students do not have to fit a standard mold (*i.e.*, have a certain opinion/copy of the lecturer's opinion) – which is a defining characteristic of the DCP.

5.2 Key Insights from the Demonstration Project

This demonstration project with a new DCP-based approach produced important results for students, the teacher, and the market. On the students' side, the insights are: gradual appropriation of the topic at stake; more spontaneous expression of their views; more emotional involvement; objectified opinions of biotechnology (development of representations); increased interest in biotechnology; actual learning; personal development; and development of dual skills. On the teacher's side, the findings are: more involved students; practical combination of both models' (TCM and LCM/PBL) advantages; and students' interest for transversal subjects such as the management of biotechnology. Finally, on the market's side the results are: developing a DCP-based educational approach to train dual skills profiles that answer to the needs of the biotechnology market; and making that approach beneficial for multidisciplinary markets that deal with social representation constraints.

6 Some Concluding Observations

In this chapter we have presented the fundamental tenets of the Development Centered Paradigm and explained how it is superior to the Teacher Centered Model and the Learning Centered Model for addressing the educational needs of current and future generations of learners. Additionally, we have described the practical application of a demonstration project at a French business school that represents an important step toward substantial implementation of the DCP philosophy.

We believe the DCP holds much promise for meaningfully addressing many of the challenges associated with the teaching/learning enterprise. We also believe that the DCP holds much promise for helping people develop into *functionally mature individuals*.

Without question, our explication of this important step toward the Development Centered Paradigm is but little more than 'a big toe in the water at the beach's edge' – but it is a movement toward what we hope will become a growing revolution in education in general, and in higher education in particular. Much work remains to be done, by ourselves as well as many others. Obviously, we believe that revolutionary transformation at all educational levels is needed – and particularly in higher education where we personally make our academic home. We invite the reader to join us in working toward revolutionary transformation of the teaching/learning enterprise based upon further development and application of the DCP.

References

Allport, G. W. (1961). *Pattern and growth in personality*. New York: Holt, Rinehart & Winston.
Argyris, C. (1957). *Personality and organization*. New York: Harper.
Argyris, C., Putman, R., & Smith, D. M. (1985). *Action science: Concepts, methods, and skills for research and Intervention*. San Francisco, CA: Jossey-Bass.

Argyris C., & Schôn, D. A. (1989). *Theory in practice: Increasing professional effectiveness.* San Francisco, CA: Jossey-Bass.

Bransford, J. D., Brown, A. L., & Cocking, R. R. (Eds.). (2000). *How people learn: Brain, mind, experience, and school.* Washington, DC : National Academy Press.

Bransford, J. D., & Stein, B. S. (1993). As cited in J. D. Bransford et al. (Eds.). (2000). *How people learn: Brain, mind, experience, and school* (p. 9). Washington, DC: National Academy Press.

Brown, K. L. (2003). From teacher-centered to learner-centered curriculum: Improving learning in diverse classrooms. *Education, 124*(1), 49–54.

Darling-Hammond, L. (2008, February 25). How they do it abroad. *Time, 171*(8), 34.

De Bie, D., & de Kleijn, J. (2001). *Wat gaan we doen? Het construeren en beoordelen van opdrachten [What are we going to do? Constructing and assessing assignments].* Houten, The Netherlands: Bohn Stafleu Van Loghum.

Dehler, G. E., & Welsh, M. A. (1997). Discovering the keys: Spirit in teaching and the journey of learning. *Journal of Management Education, 21*(4), 496–508.

Finger, M., & Asun, J. (2001). *Adult education at the crossroads. Learning our way out.* London: Zed Books.

Franz, R. S. (1998). Whatever you do, don't treat your students like customers! *Journal of Management Education, 22*(1),63–69.

Gilligan, C. (1982). *In a different voice: Psychological theory and women's development.* Cambridge, MA: Harvard University Press.

Hart, L. (1983). As cited in N. Lazeron, (2007), Leren Over en Met het Brein [Learning About and With the Brain]. *Leren in Organisaties*, 8(9),19.

Hofstede, G. (2001). *Cultures consequences: Comparing values, behaviors, institutions, and organizations across nations* (2nd ed.). Thousand Oaks, CA: Sage.

Kohlberg, L. (1976). Moral stages and moralization: The cognitive-development approach. In T. Lickona (Ed.), *Moral development and behavior: theory, research, and social issues.* New York: Holt, Rinehart and Winston.

Kohlberg, L. (1984). *The psychology of moral development: The nature and validity of moral stages.* New York: Harper and Row.

Kolb, D. A. (Ed.). (1984). *Experiential learning: Experience as the source of learning and development.* Englewood Cliffs, NJ: Prentice-Hall.

Kolb, A., & Kolb D. A. (2001). *Experiential learning theory bibliography 1971–2001.* Boston, MA: McBer.

Kunkel, S. W. (2002). Consultant learning: A model for student-directed learning in management education. *Journal of Management Education, 26*(2), 121–138.

Lazeron, N. (2007). Leren over en Met het Brein [Learning About and With the Brain]. *Leren in Organisaties*, 8(9), 16.

Lugo, J. O., & Hershey, G. L. (1974). *Human development: A multidisciplinary approach to the psychology of individual growth.* New York: Macmillan.

MacDonald, H. (1998, July 20). The flaw in student-centered learning. *New York Times*, section A, 15.

McCombs, B., & Whisler, J. (1997). *The learner-centered classroom and school: strategies for increasing student motivation and achievement.* San Francisco: Jossey-Bass.

McCuddy, M. K., Pirie, W. L., Schroeder, D. L., & Strasser, S. E. (2002). Issues in team teaching: Point and counterpoint. In T. A. Johannessen, A. Pedersen, & K. Petersen (Eds.), *Educational innovation in economics and business VI: Teaching today the knowledge of tomorrow* (pp. 63–74). Dordrecht: Kluwer.

McCuddy, M. K., & Reeb-Gruber, S. A. G. (2008). *Moving beyond teaching and learning: Arguments for a human development paradigm.* Paper presented at 2008 conference of educational innovation in economics and business (EDiNEB), Malaga, Spain.

Mezeske, B. (2004). Shifting paradigms? Don't forget to tell your students. *The Teaching Professor, 18*(7), 1–1.

Morse, K. (2007). Learning on demand: The education objective for the knowledge economy. In M. K. McCuddy, H. van den Bosch, W. B. Martz Jr., A. V. Matveev, & K. O. Morse (Eds.),

Educational innovation in economics and business X: The challenges of educating people to lead in a challenging world (pp. 33–49). Dordrecht: Springer.

Paris, C., & Combs, B. (2006). Lived meaning: What teachers mean when they say they are learner-centered. *Teachers and Teaching: Theory and Practice, 12*(5), 571–592.

Parker, M. (1998). Moral development. In R. Chadwick (Ed.-in-Chief), *Encyclopedia of applied ethics* (Vol. 3, pp. 267–273). San Diego, CA: Academic.

Piaget, J. (1932/1965). *The moral development of the child*. New York: Collier.

Pelton, J. N. (1996). Cyberlearning vs. the university: An irresistible force meets an immovable object. *The Futurist, 30*(6),17–20.

Samuelowicz, K., & Bain, J. D. (2001). Revisiting academic's beliefs about teaching and learning. *Higher Education, 41*, 299–325.

Savin-Baden M., & Howell C. (Eds.). (2004). *Foundations of problem-based learning, (Society for Research into Higher Education)*. Berkshire: Open University Press.

Van Merriënboer, J. J. G. (1997). *Training complex cognitive skills: A four component instructional design model for technical training*. Englewood Cliffs, NJ: Educational Technology Publications.

Watzlawick, P., Weakland, J. H., Fish, R., & Erickson, M. H. (1974). *Change principles of problem formation and problem resolution*. New York: W. W. Norton.

Wlodkwoski, R. J., & Ginsberg, M. B. (1995). *Diversity and motivation: Culturally responsive teaching*. San Francisco: Jossey-Bass.

Chapter 17
Leaders for the Twenty-First Century: Preparation, Experiences, and Roles in Technology Implementation

Lynne Schrum, Lyndsie M. Galizio, Mary C. English, and Patrick Ledesma

Abstract This research sought to understand perspectives of tech-savvy administrators from the US in regards to how they learned what they know and how they lead their schools in the twenty-first century. It explored this issue in light of gathered information about targeted other countries' requirements for administrator preparation. Looking through the lens of Fullan (1991), a mixed-methods survey gathered a sample of US leaders' perspectives. Findings indicate that most leaders have not been formally prepared to implement technology systemically in their school; rather, those with skills in this area have learned on their own or through other educational experiences. Successful tech-savvy leaders purposefully set goals for their school, serve as role models, and support professional development for staff.

Keywords Leadership · Technology implementation · Change process · Preparation of leaders

1 Introduction

Typically, significant effort is aimed at preparing teachers to integrate technology, through both preparation for licensure and professional development. A 2007 study (Kleiner, Thomas, & Lewis, 2007) found that 100% of teacher education institutions teach the use of Internet resources and communication tools for instruction; over 90% provide specific training on curricular integration, software, or digital content. Further, research has demonstrated that technology training for teachers does have an impact (Casey & Rakes, 2002; Ertmer, 2005; Wang, Ertmer, & Newby, 2004). Unfortunately, the same level of effort has not been given to prepare leaders in understanding the challenges they will face to support the effective

L. Schrum (✉)
George Mason University, CEHD Robinson A 337, Fairfax, VA MSN 4B3, USA
e-mail: lschrum@gmu.edu

use of educational technology in instructional ways (Holland & More-Steward, 2000; Schrum & Levin, 2009). Equally problematic is that without leadership from their administrator, professional development and training do not seem to influence teachers' ability to effectively use that technology (National Center for Educational Statistics [NCES], 2000).

This research sought to understand the perspectives of tech-savvy administrators, their technology-related skills, knowledge, and use, and how those administrators strive to lead their schools in the twenty-first century. Through a mixed methods design, and using Fullan's (1991, 2007) theoretical framework, this study explores the challenges of leading a school and preparing learners for the future.

2 Review of Literature

It seems clear that administrators are not able to lead their schools' or districts' technology integration if they do not understand what is involved in this process (Dawson & Rakes, 2003). Ritchie (1996) offered several variables that impact the implementation of educational technology for classroom use. He determined that lack of administrative support is the most important of these; without it, other variables are negatively impacted. Stegall's study (1998) found that leadership of the principal was a common thread in successful technology integration.

Dawson and Rakes (2003) addressed the need for administrators to take part in technology training and to model its use, and found that many principals are uninformed and uninvolved in the technology role of their schools. They concluded that there is a relationship between the technology training principals receive and the level of technology integration in their schools; as principals become leaders of technology and knowledgeable of its benefits, their teachers receive more support for integration. Testerman, Flowers, and Algozzine (2002) suggest 'If educational leaders continue to demonstrate developmental lags in their knowledge and technology competence, the expected benefits of innovative technology practices will likely be unrealized' (p. 60). Further, Fullan (2007) suggests that, 'The litmus test of all leadership is whether it mobilizes people's commitment to putting their energy into actions designed to improve things. It is individual commitment, but above all it is collective mobilization' (p. 9). This perspective of the need for collective mobilization guided this research study, as Fullan suggested.

In addition to leadership roles within the school, leaders have responsibilities outside the school. Moos and Johansson (2009) stated, 'Schools are profoundly dependent on their environments, be they political, administrative, community, professional, cultural or other. Therefore it is a very important practice for principals to manage and lead relations with the "outer" world. They must be able to understand and interpret signals and expectations from many stakeholders and they must also succeed in having the environments think that the school is successful...' (p. 770). Overall, it is suggested that general school outcomes can be directly tied to the effects of leadership activities (Leithwood, Jantzi, Silins, & Dart, 1993).

Given the impact of the leader's role in successful technology integration, it is important to determine how local or national requirements for school leaders' preparation relate to the larger context of administrators' and leaders' readiness to promote appropriate uses of technology, and to better grasp what may be required to lead twenty-first century schools.

2.1 Theoretical Lens

This investigation used the work of Fullan (1991, 2007) as the lens through which to examine the complexity of administrators' role in leading change and supporting teachers' use of educational technology. His notion of a complex, non-linear, and difficult process included three stages: initiation or adoption, implementation, and continuation or institutionalization. Additionally, Fullan (1991) suggests that teachers as learners require time to gain knowledge and then weave that knowledge into what they know and do in their instructional lives. He stated, 'The relationship between behavioral and belief change is reciprocal and ongoing, with change in doing or behavior a necessary experience on the way to breakthroughs in meaning and understanding' (1991, p. 91). It takes considerable practice for teachers to become technically proficient and for new behaviors to integrate with existing teaching repertoire.

Fullan (1991) maintained that in each of his three phases the school leader has responsibilities, including ongoing pressure and support, links to instruction, early rewards for educators, and raising the level of the innovation in terms of priorities. Similarly, leaders must have a deep understanding of the context of the school or district; they must know if the educators are ready for change or have the capacity for the specific change or innovation. A commitment to quality education, coupled with systematic movements toward improvement, characterize what Fullan (2007) describes as *reculturing* – a process in which community members routinely examine practices within schools that change practices as well as the culture within their professional communities. As Sergiovanni (2006) pointed out, the culture of a school is actually a negotiated product between school leadership and teachers within that school.

2.2 Transformational Leadership

For a long time, administrators were expected to be the instructional leaders of their schools; however, that form of leadership did not translate into the expectations of the 1990s and beyond (Leithwood, 1994). Instead, the notion of principals' transformational leadership was adopted. This notion that leaders must help focus on primary goals and motivate toward a shared goal has been shown to positively affect teachers' satisfaction both directly and indirectly through their occupation perceptions (Bogler, 2001).

Today, principals must deal with increasing complexity and add to the repertoire of responsibilities. Portin (2000) concluded that principals are increasingly decision-makers and continue to add managerial roles. Lauder (2000) also suggested that successful principals possess a strong knowledge base and the skill to use that knowledge effectively. Research provides evidence that leadership preparation programs do not adequately prepare school leaders. Murphy (2001) suggests that 'The problem with educational leadership preparation programs today is that they are driven by neither education nor leadership' (p. 14). Hess and Kelly (2007) surveyed 56 programs and analyzed course syllabi; they concluded that fewer than 5% included instruction on managing school improvement via data, technology, or empirical research.

When the infusion of technology is also involved in preparing leaders, change becomes even more multifaceted. The purpose of this research was to first identify the skills or requirements needed in the US to become a school leader, and then to understand perspectives of current US technology-savvy administrators on their experiences and goals, and what they report as their current skills, knowledge, and use of technology. To accomplish these goals, it began with the following question:

What do technology-savvy school administrators report about their preparation, experience, and practice in supporting, assisting, and promoting use of technology for integration into curricular

3 Methods

This study consisted of two phases. First, an in-depth investigation began to identify the requirements for leader certification from the 50 US states, and then from a small opportunity group of primarily English-speaking countries. Each of the 50 US states and eight other countries were examined. Phase Two consisted of an online survey (posted on SurveyMonkey), developed to identify the skills, knowledge, training, and experiences from a purposeful sample of administrators regarding instructional uses of technology and their interactions with their teachers regarding technology implementation. Using open-ended questions, researchers sought respondents' perspectives on preparation for being a leader, roles in schools, efforts to support technology integration and use, and ideas about the issues and challenges of technology implementation.

Participants. The goal was to gather data from technology-savvy administrators regarding their personal experiences and activities in relation to school leadership. A purposeful sample was determined to be essential. Targeted populations included members of a special interest group sponsored by the International Society for Technology in Education (ISTE) for administrators, members of the Classroom 2.0 Ning educator group, and targeted administrators who were identified through their blogs as familiar with and comfortable using educational technology.

Data from the survey provided descriptive statistical information regarding their years as leaders, their job descriptions and ages. Each researcher independently analyzed open-ended survey answers to determine a coding scheme and emergent themes (Merriam, 1998). Following the independent analysis, the researchers worked toward consensus through discussion, seeking inter-rater agreement.

4 Results

Phase One Results. As the investigation began, the research team gathered data on the fifty US states' requirements for leadership positions, the manner of licensure for those positions, and the types of requirements expected of those individuals seeking them. After a review of the US state licensure/certifications, we found that all of the states require that school principals/leaders have prior teaching experience, although some states do have 'alternative routes to certification.' The states typically follow the model used for educator licensure; that is, they allow specific institutions to prepare and recommend administrators for licensure or credentials. The institutions examined in this research have all successfully gone through a type of approval process in which the program of study is endorsed by the state. Thus, the research also sought to determine whether expectations exist for future leaders to guide their schools in educational uses of information technologies. Overall it was found that no such expectation exists in the programs or states reviewed.

Given the global focus of education today, it was also important to gather information about how similar the process of becoming a school leader in the US is to systems used by other countries. While it was not possible to find information for a large number of other countries (given language barriers and inability to locate correct information) the research team was able to uncover data for the following: Australia, Canada, Great Britain, Germany, Ireland, New Zealand, Singapore, and The Netherlands. Most of these countries require that an individual be a teacher before becoming a school leader, but other requirements vary. Table 17.1 provides the results of the countries identified through this convenience sample.

Table 17.1 Non-US countries' leadership requirements

Country	Teaching requirement	Additional training/education
Australia	• Minimum of 5 years	• University-level study of teaching or education or a Graduate Diploma of Education • Experience as a senior teacher and as a deputy principal
Canada	• Minimum of 3 years	• Each province has own rules, most require administrative training
Germany	• Minimum of 3 years	• Additional programs in school law and administrative tasks (mandatory)

Table 17.1 (continued)

Country	Teaching requirement	Additional training/education
Great Britain	• Must be a successful teacher or have some type of leadership role of some kind • No more than 12–18 months from applying to be a head teacher • Must have full support of current head teacher	• National Professional Qualification for Headship (NPQH), • Professional prerequisite of preparation for aspiring head-teachers in England and Wales • Leadership experience
Ireland	• Minimum of 5 years	• Many have master's or advanced degree
New Zealand	• Several years of teaching experience	• Take part in the National Aspiring Principals Programme to gain skills needed
Singapore	• Some teaching experience • Promoted from teacher to principal, then to Superintendent	• Department head role • Many heads of school were groomed as leaders since high school • Many 'leaders' are scholars
The Netherlands	• None required (however, most do have teaching experience)	• A certified course for school leadership exists

Phase Two Results. The survey questions focused on answering the second part of the research question. In all, 48 school-based administrators (principals, assistant principals, superintendents, central office administrators) responded to our call for participation. In addition, 102 technology leaders (central office technology leaders, school-based technology coordinators) responded to the survey. While their perspectives and data were not the initial focus of this study, these data were deemed as important both in terms of providing insight into their world and as a way to compare and contrast their perspectives with those of the school-based administrators. Those data are reported separately. School administrators who responded were primarily women (33 of 48), and fell primarily into one of two age groups: the 40–49 group (22) and over 50 group (23). Technology directors were also primarily women (56), and a majority were over the age of 50 (49) with some ranging in age from 30–39 (30), and a smaller number between 40–49 years (23). See Table 17.2 for a display

Table 17.2 Demographic information of respondents

Respondents	Women	Men	30–39 years	40–49 years	> 50 years
School based administrators	33	15	3	22	23
Technology leaders	56	46	30	23	49

of these two groups' demographic information. There were an additional 16 survey respondents who were not included in these results, since they were professors, students or others.

4.1 Learning What They Know

Participants were asked to provide information regarding how they learn about using technology for education activities. School-based administrators reported learning about technology on their own and during their teacher preparation programs. One principal stated she learned about technology, '...in my teaching through professional development opportunities and exploring on my own.' This was reiterated by an elementary school principal who described his learning experiences as, '...through reading literature, attending conferences, as well as using the equipment that is housed in our school.' In contrast, many of the survey participants who were leaders in technology within their school district noted they learned about using technology from their university course work, most typically in an educational technology master's or doctoral program. Survey respondents also reported using technology as a classroom teacher, and for managerial or clerical tasks.

Next, survey participants were asked to describe the role of technology in their school leader preparation programs. A majority of school-based administrators, as well as those in the technology director role, stated that they had had no specific instructional technology course (in their administration classes); however, a small number of participants did report that technology was emphasized within their classes with regards to assessment and data-driven decision making. One assistant principal stated, 'In my administrative coursework there was one class that was titled Educational Technology. The class had little to do with application, it was more focused on data-driven decision making.' This was further emphasized by a middle school principal who remarked, 'Very little practical technology was taught. Most was connected to research and testing.' Furthermore, some of the school-based administrators mentioned learning about technology as it was integrated into their graduate learning program. 'In my coursework, there was an understanding to use technology whenever possible, i.e., presentation software, databases, spreadsheets, and word processing,' explained one school principal. A chief school administrator stated, 'The use of technology was integrated into the (administrative) program. Instructors used it for class presentations, assignments were submitted electronically, and my research was done primarily online.' Finally, a few school-based administrators reported learning about technology as part of a doctoral program or continued advance studies. 'In my doctoral work, the role of technology was split with emphasis on technology integration into teaching, learning, and as a critical component of data-driven decision making,' explained an associate superintendent.

4.2 Current Use of Technology

The school-based administrators described many professional uses of technology in their everyday lives: communication, data analysis, professional uses (reports, spreadsheets, etc.), student management, and in their professional development for teachers. One said,

> I blog weekly as a model and a handful of teachers are becoming more regular in their postings as they find a purpose and an audience. Some members of my Leadership Team are beginning to produce podcasts of students as they explore the possibilities of this new technology.

Another reported, 'I use technology for typical office applications, organizing information, teacher appraisals, analyzing data, and for data driven decision making.' And one stated,

> As a building principal I use technology for communication in the form of email, blogs, and presentations. I just finished converting my "State of the School Address" to a podcast that will be placed on our school website. Additionally, I use technology to help my staff understand the vision of using technology as both a teaching and learning tool. Just one example is for the last two years during the "Welcome Back Breakfast" in August I show a motivational movie that I created.

Others' answers focused on tracking students and student data, as well monitoring the use of technology, and surveying stakeholders. Several school administrators described ways they model technology use, as this one who commented, 'Lead faculty meetings with a smart board. Use a blog to send out my weekly newsletter, participate in an online blog about a professional book the staff is reading, post weekly announcements to our Sharepoint site.'

As central office administrators, technology directors and coordinators reported using technology primarily for productivity and administrative applications such as email, word processing, data analysis, budgeting, presentations, and publications. They also reported integrating technology into staff development, curriculum and problem-solving efforts for technology implementation (such as interactive whiteboard implementation, etc.).

Another technology director reported, 'I am working on upgrading email, encouraging more video conferencing, and employing more technology tools in the classrooms.' And a coordinator of instructional technology stated they use technology for, 'curricular integration, formative and summative assessments, small group work, internet safety, email, virtual workspaces, video conferencing, and RSS feed readers.'

Other technology directors described using technology to assist with professional development. One said, 'As Director of Technology, I supervise staff development for teachers, administrators, and clerical staff.' Another explained they 'work with teachers on technology integration, plan staff developments, and make tech-related decisions for our district.' Another stated, 'Essentially, I provide professional development to teachers and administrators on technology integration in the classroom.'

School-based technology coordinators and resource specialists reported using technology for instructional purposes such as helping teachers to access resources and integrate new software or platforms such as blogs, wikis, and podcasts. Others reported using technology with online learning, video conferences, and webinars. As one technology specialist remarked, 'I use it continually—I look at what the teachers are teaching and I look at the curriculum – how it could all of it be delivered more effectively? Is there a tech tool that would help the teachers and/or learners?'

4.3 Encouraging Others

In general, the responses to this question fell into two main groups. Some districts or other organizational/institutional structures take a systemic approach in which the purchase, use, and support for technology is integrated into all aspects of activity. These include statements such as, '...competencies that all new teachers to the school must complete within their first three years' 'All new staff go through a Tech Boot Camp,' and 'Each of our teachers is required to have six hours of technology training every year.'

Some offer professional development for all educators in a 'one-size fits all' approach or in which teachers can pick and choose what they want to learn. Individuals reported traditional day long professional development workshops, summer tech camps, demonstration models, 'just-in-time' training as requested, and other inventive models. One school-based administrator reported, 'This year, my teachers will choose two NETS-T [standards] and focus on those. Their evaluation will depend on their achievement/growth in the identified standards.' Another commented, 'All educational community members at our school (teachers, admin[istrators], counselors, nurses) are given a laptop upon arrival at our school. They are supported from day one with PD [professional development] and online resources for learning how to use the machine.'

Other responses indicated a much more individual approach in which that one person appears to be a driving force in the development and promotion of technology use in curricular activities. One respondent described 'March Tech Madness' in which special sessions are offered throughout the month of March to coincide with the basketball tournament. Others support technology integration by encouragement or making professional development available all the time.

A few discussed ways they promote demonstration of various technology uses. For example, one stated, 'Three years ago when I made integration mandatory I set aside time at one staff meeting a month for the teachers to share what they were doing. This "positive peer pressure" did two things. One it helped the teachers learn of different techniques and programs to use, and it held them accountable to their colleagues.' Many of these described ways they try to model the technology use. One administrator commented, 'I encourage our educators by USING it, every day in every way. Our district focuses on the 4 Rs - Relationships, Rigor, Relevance, and Results.' Another stated, 'At the conclusion [of each faculty meeting], one of the teachers presents a five minute tech tip (teacher chosen at previous meeting) and shares the tool with everyone else.'

School administrators and technology directors/coordinators do have a shared sense of the importance or value of the technology. One said, 'I encourage teachers to use technology only when it makes sense. Teachers who use technology simply for technology's sake do all of us a disservice.' Another commented, 'We strongly encourage use of technology as a means to differentiate instruction and to increase student motivation.'

A small number of respondents did mention changes in their budgets in the current economic downturn and the need to scale back their spending; others talked about using [US] federal funds to continue their professional development and technology purchases. Many did mention going after grant funds to support their use of technology.

4.4 Future Uses of Technology

Many administrators believe that technology's role in education will continue to expand within the next five years as it becomes more prevalent in all school operations. One administrator commented that 'Technology is the pen and pencil and the library of the future.' Many believe that one-to-one computing will be common and every classroom will have interactive whiteboards.

These leaders believe that technology will increase the learning opportunities for students and educators. Teachers will also be able to benefit from more professional development options. The school-based leaders indicated that future would bring new challenges for them to understand technology, become role models, and develop a vision. We 'cannot inspire teachers if (we) are not technologically savvy,' remarked one. Another commented, 'Administrators must have a vision of technology use, model this vision in the professional practice, and develop teacher leaders who take a lead role in implementing said technology vision.' In addition one said, 'We need to discover what value we add to learning for students and then be thoughtful about how the use of technology fits with the process.'

According to the administrators, the next 5 years will be one of tremendous potential and challenge. As one administrator commented, 'If done right technology will become invisible in the classroom, as it will be the standard tool for learning content and communicating what the student has learned.' They cited examples such as 1:1 computing, interactive whiteboards in every classroom, handheld devices, online classes for teachers and students, and an increased online presence for classrooms that will maximize access and opportunities for learning. There will be an increase of teachers using technology to create more 'teacher created' content such as podcasts and videos, and more opportunities for students to use technology to demonstrate their learning. Others identified the increase in the use of blogs, wikis, and podcasts in the classroom. Many remarked that technology would become 'seamless' in the classroom and part of the everyday routines. Others emphasized the transformative potential of technology for student learning and the importance for educators to be prepared for those changes.

Many technology directors also noted the challenges from technology's expanding role – specifically the need for administrators to understand its potential in order to articulate a vision for the school, provide staff development opportunities, and support all teachers. The technology directors worry about the financial challenges for continued funding to maintain and expand the infrastructure to ensure equal access. One specialist commented, 'In the past ten years, my job has evolved from teaching users how to double-click to teaching them how to get the best use of data available in the data warehouse, to how to create fully integrated lessons. We've gone from 'Why do I have to do that on a computer' to 'What do you mean I can only have two student computers in my room?' The technology directors also expressed the importance of collaborating with Information Technology departments to establish proactive and instructionally appropriate procedures for Internet filtering and student use of technology.

5 Discussion

The respondents did not all meet the criteria of being administrators, and further, not everyone who is an administrator went through a traditional licensure program. These situations complicated the data collection process as not all respondents provided meaningful data. We did not ask about individuals' geographic location, which may or may not have had an impact on our analysis. Finally, the sample was purposeful and thus, we can assume that those who responded have already self-identified as technology using administrators so it would be extremely informative to gather perspectives from those school leaders who do not consider themselves tech-savvy administrators.

Given the limitations, the data do still provide insight into the state and institutional expectations and current practice. More importantly, the responses from individual practitioners provided excellent information about how and when they learned about using and supporting technology in their schools. It appears clear that these individuals take responsibility for staying current, modeling the appropriate use of technology, and supporting the professional development of their staff. They see these as some of the many roles within the larger context of being the leader of a twenty-first century school.

In light of the general ages of the respondents, and given that it does take some years as a classroom teacher prior to assuming a leadership role, it is encouraging that these school leaders have stayed current, improved their skills and experiences, and also see themselves as role models in this position. They also expend effort and resources to improve their staff's knowledge of current technologies.

It is not surprising that the technology directors learned about technology integration and support in their graduate programs, and see this as the major focus of their positions. It is interesting, however, that they see their communication and relationship with school administrators as an essential part of their role. Additionally, the school administrators and technology directors expressed such similar comments about the uses of technology, ways of encouraging teacher use of the tools, and their visions of the future of over the next few years.

Future research questions. This research was a first step in understanding the complex issues surrounding school leaders' knowledge, skills, and interest in promoting the instructional use of educational technology, by themselves and by their staff. It would be of interest to investigate students' use of the tools, as well as ways that school leaders evaluate or assess teacher and student use. And even though a great deal of research has been conducted to examine this innovation from teachers' perspectives, it might be helpful to understand what teachers see as needed from their school leaders to encourage, support, or require them to use technology in curricular ways.

Given that many school-based administrators with a high comfort level with technology have learned their skills on their own or outside their formal training, it may be helpful to investigate how administrators with lower levels of comfort with technology learn skills for their own professional use, and how this may affect their ability to make decisions regarding technology integration and staff development. It would also be helpful to understand if leaders without a strong understanding of technology perceive resulting impact on their ability to lead. If so, then who in the school or school system assumes that responsibility and what are the implications? As technology becomes a larger part of learners' and future teachers' daily lives, what does a leader need to know and do?

6 Conclusion

Research suggests that building and district level leaders are essential to the thoughtful and appropriate integration of technology into professional and curricular aspects of the education system. The purpose of this study was to take a scan of the technology-savvy leaders to determine their preparation for and approaches to leading their schools in the technology integration, and their perspectives on these experiences and challenges. The good news is that many respondents are self-taught, and see the use and support of technology as important to their ability to effectively lead schools today. The question still remains, however, regarding how those school administrators who do not learn these skills impact their teachers, students, and the larger educational community. Finally, the information gathered from the participants provided insight into the ways that school leaders are accomplishing their goals with respect to supporting the effective use and curricular applications of educational technology, and encouraging their staff to stay current. This research project provides a glimpse into one country's administrators and where they see their future; moreover, it points out some ways to improve the preparation, readiness, and actions of all administrators in our schools. It further made a beginning step toward identifying global issues regarding school leaders and administrators. This research team encourages a wider discussion and investigation into preparation, training, and requirements for these leaders to support and encourage thoughtful and appropriate uses of information technologies.

References

Bogler, R. (2001). The influence of leadership style on teacher job satisfaction. *Educational Administration Quarterly, 37*(5), 662–683.

Casey, H. B., & Rakes, G. C. (2002). An analysis of the influences of technology training on teacher stages of concern regarding the use of instructional technology in schools. *Journal of Computing in Teacher Education, 18*(4), 124–132.

Dawson, C., & Rakes, G. (2003). The influence of principals' technology training on the integration of technology into schools. *Journal of Research on Technology in Education, 36*(1), 29–49.

Ertmer, P. A. (2005). Teacher pedagogical beliefs: The final frontier in our quest for technology integration? *Educational Technology Research and Development, 53*(4), 25–39.

Fullan, M. (2007). *Leading in a culture of change* (Rev. ed.). San Francisco: Jossey-Bass.

Fullan, M. (1991). *The new meaning of educational change* (3rd ed.). New York: Teachers College Press.

Hess, F. M., & Kelly, A. P. (2007). Learning to lead: What gets taught in principal-preparation programs? *Teachers College Record, 109*(1), 244–274.

Holland, L., & Moore-Steward, T. (2000). A different divide: Preparing tech-savvy leaders. *Leadership, 30*(1), 8–10, 37–38.

Kleiner, B., Thomas, N., & Lewis, L. (2007). *Educational Technology in Teacher Education Programs for Initial Licensure* (NCES 2008–040). Washington, DC: National Center for Education Statistics, Institute of Education Sciences, U.S. Department of Education.

Lauder, A. (2000). The new look in principal preparation programs. *NASSP Bulletin, 84*(617), 23–28.

Leithwood, K. A. (1994). Leadership for school restructuring. *Educational Administration Quarterly, 30*(4), 498–518.

Leithwood, K., Jantzi, D., Silins, H., & Dart, B. (1993). Using the appraisal of school leaders as an instrument for school restructuring. *Peabody Journal of Education, 68*(2), 85–109.

Merriam, S. B. (1998). *Qualitative research and case study applications in education* (2nd ed.). San Francisco: Jossey-Bass.

Moos, L., & Johansson, O. (2009). The international successful school principalship project: Success sustained? *Journal of Educational Administration, 47*(6), 765–780.

Murphy, J. (2001). The changing face of leadership preparation. *School Administrator, 58*(10), 14–17.

National Center for Education Statistics. (2000). *Teachers' tools for the 21st century: A report on teachers' use of technology.* Jessup, MD: U.S. Department of Education.

Portin, B. (2000). The changing urban principalship. *Education and Urban Society, 32*(4), 492–505.

Ritchie, D. (1996). The administrative role in the integration of technology. *National Association of Secondary School Principals. NASSP Bulletin, 80*, 42–52.

Schrum, L., & Levin, B. B. (2009). *Leading 21st Century Schools: Harnessing Technology for Engagement and Achievement.* Thousand Oaks, CA: Corwin Press.

Sergiovanni, T. J. (2006). *The principalship: A reflective practice perspective.* Boston: Pearson Education.

Stegall, P. (1998). *The principal-key to technology implementation.* ERIC Document Reproduction Service No. ED424614.

Testerman, J. C., Flowers, C. P., & Algozzine, R. (2002). Basic technology competencies of educational administrators. *Contemporary Education, 72*(2), 58–61.

Wang, L., Ertmer, P. A., & Newby, T. J. (2004). Increasing preservice teachers' self-efficacy beliefs for technology integration. *Journal of Research on Technology in Education, 36*(3), 231–250.

Chapter 18
Pedagogy and Content Knowledge Based Podcasting Project for Preservice Teachers

Junko Yamamoto

Abstract This study examines the impact of an instruction based on the technological pedagogical content knowledge (TPACK) framework on podcasting and vodcasting for preservice teachers in the United States. Podcasting and vodcasting enhances public school learners' creativity and critical thinking as well as verbal skills. Preservice teachers enrolled in teacher preparation programs benefit from learning pedagogical reasons to implement podcasting and vodcasting. However, the conceptual knowledge is not enough. They should also have the technology skills to facilitate them in the context of the subject they are teaching. The result indicates that the research participants developed positive attitudes towards using podcasting and vodcasting in their classrooms after the instructional sequences.

Keywords Podcasting · Vodcasting · Preservice teacher · TPACK

1 Introduction

This study aimed to facilitate a pedagogy-based project in using sound files and video files within the context of the certificate areas of preservice teachers. After they created sound and video files in groups, they uploaded the files in cyber space, and shared the links to download files with their peers. Downloadable sound files are called podcasting, and downloadable video files are vodcasting.

Public school teachers need to consider teaching literacy in a multimedia format (Luce-Kapler, 2007) because their students grow up with televisions and computers. As a result, the students in public schools view literacy in the form of multimedia (Dresang, 1999; Pantaleo, 2006; Unsworth, 2008). In addition, media production including voice recording and video recording encourages students to talk with an

J. Yamamoto (✉)
Slippery Rock University of Pennsylvania, 206 McKay Education Building, Slippery Rock, PA 16057, USA
e-mail: junko.yamamoto@sru.edu

end-product in goal. Practicing to talk academically gives students an opportunity to propel their thinking (Thompson, 2008). Oral language development enhances written language development: in fact, children learn to speak before they learn to write. Injecting meaningful spoken-language-based literacy activities is an especially important concept in today's public schools in the United States where there are non-native speakers of English because English Language Learners (ELL) are thrown into an academic environment without having time to develop oral language first (Fisher, Frey, & Rothenberg, 2008).

The accommodation of diverse learners is an important academic concept for today's educators. Preservice teachers need exposure to a wide range of strategies in order to teach diverse learners, including English Language Learners in the United States. Interaction represents a crucial piece for language acquisition (Beckner, Blythe, Bybee, Christensen, Croft, Ellis, et al., 2009; Ziglari, 2008). Specifically, English Language Learners need context-rich environments to acquire academic language (Fisher, Frey, & Rothenberg, 2008). Natural language acquisition requires a great amount of input and output of spoken language. The proficiency in spoken language transitions into reading and writing skills. Language use for interaction with the environment and with peers also helps native speakers and non-native speakers of English to build critical thinking.

The production of podcasting, or audio files published on the Internet, has the potential to enhance instruction in a diverse classroom. For example, podcasting can be a great medium to enforce correct pronunciation in language instruction (Lord, 2008). Likewise, vodcasting, or online video broadcasting, strengthens the script writing and speaking of students in any subject area. Use of video in English can provide feedback to learners' performance: this reflective process can motivate them to speak better (Hung, 2009). Podcasting and vodcasting can facilitate the social interaction of students when they are assigned as group projects.

An important concept that teacher educators need to emphasize is that podcasting or vodcasting is just a means of instruction and it is up to teachers' pedagogical knowledge and content expertise to make either one of them an effective learning tool. If a group of students is mindlessly reading assigned texts and uploading a voice recording, the activity does not enhance the students' creativity or critical thinking. However, if learners write and edit their own scripts, record, and publish (Lee, McLoughlin, & Chan, 2008), podcasting can be a powerful instructional process. By the same token, if students studying German simply memorized and recited Goethe's Erlkönig (Elf King) and uploaded the voice recording to a web site, the podcasting would not enhance creativity or critical thinking. When a student is required to analyze the characters and shifting emotions in the poem and express it, or when students are required to incorporate Franz Schubert's musical interpretation of the poem and create a music video, then the students' creativity and critical thinking are nurtured. Hence, teacher educators need to impress on future teachers that they need to start with content and pedagogy prior to thinking about technology (Harris & Hofer, 2009).

Knowing pedagogical benefits and strategies is not enough for preservice teachers to successfully set up podcasting and vodcasting in their future classrooms. They have to have hands-on experience in creating podcasting and vodcasting if their students are to create them. Being confident in hardware and software promotes a positive attitude about using such technology. An ideal technology instruction for preservice teachers weaves technology, pedagogy, and content knowledge together (Harris, Mishra, & Koehler, 2009). Lacking any of the three can lead to a negative attitude about using technology in class (Lloyd & Albion, 2009). This is true even for today's college-age students who are accustomed to a variety of social networking tools. Their ability to use technology for personal enjoyment does not automatically transform to using technology for instruction (Lei, 2009). Therefore, teacher education institutions need to structure technology training around enhancing critical and creative thinking (Lambert & Cuper, 2008).

However, using technology to support learning is rather complex (Keengwe, Onchwari, & Wachira, 2008) because it entails diverse contexts (Koehler & Mishra, 2008). The technological pedagogical content knowledge (TPACK) framework is useful for designing technology instruction for teachers (Harris, Mishra, & Koehler, 2009; Koehler & Mishra, 2005).

2 Theoretical Framework

As its name represents, TPACK combines technology, pedagogy, and content knowledge in instructional planning. Since every classroom is unique and dynamic, there is no single solution that works in all cases. However, there is a common denominator that educators have to know the content to teach and know how to teach it. They also have to know how the technology can best enhance learning (Mishra & Koehler, 2006). Therefore merely using technology in the classroom does not satisfy this framework (Koehler & Mishra, 2005). Factors such as knowledge of students, knowledge of schools, the subject to be taught, and instructional strategies are all included in this framework (Niess et al., 2009).

The framework includes declarative, procedural, schematic, and strategic knowledge. Teacher education using the TPACK framework aims for an attitude change to constantly rethink and adapt to diversity and dynamic changes in classrooms (Niess, 2008). Nurturing the attitude to think that technology-enriched projects contribute to students' learning is an important role for teacher education institutions because some teachers perceive such projects as 'stop[ping] teaching' (Hofer & Swan, 2008).

When sound pedagogy and content knowledge are present, educators can take social networking tools that were not invented for education and convert them into learning agents (Mishra & Koehler, 2009). The podcasting and vodcasting projects for the preservice teachers in this research included discussion in pedagogy, project designs to promote content knowledge, and hands-on production. This paper discusses the sequencing and the impact of instruction about podcasting and vodcasting in an undergraduate level instructional technology class. This instruction occurred at the end of the semester. By the time the preservice teachers were engaged in this instruction, they were accustomed to defining learning outcomes first, making pedagogical decisions, and then thinking about how technology can enhance their learning goals.

3 Research

The research Questions include:

1. Will the preservice teachers enrolled in an undergraduate level instructional technology class gain confidence in using podcasting and vodcasting in the classroom after a group production of podcasting and vodcasting?
2. Will the preservice teachers enrolled in an undergraduate level instructional technology class consider podcasting and vodcasting as useful instructional media as the result of the instruction on podcasting and vodcasting?

3.1 Research Participants

Preservice teachers enrolled in two sections of an undergraduate level instructional technology class during the 2009 spring semester served as research participants. One section had 20 enrolled and the other section had 23. After the informed consent process, 34 preservice teachers consented to have their survey and their comments used for this study. Also, 33 agreed to have their videos and audio used. Table 18.1 illustrates the breakdown of the research participants according to certificate areas.

Table 18.1 The number of preservice teachers according to certificate area

Certificate area	Frequency	Percent
Elementary education	13	38.2
Elementary and special education	11	32.4
Elementary and early childhood	2	5.9
English	1	2.9
History	4	11.8
Spanish	1	2.9
Environmental education	1	2.9
Special education	1	2.9
Total	34	100.0

3.2 Research Instrument

Participants filled in a Likert-type scale survey comprised of questions regarding their perceptions and confidence in using podcasting and vodcasting for instructional purposes. The scaled ranged from 1 to 4, 1 being 'strongly disagree' and 4 being 'strongly agree'. They also wrote comments to explain why they chose the score for each question. The survey was taken immediately before and after the instruction for pre-post comparison.

3.3 Instruction Based on TPACK Model

The preservice teachers had the podcasting and vodcasting projects at the end of the semester. At the beginning of the semester, it was already established that successful technology integration into the classroom starts by setting learning goals first, making pedagogical decisions, and then selecting a technology solution (Harris & Hofer, 2009).

Prior to hands-on instruction, preservice teachers researched what podcasting is in a group. The groups were clustered based on the preservice teachers' certificate area. Due to the fact that there was only one history education major, English education major and Spanish education major in one section, they were put together in one group. For this group, the instructor provided some examples for how they could collaboratively pick a topic that was applicable for all subjects, such as writing on a historical event in Spain.

The instructor provided a PowerPoint template with six questions for the participants to answer as a form of scaffolding:

1. What is podcasting?
2. How will I facilitate creativity with podcasting?
3. How will I stimulate critical thinking with podcasting?
4. How will my students enhance content knowledge with podcasting?
5. What type of online broadcasting can your students create? Can your students choose from different types (news, sport casting talk show), or would you assign a specific one to your students? Why?
6. What would be the benefits if students analyzed the speech style of a talk show host, news caster, etc., and recreate the style? Can you also think of drawbacks?

In order to answer questions, some groups referred to journal articles selected by the instructor. All groups used the internet to find out what podcasting and vodcasting are. Two groups from each class gave PowerPoint presentations to their peers. Preservice teachers in the class had already connected critical thinking to Bloom's Taxonomy, and had applied the concept to other technology-based project such as WebQuest prior to this point. They had also established the relationship between creativity and the synthesis level of Bloom's Taxonomy.

After the presentations about podcasting, the class had a discussion to reinforce their ideas about pedagogy and content knowledge using podcasting. Then the instructor explained the hands-on project for podcasting to the class. The preservice teachers downloaded the explanation and the assessment rubric from Blackboard.

The pre-production planning instruction included:

- Explain how your project will enhance the content knowledge of your learners.
- Explain how your project will facilitate creative thinking and critical thinking. Refer to your textbook or other literature.

Groups discussed the content and pedagogy by answering these questions. They invited the instructor to exchange ideas with them as they made the plan.

After groups finished their pre-production plans, they downloaded the how-to manuals with graphics that the instructor prepared for creating mp3 files with Audacity and publishing the sound files through Box.net. Each group received one laptop with a built-in microphone and Audacity. They used the instruction to record, edit, and convert sounds with Audacity and to upload sound files to Box.net. All groups sought out the instructor's help in addition to the manuals at various points. All groups completed their podcasting projects within 1.5 h. The class then listened to the completed podcastings. The production path is shown in Fig. 18.1.

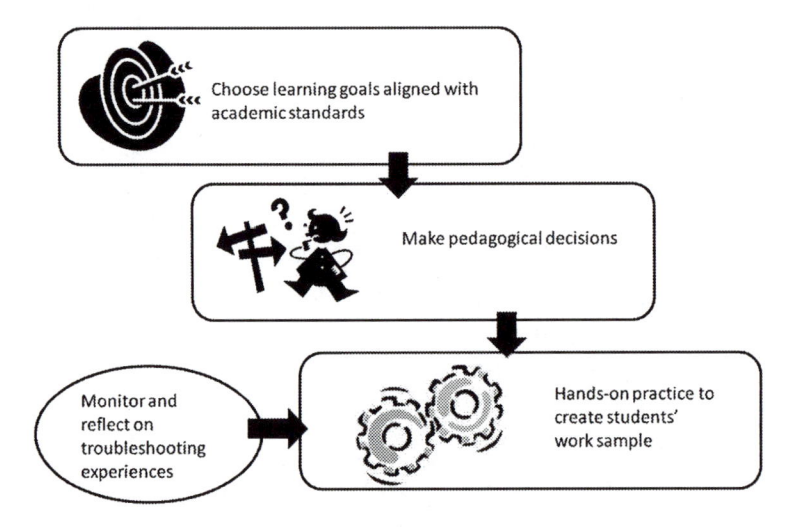

Fig. 18.1 Podcasting production path

The class then moved onto the production of vodcasting following 4 steps. First, preservice teachers started with a lesson objective aligned with academic and technology standards. Second, they created a story board. Third, each group checked out a Flip Video to record the video. Fourth, they used a laptop with Windows Movie Maker to edit the video. Since the groups started editing videos at different times, they used the Movie Maker manual that the instructor created and the instructor's assistance as needed. All groups completed their vodcasting projects within 5 hours. Some groups completed their projects much sooner and moved onto the next project, a digital portfolio while some groups experienced glitches and took time to fix the problems.

Finally, one notable aspect about this project is that podcasting and vodcasting were assigned towards the end of the semester. The participants had already learned about critical thinking and creative thinking. They had also established the habit of thinking about increasing the quality of learning and supporting it with various technologies. It appears that anything that is done toward the end of the semester is more meaningful than the earlier assignments because the web of pedagogical knowledge is more intricate.

3.3.1 Glitches: Teachable Moment

Prior to the project, the instructor informed preservice teachers that even though she prepared manuals for creating mp3 with Audacity, editing videos with Window's Movie Maker, and uploading and sharing audio and video files through Box.net, they may experience technical glitches. When they did, they monitored their approaches. They shared how they solved their problems after the project completion. Most groups in both sections experienced some kind of glitch. They orally stated that knowing how to fix problems added to their confidence in using technology. This confidence, they stated, is necessary for them to learn new technology as they constantly change.

3.4 Result

Chronbach's Alpha was used to check for the research participants' subjectivity. With Alpha = .951, it was determined that the survey tool is reliable. T-test was used to compare means for the respondents' answers for pre-instruction and post-instruction. Table 18.2 shows the result of the *t*-test.

Table 18.2 Pre-post instructional comparison of the participants' answers

	Pre mean	Post mean	Mean (Pre-post)	Std. Dev.	*t*	df	Sig. (2-tailed)
Podcasting is useful in classrooms	2.15	3.35	−1.206	1.175	−5.984	33	0.000
Vodcasting is useful in classrooms	2.00	3.47	−1.471	1.187	−7.226	33	0.000
The combination of podcasting and vodcasting is useful in classrooms	2.06	3.44	−1.382	1.326	−6.078	33	0.000
I am confident that I can create podcasting	1.91	3.53	−1.618	1.256	−7.512	33	0.000
I am confident that I can create vodcasting	1.85	3.56	−1.706	1.315	−7.565	33	0.000
I am confident that I can participate in a blog	3.03	3.15	−.118	1.008	−.681	33	0.501
I am confident that I can facilitate a blog for instructional purpose	2.62	2.97	−.353	1.252	−1.643	33	0.110
I am confident that I can facilitate podcasting in the area of my certification	2.09	3.41	−1.324	1.065	−7.245	33	0.000

Table 18.2 (continued)

	Pre mean	Post mean	Paired differences Mean (Pre-post)	Std. Dev.	t	df	Sig. (2-tailed)
I am confident that I can facilitate vodcasting in the area of my certification	2.06	3.47	−1.412	1.104	−7.455	33	0.000
I am confident that I can combine podcasting, vodcasting, and a blog in the area of my certification	1.94	3.21	−1.265	1.238	−5.954	33	0.000

3.4.1 Research Question 1

The first research question in this study was: 'Will the preservice teachers enrolled in an undergraduate level instructional technology class gain confidence in using podcasting and vodcasting in the classroom after a group production of podcasting and vodcasting?' Questions related to confidence were used in order to answer this question.

For the statement, 'I am confident that I can create podcasting,' the mean score for the pre-instructional survey was 1.91. The mean score for the post-instructional survey was 3.53. The $t(33) = -7.512$, $p < .05$. For the statement, 'I am confident that I can create vodcasting,' the mean score for the pre-instructional survey was 1.85. The mean score for the post-instructional survey was 3.56. The $t(33) = -7.565$, $p < .05$. For the statement, 'I am confident that I can facilitate podcasting in the area of my certification,' the mean score for the pre-instructional survey was 2.09. The mean score for the post-instructional survey was 3.41. The $t(33) = -7.245$, $p < .05$. For the statement, 'I am confident that I can facilitate vodcasting in the area of my certification,' the mean score for the pre-instructional survey was 2.06. The mean score for the post-instructional survey was 3.47. The $t(33) = -7.455$, $p < .05$. These results indicate that the confidence level in using podcasting and vodcasting significantly improved after the instruction.

Since podcasting and vodcasting are often embedded in blogs, there was a question regarding blogs. For the statement, 'I am confident that I can participate in a blog,' the mean score for the pre-instructional survey was 3.05. The mean score for the post-instructional survey was 3.15. The $t(33) = -681$. The p value was .501. The result was not statistically significant because the mean score prior to the instruction was already high.

Typical comments in the pre-instructional point included, 'I've seen blogs before.' Three reported that they had participated in blogs before. This explains the high mean score at the pre-instructional point. Comments regarding blogs at the post-instructional stage add another layer. To keep the instructional process simple, the preservice teachers did not go through the process of embedding podcasting and vodcasting into a blog. Therefore some answered, 'We did not have to make or participate in a blog,' and, 'I have never blogged before,' and assigned low scores for 'I am confident that I can participate in a blog.' This implies that hands-on practice and familiarity are tied to confidence.

A statement from a preservice teacher in the class supports this implication: 'I had never done vodcasting or podcasting so I was unsure of the assignment. After being instructed and walked through it, it made much more sense and I felt more comfortable with it. After doing the assignments I am confident that I can do it myself, and for my certification area. I can see how it would be helpful in the classroom.' Another participant stated, 'Before we started working on podcasting and vodcasting, I had no idea what either of them were or how to create such things. I now have a better understanding of how to create them and how I could use them in the classroom. My attitude towards them has changed significantly. At the beginning, the idea of using podcasting/ vodcasting was scary to me, but I now feel with a little practicing I could create my own!!' One also stated, 'I had never done podcasting before, but now I am confident that I can create a podcast.' As shown in these statements, 13 participants connected increased familiarity as the cause of the confidence.

Fear of glitches can negatively impact attitudes about new technology (Lloyd & Albion, 2009). With that in mind, dealing with glitches while learning new technology was woven into this instructional process. It appears that such obstacles facilitated stronger confidence in this instruction. One preservice teacher stated, 'I enjoyed using podcasting and vodcasting. I did not know how to do either of these before class but now I feel like I would be able to do this in my classroom. My group ran into a few problems while doing both the podcasting and the vodcasting but we were able to fix our mistakes and I feel that I actually learned more because of this. I found that creating these were very helpful.' To echo this statement, another said, 'I really did learn a lot from our mistakes.'

3.4.2 Research Question 2

The second research question was: 'Will the preservice teachers enrolled in an undergraduate level instructional technology class consider podcasting and vodcasting as useful instructional media as the result of the instruction on podcasting and vodcasting?' The mean scores for pre-instruction and post-instruction for the statements related to usefulness were compared.

For the statement, 'Podcasting is useful in classrooms,' the mean score for the pre-instructional survey was 2.15. The mean score for the post-instructional survey was 3.35. The $t(33) = -5.984$, $p < .05$. For the statement, 'Vodcasting is useful in classrooms,' the mean score for the pre-instructional survey was 2.00. The mean score for the post-instructional survey was 3.47. The $t(33) = -7.226$, $p < .05$. For the statement, 'The combination of podcasting and vodcasting is useful in classrooms,' the mean score for the pre-instructional survey was 2.06. The mean score for the post-instructional survey was 3.44. The $t(33) = -6.078$, $p < .05$. Thus, all the statements yielded significantly higher means for all three statements at the post-instructional point.

As for the pedagogical reasons to use podcasting and vodcasting for instruction, eight participants connected the projects to creativity. Six participants mentioned that it allows learning through audio and video. Six mentioned enjoyment in the learning process. Four participants stated that the strategy is useful to accommodate English Language Learners. Four said that the process stimulates critical thinking, and two mentioned the active engagement in the learning process. One said that podcasting and vodcasting allow different forms of assessment. Those comments were written on either the blank spaces under the survey statements or on the back of the survey sheets. For drawbacks, one participant mentioned, 'Can be useful but may be confusing for some students.' One stated that software may be hard for students to learn, and one stated that some schools may not be able to purchase the equipment.

Mixed comments on pedagogy and content included, 'Vodcasting and podcasting can be very useful in the classroom because they allow students to hear and see what they are learning about. Also students can do research on a topic and then create a vodcast or podcast. I enjoyed creating vodcasts and podcasts.' Mixed comments on technology and pedagogy included, 'At first, I was not sure how to use or create a podcast, or a vodcast. I think that both are definitely very easy to put together, and can be extremely useful. Podcasts can be used in the English classroom to help students understand readings.'

One preservice teacher stated, 'Podcasting and vodcasting were foreign terms to me before this class, but now they aren't! Both podcasting and vodcasting are untraditional ways to expose students to new ways of learning. Both techniques allow students to use creativity and critical thinking through technology. I had no idea that devices like "Flip" existed, and I was very happy to learn that they are inexpensive and easy to use. Glitches that I could not control did *not* cause me to have a bad opinion of the program. It is very beneficial.' This researcher suspects that this preservice teacher had a positive attitude about glitches because they were treated as learning opportunities: the group members collaboratively and systematically fixed glitches. After podcasting and vodcasting were completed, they orally shared how they solved their problems.

4 Discussion

While planning lessons learning goals must come first prior to selecting materials and an instructional procedure. Hence, technology should be secondary to learning (Egbert, 2009). Novice teachers can make mistakes by selecting hardware and software first and then catering their instructional plan around them. A dilemma for technology instructors at colleges of education is teaching learning-goal-centered instructional planning while all in the class practice the same technological skills.

In this instruction preservice teachers first researched what podcasting is and how it is used in their own certificate areas. After they answered five pedagogical questions related to podcasting in small groups according to their certificate areas, they had a class discussion to exchange their answers. In addition, the groups made an instructional plan starting with learning goals. They then produced podcasting. Preservice teachers in this study commented about pedagogical justifications in using podcasting for their subjects in this study. A limitation of this study is that no one in the class practiced technology without the presence of learning goals and pedagogical justification. Therefore, it is impossible to know if preservice teachers can make references to pedagogy when the scaffolding to think about it is absent.

Those who are considered digital natives did not know Flip Video and did not know how to edit a digital video. Digital video can deepen reflection on their teaching (Calandra, Brantley-Dias, Lee, & Fox, 2009), and the preservice teachers in this study were exposed to an affordable and easy-to-use video recording device prior to their student teaching. When preservice teachers move onto student teaching, they may or may not have on-site support to fix technical failures. Therefore, it seems beneficial that students in this instructional technology class not only used the digital video hardware and the software, but also reflected on how they fixed glitches.

Even though the value of 'having fun' was not explicitly taught during this project, some preservice teachers pointed it out as a pedagogical reason to implement podcasting. Enjoyment in learning can feed into motivation and it can also lower anxiety. Although correlation does not automatically suggest causation, there is a link between emotion and learning (Dörnyei & Kormos, 2000; Ewald, 2007; Lei, 2007; Zarra, 2009) and the connection between teachers' motivational practices and students' motivation is documented (Guilloteaux & Dörnyei, 2008).

5 Conclusion

5.1 Summary of This Study

This study illustrated the impact a methodical teaching approach in the development of positive attitudes about using podcasting and vodcasting for class use among preservice teachers. Podcasting and vodcasting projects for preservice teachers must begin with research on pedagogy, promote presentation and discussion on pedagogy, and finalize hands-on production in preservice teachers' content areas. Qualitative data suggest that the participants did not know how to create podcasting or vodcasting, with thirty out of thirty-three participants stated that they had never heard of it.

Preservice teachers' perceptions of the usefulness of podcasting and vodcasting increased after this instructional approach. All of them provided at least one pedagogical reason to explain why they are useful, ranging from creativity, accommodating diverse learners such as English Language Learners, enjoying the learning process, to offering different types of assessment. Pleasurable instruction was not explicitly taught or discussed during the instructional process. However, preservice teachers pointed it out as an important factor. This finding parallels a previous study that inservice teachers consider making learning fun as reason to use new technology (Kebritchi, 2010).

5.2 Limitations

Although it was an intriguing finding that research participants pointed out a benefit of podcasting that was specifically not mentioned during the lecture or discussion, it also reveals a limitation of this study. It is not clear if preservice teachers could have pointed out other pedagogical reasons on their own, or if they became aware of them as the result of this instruction. The participants might have pointed out pedagogical justifications for podcasting without lecture or discussion about podcasting prior to the production.

Another limitation of this study is that it only relied on preservice teachers as the research participants. Neiss and his colleagues (2009) identified five steps for teachers to fully engage students into learning with technologies: recognizing, accepting, adapting, exploring, and advancing. Since preservice teachers lack the classroom experiences that inservice instructors possess, the participants in this research may only have recognized and accepted the benefits of podcasting and vodcasting. They certainly have not had a chance to adapt, explore, or advance in technology integration. It is unrealistic to expect preservice teachers who have not even completed their student teaching experiences to master a seamless integration of technology into a curriculum because inservice teachers can struggle with pedagogical issues such as designing an effective lesson plan in their early years (Guzey & Roehrig, 2009).

Moreover, the participants might not have recognized the pedagogical benefits of podcasting and vodcasting if the project was implemented earlier in the semester. Since the assignment occurred towards the end of the semester, the participants had already formed the habit of thinking about learning goals aligned with academic standards prior to the use of any technology. They also had rich discussions about the pedagogical reasons to use technology for multiple projects prior to their podcasting.

Furthermore, the lack of control and experimental groups limited this study. It is possible that preservice teachers develop negative attitudes about podcasting and vodcasting if they experience technical failure but never have an opportunity to reflect on what they learn from it. The result may be different if no metacognitive process, about noting and sharing how they dealt with problem solving, had occurred. There can be a valid comparative study on the attitude to adapt a new technology if one group receives scaffolding to solve glitches and another group receives the scaffolding plus the prompt for the metacognitive process. The latter group, it is predicted, will connect trouble shooting as to the increased confidence than the former group.

5.3 Directions for Future Studies

Comparing preservice teachers' perceptions to those of inservice teachers regarding podcating can be a valid study. Specifically, a comparative study in relation to years of teaching and where they are in terms of the five steps by Neiss et al. (2009) may provide direction for a continuing education model for inservice teachers. Such a study could be useful for a graduate level instructional technology class because the diversity in teaching experience tends to increase in at that level compared to an undergraduate class: in a graduate school, there can be preservice teachers who have undergraduate degrees in their content areas who are seeking an initial teaching certificates taking courses with inservice teachers who are seeking master's degrees.

As participants used software and online tools that were new to them, all of them ran into technical difficulties. They stated that solving them actually increased their confidence in using the new technology. This qualitative data leads to new research questions:

1. Would teachers be more confident about technology if everything operated smoothly, or when they encountered unexpected problems and successfully solve them?
2. Which types of instruction tend to foster the most positive attitude about using technology among preservice teachers: no problems, troubleshooting on their own, solving glitches with the instructors' assistance and reflecting on how they dealt with the situations? It is possible the outcome depends on the preservice teachers' abilities to think logically. It can also depend on one's emotional maturity. This author has observed different responses to similar problem-solving situations. Some preservice teachers remain calm, analyze the problems, and solve them even if they never used software before. Others, however, become immediately frustrated when they encounter an unknown situation and allow their emotions to block their thinking. However, they tend to switch to problem solution mode if an instructor asks questions to help them identify the problems and solutions. From these observations, this author suspects that assisting them to create the habit to switch from frustration mode to problem-solution mode would be the best approach. However, further research is necessary to answer this question.

Finally, additional research can be conducted on the reflection of their own learning. For example, they can analyze if a project like this increased their creativity and critical thinking, content knowledge, and their ability to actively engage students in learning.

Acknowledgements The author thanks Dr. Richard Altenbaugh for formative feedback and Dr. John K. Hicks for proofreading.

References

Beckner, C., Blythe, R., Bybee, J., Christensen, M. H., Croft, W., Ellis, N. C., et al. (2009). Language is a complex adaptive system: Position paper. *Language Learning, 59*(1), 1–26.

Calandra, B., Brantley-Dias, L., Lee, J. K., & Fox, D. L. (2009). Using video editing to cultivate novice teachers' practice. *Journal of Research on Technology in Education, 42*(1), 73–94.

Dresang, E. T. (1999). *Radical change: Books for youth in a digital age*. New York: The H. W. Wilson Company.

Dörnyei, Z., & Kormos, J. (2000). The role of individual and social variables in oral task performance. *Language Teaching Research, 4*(3), 275–300.

Egbert, J. (2009). *Supporting learning with technology: Essentials of classroom practice*. Upper Saddle River, NJ: Pearson Prentice Hall.

Ewald, J. D. (2007). Foreign language learning anxiety in upper-level classes: Involving students as researchers. *Foreign Language Annals, 40*(1), 122–142.

Fisher, D., Frey, N., & Rothenberg, C. (2008). *Content-area conversations: How to plan discussion-based lessons for diverse language learners*. Alexandria, VA: Association for Supervision and Curriculum Development.

Guilloteaux, M. J., & Dörnyei, Z. (2008). Motivating language learners: A classroom-oriented investigation of the effects of motivational strategies on student motivation. *TESOL Quarterly, 42*(1), 55–77.

Guzey, S. S., & Roehrig, G. H. (2009). Teaching science with technology: Case studies of science teachers' development of technology, pedagogy, and content knowledge. *Contemporary Issues in Technology and Teacher Education, 9*(1), 25–45.

Harris, J., & Hofer, M. (2009). Grounded tech integration. *Learning & Leading with Technology, 37*(2), 22–25.

Harris, J., Mishra, P., & Koehler, M. (2009). Teachers' technological pedagogical content knowledge and learning activity types: Curriculum-based technology integration reframed. *Journal of Research on Technology in Education, 41*(4), 393–416.

Hofer, M., & Swan, K. O. (2008). Technological pedagogical content knowledge in action: A case study of a middle school digital documentary project. *Journal of Research on Technology in Education, 41*(2), 179–200.

Hung, H. T. (2009). Learners' perceived value of video as mediation in foreign language learning. *Journal of Educational Multimedia and Hypermedia, 18*(2), 171–190.

Kebritchi, M. (2010). Factors affecting teachers' adoption of educational computer games: A case study. *British Journal of Educational Technology, 41*(2), 256–270.

Keengwe, J., Onchwari, G., & Wachira, P. (2008). The use of computer tools to support meaningful learning. *AACE Journal, 16*(1), 77–92.

Koehler, M. J., & Mishra, P. (2005). What happens when teachers design educational technology? The development of technological pedagogical content knowledge. *Journal of Educational Computing Research, 32*(2), 131–152.

Koehler, M. J., & Mishra, P. (2008). Introducing TPCK. In AACTE Committee on Innovation and Technology (Ed.), *Handbook of technological pedagogical content knowledge (TPCK) for educators*. New York: Routledge. 1–29.

Lambert, J., & Cuper, P. (2008). Multimedia technologies and familiar spaces: 21st-century teaching for 21st century learners. *Contemporary Issues in Technology and Teacher Education, 8*(3), 264–276.

Lee, M. J. W., McLoughlin, C., & Chan, A. (2008). Talk the talk: Learner-generated podcasts as catalysts for knowledge creation. *British Journal of Educational Technology, 39*(3), 501–521.

Lei, J. (2009). Digital natives as preservice teachers: What technology preparation is needed? *Journal of Computing in Teacher Education, 25*(3), 87–97.

Lei, Q. (2007). EFL teachers' factors and students' affect. *US-China Education Review, 4*(3), 60–67.

Lloyd, M. M., & Albion, P. R. (2009). Altered geometry: A new angle on teacher technophobia. *Journal of Technology and Teacher Education, 17*(1), 65–84.

Lord, G. (2008). Podcasting communities and second language pronunciation. *Foreign Language Annals, 41*(2), 364–379.

Luce-Kapler, R. (2007). Radical change and wikis: Teaching new literacies. *Journal of Adolescent & Adult Literacy, 51*(3), 214–223.

Mishra, P., & Koehler, M. (2006). Technological pedagogical content knowledge: A framework for teacher knowledge. *Teachers College Record, 108*(6), 1017–1054.

Mishra, P., & Koehler, M. (2009). Too cool for school? No way! *Learning & Leading with Technology, 36*(7), 14–18.

Niess, M. L. (2008). Guiding preservice teachers in developing TPCK. In AACTE Committee on Innovation and Technology (Ed.), *Handbook of technological pedagogical content knowledge (TPCK) for educators*. New York: Routledge. 223–250.

Niess, M. L., Ronau, R. N., Shafer, K. G., Driskell, S. O., Harper, S. R., Johnston, C., et al. (2009). Mathematics teacher TPACK standards and development model. *Contemporary Issues in Technology in Teacher Education, 9*(1), 4–24.

Pantaleo, S. (2006). Readers and writers as intertexts: Exploring the intertextualities in student writing. *Australian Journal of Language and Literacy, 29*(2), 163–181.

Thompson, P. (2008). Learning through extended talk. *Language and Education, 22*(3), 241–256.

Unsworth, L. (2008). Multiliteracies, e-literature and english teaching. *Language and Education, 22*(1), 62–75.

Zarra, E. J., III. (2009). Wired up and fired up: Secondary social studies and the teenage brain. *Social Studies Review, 48*(1), 68–70.

Ziglari, L. (2008). The role of interaction in L2 acquisition: An emergentist perspective. *European Journal of Scientific Research, 23*(3), 446–453.

Part V
Virtual Environments Perspectives

Chapter 19
Simulation-Games as a Learning Experience: An Analysis of Learning Style and Attitude

Janet Lynn Sutherland and Knut Ekker

Abstract The authors explore the degree to which individual learning styles affect pre-simulation attitudes toward teamwork and post-simulation perceptions of the value of the simulation as a learning experience among third-semester university-level participants in a large-scale telematic simulation-game in Bremen (Germany). The learning style trait pairs 'academic type' and 'interpersonal type' are introduced as explanatory variables, first as categorical variables, then as continuous variables in multiple regression analyse. The results show that the pre-simulation attitude toward teamwork and interpersonal type explain variation in perceptions of the simulation experience. Qualitative data from debriefing teleconferences generally reflect the quantitative analysis.

Keywords Telematic simulation-game · learning style · academic type · interpersonal type

1 Introduction

Although literature on the pedagogical effectiveness of simulations and simulation-games[1] is abundant, the majority of these studies deal with the use of simulations in a rather limited number of specific fields: management training, business

---

J.L. Sutherland (✉)
English-Speaking Cultures, Languages and Literatures Faculty, University of Bremen, Postfach 330440, 28334, Bremen, Germany
e-mail: jsuther@uni-bremen.de

[1] In this sentence, "simulation" refers to computerized simulations – mathematical models of complex systems such as climate change or traffic flow – while "simulation-game" refers to simulations of complex systems in which the focus is on human decisions, actions and interactions, whether or not the activity is computer supported. For the remainder of the discussion, however, unless otherwise indicated, the two terms are used interchangeably to refer to human-centered simulation-games, specifically to scenarios developed and implemented by the IDEELS project team.

administration, and international relations (Gosen & Washbush, 2004; Chin, Dukes, & Gamson, 2009).

While there appears to be a broad consensus that simulation-games support and enhance learning, considerably less agreement exists regarding the nature and source of their effectiveness. Moreover, to date few studies have considered the possible effects of learning style on outcomes as assessed in terms of short-term cognitive or performance-based measures; fewer still have studied the effects of learning style not linked to such 'successful' participation. Gosen and Washbush (2004) cite five studies which find similarities between the personality characteristics and decision-making styles of successful 'real-world executives' or 'practicing middle managers' and those of successful simulation players. Golden and Smith (1989) analyze the relationship between trainer style and learner style and its effect on performance. Wheatley, Armstrong, and Madox (1989) examine the impact of leadership style (autocratic or democratic) and team cohesiveness on performance in simulations, and ultimately conclude that 'the variables that impact the results of a simulation outcome are as complex as the environmental variables that are designed into simulations.'

We tend to agree. Not infrequently, the present investigators' research models have had to be revised or rejected altogether when the predicted results proved unexpectedly elusive. Yet, as Edward de Bono (2009) astutely observes, 'perception is real, even if it is not reality.' Indeed, when assessing attitude change, perceptions are the reality which interests us.

Thus, in assessing the effectiveness of simulations in supporting learning, our primary research focus is less on whether students have internalized specific content than on the degree to which participants' perceptions of the simulation experience suggest that a constellation of communicative and 'soft' skills have been acquired and practiced, and the ability to comprehend and deal with complexity enhanced.

1.1 Background

Intercultural Dimensions in European Education through onLine Education (IDEELS) – from 1997 through 2001 a Socrates Curriculum Development project – is now in its thirteenth year of developing and running large-scale, interdisciplinary, telematic simulation scenarios for use in tertiary education. As a rule, IDEELS scenarios are set in a realistic but fictionalized world to avoid the pitfalls of stereotyping. They deal with a range of complex issues, including education reform, data access and security, immigration, Eutropian (i.e., European) identity, and sustainable development. Given the task of achieving an international agreement on the scenario's topic, simulation participants form teams and act as members of high-level government delegations, non-governmental organizations, technical consultants, or journalists. After presenting their opening positions, each team negotiates with the others to reach a consensus, which they then document in a collaboratively-written text: a treaty, a resolution, a set of policy recommendations, an action plan, or a project proposal.

Before beginning a 3-week-long IDEELS simulation-game, students familiarize themselves with the various role profiles and the thematic focus of the scenario. They also engage in a variety of preparatory activities designed to focus their attention on specific skills such as language, teamwork, effective thinking, priority setting, decision making, and effective communication. For example, language activities may concentrate on register – on learning to recognize and use the formal, diplomatic language needed during the simulation – or on the pitfalls of miscommunication and how to avoid them. Short 'paper and pencil' simulations lasting 60–90 min raise awareness of the challenges inherent in negotiations, decision-making and cross-cultural communication. Effective thinking skills are taught using Edward de Bono's Cognitive Research Trust (CoRT) Thinking Tools.[2]

Because both project members and the initial participants in IDEELS simulations came from a variety of academic disciplines, countries and institutional types, we developed a set of shared learning objectives[3] addressing four areas: cooperative/collaborative, socio-affective, interdisciplinary/cross-cultural, and cognitive learning. In addition, individual classes were encouraged to develop their own subject-specific learning objectives[4] and assessment instruments, provided these were not incompatible with the shared learning objectives. Such a two-tier approach to learning objectives gives individual groups and facilitators latitude to select pre-simulation activities and role assignments that match their group's specific objectives while preserving the cohesiveness of the simulation as a whole. Similarly, subject-specific assessments were decentralized – developed and administered by individual teachers, while the shared learning objectives were addressed in the pre- and post-simulation surveys all participants were asked to complete.

Since 2005, when the European BA was implemented by the English-Speaking Cultures Program at the University of Bremen and a language module was designed around the IDEELS simulation, we have been working almost exclusively with advanced students of English as a Foreign Language, at least half of whom plan to become teachers of the language. Thus, regardless of the thematic focus of a given scenario, language improvement (listening and reading comprehension, fluency, lexis, accuracy, register) is now an important learning objective. However, since the European BA is also intended to prepare students for the working world, we are equally interested in providing an opportunity for them to develop their 'soft skills': e.g. interdisciplinary and cross-cultural communication, team, leadership, time-management, problem-solving, negotiating and collaborative writing skills. The pre- and post-simulation activities, surveys and assessment tools reflect this broad agenda, as do the scenarios.

---

[2] For more information about the specific CoRT Thinking Tools used in IDEELS simulations, refer to http://www.ideels.uni-bremen.de/about_cort.html.

[3] A detailed list of the shared learning objectives is available at http://www.ideels.uni-bremen.de/shlobj.html.

[4] Examples of subject-specific and course-specific learning objectives are available at http://www.ideels.uni-bremen.de/splobj.html.

The range of assessment tools used reflects our desire to balance qualitative and quantitative assessments, on the one hand, and to provide students with a variety of opportunities to reflect on, 'digest' and assimilate the simulation experience, on the other.

1.2 Data Collection

In pre-simulation surveys, personal data collected includes age, sex, first language, and other languages spoken. Academic data includes the participant's year at university, the type of class through which the student is participating in the simulation, and whether the class is mandatory or optional. Participants are also asked to rate their typing ability, their proficiency in English, and to provide information about the duration and purpose of time spent in another country. Finally, the pre-simulation survey collects information about the students' use of computers and Internet resources, cross-cultural, cross-disciplinary and collaborative experience. Survey items address attitudes toward communicating in a foreign language, using computers for learning, working in teams, and issues related to the thematic focus of the simulation scenario. By arrangement with the developers of the Paragon Learning Style Inventory (PLSI), the 48-item PLSI is used to identify the learning style of each participant.[5]

In addition to collecting detailed responses to the software platform used for communication during the simulation, the post-simulation survey repeats a number of the attitude-related items in the pre-simulation survey, providing us with data on attitude change in these areas.

Beyond the 48-item Paragon Learning Style Inventory (PLSI) and pre- and post-simulation surveys on which the current study is based, students participate in a 2-week oral debriefing period (four 90-minute class periods and a 60- to 90-minute online debriefing teleconference). Individually, students write two essays, one related to the thematic focus of the simulation and a second, personal reflective essay on the simulation experience. The two essays are assessed by the teacher/facilitator according to the same criteria used in all language classes in the English-Speaking Cultures BA program, and the documents produced by the teams during the simulation, most of which are collaboratively written, are revised and corrected in a collaborative process during class meetings after the simulation has ended.

Each student also prepares and gives an in-class oral presentation on a topic related to the simulation, speaking for 10 minutes and responding to questions for an additional 5 minutes. This presentation is evaluated by the other students in the

---

[5]While budgetary considerations were a factor in choosing the short PLSI, it nevertheless serves our purpose quite well. The (free) 48-item inventory, which has 12 items for each trait pair, allows responses to be evenly split between the two traits, an outcome which is avoided by the 52-item version, which has 13 items for each of the trait pairs. Since the present study only includes those students with more pronounced traits, evenly-split responses are omitted.

class and by the teacher; the student revises it on the basis of this feedback and then gives it a second time (for a grade) at the end of the fourth semester, the semester following the simulation, as part of the module examination for the final language module in the BA program.

The quantitative assessment of skills practiced during the simulation also includes a reading comprehension test at the C-2 (mastery) level (i.e., a full level higher than the level required for admission to the English-Speaking Cultures program). Thus, students receive both qualitative and quantitative feedback from their peers and their teachers over an extended period of time through discussion and reflective writing as well as through objective tests, a process which meets both institutional requirements and the needs of individual learners.

1.3 Procedure

Prior to the present study, our publications (Sutherland, Ekker, & Eidsmo, 2006; Ekker & Sutherland, 2005; Ekker 2004) focused on background characteristics (e.g. age, gender, major subject) as predictors of attitude change. However, this approach proved less than fully satisfactory. On the recommendation of IDEELS project member Konrad Morgan, we began collecting data on participants' learning styles in 2005.

The present study is the first to utilize data from the the Paragon Learning Style Inventory in addition to previously available data from the pre- and post-simulation surveys. Statements made by students during the post-simulation debriefing teleconference add a further dimension.

Figure 19.1 shows the overall research model used in this paper. In the analysis, background variables including age, gender and native language will also be included.

Learning Style → Pre-simulation attitude toward teamwork → Post-simulation attitude toward simulation as learning experience

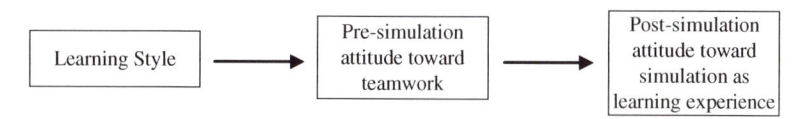

Fig. 19.1 Research model of simulation as a learning experience predicted by learning style and attitude towards teamwork

The Paragon Learning Style Inventory used in our research uses the same Jungian personality trait pairs (introversion-extroversion, sensing-intuiting, thinking-feeling, judging-perceiving) as the Myers-Briggs Type Indicator (MBTI), and was chosen for its accessibility (the formulations are suitable for non-native speakers of English), its reliability, and the ease with which it can be administered.[6] Based on

---

[6]Information about the Paragon Learning Style Inventory is available at http://www.oswego.edu/plsi/plsinfo.htm.

his own research and that of co-developer, Schindler and Yang (2009) identifies four 'academic types' derived from the four possible combinations of first two traits: Extrovert/Sensate, Extrovert/Intuitive, Introvert/Sensate, and Introvert/ Intuitive and four 'personality combinations' – referred to here as Interpersonal Type: Sensate/Perceiver, Sensate/Judging, Intuitive/Feeling, and Intuitive/Thinking.[7]

Table 19.1 shows the distribution of the two learning style characteristics used as categorical variables in this paper: academic type and interpersonal type. The distribution of characteristics is fairly consistent over the 4 years of simulations since we have begun using the Paragon Learning Style Inventory (Academic type and year: $eta^2=0.003$ and Interpersonal type and year: $eta^2=0.03$, $p>0.05$).

Table 19.1 Academic type ($n=260$) and interpersonal type ($n=262$) (percentages)

		2005	2006	2007	2008	Total
Academic type	IS: Introvert and sensate	21.2	32.0	32.5	27.4	29.2
	IN: Introvert and intuitive	30.3	19.4	10.0	16.7	18.5
	ES: Extrovert and sensate	21.2	24.3	35.0	29.8	27.3
	EN: Extrovert and intuitive	27.3	24.3	22.5	26.2	25.0
		100.0	100.0	100.0	100.0	100.0
Interpersonal type	SP: Sensate and perceiver	2.9	2.9	4.7	8.5	5.0
	SJ: Sensate and judging	44.1	55.3	67.4	50.0	54.2
	NF: Intuitive and feeling	26.5	31.1	20.9	32.9	29.4
	NT: Intuitive and thinking	26.5	10.7	7.0	8.5	11.5
		100.0	100.0	100.0	100.0	100.0

2 Analysis

2.1 Learning Style as a Categorical Variable

Table 19.2 shows the distribution by learning style of attitude toward working with other individuals in teams. The first part of the table shows the academic type, distinguishing between the IS (Introvert/Sensate), IN (Introvert/Intuitive), ES (Extrovert/Sensate) and the EN (Extrovert/Intuitive). Not surprisingly, extroverts are more likely to enjoy working with other individuals in teams – over 70% agree with the statement, compared with slightly more than 40% of introverts.

The bottom part of Table 19.2 shows the interpersonal type as the predictor. The dependent variable 'I enjoy working with other individuals in teams' is reduced to 3 categories in Table 19.2, and still the table has many cells with less than the 5 expected participants. Thus the chi-square statistic is unpredictable, and we should pay more attention to Table 19.3, which retains the complete 5-category variable.

---

[7] For concise descriptions of the trait pairs, refer to http://www.calstatela.edu/faculty/jshindl/plsi/combo1.htm.

19 Simulation-Games as a Learning Experience

Table 19.2 Attitude toward working in teams and learning style (percentages)

		Learning style				
		Academic type				
		IS	IN	ES	EN	Total
I enjoy working with other individuals in teams	Disagree	23.9	16.3	4.6	0.0	11.3
	Neutral	35.2	41.9	20.0	27.9	30.4
	Agree	40.8	41.9	75.4	72.1	58.3
		100.0	100.0	100.0	100.0	100.0
Chi-square=36.3, $p<0.001$						
		Interpersonal type				
		SP	SJ	NF	NT	Total
I enjoy working with other individuals in teams	Disagree	7.7	15.5	2.8	15.4	11.3
	Neutral	23.1	28.7	31.0	38.5	30.1
	Agree	69.2	55.8	66.2	46.2	58.6
		100.0	100.0	100.0	100.0	100.0
Chi-square=9.8, $p=0.13$						

Table 19.3 Attitude toward working in teams and learning style (analysis of variance)

Attitude toward working in teams	Mean	N	Std.dev.
Academic type			
IS: Introvert and sensate	3.21	71	0.99
IN: Introvert and intuitive	3.35	43	0.95
ES: Extrovert and sensate	3.94	65	0.79
EN: Extrovert and intuitive	3.97	61	0.73
Total	3.62	240	0.93
$F=12.7$, $p<0.001$, eta^2=0.14			
Interpersonal type			
SP: Sensate and perceiver	3.69	13	0.75
SJ: Sensate and judging	3.51	129	0.96
NF: Intuitive and feeling	3.87	71	0.81
NT: Intuitive and thinking	3.31	26	1.01
Total	3.61	239	0.93
$F=3.4$, $p=0.02$, eta^2=0.04			

Table 19.2 does not show a significant difference between the various interpersonal types in predicting enjoyment of working in teams.

Table 19.3 shows the same information as in Table 19.2, presenting the analysis of the variable 'I enjoy working with other individuals in teams' including all five response categories. The average score (1=strongly disagree; 5=strongly agree) for the extroverts is close to 4, while for the introverts the average is around

3.3 ($F=12.7$, $p<0.001$). Academic type explains 14% of the variation in the variable 'I enjoy working with other individuals in teams' ($eta^2=0.14$).

Using interpersonal type as the predictor, the NF group has the highest (most positive) score of 3.87 with respect to working in teams (Table 19.3), while the NT group has the lowest value (3.31), a significant difference ($p=0.02$). But the interpersonal type variable only explains 4% of the variance in 'I enjoy working with other individuals in teams' ($eta^2=0.04$).

The percentage agreeing with 'I enjoy working with other individuals in teams' (agree or strongly agree) is just below 70% for the SP and NF interpersonal types, while it is 56 and 46 % for the SJ and the NT interpersonal types, respectively (Table 19.2).

In order to show the effect of academic type and interpersonal type on the post-simulation variable 'This was a good learning experience,' we use analysis of variance. Table 19.4 shows that the academic type does not contribute toward explaining the post-simulation variable 'This was a good learning experience.'

Interpersonal type, however, does tend to affect the post-simulation perception of 'This was a good learning experience.' While the intuitive and thinking group has an average of 3.6, the sensate and perceiver group (SP) have an average of only 2.6; again, the difference is not significant ($p=0.08$).[8]

Table 19.4 Simulation as a learning experience and learning style (analysis of variance)

Simulation as a learning experience	Mean	N	Std.dev
Academic type			
IS: Introvert and sensate	3.29	62	1.26
IN: Introvert and intuitive	3.22	36	1.02
ES: Extrovert and sensate	3.33	60	0.98
EN: Extrovert and intuitive	3.36	56	0.99
Total	3.31	214	1.07
$F=0.13$, $p=0.94$			
Interpersonal type			
SP: Sensate and perceiver	2.64	11	0.92
SJ: Sensate and judging	3.41	117	1.14
NF: Intuitive and feeling	3.25	67	1.02
NT: Intuitive and thinking	3.60	20	0.88
Total	3.34	215	1.08
$F=2.3$, $p=0.08$			

---

[8] Interestingly, compared to the responses to simulations as a learning experience reported prior to 2005 (when students from a variety of academic disciplines participated in IDEELS simulations), these figures represent a slightly less positive attitude toward the learning experience, with the 4-year average just above the midpoint of 3 on the scale from 'strongly disagree' (1) to 'strongly agree' (5). Between 1998 and 2004, averages ranged from 3.5 to 4.39. The statistically insignificant drop in average degree of agreement with the statement 'The simulation was a good learning

The percentage agreeing with 'This was a good learning experience' (agree or strongly agree) is around 55% for the SJ and NT interpersonal type (sensate and judging; intuitive and thinking), while it is below 45% for the SP and the NF academic type (sensate and perceiver; intuitive and feeling).

The zero-order correlation between 'enjoying teamwork' and the dependent variable of 'simulation as a learning experience' shows a moderately strong association, and the higher the score on 'enjoying teamwork' the higher is the score on 'simulation as a learning experience' (beta=0.206, p=0.001).

2.2 Learning Style as a Categorical Variable: Analysis of Variance

Table 19.5 displays the analysis of variance of the simulation as a learning experience (post-simulation variable) with academic type, interpersonal type and enjoyment of teamwork as predictors. Interpersonal type and attitude toward teamwork contributes to explaining variation in the variable 'This was a good learning experience.' The variable academic type does not contribute toward explaining variation in the variable 'This was a good learning experience,' but interpersonal type and the pre-simulation variable 'I enjoy working with other individuals in teams' both contribute significantly to the model (p=0.035 and p=0.01, respectively). The differences we see in Table 19.4 are enhanced in Table 19.5 by adding the variable attitude toward teamwork, although there is no interaction effect between interpersonal type and enjoying teamwork. The intuitive and thinking group (NT) is the most

Table 19.5 Simulation as a learning experience, academic type, interpersonal type and attitude toward teamwork (ANOVA)

Source	Type III sum of squares	df	Mean square	F	Sig.
Corrected model	29.09	17	1.711	1.57	0.078
Intercept	345.990	1	345.990	317.96	< 0.001
Academic type	1.942	2	0.971	0.89	0.412
Interpersonal type	7.460	2	3.730	3.43	0.035
Enjoying teamwork	14.875	4	3.719	3.42	0.010
Interpersonal type * Enjoying teamwork (interaction)	5.710	8	0.714	0.66	0.730
Error	167.577	154	1.088		
Total	2079.000	172			
Corrected total	196.669	171			

R Squared=0.175 (Adjusted R Squared=0.040)

---

experience,' while irrelevant to the present study and possibly related to the change in user population, may also suggest a need to more closely examine the 'fit' between the learning experience we provide and the 'space' allowed for it by the European BA system.

positive with respect to the simulation as a learning experience, and the sensate and perceiver group is slightly negative (Table 19.4).

The interaction term of interpersonal type and attitude toward teamwork does not contribute toward explaining the variation in the dependent variables ('simulation as a good learning experience'). The other interaction terms are not shown in Table 19.5, since they do not contribute significantly to explaining the model. Similarly, background variables like gender, age, native language, typing ability, year in college, computer use (hours per day), and self-rated computer knowledge do not predict variation in simulation as a learning experience, and are not included in the analysis.

2.3 Learning Style as Continuous Variables: Regression Analyse

To determine whether the results presented in the preceding two sections have been influenced by the way the variable learning style has been operationalized, i.e. as two categorical variables, academic type and interpersonal type, we analyze the data with learning style as a set of four continuous variables: extrovert-introvert score, sensate-intuitive score, feeler-thinker score and judger-perceiver score. The following figure (Fig. 19.2) shows the distribution of the four variables.

In each of these four scales representing dimensions of learning style, a low value represents the first dimension mentioned, while a high score represents the second dimension. Thus in the graph on the top-left of Fig. 19.2, a low value represents the introvert personality, while a high score represents the extrovert personality.

The following analyse will use multiple regression to identify which dimension is able to predict pre-simulation attitudes towards teamwork and post-simulation attitudes towards the simulation as a learning experience. Figure 19.3 shows the distribution of these two variables.

Table 19.6 shows that only two of the four personality traits contribute significantly towards explaining variation in attitudes towards teamwork. The introvert-extrovert and the thinker-feeler personality dimension contribute significantly; together, these two variables explain 19% of the variance in attitudes towards teamwork ($R=0.44$).

Table 19.7 shows that in terms of explaining variation in the dependent variable 'This was a good learning experience', the pre-simulation attitude toward teamwork is the strongest predictor ($p<0.001$). The only other significant predictor towards explaining variation in the simulation as a learning experience is the perceiver-judger variable ($p=0.003$). This model explains 7% of the variation in the variable 'simulation as a good learning experience' ($R=0.27$).

Based on the analysis of learning style as a categorical variable (Table 19.4), where the extrovert-intuitive and the intuitive-thinking combination scored the highest on the variable 'simulation as a learning experience', we include the corresponding interaction terms in the regression analysis. That is, we construct the interaction term between the extrovert and intuitive dimension (multiplying the

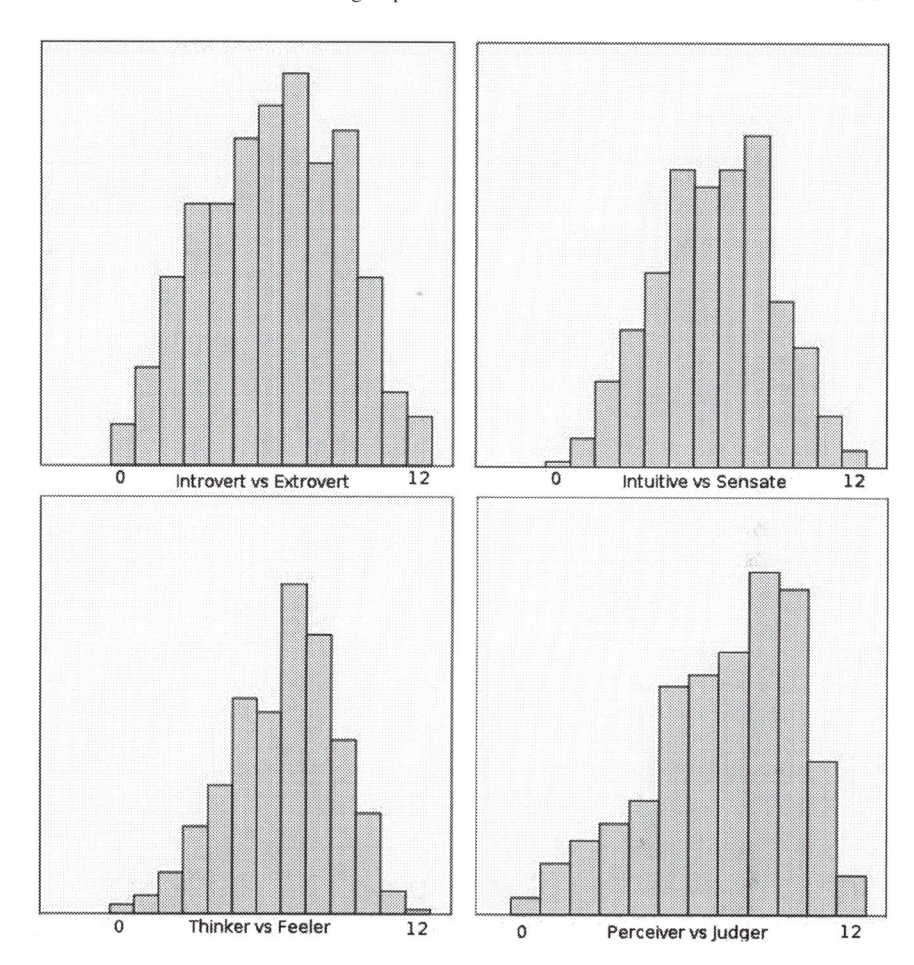

Fig. 19.2 Distribution of the four learning style variables

two individual variables). We also construct the interaction term between the intuitive and thinker dimensions. These two new interaction terms are added into the regression analysis predicting enjoyment of the simulation as a learning experience.

In order to avoid multicollinearity, the variable intuitive-sensate dimension was excluded from the regression analysis (VIF value=14.7). The remaining VIF values are all under 10 (from 1.3 to 5.9, Table 19.8) which satisfies the criterion of no multicollinearity among the explanatory variables.

Table 19.8 shows that both the perceiver-judger dimension and the previous experience with working in teams are predictors of the simulation as a good learning experience. The higher the score on the perceiver-judger dimension, the more positive the evaluation of the simulation as a learning experience is (i.e., the judgers are more positive towards the simulation as a learning experience, beta=0.175). The

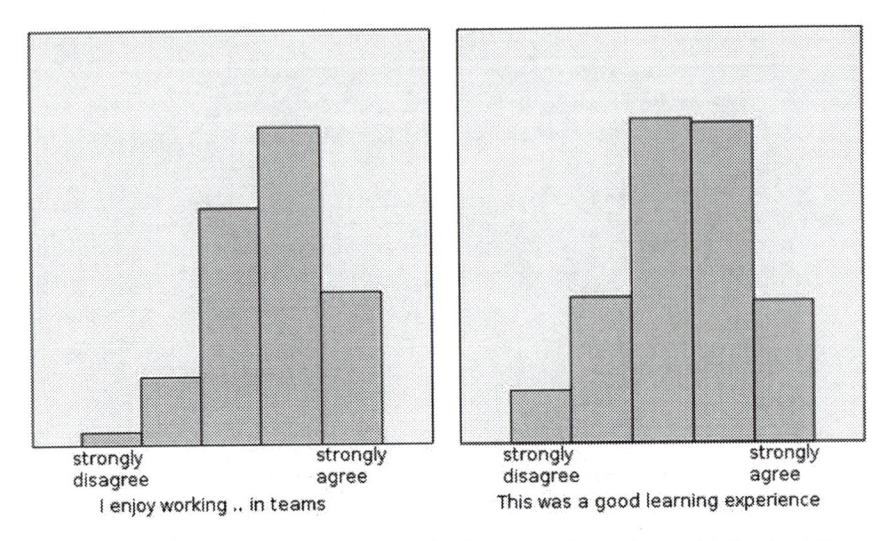

Fig. 19.3 Distribution of attitude towards working in teams and experience with the simulation

Table 19.6 Attitude toward teamwork and personality trait (regression analysis)

Model	Unstandardized coefficients B	Std. error	Standardized coefficients Beta	t	Sig.
(Constant)	2.923	0.253		11.540	0.000
Introvert vs extrovert (low vs high)	0.119	0.018	0.356	6.658	0.000
Intuitive vs sensate (low vs high)	−0.016	0.022	−0.042	−0.715	0.475
Thinker vs feeler (low vs high)	.055	0.023	0.130	2.451	0.015
Perceiver vs judger (low vs high)	−0.031	0.021	−0.084	−1.458	0.146

Dependent variable: I enjoy working with other individuals in teams
R Squared=0.175 (Adjusted R Squared=0.040)

higher the score on 'enjoying working in teams', the more positive the evaluation of the simulation as a learning experience is (beta=0.227).

The sensate-feeler interaction term also contributes to explaining the variation in perception of the simulation as a good learning experience. Individuals who score high on both the sensate and the feeler dimensions exhibit the most positive attitude with respect to the simulation as a learning experience (beta=0.281). The model explains 9% of the variation in the dependent variable (R=0.31).

Figure 19.4 shows the effect of the attitude towards teamwork and the categories of the combination of personality traits on the perception of the simulation as a

19 Simulation-Games as a Learning Experience

Table 19.7 Simulation as a learning experience, personality trait and attitude towards teamwork (regression analysis)

Model	Unstandardized coefficients B	Std. error	Standardized coefficients Beta	t	Sig.
(Constant)	2.358	0.436		11.540	<.001
Introvert vs extrovert (low vs high)	−0.006	0.026	−0.016	−0.227	0.821
Intuitive vs sensate (low vs high)	−0.021	0.031	−0.048	−0.668	0.505
Thinker vs feeler (low vs high)	−0.059	0.031	−0.123	−1.882	0.061
Perceiver vs judger (low vs high)	0.067	0.031	0.154	2.177	0.003
I enjoy working with other individuals in teams	0.283	0.080	0.249	3.533	<.001

Dependent variable: This was a good learning experience
R squared=0.07 (R squared=0.05)

Table 19.8 Simulation as a learning experience predicted with interaction terms included (regression analysis)

Model	Unstand. coeff. B	Std. error	St.Cf Beta	t	Sig	Collinearity statistics Tolerance	VVIF
(Constant)	1.138	0.612		1.860	0.064		
Introvert vs extrovert	0.044	0.046	0.118	0.954	0.341	0.251	3.984
Thinker vs feeler	0.033	0.050	0.069	0.664	0.507	0.360	2.781
Perceiver vs judger	0.076	0.030	0.175	2.493	0.013	0.777	1.287
I enjoy working with other individuals in teams	0.258	0.080	0.227	3.230	0.001	0.779	1.284
Extrovert-sensate (interaction)	−0.009	0.007	−0.200	−1.334	0.184	0.170	5.873
Sensate-Feeler (interaction)	0.017	0.007	0.281	2.343	0.020	0.267	3.752

Dependent variable: This was a good learning experience
R=0.31 (R Squared=0.09)

learning experience. We see that the intuitive-thinking category produces the highest score (estimated marginal means) of the variable 'this was a good learning experience', particularly when viewing individuals who have a positive attitude towards teamwork. In general, a positive experience toward teamwork will raise the average

Estimated Marginal Means of This was a good learning experience

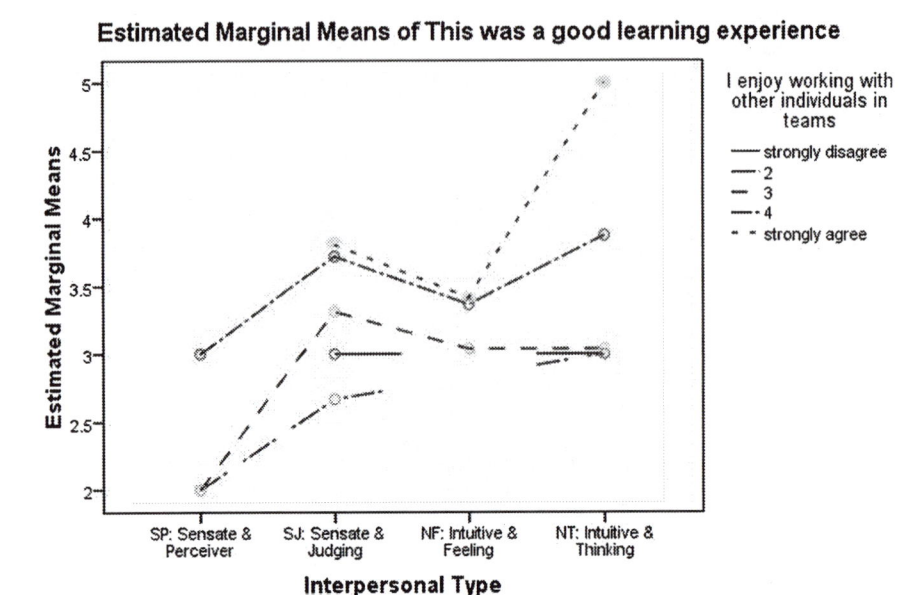

Fig. 19.4 Simulation as a learning experience, teamwork experience and learning style

score on the perception of the simulation as a learning experience; this effect is most pronounced in the intuitive-thinking group.

At the other extreme, the individuals categorized as sensate-perceiver have a much more negative perception of the simulation as a learning experience.

2.4 Analysis of Statements Made by Participants During Post-simulation Debriefing Teleconferences

The statistical analyses discussed above suggest further questions of a more qualitative nature: to what extent do personal statements made by students during post-simulation debriefing teleconferences (held in each case on the Monday following the simulation's conclusion) reveal attitudes toward teamwork and the simulation as a learning experience. Examining post-simulation teleconferences from 3 years (2006, 2007, and 2008), we find that only the 2007 debriefing teleconference explicitly addresses teamwork and the learning experience as a whole. The 2006 teleconference participants focus on the Moodle software, which was a last-minute, emergency replacement for the OPUSi platform used from 1998 through 2004 for the simulations. The 2008 post-simulation teleconference participants focus primarily on rules (the official prohibition on inter-team communication outside the Moodle software platform) and on changes in the simulation structure (the addition of student-moderated working groups).

Of a total of 137 participants in the 2007 simulation, seventeen (all female) participated in the 2007 debriefing teleconference. Of these seventeen, eight completed the PLSI inventory, leaving us with a rather small sample of the participant group; still, the statements included here appear consistent with in-class debriefing sessions as reported by the facilitators. In the discussion which follows, participants are identified by age, first language (L1), status in the English program, and learning style (PLSI).

2.4.1 Extroversion and Positive Attitude Toward 'Working with Other Individuals in Teams'

An *extrovert* female had the following to say about teamwork during the simulation (emphasis added): *We for sure felt like a team.* There would have been no possibility to have achieved everything individually. (age 23, L1=German, English major, PLSI: ESFJ)[9]

A second *extrovert* female made the following comments (emphasis added): 'The *teamwork management* in our delegation *went pretty good I think*. We divided the different tasks up per mail etc.' 'Our delegation managed to *divide the work* up in parts. As a precondition, *everyone had to trust the other members* of the group, so every member does a "proper" work.' 'It would surely have been harder to do all the work if everyone had done it on her or his own. *Team work was a better choice* in this simulation.' 'In our delegation (11 people), *leadership responsibilities were shared.* Surely, in a group *you have to compromise but also accept and tolerate* other's peoples speeches.' (L1=German, English major, PLSI: ENTP)[10]

Both of these students appear to have had a positive experience working with other individuals in their simulation team. Interestingly, while the first of these two students – a 'feeler' – expresses this in terms of how she and her fellow team members felt, the second student – a 'thinker' – comments on several specific aspects of her team's collaborative work.

The comments of an *introvert* female are comparable to those of the preceding student in that she offers specific analyses of her team's approach, but she also expresses very positive feelings about working in this particular team (emphasis added): *Our strongest experience will be the team we worked in.* It was *the best team we have ever worked!* 'We just *did not panic,* when it was unstructured.' 'As for group work, *we* have *divided the tasks* among the members–*that worked well!*' 'Our 7 members were *a nice group size.* It was not so much (we could divide the tasks well) and not little–nice group to coordinate.' 'To be honest, we did not have

---

[9]L1 refers to the first language spoken, or "mother tongue"; E = extrovert; S = sensate; F = feeler; J = judger.
[10]N = intuitive; T = thinker; P = perceiver.

a leader–*our leadership was shared* somehow.' *We did not have any problems concerning different working styles. The results were important.* 'We did not probably notice that we were working in different ways–*we just worked and were satisfied with our results*... Maybe these [sic] *our different methods of work complemented one another* as we realize it now.' (age 23, L1=Russian, English major, PLSI: ISTJ)[11]

While the determining factor in selecting these three examples is the introvert-extrovert pair, they also illustrate both the association of the feeler trait with a positive attitude toward teamwork and the effect this trait can have on the manner in which this attitude finds expression, i.e. more concrete and specific in identifying what made the experience positive.

2.4.2 Introversion and Positive Attitude Toward the Simulation as 'a Good Learning Experience'

The *introvert* female quoted above also commented on the simulation as a good learning experience; again, her statements are both positive and specific, as might be expected from a thinker: 'We really made progress, we created an action plan, and we have improved our language skills...' 'We think it is not only about creating something new, but about making own decisions, working in [a] team, taking responsibility...' (age 23, L1=Russian, English major, PLSI: ISTJ)

This *extrovert* female appears to have been less than satisfied with the simulation as a learning experience: 'Weren't we supposed to develop a new Education system? I would have liked to really develop something. What we did now was just copying something we in reality have because time did not allow us to do anything else.' (age 23, L1=German, English minor for primary school, PLSI: ENFJ)

A second *extrovert* female, however, clearly felt the simulation had been a positive learning experience: 'I found the simulation to be very productive. What I liked most was the strictly formal character of the simulation. Policy-making was a good way to improve skills of formal contacts.' 'I also think, [t]hat it showed us very clearly how policy making works, bringing certain other entities into discussions such as NGO's and the press.' 'We did create a basis for education? Didn't we? I think putting these ideas toget[h]er in Action Plans have already been the first step of defining how a Eutropian Identity should be and how those should be represented in the educational system.' (age 21, L1=German and Turkish, English major, PLSI: ENF+TP)

While the third student's responses are not predicted by our statistical data, they serve to remind us that in the classroom, we are working with individuals, not statistics.

Just as our students are individuals with unique personalities, so are the facilitators who guide the teams. While some teachers may find the role of a facilitator closer to their own classroom style than others might, anyone who has facilitated

---

[11] I = introvert

19 Simulation-Games as a Learning Experience

simulations more than once knows how seemingly unpredictable the interactional dynamics of groups can be. To begin exploring this aspect, we make two further comparisons: 1) two students with contrasting responses to the survey items, and 2) three groups facilitated by the same faculty member.

2.4.3 Comparison of Two Students' Debriefing Comments with Contrasting Responses to the Survey Items

A female who posted five of her team's documents and was a very active participant in at least two teleconferences during the simulation made the following statements about the experience during the post-simulation debriefing conference: 'yes, it was [a good idea to prohibit contact between teams outside Moodle], Janet.' Responding to the question, 'Was it difficult to maintain the required level of decorum during the conferences,' she said, 'Janet, we sometimes got a little annoyed and had to hold back, but most of the time it worked out quite well.'

Responding to a question about the experience of student-moderated working groups, this participant agreed explicitly with statements made by two others who said they thought student-moderated working groups had been a good experience, liked having the responsibility and felt it was a good challenge. When asked what it was like to moderate a group, she responded that 'the moderation of our group was very frustrating...we tried to stick to the agenda but the other countries ignored it.' (age 21, L1=German, English major, no PLSI)

An extrovert male student who posted four of his team's eight documents and messages but who did not appear on the lists of participants for any of the teleconferences or working groups during the simulation disagreed with the statements 'I enjoy working with other individuals in teams' and 'The simulation was a good learning experience.' During the debriefing conference, he expressed skepticism about the effectiveness of the rule prohibiting teams from communicating with each other outside the software: 'seems ineffective, because obviously people will talk to each other outside of the university' – a statement with which four others quickly agreed, incidentally. Other comments during the debriefing teleconference were similar in tone. Asked whether participants 'got more English practice by talking directly to the other teams,' this student responded, 'A wee bit.' He said he 'understood why this particular medium [Moodle] was chosen. It trains certain skills that would not be enhanced in face-to-face encounters,' and when another student expressed skepticism about the value of the student-moderated working groups ('I'm not sure what new skills chatroom conversations are teaching.'), he responded 'Reacting on the spot to questions, being forced to think and work under pressure.'

Responding to the statement that 'Most of us feel some degree of insecurity that is eliminated when we sit at a keyboard and the "other" cannot see us,' he added, '...the anonymity tears down certain inhibitions.' Commenting on the less-than-polite tone in some of the student-moderated working group sessions, he observed, 'I think the tone often turned fairly nasty, maybe in the heat of the moment.' Still, he felt that having student-moderated working groups 'certainly promoted indepe[n]dent work,' although 'a little guidance probably would have helped.' (age 20, L1=German, English minor, PLSI: ENFJ+P)

The first student, with strongly positive responses to both the teamwork and the learning experience survey items, experienced frustration and annoyance at times, but nevertheless felt the experience of moderating had been positive.

The second student, who disagreed with both survey items used in this study, expressed skepticism regarding the prohibition on communication outside Moodle and criticism of the tone of some student-moderated working groups, but also demonstrated an awareness of several of the potential opportunities for learning: thinking, working, and responding to questions under pressure, as well as learning to work independently. In view of this, this student's negative response to the item 'This was a good learning experience' is somewhat unexpected. One possible explanation is his involvement in a potentially unpleasant exchange during a teleconference in which he (acting on behalf of his team) accused another delegation of plagiarizing parts of a document. Asked by the moderator to substantiate his claims, he did so in a long Forum message following the teleconference. In subsequent conversations (in February, 2010), he mentioned this situation as proof that he had indeed played an active role in the simulation. In a subsequent conversation in March, 2010, sixteen months after he participated in the simulation, this student reported that the simulation in fact had been a good learning experience. Asked about his negative survey responses, he attributed them to a conflict he had had with one of his teammates which had temporarily affected his overall reaction to the experience.

As teachers, we tend to assume not only that the more active students in a class derive greater benefit from their participation, but also that they are aware that they are learning. However, these two students, both of whom appear to have been among the more active individuals in their teams (based on their individual activity reports in Moodle), initially report strikingly different perceptions of their learning experience in the post-simulation survey, and these perceptions also find expression in the debriefing teleconference. Does this suggest that the students' attitudes and perceptions going into the simulation may be more relevant to their post-simulation perceptions than the experience itself, or that a negative experience during the simulation may be perceived with greater or lesser intensity, depending on the pre-simulation attitude? While an answer to this question remains elusive, it serves to remind us of the complexity of the factors that can influence the perceived outcome of the simulation experience for a given individual, as well as how these perceptions can evolve over time.

2.4.4 Comparison of Three Teams Facilitated by the Same Person

The three teams chosen (Eastland, Highland, and Idanialand) were facilitated by Sutherland, two in one class and one in another. Each of the teams had nine members.

The Eastland group ranged in age from 21 to 30 and consisted of seven females and two males. Seven group members were L1 German speakers; one male listed both German and Turkish as his first languages, and one female listed Persian as her first language. These two also reported having migrated from one country to another. English skills levels were reported as good to very good, with the exception of two students who reported fair written English skills and one student who reported excellent English reading skills. Seven members of the team were English majors, one an English minor, and one an English minor for primary school teachers.[12]

Highland's members ranged in age from 19 to 28 years old; all were female, L1 German speakers with good to excellent self-assessed English skills levels. Four were English majors, three English minors, and two English minors for primary school. One student reported having a migration background.

The Idanialand team ranged in age from 21 to 25 and was comprised of eight females (L1 German) and one male (L1 Polish). Self-assessed English skills levels ranged from good to very good, with one student reporting excellent listening and reading skills, one reporting fair speaking skills, and one reporting fair writing skills. Four students were English majors, two were English minors, and three were English minors for primary school teachers. Four students reported having a migration background.

During the simulation, two of the teams (Highland and Idanialand) appeared to be collaborating effectively, consistently attending to both 'task behaviors' and 'maintenance behaviors' (Morgan, 2001), while the third (Eastland) did not. In-class debriefing sessions confirmed this; both Highland and Idanialand expressed satisfaction with their teamwork and with the learning experience. In contrast, several members of the Eastland group expressed high levels of dissatisfaction and frustration – with the role profile they had been given,[13] the dynamics within the group, and the overall learning experience (factors mentioned included the uneven distribution of work, poor communication within the group, and the feeling that they had not learned anything).

Both Highland and Idanialand participated in the post-simulation debriefing teleconference. Highland was represented by three members and Idanialand by two; none of Eastland's members participated.

During the debriefing conference, both Highland and Idanialand commented on aspects they found challenging or frustrating (keeping up with the speed of

---

[12] Although all students in the English-Speaking Cultures BA program are required to take the same number of hours of language classes in the first four semesters, the distinction between major, on the one hand, and minor and minor for primary school teachers, on the other hand, appears to have some bearing on attitudes toward the workload, which we have not yet explored.

[13] The Eastland profile, which is based on Turkey, is not yet a full member of the scenario's Eutropian Federation, a situation which gives rise to challenges not faced by teams representing member countries.

the teleconference discussions, dealing with 'interruptions' in teleconferences, avoiding misunderstandings, moderating the working groups), but also mentioned solutions they had tried or wanted to recommend (think faster, prepare statements beforehand, let the fastest typist do the typing, use more concise formulations, have the moderators do more to regulate the speed of the discussion). Idanialand also emphasized their group's tendency to concentrate on their own concerns: 'We were a well-working [sic] group and, honestly, we weren't interest[ed] in other teams very much… We were interest[ed] in our own topics and problems….'

To what extent was the satisfaction or dissatisfaction of each group as reported in debriefing sessions reflected in the survey data? Responding to the pre-simulation item 'I enjoy working with other individuals in teams,' Highland's average score was 4.0, while both Idanialand and Eastland averaged 3.89 on the same item. The average scores of the three groups on the post-simulation item 'This was a good learning experience' reflected their comments during the debriefing process. The Idanialand team, whose comments were the most positive during debriefing, had an average score of 4.25 on the simulation as a good learning experience. The Eastland team, whose members expressed the greatest dissatisfaction with the experience, had an average score of 3.56 on the item 'This was a good learning experience,' a response only slightly above neutral. Finally, the Highland team, which expressed the most positive attitude toward teamwork before the simulation, had an average score of 3.75 on the simulation as a good learning experience. This was slightly higher than that of the least satisfied team, but still lower than the most satisfied team.

While Eastland and Idanialand entered the simulation with statistically identical attitudes toward teamwork, their perceptions of the simulation as a learning experience, expressed in the post-simulation survey and in-class debriefings were quite different.

Looking for possible explanations, we identify the number of students with pronounced personality traits (N>8) in each team.

Figure 19.5 shows the total number of individuals in each team with individual trait scores above 8 for each trait pair; the lighter gray indicates the number with high scores on the second trait in each pair (e.g. Highland has a total of six high scores on the judger-perceiver trait pair: five judgers and one perceiver). Interestingly, the two groups reporting positive teamwork experiences during the simulation have a total of fourteen (Highland) and fifteen (Idanialand) high scores, while the group reporting negative experiences with teamwork (Eastland) has a total of eleven. While the evidence is not conclusive, it nevertheless suggests a potentially interesting area for further research.

While the extent to which the full debriefing process allowed the Eastland team members to extract useful lessons from the experience remains unknown, we know that initial perceptions often evolve over the course of the debriefing process – and beyond – as participants assimilate the experience and gain insights into their behavior and consider alternatives.

19 Simulation-Games as a Learning Experience

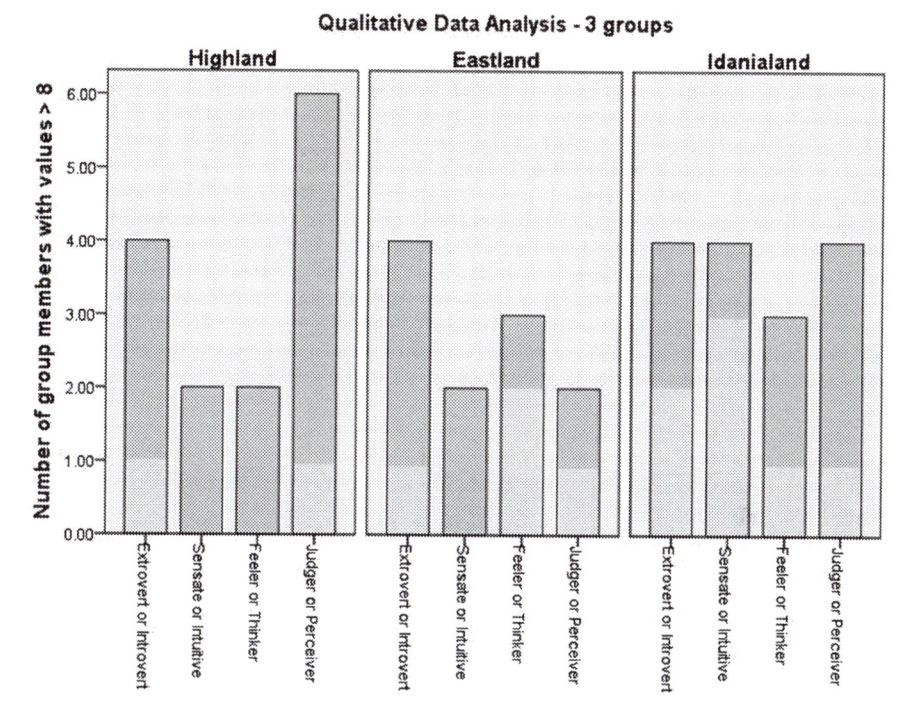

Fig. 19.5 Team members with individual trait scores above 8 for each trait pair (number of individuals)

3 Conclusion

In IDEELS simulations, the pre-simulation attitude toward teamwork and interpersonal type are predictors of the post-simulation variable 'This was a good learning experience.' Academic type does not contribute toward explaining variation in the variable 'This was a good learning experience.'

To a large extent, the qualitative data (statements made during the debriefing process) are consistent with these statistical findings. Debriefing statements made by participants selected for introversion-extroversion illustrate not only the association of the 'feeler' trait with a positive attitude toward teamwork but also the effect this trait can have on the manner (concreteness, level of detail) in which the student expresses an attitude. Introversion is associated in both quantitative and qualitative data with a positive perception of the simulation as a learning experience, but this does not preclude positive perceptions on the part of extroverts. Neither low responses to survey items nor extremely high ones necessarily prevent students from seeing both positive and negative aspects to the experience.

Most responses in debriefing conferences – but not all – mirror our statistical data. Those that differ serve to remind us that in the classroom, we work with students, not numbers. The concatenation of events which determine each individual participant's simulation experience, perceptions and reactions cannot be predicted. Thus, it is important to provide a variety of both extensive and intensive debriefing opportunities to ensure that the necessary reflection and assimilation of the experience can occur. That said, this study at least suggests that the combination of physical and virtual environments, as well as the opportunities for individual and collaborative work provided by IDEELS simulations works well for a wide range of learning types.

Acknowledgements The authors wish to thank John Schindler for permission to use the Paragon Learning Style Inventory he and Harrison Yang developed. We also owe a debt of gratitude the European Union's Socrates Program for funding IDEELS as a curriculum development project from 1997 through 2001.

References

Chin, J., Dukes, R., & Gamson, W. (2009). Assessment in simulation and gaming: A review of the last 40 years. *Simulation & Gaming, 40*, 553–568.
de Bono, E. (2009). Edward de Bono personal web site. Retrieved April 14, 2010, from http://www.edwarddebono.com/Default.php
Ekker, K. (2004). User satisfaction and attitudes towards an I-based simulation. *Proceedings of the IADIS International Conference: Cognition and Exploratory Learning in Digital Age (CELDA 2004).* (pp. 224–232). Lisbon, Portugal: IADIS.
Ekker, K., & Sutherland, J. (2005). Telematic simulations and changes in attitudes towards simulation topics. In G. Richards (Ed.), *Proceedings of E-Learn 2005: World Conference on E-Learning in Corporate, Government, Healthcare, and Higher Education 2005* (pp. 2034–2041). Chesapeake, VA: AACE.
Golden, P. A., & Smith, J. R. (1989). Simulation performance revisited: The fit between instructor style and learning style. *Developments in Business Simulation & Experiential Exercises, 16*, 89–91.
Gosen, J., & Washbush, J. (2004). A review of scholarship on assessing experiential learning effectiveness. *Simulation & Gaming, 35*, 270–293.
Morgan, K. (2001) *What does a group need to be successful?* Retrieved April 14, 2010, from http://www.ideels.uni-bremen.de/narg_discussion.html
Schindler, J., & Yang, H. (2009). Paragon Learning Style Inventory. Retrieved April 14, 2010, from http://www.calstatela.edu/faculty/jshindl/plsi /index.html and http://www.oswego.edu/plsi/
Project IDEELS (2001a). *Shared learning objectives.* Retrieved April 14, 2010, from http://www.ideels.uni-bremen.de/shlobj.html
Project IDEELS (2001b). *Specific learning objectives.* Retrieved April 14, 2010, from http://www.ideels.uni-bremen.de/splobj.html
Sutherland, J. L., Ekker, K., & Eidsmo, A. (2006). Telematic simulation in the post-September 11 world. In Reeves, T. C., & Yamashita, S. F. (Eds.), *Proceedings of E-Learn 2006. World Conference on E-Learning in Corporate, Government, Healthcare, and Higher Education* (pp. 2650–2657). Chesapeake, VA: AACE.
Wheatley, W. J., Armstrong, T. R., & Madox, E. N. (1989). The impact of leader and team member characteristics upon simulation performance: A start-up study. *Developments in Business Simulation & Experiential Exercises, 16*, 13–16.

Chapter 20
Implementation of an Online Social Annotation Tool in a College English Course

Anne Mendenhall, Chanmin Kim, and Tristan E. Johnson

Abstract An online social annotation tool was implemented in the context of utilizing question-answering tasks with reading documents. The tool and tasks were used in order to foster students' cognitive development with higher-order thinking, critical analysis, and development of sophisticated arguments in English writing. The effects of the tool on students' mental models as well as their motivation for and achievement in a college argument and persuasion course were investigated. The findings are discussed along with implications and possibilities for future studies.

Keywords Social annotation tool · Question-answering · English education · Mental model · Motivation · Community college

1 Introduction

The fundamental goals of college English courses are three-fold. First, the goal is to enhance students' ability to write effectively by fostering higher-order thinking ability. Second, is to promote critical analysis of information and third, is to increase students' abilities to develop arguments (Campbell, Smith, & Brooker, 1998). Students' critical thinking and analysis ability can be enhanced by question-answering tasks associated with assigned readings since such tasks require (a) a process of information discrimination (e.g., relevant vs. irrelevant information), (b) understanding the contextual meaning of questions, and (c) comprehending reading materials (Cerdán, Vidal-Abarca, Martínez, Gilabert,& Gil, 2009).

A. Mendenhall (✉)
Department of Educational Psychology Learning System, Florida State University, 3210 Stone Building, Tallahassee, FL 32306, USA
e-mail: anne.mendenhall@gmail.com

Although question-answering tasks with reading documents are commonly used in English courses, they do not necessarily help students develop sophisticated arguments. A critical problem is that students have difficulty in developing arguments and persuasive essays for a particular audience (Crammand, 1998). Without an understanding of their audience, it is hard for students to explain and justify the links between data and claims and establish a shared context with the audience. Incorporating multiple perspectives of reality into their own world views is necessary in order to be able to develop sophisticated arguments that recognize multiple perspectives of audience (Shapiro, 1985).

Online teaching and learning environments have the potential to capture the mental processes of students' who read and answer questions (Cerdán et al., 2009; Rouet, Vidal-Abarca, Bert-Erboul, & Millogo, 2001). Online question-answering tasks along with opportunities to interact with multiple perspectives should foster cognitive development for effective writing. However, too often online English courses and tools are used for drill and practice of basic skills and not for developing more complex cognitive skills. In addition, a quick and unplanned transition from traditional classroom instruction to relying solely on online teaching and learning environments may not provide an optimal environment for efficient, effective and engaging learning (e3-learning; see Spector & Merrill, 2008). Rather, a more gradual and planned integration of e-learning tools, either as supplements or in a blended setting, may offer learners tangible benefits without risking loss of effectiveness or efficiency while increasing learner engagement (Rivera, McAlister, & Rice, 2002).

This study implemented a structured method to engage students in online question-answering tasks in the context of a face-to-face English course and made use of an online social annotation tool called HyLighter (www.hylighter.com). HyLighter is designed to improve students' metacognition, reading comprehension, critical thinking, and writing skills. HyLighter has two major functions, annotating an electronic document (question-answering tasks) and commenting on peers' annotations. These functions require students to engage in the processes of reflection, analysis, deliberation, and judgment of multiple perspectives in peers' contribution. Unlike many other annotation tools, HyLighter allows any number of users to synchronously engage in collaborative conversations. The specific functions and features of HyLighter are described in the Method section.

The specific purposes of this study were to (1) implement an online social annotation tool, HyLighter, for question-answering tasks in a college argument and persuasion course, and (2) investigate the effects of HyLighter on the students' mental models, motivation for the course, and achievement in the course, compared to the students who engaged in question-answering tasks without using HyLighter.

First, it was expected that the mental models of students using HyLighter would become more expert than students not using HyLighter, because interactions with peers in HyLighter would facilitate the development of students' mental models for sophisticated arguments (Merrill & Gilbert, 2008). Second, it was expected that motivation for the course would be higher among those completing question-answering tasks using HyLighter than among those completing question-answering tasks without HyLighter, because the presence of peers would cultivate motivation to succeed with attentions to the quality of their work (Kim, Mendenhall, & Johnson, in press). Due to the developed mental models and cultivated motivation, it was expected that students completing question-answering tasks using HyLighter would perform better on the final exam than those completing question-answering tasks without HyLighter.

2 Method

2.1 Participants

The participants in the study consisted of students enrolled in two sections of an "Argument and Persuasion" course at a southeastern community college. The purpose of the course was to help students synthesize reading and writing experiences, practice analytical response, and nurture/sharpen critical thinking skills as well as identify and understand concepts of argument and persuasion. The majority of participants were freshmen and sophomores and the course was required for all of them. Some participants were recent high school graduates while others were reentry or non-traditional students (i.e., older students and working full-time). They voluntarily participated in this study and did not receive extra credit for their participation. Each section was randomly assigned to one of two conditions: one completing question-answering tasks using an online social annotation tool (HyLighter Group) and the other completing question-answering tasks without using an online social annotation tool (Non-HyLighter Group). The initial number of participants was 46 (HyLighter Group: $n=20$; Non-HyLighter Group: $n=26$); however, 16 participants were excluded from the data analysis because they missed one or more of the question/answer tasks.

2.2 Materials

For this study, there were four articles in which participants read and answered questions relating to the content of the article. Since the course is about arguments and persuasion the content for the activities were selected articles relating to recent controversial subjects. The first task article was from the New York Times (1996) titled "Gay Marriage, an Oxymoron" by Lisa Schiffen. The second task article was "Put on a Happy Face: Masking the Differences Between Blacks and Whites" by Benjamin DeMott (1995). The third task article was from Time Magazine and was written by Barrett Seaman (2005) titled " How Bingeing Became the New College Sport". The final task article was titled "On Being a Fan" by Murray Sperber (2007) from the Chronicle Review. The tasks consisted of twelve to fourteen reading comprehension questions and a thesis activity where students are asked to write their own version of the thesis. Additionally, there were three to four critical thinking questions that asked students to think about, relate, and apply concepts in the current article to previous concepts illustrated in previous articles and in-class discussions.

2.3 Independent Variable

The independent variable was a type of question-answering task with two levels: one was a question-answering task using an online social annotation tool (HyLighter); and the other was a question-answering task that did not use an online social annotation tool (Non-HyLighter).

Hylighter is a social annotation tool where the instructor and students are able to collaborate online to review and mark-up a single document. The instructor loads a DOC, PDF, JPG or HTML file into HyLighter. The instructor then invites the student to have access to and annotate the document. A unique feature of HyLighter that distinguishes it from other existing annotation tools (e.g., Microsoft Office, iMarkUp, Proof-It Online, etc.) is that it allows instructors to create synchronous or asynchronous text-dependent socio-intellectual interactions among students (see Fig. 20.1).

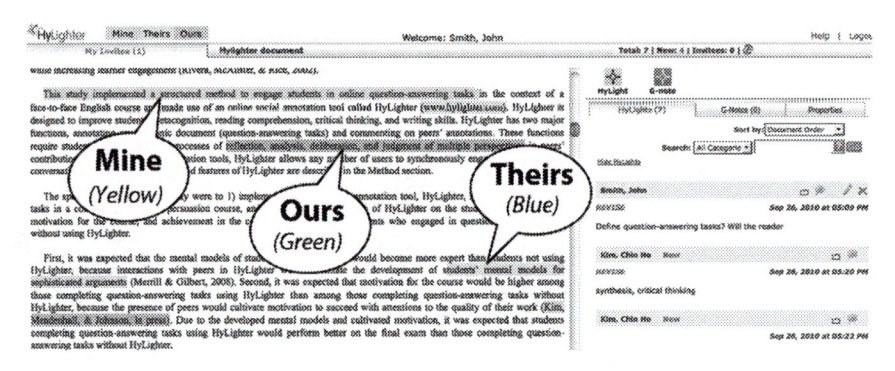

Fig. 20.1 Sample HyLighter screen with color coding to indicate contributions

The capabilities of HyLighter to display shared annotation are supported by four main functions including provisions to compare hylights of a selected individual to all contributors or selected contributors using color-coding or other forms of emphasis. As illustrated in Fig. 20.1, a contributor can compare the parts of the text they hylighted with what other contributors hylighted. "My" hylights are represented in yellow while "theirs" is in blue and the portions we both selected ("ours") are represented in green.

The second main function is to compare g-notes of a selected individual to all or selected other contributors. G-notes are general comments or summarizations not tied to specific sections of the document. For example, the instructor asked the students, in a g-note, a critical thinking question about the overall theme and sub-themes of the article and how it related to themes and sub-themes previously discussed in class. Students responded to the g-note, read other contributors' responses, and then replied to those contributors' g-notes.

The third main function is to view threaded comments (i.e., comments on the comments of others using a markover). Contributors can tag comments for future reference and they can filter through the comments to make their desired comparisons (i.e., to all or selected individual contributors). The threaded comments are similar to a discussion forum; however, the threaded comments from all contributors appear immediately after they are posted, creating a synchronous social experience.

The fourth main function is to display the annotation of a group in various table formats. HyLighter uses color-coding to create a cumulative map of multiple students' intellectual travels through a document and, additionally, to single out an individual student's journey and compare it with the whole group of students or with the paths of another individual student (Lebow, Lick, Hartman, & Marks, 2007).

2.4 Measures

Mental models were measured using parts of HIMATT (Highly Interactive Model-based Assessment Tools and Technologies) that analyzed structural and conceptual aspects of a student's mental models and then used analytical methods to compare the student's mental models with an expert's mental models in order to assess the level of conceptual and structural similarity of the two models. The tasks completed by students (i.e., question-answering tasks) were used for the mental model analysis (Kim, Mendenhall, & Johnson, in press) and compared with the expert's responses to the same tasks. The four completed tasks were chosen due to their complexity and the tasks could reflect the progress of students' development of mental models.

Specifically, (1) Surface, Matching, and Deep Structure (SMD) Methodology (Ifenthaler, 2006; Seel, Ifenthaler, & Pirnay-Dummer, 2009) and (2) Model Inspection Trace of Concepts and Relations (MITOCAR) Methodology (Dummer & Ifenthaler, 2005; Seel, 1999) of HIMATT were used. The analysis produces six different measures for the comparison between the mental models of a student and an expert as follows (Kim, Mendenhall, & Johnson, in press): (1) Propositional Matching (SMD), which compares identical propositions (semantic similarity) between two mental models graphs; (2) Concept Matching (MITOCAR), which compares the sets of concepts (vertices) within a mental model graph to determine the use of terms. This measure determines differences in language use between the models; (3) Surface Structure (SMD), which compares the number of vertices within two graphs and represents the values for surface complexity; (4) Graphical Structure (SMD), in which the diameters of the spanning trees of the mental model graphs are compared; (5) Density of Vertices (MITOCAR) – density of vertices describes the quotient of terms per vertex within a graph. Medium density models are considered good models. Weak models include both graphs that connect every term with each other term and graphs that only connect pairs of terms; and (6) Structural Matching (MITOCAR), which compares the complete structures of two mental model graphs without regard to their content. This measure is necessary for all hypotheses that make assumptions about general features of structure (e.g., assumptions which state that expert knowledge is structured differently from novice knowledge).

Achievement was measured by students' final exam scores. In the final exam, a newspaper article was provided, accompanied by questions related to a) reading comprehension (i.e., questioning about certain information embedded in the article), b) critical thinking (i.e., questioning students' thoughts about logical structure and arguments in the article), and c) a thesis (i.e., asking to write a short thesis in regard to arguments in the article). Students could earn 0–100 points.

Motivation was measured using the Course Interest Survey (CIS) (Keller & Subhiyah, 1993). The CIS was designed to measure students' reactions to classroom instruction. The present study used an abbreviated version of the survey, which contained 16 items and responses were made on a five-point Likert type scale.

2.4.1 Procedures

One participating section was randomly assigned to the experimental group (completing question-answering tasks using the online social annotation tool, HyLighter). The other class section was assigned to be the control group (completing question-answering tasks without HyLighter). At the beginning of the first week, researchers attended each class section to recruit participants. For the experimental group, they provided a 20-min tutorial session on the use of HyLighter. The tutorial was given prior to the study so students' time was optimized during the class periods when the study was conducted. Students from both groups worked individually at their own computer workstation in a computer laboratory.

Each group participated in the study for 4 months. There were four question-answering tasks with four different reading documents. The questions within each task pertained to a) reading comprehension (i.e., questioning about certain information embedded in the reading material), b) critical thinking (i.e., questioning students' thoughts about logical structure and arguments in the reading material such as overgeneralization, oversimplification, clichés, etc.), and c) a thesis (i.e., asking to write a short thesis in regard to arguments in the reading material). Unlike the experimental group, students in the control group did not have an opportunity to see or make comments on each other's answers to the questions since they did not use HyLighter.

Each task was given to both groups on the same day. The students were given 50-min of a 60-min class period to complete one task. The additional 10 min were for instructor announcements and instructions. This process was repeated four times over a 4-month period of time. After students completed the fourth question-answering task, each group responded to the Course Interest Survey (CIS) measuring motivation for the course for about 10 min and then took the final exam for 50 min.

2.5 *Data Analysis*

The data were analyzed according to three dependent measures: (a) mental models, (b) motivation, and (c) achievement. Mental models (Surface Structure,

Graphical Structure, Structural Matching, Density of Vertices, Concept Matching, and Propositional Matching) were assessed via a one-factor MANOVA (Type of question-answering tasks: HyLighter, Non-HyLighter). Motivation and achievement were evaluated by one-way ANOVAs.

3 Results

A review of data for all three dependent variables indicated that there was no serious violation of the assumptions of normality. Means and standard deviations for all the measures are shown in Table 20.1.

Mental Models were analyzed through a one-factor MANOVA, with Surface Structure, Graphical Structure, Structural Matching, Density of Vertices, Concept Matching, and Propositional Matching, and with condition (Treatment, $N=12$; Control, $N=18$) as the between-subject factor. The MANOVA indicated that there was no significant effect of the treatment condition on mental models, Wilk's Lambda $= 0.924$, $F(7, 22) = 1.835$, $p = 0.131$. Follow-up ANOVAs indicated that significant differences occurred only for Surface Structure, $F(1, 28) = 6.184$, $p = 0.19$, and Concept Matching, $F(1, 28) = 7.38$, $p = 0.011$. The effect size estimates were $d = 0.99$ for Surface Structure, $d = 0.28$ for Graphical Structure, $d = 0.42$ for Structural Matching, $d = 0.36$ for Density of Vertices, $d = 0.95$ for Concept Matching, and $d = 0.71$ for Propositional Matching, indicating a medium effect (Cohen, 1988).

Achievement was analyzed through one-way ANOVA and no significant difference in achievement between the two groups was detected, $F(1, 28) = 1.961$, $p = 0.172$. The effect size estimates were $d = 0.54$, indicating a medium effect (Cohen, 1988). Levene's test revealed appropriate homogeneity of the final exam scores, $F(1, 28) = 0.452$, $p = 0.507$.

Motivation was analyzed with a one-way ANOVA and no significant difference in achievement between the two groups was detected, $F(1, 28) = 0.066$, $p = 0.799$. The effect size estimate was $d = 0.09$, indicating a small effect (Cohen, 1988). Levene's test revealed appropriate homogeneity of the posttest scores, $F(1, 28) = 0.722$, $p = 0.403$.

4 Discussion

The purpose of this study was to document the impact of an online social annotation tool, HyLighter, on students' mental models, motivation for the course, and achievement in the course.

Tasks completed by participants, in four different question-answering tasks, with the HyLighter group (collaborative experience) would be more similar with expert's than the Non-HyLighter group (individual work) in terms of *Surface Complexity* and *Concept Matching*. When students are required to collaborate and critique the work

Table 20.1 Means and standard deviations for the dependent variables

Group	Mental model (similarity-with-expert score)[a]						Achievement (final exam score)[b]	Motivation (CIS score)[c]
	Surface structure	Graphical structure	Structural matching	Density of vertices	Concept matching	Propositional matching		
HyLighter ($n=12$)	0.78 (0.17)	0.78 (0.17)	0.69 (0.12)	0.78 (0.18)	0.42 (0.09)	0.20 (0.07)	80.08 (7.20)	2.72 (0.56)
Non-HyLighter ($n=18$)	0.55 (0.28)	0.72 (0.25)	0.63 (0.16)	0.71 (0.21)	0.33 (0.10)	0.15 (0.07)	75.00 (11.08)	2.67 (0.50)

[a]Possible range for similarity-with-expert score (0–1)
[b]Possible range for final exam score (0–100)
[c]Possible range for CIS score (1–5)

of their peers the student assesses his or her own mental model of the "phenomena against the product resulting from the mental model of the peer" (Merrill & Gilbert, 2008, p. 202). The students are required to process more deeply their own understandings and to modify their mental model (Merrill & Gilbert, 2008). Outcomes of this process include greater sharedness of mental models with peers and experts. This finding is consistent with previous research showing collaboration with peers is effective for developing novice learners' mental models (Seel, 2004).

There was no statistically significant impact of the improved mental models on achievement. Considering the slightly higher exam score and smaller standard deviation in the HyLighter group than in the Non-HyLighter group, although it is not statistically significant result, if we had a bigger sample size, the power would have increased. Another explanation for non-significant results could be because the students were not consistently using the software for other in-class and out-of-class assignments. Prolonged usage and collaboration among peers in addition to a bigger sample size may lead to improved results. Further research with a larger sample size and more activities is recommended.

In addition to the unexpected, non-significant finding on achievement, there was no statistically significant difference in motivation between the two groups as well. This is a good example that it should not be expected that a new technology tool alone (HyLighter in this context) can be a motivator for students' study. Aspects that can meet students' needs and enhance their motivation should be integrated into the use of technology (Keller, 2009). In fact, both groups show lower levels of motivation than desirable (less than 3 out of 5), which should be taken into consideration when designing a course like this where many students are non-traditional and have full time jobs. Low levels of motivation can be caused by many factors. The theory of involvement (Astin, 1999) states that the environment in which the student resides affects their motivation. Moreover, students who spend much of their time on a college campus (e.g. residential students at 4-year institutions) are more likely to develop an attachment and identify undergraduate life than commuter or part-time students. Community college students are often commuter and/or part-time students where most of their time is spent away from campus thus, "presumably manifest[ing] less involvement simply because of their part-time status" (Astin, 1999, p. 7) resulting in overall lower motivation.

Additional factors that can affect the motivation of the students can be the time of day the course is taught and the fact this course was a required general education course and not an elective. The instructor indicated that the early morning courses were less preferred and often the only section open for students who register for the course late.

There are several limitations in our present study to be considered for future research. First, the assignment of the participants was not completely random since we used intact classes – one section of the course for the treatment group (HyLighter) and the other section (Non-HyLighter). One should be aware of the threat to internal validity due to this non-random assignment. Both sections of the course were morning classes and they were taught by one instructor. However, there might have been different characteristics between them: 40% of the HyLighter group did not complete at least one of the four question-answering tasks and 30% of the Non-HyLighter group did not complete at least one of the four question-answering tasks. These participants were excluded from the data analysis. The section with the HyLighter participants began at 8 am and the other section with non-HyLighter participants began at 10 am. The instructor mentioned that students in the earlier class tend to be absent more often than student in the later class and they are more likely to have full-time jobs as well. Second, if there were more participants as well as equal numbers in each group, data analyses could have had greater power. Third, the treatment and control conditions were not completely under full control owing to the length of our study – 4 months. In addition, the quality and quantity of interactions within the HyLighter group was not controlled.

The findings and limitations of this study provide several directions for future research. Studies should be conducted to verify persistence of the positive effects on the mental model (Surface Structure & Concept Matching) as well as design and develop methods to positively influence the mental models (Graphical Structure, Structural Matching, Density of Vertices, and Propositional Matching). In addition, future research should investigate methods to improve students' motivation in community college English courses. Last, future research might consider a provision of incentives to participants in order to obtain complete datasets, especially for a semester-long study. Keeping as many participants as possible would secure statistical power to analyze data so that the researcher would have high probabilities to see the actual effectiveness of the treatment.

Despite the limitations, this study is significant in that it reports: a) the implementation of an online social annotation tool into a face-to-face course; and b) a variety of ways of looking into the effects of the tool, especially in students' mental models.

References

Astin, A. W. (1999). Student Involvement: A developmental theory for higher education. *Journal of College Student Development, 40*(5), 518–529.

Campbell, J., Smith, D., & Brooker, R. (1998). From conception to performance: How undergraduate students conceptualise and construct essays. *Higher Education, 36*, 449–469.

Cerdán, R., Vidal-Abarca, E., Martínez, T., Gilabert, R., & Gil, L. (2009). Impact of question-answering tasks on search processes and reading comprehension. *Learning and Instruction, 19*(1), 13–27.

DeMott, B. (1995). Put on a happy face: Masking the differences between black and whites. *Harper's Magazine, 291*(1744), 31–38.

Dummer, P., & Ifenthaler, D. (2005). Planning and assessing navigation in model-centered learning environments. Why learners often do not follow the path laid out for them. In G. Chiazzese, M. Allegra, A. Chifari, & S. Ottaviano (Eds.), *Methods and technologies for learning* (pp. 327–334). Southampton, Boston: WIT Press.

Ifenthaler, D. (2006). *Diagnosis of the learning-dependent progression of mental models. Development of the SMD-Technology as a methodology for assessing individual models on relational, structural and semantic levels.* Freiburg: Universitäts-Dissertation.

Keller, J. M. (2009). *Motivational design for learning and performance: The ARCS model approach.* New York: Springer.

Keller, J. M., & Subhiyah, R. (1993). *Course interest survey*. Tallahassee, FL: Instructional Systems Program, Florida State University.

Kim, C., Mendenhall, A., & Johnson, T. E. 2010. A design framework for an online English writing course. In J. M. Spector, D. Ifenthaler, P. Isaías, Kinshuk, & D. G. Sampson (Eds.), *Learning and instruction in the digital age: Making a difference through cognitive approaches, technology-facilitated collaboration and assessment, and personalized communications*. New YorK: Springer.

Lebow, D. G., Lick, D. W., and Hartman, H. (2009) New technology for empowering virtual communities. In M. Pagani (Ed.), *Encyclopedia of multimedia and technology* (2nd ed., pp. 1066–1071). Hershey, PA: IGI Global.

Merrill, M. D., & Gilbert, C. G. (2008). Effective peer interaction in a problem-centered instructional strategy. *Distance Education, 29*(2), 199–207.

Rivera, J., McAlister, K., & Rice, M. (2002). A comparison of student outcomes & satisfaction between traditional & web based course offerings. *Online Journal of Distance Learning Administration, 5*, 151–179.

Rouet, J.-F., Vidal-Abarca, E., Bert-Erboul, A., & Millogo, V. (2001). Effects of information search tasks on the comprehension of instructional text. *Discourse Processes, 31*(2), 163–186.

Schiffren, L. (1996). Gay marriage, an oxymoron. (1996, March 23). *New York Times*. New York, p. A21.

Seaman, B. (2005). How bingeing became the new college sport. *Time, 166*(9), 80.

Seel, N. M. (1999). Educational diagnosis of mental models: Assessment problems and technology-based solutions. *Journal of Structural Learning and Intelligent Systems, 14*(2), 153–185.

Seel, N. M. (2004). Model-centered learning environment: Theory, instructional design and effects. In N. M. Seel, R. Marr, & S. Dijkstra (Eds.), *Curriculum, loans and processes in instructional design* (pp. 49–74). Mahwah, NJ: Lawrence Erlbaum.

Seel, N. M., Ifenthaler, D., & Pirnay-Dummer, P. (2009). Mental models and problem solving: Technological solutions for measurement and assessment of the development of expertise. In P. Blumschein, W. Hung, D. H. Jonassen & J. Strobel (Eds.), *Model-based approaches to learning: Using systems models and simulations to improve understanding and problem solving in complex domains* (pp. 17–40). Rotterdam: Sense Publishers.

Spector, J. M., & Merrill, M. D. (2008). Special issue: Effective, efficient and engaging learning. *Distance Education, 29*(2), 123–126.

Sperber, M. (2007). On being a fan. *Chronicle of Higher Education, 54*(6), 19–21.

Chapter 21
Self-Direction Indicators for Evaluating the Design-Based Elearning Course with Social Software

Kai Pata and Sonja Merisalo

Abstract This paper discusses the development of self-direction indicators for evaluating the e-learning course using students' self reflections with social software. Fifty five students of the international Design-based eLearning course wrote in blogs weekly self-reflections during 14 study weeks. Data were qualitatively categorized using the classification scheme of self-direction indicators. Linear Regression demonstrated the dependence of some self-direction indicators on the study weeks. Bayesian dependency modeling revealed the significant causal interrelations of the self-direction indicators, representing a system in which various types of mediators (social software tools, self-direction as a tool, and group-work as a tool) were used as possible paths for reaching individual and group goals.

Keywords Self-direction · Self-reflection · Design-based learning

1 Introduction

The explosion of social software in recent years has created a new environment for formal and informal learning. Characteristic to this is that it enables people to actively reflect, publish and share experiences; gain awareness and monitor other individuals, communities and networks; publicly store and maintain artifacts and gain from retrieving the socially gathered information; and autonomously combine various tools, material- and human resources into personal and group environments (Constantinides & Fountain, 2008). At the time when life-long learning is a key for social and economic survival and co-evolvement, the development of the designing competences for personal and group interaction and learning environments must be promoted. Maintaining Personal Learning Environments can offer learners the opportunity to plan their own learning trajectory by providing them a certain

K. Pata (✉)
Institute of Informatics, Tallinn University, Narva road 25, 10120 Tallinn, Estonia
e-mail: kpata@tlu.ee

amount of freedom to choose what they want to learn (i.e., selecting a topic) and how they want to learn this (i.e., selecting particular learning tasks) (Attwell, 2007; Underwood & Banyard, 2008). The design process at a cognitive and metacognitive level attributes to the development of self-direction and self-reflection habits as part of the design process.

This paper discusses the development of self-direction indicators for evaluating the e-learning course using students self reflections with social software. Knowing the recognizable indicators of self-direction in self-reflections would enable facilitators and course developers to evaluate learner progress at Design-based Learning course. This paper aimed at creating and validating such indicators. The following research questions were formulated: Which are the indicators of the self-direction in students' self-reflection blogs-posts? What is their application during the Design-based learning course? Which are the interrelations between the indicators of self-direction?

1.1 Design-Based Learning with Social Software

Wijnen (2000) defines design-based learning as an educational model in which the study program is aimed at learning to design. He assumes that Design-Based Learning is not only the type of education with an emphasis on products that are created within the framework of education, but the underlying design processes are of same relevance. Ning, Williams, Slocum and Sanchez (2004) write that design-oriented learning takes a unique approach of a combination of objectivism/behaviorism and constructivism because it is a mix of understanding of explicit design parameters and conducting conscious and yet implicit creative activity. Such courses are becoming more and more practiced at upper bachelor and master level education. Creating design solutions that are targeted for learning and work follows Instructional Design process. Instructional Design is the systematic and reflective process of translating principles of learning and instruction into plans for instructional materials, activities, information resources and evaluation (Smith & Ragan, 1999).

The process of developing an Instructional Design, and the process of self-directing learning are guided by the questions of similar nature (see Table 21.1). The activities of self-direction contain diagnosing and formulating needs, identifying resources, choosing and implementing suitable strategies and evaluating outcomes (Knowles, 1975). Therefore, it makes sense for learners to target Instructional Designs towards their own needs. If learners develop Personal or Collaborative Learning Environments from social software, they must simultaneously take an insight into themselves, and find what they perceive as a mediator for taking action. They can monitor themselves within their teams and analyze their needs and actions in these settings using these tools. On the other hand, while the learning environment is developed, it is simultaneously tested and adapted to better meet their needs. Some critical aspects of self-direction may become evident in this design process.

Table 21.1 Comparison of the phases of self-direction and instructional design process

Phases for planning	Questions in instructional design phases (Smith & Ragan, 1999)	Components of self-directed learning (Knowles, 1975; Pressley, 1995)
Diagnose	Where are we going?	Diagnosing learning needs in the light of given performance standard
Set goals	What are the goals of the instruction?	Formulating meaningful goals for learning
Develop strategy	How will we get there? (What is the instructional strategy?)	Developing and using a wide range of learning strategies appropriate to different learning tasks
Select resources	What is the instructional medium?	Identifying resources for accomplishing various kinds of learning objectives
Implement	Instructional design is developed	Carrying out a learning plan systematically and sequentially
Evaluate	How will we know when we have arrived? (What should our tests look like? How will we evaluate and revise the instructional materials?)	Diagnosing and monitoring performance

Simultaneously, learners can decide which tools might compensate these limitations of self-direction. The learner's self-directing competences will be embedded into the Instructional design and adjusted with it during the design process. In each phase learners will have to ask the same questions about the Instructional Design that they are developing, and of self-directing their own learning. Thus, the Design-based learning course, in which students develop an Instructional Design for aiding their learning, can serve for advancing learners' self-directing competences and may be preparing them for design-oriented thinking in future workplaces.

1.2 Self-Reflection at Design-Based Learning

Self-reflection at individual and team level is a natural part of the Design-based learning and self-directed learning activities. Smith and Ragan (1999) emphasize reflective processes of translating principles of learning and instruction into plans for instructional materials, activities, information resources and evaluation that occur as part of the Instructional Design process. Self-reflection activities are part of our strategies for coping with problems in situations where we need to direct our action plans during self-directed learning. Self-reflection enables to structure and externalize for our own needs parts of the self-direction process, reducing the cognitive load.

In addition to internal self-reflection and self-directed actions, social software applications enable people to record their reflections externally, enabling them and their facilitators to keep track of their self-directed learning. For technologically aiding self-directing and reflecting learning, conversational learning diaries in blogs may be used. Scaffolding elements to support self-reflection can be added to blogs, such as guiding questions.

For identifying self-reflection indicators we can elaborate activity theory (Engeström, 1987) that uses the tool concept as central for signifying various mediators that enable learners and teams to fulfill objectives. Original model considers the material tools, language, and the organization of group-work as the mediating tools to achieve the objectives. In this paper we assume that self-directing individuals are aware of, and use consciously various diagnosing, planning and evaluating activities, while working individually and in groups. Thereby, this self-directing competence becomes a cognitive tool, and may serve as another mediator of actions. Thus, three types of tools are available for individuals: a) material tools (eg. software); b) team as the tool to reach personal and group goals during the activity; and c) the person itself with its aresenal of self-direction competences. We can consider the following groups of indicators of self-direction:

I. Tool-Use: A common way in using social software in Design-based courses has been moving from the establishment of initial Personal Learning Environments (PLE) towards combining these with other people's PLEs in order to carry out some joint learning activities (Fiedler & Pata, 2009; Pata, 2009). This often means changing and expanding each individual's PLEs, and integrating new tools, resources and people to their PLEs, while suppressing the use of others in the sake of forming a shared learning environment where all the tools can be used equally by the group members for collaborative tasks. Moreover, the components of PLE and collaborative environment are continuously changed during learning process, while adopting better to the learners' needs. Indicators of learners' confidence in using tools in PLE and collaborative environment can be: their initiative in using new tools, using the same set of tools, dropping the tools, and starting to use the tools again. The expressed difficulty of using tools is also a meaningful indicator.

II. Clarity of the Learning Process: The learning process at Design-based courses is messy. Learners, and not the instructor determine the nature and components of the Instructional Design, which makes pre-planning of course tools, resources and activities difficult. The unclear learning process represents similar challenging situations that learner must face in real life situations where design-based approach becomes usable. However, participating in design process first time, may leave many aspects unclear for learner. So if learner is mentioning clear or unclear learning process aspects in his refections, this could be used as an indicator of clarity.

III. Observed Change: As any learning is an observed change, inference has to be made from evidence that there has been some significant change in somebody else's, or our own, way of thinking, perceiving, and doing something

(Harri-Augstein & Thomas, 1991). For making such observations of change one has to consciously observe and reflect on the learning process. Indicators of observed change can be: change that learner monitors himself or the change that is observed in other learners of the team.

IV: *Origin of Ruptured Situations*: The self, according to Hermans (1996), is organized as a dialogical interchange between relatively autonomous and mutually influencing selves. By allowing the various positions to be internally voiced, one reaches decisions and self-directs ones actions. Gillespie (2007) has brought out some of the theories of the origin of self-reflection: a) ruptured situations, in which actors have more than one response to the situation that needs decision-making, and thus self-reflection of our own arguments is induced; b) the presence of others who provide feedback to the sides of the self we are not so aware of, and thus make us to reflect upon these sides; and c) in groups and communities the reflection upon the rules and conditions of the ongoing interaction that leads to the personal self-reflection. Conscious self-reflection is always part of our decision-making activities internally, but people seldom express these contraversial arguments if alone, neither do they make them public to other people. Conversations with others or with oneself (by explicit process monitoring) enable us to clearly formulate our responses to the ruptured situations. This makes our own thinking clearer to us. Thus, both self-reflecting individually in problem situations and learning in social settings provide conditions for the ruptured situations and self-directed actions. Indicators of ruptured situations can be noticed difference between old and new knowledge and competences in self or noticed difference of knowledge and competences between self and the group.

V: *Self-Directing Oneself*: The processes of self-direction (see Knowles, 1975) and planning for Instructional Design development (Smith & Ragan, 1999) consists of same phases: diagnosing what one can/cannot do and know, formulating the needs, setting the goals, finding the strategy, creating an agenda, identifying resources, implementing strategies, and evaluating outcomes. The presence of these phases in reflections may be used as indicators of planning for self-direction.

VI: *Directing the Group*: Most of the Design-based Learning is conducted in group-work. Therefore, learners' self-reflections may represent their expectations towards group-work. Team may serve as a tool for promoting learners' individual goals in the group. Such indicators of directing the group as part of operationalizing self-direction are: organizing the team or expecting the team to work.

VII: *Reflecting Voice*: One important indicator demonstrating if learner is focusing at himself while performing self-direction or if learner perceives himself as part of the group when self-directing is the reflecting voice. Kieslinger and Pata (2008) have identified three different addressees the reflection may be directed to: towards the self, towards the self in the group, and towards the group. Self-directed reflection mode was usually very general and occurred at the beginning of a course when learners faced difficulties in explicitly distinguishing how their planning is part of the group-work. When starting to work collaboratively, the voice changed and learners associated their reflections with the group work. In self-reflections two main arguments were used: entries related to how the individual can contribute to the group, and the second that referred to how the group could contribute to the individual's learning. Thus, the reflecting voice as an indicator of self-reflection mode may be directed towards self and towards the group.

2 The Design-Based Learning Course 'Elearning'

The international master course of EMIM (European Master of Interactive Media) curriculum, coordinated by Tallinn University, was expanded to integrate more interested counterparts from other universities for conducting an experimental teaching in the frames of the IST 6th Framework project iCamp (http://icamp.eu). Students from 10 universities were enrolled to the international course of eLearning dedicated to teach the principles of planning an eLearning course in the distributed social software settings. Initially 86 BA, MA and PhD students from 10 universities were involved, however, the majority of them were master students. The team facilitators were lecturers and researchers from the involved universities in Estonia, Spain, Poland, Croatia, Lithuania and Finland. The authors of this paper acted as a facilitator and a student in this course.

The course framework was developed for Design-based learning (see Fig. 21.1). The objective was to understand the principles of planning e-learning courses, while developing jointly a prototype of an e-learning course.

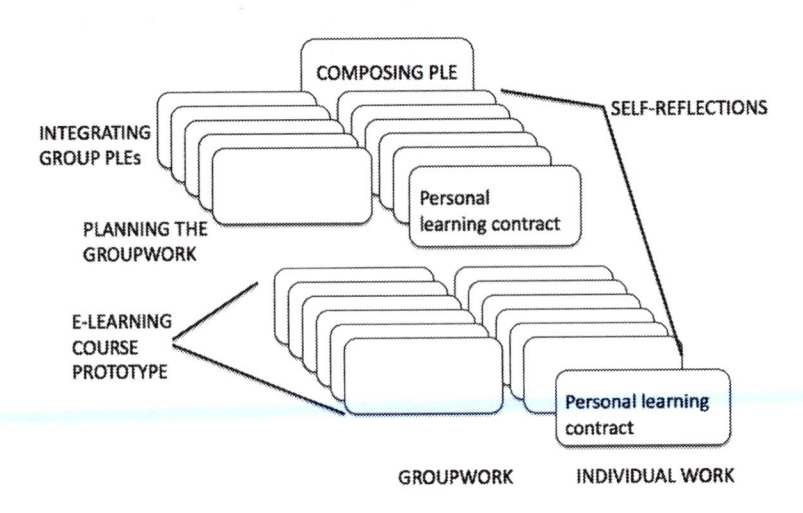

Fig. 21.1 Outline of the course for design-based learning

Outline of the course tasks was the following:

Week 1: Individual work, assembling PLE. Individual reflective assignments.
Week 2: Forming the groups. Assembling group environment. Individual reflective assignments.
Week 3: Group work, preparing the group work for prototype development. Individual reflective assignments.
Week 4: Group work, preparing the group work for prototype development. Individual reflective assignments.
Week 5: Individual work, creating personal learning contract. Individual reflective assignments.
Week 6: Group work, networking for learning about e-learning courses. Individual reflective assignments.
Week 7: Group work, finding/composing learning environment for the prototype. Individual reflective assignments.
Week 8: Group work, planning and preparing materials for prototype. Individual reflective assignments.
Week 9: Individual work, peer-reviews about personal learning contracts. Individual reflective assignments.
Week 10: Group work, preparing the description of the prototype. Individual reflective assignments.
Week 11: Group work, developing formative evaluation plans for the prototype. Individual reflective assignments.
Week 12: Group work, analyzing the outcomes of the prototype evaluation. Individual reflective assignments.
Week 13: Individual work, self-evaluating personal learning contract. Individual reflective assignments.
Week 14: Individual work, reflecting of the course, and own goals. Individual reflective assignments.

Students were registered to the course in the EMIM Moodle environment. This institutional environment was used for centrally presenting the learning tasks and materials as required in EMIM consortium. This initial EMIM course setting was expanded with the variety of social software tools, and the actual coursework activities were conducted in the personal and group environments composed of social software. This enabled to compose an expanded learning landscape, which provided a possibility to test one of the iCamp project aims: how could teaching and learning be organized in the settings that go beyond the institutional learning management systems. The course materials and links to the web-based materials were embedded to Moodle, but alternatively, students could use a Scuttle social bookmarking tool where materials were organized with tags. A set of possible social software tools (Wordpress blog running at university server, various free wiki services, Skype.com, Doodle.com) was suggested for students, but they had freedom to try out other social software tools.

One of the environments for providing centrally the course outline and giving feedback of progress and critical aspects in the groups was a course weblog (http://htk.tlu.ee/elearning). The access to make postings to this weblog was exclusively with the course organizers – the two facilitators from the iCamp project. The other facilitators and students could leave comments on the weblog postings, but not post something new. This weblog served also as an alternative central space where course participants and facilitators' weblog links were centrally collected. It offered links to other course materials – social bookmarking site with the tag-cloud with various course materials and to the Help-centre providing technical information about tools. The links to the joint group prototypes were added to the weblog.

Each facilitator and student was required to keep a personal weblog. The addresses of facilitators' personal weblogs were announced in the Moodle wiki page. Students were asked to select a preferred facilitator and join one of the groups, leaving their weblog addresses and contacts in this wiki page. The only constraint in the group formation rules was that students could not form national-based workgroups but they could form teams with participants from different universities. The initially planned group size was 8 people. After receiving contacts and weblog addresses from the students, each facilitator organized his or her facilitator weblog and added the links and feeds of students' weblogs to their page. The facilitators also had to monitor the central course weblog and accommodate the centrally provided course information for the needs of their group.

The learning tasks supported both individual development through obtaining self-directing competences, as well as, the competences of collaboration and networking when working with the joint aims. Students had to make weekly postings in their personal weblog about their progress in this week. A scaffolding framework for these self-reflection postings was developed (see in Section 3). It was intended to on a weekly basis raise students' awareness of their learning process, achievements and problems. This reflection enabled students to monitor the development of their own and their group-mates' PLEs and the joint environment. They could become more aware of the affordances each student perceived in relation to used social software. This is especially important as the group members do not work only in the shared learning environment, but their environment consists of PLEs with various elements. Therefore, the awareness of perceived affordances of this distributed environment is important and helps to find out commonly preferred tool functionalities that support joint work. The reflection postings provided the facilitators a monitoring tool to view and trigger students' self-directed learning progress. It was required that facilitators would comment these weekly reflection postings.

Besides structured reflection postings, students were on a weekly basis asked to read some materials and reflect on some questions. From week 7 these individual tasks were changed to collaborative actions related with the preparation of their prototype that were required in the second half of the course. The second optional activity of the course was to maintain a personal conversational learning contract, filling it in at least three times in the beginning, in the middle and in the end of the course.

The collaborative task was generally defined by the course requirements. Each team had to develop a prototype of an e-learning course. The teams could modify this task. As the first challenge, each team could decide the topic, the activities and the learning environment of their course. It was recommended to try out the course in distributed social software-based settings for developing these prototypes. Second challenge was to find a suitable collaborative space for coordinating their group-work. The student group could initiate a joint weblog, wiki or use some other distributed environments to work in asynchronous and synchronous mode. However, the students' and facilitators' attempts to use Moodle forums for their group-work were not encouraged. This was due to make participants try out authentic settings where institutional learning management systems might not be available after they leave university and start their work and wish to participate in various teams. Collaboratively developed prototypes were to be introduced among other groups for getting evaluations. Each group developed a formative evaluation plan (usually questionnaire) of their course and sent an invitation to the other groups to fill it in and give them feedback. The peer- and facilitator-evaluation of joint group outcomes formed part of the grading. The course lasted 14 weeks.

3 Methods

The data were gathered from the students' blogs, from the weekly reflection templates. Besides these reflections students posted into the blogs the reflections assigned to them individually, and sometimes they made posts about these aspects that they noticed or became interested in. Each template consisted of the following questions:

1. What was the most important thing you learned this week?
2. What was particularly interesting/boring in this week?
3. Was there something you did not quite understand and want to know more about it?
4. What kind of questions/ideas/experiences this week's activities raised for you?
5. Which tools did you use this week? Explain what was the purpose of using these tools (e.g. social talk, to regulate my team activities, to work on my documents)?
6. With whom did you communicate during this week, how many times, with which tools, and for what purposes?

The initial sample of course participants consisted of 86 students, however, 55 students used the reflection template at least once per week. Fifteen students posted to their blogs 1–3 times per week, 4 just created the blog but never wrote to it, and one posted several times and participated in the whole course but never used the reflection template. These students who did not use the reflection template were removed from the sample of this paper. Final sample for analysis consisted of 55 students who reflected weekly through the proposed reflection template during the course. There were 14 students who reflected only at the first week, but 74.5% of the students reflected more than 1 week. 45.5% of the students reflected also after the half way of the course, and 34.5% in the last 3 weeks.

From students' blog the answers to the questions of the template were copied to excel-files. Each student's responses were organized initially into one excel-sheet; the reflection template questions were presented in rows, the text responses for each week were presented in columns. The exact categorization of responses according to the reflection template elements was grounded between the two researchers. The table of self-directing indicators (see Table 21.2) was composed based on theoretical considerations, and modified using the content analysis of students' reflections. The table of indicators and examples (not presented here) were used for categorizing the presence of self-direction in posts. The presence of a certain indicator was recorded once per post, using the binary system (0/1). To test the categorization reliability, two researchers simultaneously categorized five students' data and compared the results, finding 95% of similarity. Next, the data matrixes, consisting of all students' self-direction indicators, were compiled. Individual students' progress in study weeks was collected into the matrix in which the presence of the category in each week for each student was indicated in columns using the binary (0/1) system. A second data matrix was compiled in which the weekly frequencies of each category were presented in columns.

Table 21.2 Self-reflection indicators in blog reflections

Category	Explanation
Tool usage	Student starts to use new tools
	Student uses same tools
	Student stops using certain tools
	Student starts to use some tools again
	Student has difficulties in using tools
Clarity of the course	Un-clarity with the course
	Course is clear
Observed change	Student notices change in oneself
	Student notices a change in some of the group members
Ruptured situation	Different voices of oneself
	Different voices between oneself and the group
Strategy	Student is diagnosing what he does not know, can not do
	Student set up goals for himself
	Student formulates the needs, identifying the objective
	Student is identifying resources needed to get to the goal
	Student finds strategies to cope
	Student creates an agenda
	Student is implementing to achieve the goal
	Student evaluates if he succeeded or not
Team as a tool	Student expects the others to work
	Student organizes the team
The voice of the writer	Student is writing as 'I'
	Student is writing as 'I' in the group

The linear regression analysis was conducted, using the week variable as the dependent and the self-direction indicators as independent variables. The regression analysis terminated when the significance level was higher than 0.10. The weekly frequency data matrix was analyzed using the web-based Bayesian dependency-modeling tool D-trail (Myllymäki, Silander, Tirri, & Uronen, 2002). The causal dependency model was drawn. Causal model takes into account also the possibility that the dependencies can be caused by unmeasured variables. During the search, 133921 candidate models were evaluated. The last 89701 evaluations did not result in finding better models. Figure 21.2 presents the simplified model with important arcs (dependencies) between causally dependent components. Removing these arcs would result in decreasing the probability of the model to less than 1/1000000 (strong dependency), 1/1000 (medium dependency) and 1/100 (weak dependency) of the probability of the original model.

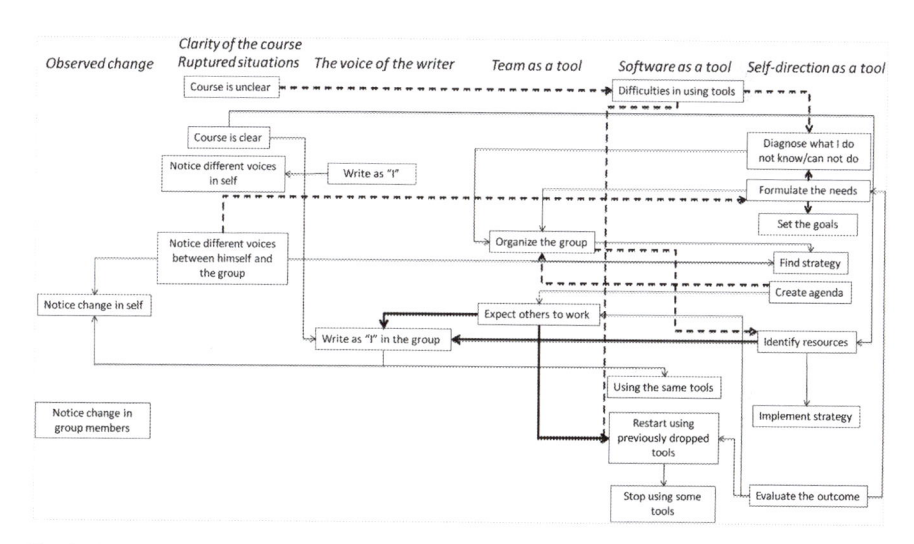

Fig. 21.2 Dependency model of causally related self-directed learning indicators (Note: *bold line arcs* – strong dependency, *medium line arcs* – medium dependency, *dashed line arcs* – weak dependency)

4 Results

4.1 The Indicators of the Self-Direction in Students' Self-Reflection Blog-Posts

The categories of self-reflection indicators were composed considering theory in one hand (presented in Section 1.2), and content analysis from blog reflections in another hand. Table 21.2 presents only the main categories, the qualitative examples can be found in the master dissertation (Merisalo, 2009). We found that the rate of self-reflections decreased towards the end of the course. However, this indicates that students did not need the externalization of self-direction processes anymore.

4.2 The Week-Dependent Indicators of Self-Direction

The occurrence of self-direction indicators in blog posts depended on the tasks of the study weeks (see Table 21.3). Significant dependence ($p>0.001$) was found with the students' reflecting voice – students wrote from 'I' perspective in the beginning of the course when the tasks were more individual, and the usage of this reflection mode decreased in time when collaborative tasks appeared. However, the usage of another perspective, when the student reflected as a part of the group, was not significantly week-dependent. Starting to use new tools and feeling difficulties with using new tools was also significantly ($p>0.05$) dependent on the course weeks, prevailing during the first weeks. Continuing to use tools, dropping tools, and restarting to use tools were not time-dependent indicators.

Table 21.3 Regression analysis results of the week-dependent indicators of self-direction in self-reflecting posts

Self-direction indicators	R^2	F	p
Student starts to use new tools	0.543	14.32	0.003*
Student uses same tools	0.012	0.144	0.71
Student stops using certain tools	0.178	2.592	0.133
Student starts to use some tools again	0.082	1.073	0.321
Student had difficulties in using tools	0.442	9.523	0.009*
Un-clarity with the course	0.530	13.509	0.003*
Course is clear	0.350	6.459	0.026*
Student notices a change in oneself	0.046	0.574	0.463
Student notices a change in some of the group members	0.062	0.799	0.389
Different voices of oneself	0.380	7.352	0.019*
Different voices between student and the group.	0.001	0.006	0.940
Student is diagnosing what he does not know, can't do	0.577	16.377	0.002*
Student set up goals for himself	0.555	14.966	0.002*
Student formulates the needs, identifying the objective	0.456	10.066	0.008*
Student is identifying resources needed to get to the goal	0.130	1.788	0.206
Student finds strategies to cope	0.104	1.386	0.262
Student creates an agenda	0.186	2.745	0.123
Student is implementing to achieve the goal	0.177	2.580	0.134
Student evaluates if he succeeded or not	0.414	8.485	0.013*
Student sees that the others should do things what he does	0.019	0.231	0.639
Student tries to organize the team, make it a better tool	0.671	24.419	0.001**
Student is writing as 'I'	0.755	36.944	0.001**
Student is writing as 'I' in the group	0.002	0.021	0.887

Note: *$p>0.05$, **$p>0.001$

As the study weeks progressed and the collaborative tasks became prevalent, students tried to organize teams as their tools (p>0.001). However, no significant weekly dependence was found with students' expectation that other team-members should do some tasks that the student was doing. The ruptured situations, when different voices were perceived between the student and the group, were dependent on study weeks ($p<0.05$) and increased during collaborative tasks in the second half of the course. Perception of different voices in oneself was not time-dependent. For students diagnosing known and unknown aspects or possible activities, setting up goals for themselves, formulating needs, and identifying objectives were significantly (p>0.05) dependent on these study weeks, when the team planned collaborative work and designed their course prototype. Evaluating success appeared significantly ($p>0.05$) at later study weeks, when the group assignment and personal learning contracts were to be evaluated. Nevertheless, identifying resources, finding strategies to cope, creating agenda, and implementing the assignment did not depend on the particular tasks of the particular study weeks. Observed change in oneself, and in other team-members, were not weekly dependent self-direction indicators. In order to get more information about self-direction, and use the self-direction indicators to monitor courses, students should be taught and advised to use self-reflections regularly.

4.3 The Interrelations Between the Indicators of Self-Direction

We discovered that the self-direction indicators (Table 21.2) were meaningfully interrelated in the collected dataset, representing a model system in which various types of 'tools' (social software tools, self-direction as a tool and team as a tool) were used as possible mediators for reaching individual and group goals. We investigated the potential causal dependencies between the self-direction indicators using Bayesian modeling (see Fig. 21.2). Such dependency model could be used for explaining how different mediators might be causally interrelated and influencing learning situations in e-learning courses that involve parallel individual and group assignments with social software.

The dependency model (see Fig. 21.2) revealed the following potential causal interrelations:

I. Ruptured situations as triggers for using software as a tool and self-direction as a tool

If the learning process at the course was perceived as unclear, students reflected on difficulties in using software tools. Perceiving difficulties with software tools could influence them to restart using some previously used but now neglected tools. Possibly, they returned to using those software tools, which had given them successful performance experiences previously, whereas new software seemed too complicated. Secondly, difficulties with tools triggered them to use self-direction as a tool – students diagnosed what they do not know or cannot do.

If the learning process at the course was perceived as clear, students started to use self-direction as a mediator of action – they identified the resources and implemented the strategy. The 'voice' of such reflections related learner's actions with his/her group-members ('I' as part of the group). Students who reflected as part of the group were using mainly the same software tools. Possibly, working with these tools did not cause any perceived difficulties that could have hindered the work process. The reflection mode 'I' as part of the group was causally related with observed change in oneself, indicating learning.

Noticing 'different voices' between oneself and the group triggered using the self-direction as a tool – formulating the needs, setting the goals, formulating what he/she knows or does not know or what he/she can or cannot do, and finding the strategy. This ruptured situation, when difference was perceived between own and the others' knowledge and competences were causally related with noticing the change in oneself.

However, another ruptured situation, described by Gillespie (2007) as noticing different 'voices' in oneself, appeared not to be triggering the use of any mediators of action – software, self-direction and team as the tools. Students, who used the self-centered reflection style tended to reflect about differences in their knowledge and competences compared with what they wanted to have or needed (notice different voices in self).

II. Self-direction actions as hubs to redirect mediation of action towards team as a tool

Several self-direction actions served as hubs redirecting mediation of action from the self-direction tools to the team as a tool. The most important causal arcs started from 'diagnosing one's knowledge/competences' and 'formulating the needs' and ended both at 'organizing the group'.

'Creating the agenda' was a self-directed action that was not caused by other investigated indicators. 'Creating an agenda' was causally related with 'organizing the group' and 'expecting others to work'. This action was strongly influencing whether students started the goal-directed work in a team (organizing the group) or if they perceived problems in teamwork (expecting others to work) (see below).

'Evaluating the outcome' was another self-directed action that was not caused by other investigated indicators. 'Evaluating the outcome' redirected learners back to 'formulating the needs', 'expecting others to work' and 'changing the used software tools with some previously used tools' or 'dropping the tools'. Thus, the evaluation served as a feedback loop to restart using some mediators of action again.

III. Team as a tool as a type of mediator indicating if learners face problems or not

If the students were 'organizing the group' they started to use self-direction tools –'identifying the resources' and 'finding the strategy'.

If students were 'expecting others to work in team', they started to reconsider the software tools –'restarting to use previously used tools' and 'stopping to use some tools'. Possibly, they returned to using those software tools, which had given them successful performance experiences previously, whereas new software seemed not to be useful for the team members. Pata and Väljataga (2007) observed similar behavior in the course environment where students dropped using several social media tools if the team had communication problems and returned to using only a blog as a central communication medium.

Secondly, there was a causal arc leading to 'group-directed writing mode'. Above, we have described that this arc would lead to 'using same software tools' on one hand (that might indicate that team is satisfied with their tools) and 'noticing a change in oneself' (meaning learning). It may be assumed that 'expecting others to work' is an ambiguous indicator of a) problems in teamwork or b) trust that team members will do expected actions (relying on others).

5 Discussion

This paper is inspired by the growing usage of social software at learning courses. Such courses are learner-designed to a great extent – each individual is changing and expanding their personal learning environments, integrating new tools, resources, people and self-directing their own learning individually and in teams (Pata, 2009). The components in these learning environments are dynamically changing during the learning process to better meet the needs of the learners (Pata & Väljataga, 2007; Fiedler & Pata, 2009). The self-reflections are used as an integral part of the learning process. Self-reflections are giving feedback to other learners and facilitator about the learners' self-regulations, and serving simultaneously for the learner as the tools aiding his self-directed actions. Hermans (1996) says that in self there is a dialogical interchange going on between relatively autonomous and mutually influencing selves. Self-direction is reached when the individual allows the various positions to be internally voiced. In order to observe changes in own or others' way of thinking, perceiving and doing, the individual needs to consciously observe but also to reflect about his thinking processes. Thus, there is an intention to use students' reflections as diagnostic instruments for evaluating the learning situation. In this paper we proposed a set of such indicators of self-direction and validated them using the dataset from the Design-Based eLearning course.

We found that these indicators may be grouped as triggers that activate three types of mediators of self-directed actions, and may end in learning as an observed change in oneself. Figure 21.3 generalizes the interrelations between the types

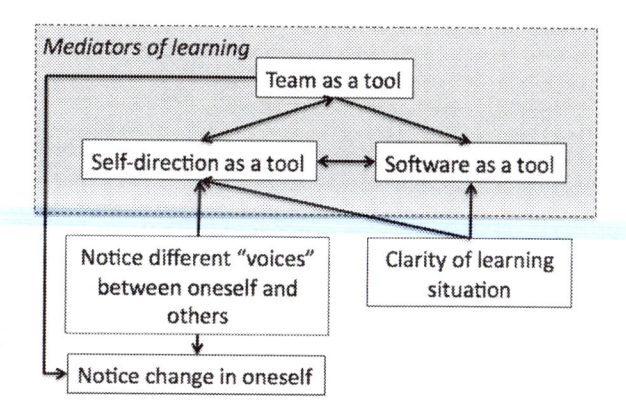

Fig. 21.3 Generalized model of self-direction components at learning situations

of self-direction indicators. This model generalizes the results of Bayesian causal dependency model.

Brockett and Hiemstra (1991) assume that self-directed learning is a combination of forces inside and outside of the individual, making the individual take responsibility for decisions associated with the learning process.

The whole learning process in Design-Based courses with social media is highly challenging and not structured in details in advance, when learning begins. Pre-planning of course tools, resources and activities is hard since learners determine the nature of learning, and the tools and resources they need. Participating in the design process for the first time can be difficult to some students and may leave many aspects unclear. Clarity of the course is related with the outside factors influencing self-direction. If the student has un-clarities with the course he/she does not feel him/herself in charge of the situation and learning, and most likely feels uncertain. To some students un-clarity can be a trigger to be more self-directive and find out issues that can help them to clear the situation. Some other students may get 'locked' if they face unclear situations, and would need the help of the teacher or other students to activate themselves again. Un-clarities can also make some students to drop the usage of certain tools and make them try other tools and procedures to clear the situation.

Ruptured situations described by Gillespie (2007) – 'noticing different voices in oneself', and 'noticing different voices between self and others' represent the inside forces that influence self-direction.

We found that clarity and ruptured situations are external and internal factors that trigger learners to activate mainly two types of mediators of action – software as external tools to carry out learning actions and self-directed actions as the internal tools to drive their learning process. Both types of mediators could have some causal influence to each other.

The role of self-directing actions appeared to be important in triggering the third type of mediator – the team as a tool. Thus, without self-directed actions it is difficult to enter actively into collaborative learning situations. Success in activating the team as a tool in collaborative activities enabled again to use more the self-direction as a tool. Thus, we may predict that successful activation of teamwork might lead to better self-direction. The failures in team ('expecting team to work') could lead either to simplifying/modifying the software tools or noticing the change in oneself. Accordingly, Engeström (1987) assumes that problems are introduced through the perspective of others when the group is in problematic situation.

Some self-direction indicators, such as 'noticing different voices in oneself' in 'self-centered reflection mode' appeared not to be causally related with other indicators. One reason could be simply that such reflections appeared in the first weeks of the course when collaborative work had not started yet and students reflected their progress in individual assignments.

Another finding was that reflection about 'noticing change in oneself' could not be interpreted in the causal model so much as an outcome of learning but rather it was caused by dissatisfactions with the team ('noticing difference between self and the group' and 'expecting others to work'). This result was surprising also because the reflection templates particularly addressed what was the most important thing that was learned during the study week. Similarly, 'noticing change in group members' was not causally related to other indicators of self-direction. Interpreting these results needs further investigations.

6 Conclusions

This paper presented the results of developing the self-direction indicators for analyzing reflective blog postings of the Design-based eLearning course. We discovered that the indicators were meaningfully interrelated in the dataset, representing a model system in which various types of 'tools' (social software tools, self-direction as a tool, and group-work as a tool) were used as possible paths for reaching individual and group goals. Such model could be used for evaluating the progress and constraints in e-learning courses that involve parallel individual and group assignments with social software. For example, expecting team members to work and simplification of software environments for learning might indicate difficulties in teamwork, while missing self-direction actions might predict difficulties in entering the collaborative learning situations. In order to use indicators of self-direction for monitoring purposes while course is running, the regular self-reflections should be added as required/suggested assignments into eLearning courses.

Acknowledgements This study was partly funded by the iCamp project (027168) under the 6th framework programme of the EU, ESF grant 7663 and MER targeted research 0130159s08.

References

Attwell, G. (2007). Personal learning environments – the future of eLearning? *eLearning Papers*, 2. Retrieved from http://www.elearningpapers.eu/index.php?page=doc&doc_id=8553&doclng=6. Accessed on March 10, 2009.

Brockett, R. G., & Hiemstra, R. (1991). *Self-direction in adult learning. Perspectives on theory, research and practice.* London: Routledge.

Constantinides, E., & Fountain, S. J. (2008). Web 2.0: Conceptual foundations and marketing issues. *Journal of Direct, Data and Digital Marketing Practice, 9*, 231–244.

Engeström, Y. (1987). *Learning by expanding: An activity-theoretical approach to developmental research.* Helsinki: Orienta-Konsultit.

Fiedler, S., & Pata, K. (2009). Distributed learning environments and social software: In search for a framework of design. S. Hatzipanagos and S. Warburton (Eds.), *Handbook of research on social software and developing. Community Ontologies* (pp. 145–158). Hershey, PA: IGI Global.

Gillespie, A. (2007). Social basis of self-reflection. In V. Jaan & R. Alberto (Eds.), *Cambridge handbook of sociocultural psychology* (pp. 678–691). Cambridge: Cambridge University Press.

Harri-Augstein, S., & Thomas, L. (1991). *Learning conversations: The self-organised way to personal and organisational growth.* London: Routledge.

Hermans, H. J. M. (1996). Voicing the self: From information processing to dialogical interchange. *Psychological Bulletin, 119*(1), 31–50.

Kieslinger, B., & Pata, K. (2008). Am i alone? The competitive nature of self-reflective activities in groups and individually. *Ed-Media 2008 Proceedings* (pp. 6337–6342), Vienna, AACE.

Knowles, M. (1975). *Self-Directed learning. A guide for learners and teachers*. Englewood Cliffs, NJ: Prentice Hall/Cambridge.

Merisalo, S. (2009). *The development of self-direction in self-reflections in an elearning course*. Master thesis, Tallinn University. Retrieved from http://www.cs.tlu.ee/instituut/opilaste_tood/magistri_tood/2009_kevad/sonja_merisalo_magistritoo.pdf. Accessed on July 10, 2009.

Myllymäki, P., Silander, T., Tirri, H., & Uronen, P. (2002). B-Course: A web-based tool for bayesian and causal data analysis. *International Journal on Artificial Intelligence Tools, 11*(3), 369–387.

Ning, H., Williams, J. R., Slocum, A. H., & Sanchez, A. (2004). InkBoard – Tablet PC enabled design-oriented learning. *Proceeding (428) Computers and Advanced Technology in Education*. Retrieved from http://www.actapress.com/Abstract.aspx?paperId=17075. Accessed on March 10, 2009

Pata, K. (2009). Modeling spaces for self-directed learning at university courses. *Journal of Educational Technology and Society, 12*, 23–43.

Pata, K., & Väljataga, T. (2007). Collaborating across national and institutional boundaries in higher education – the decentralized iCamp approach. In C. Montgomerie, J. Seale (Eds.), *Proceedings of Ed-Media 2007*, World Conference on Educational Multimedia, Hypermedia & Telecommunications (pp. 353–362).Vancouver, Canada: 24–29 June, 2007. VA: Association for the Advancement of Computing in Education (AACE)

Pressley, M. (1995). More about the development of self-regulation: Complex, long-term, and thoroughly social. *Educational Psychologist, 30*(4), 207–212.

Smith, P., & Ragan, T. J. (1999). *Instructional design (2nd ed.)*. New York: Wiley.

Underwood, J., & Banyard, P. E. (2008). Understanding the learning space. *eLearning papers*, 9. Retrieved from http://www.elearningpapers.eu/index.php?page=doc&doc_id=11937&doclng=6. Accessed on March 10, 2009.

Wijnen, W. H. F. W. (2000). *Towards design-based learning*. Retrieved from http://w3.tue.nl/fileadmin/stu/stu_oo/doc/OGO_brochure_1_EN.pdf. Accessed on March 10, 2009.

Chapter 22
Employing Virtual Collaborative Exchanges to Expand Global Awareness

A Multi-discipline, Three-Year Effort

Sandra Poindexter, Ray Amtmann, and Tawni Ferrarini

Abstract Universities commonly mention global components in their mission statements. Many governments endorse the concept of global preparedness for its industry and people, and support student and faculty mobility. Yet not all students have the resources or motivation to study abroad, though still value an international experience. This 3-year study, based in the United States and Finland, explores the use of the Internet to connect university students in equivalent classes across international borders, completing collaborative assignments requiring student-student virtual dialog and cross-cultural reflection. After 10 repetitions of virtual exchanges between U.S. and European undergraduate students, quantitative and qualitative results indicate that virtual exchanges, like actual student exchanges, can provide learning opportunities for global awareness. Students, regardless of prior international experience, recommend virtual exchanges. No single pedagogy achieves 100% success and improvements are underway. This paper identifies virtual exchange goals, describes pedagogical activities, presents results, identifies areas for improvement and offers research suggestions. The approach can apply to any discipline at any level. Faculty hesitant about either technology or interference with course structure may be motivated to try this easy-to-use, cost-effective pedagogy to broaden global perspectives that can be scaled up, down, or custom-tailored.

Keywords Collaborative learning · Virtual exchanges · Global awareness · International teams · International collaboration

1 Introduction

Integrating cross-cultural awareness and education is an expressed objective for the United States. A 2008 amendment of the Higher Education Act supports foreign language and cultural awareness; global preparedness is mentioned in

---

S. Poindexter (✉)
College of Business, Northern Michigan University, Marquette, MI 49855, USA
e-mail: spoindex@nmu.edu

the mission statement of the Office of Postsecondary Education of the U.S. Department of Education; and international study and exchange activities are sponsored through Fund for Improvement of Postsecondary Education or FIPSE (Office of Postsecondary Education, 2010). The *Open Doors 2009 Report* on International Educational Exchange states the United States has seen a 150% growth over the past decade in the number of U.S. students studying abroad (Institute of International Education, 2009), citing increased programming by government and institutions of higher education. However, figures on U.S. undergraduate students studying abroad given in *Digest of Educational Statistics* reveal that only 1.4% of all students in U.S. institutions studied abroad in 2007/2008 (National Center for Education Statistics, 2008). In comparing these two reports on U.S. undergraduate students, there is a gap offering huge growth opportunities in the number of international experiences realized by U.S. students.

Not all students have the funding, mobility or motivation to study abroad, yet still value some type of international experience. By turning to virtual communities, we wished to explore the viability of creating a collaborative learning environment for cultural awareness, which we termed 'virtual exchanges,' that simulates the person-person experience seen in a short study abroad.

There are documented studies of U.S. schools collaborating virtually with schools in other areas of the world towards a cultural awareness goal. The Runestone Project between Sweden, U.K. and U.S. was collaborative and evolutionary over multiple years, similar to that documented in this paper. The primary goal in the problem-based Runestone Project was to introduce students to international contacts and give them experience working in teams with people from a foreign culture. (Daniels, 2000; Last, Daniels, Hause, & Woodroffe, 2002). Teng documents a virtual exchange between Taiwan and U.S. schools that used discussion forums and international group projects to study motivation for success as well as the acquisition of cross-cultural communication skills (2005). Campbell describes the use of email to facilitate a 5-week project of jointly analyzed case studies assigned to pairs of intercultural communications students in a virtual exchange between New Zealand and the U.S. (2008). Technology students in Romania and the U.S. collaborated on multimedia projects related to technology and culture (Andone & Frydenberg, 2009). European countries, whose citizens are far more advanced in global awareness, are pursuing such technologies to support global advancement on a broader scale. The European-funded *iCamp Project* (http://www.icamp.eu) is well documented by numerous researchers for its collaborative and self-directed social networking across borders involving nine countries. Nguyen-Ngoc and Law (2007) and Kieslinger and Fiedler (2006), in particular, have studied and reported on the cross-cultural collaborative component of iCamp.

The Horizon Project is a collaboration between New Media Consortium and the EDUCAUSE Learning Initiative (ELI), which reports annually on the state of emerging technologies in teaching and learning. The *2008 Horizon Report* states, 'With the increasing availability of tools to connect learners and scholars all over the world – online collaborative workspaces, social networking tools, mobiles, Skype, and more – it is increasingly common to see courses that include international students who meet online or incorporate connections between classrooms in different areas of the world' (Johnson, Levine, & Smith, 2008, p. 6). In examining five documented case studies involving technology and cultural learning, Levy formulated a pedagogical framework to align five components of his culture concept with specific pedagogical designs and technologies, e.g., discussion forums, email and web-based projects. (2007, p. 120)

This paper highlights ten virtual exchanges between higher education students at a U.S. and a Finnish school. It describes methods, pedagogies, research questions and outcomes of student surveys. Results indicate some success in improving global awareness at both the academic discipline and personal levels.

2 The Study

The basis for this extended study was to examine the impact of virtual exchanges and to determine whether there is evidence to support the following four research questions, worded as null hypotheses.

> $H1_0$ - There are no indicators for overall positive student recommendation for a virtual exchange.
> $H2_0$ - Results for the virtual exchange are irrespective as to location.
> $H3_0$ - A virtual exchange cannot be a substitute for a short-term study abroad.
> $H4_0$ - Results for the virtual exchange are irrespective of chosen pedagogical activity.

2.1 Setting

The U.S. partner is a regional, public university in the upper Midwest of the U.S. and located in a geographically remote community of Scandinavian heritage. Many students attending the university come from rural areas that lack significant diversity, do not typically have personal exposure to international travel and are often first generation university students within their families. These students have opportunities to study abroad via faculty-led intensive courses or longer exchange options, but work schedules, costs and other barriers exist.

By contrast, the Finnish partner is a University of Applied Sciences located in the large and diverse capital, Helsinki. In addition to its Finnish curricula, the Finnish university has several international programs taught in English that draw a diverse population of students from elsewhere in Europe and around the world. Therefore, the Finnish participants are a mixture of Finnish natives and international students. They know multiple languages, have regular access to international culture and news through local media and entertainment and are likely to have traveled to other countries. The exact numbers of the population mix are not available; asking country of residence would not have permitted anonymous surveys.

While both universities offer a broad range of programs of study, these virtual exchanges were conducted in business or information technology courses. In January 2006, taking advantage of an existing bilateral exchange agreement, two instructors paired similar undergraduate upper division courses to conduct a virtual experience. The secured Internet class space provided a forum for students to exchange views internationally on current topics germane to their studies without leaving home. That initial trial expanded to six instructors and nine different courses over ten exchanges between January 2006 and October 2009.

2.2 Pedagogies Employed

Our virtual exchange strategy used the Internet to connect business and information technology students across international borders. The core objective of our virtual exchanges was to present stay-at-home students with a problem solving or research activity that could be completed jointly or evaluated from the perspective of their international counterpart. Each pair of instructors was allowed to select the specific joint task or assignment that best fit their schedules, subject matter and style of teaching. However, it was agreed that collaborative assignments should employ two important components: student-student dialog and some type of cross-cultural reflection, i.e. students must reflect upon comments and writings done by students in the opposite location.

The instructors chose variations of four pedagogical activities for their online collaboration: discussion board dialog, joint research paper, live video conference and a joint online course using a social network venue. An early decision to restrict ourselves to commonly known technologies, such as email and discussion boards, was made to eliminate technical barriers and encourage student participation. In 2008, that decision was expanded to include a live video conference. In 2009, a joint online course was delivered. Table 22.1 provides the distribution of pedagogies and

Table 22.1 Student study populations by pedagogies

Virtual exchanges	Term	Collaborative online activity	Duration	No. student responses Finland	U.S.
1	Spring 2006	Discussion Board + Joint Report	1 wk / 6 wks	10	18
2	Fall 2006	Discussion Board	1 week	15	18
3	Fall 2007	Discussion Board	2 weeks	10	17
4	Spring 2008	Joint Report	4 weeks	12	31
5	Spring 2008	Discussion Board	2 weeks	–	25
6	Fall 2008	Discussion Board	1 week	13	16
7	Fall 2008	Live Video Conference	2 h	10	21
8	Spring 2009	Discussion Board	1 week	3	10
9	Spring 2009	Live Video Conference	2 h	5	8
10	Fall 2009	Social Network Online Course	1 term	4	3
Total				82	167

the numbers of student participants responding to surveys for each of the ten virtual exchanges. A detailed description of these pedagogies follows Table 22.1.

The first nine exchanges occurred in courses delivered in a face-to-face mode where a content management system was used for delivery of materials and course management. The U.S. instructors, using the WebCT course management system, added all participating students from the Finnish school as guests into their course module in which all activity took place. Students were free to use any other means of Internet communication such as email, chat, voice and shared file services.

In the *discussion board* experiences, students in each class either read a common article or watched a common video and then discussed the topic within a specific time span, generally one to two weeks. Usually, instructors provided starter questions on the discussion board, but did not restrict comments to those starters. Students in the U.S. were given a short deadline to post their own comments, students in Finland were to review and respond to those postings within 48 h; in some cases the cycle was repeated a second time. Students were shown how to compile all the postings into one document to make reading easier. The total number of postings for each discussion board activities were 71 (Spring 2006), 80 (Fall 2006), 156 (Fall 2007), 153 (Spring 2008), 158 (Fall 2008), and 133 (Spring 2009). Discussion board logs were archived and viewable by both instructors to assess the depth of dialog. The U.S. student entries were treated as a scored assignment; the Finnish instructors treated them as class participation and not specifically scored.

The *video conference* activity had a similar preparatory reading, but dialog occurred in a 1–1 ½ h live video conference. Logistics for a video conference are much more complex, requiring advanced technology to exist at each location, rescheduling of class time to accommodate the 7-h time difference and accounting for unplanned events – a third video conference was canceled due to a snowstorm that closed the university on the schedule day. Only the first video conference was recorded and has been reused by the instructor in other courses to prompt further dialog.

A *joint research paper* was used in two virtual exchanges; one involved upper level students and one involved lower-level students. For this research paper, students from each institution were partnered based on their selection of topic choices, such as the adoption of online banking. Three-person teams were created for uneven class rosters. The assignment had four parts: (1) research and write on trends in one's own country; (2) receive and review partner's paper; (3) together reflect and write on similarities and differences identified in the two drafts; (4) consolidate all parts into one paper and submit to both instructors. This activity was the most time-intensive, taking 3–5 weeks to complete. Much more coordination between the instructors was required as students were paired, topics approved, academic schedules accommodated, and problems resolved. Most of the problems involved non-compliance of deadlines and handling poor quality work. A workable solution was found by having the instructor serve as a clearinghouse of all communication, i.e. being copied on emails. In instances where no work was submitted by a student partner, the submission by another person researching the same topic was substituted and a three-way partnership was created. Students in the joint report activities were free to select their own communication mode; most chose email attachments due to the 7-h time difference, but a few mentioned using synchronized options like chat rooms.

The *social network online course* in the last virtual exchange conducted in Fall 2009 deviated from the pedagogical framework in several substantial ways: there was only one instructor; the course was taught entirely online to a single international group of students; and students could collaborate with any combination of their international peers for the duration of the 8-week course, but were not required to do so. The course venue was Facebook; the instructor created a Facebook 'group' entity and invited students to join in order to allow two-way access to the content. The group was open so that anyone could join and/or members could invite others to join. Group information and content could be viewed by anyone in or outside the class; this did occur. A social networking system was chosen over a formal course management system in part to encourage a friendly and more casual learning environment and help overcome the lack of any face-to-face contact. The instructor also believed that capitalizing on a medium well known to students would minimize technology barriers that exist with formal course management systems. Materials were delivered via short, recorded video clips, digital handouts and resources. The standard Facebook wall was used by students to post and answer each other's questions; the instructor also participated in this Q & A. All participants regularly viewed these dialogs.

2.3 Evaluation

2.3.1 Survey

Students were surveyed within two weeks of the activity completion. In Virtual Exchange (VE) 1, only one survey was administered that combined the discussion board and joint report question. In VE 6–9, two activities occurred in each course and each activity had its own survey.

Although the surveys varied in number of questions, some common questions applied to the cultural aspect. Table 22.2 provides a list of these questions. The scale for each question was Agree Strongly (5) – Disagree Strongly (1) with the exception of Prior Experience.

Table 22.2 Survey questions

Question	Chart legend	VEs
I would like to see more of this kind of activity	Recommend	All
I gained international perspective on these issues	Gain int'l view	All
I told other students who are not in this class about this international cooperation	Told students	All
I told friends/family who are not students about this international cooperation	Told family	All

Table 22.2 (continued)

Question	Chart legend	VEs
This virtual international experience made the class more interesting	Inc. class interest	All
Doing this course made it seem as though I actually met people from the other schools	Virtual reality	1–5, 10
I do a lot of reading about events / trends in other countries	Keep abreast	1–5, 10
I have studied/lived as a youth or adult in another country. (Y/N)	Prior exp	All
This experience made me more interested in studying abroad	Encourage study abroad	6–10

The questions related to sharing with family/friends were included to measure a behavior, rather than perception. When students study abroad on location and share those experiences with others at home, it multiplies the overall global awareness gain and possibly reflects the impact of the experience on the student. If virtual exchange students similarly shared the experience, it may indicate a similar impact as the study abroad.

2.3.2 Overall Results

Two questions involved past international experiences and knowledge. As expected, the U.S. student respondents had significantly less prior experience in terms of travel or study abroad than did their counterparts at the Finnish school (21% v. 54%, respectively). Their self-perception of keeping current and aware of international issues was closer, but still significantly different: 62% (U.S.) and 83% (Finland).

The survey response frequency distribution of all VEs (combined), shown in Fig. 22.1, indicate overall satisfaction with the experience; 73% of the respondents agreed or strongly agreed that they would recommend this concept be used in other

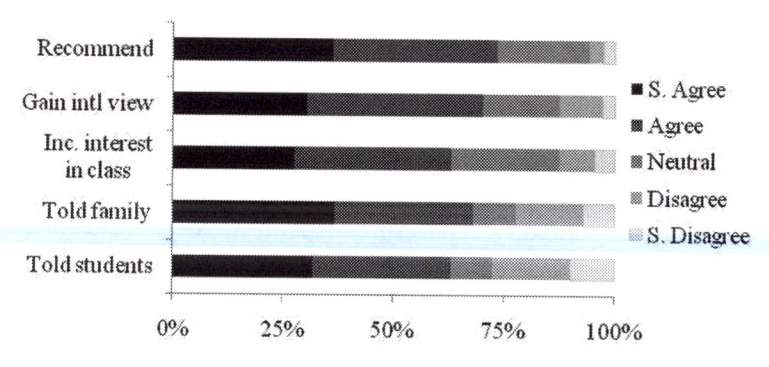

Fig. 22.1 Student feedback – all virtual exchanges combined

courses and only 5% would not. The experience increased interest in the course; 63% agreed or strongly agreed.

2.3.3 Analysis

The research question behind $H1_0$, There are no indicators for overall positive student recommendation for a virtual exchange, asks whether certain situations, such as little prior international experience, might lead to a greater success of a virtual exchange. Pearson correlations computed in SPSS are given in Table 22.3.

Table 22.3 Correlation coefficients on variable recommendation

	Location	Prior abroad	Keep abreast	Inc. class interest	Gain int'l view	Told students	Told family
Pearson coeff.	0.101	−0.087	0.041	0.533*	0.368*	0.462*	0.343*
Sig. (2-tailed)	0.112	0.173	0.602	0.000	0.000	0.000	0.000
N	249	249	0.163	249	249	249	249

*Correlation is significant at the 0.01 level (2-tailed)

The pre-existing factors of location (U.S. or Finland), prior study abroad experience and level of keeping abreast of international affairs, do not show a high correlation to overall satisfaction and recommendation. Students' perceptions (Increased class interest and Gained int'l view) and their sharing of the experience (Told other students and Told family) are positively correlated with Recommendation for similar activities. One could argue that they reflect post-experience factors – the reasons behind the recommendation valuation rather than indictors that could be used in advance to help increase success. An R Square of 0.352 from a multiple regression using the same variables does not give strong support for predictors. However, a backward regression retained Increased Interest in Class and Told Other Students as predictors.

These variables on sharing and interest are consistent with Instructors perceptions that student excitement in the virtual exchange upon its announcement may have carried through to the high valuation on the survey. 'I liked the discussion board, and it was nice to get different opinions. We hear the class opinions twice a week, sometimes we need a change.' 'I was excited [about] the video conference. This was a clear evidence what can be achieved with the modern technology.' 'I LOVED the experience and wanted to have it occur more often in class.' 'I like this kind of discussion.' 'I was really excited to take part in this process, and really would like to do it again sometime!' 'Loved it! This is absolutely needs to happen in more classes!!!' No students commented that they disliked the idea from the outset or anticipated a negative experience. Considering this positive expectation was supported in the written comments and the correlations that do exist, $H1_0$, There are no indicators for overall positive student recommendation, is partially rejected.

The research question behind $H2_0$, Results for the virtual exchange are irrespective as to location, asks whether students from the U.S. and Finnish universities will have similar opinions about the virtual exchange. In regards to the impact of location, there was some early discussion between participating U.S. instructors that the more traveled Europeans might find this virtual exchange of less interest. The results of mean and variance analyses for Location, shown in Tables 22.4 and 22.5, indicate that geographically remote U.S. students report the virtual exchange had higher positive impact on their interest in the course in general and on gain of international perspective. Given the disparity in prior study/travel abroad experiences between U.S. and European students (21% v. 54%), there was more to gain for the U.S. students. However, the Recommendation factor does not show a significant difference between Location. The novelty of this type of international experience on the students who lacked other benchmarks, may have contributed to their perceptions on interest and gain of international perspectives.

Therefore, $H2_0$, Results for the virtual exchange are irrespective as to location is rejected as there are some variations in student perceptions between location groups.

Table 22.4 Means comparison for location

Location		Recommend more	Gain intl view	Inc. interest in class	Told other students	Told family
FI	Mean	3.88	3.45	3.46	3.38	3.70
$N=82$	Variance	0.948	1.189	1.116	1.917	1.548
US	Mean	4.08	4.05	3.87	3.67	3.78
$N=167$	Variance	0.897	0.937	1.151	1.776	1.676

Table 22.5 Anova results for location

		Sum of squares	df	Mean square	F	Sig.
Recommend more	Between groups	2.329	1	2.329	2.550	.112
	Within groups	225.607	247	0.913		
	Total	227.936	248			
Gain intl view	Between groups	19.580	1	19.580	19.198	0.000
	Within groups	251.922	247	1.020		
	Total	271.502	248			
Inc. interest in class	Between groups	9.014	1	9.014	7.909	0.005
	Within groups	281.492	247	1.140		
	Total	290.506	248			
Told other students	Between groups	4.709	1	4.709	2.584	0.109
	Within Groups	450.167	247	1.823		
	Total	454.876	248			
Told family	Between groups	0.439	1	0.439	0.268	0.605
	Within groups	403.618	247	1.634		
	Total	404.056	248			

H3₀. A virtual exchange cannot be a substitute for a short-term study abroad, implies that in order to get a personal international experience a student must travel abroad. The possibility that a virtual exchange can simulate a short study abroad gets some support. Students report gaining an international view (70%) and sharing their VE experiences by telling other students (63%) and family (68%). Figure 22.2 shows distribution of responses to questions posed on some VE surveys. The experience gave 43% of participants some encouragement to consider a study abroad. However, the virtual reality, i.e. that it really felt like they had actually met students from the other school, was polarized: 39% agreed and 36% did not.

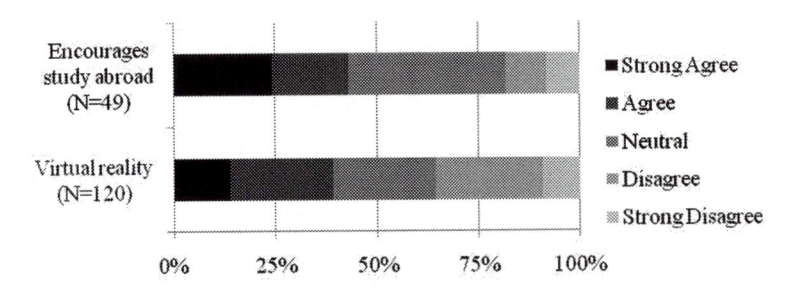

Fig. 22.2 Perceptions of global involvement

Written comments in the responses from both groups also indicate gain in cultural awareness. 'It was nice working in such a project. It gave me the opportunity to know not only my fellow mates but other students studying in another continent.' 'I really liked the discussion board. It gave a different perspective with the international students and shows the differences in the day to day operation of lives.' 'I thought that it was very interesting to hear what effect other areas ethics and values played in their thoughts on this particular topic.' 'The discussion was nice in a way that we were given an article and everybody was suggesting his own opinion freely.' 'Well. I think this project was good. At least I got to know more information about countries I knew already and those that I never knew. This information not only helps one to conduct business but to also behave properly to prevent conflicts.' 'It was more interesting to study with a teacher from a foreign country.' 'It was a great experience to get an outsiders perspective on what's going on in our country and the rest of the world. It would be great if we had more opportunities to partake in experiences like this.' 'Actually I have gained a lot of idea about that particular topic [from] other students who are from a different nationality.' 'I feel like experiences like these really broaden our perspectives!!!'

Students' comments about the similarity of opinion could also be considered valuable learning in that people and places are not always different. 'I honestly could not tell much of a difference between the discussion board comments from students at my school and the international students' and 'I read most of the opinions and postings and in fact approx. 99% have the same opinion. There was no real discussion about the topic. I figured out that everyone agrees with the opinion.' Only

13% of respondents disagreed or strongly disagreed that were was a gain in international awareness (see Fig. 22.1). 'With my team we got along from the beginning and had no problems at all. I should say we had fun... but other ways, it was not a real cooperation with foreign students.'

While it appears the virtual exchange may offer gains in international awareness and behaviors are elicited that are similar to a study abroad, i.e. sharing, there is no corresponding data from a short-term study abroad to verify its comparison to an actual study abroad. Therefore, $H3_0$ as stated, 'A virtual exchange cannot be a substitute for a short-term study abroad,' cannot be directly determined by this study.

$H4_0$, Results for the virtual exchange are irrespective of chosen pedagogical activity, attempts to determine whether a particular pedagogy was superior in terms of gains in international awareness or satisfaction with the virtual exchange. By attempting flexibility, we believe too many uncontrolled variables surfaced: delivery, instructor enthusiasm and integration into course content, time given to the exchange, and assignment versus voluntary task. Figure 22.3 illustrates data that can be gleaned from the survey responses. Means for five variables are given for each of the five pedagogical scenarios.

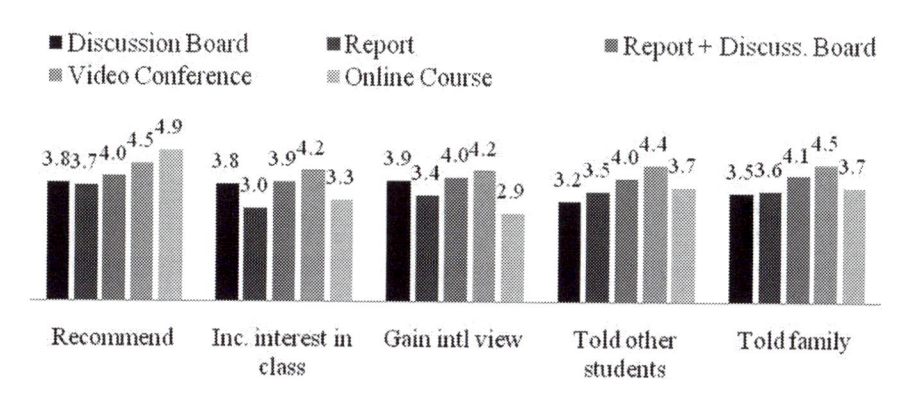

Fig. 22.3 Impact of pedagogy – variable means

Qualitative data on pedagogy comes from the written comments to open-end questions and class discussion. All five instructors were willing participators, but each was committed to teaching their particular course. At times, other portions of the course or tight timetables took precedence over the discussion board dialog that became rushed or too unstructured. Most U.S. instructors assessed the discussion board dialogs, which were part of the students' coursework. This was not true at the Finnish school, as noted by a Finnish student. 'Participating in the discussion had no part in the grade evaluation one gets from this course. Hence, people were not that enthusiastic about participating: it was all extra work not required for completing the course. Of course, it is nice to discuss with others.'

Student comments in some virtual exchanges reflected dissatisfaction with delivery, instructions, timing or topic, but rarely the concept. 'Please prepare this intervention earlier. I would like to know more beforehand,' was one student's comment. 'I think that there needs to be more instruction on what is actually required of both partners, especially on the paper.' 'I love the idea of discussion on an international level. I feel that the articles weren't interesting enough to put it bluntly. When reading through the articles I wasn't excited to discuss them.' 'I think this [discussion board] assignment had potential, but kind of fell short. I know the beginning of the semester we were planning on doing a joint paper with a foreign class, and I believe that would be been more beneficial as far as actually communicating.' 'Earlier notice about the assignment, longer period of time for the interaction (discussion), and broader questions or no questions at all for the articles would bring more opinions and discussion...the questions were pretty straightforward and obvious.'

One U.S. student who participated in a discussion board and research paper acknowledged that encouraging communications between international students on the similarities and differences between countries is a good way to open up the boundaries of education. However, the student's experience with the research report wasn't very beneficial. Conversely, a Finnish student in the same group felt the research paper made the topic more interesting. A U.S. student felt, 'This paper was not only informative, but also eye-opening. I would have liked it if our partner country had written about our country instead of their own, and we could have corrected their statements of fact instead of their grammar'.

The video conference had higher mean responses on the survey than any other type of activity, but in both cases, the video was the second intervention in the respective classes. Students in the video conference wrote, 'I really enjoyed partaking in this activity, and I wish we could do it more often. I think it seemed to have a rough (or rather quiet start) because we didn't know what we were supposed to be talking about. I think a little bit more guidance/preparation next time will help to alleviate that situation. But, overall, I was really excited to take part in this process, and really would like to do it again sometime!' These comments echo the instructor opinions that video conferencing may have the greatest potential, but it also has the highest risk and cost; it took more effort to get students actively engaged within the brief live video and could highlight unpreparedness.

Interestingly, the last virtual exchange which had the most opportunity to interact in a very familiar Facebook setting rated Recommendation very high, but the international perspective issues lower. They did not feel as though they were in an international class despite the frequent postings and occasional outside international drop-in student and were neutral on having gained international awareness. The connection bond was student-instructor rather than student-student. When asked to comment on increased student-student joint activity, responses were mixed. 'This is a great idea. It would certainly help to enhance language and team working skills.' 'Sure, if participants' english skills and education levels meet well enough.' 'It would motivate me BUT there are many questions: How does the cultural differences, the different level of experiences (of subject), motivation affect the outcome of assignment?'

These situational and instructional differences can influence the correlations between type of activity and other measured factors. More responses and more analysis are needed; more guidance and collaboration may be needed for the participating instructors. Therefore, H_4, Results for the virtual exchange are irrespective of chosen pedagogical activity, cannot be determined. However, based upon written comments, the discussion board seemed easiest to implement, the joint research paper forced more in-depth discussion and uncovered some of these misconceptions, and video conferencing offered high interchange at a high cost.

3 Discussion and Limitations

The goals of the virtual exchange strategy were to, in an easy to use, cost-effective pedagogy, help students view a situation from the viewpoint of students in other nations and realize different value judgments may affect various solutions. Class discussions after international collaborative assignments were found to result in a much deeper dialog than generally occurs domestically. Campbell's article, 'You've Got Mail' describes the use of email to facilitate a 5-week project of jointly analyzed case studies assigned to pairs of students in a virtual exchange. Her findings were very similar, i.e. the majority of the students felt it was a good method for learning intercultural communication (2008).

One significant limitation in evaluating the results lies in the lack of consistency in instructor administration of the virtual exchanges and subsequent data collection. Our results were similar to iCamp Trial–1, as reported by Nguyen-Ngoc and Law (2007) – there were too many factors undermining the effectiveness of the pedagogical portion of the study. In a virtual exchange between communications courses at Taiwan and U.S. schools documented by Teng, the number of discussion board dialogs was greater (five topics), but encountered similar variations in instructor expectations and instructions for the discussion board dialog (2005). From student comments, it seems clear that instructors must more carefully integrate the virtual exchange into their course rather than tack it on. For increased learning benefits, instructors should follow-up with class discussion or other reflective exercise.

One factor that differentiates our study from others is the academic discipline of business, rather than communications, culture or language. Several student comments acknowledged the discipline aspect, 'I greatly believe that this project should be kept in this course. It shows business students how to work [in teams] with other countries, which is important to learn in today's world.' 'Great experience, this should happen more often to understand business on a global perspective.' The Runestone Project (1998–2001) is the most similar in its academic discipline, duration, number of students and evolutionary-based nature. As with Runestone, there were no negative content learning results related to the virtual exchange when carried out in a planned and deliberate manner (Daniels et al., 1998; Last et al., 2002).

Without surveying students who have been on a short study abroad or use of pre- and post- surveys, the seemingly positive data lacks evidence that virtual exchanges simulate real exchanges. While acknowledging this limitation, it is also recognized that other research endorses the benefits of the virtual. O'Dowd, in a study of yearlong e-mail exchanges between students in university language courses (English and Spanish), employed student interviews as a data collection method and was able to document intercultural learning taking place and probable causes (2003).

Students and faculty alike were surprised at the diversity in thought on what was assumed to be commonly held facts and values about business and economic issues; yet note their many similarities provide a starting point for open communication. Inclusion of the reflective discussions had the greatest impact on the most students yielding comments such as 'I wouldn't have guessed that...' and 'When I think about the whole picture, it does make sense they would have a different approach...' Not all students felt there were differences between the two sets of students; some may be more aware of the opposite culture and have less of a gap to close.

These observations directly correspond to three cultural levels identified by Levy: culture as elemental, culture as relative and culture as individual. Levy also supports the possibility that virtual exchanges can simulate physical cultural interchange. In analyzing one of the five case studies which used email as the communication tool, Levy states that, 'describing their image of the respective cultures were helpful in differentiating personal opinions and viewpoints with what was believed to be widely-held views of their country/culture' (2007, p.114). Further, he supports a reflection component as required in our study in order to put one's own culture into context. Levy posits that regular online participation in international online communities both 'dilutes and expands our individual cultural orientation and mix. Overseas travel can also exert the same effect' (2007, p. 111). Longer collaborative projects facilitated by the web can also help understand culture as relative to another (comparing and contrasting as done in the research paper pedagogy) (2007, p. 120). Though not included in his case studies analyzed, Levy believes asynchronous technology (such as the discussion board, research paper, and online course pedagogies) are easier and less risky to implement than synchronous technologies (such as the virtual conference). Thus, the work by Levy supports the virtual cultural learning research question of this study.

One limitation involves variation in data collection. When courses did more two activities, some cases used a combined survey with separate sections and others used a separate survey after each activity. Further, little data collected specifically relates to the activity. Further implementations of these virtual exchanges are underway; two marketing instructors from the respective schools are collaborating on a joint project using a wiki tool for a common assignment. The survey instrument has been revised to incorporate more data gathering on pedagogical methods and questions on study abroad encouragement and sense of reality of the virtual exchange, which were included on some, but not all, surveys have been added.

4 Conclusion

Other literature was found relating to use of international virtual teams that emphasized interpersonal relationships and trust building over global awareness and cultural learning. Literature on iCamp and proceedings from educational technology conferences concentrate more on the technical logistics. The contribution of this paper is on the practical nature of a virtual strategy. It describes a logical extension of existing bilateral exchanges and communication technologies that can unite classrooms and bring together students from different countries in a common learning situation.

This virtual collaborative exchange appeared to aid global awareness, while reaching a large number of students at a low cost and faculty time commitment. Students from all locations and regardless of prior study abroad or cultural currency consistently recommended the virtual exchanges using any of the tried pedagogies. There is no evidence that the experiment harmed either the course content learning or international views. Faculty hesitant about either technology or interference with course structure may be motivated to try this pedagogy to broaden global perspectives that can be scaled up or down, and applies to any discipline.

Acknowledgements The authors wish to acknowledge participating instructors from Haaga-Helia University of Applied Sciences of Helsinki, Finland.

References

Andone, D., & Frydenberg, M. (2009). One idea, one ocean, two countries and tens of students the implications of virtual mobility. *Proceedings of IADIS international conference on cognition and exploratory learning in digital age (CELDA 2009)* (pp. 388–391), Rome, Italy.

Campbell, N. (2008). You've got mail! Using email technology to enhance intercultural communication learning. *Journal of Intercultural Communication, 16*. Retrieved September 2008, from http://www.immi.se/intercultural

Daniels, M., Petre, M., Almstrum, V., Asplund, L., Björkman, C., Erikson, et al. (1998). RUNESTONE, an international student collaboration project. *Proceedings of IEEE 1998 Frontiers in education conference* (pp. 727–732), Tempe, AZ, doi:10.1109/FIE.1998.738780

Institute of International Education. (2009). *Open Doors 2009 Report on International Educational Exchange.* New York: Institute of International Education, Table 22. Retrieved November 2009, from http://opendoors.iienetwork.org

Johnson, L., Levine, A., & Smith, R. (2008). *2008 Horizon report,* Austin, TX: The new media consortium, 6. Retrieved January 2010, from http://www.nmc.org/horizon

Kiesliinger, B., & Fiedler, S. (2006). iCamp: A cross-cultural research approach for a cross-cultural learning design. *Proceedings of the third international conference on eLearning for knowledge-based society,* Bangkok, Thailand. Retrieved from http://www.icamp.eu/wp-content/uploads/2007/05/ap06_paper_final.pdf

Last, M., Daniels, M., Hause, M., & Woodroffe, M. (2002). Learning from students: Continuous improvement in international collaboration. Annual Joint Conference Integrating Technology into Computer Science Education: *Proceedings of the 7th annual conference on innovation and technology in computer science education* (pp.136–140), Aarhus, Denmark.

Levy, M. (2007). Culture, culture learning and new technologies: Towards a pedagogical framework. *Language Learning and Technology, 11*(2), 104–127. Retrieved from http://llt.msu.edu/vol11num2/levy

National Center for Education Statistics. (2008). *Digest of education statistics: 2008*. Washington, DC: Institute of Education Sciences, Table 189. Retrieved from http://nces.ed.gov/programs/digest/d08

Nguyen-Ngoc, A. V., & Law, E. (2007). Evaluation of cross-cultural computer-supported collaborative learning: Preliminary findings for iCamp challenges. *Proceedings of the world conference on educational multimedia. Hypermedia and telecommunications 2007* (pp. 1887–1996), Vancouver, Canada.

O'Dowd, R. (2003). Understanding the 'Other Side': Intercultural learning in a spanish-english e-mail exchange. *Language, Learning and Technology, 7*(3), 118–144.

Office of Postsecondary Education. (2010). U.S. Department of education. Retrieved from http://www.ed.gov/about/offices/list/ope

Teng, Y-W. (2005). A cross-cultural communication experience at a higher education institution in Taiwan. *Journal of Intercultural Communication, 10*. Retrieved from http://www.immi.se/intercultural

Chapter 23
Ideas and Concepts of ViCaDiS – A Virtual Learning Environment for Digital Students

Radu Vasiu and Diana Andone

Abstract The main purpose of the Virtual Campus for Digital Students – ViCaDiS Project (2007–2009) is to assist international cooperation in learning by using social media and open source applications. ViCaDiS facilitates a shift from Institutional Learning Environments towards Personal Learning Environments. Digital students are young adults who have grown up with digital technologies integrated as an everyday feature of their lives. The chapter describes the development of an online – mobile phone environment -ViCaDiS – Virtual Campus for Digital Students, as a co-operation between 6 universities from European Union to develop a common online learning environment enhanced with web 2.0 tools for supporting the online international co-operation at academic level. It presents also the evaluation of this new learning environment for digital students.

Keywords Digital students · Virtual campus · Social media · Higher education · Learning environment

1 Introduction

This chapter describes the main ideas of a collaborative project between 6 universities from European Union to develop a common online learning environment enhanced with web 2.0 tools for supporting the online international co-operation at academic level: ViCaDiS – Virtual Campus for Digital Students.

The project is based on the article of faith that underpins our work is that "technology makes it possible to design learning situations that actively engage and guide learners while allowing them to choose their style of learning and organize their knowledge outcomes". This conceptualization of the learning environment allows learners to make the transition from learning in a physical space such as the lab or

R. Vasiu (✉)
"Politehnica" University of Timisoara, Bd. Vasile Parvan, nr. 2, Timisoara 300223, Romania
e-mail: radu.vasiu@cm.upt.ro

lecture theatre to learning in a student-centered learning environment in cyberspace. Technology can change the education setting from a physical one to a virtual one. Virtual spaces may be in constant flux: they can be instantaneous, deliberate, mobile, synchronous and asynchronous. The student's relationship with virtual space can shift rapidly and they may co-exist in several spaces at a time. These virtual spaces can play a bigger role in all aspects of higher education through the use and integration of technology (laptops, handhelds, mobile phones) and communication (wiki, blogs, SMS, podcasting, etc) (Andone, 2008). We planned to extend this concept by the development of an international virtual campus where several universities to join in creating an open space for formal and informal learning. This campus allows multiple international co-operation between students and tutors in creating common project work, self-assessment exercises, and multiple examples for the improvement of formal learning. They will also be able to co-operate in creating a common space of sharing information and knowledge about subjects related with academic life and with the EU values (Erasmus mobilities, cities, countries, travelling, studying in EU).

In ViCaDiS (Virtual Campus for Digital Students) a wide range of Open and Distance Learning actors from EU countries (Romania, Italy, Finland, Hungary, Lithuania and UK) focus on developing an innovative approach for enhancing international eLearning by moving the strength from the institutional learning environment to the personal learning environment (PLE) (5) with focus on students. It produces an instructional or pedagogical shift inside universities eLearning moving the focus from the education materials and technology to the user-student, to user generated content. The partners in ViCaDiS are: "Politehnica" University of Timisoara – RO – co-ordinator, Università degli Studi di Palermo – IT, Baltijos edukacini technologij institutas – LT, University of Miskolc – NHRDEC – HU, Oulu University of Applied Sciences, School of Engineering – FI, University of Brighton – UK, Visioni di Caro arch. Ernesta – IT, Euro-Contact Business School – HU, Bridgeman – RO, JME Associates – UK.

1.1 *Digital Students*

For the generation born after 1980 the digital world is even more present and pervasive than for the rest of us: for them it is the only world they know. They are the "digital" or "Net" Generation (Tapscott, 1998): children or teenagers who have lived all their lives in a changing but (from their perspective) a predominantly digital world. Significantly, most students in higher education now belong to this group. We have identified these students as a special group due to their characteristics (Andone et al., 2007) and we consider that this community has different learning habits from students of previous generations. The final target of the project is to build and test an eLearning environment targeted at their needs, based on the assumption of an "ecology" of learning (Seely Brown & Duguid, 2000) and which will complement their usual online environments from each university by allowing them to connect, study, work and get together at international level.

The full results of the early studies are presented in (Andone, Boyne, Dron, Pemberton, 2005; Andone, Dron, Boyne, Pemberton, 2006a; Andone, Dron, Boyne, Pemberton, 2006b), The main characteristics of the digital student were identified as a result of this research. The characteristics of the technological confident digital students were found to include a strong need for instantaneity, a desire to control their environment and to have a technology based social life (or – to communicate socially by an extensive use of technology).

From our research perspective, "digital students" are defined as young adult students who have grown up with active participation in technology as an everyday feature of their lives. Among the characteristics that define digital students are that they take the availability of email, instant messaging and text messaging for granted, and use unlimited online resources. The digital world has had a significant impact on their habits and behaviour. They expect to try things rather than hear about them. They want to learn by doing – usually just by trying things out (Tapscott, 1998) from which they develop understanding by synthesis. They tend to learn visually and socially. Using technology to organize and integrate knowledge feels normal to them, as well as "doing rather then knowing" (Frand, 2000).

They have very specific needs and expectations from their learning environments. They will enjoy enhanced interactivity and connectivity with others, and expect to learn in groups that may be physical or virtual. Papert (1996) says that young people's "access to information is more interactive and non-sequential" and they learn for "the pleasure and benefit of discovery".

As a result of their powerful access to digital media and to the endless information on the Internet they have learned to access facts and to assess them in particular ways, and to synthesize. However, digital students will engage in searching for information sources and, quite often, for other people on the Internet and based on this they will construct new structures and new information. Their learning expectations are different due to new patterns of behaviour developed over their school years. They use the Web for research, collaboration with other students, and as a resource for information passed on to them by other students or teachers. Students also use it as a "virtual guidance counsellor" and as a way to store important school-related materials.

Treating the Internet and mobile phones as normal tools means that collaboration is an area of great potential for digital students. Using instant messaging, e-mail and text messages via mobile phones they're able to create, join, leave and rejoin at will, what the Pew Internet group calls "virtual study groups" (Jones & Madden, 2002). These groups can be synchronous or asynchronous but the "feeling" is of instant communication. This has led to a continuous need for instant feedback which is also found in their learning attitudes (Andone, Dron et al., 2007).

Despite the traditionally restrictive educational settings in which they often have to function, today's students perceive their learning environments as boundless. They tend to use physical space differently from prior generations and they blur the boundaries between physical and cyber space and between mine, yours, ours, and everyone's (Andone, Boyne et al., 2005).

They tend to use the Internet to search both for educational purposes and for information about their hobbies and interests. They use SMS (mobile text messaging) extensively for contacting their friends and colleagues, as well as IM – instant messaging. These results show that the use of multiple media and technologies is directly connected to their use in education, home and entertainment (Andone, Dron et al., 2006; Pemberton, 2006c).

Though lagging very slightly behind their UK and Finnish counterparts, the students from Eastern European countries are becoming stronger in their ICT use and understanding and have jumped several technological steps. They started using the computer, the Internet and the mobile phone at around the same time, and after just a few years they are using similar tools (SMS, Instant messaging, search engines, online playing) at much the same level as their Western colleagues (Andone, Dron et al., 2006; Pemberton, 2006a). They use the Internet for research, collaboration with other students, and as a resource for information passed on to them by other students or teachers (Andone, 2008).

A large number of desirable attributes for e-learning environment emerged from the research, some of them contradictory. For instance, while participants generally want to have "things coming to them" in a "rapid, fast way", receiving un-requested learning objects disturbs them. It was clear that no single approach would be likely to satisfy all requirements, and an e-learning environment for digital student will need to use complementary methods and technology and leave the power of choice of the "right one" to the student.

2 ViCaDiS Environment

The main scope of ViCaDiS is to provide an accessible and attractive environment for all students within the Member States, using already existing tools enhanced with new tools wanted by the new generation of students. By providing students the tools which they use anyway extensively outside the institutional framework of learning (wiki, blogs, forums, IM, podcasting, RSS) ViCaDiS supports the learning attractiveness of the university curricula, and we suppose will improve the quality of the learning process by encouraging the exchange of information/knowledge between students from different universities, and will reduce university drop-out or student de-motivation for learning. It also produces an instructional or pedagogical shift inside the universities eLearning moving the focus from the education materials and technology to the user- student, to user generated content.

ViCaDiS is an interoperable dual-device (Internet and mobile phone) environment which brings together partner universities into one single place as they are already using different eLearning environments for distance education or blended learning which is either open source (Moodle) or large Learning Management Software (LMS) (Blackboard). Some of them are using social software to improve the education level of students and to create an integrated online "community". The virtual campus encompasses the partners' experience in using or developing these eLearning environments and provides a unique set of Open Educational Resources (OER) desired by the digital students. The OER mainly concentrate on tools that allow a user-content driven environment where students move from being simple users to becoming content providers. ViCaDiS is in essence a "community", a virtual campus that contains a blend of Internet and mobile technologies to enhance the student-tutor communication, the quick response of the environment to the student needs (by setting up his own settings and accessing information using this system, transfer learning objects to mobile devices) and the environment's flexibility (by using learning objects other than the traditional text, images and animations: blogs, podcasting, wikis).

The ViCaDiS Campus is based around four aspects of development:

- Technical: the development of the virtual campus ViCaDiS, as an OER with an interoperable interface, social software implementation and new tools for mobile learning. The interoperability is defined here by the ViCaDiS capacity to give instant access to students from their own university learning environment (which is in these cases Moodle or Blackboard), without any other log in and by recognizing their profiles into ViCaDiS.
- Pedagogy: to encourage informal learning as a viable method for Higher Education, to change Virtual Learning Environments (VLE) into Personal Learning Environments (PLE), to envisage possible ideas and solution for student-generated educational materials.
- Management: to bring a change in the management of VLE with more distribution of responsibility both at a conceptual level (teachers and students as equal participants) and a practical one, allowing joint participation from different institutions in an open, free educational environment.
- Social and cultural: ViCaDiS is an online community space, a meeting room where all users (students and teachers) are equal and contribute freely and actively. It uses all partner languages (EN, IT, LT, HU, RO, FI) and brings "the outside world" of social media into the "education world" and extends the real world of the student campus into virtual space.

The ViCaDiS Server is multiplied in all 6 universities as a network with partially mirroring information. All students and tutors access the environment from the same place, without taking into consideration from which University online campus they migrate (interoperability of ViCaDiS). They see similar things but all of their information, data and work are stored in their university server. This network of servers was a project challenge as it needed to overcome barriers in data protection, in student work or course material copyright, all subject to internal university policies of each of the 6 universities involved.

The ViCaDiS content is subject and interest based and is mainly in conjunction with their curricula but supplement rather than replace the normal curricula. The students are able to access ViCaDiS free-of-charge just by proof of their student status.

The ViCaDiS core structure is around the "groups" which identifies the objects, projects and tasks in (www.vicadis.net/campus):

- language (EN, RO, IT, HU, LT, FI),
- university (each university involved in the project and a user can belong to one university group)
- course (part of the piloting: Web 2.0 Technologies, Multimedia Technologies, Technical English, e-learning, practical placement),
- subject (ICT, Web 2.0, graphics, research, social media & nonprofits),
- interests (countries, cities, Erasmus mobilities, studying in EU),
- life (sport, financial issues, travel).

The piloting and evaluation of the idea is based on the activities run within these groups.

The environment can be used by students to learn and work together in structured projects, or simply to find information on their subjects of interest. *ViCaDiS is open and free to all students and teachers within the EU.*

3 Piloting ViCaDiS

In the ViCaDiS project the development of social media tools layers have been the starting point (see Fig. 23.1). In the core of the ViCaDiS Campus we have also a mobile interface. Social media tools not-integrated in the learning environment have been considered by adding social media related IDs in user profiles to facilitate ad-hoc use. Pedagogical paradigms, teaching and learning competences, technology related competences, existing culture and available technology are affecting how mobile technology and social tools are used or will be used.

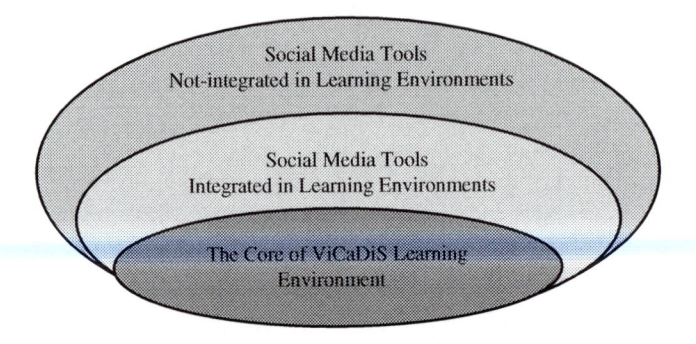

Fig. 23.1 Mobile and social media tools

Students need mobile features that support them to keep on track of the learning process and changes in the learning process. Mobile Tools and Social Tools may be available on three layers. The use of Mobile Tools and Social Media Tools can be preplanned or ad-hoc by nature. It is beneficial to see educational use of mobile and social technologies as an innovation process which includes: discovering of possibilities in learning, teaching and cooperation, developing related resources and implementation of resources to facilitate learning, teaching and related cooperation.

ViCaDiS Piloting Activities can be classified into three levels depending on deployment of the main idea of the ViCaDiS Project – the integration of social media tools for student international co-operation at academic level.

– Level 1: *Inter-university cooperation.* This is the most valuable level for ViCaDiS. On this level: Cooperation areas on the ViCaDiS Campus have been agreed between universities. Social media based learning and cooperation is partly designed by educational designers and teachers. Social media based ad-hoc cooperation between students plays an essential role. Students can use preselected or other freely available social media tools in their cooperation.
– Level 2: *Educational use of social media inside one course.* On this level: Cooperation is restricted to one university and one course on the ViCaDiS Campus. Students can use preselected or any other social media tools in their cooperation.
– Level 3: *Courses without use of social media.* On this level the ViCaDiS Campus is used as a learning environment, but the use of social media is not included.

Levels 1 and 2 are relevant for ViCaDiS Piloting and testing. Level 3 is not very relevant for ViCaDiS because it does not have a match to the main idea of the ViCaDiS Project. The research is focused on Level 1 and Level 2 piloting cases.

The evaluation and piloting is based on the socio-engineering methodology, which aims to involve the potential users by incorporating their knowledge in the design process and has a number of interrelated design stages. It mainly consists of two stages: a stage of analysis which sets up the constraints of the second stage – the design of the new environment. The entire process is based on the idea that "users are important sources of design information and may be partners in the design process" introduced by Sharples in (2002). The results are evaluated against initial requirements, but also for usability, usefulness, desirability, elegance, and acceptance by the user groups. The Evaluation strategy is part of the socio-cognitive engineering and is a continuing process. The evaluation will consist of different stages: to test ViCaDiS against its own requirements, for usability and desirability by the users (technical testing done using accredited methodologies from Isometrics and the Usability Lab of Microsoft) (Benedek & Miner, 2002); to evaluate ViCaDiS environment – against students learning attributes, user satisfaction, also an evaluation of the users needs will be repeated to seek the user new characteristics using the ZEF method and tool (www.zef.fi) which grows from creative strategic thinking in a web-based environment, a very new and innovative method. The ZEF-tool and method makes it possible to evaluate the most effective way the project progress, tools, services, content, usability, effectiveness etc. The ZEF method includes the "four-square" table and it makes it possible to evaluate each item in two-dimensional ways in real time. ZEF reports will show and guide the project to concentrate and to do the "Right Things Right".

4 The Piloting Evaluation

We studied the impact of the various features on the experience of the new student generation. The environment was used in normal University course (Technical English and Multimedia Technologies) and during the Technical Placement in the Industry by groups of both "digital" and "non-digital" students. Another use for informal learning was to gain information and share the experiences of student mobilities between the partner universities in the EU ERASMUS programme. The usage made of the environment was measured, and qualitative evaluation (interviews) were carried out to establish attitudes and preferences. The evaluation process took place until the end of December 2009, when the academic semester ends and the final evaluation (a questionnaire using the ZEF methodology) was used. A Pre-piloting questionnaire was also run. The Pre-Piloting Questionnaire was divided into three sets of questions: Background Information, Social Media and Tools and Social Networking and Learning.

The results are presented in Fig. 23.2a in normalised form and in Fig. 23.2b. in z-scored form (From the top-right corner of the Z-Scored diagram one can see where the greatest potential is; from the bottom-right corner one can see where better competence is needed; from the bottom-left corner one can identify features where low competence levels have probably prevented recognition of any potential for learning.). The strong use and potential for learning, as identified by the students, for instant messaging and the share of resources influenced the pedagogical patterns for the piloting cases.

4.1 Erasmus Mobility Case – Outgoing Students at OUAS (INMO)

The Erasmus Mobility case (INMO) was piloted May–December 2009 in order to support students' outgoing mobility through the ViCaDiS *virtual learning environment*. It offers various *activities* for outgoing students and international coordinators of the Oulu University of Applied Sciences (OUAS). The VLE activities are structured chronologically, and they facilitate the preparation, documentation and reflection of students' international mobility periods by means of *social media* (Kurkela, Fähnrich, & Kocsis-Baan, 2009).

Students who have been accepted for studies or a placement abroad join the VLE and *prepare a home country presentation* about Finland, which they share as a PowerPoint-*file* in a *forum*. In addition, they update their VLE profiles and thus indicate their abilities to use further social media (Skype, MSN etc.). Before going

Fig. 23.2 (a) and (b): Results of the pre-pilot questionnaire

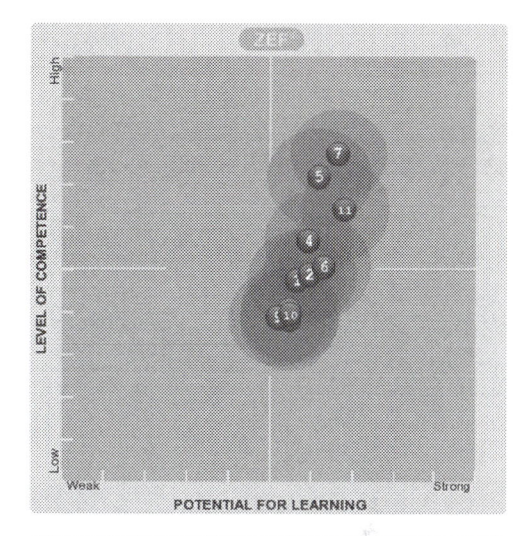

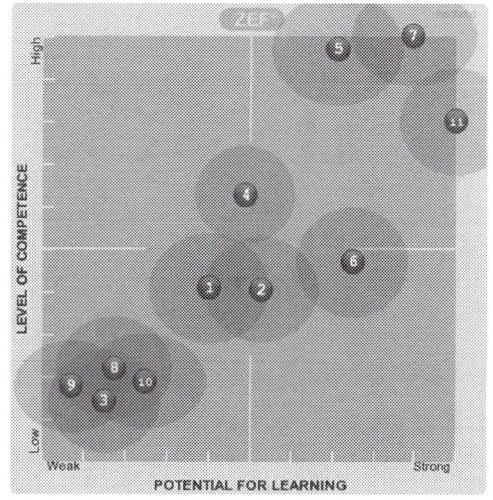

abroad, students also *prepare a target country wiki*, which aims at developing students' language and intercultural competence and orientation towards their target country. Students may use various sources such as *texts, pictures, videos, tables, links, and social bookmarks*. At this stage students also establish *a blog* or *learning diary*. The objective of a blog is to facilitate students' reflection on their learning process. Students benefit from keeping a blog both individually and collectively, as they document their experiences for themselves, and share them with other students and staff members.

The students at OUAS found that using the ViCaDiS Blog or OU Blog the most beneficial (clearly apart from any other tools used) and the less attractive one the Video Aula (which had some videos about the country of their mobility). The successful implementation of the solutions provided in the INMO case requires, above all, an appropriate pedagogical and organisational paradigm or settings by which staff is enabled to guide and support outgoing students and trainees at various stages of their mobility period. In addition, it requires sufficient technical competence by both staff and students and/or trainees as well as technical devices, facilities and infrastructure such as computers, phones, mobile or local Internet connection, the ViCaDiS Campus', integrated and additional social media and networking tools for synchronous and asynchronous online activities, or rooms for face-to-face meetings at the home and/or host organisations/enterprises etc.

Fig. 23.3 The use of ViCaDiS features from OUAS Erasmus students

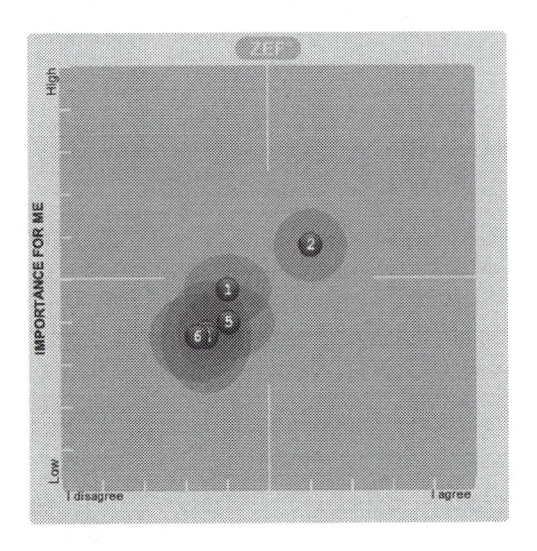

Based on post-piloting interviews, the blogs have served well as learning diaries for some of the students. Some of the participants in the post-piloting interview mentioned that additional group blogs could be used, dealing with particular topics that come up or need to be dealt with for the purpose of individual and collective learning at certain stages of a mobility period. Students and trainees reported in the post-piloting questionnaire and interviews that the INMO design and chronological approach was well structured, but getting used to it required additional effort and time in the starting phase, as is usually the case with VLE's in higher education and other contexts.

4.2 The Students' Technical Placement – Summer Practice

Technical placement – Summer Industrial Practice course was piloted 29 June–07 August 2009 at University of Miskolc, offered for a group of 11 final year BSc students. According to their official curricula, they had to pass a 6-week industrial practice period, while working on their individual project work. These project activities were supervised by lecturers of the Department of Mechanical Technologies and were expected to lead to the Final Project Work (or Diploma thesis) of the students, within a very short period, having a demanding, strict deadline of 27 November 2009 for submitting the Diploma work. Students were sent to different industrial firms all over the country, and at each firm a local industrial instructor supported their work as well. Students received detailed instructions on how to prepare the summer practice report, but it was also advised, that these documents should be adequate for integrating them into the Diploma work as well. The Summer Practice reports were due to the beginning of September and evaluated by the academic supervisor. No credit is given for fulfilling this requirement however it is compulsory for all of the students. A pre-course training in the use of ViCaDiS was done.

The ViCaDiS pilot case Technical placement – Summer Industrial Practice course area has been structured according to the individual students and their supporting academic and industrial team (Kurkela, Fähnrich, & Kocsis-Baan, 2009). The social media in the course was expected to be used as the medium for collaborative learning, supporting each other in understanding, developing their own project work, using jointly developed resource-lists and motivating each other by keeping in touch, consulting their problems – as they usually do in the classroom. Based on the pre-questionnaire the following social media tools were introduced to students for improving the efficiency of project-based learning activity:

- Forums and Chat for communication – although students work on individual tasks, they may support each other in sharing information on resources and methodology.
- WIKI documents for developing and publishing project report.
- Blog, to make records on working process, diary of practical placement.

Students showed high interest to use the tools of ViCaDiS environment at the beginning, when we organised a demonstration about its applications and functions. However when arriving the venue of their technical placement they faced much more technical problems as we had foreseen: in many industrial firm internet cannot be freely used by staff members, because of closed, safety intranet applications. Another technical problem was recognised with regarding using wikis. Students received strict formal requirement to be followed when submitting their summer practice report, and even more importantly, when preparing their diploma-work. Regarding the time-pressure they suffered from, they found it useless to edit their reports in wikis and later in the requested word format. From this piloting case we should learn that in a very tight, demanding period of their studies students cannot be expected to invest time and energy to use new methodology and tools – they focus on well-known, routine tools and solutions. Moreover the group which has been invited to join this ViCaDiS pilot is the first group learning in engineering management course according to the Bologna system and they suffered from too many uncertainties during their studies and also changing requirements regarding the

Diploma-work. So timing of this initiative cannot be considered as an appropriate possibility for innovation.

In the future Summer Industrial Practice course could be offered only after introducing the methodology within a mid-semester project-work type course and when students become familiar with the wide range of social media tools, they can be invite to apply these tools in their remote project-based work and practical placement. Another necessary preparatory step is to clarify the IT access-policy of the industrial firms, moreover industrial instructors should be inform about these possibilities in more detailed pre-training – or more feasible could be the production of tutorials as an introductory training and help service.

Another consideration can be for the future to use the ViCaDiS environment for supporting project-based work of students also in abroad – mobility programs may include joint research activities of student from different countries, which may be realised via networking tools before or after physical mobility and placement, moreover, teachers sending their students to abroad may get more insight to the activities and performance of their students by using ViCaDiS as a collaborative working area (Vasiu & Andone, 2009).

4.3 The TalkTech'09 Course Module

The TalkTech'09 course module was a second edition of the similar project run in 2008 (Frydenberg & Andone, 2009). TalkTech'09 – Multimedia Technologies focuses on how computer mediated communication over the Internet may be used to foster information technology and web 2.0 literacy skills of students enrolled at business and technical universities, while at the same time, promote cross-cultural awareness. It is a partnership between first year business students in IT 101, an introductory information technology course at Bentley University in the United States, and Bachelor in Telecommunications students in the Technologies of Multimedia (TMM) course, in their final year at the "Politehnica" University of Timisoara in Romania, as well as towards the final, students in the second year from University of Palermo, Italy studying The Use of technologies in Linguistic. These students partnered over a period of semester in 2009, to explore a variety of web-based collaboration and communication tools to create a multimedia presentation on a topic related to technology, and culture. The tutors introduced the proposed topics and at the end they needed to present as a group their project result. Their activity was marked and they earned credits for it. Approximately 12 American and 37 Romanian and 22 Italian students participated in the project, with six students per group. All of the Romanian students, who volunteered out of the 75 students enrolled in the TMM course, spoke English comfortably. http://www.vicadis.net/campus/course/view.php?id=56

The main aim of this pilot was to generate a familiar context for digital students in which they had to work effectively with international partners in a project, and to analyze the implications of such an experiment of international collaboration on digital students.

During this course the students have different tasks to do: to use multimedia technologies in new ways and to develop a full, multimedia interactive website. Prior to this project, students in both classes have accomplished similar technical tasks: they made personal web pages, posted online videos, and created PowerPoint presentations; they are web literate; they are familiar with social networking sites, search engines, email, instant messaging, and other applications. The pre-project survey given to both students groups made it clear that these students belong to the group of digital students (Andone, 2008). This project introduced many of them to virtual campus as new collaboration tools that many had not used previously.

The goals of this project were to create a virtual learning environment which encouraged students to:

- work with students from another country (Romania, Italy and the USA) to create a multimedia presentation showcasing research on a topic related to technology and culture
- choose and use both synchronous and asynchronous computer-mediated-communication tools to communicate with international partners
- choose and use Web 2.0 collaborative tools to facilitate and chronicle group process, progress, and collaboration to produce a tangible work product within a designated period of time.

The students' goal was to use these different technologies to work together to create a multimedia presentation that shared their understanding of a current issue in technology and culture. Sample topics included "what are the mobile phones of the future and why", "how does the Internet change the way people communicate," and "how a green computer can be built?" The format of their final deliverables was left open to the students, but could take the form a web page with images, a video, a PowerPoint, or a combination of any of these. By introducing these principles, both course leaders tried to match the ideas of learning ecology (Seely Brown, & Duguid, 2000) and of the virtual campuses and open personal learning environment as introduced by (Andone, Dron, Pemberton, 2009).

Social media related competences (by students and teachers) can be either synergy enablers or synergy disablers. Educational designers, teachers and tutors need competencies and experiences from the use of social media services available in the ViCaDiS Campus and also services available outside the Campus. For this we run a Pre-piloting questionnaire where the students gave their initial feedback about what social media tools they use and how. As the results showed that students used extensively the instant messaging, audio conferencing, blogs, and wikis in their life in and out of the university campus, we focused mainly on these tools to be used in the TalkTech'09.

It has an News forum where the students or the instructors could post announcements, a home page with a description of the project and related milestones, and a groups modules, where students signed up for groups and selected topics. These modules included a blog, a forum, a wiki and an upload section. The tutor continuously supported the students online during the project. The upload are served

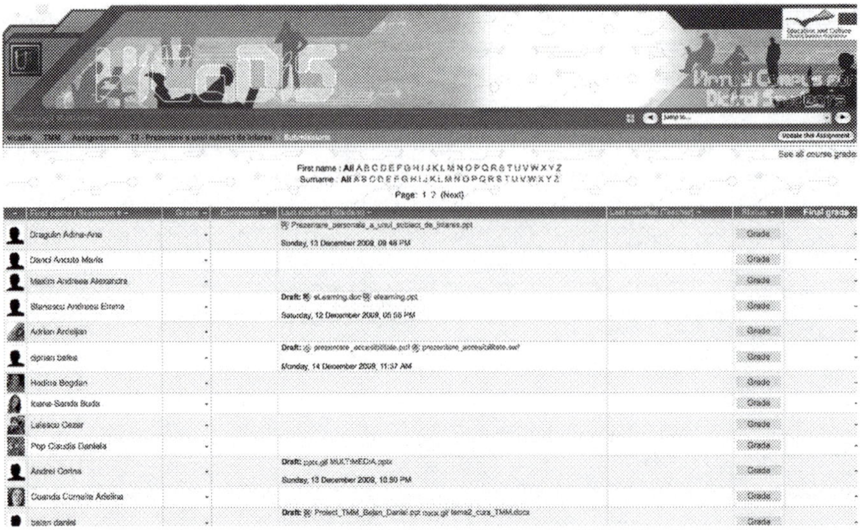

Fig. 23.4 The upload area for TalkTech'09 for joint student work

as a common online repository for students to share images, videos, presentations, and other files that they generated as part of their work on this project. Students used their group's Forum and Blog to present their findings, include links to references or other resources and to embed multimedia that they created as part of the project. Some groups simply provided hyperlinks to their final documents, which were external files or websites.

Of the 16 groups, 13 described on the blog their methods of communication online: the most preferred one being synchronous meeting using instant messaging (IM) (such as AIM, Yahoo messenger or Google Talk) or VoIP (Skype). The use of IM was also reported in the open question as the preferred beside the live VoIP especially by the Romanian students: "it was easier to write then to talk", "writing it gives you time to think a bit what are you saying". Several students also reported that the most important decisions regarding the project work were taken during live IM chats and not in emails. During the instant messaging communication they discussed about the division of tasks, organizational details (when to 'meet again' and how), "getting to know you", and "difficulties we were facing". Instant messenger conversations focused on several areas: personal relationship building between partners, project management skills (brainstorming and delegation), consensus building (a student proposes a plan to structure the presentation, but another suggests an alternative approach), and technical difficulties. Their liberal use of smiley faces suggests and terms such as "excellent!" and "great!" suggests they formed a collegial relationship. By placing them in an environment that both required and supported Web-based collaboration, students were able to conceptually understand and really participate in a process that linked them with international student partners. Observed one student, "Technology can help you communicate no matter

23 Ideas and Concepts of ViCaDiS

Fig. 23.5 The use of ViCaDiS social media tools from TalkTech'09 students

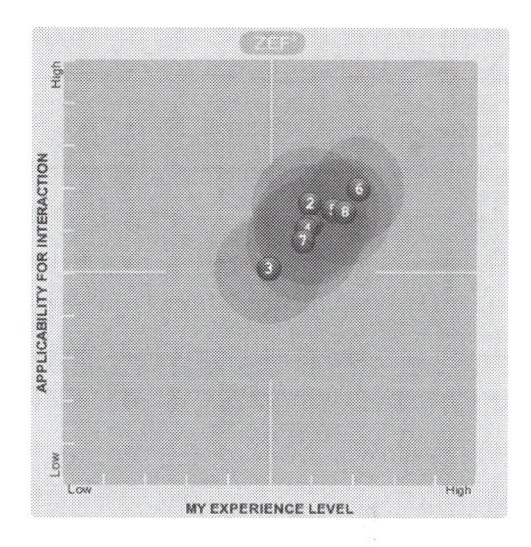

where you are in the world. You don't need to be face to face in order to do a project together.".

Almost all the students found working across time zones and the process of finding compatible synchronous meeting times on their own to be difficult (all 16 groups listed this). Several students had similar sentiments that it is "hard ... to coordinate a meeting schedule with 5 different students with different schedules when two of them are 7 hours ahead. We sometimes didn't meet as a whole group but usually had at least 4 or the 5 people present." They enjoyed the freedom using any tools they wanted for communication but, as their project result was graded, they wanted to know exactly how their work would be evaluated. Some complained about their work being more complicated and challenging than that of other groups, with a direct sense of competition between them. One Romanian student mentioned that the most important aspect on this project was the motivation to do it and to "show how good you are... to identify yourself with the work you've done and the quality of the final product". The biggest impact of this project on students was a tangible lesson in the global reach of the Internet and the global impact of technology. Some students noted the differences in language and reported that they had to be careful when communicating with their international partners to be sure everyone was clear on their tasks (full results of the questionnaires at http://kysy.oamk.fi/zef7/reports/1d4a22bab505d28fea405f61eea41670/).

By placing them in an environment that both required and supported Web-based collaboration, students were able to conceptually understand and really participate in a process that linked them with international student partners. The course leaders observed that almost half of the groups weren't fulfilling equally their work. The groups that spent the most reported time communicating with each other, or who were gossiping about different issues online, have had the most accomplished, structured and comprehensive final projects. Better communication between the partners on the same project ("got new friends"), leads to better work results even if they never met face-to-face and their communication is just online. They all reported that this project was interesting and that they learned "a lot of new things". They described the experience of using all the instant communication tools to be fast and efficient, as was the pace of the project: "we learned more things in a month that in a year." They found the project useful and high quality as trying "to use new tools made the project experience better"; TalkTech2009 was a social environment to share ideas with peers, see what others are doing and, as one student said, "give" them "confidence that they are on the right track" with their studies and understanding of technology.

It is significant that the students placed great value in tools that enabled communication not just between themselves but also with the course leaders, who used the same tools to plan this project. This project entrusted confidence into the students' online abilities and skills especially for using them in an international context.

Throughout the project, the instructors worked to provide support, build a common learning-communication environment through the TalkTech module. Despite these efforts, the fact that students sometime found other alternatives (such as in the use of Yahoo Briefcase for file sharing, or tools to create their own websites, or Wikipedia to show cast their result) shows that, even within a rigid institutional setting, it is increasingly they and not us who create and control their learning ecologies. In a sense, it may be seen that they are creating their own classrooms and project spaces, using the tools and virtual spaces that work best for them. Rather than expecting students to adapt to the spaces we create for them, it is increasingly that we must adapt to the spaces they choose to create and inhabit.

5 Conclusion

In ViCaDIS piloting wiki, blogs and chat/forums were used extensively for fulfilling the given academic task. The Wiki, OU Blog and Chat/Forums were seen as the most important ViCaDiS features for users, as resulted from the post-piloting analysis. They were also included in pedagogical settings of the piloting cases. . It clearly resulted that students preferred blogs and chats for communicating their thoughts, reflections or working in groups for the same tasks. According to these answers ViCaDiS was considered particularly good at facilitating international communication between students, which was one of the main goals of the project. In some piloting cases students worked internationally in fulfilling the same tasks (the TalkTech'09 and Technical English). This allowed them to get to know each other better and to interact in ways which weren't the usual in their universities settings. Only some of the piloting students used ViCaDiS through a mobile interface. None of the piloting cases was specifically based on mobile communication, but about 12% of users connected to ViCaDiS via their mobile phones. The answers on ViCaDiS Error Tolerance and interviews for the piloting suggest that the environment as tested was easy to use and highly reliable. The only problems were related to a couple of virus attacks and electric power interruptions in Timisoara. Romanian partners sorted out the virus problems very fast, which were caused by an entirely separate server on the same network. Most of the piloting students were familiar with social media tools, and they considered them appropriate for interaction in an educational environment. The students also appreciated the high educational value of online video connection with peers or tutors during a course. This tool was extensively used in 2 piloting cases and better academic results were obtained by the group of students which used it. It is significant that the students placed great value in tools that enabled communication not just between themselves but also with the course tutors. This project entrusted confidence into the students' online abilities and skills especially for using them in an international context (Vasiu & Andone, 2009).

The ViCaDiS ideas, concepts and the Campus contain many interesting examples of good pedagogy, good uses of technology and evidence of rich interactions. While there are many ways in which the Campus could be improved in order to better achieve the stated goals, as a research effort it raises many interesting questions and helps to move knowledge forward in the field of technology-enhanced learning. The ViCaDiS Campus is aligned to be used to support blended learning rather than purely distance learning. The activities provided, for the most part, are not complete courses or learning activities, but instead have a strong reliance on other activities, courses and processes that are happening outside the system. It is a toolset for face-to-face teachers rather than a comprehensive online learning environment. This is in keeping with the notion of the digital student, who is expected to not only make use of multiple media and multiple channels of communication, but to prefer that way of working. However, technologies can make things easier to manage this multiplicity, and there are opportunities to take this further to support more collaboration across nations and sites. A good start has been made on this already in some course modules (as described here), where the system itself acts as a communication channel, link space and repository for different teaching and learning activities.

The results indicate that an eLearning environment that has the described tools and involves student control leads to greater engagement in the learning process and a higher level of satisfaction of the group which we identified as digital students. Inter-university cooperation requires to agree and to build on the very same paradigms, settings, abilities and facilities. The ViCaDiS pilot results played a key role in directing our eLearning environment development strategy and influence some major decisions. One such decision concerned the appropriateness of formal learning structures for Internet and Mobile phone based services. For the near future the ViCaDiS consortium intends to approach different universities to take part, as a future possibility for their students and tutors to join and re-join an open, free, international virtual campus where they can find common interest and develop new and innovative content to add-value to the formal and informal learning process.

Acknowledgment The environment described here is named ViCaDiS – Virtual Campus for Digital Students and is supported by the EU Lifelong Learning Erasmus Virtual Campus Programme www.vicadis.net.

References

Andone, D., Boyne C., Dron, J., & Pemberton, L. (2005). *What is it to be a digital student in a British university?* ICALT 2005 The 5th International Conference on Advanced Learning Technologies, Kaohsiung, Taiwan, IEEE Computer Science, 925–927.

Andone, D., Dron, J., Boyne, C., & Pemberton, L. (2006a). *Are our students digital students?* 13th association for learning technology conference (ALT-C 2006): The next generation, Heriot-Watt University, Edinburgh, Scotland, UK, Association for Learning Technology, 82–96.

Andone, D., Dron, J., Boyne, C., & Pemberton, L. (2006b). *Digital Students Across Europe*. World Conference on Educational Multimedia, Hypermedia and Telecommunications ED-MEDIA 2006, Florida, USA, AACE, 1741–1749.

Andone, D., Dron, J., Boyne, C., & Pemberton, L. (2007). E-Learning Environments for Digitally-Minded Students. *Journal of Interactive Learning Research, 18*(1), 41–53.

Andone, D. (2008). *Web 2.0 Technologies for Digital Students*. IADIS International Conference e-Learning 2008 (part of MCCSIS 2008), Amsterdam, NL, IADIS, 287–294.

Andone, D., Dron, J., & Pemberton, L. (2009). Developing a Desirable Learning Environment for Digital Students. *Journal of Technology, Instruction, Cognition and Learning (TICL), 6*(4), ISSN: 1540-0182, 253–271.

Benedek, J., & Miner, T. (2002). *Measuring Desirability: New methods for evaluating desirability in a usability lab setting*. Proceedings of Usability Professionals Association, Orlando, USA.

Frydenberg, M., & Andone, D. (2009). *Two screens and an ocean: Collaborating across Continents and Cultures with Web-Based Tools*. ISECON (Information Systems Education Conference) 2009, Washington, DC, USA, EDSIG, § 3162 9 p, ISSN: 1542–7382.

Kurkela, L., Fähnrich, B., & Kocsis-Baan, M. (2009). *Piloting of a Virtual Campus for Interuniversity Cooperation*. Presentation and paper in the IADIS International Conference on Cognition and Exploratory Learning in Digital Age – CELDA, 2009.

Jones, S., & Madden, M. (2002). *The Internet Goes to College: How Students are Living in the Future with Today's Technology*. P. I. A. L. Project, Pew Internet & American Life Project.

Livingstone, S., Bober M., Helsper, E.J. (2005). "Active Participation or just More Information? Young people's take-up of opportunities to act and interact on the Internet". *Information, Communication & Society, 8*(3): ISSN 1369-118x print/ISSN 1468-4462, 278–314.

Papert, S. (1996). *The connected family: Bridging the generation gap*. Athens, GA: Longstreet Press.

Seely Brown, J., & Duguid, P. (2000). *The Social Life of Information*. Boston, MA: Harvard Bussines School Press.

Sharples, M., Jeffery N., du Boulay, J.B.H., Teather, D., Teather, B., & du Boulay. (2002). "Socio-cognitive engineering: a methodology for the design of human-centred technology". *European Journal of Operational Research, 136*(2): 310–323.

Tapscott, D. (1998). *Growing up digital: The rise of the Net Generation*. New York: McGraw Hill.

Vasiu, R., & Andone, D. (2009). *The development of a Virtual Campus for Digital Students (ViCaDiS)*. In Proceedings of World Conference on E-Learning in Corporate, Government, Healthcare, and Higher Education 2009 (pp. 819–826). Chesapeake, VA: AACE.

Vasiu R., & Andone D. (Eds.). (2009). *ViCaDiS Virtual Campus for Digital Students – Set of Guidelines*. Timisoara: Ed. Politehnica. ISBN 978-606-554-061-3.

Index

A
Abma, H. J., 232
Abrami, P. C., 144
Absorption view-of-learning, 12
Academic type, 296–300, 311
ACAT system, 151, 154–155
    calculated cumulated score for, 152
    vs. Cambridge thinking skills assessment score, 153
    coding transcripts, 149
    vs. human coder, 150–151
Accountability, 92
Ackerman, P. L., 29, 32
Acquisition of expertise, 49
Actions and timeline (ACT) tool, 133
    cognitive functions, 133–134
Activities and learning monitoring tool, Meshat, 60
Adaptive intelligent knowledge assessment system (IKAS), 179–181, 185–195
Adobe Captivate, web-based training course, 234
Affect, 17, 46, 89–106, 261, 270, 298, 321, 354–355
AGENT-UM, 195
Ahlberg, M., 183
Albion, P. R., 275, 281
Aleven, V., 218
Alexander, P. A., 29, 32
Algozzine, R., 260
Allison-Bunnell, S., 15
Allport, G. W., 250
Almond, R. G., 163
Alvarez Valdivia, I. M., 111–124
Alwi, A., 11–20
Amelang, M., 223
American Society for Training & Development (ASTD), 233
Amtmann, R., 343–357

Anderson, J. R., 25, 27–28, 106, 180
Anderson, L., 201–202, 204–205, 209
Anderson, L. W., 27
Anderson, R., 116
Anderson, R. C., 93–95
Anderson, T., 12, 113, 115–116, 143, 147
Andone, D., 344, 359–375
Angeli, C., 116, 143
Annotated causal representation, 170
    coding and analysis of, 172
Anohina, A., 179–181, 185, 187, 189, 192
Anyouzoa, A., 56
Archer, W., 116, 143, 147
Argyris, C., 250–252
Aristotle, 78, 244, 245
Armstrong, T. R., 292
Arvaja, M., 116
Assessment, 5, 31, 83–87, 143–155, 159–174, 179–195, 199–214, 217–224, 317
Assessment module (AM), 86
    elaborate, 86
Assessment of complex learning in capstone units, 199–200
    capstone units, 200–203
    child development (case study), 208
        assessment, 210–211
        learning outcomes, 208–209
        scaffolding, 209–210
        technologies, 211–212
    comments, 214
    common themes, 212–213
    computing science (case study), 205
        assessment, 206–207
        learning outcomes, 205
        scaffolding, 205–206
        technologies, 208
    study, 204–205
    technologies to support assessment, 203
Astin, A. W., 321

Astleitner, H., 202
Asun, J., 252
Athanasiou, T., 106
Attitude toward working in teams and learning style, 297
Attwell, G., 326
Australian Qualifications Framework Council, 199
Ausubel, D. P., 95, 181
Automated online-coaching, 223–224
Automatic Content Analysis Tool (ACAT), 144
    development and use, 147
Automating measurement of critical thinking, 143–144
    critical thinking, 144–146
    discussion, 153–155
    discussion forums, 146–149
    methodology, 149–150
    results and findings, 150–153
Autonomisers, 53
Avouris, N., 38
Azevedo, R., 57

B
Bailin, S., 144
Bain, J., 202–204, 207
Bain, J. D., 244, 246
Baker, E. L., 164, 166
Banyard, P. E., 326
Barab, S. A., 161–162
Barker, P., 38
Barrett, L. F., 96, 102
Bartell, E., 145
Bartlett, F. C., 97
Barton, E. E., 161
Bastiaens, T. J., 232
Bath, D., 202
Baudet, S., 69
Beach, R. W., 217
Beckner, C., 274
Behavioral view-of-learning, 12
Béler, C., 57
Belland, B. R., 39
Bendixen, L. D., 163
Benedek, J., 365
Benmahamed, D., 53
Benson, B., 201
Berardi-Coletta, B., 213
Bereiter, C., 132, 144, 246
Berggren, C., 51–52, 57
Berliner, D., 3
Berliner, D. C., 105
Bernard, R. M., 144

Berry, L. H., 15–16
Bert-Erboul, 314
Biggs, J., 24, 203
Biofunctional embodiment, 92
Biofunctional schemas, 95
    theory, 94–96
Biotechnology course, DCP-based structure of management of, 253
Biotechnology education, 243
Black, G., 15, 19
Blanchard, H. E., 96
Blitsas, P., 67–87
Blogs, Meshat, 60
Bloom, B. S., 89, 181, 201
Bloom's taxonomy, 181, 201, 277
    categories in, 201
    revised, 201
Blythe, R., 274
Boakaerts, M., 116
Bogler, R., 261
Boix-Mansilla, V., 105
Bonk, C. J., 116, 143
Borokhovski, E., 144
Borun, M., 15
Boud, D., 218
Boulos, M. K., 28, 203
Bower, M., 24, 28
Boyne, C., 361–362
Bransford, J. D., 92–94, 245–246, 248–249, 252–253
Brantley-Dias, L., 283
Brinck, T., 38
Brito Mírian, C. A., 58
Brockett, R. G., 340
Brook, C., 202
Brooker, R., 313
Brookshear, G., 77
Brown, A. H., 201
Brown, A. L., 245
Brown, B., 232–333
Brown, J. S., 3, 160–161, 180
Brown, K. L., 244–246
Brown, S., 14
Brown, S. I., 2
Brown, S. J., 360, 371
Bruner, J., 130
Brunstein, J. C., 218
Brush, T., 231
Bryan, C., 202
Budd, 116
Burgess, C., 68
Burns, M., 24, 202
Burtis, J., 132

Index

Burton, R. R., 180
Butler, D. L., 209, 213
Buyer, L. S., 213
Bybee, J., 274
Byrnes, R., 203

C
Cagnat, J., 55
Calandra, B., 283
Cambridge thinking skills assessment, 152
    and ACAT system weighted score, 153
Campbell, J., 313
Campbell, J. P., 202
Campbell, N., 355
Cañas, A. J., 183
Capacity of adaptation, 189
Caperton, G., 161
Capstone units, 29, 199–214
    assessment of complex learning in,
        199–200
    child development (case study), 208
        assessment, 210–211
        learning outcomes, 208–209
        scaffolding, 209–210
        technologies, 211–212
    common themes, 212–213
    computing science (case study), 205
        assessment, 206–207
        learning outcomes, 205
        scaffolding, 205–206
        technologies, 208
    study, 204–205
    technologies to support assessment, 203
Carey, 248
Carlson, S., 128, 130
Carroll, J. M., 230
Carteaux, R., 162
Casanova, M., 120
Casey, H. B., 259
Categorization unit, 115–116
Cates, W. M., 39
Causal representations
    in vivo codes, 172
CELDA conference (2004), 1
Cerdán, R., 313–314
Chambers, M., 15
Chan, A., 274
Chan, C., 132
Change process, 259
Chan, J. C. Y., 218
Cheema, I., 16–17
Chen, N.-S., 6
Chen, S., 161

Chiarelli, S., 113, 120
Child development (case study), 208
    assessment, 210–211
    learning outcomes, 208–209
    scaffolding, 209–210
    technologies, 211–212
Chi, M. T. H., 163, 165, 171
Chin, J., 163, 165, 292
Cho, K., 218
Christensen, M. H., 274
Chronbach, 279
Chudowsky, N., 163
Chung, G. K. W. K., 164, 166
Churchill, D., 203
Cimolino, L., 181
Clancey, W. J., 180
Clariana, R. B., 165, 167
Clark, R. C., 12–14
Clarkson, B., 202
Clegg, K., 202
Clements, A. C., 93
Clore, G. L., 105
Cochrane, C., 147
Cocking, R. R., 245
Coding unit, 116
Coffinet, T., 56
Cognitive activator, 132
Cognitive preferences, 15–17
Cognitive regulation, 114
    with descriptors, categories of, 117
Cognitive styles, 16
    construct, 16–17
    doctoral-study, experimental design of, 18
Cognitive Styles Analysis (CSA) tool, 18
Cognitive tools, 127–138, 328
    defined, 130
Cognitive view-of-learning, 12
Cohen, 319
Cole, 112
Collaborative annual action planning process
    (CAP), 128
Collaborative cognitive tools (CCT), 127,
        129–130
    CAP with, 129
    collaborative strategy process, 131
    for shared representations, 127–138
Collaborative cognitive tools for shared
        representations, 127–129
    cognitive tools for collaborative shared
        representations, 130–131
    collaborative construction of
        development goals, 132–133

Collaborative cognitive tools (*cont.*)
    identifying development needs, 131–132
    mapping teachers' combined pedagogical skills in use of ICT, 134
    practical alignment of development goals, 133–134
    collaboratively created and shared representation, 135–136
        implementation of national information strategy and policies, 136–137
    information strategy process and collaborative cognitive tools, 129–130
Collaborative construction of development goals, tools for, 132–133
Collaborative learning, 39, 46, 112–115, 119, 135, 143, 159, 326, 340–341, 344, 369
    computer conferencing as environment for encouraging, 143
Collaboratively created and shared representation, 135–136
    implementation of national information strategy and policies, 136–137
Collaborative strategy process, 131
Collier, P., 200
Collins, A., 3, 161, 180
Combs, B., 246
Comments, 214
Communities of practice (CoPs), 58
Community college, 315, 321–322
Complex learning, 26, 49, 199–214
    See also Ill-structured problems
Complex problem solving, 162, 167–170
    alternative assessment strategies for, 159–160
    assessment of game-based learning, 163–165
        external assessment, 165–166
        internal assessment, 166–167
        game-based learning in digital age, 160–162
    methods for external and internal game-based assessment, 167
        coding and analysis, 171–172
        external assessment strategies, 169–170
        internal assessment strategies, 170
    Study on Surviving in Space, 167–168
"Computational system," teleological structure describing, 76

Computer networks, search entry example of, 82
Computer supported collaborative learning (CSCL), 113, 115
Computing science (case study), 205
    assessment, 206–207
    learning outcomes, 205
    scaffolding, 205–206
    technologies, 208
Concept map based intelligent knowledge assessment system, 179–181
    concept maps as knowledge assessment tools, 181–182
        concept map tasks, 183–184
        representation of concept maps, 182–183
        response format and scoring system, 184–185
    IKAS
        operation scenario, 187–189
        principles of IKAS, 185–186
    results of practical use of IKAS
        change of degree of task difficulty, 192
        feedback provided to students, 193–194
        improvements of functionality of IKAS, 192
        organization of practical testing, 190
        student opinions about concept maps as knowledge assessment tools, 190–192
Concept map/mapping, 68, 71–77, 83–87, 165, 179–195
    assessment, 83–85
    based IKAS, evolution of, 188
    concept map constructing procedure, 71–77
        expert's relational structure representation, 73
        expert's teleological structure representation, 75–77
        expert's transformational structure representation, 74
        hyponymic and hypernymic relations, 72
        meronymic relations, 72
    constructed by Cmaptools, 72
    defined, 71
    describing different kinds of meronymy, 74
    as knowledge assessment tools, 181–182, 190–192
    as pedagogical tools, 181
    representation of, 182–183
    represented as directed graph, 182
    represented as heterogeneous graph, 183

Index

represented as homogeneous attribute graph, 183
represented as undirected graph, 182
shallow assessment by Semandix, 84
tasks, 183–184
theoretical basis of, 181
Conceptual research design model, 17
Conlon, T., 181
Constantinides, 325
Constructive alignment, constructive alignment, 24
Constructivist-museum context, 19
Content analysis, 30, 135, 144, 146–147, 153, 334–335
Contextual prerequisite, 92
Cooperation and collaboration process, 112
Cooperative learning, 111–124
  regulated learning in, 114
  tasks/activities, 113
    language, 112
Copeland, C. R., 14
Corbin, J., 135
Corich, S., 143–155
Corich, S. P., 147, 151
Cortez, C., 50, 56–57
Costich, C., 113
Coudert, T., 57
Covarrubias, M. A., 114
Crammand, 314
Creswell, J., 204
Crisp, G., 203
Critical thinkers, 145
Critical thinking, 30, 143–155, 160, 200, 274, 277–278, 282, 285, 313–316, 318
  automating measurement of, 143–144
  discussion, 153–155
  discussion forums, 146–149
  methodology, 149–150
  models, 148
    for identifying engagement in, 148
  results and findings, 150–153
  tools, 146
'Critical Thinking: What It Is and Why It Counts,' 144
Croft, W., 274
Cronbach, 223–224, 236
Cuper, P., 275
Curriculum design, 34, 203–204, 214
Cuthell, J. P., 58
"Cyclic definition," 81

D

Daniels, M., 344, 355
Da Nóbrega, G. M., 58
Darling-Hammond, L., 245
Da Rocha, F. E. L., 180–181, 191
Dart, B., 260
Data bases, search entry example of, 81
Davidsen, P. I., 3
Davis, J., 32
Dawes, L., 112, 116
Dawson, C., 260
DCP-based structure of management of biotechnology course, 253
DCP, demonstration project applying, 250–252
  description, 252–254
  key insights from demonstration project, 255
De Bie, D., 246
De Bono, E., 292–293
Dee-Lucas, D., 28
Deese, J., 181
Dehler, G. E., 245–246
De Jong, T., 28
De Kleer, J., 180
De Kleijn, J., 246
Delacruz, G. C., 166
De la Teja, I., 145
Demetriou, A., 173
DeMott, B., 315
Denhière, G., 69
Dennen, V. P., 58
Dennon, 166
De Oliveira, K. M., 58
Department of Systems Theory and Design of Riga Technical University, 179
Dependency model of causally related self-directed learning indicators, 335
Der-Thanq, Ch, 112
Descartes, R., 2
Design-based Elearning course, self-direction indicators for evaluating, 325–326
  discussion, 339–341
  'Elearning,' 330–333
  methods, 333–335
  results
    indicators of self-direction in students' self-reflection blog-posts, 335–336
    interrelations between indicators of self-direction, 337–339
    week-dependent indicators of self-direction, 336–337

Design-based Elearning (*cont.*)
    self-reflection at design-based learning, 327–330
    with social software, 326–327
Design-based learning, 326–333
    defined, 326
    outline of course for, 330
Design of curricula, 26
De Souza, F. S. L., 183
Després, C., 55–56
Development centered paradigm (DCP), 248–255, 247–250, 255
    considering beneficiaries of education, 247–248
    considering purposes of education, 247
    cultural transcendence in education, 248
    transcending TCM and LCM with, 247–248
Development goals (GOALS) tool, *see* GOALS tool
Development goals set by schools, focuses of, 135
Dewey, J., 144–145
Dewey, K., 144–145
Dickey, M., 28
Dickey, M. D., 162
Diener, E., 105
Dierking, L. D., 19
Digital age
    advantage, 90
    learning to solve problems in, 1–2
        developing problem solving expertise, 3–4
        problem solving, 2–3
        problem solving in digital age, 4–5
        tools and technologies, 5–6
Digital literacy, 42
Digital students, 359–375
    defined, 361
Dijkstra, E. W., 4
Dillenbourg, P., 113, 116
Directive architecture, 13
Discussion forums, 143–155, 206–208, 211, 317, 344–345
Distributed database administration system, 81–82
Dodge, T., 162
Doherty, J. J., 144
Dolores, P., 217
Domain knowledge, 25
Dominowski, R. L., 213
Dondlinger, M. J., 162

Donohue, 116
Dörner, D., 2, 4–5
Dörnyei, Z., 283
Dorsey, L. T., 231
"DRAM-read Operation," 74
    transformational structure describing, 75
Dresang, E. T., 273
Dreyfus, H. L., 3, 20, 106
Dreyfus, S. E., 3, 20, 106
Dron J., 361–362
Dudley, C., 27
Duffy, T., 161
Duguid, P., 161, 360, 371
Dukes, R., 163, 292
Dumais, S., 67
Dummer, P., 5, 163–167, 172–174, 181, 217–224, 317
Dunkle, M. E., 163
Dunlap, J. C., 200
Durán, D., 111
Dyke, R. B., 16
Dynamic evaluation of enhanced problem-solving (DEEP) method, 165–166

E
ECTS (European Credit Transfer System), 115
Educational assessment, 163
    within game-based learning environments, 164
Educational practice, thematic organizer for two approaches to, 106
Educational technologies, 14, 128, 154, 260–262, 265, 270, 357
Education, essential elements of
    2nd/3rd-person, 90
    1st-person, 91–92
Edward de Bono, 292
Edward de Bono's Cognitive Research Trust (CoRT), 293
Efklides, A., 111
Egbert, J., 282
Eidsmo, A., 295
Eigler, G., 166, 217
Ekker, K., 291–312
Elder, L., 145
'Elearning,' design-based learning course, 330–333
Electronic performance support, 229–240
    discussion, 238–240
    method
        criterion and enroute measures, 235–236
        materials, 234–235

Index

participants, 233
procedures, 236
purpose, 233
results, 237–238
and WBT, comparing impact of, 229–233
Electronic performance support systems (EPSS), 230, 238–240
Eliaa, I., 173
Elliot, G. J., 38
Ellis, A., 203
Ellis, N. C., 274
Ellis, R., 24
Ellis, R. A., 203
Elloumi, F., 12
Elsom-Cook, M., 14
Engeström, Y., 328, 340
Englehart, M. D., 89
English education, 315
English, M. C., 259–271
Ennis, R. H., 146
Enrichment Module (EnM), 86
'Epistemic games,' 161
Erasmus mobility case, ViCaDiS, piloting evaluation, 366–368
ERIC databases, 162
Ericsson, K. A., 2–4, 26, 165, 171, 174
Ericsson, K. C., 26
Eric Wier, 146
Ermine, J.-L., 53
Erstad, O., 42
Ertmer, P. A., 259
Eseryel, D., 159–174
ESSAIM (learning tools), 55
Estrevel, L. B., 114
European Commission, 128
European master of interactive media (EMIM), 330
Moodle environment, 331
European Union, 359
Eutropian Federation, 309
Evans, W., 147
Ewald, J. D., 283
Expanded learning circle, 52
Expanding global awareness, employing virtual collaborative exchanges for, 344–345
discussion and limitations, 355–356
study, 345
evaluation, 348–355
pedagogies employed, 346–348
setting, 345–346
Experience sharing, 49–62

Expertise, 2–6, 23–34, 38, 50, 55–58, 60–61, 106, 164, 181, 201, 203, 206, 208, 212–214, 218, 231, 244, 246, 251, 274
cognitive measure of, 4
development, 3–4
Expert's relational structure representation, 73
Expert's teleological structure representation, 75–77
Expert's transformational structure representation, 74
Exploratory architecture, 14
Extrinsic performance support, 230

F
Face-to-face coaching, 218
Facione, P., 144
Facione, P. A., 144–145
Fähnrich, B., 366, 369
Falk, J. H., 19
Feedback, 1, 4, 12–13, 27, 40, 53–54, 56, 60, 62, 155, 163–164, 166, 171, 173–174, 180, 186, 188–190, 192–195, 202, 204, 206–209, 211–214, 218, 220–224, 234, 274, 294–295, 329, 332–333, 338–339, 349, 361, 371
Ferrarini, T., 343–357
Fetterman, D. M., 218
Fiedler, S., 328, 339, 344
Finger, M., 252
First-person education, 89–92, 105
goal of, 91
knowledge acquisition, 89
in 2nd/3rd-person education, 92–93
methodology, 97–98
knower and understanding statements, 101–104
participants' first person-related intuitions, 98–100
from 2nd/3rd-person prior knowledge to 1st-person prior understanding, 93–94
structural and biofunctional schema theories of knowledge acquisition, 94–95
understanding as embodied form following function, 95–96
wholetheme, whole-body, biofunctional activity, 96–97
First person-related intuitions about knowing, knower, and understanding processes

First person-related intuitions (*cont.*)
  discussion, 99–100
  participants, design, and material, 98
  Pearson correlations among, 99
  procedure, 98
  results, 99
Fischer, F., 113, 116, 165
Fisher, D., 274
Fletcher-Flinn, C. M., 27
Flower, L., 218
Flowers, C. P., 260
Foguem, K. B., 57
FORMID (learning tools), 55
Fountain, S. J., 325
Fowler, C. J., 38
Fox, D. L., 283
Frand, 361
Franz, R. S., 245
Free-text response, LSA, 68
  assessment system, architecture of, 85
Frey, N., 274
Frydenberg, M., 344, 370
Fullan, M., 260–261
Functionally mature individual, 247
Functional schema theory of understanding, 94
Functional system, 70
Functional system module (FSM), 85
"Fundamentals of Artificial Intelligence," 195
Funke, J., 172
Furst, E. J., 89
Fusco, J., 58

G
Gabriel, 96
Gadanidis, 46
Gadio, C. T., 128, 130
Gagatsisa, A., 173
Galarneau, L., 161
Galizio, L. M., 259–271
Gallini, J. K., 28
Game-based assessment, methods for external/internal, 167
  coding and analysis, 171–172
  external assessment strategies, 169–170
  internal assessment strategies, 170
  Study on Surviving in Space, 167–168
Game-based environment, goals of, 167
Game-based learning, 159–174
  assessment of, 163–165
    external assessment, 165–166
    internal assessment, 166–167
  in digital age, 160–162
  See also Simulation-games as learning experience

Games, 161
Gamson, W., 163, 292
Garbowski, 145
Gardiner, J., 200
Gardner, H., 105, 248
Garner, B. J., 20
Garrison, D., 113, 116
Garrison, D. R., 143, 147–149, 151
Garrot, E., 53, 57
Garrot-Lavoué, E., 58
Garrot's taxonomy, 53
Gee, J. P., 161–162
Gelman, 248
Geneste, L., 57
Genuine understanding processes, 105–106
George, S., 53, 57
Gergle, D., 38
Gery, G., 230–231
Ge, X., 168, 159–174
Giancarlo, C. A., 145
Gick, M. L., 163
Gilabert, R., 313
Gilbert, C. G., 314, 321
Gil, L., 313
Gillespie, A., 329, 338, 340
Gilligan, C., 250
Ginsberg, M. B., 253
Glaser, B., 135
Glaser, C., 218
Glaser, R., 33, 163, 171
Glina, M., 116
Global awareness, 343–357
Global environmental crises, 30
  procedure, 30
  results, 30–34
    activities and resources, 32
    aims/outcomes in relation to phases of acquisition, 31
    discussion and recommendations, 32–34
    learner characteristics, 32
GOALS tool, 132
  cognitive functions, 132–133
Goethe's Erlkönig, 274
Golden, P. A., 292
Goodell, J., 143
Goodman, D. R., 16
Goodrum, D. A., 231
Goodyear, P., 24, 203
Gosen, J., 292
Gosper, M., 23–34, 203–204
Gould, S., 32
Gouli, E., M., 181

Gowin, B., 71
Gowin, D. B., 181, 185
Graesser, A., 67
Graf, S., 6
Graham, S., 217
Grammatical/syntax analyzer, interconnection between Semandix normalization module and, 86
Graph patterns, operation scenario, 187
　examples, 187
Graudina, V., 187
Gravatt, B., 27
Greene, J., 113
Gregg, M., 91, 97, 100
Grigoriadou, M., 67–87
Groeben, N., 172
Grounded theory, 135
Grundspenkis, J., 179–195
Grundspenkis, K., 179–195
Guéraud, V., 55
Gueye, O., 56
Guided-discovery architecture, 13
Guilford, J., 16
Guilloteaux, M. J., 283
Gunawardena, C., 115, 118, 147
Guzey, S. S., 284

H

Hadjerrouit, S., 37–47
Hakkarainen, K., 112
Hakkinen, P., 116
Halpern, D. F., 145
Hanesian, H., 95
Hanna, S. E., 231
Hansen, M. A., 144
Hara, N., 143, 147
Hardy, I., 173
Harmon, S. W., 147
Harri-Augstein, S., 329
Harris, J., 274–275, 277
Hart, L., 249
Hartman, H., 317
Haswell, R. H., 217
Hause, M., 344
Hayes, J. R., 218
Haynes, R. B., 231
Hedberg, J., 24, 204
Hein, G. E., 19
Henri, F., 116, 147
Herl, H. E., 166
Hermans, H. J. M., 329, 339
Hershey, G. L., 249
Hesketh, B., 28

Hess, F. M., 262
Hetherington, L., 28
Hewitt, J., 203
Hiemstra, R., 340
Higgins, J. M., 131
Higher education, 25, 39, 103, 190, 199–200, 203, 243–245, 247, 255, 343–345, 360, 363, 368
Hill, W. H., 90
HILVE, 223–224
HIMATT, 5
Hiragana, 27
Hofer, M., 274–275, 277
Hofstede, G., 250–251
Holland, L., 260
Holzman, P., 16
Hong, N. S., 163
Horizon Project, 344–345
Howell, C., 252
Hsieh, I.-L., 181
Hubbard, L., 181
Huber, B., 231
Hughes, G., 146
Huizinga, K., 160
Hull, D. A., 86
Human cognitive preferences, see Learning style
Human-computer interaction (HCI), 11–20, 38
Human development, 106, 243–255
　demonstration project applying DCP, 250–252
　　description, 252–254
　　key insights from demonstration project, 255
　Learning Centered Model (LCM) of education, 245–247
　paradigm, moving beyond teaching and learning into, 243–244
　Teaching Centered Model (TCM) of education, 243–244
　transcending TCM and LCM with DCP, 247–248
　　development centered paradigm (DCP), 248–250
Humans' processing information, research terms for, 16
Hung, D., 112
Hung, H. T., 274
Hunt, D. L., 231
Hunt, E., 20
Hunt, L. M., 147
Hutchison, D., 28

HyLighter, 314, 316
  capabilities of, 316
  screen with color coding, 316

I

ICT tools, *see* Information and communications technology (ICT) tools
Identifying development needs (NEEDS) tool, 131
  cognitive functions, 132
Ifenthaler, D., 5, 159–174, 217–224, 317
Iiskala, T., 113
IKAS, *see* Intelligent knowledge assessment system (IKAS)
Ill-structured problems, 2
Immaturity–maturity theory, 250
Individualisers, 53
Information and communications technology (ICT) tools, 11–12
  educational process, influence and change in, 180
  students' competences, 134
  use of, tool for mapping teachers' combined pedagogical skills in, 134
  use to enhance museum learning experience, 15
Information and communication technologies (ICTs)., 2, 115, 180
Information, Constraint, Activity, Rule, Entity (ICARE), 53
Information society program, 128
Information strategy, 127–138
  process, 129–130
Inglis, A., 16, 19
Ingram, A., 38
Instructional architecture, 12–14
Instructional design, 3–4, 6, 11–20, 23–34, 37–47, 49–62, 160, 162–163, 233, 238, 326–329
  process, comparison of phases of self-direction and, 327
Instructional environments, 13
Intellectual skill development, 25–26
  domain knowledge, 25
  intermediate/procedural phase, 25
  VanLehn's model, 25
Intelligent knowledge assessment system (IKAS)
  concept map based, 179–181
    examples of graph patterns, 187
  concept maps as knowledge assessment tools, 181–182
  concept map tasks, 183–184
  representation of concept maps, 182–183
  response format and scoring system, 184–185
  evolution of CM based, 188
  and its environment, 186
  numerical data of practical testing of, 190
  operation scenario, 187–189
  principles of, 185–186
  results of, practical use of
    change of degree of task difficulty, 192
    feedback provided to students, 193–194
    improvements of functionality of, 192
    organization of practical testing, 190
    student opinions about concept maps as knowledge assessment tools, 190–192
Intelligent tutoring systems (ITS), 180
  functional architecture of, 180
Intercultural dimensions in European education through onLine Education (IDEELS), 292
International association for development of the internet society (IADIS), 1
International collaboration, 370
International society for performance improvement (ISPI), 233
International society for technology in education (ISTE), 262
International teams, 357
Interpersonal type, 296–300, 311
Intuition, 97–98, 100–102, 105–106
Iran-Nejad, A., 89–106
Irrational or animalistic affect/emotion *vs.* rational or intellectual knowing and understanding, 96

J

Jacobson, C., 28
Jacobson, M. J., 28, 33
Jamieson-Proctor, R., 39
Jan, 123
Janet, 307
Jantzi, D., 260
Järvelä, S., 111, 113, 116
Jarvenoja, 111
Ježek, K., 67
Jeffrey, L., 143–155
Jelsma, O., 28
Jhon, 122
Jim, 121
Johansson, O., 260
John, P., 39, 45

Index

Johnson, D., 112
Johnson, L., 345
Johnson-Laird, P. N., 164
Johnson, M. K., 92–94
Johnson, R., 112
Johnson, T. E., 165, 313–322
Jonas, A., 114
Jonassen, D. H., 2, 19, 24, 28, 130, 163, 202–203
Jones, 38, 147, 361
Joosten, V., 16, 19
Journal of Management Education, 245
Judy, J. E., 29, 32
Jutti, 130

K

Kaftarian, S. J., 218
Kagan, J., 16
Kajamies, A., 113
Kanejiya, D., 67
Kanfer, R., 29, 32
Kantaro (multimedia CD), 27
Kanuka, H., 143
Karacapilidis, N., 58
Karasavvidis, I., 130
Karl, 122
Kasvi, J. J., 232
Katakana, 27
Kate, 122
Kaya, K. K., 144
Kebritchi, M., 284
Keengwe, J., 275
Keller, J. M., 318, 321
Kelly, A. P., 262
Kemp, D. R., 16
Khalifa, M., 28, 33
Kim, C., 313–322
Kinnunen, R., 113
Kinshuk, D. G., 1–6, 143–155
Kintsch, E., 218
Kintsch, W., 68
Kirschner, P., 112
Kirschner, P. A., 2–4
Klabbers, J. H., 165
Klawe, M., 38
Kleiner, B., 259
Klein, G., 16
Klein, G. A., 2, 4
Klein, J. D., 145, 229–240
Kline, P., 20
Knapczyk, D., 231
Knower and understanding statements, intuitions

educational psychology class, undergraduates
    discussion, 102–103
    materials, design, and instrument, 101
    mean consistency ratings for knower, understanding, and affective processes, 102
    participants, 101
    procedure, 101
    results, 102
educational psychology class, undergraduates and graduate students
    pair-wise Pearson correlations among marker knower, 104
    participants, material, and procedure, 103
    results, 103–104
Knowing, 51, 57, 89–106, 113, 154, 246, 274, 279, 326, 361
Knowledge, 91
    acquisition
        biofunctional schema theory, 94–96
        human development and, 106
        in 2nd/3rd-person education, 92–93
        theory of, 92
    definition of, 90
    domain, 25
    2nd/3rd-person source of, 90
Knowledge assessment, 166, 179–195, 218
    tools, concept maps as, 181–182
        concept map tasks, 183–184
        representation of concept maps, 182–183
        response format and scoring system, 184–185
Knowledge base, 4, 25, 29, 57, 67–87, 91, 254, 262, 273–285
    administration module, 70–82
Knowledge based systems (KBS), 57–58
Knowledge management (KM), 49
    in schools, 128
Knowles, M., 326, 329
Kocsis-Baan, M., 366, 369
Koedinger, K. R., 218
Koehler, M., 275
Koehler, M. J., 275
Kohlberg, L., 250
Kolb, A. Y., 51
Kolb D. A., 51, 253
Kolb's theory, 15
Komis, V., 38
Kommers, P., 130

Kormos, J., 283
Koschmann, T., 159–160
Koszalka, T. A., 4, 165–166
Krathwohl, D., 202
Krathwohl, D. R., 27, 90
Kreijns, K., 112
Kremizis, A., 77
Kukusska-Hulme, A., 38
Kulik, C. C., 27
Kulik, J., 27
Kumar, A., 67
Kunkel, S. W., 245
Kuo, L.-J., 116
Kurkela, L., 366, 369
Kurshan, R., 91
Kuswara, A., 24
Kwok, R. C.-W., 28, 33, 213
Kylämä, M., 128

L
Laffey, J., 231
Lambert, J., 275
LaMont Johnson, D., 39, 41
Lam, S.-F., 218
Landauer, T., 67
Landauer, T. K., 68
Language, cooperative learning tasks, 112
Laperrousaz, C., 56
Laru, J., 113
Last, M., 344, 355
Latent semantic analysis (LSA), 68
  drawback, 68
Latto, 130
Lauder, A., 262
Laurillard, D., 38
Lavelle, E., 217
Lavendelis, E., 195
Lavonen, J., 130
Lavoué, É., 49–62
Law, E., 344–345
Lazeron, N., 249
LCC (Learning to Collaborate by Collaborating), 56
Leacock, T., 38–39
Leaders for twenty-first century, 259–260
  discussion, 269–270
  literature review, 260–261
    theoretical lens, 261
    transformational leadership, 261–262
  methods, 262–263
  results, 263–265
    encouraging others, 267–268
    learning, 265
  use of technology, 266–267
  uses of technology, future, 268–269
Leadership, 51, 56, 60–61, 128, 138, 168, 202, 260–264, 266, 269, 292–293, 305–306
  requirements, non-US countries', 263–264
Learner centered instruction/education, 245
Learning, 91
  activities, Meshat tools to support, 55
    experience sharing tools, 57–58
    monitoring tools, 55–57
  contract, 57
  definition of, 90
  environment, 11, 13–14, 19–20, 24, 58, 112, 114–115, 118–124, 137, 149, 159–174, 217, 223, 244, 314, 325–328, 331–333, 339, 344, 348, 359–375
  management systems, 23
  progression, 223–224
  style, 15, 45–46, 51, 291–312
  system/perspective, 24–25
  theory, 46, 51, 61, 161
  types, 12
Learning Centered Model (LCM), 243–255
  characteristics of, 246–247
  of education, 245–247
  with DCP, transcending TCM and, 247–248
Learning experience, simulation-games as, 291–292
  analysis
    analysis of variance, 299–300
    learning style as categorical variable, 296–299
    learning style as continuous variables: regression analysis, 300–304
    statements made by participants during post-simulation debriefing teleconferences, 304–310
  background, 292–294
  data collection, 294–295
  procedure, 295–296
Learning style, 15
  attitude toward working in teams and, 297
  as categorical variable
    analysis of variance, 299–300
  as continuous variables: regression analysis, 300–304
  simulation as learning experience and, 298
    experience, academic type, interpersonal type and attitude toward teamwork, 299

personality trait and attitude towards teamwork, 303
predicted with interaction terms, 303
simulation-games
as categorical variable, 296–299
variables, 301
Lebow, D. G., 317
Ledesma, P., 259–271
Lee, J. K., 283
Lee, M. J. W., 274
Lehmann, A. C., 26
Lehtinen, E., 113
Lei, J., 123, 275
Lei, Q., 283
Leithwood, K., 260–261
Leroux, P., 56
Levene, 319
Levin, B. B., 260
Levine, A., 345
Levine, J. M., 345
Levy, M., 345, 356
Lewis, L., 259
Lick, D. W., 317
Li, H., 46
Li, M., 167
Ling, P., 16, 19
Lin, T., 6
Lippincott, J., 231
Lipponen, L., 112, 120
Littleton, K., 112
Liu, T.-C., 6, 39, 41
Lloyd, M. M., 275, 281
López Benavides, D. M., 111–124
Lord, G., 274
Lovins, J. B., 86
Lowe, C., 115, 147
Lowe, K., 203
Luce-Kapler, R., 273
Lugo, J. O., 249
Lukashenko, R., 181, 195
Lund, K., 68
Luokkanen, T., 113

M
MacDonald, H., 247
Macy, M., 161
Madden, 361
Maddux, C. D., 39
Madox, E. N., 292
Mandl, H., 165
Mao, J., 232–233
MAPLET, 23–25
case study, 30

procedure, 30
results, 30–34
framework, 26–27
in action, 29–30
alignment along horizontal axis, 26–28
analysis of global environmental crises guided by, 31
sequencing down vertical axis, 29
intellectual skill development, 25–26
Mapping teachers' combined pedagogical skills in use of ICT, tools for, 134
Maramba, I., 203
Marilyn, 96
Marks, P., 317
Marsh, E. E., 146
Marsh, G. E., 93, 105
Martínez, T., 313
Martinidale, T., 39
Marty, P. F., 14
Masduki, I., 166
MASK, 53
Mason, R., 143
Massey, W., 203
Massively multiplayer online games (MMOGs), 159–160, 162
Surviving in Space, 167
Matching aims, processes, learner expertise and technologies, *see* MAPLET
Mayer, R. E., 12, 15–16, 28, 33, 145
Mayes, J. T., 38
Mayes, T., 130
Mbala, A., 56
McAlister, K., 314
McCombs, B., 246
Mccuddy, M. K., 243–255
McFarlane, A., 163
McGee, S., 163
McKay, E., 11–20
McKeachie, W. J., 105
McKlin, T., 147
McLarin, K., 169, 171
McLoughlin, C., 274
McMahon, C., 231
McManus, P., 232
McNab, P., 6
McNamara, S. E., 20
McNeill, M., 26, 199–214
Meisalo, V., 130
Mel, 123
Mendenhall, A., 313–322
Mengel, T., 50
Mental model, 14–15, 19, 164, 218, 314–315, 317–322

Mercer, N., 112, 116, 120
Merisalo, S., 325–341
Meronymy
  concept map/mapping describing different kinds of, 74
  different types of, 73
  meronymic relations, concept map constructing procedure, 72–73
  examples of, 73
Merriam, S. B., 263
Merrill, M. D., 3, 314, 321
Meshat (KM and WEB 2.0 methods for project-based learning), 49–50, 59
  case study: project management training course
    course organisation, 50–53
    observed problems, 53–55
    dashboards, 59–60
    interface, 59
    platform for tutors and students, 58–61
    tools to support learning activities, 55
      experience sharing tools, 57–58
      monitoring tools, 55–57
Metacognition, 57, 59, 204, 314
Metacognitive tool, Meshat, 59
Method for Knowledge System Management (MASK) approach, 53
Meyer, K., 143
Meyer, K. A., 146
Mezeske, B., 244, 246
Michael, D., 161
Michel, C., 49–62
Mike, 122
Millan, K., 146
Miller, R. B., 168
Milligan, C., 203
Millogo, 314
Milrad, M., 3
Miner, T., 365
Minnaert, A., 116
MIPITS, 195
Mishra, P., 275
Mislevy, R. J., 163
MMOG, 159–160, 162, 167–168, 170
Mobile and social media tools, 364
Model-facilitated learning, 3
Momentary constellation firing (MCF), 94
Monereo, C., 111
Monitoring tools, 50, 55–62, 332
Monitor, ITU, 39
Moodle learning management system, 149–150
Moore-Steward, T., 260
Moos, L., 260

Moral development, 250
Moreno, R., 15–16
Morgan, 295, 309
Morgan, K., 295
Morse, K., 246
Morse, K. O., 246
Motivation, 34, 40, 43–45, 57, 59, 61, 113, 117, 160, 164, 168, 219, 224, 249, 268, 283, 314–315, 318–322, 344, 354, 362, 373
Muir, H., 27
Multi-agent system, 186
Murphy, E., 147–151, 154
Murphy, J., 262
Museums Australia Constitution, 15
Musonda, D., 71
Myers, M. T., 145
Myllymäki, P., 335

N
Nakazawa, K., 27
Nam, C. S., 38
Namjoshi, K., 81
National Center for Educational Statistics (NCES), 260, 344
National information strategy
  and policies, implementation of, 136–137
  in schools, implementation of, 136
National Professional Qualification for Headship (NPQH), 264
National Transportation Safety Board, 3
Näykki, P., 113
Neiss, 284–285
Nesbit, J. C., 38–39
Newby, T. J., 259
Newell, A., 2, 163
Newman, G., 147
Newman, S. E., 3
New Zealand Ministry of Education, 145
Nguyen, F., 229–240, 355
Nguyen-Ngoc, A. V., 344, 355
Nicholson, P., 112
Nicol, D. J., 203
Nielsen, J., 37–39
Niemi, D., 166
Niess, M. L., 275
Nijhof, W. J., 232
Ning, H., 326
Nisbett, R. E., 165
Nokelainen, P., 37–40, 45
Normalization Module (NoM), 85
  implementation, 86
Northcote, M., 203

Novak, J., 71, 95, 181, 185
Novak, J. D., 181, 185
Novice learner, 90
Nussbaum, M., 50

O

Oblinger, D., 28
O'Dowd, R., 356
OECD, 128
Onchwari, G., 275
O'Neil, H., 181
Ongoing biofunctional activity (OBA), 94–95
Online museums, 11–20
    constructivist environment, 19
    information system, 14–15
        cognitive style construct, 16–17
        considering learners' differences, 15–16
        discussion and conclusions, 19–20
        experimental design, 17–19
        investigating, 11–14
        preparing cognitive space in online exhibits, 15
        validation and reliability testing, 19
Online social annotation tool in college english course, implementation, 313–315
    discussion, 319–322
    method
        data analysis, 318–319
        independent variable, 316–317
        materials, 315
        measures, 317–318
        participants, 315
    results, 319
Open-ended learning, *see* Exploratory architecture
Orava, K., 127–138
Ortony, A., 94–95

P

Paas, F., 201
Paas, F. G., 25–26, 28
Page turners, 13
Palinscar, 246
Palonen, T., 112
Panitz, T., 112
Panksepp, J., 96, 102
Pantaleo, S., 273
Papadopoulos, G., 71
Papakostas, E., 86
Papanastasiou, E. C., 181
Papert, S., 161, 361
Paragon Learning Style Inventory (PLSI), 294–295
Paris, C., 246
Parisot, X., 243–255
Parker, M., 250
Pashnyak, T. G., 58
Pask, G., 16
Pata, K., 123, 325–341
Patel, A., 6
Pattern and Growth in Personality (Gordon W. Allport), 250
Patterson, H. F., 16
Paul, R., 145
Peacock, D., 14
Pea, R. D., 130
Pearson, P. D., 105, 153
Peck, K. L., 19
Pedagogical leadership, 128, 138
Pedagogical team and course organisation, 51
Pedagogical usability of WBLOs, 37–47
    autonomy, 40
    collaboration, 40
    criteria, 39–40
    differentiation, 40
    flexibility, 40
    goal-orientation, 40
    interactivity, 40
    learner-control, 40
    motivation, 40
    multiple representation information, 40
    students' perceptions of, 44
        difference in, 44–45
    time, 40
    understandability, 40
    variation, 40
Pedagogical value of WBLOs, 42
    learning objectives, 42
        methods, 42–43
    survey questionnaire, 43
Pedagogies
    impact of, 353
    student study populations by, 346
Pedagogy and content knowledge based podcasting project, 273–275
    discussion, 282–283
    research, 276
        instruction based on TPACK model, 277–279
        instrument, 276
        participants, 276
        result, 279–282
    theoretical framework, 275
Pellegrino, J. W., 163
Pelton, J. N., 244–245
Perfetti, C. A., 68
Performance interventions, 233, 240

Performance measures, 4
Perkins, C., 147, 149–151, 154
Perkins, D. N., 130
Personality and Organization (Chris Argyris), 250
Personality development, theory of, 250
Personality trait and teamwork (attitude toward), 302
Personal reflexivity, 251
Peters, V., 203
Philips, R., 203
Piaget, J., 250
Piaget, K., 250
Piano Clark, V., 204
Pichert, J. W., 94
Pirie, W. L., 246
Pirnay-Dummer, P., 5, 163, 165–167, 172–174, 181, 217–224, 317
Plato, 145, 244–245
Podcasting, 229, 273–285, 360, 362–363
    production path, 278
Podcasting project, pedagogy and content knowledge based, 273–275
    discussion, 282–283
    research, 276
        instruction based on TPACK model, 277–279
        instrument, 276
        participants, 276
        result, 279–282
    theoretical framework, 275
Poindexter, S., 343–357
Politehnica, 360, 370
Polya, G., 2
Portin, B., 262
Pozdnakovs, D., 192
Practical alignment of development goals, tools for, 133–134
Prasad, S., 67
Prawat, R. S., 95, 100
Preece, J., 14, 39
Preflection, 218, 222–224
Prensky, M., 161–162
Preparation of leaders, 262
Preservice teacher, 273–285
Pressley, M., 327
Prévot, P., 50–51, 53, 57
Prior knowledge
    hypothesis, 93
    to 1st-person prior understanding, 2nd/3rd-person, 93–94
Problem based learning (PBL), 251
Problem centered instructional models, 3

Problem scenario, 169
Problem solving, 2
    developing expertise, 3–4
    in digital age, 4–5
    effective use of technologies in, challenges, 5
    phases/principles, 2
    protocols, coding and analysis of, 171
Procedural knowledge, 98
Prochaska, M., 224
Project-based learning, 49–62, 247, 369
    problems, 50
Project management training course (Meshat case study)
    case study: project management training course
        articulation phase, 52
        expanded learning circle, 52
        investigation/enaction and diffusion, 52
        observed problems, 52–55
        pedagogical team and course organisation, 51
        personal and social actions, 52
        personal experience as result, 52
        phases, 51
        reflection phase, 52
    course organisation, 50–53
Project monitoring dashboard, Meshat, 59
PsycINFO databases, 162

Q
Qian, Y., 39
Qualimetrors, 53
Quantitative content analysis (QCA), 146–147
Question-answering, 314–319, 322

R
Race, P., 202
Rahikainen, M., 112
Raitman, R., 112
Rakes, G., 260
Rakes, G. C., 259
Raths, L. E., 144
Rational or intellectual knowing and understanding *vs.* irrational or animalistic affect/emotion, 96
Raybould, B., 231
Receptive architecture, 13
Reculturing, 261
Reeb-Gruber, S., 243–255
Reeb-Gruber, S. A. G., 247, 249
Reeves, T., 203
Reeves, T. C., 130
Reffay, C., 56

Reflection, 97, 99–100, 105, 113, 132–133, 138, 145–146, 166, 181, 206, 218–220, 223–224, 251–252, 283, 285, 312, 314, 326–330, 332–336, 338, 340–341, 346, 356, 366–367
Reflective thinking, 145
Reflexivity, 251
Regulated learning in cooperative learning tasks in VLE, 114
Regulation models during cooperative tasks in VLE, 118–123
  regulation strategies used by students during cooperative work, 119
Reif, F., 2
Reiser, B. J., 180
Relational structure, Semandix, 69
Rellinger, E. R., 213
Renkl, A., 25
Research model of simulation as learning experience, 295
Research terms for humans' processing information, 16
Response format, 184
RESU, 128, 136
Reuse, Improve and Share Experiment (RISE), 53
Reviewing theory, purpose of, 114
Reznitskaya, A., 116
Rice, M., 314
Rich, D. C., 32
Riding, R., 16–18
Rieber, L. P., 28
Rinaldi, F., 67
Rindermann, H., 223
Ritchie, D., 260
Rittel, H., 2, 5
Rivera, J., 314
Rocha, F. E. L., 180–181, 191
Roehrig, G. H., 284
Rogers, Y., 14
Rohde, J., 166
Romiszowski, A. J., 143
Rose, M., 217
Rossett, A., 232
Ross, G., 130
Rossi, D., 243–255
Rosson, M. B., 230
Rothenberg, C., 274
Rothstein, A., 144
Rouet, J. R., 315
Rourke, L., 116, 147
Ruiz-Primo, M. A., 167, 173, 181, 184–185
Rumelhart, D. E., 94–95

S

Salas, E., 2
Salmon, G., 113, 213
Salonen, P., 111, 113, 116
Salovaara, H., 116
Samuelowicz, K., 202–204, 207, 244, 246
Sanchez, A., 326
Savin-Baden M., 252
Scaffolding, 13
Scandura, J. M., 163
Scarmadalia, 246
Schaller, D. T., 15
Scheele, B., 172
Schegloff, E. A., 130
'The schema: A structural or functional pattern,' 94
Schiffen, L., 315
Schindler, J., 295
Schindler, K., 46, 295
Schlager, M., 58
Schneider, D., 113
Schneider, W., 113
Schôn, D. A., 251
Schön, D. A., 161
School education, WBLOs in, 37
Schooling and the acquisition of knowledge, 93
School subjects and associated WBLOs, 42
Schraw, G., 163
Schroeder, D. L., 246
Schrum, L., 259–271
Schubert, F., 274
Schuler, H., 224
Schultz, S. E., 167
Schunn, C. D., 218
Schweibenz, W., 15
Schwen, T. M., 231
Scott, B. C. E., 16
Seaman, B., 315
Search entry
  example of computer networks, 82
  example of data bases, 81
Second/third-person education, 105
  essential elements of, 90
  knowledge acquisition, 89
Sedig, K., 38
Seel, N. M., 3, 163–164, 166–167, 172, 218, 223, 317, 321
Self-assessment, 138, 189–190, 218–222, 224, 360
  coaching to, 218
Self assessment, text-guided automated, 217–224

Self-direction, 325–341
　generalized model of, 339
　indicators, 336
　　groups of, 328–329
　　and instructional design process, comparison of phases of, 327
　　interrelations between indicators of, 337–339
　　students' self-reflection blog-posts, 335–336
　　week-dependent indicators of, 336–337
Self-direction indicators for evaluating design-based elearning course, 325–326
　design-based learning course 'Elearning,' 330–333
　design-based learning with social software, 326–327
　discussion, 339–341
　methods, 333–335
　results
　　indicators of self-direction in students' self-reflection blog-posts, 335–336
　　interrelations between indicators of self-direction, 337–339
　　week-dependent indicators of self-direction, 336–337
　self-reflection at design-based learning, 327–330
Self-reflection, 122, 326–330, 332, 334–337, 339, 341
　indicators in blog reflections, 334
Self-regulation, 113
　sources of, 91
Semandix, 69
　administration options, 71
　concept map/mapping, shallow assessment by, 84
　concept map shallow assessment by, 84
　database building, 70
　description, 69–70
　entity/state/event/action, 69
　knowledge-base administration module, 70–82
　　concept map constructing procedure, 71–77
　　WordNet extension procedure, 77–82
　normalization module and grammatical/syntax analyzer, interconnection between, 86
Semandix – constructing knowledge base according to text comprehension model, 67–69

concept map assessment, 83–85
description, 69–70
discussion, 85–87
knowledge-base administration module, 70–82
Semandix Semantic Dictionary, 82–83
text semantic analysis, 83
Semandix Semantic Dictionary, 82–83
Semantic cyclic reference, 81
Semantic dictionary, concept searching in, 83
Sergiovanni, T. J., 261
'Serious games,' 161
Shaffer, D. W., 161–162
Shapiro, 314
Shared regulation, 113
Shared representations, 127–138
Sharp, H., 14
Sharples, M.,365
Shavelson, R. J., 167, 181, 184, 185
Shepherd, 202
Shield, L., 38
Short text semantic analysis, 84
Shuell, T. J., 106
Shute, V. J., 164, 171
Siegel, H., 144
SIGFAD (learning tools), 56
Silander, P., 127–138
Silander, T., 335
Silins, H., 260
Simon, H. A., 2, 163, 165, 171, 174
Simulation, 291
　game, 291
　as learning experience
　　and learning style, 298
　　research model of, 295
　　teamwork experience and learning style, 304
Simulation-games as learning experience, 291–292
　analysis
　　analysis of statements made by participants during post-simulation debriefing teleconferences, 304–310
　　analysis of variance, 299–300
　　learning style as categorical variable, 296–299
　　learning style as continuous variables: regression analysis, 300–304
　background, 292–294
　data collection, 294–295
　procedure, 295–296
Skills, 53
Slocum, A. H., 326

Index

Smith, C., 202
Smith, D., 313
Smith, J., 2–3, 26
Smith-Jackson, T. L., 38
Smith, J. R., 292
Smith, K., 231
Smith, P., 326–327, 329
Smith, R., 345
Social annotation tool, 313–322
Social media, 137, 338, 340, 363–366, 368–371, 373, 375
Social regulation, 114
 with descriptors, categories of, 117
Social Reinforcements (RS), 120
Social software, design-based learning with, 326–327
Social strategies, 120
Socio-cognitive regulation, 111–124
 strategies in cooperative learning, 111–115
  categorization unit, coding system, inter-judge reliability, 115–116
  inter-judge reliability, 116–118
  methods and procedure, data, 115
  regulation models during cooperative tasks in VLE, 118–123
Söderlund, J., 51–52, 57
Soren, B., 14
Spector, J. M., 1–6, 145, 164–167, 171, 314
Sperber, M., 315
Sperry, R. W., 96
Spiro, R. J., 28, 33
Squire, K., 162
Squires, D., 39
Squires, J. K., 161
Stadelhofer, B., 173
Stahl, G., 218
Stavropoulos, S., 86
Stegall, P., 260
Steinberger, J., 67
Steinberg, L. S., 163
Stein, B. S., 246, 248–249, 253
Steinhart, D., 218
Stein, S., 202
Stephenson, J., 200
Sterman, J. D., 162
Stevens, A., 180
Stewart, W., 89–106
Stoyanova, N., 130
Strasser, S. E., 246
Strauss, A., 135
Strautmane, M., 187, 189
Stremer, 232

Structural schema theory of knowledge acquisition, 94–95
Student feedback – virtual exchanges combined, 349
Students' technical placement, ViCaDiS, piloting evaluation, 368–370
Subhiyah, R., 318
Sullivan, H., 231, 235, 239
Summers, M., 113
Sun, X., 46
Surface complexity, 319
Surkes, M. A., 144
Survey questions, virtual exchange (VE), 348–349
Surviving in Space, 168
Sutherland, J. L., 291–312
Sutherland, R., 39, 45
Swan, K. O., 275
Swann, R., 202
Swearingen, D., 168
Sweller, J., 5, 20, 25, 33
Synteta, P., 113

T
TACSI (learning tools), 56
Tait, S., 14
TalkTech'09 course module, ViCaDiS, piloting evaluation, 370–374
 upload area for, 372
 use of ViCaDiS social media tools from TalkTech'09 students, 373
Tamin, 144
Tapscott, D., 360–361
Tarciani, E. M., 165, 167
TASA environment, evaluation of learning progression within, 223
 discussion, 224
 method, 223
 results, 223–224
TASA reflection output, 219
 different set models as derived from the graph, 222
 text feedback composition modules, 221
TASA (text-guided automated self-assessment), 218
 preflection, 222
 reflection, 220–222
Task constraints, 184
Taylor, B. M., 217
Tchounikine, P., 53
Teaching and learning into human development paradigm, moving beyond, 243–244
 demonstration project applying DCP, 250–252

Teaching and learning (cont.)
    description, 252–254
        key insights from demonstration project, 255
    LCM of education, 245–247
    TCM of education, 243–244
    transcending TCM and LCM with DCP, 247–248
    DCP, 248–250
Teaching Centered Model (TCM), 243–245, 247–255
    of education, 243–244
        with DCP, transcending LCM and, 247–248
Teaching system, 24
Teamwork (attitude toward) and personality trait, 302
TE-Cap, Meshat, 60
Technical usability, 37–38, 46
    defined, 37
    goal, 37
    WBLOs, 37–38
Technology
    affordances, 28, 161, 332
    implementation, 259–271
    information and communication, 2, 5, 11, 115, 127–129, 180, 269, 346, 370
    instructional, 159, 265–266, 275–276, 280–281, 283, 285
    tools for problem-solving, 6
    uses of, 204, 261–262, 266, 268–270, 375
        current, 266–267
        future, 268–269
Telematic simulation-game, 292
Teleological structure
    describing "computational system," 76
    Semandix, 69–70
Teng, Y-W., 344, 355
Testerman, J. C., 260
Teutsch, P., 56
Text comprehension model, 67–87
Text-guided automated self assessment, 217–218
    coaching to self-assessment, 218
    evaluation of learning progression within TASA environment, 223
        discussion, 224
        method, 223
        results, 223–224
    TASA: text-guided automated self-assessment, 218
        preflection, 222
        reflection, 220–222

Text semantic analysis – Semandix, 83
    example of short, 84
Think-aloud method, 165, 169–170, 173
Thomas, D., 160–161
Thomas, J., 50
Thomas, L., 329
Thomas, N., 259
Thompson, P., 274
Thompson, S., 105
Thorndike, E. L., 3
Thorp, 116
Thurman, J., 113
Thurmond, P. J., 96
Tillmann, R., 326–327, 329
Timpson, C., 14
Tipping, P., 67
Tirri, H., 335
Tomas, M., 162
Toohey, S., 25
Tools and technologies, 5–6
Tools for collaborative shared representations, 130–131
    collaborative construction of development goals, 132–133
    identifying development needs, 131–132
    mapping teachers' combined pedagogical skills in use of ICT, 134
    practical alignment of development goals, 133–134
TPACK, 275, 277
    model, 277–279
Transformational leadership, 261–262
Transformational structure, Semandix, 69
Tselios, N., 38
Tsikalas, K., 113, 120
Tuma, D., 2
Tuovinen, J. E., 20, 25
Tuzun, H., 162
Twenty-first century, leaders, 259–270
Tzagarakis, M., 58

U
Understanding, 31, 89–106, 119, 246
    definition of, 90
    as embodied form, 95–96
    nervous system as organ of, 91
Underwood, J., 326
Unsworth, L., 273
Uronen, P., 335

V
Valanides, N., 116
Väljataga, T., 338–339
Van Gog, T., 201

Index

VanLehn, K., 25, 27
VanLehn's model, 25
Van Merrienboer J., 5, 28, 201, 238, 246
Van Merriënboer, J. J. G., 2, 28, 238, 246
Vartiainen, M., 232
Vasiu, R., 359–375
Vauras, M., 111, 113, 116
Veermans, 111
Verbal-Imagery and Wholist-Analytic, 16
ViCaDiS
   digital students, 360–362
   environment, 362–364
   ideas and concepts of, 359–360
   piloting, 364–366
   piloting evaluation, 366
      erasmus mobility case, 366–368
      students' technical placement, 368–370
      TalkTech'09 course module, 370–374
   use of features from OUAS Erasmus students, 368
   use of ViCaDiS social media tools from TalkTech'09 students, 373
Vidal-Abarca, E., 313
Virtual campus, 359–360, 363, 371, 375
Virtual collaborative exchanges to expand global awareness, employing, 344–345
   discussion and limitations, 355–356
   study, 345
      evaluation, 348–355
      pedagogies employed, 346–348
      setting, 345–346
Virtual exchanges, 344, 347, 356
   global involvement, perceptions of, 352
   social network online course, 348
Virtual learning environment (VLE), 112, 114–115, 118–124, 359–375
   for digital students, 359–374
   regulated learning in cooperative learning tasks in, 114
   regulation models during cooperative tasks in, 118–123
Virtual Museum of Canada (VMC), 14
Visdic editor, 77
   adding new terms on, 80
   search entry example of data bases, 81
   searching concepts and their hyper and hyponyms on, 78
VLE, *see* Virtual learning environment (VLE)
Vodcasting, 273–284
Volet, S., 113–114, 116, 119
Vondruska, R. J., 105
Vygostky's theory, 112–113
of Zone of Proximal Development (ZPD), 46
Vygotsky, L., 113, 120
Vygotsky, L. S., 29, 46

W

Wachira, P., 275
Wade, A., 144
Wagner, S. U., 164
Wagner, W., 164
Walter, M. I., 2
Wandersman, A., 218
Wang, L., 259
Warren, S. J., 162
Washbush, J., 292
Wassermann, S., 144
Waterhouse, S., 180
Watson, D. M., 128
Watzlawick, P., 251
WBLO architecture, 41
WBLOs (Pedagogical Usability Issues), 37
   case study
      learning objectives, 42
      methods, 42–43
   collaboration, 46
   defined, 41
   differentiation, 45
   discussion, 45–46
   findings, 43–45
   issues in design and evaluation, 38–39
   learning activities and tasks, 45
   literature review, 38–39
   motivation, 45
   pedagogical usability criteria, 39–40
   school subjects and associated, 42
   and technical usability, 37–38
   technologies used for implementing, 41
   WBLO architecture, 41
WBT and electronic performance support, comparing impact of, 229–233
   discussion, 238–240
   method
      criterion and enroute measures, 235–236
      materials, 234–235
      participants, 233
      procedures, 236
   purpose, 233
   results, 237–238
Web 2.0., 49–62, 137, 359, 364, 370–371
Web-based learning objects WBLOs, *see* WBLOs (Pedagogical Usability Issues)

Web-based lecture technologies, 23
Web-based Training (WBT), 229–240
Webb, B., 147
Webber, M., 2, 5
Wegerif, R., 112, 116
Weinberger, A., 113, 116
Wellman, 248
Well-structured problems, 2
　solving, 163
Welsh, M. A., 245–246
Wenger, E., 58
Wertsch J., 29, 112
Wertsch, J. V., 29
Westrom, M., 38
Wheatley, W. J., 292
Wheeler, S., 28, 203
Whipp, J., 113, 120
Whisler, J., 246
White, M. D., 146
Wholetheme biofunctional reorganization, 91
Wholetheme developmental education, 92
Wijnen, W. H. F. W., 326
Wikipedia (online encyclopedia), 28
Willett, J. B., 164, 223
Williams, D., 200
Williams, J. R., 326
Wilson, B. G., 19
Wilson, T. D., 165
Winne, P. H., 209, 213
Winsler, A., 94
Winston, 72
Winters, F., 113, 120
Witcomb, A., 15
Witkin, H. A., 16
Witt, C., 232

Wlodkwoski, R. J., 253
Wood, D., 130, 133
Woodroffe, M., 344
Wood, S. D., 38
Woo, K., 27
WordNets, 86
　extension procedure, 77–82
　　new relation types examples, 79
　　.inf file, relations enrichment examples on, 79
　searching concept and its hypernyms on, 78
Woywood, G., 50
Writing, 15, 115, 122, 166, 169–170, 208, 217–224, 245, 250, 274, 277, 293, 295, 309, 314–315, 334, 336, 339, 346, 372

Y

Yamamoto, J., 273–286
Yang, H., 295, 299
Yang, S. J. H., 6
Yorke, M., 200
Yusko, B., 143

Z

Zarra, E. J., 283
Zemsky, R., 203
Zhang, 144
Zhang, K., 46
Zhou, W., 112
Zibit, M., 161
Ziglari, L., 274
Zimmerman, B., 113, 116, 120, 124
Zuercher, N., 217